THE LETTERS OF
THOMAS BABINGTON MACAULAY

VOLUME VI

Volumes in the series

Above: Thomas Flower Ellis, Macaulay's most intimate friend throughout his adult life; photograph probably taken in the 1850s (Trinity College).

Left: Margaret Trevelyan Holland, Lady Knutsford; Macaulay's beloved niece, 'Baba.'

THE LETTERS OF THOMAS BABINGTON MACAULAY

EDITED BY

THOMAS PINNEY

PROFESSOR OF ENGLISH

POMONA COLLEGE, THE CLAREMONT COLLEGES

CLAREMONT, CALIFORNIA

VOLUME VI

JANUARY 1856—DECEMBER 1859

CAMBRIDGE UNIVERSITY PRESS

CAMBRIDGE

LONDON · NEW YORK · NEW ROCHELLE

MELBOURNE · SYDNEY

Published by the Press Syndicate of the University of Cambridge
The Pitt Building, Trumpington Street, Cambridge CB2 1RP
32 East 57th Street, New York, NY 10022, USA
296 Beaconsfield Parade, Middle Park, Melbourne 3206, Australia

First published 1981

Printed in Great Britain
by Western Printing Services, Bristol

Library of Congress Cataloguing in Publication Data
Macaulay, Thomas Babington Macaulay, Baron, 1800–1859.
The Letters of Thomas Babington Macaulay.
On spine: The letters of Macaulay
Includes indexes.
Contents: v. 1. 1807–February 1831 – v. 2. March 1831–December 1833 – v. 3. January 1834–August 1841 – v. 4. September 1841–December 1848 – v. 5. January 1849–December 1855 – v. 6. January 1856–December 1859.
I. Pinney, Thomas, ed. II. Title. III. Title: The letters of Macaulay.

DA3.M3A4 828′.8′09 [B] 73–75860

ISBN 0 521 22750 X

The title-page device is
the Macaulay coat of arms, taken from Macaulay's seal
on a letter of 17 December 1833;
it was later the basis of Macaulay's arms as Baron Macaulay.
Acknowledgement is made to the Master and Fellows of
Trinity College, Cambridge.

CONTENTS

T. F. Ellis and
Margaret Trevelyan Holland — *frontispiece*

Preface — vii

Biographical Chronology — xi

THE LETTERS

At Holly Lodge,
1 January 1856–25 August 1857 — 3

Baron Macaulay of Rothley,
29 August 1857–29 December 1858 — 111

The Final Year,
3 January–25 December 1859 — 183

Letters of Uncertain Date,
1839–1859? — 263

Additional Letters,
4 March 1831–16 December 1848 — 273

Appendixes
Additions and Corrections, vols. I—IV — 287
A List of Macaulay's Published Writings — 289

Indexes
Sources of Text — 303
General Index — 307

PREFACE

After the second part of the *History* was published at the end of 1855 Macaulay was not quite prepared to say *nunc dimittis*. Despite his infirmities, he went on enjoying life, by which he meant the life of books, of friends, and of domestic affections. As he repeatedly puts it in his Journal, so long as his head was clear and his heart warm he was content. Macaulay the historian, however, seems not to have felt any further pressure to add to the monument he had constructed, incomplete though it was. Not until October of 1856 did he resume writing; a year later he speaks of the work as 'hardly begun,' and two years after that, only a few months before his death, he wrote that 'it will be long before I shall be able to say with confidence when another portion of my history will be published.' It is fair to say that in the last four years of his life, the *History* was no longer his main occupation, as it had been for a decade, but rather an occasional amusement.

There were two major novelties for Macaulay to enjoy in these years: a house of his own, and a peerage. It would not be easy to say which pleased him more. The house, Holly Lodge, on Campden Hill, adjacent to the grounds of Holland House, came about because he was now indisputably wealthy and could afford it, because his sisters pressed him to provide easier and more spacious quarters for himself, removed from the coal smoke and fog of central London, and because Macaulay himself liked the idea of a new habitation, in, yet not wholly of, London. The walk from Kensington to Pall Mall was one that he could still manage readily, yet his retreat high on Campden Hill, backed by a large garden where he could contemplate his turf, roses, and thorn trees, provided an agreeable world apart. There Macaulay spent the last three and a half years of his life in an establishment of unaccustomed expansiveness, with a butler, cook, housemaids, a gardener, and a coachman (the coach house is all that now survives of Holly Lodge: the rest has given way to the Atkins Laboratories of Queen Elizabeth College). Here he gave dinners, as he had not been able to do since the days of his residence in ministerial style; here he could refresh his vulnerable lungs with the rural air of the Kensington heights; and here he could acquire the latest gossip of the

great world from his next neighbor, the Duke of Argyll. His pleasure in Holly Lodge seems to have been pure and uninterrupted.

The pleasure he got from his peerage, though of a rather different kind, was also unmixed. As his sister Hannah wrote, 'he enjoyed it himself as he did every thing – simply and cordially.' The offer came to him without any preparation one evening in August 1857 and took him entirely by surprise. He made up his mind at once, he tells us, that the honor was one he could accept without apology, especially since it would reflect glory on his family without entailing any burden upon it: he would be the first and last Lord Macaulay. The peerage was the first ever bestowed for literature, and Macaulay felt the attraction of such a distinction: 'Perhaps: no such offer was ever made, without the slightest solicitation, direct or indirect, to a man of humble origin and moderate fortune, who had long quitted public life' (Journal, 28 August 1857). The English public seemed rather pleased to have such a gesture made to one of its favorites, and Baron Macaulay of Rothley, though possessed of no landed estates, was certainly equal in public esteem to his neighbor peers in Kensington, the Duke of Argyll and the Baron Holland.

Macaulay duly took his seat in the House of Lords in December of 1857, but, as Trevelyan remarks, his interest in the proceedings of the House was more personal than political. The one occasion on which he seriously meditated making a speech in the House of Lords was in June of 1858, on the question of the settlement of India. When the day came, however, he found himself too weak to go down to the House, and so the history of Macaulay as a parliamentary speaker is to be found exclusively in the records of the Commons.

He made only one speech of any kind after his parliamentary speeches of 1853; this was on his installation as High Steward of the Borough of Cambridge on 11 May 1858, and is a very brief effort. He wrote a life of Johnson for Adam Black's *Encyclopaedia Britannica* in the summer of 1856, and, for the same publication, a life of Pitt. This, though the result pleased him, took a remarkably long time in the writing: Macaulay began thinking about it in September 1857, worked on it at frequent intervals through seven months, and did not entirely finish it until August 1858 – nearly a year after he began. The internal pressure to write was clearly much diminished.

Apart from his intermittent work on the continuation of the *History* the only other literary labor of these years worth mentioning is the careful preparation of a revised text of the first four volumes of the *History*. For this Macaulay began revising and correcting in May of 1856 and protracted the work a full two years, hoping, as he wrote, 'that the printing will be almost faultless.' Besides his scrupulous attention to

proof-reading, he 'removed many small blemishes, retouched the style, and added some notes, particularly about Penn' (25 August 1857).

India, which had made a decisive difference in Macaulay's earlier life, returned to play a crucial part at its end. The Mutiny in 1857 had been bad enough; Macaulay, in common with all other Englishmen, had been horrified and fascinated by the inflamed reporting of that disastrous episode. But the worst blow was to take quite a different form. When Macaulay had returned from India in 1838 with his sister Hannah and her husband Charles Trevelyan he had been constantly anxious and unhappy until he had secured such a position in London for his brother-in-law that Trevelyan could not reasonably refuse it in order to return to India. Trevelyan, however, had never ceased to yearn after India. His chance came early in 1859, when Lord Stanley offered him the Governorship of Madras. Trevelyan was determined to go, and Macaulay could not advise him otherwise, but this development at once raised the specter that had haunted Macaulay in 1838 – that Hannah, too, would return to India and so leave him desolate. As he confided to his Journal on the day that Trevelyan announced his news, 'if she were to go I should die of a broken heart, I think.'

At first everyone agreed that there was no question of Hannah's going at all – no doubt the family were thinking of Macaulay in taking this position. But gradually their way of talking changed. Trevelyan sailed for Madras in February. By April he was writing in such a way as to show that he expected to see his family in India 'some time hence.' In May Hannah told Macaulay that she meant to join her husband in November of 1860, and begged Macaulay to go with her then. At last, on the 15th of October, Hannah sent Macaulay a letter telling him that she would sail for India in February – it was evidently news that she did not dare to break to him in person, and she was certainly right as to its effect. 'I wish I were dead,' Macaulay wrote in his Journal on the next day; he got his wish two months later, and all of those closest to him felt his death as an almost providential release. As his nephew George wrote to Sir Walter Trevelyan:

> Our great comfort is in the knowledge that my dear uncle was taken at a time when his happiness was already overclouded by the shadow of a great sorrow: my mother's separation from him he always feared more than death. Never did I witness greater mental agony than he suffered since she declared her intention of joining my father.*

Macaulay died on the evening of December 28, alone, at Holly Lodge,

* Undated letter [December 1859-January 1860?]: MS, University of Newcastle.

with a book before him. He was buried in Westminster Abbey on 9 January 1860.

This edition having reached its final volume, a brief retrospect of its contents is now possible. The estimate made in Volume 1 (p. xv), that the number of letters would run to around 2,500, has proven to be close but not quite on the mark. The total is in fact 2,440; all of these are letters, or parts of letters, by Macaulay. Of this total, 1,658 have never, so far as I know, been published before; 478 have been published in full, and 304 in part. The sources of manuscript, including libraries, institutions, and private collectors, number 128, scattered over five continents. Printed texts are drawn from 62 different volumes, including sale catalogues, periodicals, and printed books. It would be foolish to conclude that no further significant numbers of Macaulay's letters, as yet unaccounted for, are likely to appear; but it is, I think, safe to say that the collection embodied in this edition illustrates the main relations of Macaulay's life and work with reasonable fullness.

The completion of a lengthy work is perhaps a better occasion on which to make one's acknowledgments than the beginning, yet there would be no stopping point on the long, long list of those upon whose help I have depended if I were to begin naming them. But I cannot resist repeating here my special thanks to two among those many: to my wife, Sherrill Pinney, who might very well claim title-page credit but who is too generous to do so; and to my friend John Clive, who knows more about Macaulay than anybody else does and who has contributed to this work in every possible way.

BIOGRAPHICAL CHRONOLOGY

1856 January 31
Retires from House of Commons
- January–February
Negotiating for Holly Lodge, Campden Hill
- March 13
Longman pays £20,000 to TBM's account
- March 20–24
Easter tour to Rochester and Canterbury
- May 2
Leaves the Albany for Holly Lodge
- May
Begins preparation of corrected reprint of *History*, published in 7 vols., 1857–8, and intended to be the final text
- July 30
Finishes life of Johnson for *Encyclopaedia Britannica*
- August 20–September 27
Italian tour with Ellis: Turin, Milan, Verona, Venice
- October 1
Begins vol. 5 of *History*

1857 February
Appointed trustee of National Portrait Gallery
- April 9–13
Easter tour to Salisbury, Stonehenge, Longleat
- July 20–23
Attends Manchester Exhibition of the Art Treasures of the United Kingdom
- August 28
Receives offer of peerage from Palmerston
- August 30–September 14
Continental tour with Ellis: Paris, Rheims, Trèves, Brussels
- October 22
Elected High Steward of Cambridge
- December 3
Takes seat in House of Lords

1858 April 1–5
Easter tour to Lichfield and Oxford
- May 11
Speech on installation as High Steward of Cambridge
- August 9
Finishes life of Pitt for *Encyclopaedia Britannica*
- August 28–September 14
French tour with Ellis: Paris, Lyons, Avignon, Montpellier, Toulouse, Bordeaux
- November 25
Marriage of Margaret Trevelyan to Henry Holland

1859 January 6
Learns of offer to Trevelyan of Madras appointment
- February 18
Trevelyan leaves for India
- April 30–May 2
Family party at Cambridge
- May 1
Learns that Hannah, Alice, and George plan to join Trevelyan at Madras in the next year

– July 28–August 17
Northern tour with Hannah: Windermere, Glasgow, Inverary, Stirling, Edinburgh

– October 1–8
Tour of South of England with Ellis: Weymouth, Lyme, Sidmouth, Exeter, Ilfracombe. TBM looking for retirement home

– October 15
Learns that Hannah will leave for India in February

– December 15
Suffers heart attack

– December 28
Death

1860 January 9
Burial in Westminster Abbey

1861 March
History of England, vol. 5, published

THE LETTERS

AT HOLLY LODGE
1 JANUARY 1856–25 AUGUST 1857

1856 January 31
Retires from House of Commons

– January–February
Negotiating for Holly Lodge, Campden Hill

– March 13
Longman pays £20,000 to TBM's account

– March 20–24
Easter tour to Rochester and Canterbury

– May 2
Leaves the Albany for Holly Lodge

– May
Begins preparation of corrected reprint of *History*, published in 7 vols., 1857–8, and intended to be the final text

– July 30
Finishes life of Johnson for *Encyclopaedia Britannica*

– August 20–September 27
Italian tour with Ellis: Turin, Milan, Verona, Venice

– October 1
Begins vol. 5 of *History*

1857 February
Appointed trustee of National Portrait Gallery

– April 9–13
Easter tour to Salisbury, Stonehenge, Longleat

– July 20–23
Attends Manchester Exhibition of the Art Treasures of the United Kingdom

TO FRANCES MACAULAY, 1 JANUARY 1856

MS: Trinity College.

Albany London Jany. 1. 1856

Dearest Fanny,

I am astonished at what you tell me.[1] There ought to be a thanksgiving day for my book, and a service prepared by the Archbishop.

We at least have reason to be thankful: for the success has certainly been great, under every disadvantage. Expectation was so extravagant that not to have altogether disappointed it is a triumph. I have a great drawer full of criticisms which Longman sends me. They are generally very laudatory with a mixture of acid. The people of Londonderry seem to be out of their wits.

I shall not give anything to Mr. What d'ye call- [. . . . .][2] Glamorganshire or Caithnessshire? If he speaks to you again say that I am forced to confine my charities to places with which I have some special connection. Love to Selina. A happy new year to [. . . .][2]

TO SELINA MACAULAY, 2 JANUARY 185[6]

MS: Trinity College.

Albany Jany. 2. 1855

Dearest Selina,

So poor George is gone.[3] I have been much affected by his death, though, during the last twelve or thirteen years, I had scarcely seen him – not from any fault of mine.

I inclose a letter from a lady whose surname I cannot make out. Is it Daniell? And who is she? Send me a line, or make Fanny send me a line to tell me how to direct my answer; and be so kind as to return the letter.

Love to dear Fanny. She forgot when she wrote last to tell me how you were going on.

Ever yours
T B Macaulay

[1] That 'a sermon was preached at Brighton to my praise and glory last Sunday' (Trevelyan, II, 387).

[2] The central third of the last leaf has been cut away, taking about four lines on the recto and the closing and signature on the verso.

[3] George Babington died on 1 January.

TO HENRY REEVE, 2 JANUARY 185[6]

MS: Berg Collection, New York Public Library.

Albany Jany. 2. 1855

My dear Sir,

You are quite right in saying that Schomberg was not buried in the Abbey.[1] But I am quite right in saying that it was intended that he should be buried in the Abbey, and that the intention was announced. I had meant to add in another place, a few pages later, that his corpse was deposited in St Patrick's Cathedral, and had not been moved thence. But I forgot to do this. I feel that the omission is a blemish; and I will take an opportunity of removing it. Many thanks for your kind interest in my book.

Very truly yours
T B Macaulay

H Reeve Esq / etc. etc. etc.

TO ADAM BLACK, 3 JANUARY 1856

MS: National Library of Scotland.

Albany London / January 3. 1856

My dear Sir,

I very much wish for your advice as to the precise time at which I ought to announce to the people of Edinburgh my intention to vacate my seat. As to the thing itself I ask no advice, – not even from you; –for my mind is unalterably made up; and on the first day of the Session, the 31st of the month, the writ will be moved for. But it seems to me that I ought to declare my purpose some days earlier, and not to do anything which might have the look of a surprise. What do you say to the 20th or the 21st?[2] I write by this post to Craig, with whom, I have no doubt, you will communicate. I am almost a prisoner to my room. When the wind is in the South West, I go out, well wrapped up for an hour in the warmest part of the day.

Ever yours truly,
T B Macaulay

[1] TBM says that, after Schomberg's death at the Boyne, 'It was announced that the brave veteran should have a public funeral at Westminster' (*History*, III, 638: ch. 16). The text was unchanged in subsequent editions, and thus furnished Paget with one of his points about TBM's inaccuracy (*Paradoxes and Puzzles*, Edinburgh, 1874, p. 182n).

[2] See 19 January.

TO ADAM BLACK, 8 JANUARY 1856

MS: National Library of Scotland.

Albany London / January 8. 1856

My dear Sir,

Yesterday I received your letter. To day I received Craig's. Both have given me much pleasure.[1] I should have felt some vexation and perhaps even some self reproach, if, in consequence of my retirement, a fanatical blockhead or a radical agitator had been sent up to Parliament by Edinburgh. I now look forward to the pleasure of hearing my successor spoken of by men of all parties as one of the most useful, prudent, temperate and independent members of the House of Commons.

I will send off my Address to you on Saturday the 19th. You can then publish it on the 21st, 22nd or 23d, as you think best.

Ever yours truly,
T B Macaulay

TO UNIDENTIFIED RECIPIENT, 8 JANUARY 1856

MS: Trinity College.

Albany Jany. 8. 1856

Sir,

I never sate to Mr. Frith[2] for my portrait.

I know nothing about the lampoons which you mention except that they are utterly worthless, and that Junius had nothing to do with either of them. / I am, Sir,

Your obedient Servant
T B Macaulay

TO FRANCES MACAULAY, 13 JANUARY 1856

MS: Trinity College.

Albany London / January 13. 1856

Dearest Fanny,

Thanks for your letters. I am glad that you are so well pleased with my book. I am more than satisfied with the share of public favour that I

[1] Craig refused to become a candidate but Black agreed and was elected as TBM's successor Black was already 73 years old, but he sat for nine years.

[2] William Powell Frith (1819–1909: *DNB*), one of the most popular of Victorian painters.

enjoy. Against a little captious censure I have to set off an immense quantity of praise which is much beyond my desert. I sometimes think that I should very willingly barter some fame for a little better health, if such dealings were possible. Then I remember Addison's Mountain of Miseries,[1] and ask myself whether I would consent to be thought a very middling writer on condition of breathing as freely as I did at twenty. There are moments when I might make such a bargain: but I should soon repent it, and long to change back again.

I shall not stir out till there is a change in the weather. In a few days I shall take the Chiltern Hundreds. But this is a secret. Pray keep it as such. Love to dear Selina.

Yours ever
T B Macaulay

To Sir Henry Rawlinson,[2] 16 January 1856

MS: Trinity College.

Albany January 16. 1856

My dear Sir,

My lease of these chambers will expire next December; and I should [. . . . .][3] venture to expose mys[elf][4] to the inconveniences inseparable from a change of residence. As soon as I see my way clearly, I will let you know; and, if you should then be of your present [. . . .][3]

[1] *Spectator*, Numbers 558 and 559.

[2] TBM's Journal for this day records a 'note from Rawlinson. He wants to take my chambers – answered him civilly' (IX, 34). Sir Henry Rawlinson (1810–95: *DNB*), after a career in the East India Company's service as interpreter, political agent, and soldier, became consul at Baghdad, where he succeeded in deciphering the Assyrian cuneiform writing for the first time. He had finally returned to England in 1855, where he afterwards sat in the House of Commons, was on the India Council, and was President of the Royal Asiatic Society. TBM, who must have seen much of Rawlinson through Rawlinson's work for the British Museum, had a poor opinion of him, calling him 'a humbug and a bore' (Journal, III, 75: 14 November 1850) and 'that prince of charlatans' (Journal, IV, 275: 4 October 1851).

[3] The letter is a fragment: several lines seem to be missing here.

[4] Letter torn.

TO THE ELECTORS OF EDINBURGH, 19 JANUARY 1856

MS: National Library of Scotland. *Published: Scotsman,* 23 January 1856.

To the Electors of Edinburgh

Gentlemen,

Very soon after you had done me the high honor of chusing me, without any solicitation on my part, to represent you in the present Parliament, I began to entertain apprehensions that the state of my health would make it impossible for me to repay your kindness by efficient service. During some time I flattered myself with the hope that I might be able to be present at important divisions and occasionally to take a part in important debates. But the experience of the last two years has convinced me that I cannot reasonably expect to be ever again capable of performing, even in an imperfect manner, those duties which the public has a right to expect from every member of the House of Commons.

You meanwhile have borne with me in a manner which entitles you to my warmest gratitude. Had even a small number of my constituents hinted to me a wish that I would vacate my seat, I should have thought it my duty to comply with that wish. But from not one single elector have I ever received a line of reproach or complaint. If I were disposed to abuse your generosity and delicacy, I might perhaps continue to bear the honorable title of Member for Edinburgh till the dissolution of the Parliament. But I feel that, by trespassing longer on your indulgence, I should prove myself unworthy of it. I have therefore determined to dissolve our connection, and to put it in your power to chuse a better servant than I have been.

I have applied to the Chancellor of the Exchequer for the Stewardship of the Chiltern Hundreds;[1] and I have every reason to believe that the new writ will issue on the first day of the approaching Session. This notice will, I trust, be long enough to enable you to make a thoroughly satisfactory choice.

And now, my friends, with sincere thanks for all your kindness, and with fervent wishes for the peace, honor and prosperity of your noble city, I, for the last time, bid you farewell.

T B Macaulay

London January 19. 1856

[1] TBM wrote to the Chancellor, Sir George Cornewall Lewis, on the 18th (Journal, IX, 38).

TO HENRY HART MILMAN, 22 JANUARY 1856

MS: McGill University.

Albany Jany. 22. 1856

My dear Dean,

I will make inquiries without delay about the house[1] which you mention. Thanks for your kindness.

I have begun the History of Latin Xtianity again,[2] and am reading with great interest. Can the Clementina[3] be got separately? And in what sort of an edition?

Ever yours truly
T B Macaulay

TO FRANCES MACAULAY, 25 JANUARY 1856

MS: Trinity College.

Albany January 25. 1856

Dearest Fanny,

Thanks for your letter. I am so well that, if the mild weather continues, I shall, in obedience to the Queen's commands, go to Windsor on Monday and stay till Wednesday.[4] I wish that the visit were over.

Teague was a hundred and sixty years ago and long after a contemptuous nickname for an Irishman. What the etymology is I do not know. I

1 TBM received a letter from Milman on the day before 'about a house on Camden Hill' (Journal, IX, 40). This is the first mention of the house, called Holly Lodge, to which TBM moved in early May and where he remained until his death. Its neighbor house, formerly called Bedford Lodge and at this time Argyll Lodge, was the residence of the Duke of Argyll; his description of the place in *Autobiography and Memoirs*, I, 391–2, gives an idea of the rural character of the region, on the high ground above Holland House called Campden Hill. Holly Lodge, built about 1814, was demolished in 1959 to make way for the Atkins Laboratory Building of Queen Elizabeth College, University of London. The plaque commemorating TBM's residence – the first such plaque sponsored by the London County Council – has been put up on the new building.

2 According to his earlier promise: see *to* Milman, 29 December 1855.

3 The religious and philosophical romance attributed to Pope Clement I: Milman says of it that 'a good critical edition . . . is much to be desired' (*History of Latin Christianity*, 2nd edn, New York, 1860, I, 61n). A later note adds that the edition by Dressel, 1853, is now the best available (*ibid.*); a copy of this is item 186 in the sale catalogue of TBM's library.

4 28–30 January. On the first evening the company were entertained by a production of Tom Taylor's *Still Waters*; next day TBM was forced to meet the Prince of Wales and 'to stand before a boy of fourteen. Sirring him and bowing to him. Wretched work!' The guests were Lord and Lady Stanhope, Lord and Lady John Russell, Lord and Lady Stanley of Alderley, and Pemberton Leigh (Journal, IX, 50–5).

suppose that the word is Irish, and was often used in conversation. In the first line of Lillibullero, one Popish Celt accosts another thus

"Ho, brother Teague, have you heard the decree?"

Kerne is the Irish word for a footsoldier.[1] You may find it in Shakspeare. The Duke of York in the Second Part of Henry the Sixth says of Jack Cade,

"In Ireland have I seen this stubborn Cade
Oppose himself against a troop of Kernes."[2]

And again,

"Full often, like a shaghaired crafty Kerne,
Hath he conversed with the enemy."[3]

Love to Selina.

Ever yours,
T B Macaulay

TO UNIDENTIFIED RECIPIENT, 30 JANUARY 1856

MS: Trinity College.

Albany London / Jany. 30. 1856

Sir,

I am much obliged to you for the trouble which you have taken: but I will not trespass further on your time. Almost all the tracts which you mention, – indeed probably all, – are in the immense collection at the British Museum. / I have the honor to be, / Sir,

Your most obedient Servant,
T B Macaulay

TO UNIDENTIFIED RECIPIENT, 30 JANUARY 1856

MS: New York University.

Albany January 30 / 1856

Dear Sir,

I am much gratified by your approbation and by the kindness with which you express it.

[1] Perhaps Fanny had been reading ch. 16 of the *History*: 'kerne' occurs twice there (III, 624, 666), though I have not found 'Teague.'

[2] III, i, 360–1.

[3] III, i, 367–8.

The discourse concerning Generosity is certainly not Somers's.[1] / Believe me, / Dear Sir,

Your faithful Servant
T B Macaulay

TO WILLIAM WHEWELL, 1 FEBRUARY 1856

MS: Trinity College.

Albany London / February 1. 1856

My dear Whewell,

Thanks for your very kind letter. I am truly glad that my book has given you pleasure. You do me no more than justice in acquitting me of the Index. It is the very worst that I ever saw.

My retirement from parliament will make little difference in my way of life. For during the last two years I have scarcely been two hours in the House of Commons. The only change will be that I shall cease to feel the uneasy sensation of being charged with a duty which I am unable to fulfil.

I am about to leave the Albany; and I shall probably take up my quarters on Campden Hill, within twenty minutes' drive of Hyde Park Corner, and yet out of the London smoke, and among hollies, turf, roses and lilacs. I shall hope sometimes to see you in my library and on my lawn.

Ever yours most truly,
T B Macaulay

TO THOMAS ELLIS, 1 FEBRUARY 1856

MS: Trinity College.

Albany Feby. 1. 1856

Dear Ellis,

I was not the worse for my trip to Windsor. I have suffered since I came back; but not more than was to have been expected.

I shall expect you on Sunday at ½ past 7.

Ever yours,
T B Macaulay

[1] 1693; it is now attributed to Somers.

TO JOHN MELVILLE,[1] 2 FEBRUARY 1856

Text: Scotsman, 6 February 1856.

Albany, London, February 2, 1856.

My Lord,

I must have been of a very insensible nature if I had not been deeply affected by the letter which I this morning received from your Lordship, and by the Address which that letter contained.[2] It is unspeakably gratifying to me to think that I carry with me into retirement the good opinion and the good wishes of a great community to which I have stood in an intimate political relation during many years of political turmoil. While I live, I shall never forget the debt of gratitude which I owe to the Citizens of Edinburgh; and I feel assured that, long after my death, the Address which bears your signature will be carefully treasured by some who are dear to me, and to whom my memory will be dear.

With warm thanks for your Lordship's great kindness, I have the honour to be, my Lord, your Lordship's most obedient and most faithful Servant,

T. B. Macaulay.

The Lord Provost of Edinburgh, / etc. etc. etc.

TO FRANCES MACAULAY, 3 FEBRUARY 1856

MS: Trinity College.

Albany London / February 3. 1856

Dearest Fanny,

I have Fleming's panegyric on William.[3] The Record is, to be sure, absurd beyond its ordinary absurdity.[4] Longman sends me everything that comes out about my book; and I have quite a library of reviews. The praise greatly preponderates; but there is much censure and some abuse.

I did not suffer so much as I expected from my visit to Windsor. Indeed I was better there than in London, though the weather was

[1] (Sir) John Melville (1802–60: *Boase*), Writer to the Signet, was Lord Provost of Edinburgh, 1854–9, and was knighted in the latter year.

[2] The address, voted at a meeting of Black's supporters on 31 January, expressed the electors' 'deep sorrow and regret' on TBM's resignation (*Scotsman*, 6 February).

[3] Robert Fleming, the Younger, *The Blessedness of Those Who Die in the Lord: A Practical Discourse Occasioned by the Death of King William*, 1702.

[4] On 25 January TBM had been surprised to see 'praise of myself where I expected none – in the Record' (Journal, IX, 44–5). The review prophesied that the *History* 'will ever take a place high amongst British classics.'

frosty, and this leads me to think that my chest is more affected by the town fog than by the mere coldness of the atmosphere. I am in treaty for a very pleasant house on Campden Hill; – not [far from Ho][1]lland House. [. . . . .][1] as freely as if I were a hundred miles from London, and yet should be within half an hour's drive of the Athenæum and the British Museum.

Love to Selina. [. . .][1]

TO HENRY THORNTON, 4 FEBRUARY 1856

MS: American Philosophical Society Library.

Albany February 4 / 1856

Dear Thornton,

I am taking a house on Campden Hill, and shall want [more][2] than is [. . . . .][2] you be kind enough to let me know when I shall attend for that purpose.[3]

Ever yours truly,

T B Macaulay

TO SIR WILLIAM GIBSON CRAIG, 7 FEBRUARY 1856

MS: Trinity College.

Albany London / Feby. 7. 1856

Dear Craig,

Thanks to you for keeping me apprised of what is going on. I have been more mortified than I can express by the conduct of a large part of the constituent body to which I owe and for which I feel so much kindness. I shall not be free from anxiety till our friend is fairly returned.[4]

It passes my comprehension how any body can maintain that the citizens of Edinburgh have been taken by surprise, or that it would have

[1] The signature has been torn away, removing about four lines and a part of a fifth on the other side.

[2] The lower part of this brief note on a single leaf is missing.

[3] On the next day TBM went to the City and 'ordered the sale of 1000£ 3 per Cents' (Journal, IX, 66).

[4] An opposition of very mixed elements, led by Duncan McLaren, was got up against Black and brought forward a candidate, F. Brown Douglas; he was defeated by a large majority on 8 February.

been for the general good that the bustle, the quarrelling and the railing of the last fortnight should have extended over three months.

Kindest regards to all your family and to our friend Black.

Ever yours
T B Macaulay

TO FRANCIS KYFFIN LENTHALL, 13 FEBRUARY 1856

MS: Trinity College.

Albany February 13. 1856

Sir,

I return the Hopkins M.S., with many thanks to you and to Mr. Northey.[1] It is highly interesting. I have made an abridgement of it which extends to twenty six pages.

I suppose that it was as a Privy Councillor of the Kingdom of Ireland that Edward Hopkins was Right Honorable. He never was a Privy Councillor here. / I have the honor to be, / Sir,

Your faithful Servant,
T B Macaulay

F K Lenthall Esq / etc. etc. etc.

TO DERWENT COLERIDGE, 16 FEBRUARY 1856

MS: Cornell University.

Albany Feby. 16. 1856

Dear Derwent,

As soon as you had left me I wrote to Lord Granville.[2] I send you his answer. I most earnestly hope that he may be successful. But you must not be sanguine. If we fail now, we may have laid the ground for a more prosperous application hereafter.[3]

Ever yours,
T B Macaulay

[1] Edward Richard Northey (1795–1878), of Woodcote House, Epsom, Surrey, was descended from Edward Hopkins, M.P., Secretary of State for Ireland (Burke, *Landed Gentry*, 1863; 1886). On 11 February TBM says that he 'went through the curious M.S. of Edward Hopkins's travels' (Journal, IX, 82); I find no reference to it in the *History*.

[2] Granville George Leveson-Gower (1815–91: *DNB*), second Earl Granville, Lord President of the Council in Palmerston's cabinet, held many offices under various liberal administrations and was thrice Minister for Foreign Affairs. He was one of TBM's favorites: 'I like him much, and think him a very able man' (Journal, XI, 511: 11 June 1859).

[3] The letter is endorsed: 're a Canonry at S. Paul's then vacant.' Coleridge did not get it.

TO THOMAS FLOWER ELLIS, 17 FEBRUARY 1856

MS: Trinity College.

Albany Feb 17. 1856

Dear Ellis,

I shall be delighted to see you to dinner on Thursday.

I really do think that out of these discussions about Codification,[1] something may turn up which may suit you. As to your photographer[2] I reserve my judgment till I see a specimen of his art.

I went to the Athenæum, and looked for your friend's name: but he is not among the candidates who stand for the next ballot.

Ever yours
T B Macaulay

TO THOMAS FLOWER ELLIS, 23 FEBRUARY 1856

MS: Trinity College.

Albany February 23. 1856

Dear Ellis,

I have put down my name among your friend's sponsors at the Athenæum.

Be so kind as to send me the letter which you took away on Thursday. I must answer the gentleman who offers me the dog.[3]

When will you dine here?

Ever yours
T B Macaulay

I find that I must pass a month at a hotel,[4] as I did more than nine years ago when I was changing my residence. This is, I hope, my last move.

1 In the Commission on the Laws of India.

2 Antoine Claudet (1797–1867: *DNB*), who operated a photographic studio in London from 1840. On 8 August Ellis took TBM to Claudet, and on the 15th TBM was shown the result: 'a hideous likeness' he called it (Journal, XI, 38). But his brother Charles later declared that it was 'unquestionably the best likeness' (to Mary Macaulay, 9 July 1879: MS, University of London), and Montgomery Stuart speaks of its 'scrupulous fidelity' (*Reminiscences and Essays*, 1884, p. 35). The photograph was first engraved as the frontispiece to volume I of Ellis's edition of TBM's *Miscellaneous Writings*, 1860, but is most familiar as the frontispiece to Trevelyan's *Life*.

3 See *to* Alfred Edward Chalon, 25 February.

4 In the event, he did not, apparently because instead of dismantling his book cases and moving them to Holly Lodge he had new ones built there. This plan for handling the 10,000 volumes of his library greatly reduced the turmoil of the move (Journal, IX, 108: 25 February).

TO JOHN PENDLETON KENNEDY,[1] 23 FEBRUARY 1856

MS: George Peabody Department, Enoch Pratt Free Library, Baltimore.

Albany London / February 23. 1856

Sir,

My friend Mr. Thackeray[2] has sent me a letter written by you to him, and has requested me to furnish you with any information which I may be able to obtain about the fate of a Colonel George Talbot[3] who was sent from Virginia to England as a prisoner on a charge of murder in 1685. I have been almost entirely confined to my room during some weeks, and have not been able to make any researches. I can, however, I think, with confidence say that Colonel Talbot escaped with life. For if a man of his rank had been hanged, there would undoubtedly have been some notice of his end in the Diary of Narcissus Luttrell, who was a very accurate chronicler of executions.

There is a weekly publication here entitled Notes and Queries.[4] Any person who wishes for information on any historical or literary point can send a question to the editor, and may, in this way, learn much that is not to be learned from books. I have sent a question about Colonel Talbot;[5] and it is not impossible that some member of the Talbot family may be able to give an answer. / I have the honor to be, / Sir,

Your most obedient servant,

T B Macaulay

The Honorable J P Kennedy / etc. etc. etc.

[1] Kennedy (1795–1870), American writer and politician, a native and resident of Baltimore, was Secretary of the Navy, 1852–3, and the author of several volumes of historical novels and sketches. Kennedy called on TBM in June, when they had a 'long talk and not uninteresting' (Journal, XI, 9).

[2] Thackeray was then on his second American tour and had been entertained in January by Kennedy, 'exceedingly pleasant natural and good-natured' (Ray, ed., *Letters of Thackeray*, III, 543).

[3] Talbot, who was convicted of murder but pardoned, is the hero of Kennedy's 'A Legend of Maryland,' published posthumously in *At Home and Abroad*, 1872.

[4] Founded in 1849 by TBM's acquaintance, the antiquary W. J. Thoms: see 6 August 1857.

[5] The query appears in *Notes and Queries*, 1 March 1856, over the initials 'K.P.J.' – Kennedy's reversed. It produced no published answer.

TO EDWARD EVERETT, 25 FEBRUARY 1856

MS: Massachusetts Historical Society. *Mostly published: New York Ledger*, 25 February 1860.

Albany London February 25. 1856

My dear Everett,

I am in your debt for two letters. The second arrived this morning. Thanks for all your kindness, and for the two specimens of American typography,[1] which had the good luck to elude the vigilance of our custom house officers.

I am much gratified by your approbation, though I know that your judgment, where I am concerned, is not quite impartial. The reception of my book here has been far more favourable than, in my most sanguine moments, I had expected. I have as yet heard little from the Continent: but the little that I have heard is encouraging. I attach great importance to the verdict of foreigners: for it indicates what the verdict of posterity is likely to be.

Thank God, I have done for ever with public business, and am free to enjoy letters and the society of those whom I love without any restraint. I have determined to fix my abode in a place which seems to have been made for me. On the same rising ground on which Holland House stands, and at the distance of perhaps two hundred yards from that dear old building is a villa with two acres of turf and flowerbed, called Holly Lodge. Even at this season it looks pretty; and in the summer I shall be able to hide myself among my rosebushes and to imagine that I am in a rural solitude, though in truth I shall be only two miles from Hyde Park Corner. I have ample room for ten thousand volumes, good air, a good gravel soil, and good water. I may add good neighbours: for the Duke[2] and Duchess of Argyle, whose grounds are divided by a paling from mine, are excellent people. Here I hope to breathe more freely than in this great cloud of river fog and sea coal. How glad I shall be to have a walk with you on the grass before my library window; and I will not suffer myself to doubt that this pleasure is in store for me.

Ever affectionately yours,
T B Macaulay

[1] Everett's earlier letter arrived on 13 February with 'two copies of my book printed in America – the best and the meanest editions' (Journal, IX, 86).

[2] George Douglas Campbell (1823–1900: *DNB*), eighth Duke of Argyll; an active Whig politician, a notable Parliamentary orator, and an amateur naturalist. After his move to Holly Lodge TBM saw a good deal of his neighbor the Duke. Cockburn described him in 1852 as 'a very singular youth, studious, thoughtful, benevolent, and ambitious. Without the least forwardness, he is always ready both with the pen and the tongue. . . . The only thing I cannot forgive him for is his small stature' (*Journal*, II, 276–7).

TO ALFRED EDWARD CHALON,[1] 25 FEBRUARY 1856

Text: S. M. Ellis, ed., *Unpublished Letters of Lady Bulwer Lytton to A. E. Chalon, R.A.*, 1914, p. 311.

February 25, 1856.

Sir,

I am very sensible of your kindness and shall be most happy to see you when we are neighbours. I hope I shall be able to dispense with the service of a yard dog![2] / I have the honour to be,

Your faithful friend,[3]
T. B. Macaulay.

TO LORD STANHOPE, 27 FEBRUARY 1856

MS: Stanhope Papers, Chevening.

Albany Feby. 27. 1856

My dear Stanhope,

I have seen Owen.[4] He had tears in his eyes, and brought tears into mine. I was touched by learning that a great natural philosopher, whose name is mentioned with honor at Petersburg, Florence, Philadelphia, should be growing old in distress and anxiety. What he asks would, in my judgment, be not merely a boon to himself, but a great public benefit.

He knows that he has no chance of the Principal Librarianship.[5] That place, he is aware, is disposed of. But he asks whether the government might not be induced to do something like what was recommended by the Commission, – to appoint a new officer with the general superintendence of the various departments of Natural History?[6] He does not demand to be put on a footing of equality with the Principal Librarian, who would still be the head of the House, and the organ of communication with the trustees. If such an office should be created, Owen would certainly be the very man for it. He would be delighted to give his services for 800£ a

[1] Chalon (1780–1860: *DNB*), R.A., was a fashionable portrait artist; he lived in a house called 'El Retiro' on Campden Hill.

[2] But he did get one: see 25 December 1856.

[3] TBM certainly never wrote 'friend,' but an editor might.

[4] He called on TBM this day about the 'possibility of doing something for him in the Museum' (Journal, IX, 112). Sir Henry Ellis, the Principal Librarian of the Museum, had just resigned.

[5] It went to Panizzi.

[6] This was the arrangement adopted – it had been recommended by the Royal Commission on the British Museum of 1847–9 – and Owen was appointed Superintendent of the Natural History Departments on 13 March (Edward Miller, *Prince of Librarians*, 1967, p. 272).

year without a house. Such an income, he declares, is the highest worldly good that he ventures even to desire. Surely his skill and knowledge would be very cheaply purchased at that rate. It seems to me also that such an arrangement would, – to say nothing of other advantages, – be a popular one, and would do much to quiet the clamour which Panizzi's promotion can hardly fail to raise.[1]

I have written to the Chancellor of the Exchequer.[2] If you see this matter in the light in which I see it, I wish that you would speak or write to the Archbishop. I really think that the welfare of the Museum and the honor of the country, as well as the happiness of a very eminent and deserving man, are concerned.

Ever yours truly,
T B Macaulay

I sent Owen straight to Murchison who is probably by this time dancing with excitement.

TO SIR GEORGE CORNEWALL LEWIS, 27 FEBRUARY 1856

MS: National Library of Wales.

Albany Feby. 27. 1856

Dear Lewis,

It is, I suppose, certain that Panizzi will be Principal Librarian and Secretary of the Museum. In many respects the appointment will be an excellent one; and from regard for him I rejoice at his good fortune. But you cannot be ignorant that he has many enemies; and I apprehend that there will be a great outcry. You might, I think, allay the ill feeling which his promotion is likely to produce, and, at the same time, render a great service to the Museum and to science, at a small expense, by taking a course which was recommended some years ago by the Commission. There certainly ought to be an officer charged with the general Superintendence of the scientific departments. Owen is the very man for such a situation. I am quite confident that if his services were secured, as they might be by a salary of 800£ a year, the public and the House of Commons would applaud the arrangement. It is, I must say, a scandal that a

[1] It raised some but not much: 'Criticism of Panizzi's appointment quickly faded to half-hearted sniping in obscure periodicals' (Miller, *Prince of Librarians*, p. 220); but there had been much public criticism of Panizzi before the appointment (*ibid.* p. 215). TBM's choice for the position was J. M. Kemble, but the objection to Kemble's drunkenness was unanswerable (Journal, IX, 104: 23 February).

[2] Sir George Cornewall Lewis: see next letter.

person whose fame is so great throughout Europe should be in need of such a provision.

I earnestly beg you to consider this matter. I hardly know Owen; and I have all my life neglected too much those branches of knowledge in which he excels. But the welfare of the Museum and the credit of the country are at stake; and I should be deeply concerned if this opportunity of placing the national museum of physical science under the care of a philosopher worthy of such a trust were suffered to pass away.[1]

Ever yours truly,
T B Macaulay

TO LORD STANHOPE, 29 FEBRUARY 1856

MS: Stanhope Papers, Chevening.

Albany February 29. 1856

My dear Stanhope,

I do not think that you understand Lewis's answer correctly; and you will be of the same opinion when you have read the inclosed letter which I received from him this morning. I have written to Lord Lansdowne to beg him to lend a helping hand. What I propose may, as Lewis says, be done without any authority from Parliament. It is important that the Archbishop should understand this.

If we fail, we must, as you say, do what we can do to get Owen a pension.

Ever yours truly,
T B Macaulay

TO LORD LANSDOWNE, 29 FEBRUARY 1856

MS: The Marquess of Lansdowne. *Partly published:* Trevelyan, II, 439–41.

Albany February 29. 1856

Dear Lord Lansdowne,

I venture to ask for your good offices in a matter which much concerns the interests of the British Museum and the honor of the country.

It is, I apprehend, certain that Panizzi will be appointed Secretary and Principal Librarian. I am glad of this both on public and private grounds. Yet I fear that the appointment will be unpopular both within and without the walls of the Museum. There is a growing jealousy among men of

[1] On 2 March TBM learned from Lewis that this letter 'was read in the cabinet yesterday, and generally approved' (Journal, IX, 121–2).

science which, between ourselves, appears even at the board of Trustees. There is a notion that the department of Natural History is neglected, and that the library and sculpture gallery are unduly favoured. This feeling will certainly not be allayed by the appointment of Panizzi, whose great object, during many years, has been to make our library the best in Europe, and who would at any time give three mammoths for an Aldus. The Royal Commissioners recommended an arrangement to which there would have been grave objections. They proposed that there should be two equal Chiefs of the Museum, – two Consuls, – one for literature and antiquities, the other for Natural History. It was determined, and, I think, wisely determined not to take this course. But I cannot help thinking that something of the kind ought to be done; and there is now an excellent opportunity.

What I propose is that Owen should be appointed Superintendent of the whole department of Natural history, including geology, zoology, mineralogy, and botany. He should be subordinate to the Principal Librarian, so that there would be no danger of the inconveniences which an Institution governed by two equal heads can scarcely fail to experience.

I cannot but think that this arrangement would be beneficial in the highest degree to the Museum. I am sure that it would be popular. I must add that I am extremely desirous that something should be done for Owen. I hardly know him to speak to. His pursuits are not mine. But his fame is spread over Europe. He is an honor to our country; and it is painful to me to think that a man of his merit should be approaching old age amidst anxieties and distresses. He told me, with tears in his eyes, that eight hundred a year, without a house in the Museum, would be opulence to him. He did not, he said, even wish for more. His seems to me to be a case for public patronage. Such patronage is not needed by eminent literary men or artists. A poet, a novellist, a historian, a painter, a sculptor, who stood in his own line as high as Owen stands among men of science, could never be in want except by his own fault. But the greatest natural philosopher may starve, while his countrymen are boasting of his discoveries, and while foreign Academies are begging for the honor of being allowed to add his name to their lists.

I feel this so strongly that I have written to the Chancellor of the Exchequer on the subject. He quite agrees with me, and has promised to speak to Lord Palmerston. Lord Stanhope is zealous in the cause, and has written to the Archbishop. If you take the same view, I should hope that you would have no objection to lend a helping hand. At any rate, pardon this long letter. / Ever, dear Lord Lansdowne,

Yours most truly,
T B Macaulay

TO RICHARD MONCKTON MILNES, 1 MARCH 1856

MS: Trinity College.

Albany March 1. 1856

Dear Milnes,

I ought to have sent you an excuse. But really it was not till a quarter past ten that I made up my mind not to venture to you. I will call the first fine morning.

Ever yours,
T B Macaulay

TO LORD STANHOPE, 3 MARCH 1856

MS: Stanhope Papers, Chevening.

Albany March 3. 1856

My dear Stanhope,

I am truly sorry that I cannot breakfast with you. The wind and the fog oppress me grievously.

I really hope that we shall be able to manage this matter at the Museum. The Chancellor of the Exchequer called here yesterday afternoon and told me that there would be no difficulty on the part of the government. We are likely, I rejoice to find, to get rid of Hawkins.[1] Either Birch[2] or Newton[3] would be a good successor.

I am truly glad that we are to have Gladstone[4] for a colleague.

Ever yours truly
T B Macaulay

[1] He had this news from Lewis too. Hawkins did not finally retire until 1860.

[2] Samuel Birch (1813–85: *DNB*), assistant to Hawkins since 1844; on the reorganization of the Department of Antiquities following Hawkins' departure Birch became Keeper of Oriental Antiquities.

[3] (Sir) Charles Newton (1816–94: *DNB*), archaeologist, formerly on the Museum staff and now in the consular service; he returned to the Museum as Keeper of Greek and Roman Antiquities in 1861.

[4] He was appointed in this year.

TO [THOMAS LONGMAN], 3 MARCH 1856

MS: Trinity College.

Albany March 3. 1856

My dear Sir,

I have corrected the third Volume for a second edition.[1] I should be glad, when it suits you, to have a word with you about the corrections. I am close prisoner till the wind changes.

Ever yours truly,
T B Macaulay

TO HENRY THORNTON, 7 MARCH 1856

MS: Longman Group Ltd.

Albany March 7. 1856

Dear Thornton,

I expect that, in a very few days, twenty thousand pounds will be paid into your house, on my account, by the Longmans.[2] A tolerable sum to have cleared in less than three months. I wish you to add a thousand pounds to the balance in your hands, as I shall soon be forced to draw largely on you for the expenses of my removal. About the disposal of the remaining nineteen thousand pounds, I shall need your kind and most judicious counsel. But, as some time may pass before I can decide how I will permanently invest the whole, I shall be obliged to you to put the whole, as soon as you receive it, into the 3 per Cents in my name.

This horrible East wind keeps me close prisoner. But, on so important an occasion, I shall try to find my way to the City soon.

Ever yours truly
T B Macaulay

1 The second edition was scheduled to appear 'after the trade sales of April' (Journal, IX, 125: 4 March). But according to Longman's records there was a printing of 2,000 copies of volumes 3 and 4 in January and none thereafter until October 1856, when a further 1,000 was printed.

2 Longman called on this day: 'He and his partners find that they are overflowing with money and think that they cannot invest it better than by advancing to me, on the usual terms of course, part of what will be due to me in December. We agreed that they shall pay twenty thousand pounds into Williams's Bank next week' (Journal, in Trevelyan, II, 410). Trevelyan adds that the 'cheque is still preserved as a curiosity among the archives of Messrs. Longman's firm.' It is still there.

TO THOMAS FLOWER ELLIS, 11 MARCH 1856

MS: Trinity College. *Extract published:* Trevelyan, II, 410.

Albany London March 11 / 1856

Dear Ellis,

I am still busy with upholsterers, linendrapers, silversmiths and dealers in China. My servants are all engaged. Hannah has chosen carpets and curtains for the rooms which require such articles, and has chosen, in my opinion, with great taste. I shall enter into possession on Monday next. Rawlinson has played me a pretty trick. After asking me to leave him my book cases, and thus inducing me to order a perfectly new set, he writes to say that he has changed his mind, and does not know that he shall take the chambers at all. He offers to pay for my new book cases: but that of course is an offer which it would not become me to accept; so that I shall be a loser of at least 200£ by his vacillation. However I shall now have a right to laugh at his theories about Nineveh and Ecbatana without restraint. Confound his winged bulls and cuneiform characters!

As some small set off against this loss, I am glad to tell you that on Thursday 20000£ are to be paid into my banker's hands by the Longmans. The payment need not have been made till December: but the Longmans are flush of money, and thought that they could not invest it better than by clearing off a debt, and getting nine months' discount. The transaction is quite unparalleled in the history of the book trade; and both the people at Smith Payne and Smith's who are to pay the money and my friends who are to receive it have been much amused. I went into the City to day to give instructions, and was most warmly congratulated on being a great moneyed man. I said that I had some thoughts of going to the Chancellor of the Exchequer as a bidder for the next loan. In the meantime I have given orders for investing nineteen thousand pounds in a way which will bring up my certain income to three thousand a year,[1] and leave a balance of two thousand five hundred at my banker's. My arms therefore are dangling in a most significant way; and, if the sight of them should affect you as the sight of Vellum's arms affected Tinsel,[2] I hope that you will imitate Tinsel's frankness.[3]

On Thursday week, if the weather be tolerable, I should make a short tour with the Trevelyans. We shall go first to Rochester, pass Good

[1] The 'certain income' is exclusive, TBM notes in his Journal, of 'a *casuel*, which, judging from the experience of the last seven years, I should estimate at not less than 1500£ a year. I am therefore a very opulent man' (IX, 124–5: 4 March).

[2] Addison, *The Drummer*, IV: 'Thou'rt confounded rich, I see, by that dangling of thine arms.'

[3] TBM was concerned about Ellis's financial difficulties: see 16 March.

Friday there, go to Canterbury on the Saturday, attend the service in the Cathedral on Sunday, and return on Easter Monday.

I meditate a longer tour for the autumn. I mean to run across France to Marseilles, to go to Genoa by the cornice, and to see the principal cities of northern Italy which are accessible by railway. In a fortnight one can see Milan, Vicenza, Verona, Padua and Venice. Then I think of returning by the lake of Como, by the sublime pass of St Gothard, and by Zurich, to our old friend Basle. Thence there is railway to Boulogne. I shall be grievously disappointed and vexed if I have not your company in this expedition. Franz, of course, if he is to be had.

Ever yours
T B Macaulay

TO SIR HENRY RAWLINSON, 11 MARCH 1856

MS: Mr Joseph Hamburger.

Albany March 11. / 1856

Dear Sir Henry Rawlinson,

The person to whom you ought to apply about these chambers is Mr. E A Sanford of 77 Pall Mall.

Perhaps the most convenient arrangement would be that I should surrender my lease, and that you should have another from Midsummer next. You and I could settle between us for the rent from April 21[1] to Midsummer. But this as you please. / Believe me

Yours very truly
T B Macaulay

Sir H Rawlinson / etc. etc. etc.

TO [HERMANN HETTNER],[2] 13[3] MARCH 1856

MS: Huntington Library. *Published: Catalogue* of the Alfred Morrison Collection, IV, 4.

Albany London / March 13. 1856

Sir,

My friend Sir Henry Holland sent me, a few hours ago, your volume

1 When TBM hoped to be in Holly Lodge (Journal, IX, 109: 25 February).

2 Hettner (1821–82), Professor in the Dresden Academy of Fine Arts, had just published the first volume of his *Literaturgeschichte des Achtzehnten Jahrhunderts*, Braunschweig, 1856–70, treating English literature from 1660 to 1770; it is item 430 in the sale catalogue of TBM's library.

3 In his Journal TBM records this letter on 12 March (IX, 145).

and your very obliging letter. I read German, but not very rapidly; and it will, I am afraid, be some time before I shall have leisure to peruse your book connectedly. I have looked at several passages, which suffice to show that your knowledge of our literature is such as only very curious students among ourselves [possess].[1]

With sincere thanks for your courtesy and kindness, I have the honor to be, / Sir,

Your faithful Servant
T B Macaulay

TO THOMAS FLOWER ELLIS, 16 MARCH 1856

MS: Trinity College.

Albany March 16. 1856

Dear Ellis,

I am not going to change my abode quite so soon as you seem to think. I come into possession of Holly Lodge to morrow. But near a month of whitewashing, bricklayer's work and carpenter's work must be done before I move. My new book cases will be up in little more than a week. All that I hear is greatly in favour of the place. The air, water, soil, are all pronounced excellent both by medical men and by the families which live on the spot; and my bargain is spoken of as a remarkably good one.

I was much amused by your account of Preston's[2] achievements. He seems to be a perfect Satyr – Nympharum fugientum Amator.[3]

I shall be sorry if you cannot go with me to Italy. If Walter really requires your tuition in the autumn, there is nothing more to be said. But I cannot admit the validity of your other reason. I am quite sure that you will yourself feel, on reflection, how unwise it would be, and how unworthy of a man of your abilities and principles, to sink into dejection, and to turn away with disgust from the beauties of nature, the masterpieces of art and the remains of antiquity, because every thing in this capricious lottery of life does not go as you could wish.[4] You know how

1 'I wrote a short civil letter to the author, praising, as I could with truth praise, his knowledge of our writers, but saying nothing about his taste and his judgment' (Journal, IX, 145).

2 There were two Prestons on the Northern Circuit at this time: Charles James, of 1 Mitre Court Buildings, and William Thomas, of 2 Fig Tree Court (*Law List*, 1857); one or the other was the hero of the 'strange circuit story' that TBM received from Ellis on 12 March (Journal, IX, 146).

3 Horace, *Odes*, III, xviii, 1.

4 Ellis had been anxious about money matters for some time. On 3 February TBM learned from Ellis that the sale of Law Reports, on which Ellis apparently depended for a good part of his income, was down (Journal, IX, 65); on 21 February TBM wrote penitentially in his

sincerely I feel for you. And you will not suspect me of speaking from any want of tenderness for your anxieties. But, for God's sake, do not make the evil ten times as great as it is by moping and pining and eating your heart. Remember how happy a man you are at the very worst – competence – security as to the prospects of your children – an attached family, affectionate friends who only wish to know how they can serve you, – an unsullied character, and all the enjoyments of the intellect – surely these are blessings of which you ought to think more. I forgot to mention health. But I assure you that I am much more inclined to envy you your lungs and limbs than to pity your misfortunes. Therefore *sursum corda*. Do not give those who love and value you the pain of thinking that your spirits are broken by a mishap which does not blemish your honor, which does not wound your affections, which leaves all your powers of body and mind unimpaired, and which does not deprive you of the means of living in the enjoyment of every comfort. The case is not one which requires the higher remedies of religion and philosophy. It is a case as Juvenal says

"Multis cognitus, et jam
Tritus, et e medio fortunae ductus acervo."[1]

It would be unbecoming in a man like you not to meet ill luck of this sort with fortitude and even with cheerfulness. I am quite confident that I have not written a word on this subject which Marian would not subscribe. I only wish that you would speak to her with perfect frankness. I am certain that she would see the matter exactly as I do. / Ever my dear fellow

Yours affectionately

T B Macaulay

TO SELINA MACAULAY, 19 MARCH 1856

MS: Trinity College.

Albany London / March 19. 1856

Dearest Selina,

I have ordered my bankers to pay every quarter-day, beginning at

Journal, after the excitement of his £20,000 payment from Longmans, that he was 'sad and anxious' about Ellis: 'I feel much for him, and the more because I am afraid that, before I knew of his vexations, I exulted in my own recent prosperity in a way which must have hurt him' (IX, 101–2). TBM also feared that Walter Ellis, at Cambridge, might be a drain on his father (*ibid.*, 103). On 30 June TBM gave Ellis £600, which Ellis had repaid by December 1858 (Journal, XI, 16; 404).

1 *Satires*, XIII, 9–10: 'Such a mishap has been known to many; it is one of the common kind, plucked at random out of Fortune's heap' (Loeb Library translation).

Lady day next week, fifty pounds into the Bank of Hall West and Co at Brighton to your credit. I hope that this arrangement will suit you. It will insure punctuality, whether I happen to be in England or abroad.

I have just seen Fanny. She does not give quite so good an account of you as I could wish. But I hope that fine weather is coming to set you up.

Ever yours,
T B Macaulay

TO THOMAS FLOWER ELLIS, 24 MARCH 1856

MS: Trinity College.

Albany London / March 24. 1856

Dear Ellis,

I have been with the Trevelyans to Rochester and Canterbury, and am here again, not at all the worse for a very pleasant tour.[1] I had to take great care of myself, and did not venture to attend the service in either Cathedral.[2] Canterbury is a most curious and interesting place. If you do not know it, we will run down thither some day.

To day I take possession; and the next three weeks will be three weeks of confusion. By the end of that time, I hope, your room will be ready, and my kitchen fire will be blazing. Meanwhile I can settle to no hard work. But I have promised Black an article on Johnson for the Encyclopædia; and this I think a good opportunity for performing the promise.[3]

Bunbury[4] – hang him – has sent to ask me to subscribe for the expenses of Denman's election.[5] I shall do so. But I really think that, when a young

1 They went to Rochester on the 20th, to Canterbury on the 22nd, where they spent Easter Sunday, the 23rd, and returned to London on the 24th (Journal, IX, 152–9). At Rochester they read aloud the Rochester sections of *Pickwick*.

2 At Canterbury cathedral the cold was so intense that TBM put on his hat, to which their guide objected, saying that 'Archdeacon Harrison's orders were positive. A fool!' (Journal, IX, 156). Harrison was the husband of TBM's old Clapham contemporary, Isabella Thornton.

3 TBM began the article on 8 April and finished it on 30 July, in the confusion between his leaving the Albany and settling in Holly Lodge (Journal, IX, 187; XI, 29). Volume 12 of the *Encyclopaedia Britannica* containing it was published in early December.

4 (Sir) Edward Herbert Bunbury (1811–95: *Boase*), B.A., Trinity, 1833, where he was Senior Classic and Chancellor's Medallist; M.P. for Bury St Edmunds, 1847–52.

5 George Denman (1819–96: *DNB*), fourth son of Lord Denman, B.A. and Fellow of Trinity; he stood for election at Cambridge University against Spencer Walpole after the death of Goulburn. At the poll in February the undergraduates created serious disturbances and Denman withdrew after a three-day contest (Winstanley, *Early Victorian Cambridge*, pp. 418–20). TBM was one of Denman's committee, together with Ellis, Frank Ellis, and John Kemble (Journal, IX, 73).

man stands uninvited, he should pay his own expenses. I shall certainly think twice before I consent to be on his Committee again.

Of course you have seen the articles on your Indian Commission in the Times.[1] I suppose that they are Lowe's,[2] – or that, at all events, he got them admitted. I am surprised at the civility with which I am mentioned.[3]

When shall you be in town again?

Ever yours,
T B Macaulay

TO LORD LYTTELTON,[4] 24 MARCH 1856

MS: University of Newcastle.

Albany London / March 24. 1856

Dear Lord Lyttelton,

Thanks for your kind letter and for your interesting lecture.[5] I will not enter into any discussion of the questions which you have treated: for, if I begin to write about them, I shall never have done. I hope that we may, some day, have an opportunity of talking them over.

Ever yours truly,
T B Macaulay

1 19 and 24 March, reviewing the Reports of the Commission just published.

2 Robert Lowe (1811–92: *DNB*), afterwards first Viscount Sherbrooke, first practiced as a barrister in Australia. He returned to England in 1850, wrote leading articles for *The Times* for many years, and entered Parliament in 1852. After holding minor offices from 1852, he was Gladstone's Chancellor of the Exchequer, 1868–73, and Home Secretary, 1873–4. As Secretary to the Board of Control under Sir Charles Wood, Lowe had worked with TBM in the matter of the Indian Civil Service examinations; TBM, in common with everyone else, thought him 'clever' (Journal, VI, 26: 27 January 1853). Lowe was a member of the Commission on the Laws of India.

3 'Years of oppression and injustice have gone by, the whole face of English politics is altered, and yet for the people of India Mr. Macaulay's wonderful Penal Code is still a dead letter' (24 March).

4 George William Lyttelton (1817–76: *DNB*), fourth Baron Lyttelton; B.A., Trinity College, Cambridge; a scholar, he was both Chancellor's Medallist and Senior Classic and later published a volume of translations with his brother-in-law, Gladstone. He was active in promoting popular education, and in colonial affairs.

5 'A Few Thoughts about Shakspeare,' privately printed, Stourbridge, 1855; a presentation copy of this is item 806 in the sale catalogue of TBM's library. The lecture, a discussion of the excellences and defects of Shakespeare as a poet, quotes the 'magnificent sentence in which Mr. Macaulay notices the signal exception of Milton to the impurity of his age' (p. 42).

TO THOMAS FLOWER ELLIS, 29 MARCH 1856

MS: Trinity College.

Albany London / March 29. 1856

Dear Ellis,

I shall be glad to see you again. Dinner shall be ready for you at half past seven next Thursday, unless I hear to the contrary from you. Our dinners here will be but few. I cannot fix the exact time of my migration. But I think that it will be about the 20th of next month. I find that I must have a dog, or rather a bitch, a little, sharp, yelping terrier, to deter those whom my old master Preston used, in his evening prayer, to describe as "the Sons of Violence and Plunder." Àpropos of dogs, I have just picked up a French novel by Paul Féval, in which there is a charming Englishwoman, Miladi Ophélie Dog.[1] Àpropos again of dogs, I shall certainly not take any notice of Mr. Hepworth or Hebworth Dixon.[2] He is a great fool. I should have thought that you must have heard of the two Penns – the Menæchmi. That point was raised five or six years ago. I still believe in my own twin. But I allow that there is something to be said on the other side. This is absolutely the only issue in the controversy which bears dispute. If people doubt, they doubt only because they will not take the trouble to examine with care the authorities to which I have referred them.

I am delighted with the tone of your letter. I most readily admit that you have had in one or two respects very bad luck. At Cambridge you are still mentioned as the best scholar that did not get a medal: and by lawyers you are mentioned as the ablest man in your profession who has not risen high. But, let the worst come to the worst, you are quite sure, I think, of a life income of two thousand a year. Your children are decently provided for. As to any extraordinary call, there are a thousand pounds, which I shall never miss, lying ready for you at a day's notice. My chief anxiety is about Walter. All that I hear of him is favourable. But I look forward with some trepidation to the Summer examination.[3]

[1] Probably Féval's *Les Bandits de Londres*, 1847, which TBM was reading in April (Journal, IX, 193; 203). I have not been able to see the book.

[2] A new edition of Dixon's *Penn* (see *to* Frances Macaulay, 14 April 1851) was published in February with a preface complaining of TBM's failure to respond to the arguments of the original edition of the book. When TBM learned of what Dixon had written he wrote: 'He will go to his grave with that grievance' (Journal, IX, 105: 23 February). He also determined not to buy the book: 'I shall not buy such rubbish' (IX, 107). But *The Times*, 26 March, reviewing the case between TBM and Dixon, concluded that TBM owed his critic an answer; and so, finally, did TBM. He had the book sent to him when he was writing the long footnote to the *History* on Penn (see 28 October 1856) which is his last word on the subject (Journal XI, 50: 22 October 1856).

[3] Walter went from bad to worse. TBM called on him in Cambridge in April in the room that

I have changed my mind about Denman, and shall not give a farthing. I find that he is very well off; and it seems to me quite monstrous that men like you, far his superiors in ability and learning, much his seniors, and not so rich as he is, should be expected to bear the charges of a foolish enterprise, about which you were never consulted, of which you have already borne much of the trouble, and of which, if it had succeeded, he would have had all the fruits. I repeat that I shall give nothing.

Ever yours
T B M

TO HENRY BOWIE, 29 MARCH 1856

MS: Edinburgh Central Public Library.

Albany London / March 29. 1856

Dear Sir,

You do me no more than justice in supposing that I should be truly glad to be able to render any service to the Philosophical Institution. But I am afraid that I can be of no use to you. Consider that the task which you wish M. Guizot to undertake is nothing less than that of preparing and delivering a course of lectures in a foreign language, a language which he reads indeed as easily as if it were his own, but which he never writes or speaks when he can avoid it. In my conversations and correspondence with him, I always use English, and he uses French. He can indeed speak English, and that very well; but not without effort. Now it seems hardly reasonable to ask a man of his eminence, who is also well known not to be a rich man, and whose time is valuable in the light of property, to make a present of the labour of months, – for it can hardly be less, – to the inhabitants of a foreign city with which he has no connection. You very properly say that the charge of his journey ought to be borne by the Institution. But the charge of his journey would be the smallest part of the charge. And his spirit is so high, and his delicacy about money matters so great, that I, at least, should not venture to hint anything to him on that subject.

All that I can do is to write to him, and to tell him, as I can with truth,

had once been Stainforth's and then Malden's: 'But W E had furnished it much better than his predecessors – too well indeed, all things considered' (Journal, IX, 194–5). In June, after Walter had been placed in the second class by the summer examinations, TBM wrote: 'I fear that he will do nothing' (Journal, XI, 11: 17 June). In the next year TBM got 'a bad account of the set in which Walter lives – idle – unintellectual – frivolous – nothing but smoking and talking ribaldry' (XI, 109–10: 25 April 1857). After leaving Cambridge, Walter went to India and then to New Zealand, where he died, aged thirty-nine, an alcoholic.

that the body which invites him to Edinburgh is most respectable, that his compliance would be felt as a great obligation, and that his reception would be in the highest degree honorable. The rest of the negotiation I must leave to others.

I am glad to hear so good an account of the state of our affairs, and am most sensible of the kindness of the members of the Institution. That kindness has indeed never varied. I only wish that it were better merited. / Believe me, / Dear Sir,

Yours very truly,
T B Macaulay

H Bowie Esq / etc. etc. etc.

TO [HERBERT FRY],[1] 3 APRIL 1856

MS: National Portrait Gallery.

Albany April 3. 1856

Sir,

I have forgotten the number of the House in Gracechurch Street.[2] If you will let me know it, I will try to call between eleven and twelve on Monday, unless the weather should be bad on that day. / I have the honor to be, / Sir,

Your obedient Servant,
T B Macaulay

[1] Fry (1830–85: *Boase*), author of numerous guides and compilations, and later Secretary of the Pall Mall Club, was editing a series of photographic portraits of celebrities accompanied by biographical sketches. That of TBM was published under the title 'Photographic Portraits of Living Celebrities Executed by Maull and Polyblank. No. 2, June, 1856, Price 5s.' (copy, National Portrait Gallery). The photograph, showing TBM at three-quarter length standing, and resting on a table a book held in his right hand, is the frontispiece to Black's edition of the *Biographies*, 1860, and, variously engraved, has often been published – e.g., *Illustrated London News*, 7 January 1860. TBM, as usual, did not care for the picture, calling it 'hideous . . . ugly beyond all names of ugliness' (Journal, IX, 207: 21 April).

[2] The photographers Maull and Polyblank were at 55 Gracechurch Street. TBM did not enjoy the sitting: 'I had to climb to the top of a house in Grace Church Street – half the height of the monument. Then I was smothered and stunk to death with æther and other chemical abominations. I was hard put to it to keep my temper' (Journal, IX, 185: 7 April). This is apparent from the photograph.

TO BISHOP SAMUEL WILBERFORCE, 9 APRIL 1856

MS: National Library of Scotland.

Albany London / April 9. 1856

My dear Bishop of Oxford,

Mrs. Walker[1] is a very proper object of charity. Her brother was a man of great abilities and attainments, and was, as she says, kindly assisted by your father. I return her papers.

This fine weather has had a reviving effect on me. I am about to leave my chambers for a house which I have taken on Campden Hill, next to the Duke of Argyle's, where we had a pleasant breakfast last summer.

Ever yours truly,
T B Macaulay

TO FRANCES MACAULAY, 12 APRIL 1856

MS: Trinity College.

Albany April 12. 1856

Dearest Fanny,

I am not sure that the Life of Sydney Smith is at the Albany. I rather think that it is among the books which are lying at a warehouse till my new bookcases are ready. If I have the volume it shall be sent to Westbourne Terrace.

I shall hardly be settled in my new quarters till May.

I have some recollection of the lines on Buchanan.[2] Very poor they were. Pray do not show such
[. . . . .][3]
the kind were destroyed. Nothing lowers a man so much as the preserving and parading of such puerilities. Love
[. . . .][3]

1 The sister of TBM's old Trinity acquaintance William Sidney Walker, who died destitute in 1846, and who had been encouraged, in vain, by the elder Wilberforce at the beginning of the religious doubts that ultimately led Walker to resign his Trinity fellowship. On 2 February of this year TBM had sent £10 to 'the sister of poor Sidney Walker' (Journal, IX, 61); on 14 June 1857 he sent 'Ten pounds to poor Mrs. Walker' (XI, 131); and in March 1859, £20 (XI, 455).

2 Not identified; perhaps they were written on the death of Claudius Buchanan in 1815: see 27 June 1834.

3 The top third of the second leaf has been torn away for the signature, taking about three lines on the recto.

TO UNIDENTIFIED RECIPIENT, 16 APRIL 1856

MS: Nationa lLibrary of Scotland.

Albany April 16. 1856

My dear Sir,

Mr. Donne[1] would be an excellent Registrar, and I should be glad to serve him. But I think myself bound to give my vote to Professor Heaviside,[2] who is, I believe, not less fit for the post which he solicits than Mr. Donne, and who has a peculiarly strong claim on me. I am not acquainted with Professor Heaviside: but I know him to be a man of great merit; and he is about to be removed from a comfortable situation, not for any fault of his, but in consequence of an arrangement which I, on public grounds, felt it to be my duty to urge on the government.[3] I am therefore naturally desirous to make him amends, as far as I justly can. It is possible that I may find that Professor Heaviside has no chance. Should this be the case, there is no candidate, as far as I am aware, whom I should prefer to Mr. Donne.[4]

Very truly yours
T B Macaulay

TO I. LIST,[5] 21 APRIL 1856

MS: New York Public Library. *Envelope:* I List Esq / 12 Cecil Street / Strand. *Subscription:* T B M.

Albany April 21 / 1856

Sir,

Mr. Einhorn is not justified in saying that I have given any special sanction to his translation.[6] I told him that I should permit everybody

1 William Bodham Donne (1807–82: *DNB*), then librarian of the London Library, succeeded John Mitchell Kemble as examiner of plays in the Lord Chamberlain's office in 1857. He was now in competition (unsuccessfully) for the position of Registrar of the University of London.

2 James Heaviside (1808–97: *Boase*), Professor of Mathematics at Haileybury, 1838–57; examiner in mathematics for the University of London, 1843–60, and for the Council of Military Education from 1858: Canon of Norwich Cathedral from 1860.

3 In consequence of the new standards of qualification for the Indian Civil Service introduced by open competitive examination, Haileybury, where boys appointed through patronage were prepared by the East India Company, had lost its usefulness; it was closed at the end of 1857.

4 The appointment went to William Benjamin Carpenter (1813–85: *DNB*).

5 A clerk in the Leipzig publishing house of Weigel. He had called on TBM on 17 April, bringing the translation by Prof. Friedrich Bülau of TBM's *History*, vols. 3 and 4, published by his firm.

6 I have not identified Einhorn. On 7 April TBM wrote that 'six translations of my new Vols

who chose to translate my book. He asked for a more special authorisation, and I refused it. / I have the honor to be, / Sir,

Your obedient Servant,
T B Macaulay

TO CHRISTOPHER WALTON,[1] 21 APRIL 1856

MS: Dr Williams's Library. *Envelope:* C Walton Esq / 9 Southwood Terrace / Highgate. *Subscription:* T B M.

Albany April 21. 1856

Sir,

I retain a very lively and pleasing recollection of my grandfather, and have a great respect for his memory. He was a truly excellent man. His M.S.S. I well remember. Indeed I heard him read much more from them than, in my boyish days, I at all wished to hear. I have, since that time, become pretty well acquainted with the works of some of his favourite divines. But my estimate of them by no means agrees with his. To me therefore his M.S.S. would have been of little value. I am truly glad that they have fallen into the hands of one whom he would have thought worthy to possess such a treasure. I beg you to accept my thanks for your courtesy and kindness, and to believe me, / Sir,

Your faithful Servant,
T B Macaulay

C Walton Esq / etc. etc. etc.

into German are coming out at once' (Journal, IX, 186). They were those by Beseler, published at Braunschweig; by Lemcke at Braunschweig; by Paret at Stuttgart; by Rödiger and Kretzschmar at Vienna; by Bülau at Leipzig; and by an unidentified translator, also at Leipzig. Perhaps it was with this last that Einhorn was associated.

1 Walton (1809–77: *DNB*), a London jeweller and goldsmith, took up the theosophical writings of Law, Boehme, and Freher. He was led by his interest to the MSS of these writers collected by TBM's grandfather, Thomas Mills, and then in the possession of his son John, the Bristol editor. Having acquired the MSS, Walton wrote to TBM wishing to know 'whether I care about such theosophic lore, as he calls it. I answered him very civilly, but in a way to show that I was no follower of Jacob and Law' (Journal, IX, 209). The MSS are now in Dr Williams's Library, London.

TO RICHARD MONCKTON MILNES, 2[2][1] APRIL 1856

MS: Trinity College.

Albany April 21. 1856

Dear Milnes,

I hoped till this morning that I should have been able to join your party[2] to day as a spectator. But I find that some business which will take me out of town is likely to detain me till late. I send my cordial good wishes to you, to Mrs. Milnes and to the little girl.

Very truly yours
T B Macaulay

TO MRS HENRY HART MILMAN, 22 APRIL 1856

MS: McGill University.

Albany April 22 / 1856

Dear Mrs. Milman,

I fear that I was too sanguine when I hoped that I should be able to welcome my friends to my turf and flowers on the first of May. But on Wednesday the seventh of May I confidently expect to have every thing in order; and I do trust that you will condescend to grace my first breakfast party, and that the Dean will accompany you.[3]

Ever yours truly,
T B Macaulay

TO CHRISTIAN BERNHARD TAUCHNITZ, 29 APRIL 1856

Text: Bernhard Tauchnitz, 1837–1887, p. 110.

Albany, London, April 29, 1856.

I write two lines merely to inform you that I am changing my residence. Be so kind as to address your letters in future to me at Holly Lodge, Campden Hill, London.

[1] The date is given as 22 April in TBM's Journal, and this seems the more likely date; he went to Holly Lodge that day – 'out of town' – but had no engagement on the 21st.

[2] 'A lunch which he gives in honor of his child's christening' (Journal, IX, 210). The child was Milnes's second daughter, Florence.

[3] The guests were Hannah and Margaret, the Duke and Duchess of Argyll, Lord and Lady Stanhope, Lord Glenelg, the Bishop of Oxford, and Dean and Mrs Milman (Journal, IX, 245–6).

TO [EDWARD RUPERT HUMPHREYS],[1] [APRIL? 1856]

MS: Yale University.

[London]

[. . .] saying that there is only one Bishop in India. There have long been three, one for each presidency.

In page 15 you confound the Ameers of Scinde with the Sikhs. The Ameers were Mahometans, and quite as distinct from the Sikhs as France from Prussia. We had no war with the Sikhs till Hardinge's administration. You ought not to call Dwarkanauth Tagore[2] a high caste Hindoo. His ancestors lost caste in the days of Surajah Dowla; and he was a mere Pariah.

It is not correct to say that Metcalfe was superseded on account of his liberality. He was not superseded at all. He was appointed to govern India during the interval between Lord William's departure and Lord Auckland's arrival; and he did so. When Lord Auckland was sent out, nothing was known in England about those liberal acts which, no doubt, brought the disapprobation of the home authorities on Metcalfe.

In page 12, you are mistaken in supposing that the name and authority of the Rajah of Nagpore were extinguished by Lord Hastings. Appa Sahib was deposed: but a boy of ten years old, belonging to the reigning family, was declared Rajah; and, when I was in India, the state of Nagpore was in the same position with the other subsidiary states.

You had better, I think, revise this chapter carefully, and verify your statements.

Very truly yours,
T B Macaulay

[1] Humphreys (1820–93), headmaster of Cheltenham Grammar School, published a *Manual of British Government in India*, 2nd edn, 1857, based on an earlier version that TBM discusses in this letter. The result of TBM's remarks was that Humphreys tried to advertise the second edition of his *Manual* as 'revised and corrected by Lord Macaulay': see 28 October 1857, and Trevelyan, II, 453. I have tentatively dated the letter from TBM's reference in his Journal for 27 October 1857 that Humphreys had 'sent some trash about India more than eighteen months ago' (XI, 201). Humphreys says that the first edition of his book, which TBM describes as 'a small edition for the use of schools' (1 November 1858), appeared in 1855 (Preface to second edition): I have not found any other record of it.

[2] Dwarkanath Tagore (1794–1846), a Calcutta banker and philanthropist, prominent in the liberal Hindu community; he was the grandfather of the poet Rabindranath Tagore. A party at which he was host and TBM among the guests is described in the *Bengal Hurkaru*, 30 November 1836.

TO H. ALLEN,[1] 1 MAY 1856

MS: Mr F. R. Cowell.

Albany May 1. 1856

Sir,

I am much obliged to you for the extract which you have been so good as to send me. It is scarcely possible to turn over any collection of papers of 1695 or 1696 without coming across evidence of the state of the currency at that time. / I have the honor to be, / Sir,

Your obedient Servant

T B Macaulay

The Reverend H Allen / etc. etc. etc.

TO FRANCES MACAULAY, 10 MAY 1856

MS: Trinity College.

Holly Lodge / Campden Hill / May 10. 1856

Dearest Fanny,

Thanks for your kind letter. I am glad that you are able to make a new arrangement which, I think, must add to your comfort.

I am not quite settled.[2] I still hear hammering and sawing: there are mats to be laid down and bells to be hung; and the ungenial weather has not, till this morning, suffered me to enjoy my pretty garden. But I believe that, as far as comfort depends on rooms, furniture and grounds, I shall be very comfortable.

Hannah and her household are just about to move.[3] Their migration will, I imagine, be a less tedious and a less costly affair than mine. Love to Selina. You do not mention her health. I hope that I may infer that she is, at least, not worse than usual.

Ever yours,

T B Macaulay

[1] There are three H. Allens in the *Clergy List* at this time. I have no evidence to enable me to decide among them.

[2] TBM spent his first night at Holly Lodge on 2 May (Journal, IX, 237).

[3] The Trevelyans moved to 8 Grosvenor Crescent on 4 June (Journal, XI, 7).

TO MRS THOMAS DRUMMOND, 10 MAY 1856

MS: Huntington Library.

Holly Lodge, Campden Hill. / May 10. 1856

Dear Mrs. Drummond,

I will with great pleasure join your party on Tuesday the 27th.[1] By that time I hope that we shall have spring, if not summer.

Ever yours truly,
T B Macaulay

TO RICHARD MONCKTON MILNES, 12 MAY 1856

MS: Trinity College.

Holly Lodge Campden Hill / May 12. 1856

Dear Milnes,

I shall have much pleasure in breakfasting with you on Tuesday fortnight.[2] Can you breakfast here next Saturday at ten?[3]

Ever yours truly,
T B Macaulay

TO SYLVAIN VAN DE WEYER, 13 MAY 1856

MS: Bodleian Library.

Holly Lodge Campden Hill / May 13. 1856

My dear Van de Weyer,

Will you breakfast here at ten next Saturday? And will you do me the great favour to use your influence with Madame Van de Weyer for the purpose of inducing her to accompany you?[4] It would be a great pleasure and a great honor.

Ever yours truly
T B Macaulay

1 There is no evidence in the Journal that he did: he sprained his ankle on the 25th and seems not to have gone out again until the 30th (XI, 4).

2 See 26 May.

3 Milnes did not but Hannah, Margaret, Lord John Russell, Dundas, Hallam, Vernon Smith and his wife did (Journal, IX, 265).

4 The Van de Weyers did not come this time, but they were TBM's guests on the 28th: see 23 May, note.

TO HERBERT FRY, 13 MAY 1856

MS: National Portrait Gallery. *Extract published: Times Literary Supplement*, 18 September 1970, p. 1039.

Holly Lodge Campden Hill / May 13. 1856

Sir,

Everything about me which it concerns the public to know[1] may be found in the Cambridge Calendar, in Beatson's Political Index,[2] in the Parliamentary History, and in my own writings. I have no objection to add that I was born on the 25th of October 1800 at Rothley Temple in Leicestershire. But you really must excuse me from furnishing anecdotes about my early home, my schooldays and my family connections. / I have the honor to be, / Sir,

Your most obedient Servant,
T B Macaulay

H Fry Esq / etc. etc. etc.

TO RICHARD MONCKTON MILNES, 14 MAY 1856

MS: Trinity College.

Holly Lodge / Campden Hill / May 14. 1856

Dear Milnes,

I am very sorry that I cannot dine with you on Sunday week.

Ever yours truly
T B Macaulay

TO LORD STANHOPE, 16 MAY 1856

MS: Stanhope Papers, Chevening.

Holly Lodge / May 16. 1856

Dear Lord Stanhope,

I leave the book for your boy.

Many thanks for the Peel papers.[3] I read them at a sitting with much interest. I should like to talk with you about them.

Ever yours,
T B Macaulay

[1] See 3 April: when he delivered the photograph to TBM for which he was to write an accompanying biographical sketch, Fry 'had the face . . . to ask me for a sketch of my life. Brazen impudence!' (Journal, IX, 207); this letter is evidently a response to another effort by Fry to get a little help from his subject.

[2] Better known in its form after 1851 as Haydn's *Book of Dignities*.

[3] The first volume of *Memoirs of Sir Robert Peel*, edited by his literary executors, Stanhope

TO SIR GEORGE CORNEWALL LEWIS, 17 MAY 1856

MS: National Library of Wales.

Holly Lodge / May 17. 1856

My dear Lewis,

I am strongly for the gilding.[1] Remember what a noble object the dome will be – about the size of the Pantheon. It will be occasionally seen by the public. It will be the daily resort of perhaps three hundred people of highly cultivated minds, among whom will be learned and accomplished men from every country in the civilised world. It is true that these people go thither to study. But they will have many minutes, as I can attest, to look about them, while waiting for books; and it is surely desirable that what they see should be magnificent rather than mean, when an outlay of 5000£ is sufficient to make the difference between magnificence and meanness. I doubt whether it be possible to expend 5000£ in a way which will do the nation more honor in the eyes of foreigners.

Ever yours truly
T B Macaulay

TO CHARLES MILLER,[2] 22 MAY 1856

MS: Trinity College.

Holly Lodge Campden Hill / May 22. 1856

Sir,

I have received your letter and the inclosed document; and I beg you to accept my thanks for the trouble which you have been so kind as to take on my account. / I have the honor to be, / Sir,

Your faithful Servant
T B Macaulay

C Miller Esq / etc. etc. etc.

and Edward Cardwell; a second volume appeared in 1857. Stanhope sent the book to TBM on the 14th; his remarks on it are in Trevelyan, II, 455–6.

1 The budget for the new reading room at the British Museum had already been exceeded, so Panizzi's plan to gild the dome had to meet opposition from the Treasury. Letters such as this to Lewis, then Chancellor of the Exchequer, finally prevailed, and the dome was gilded as originally planned. See Fagan, *Life of Panizzi*, II, 360–2.

2 Miller was a senior clerk in the Paymaster-General's office. TBM had received a bill for £67.10.0, 'the fruits of my copyright in the colonies' (Journal, XI, 2). He had attempted earlier to collect the sum from the Pay Office but found 'some hitch. The people most civil – promised to send me the needful papers as soon as possible' (Journal, IX, 253: 10 May).

TO JOHN EVELYN DENISON, 23 MAY 1856

MS: University of Nottingham.

Holly Lodge Campden Hill / May 23. 1856

Dear Denison,

As I suppose that you will not be engaged by the Derby next Wednesday, will you give me the pleasure of your company to breakfast at ten?[1]

Ever yours truly
T B Macaulay

TO ROBERT VERNON SMITH, 24 MAY 1856

MS: Trinity College.

Holly Lodge Campden Hill / May 24. 1856

Dear Vernon Smith,

The official letter which I have received from you does not require a formal answer. But I cannot refrain from telling you that I heartily approve of the course which you propose to take. I have no doubt that Lefevre will feel as I do.[2]

Very truly yours,
T B Macaulay

TO RICHARD MONCKTON MILNES, 26 MAY 1856

MS: Trinity College.

Holly Lodge / May 26. 1856

Dear Milnes,

I had an accident yesterday which has confined me to my sofa.[3] It is not without difficulty and pain that I write. I must give up all hope of breakfasting with you to morrow. If you would breakfast here on Wednesday, and meet Thirlwall and the Van De Weyers, it would be an act of charity.[4]

Ever yours,
T B Macaulay

[1] The party were Hannah and Margaret, Van de Weyer and his wife, Mrs Drummond, Bishop Thirlwall, and Longman (Journal, XI, 3).

[2] The likeliest guess is that this refers to some decision affecting the examinations for the Indian Civil Service. Smith was then President of the Board of Control, and Lefevre had been a member of TBM's committee on the matter.

[3] While walking in the verandah TBM slipped and fell, spraining his ankle and hurting his wrist (Journal, XI, 3).

[4] Milnes did not: see 23 May, note.

TO MAURICE LOTHIAN,[1] 28 MAY 1856

MS: National Library of Scotland.

Holly Lodge Campden Hill London / May 28. 1856

My dear Sir,

Yesterday I received your letter from our friend Mr. Black, and had some conversation with him about it. If anything could induce me to travel northward in the winter, and to address a large meeting, it would be the respect, gratitude and good will which I feel for the Philosophical Institution. But it is only by carefully avoiding all exposure that I am able to live with any comfort, or indeed to live at all, during the cold months; and, even in the summer, I am forced to deny myself the pleasure of reading aloud to my own family, because the sustained exertion of the voice during half an hour is more than my chest will bear. I have just retreated from the smoke of London, in the hope that, in my new abode, I may be able to respire freely. If I should suffer as much next year as I have suffered during the last three years, I shall submit to necessity, and pass my winters in Italy.

I feel, however, very strongly that I ought not to retain an honorable office the duties of which I am unable to perform. There is no man, however eminent in politics, in literature, or in science, who would not be proud to fill the chair which I am sensible that I ought to resign. As to the time and manner of resigning, I should be much obliged to you to give me your advice.

Let me beg you to convey to the Committee my thanks for their constant kindness and indulgence, and to believe me ever

Yours very faithfully
T B Macaulay

M Lothian Esq / etc. etc. etc.

TO DERWENT COLERIDGE, 30 MAY 1856

MS: Cornell University.

Holly Lodge May 30. 1856

Dear Coleridge,

I am truly sorry that I have an engagement which will make it impossible for me to get to St Mark's on Monday afternoon. If by any chance I should be at liberty, I will snatch one look at your holiday party.

Ever yours truly
T B Macaulay

[1] Lothian (d. 1880), Solicitor at Law and Procurator-Fiscal for the County of Edinburgh was a vice-president of the Edinburgh Philosophical Institution.

TO BISHOP SAMUEL WILBERFORCE, 31 MAY 1856

MS: Bodleian Library.

Holly Lodge May 31. 1856

Dear Bishop of Oxford,

I am extremely vexed by finding that I shall not be able to breakfast with you on Saturday next.[1]

Ever yours truly,
T B Macaulay

TO MRS JOHN BENJAMIN HEATH,[2] [MAY 1856]

MS: National Library of Ireland.

Holly Lodge Campden Hill

My dear Mrs. Heath,

I am very grateful for the kind interest which you take in my health. The fine weather and the fresh air have done me so much good that I hope to be able to have the pleasure of dining with you on Saturday the 14th of next month.[3]

Ever very truly yours,
T B Macaulay

TO BENSON BLUNDELL,[4] 12 [JUNE][5] 1856

Text: S. J. Davey Catalogue 39 (1893), item 6376, 2pp. 8vo: dated 12 July 1856.

[London]

I cannot help telling you . . . how much I was gratified by your letter which appeared in the Globe of Monday.[6] Long use has made me indifferent to vulgar praise and blame. But I cannot but be pleased to see my narrative vindicated by an intelligent writer. . . .

[1] Because he was giving a breakfast of his own to Hannah, Margaret, Senior, Labouchere, Grey, Charles Howard, and Lord Hatherton (Journal, XI, 8: 7 June).

[2] Sophia Bland (1793–1863) married John Benjamin Heath in 1811. Heath (1790–1879: *Boase*) was a London merchant and banker.

[3] TBM did: 'Fine house and fine dinner. . . . but I had rather be at home. I hardly knew any body, and nobody well' (Journal, XI, 10: 14 June 1856).

[4] Blundell (b. 1806) was a barrister of the Middle Temple.

[5] Dated July in the Davey Catalogue but clearly in error for June: see next note.

[6] Blundell's letter in the *Globe*, 9 June, defends TBM against Dixon's charges (see *to* Ellis, 29 March) by arguing that Dixon distorts the documentary evidence to which he appeals.

TO MRS JOHN BENJAMIN HEATH, 23 JUNE 1856

MS: Haverford College.

Holly Lodge June 23. 1856

Dear Mrs. Heath,

Many thanks for your beautiful present. I well remember with how much pleasure I read your brother's translations[1] thirty six years ago in one of the libraries of Cambridge; and I am truly glad that your kindness has enabled me to renew my acquaintance with them.

Ever yours truly
T B Macaulay

TO LORD STANHOPE, 2 JULY 1856

MS: Stanhope Papers, Chevening.

Holly Lodge July 2. 1856

My dear Stanhope,

I shall have great pleasure in breakfasting with you on Monday. Tuesday week, the 15th, would be the day which would suit me best for a visit to Chevening.[2] I could then, if it were perfectly convenient to you, pass the Wednesday and Thursday there. On Friday the 18th I must be in town again.

Ever yours truly
T B Macaulay

P.S. Ticknor[3] has just called on me, and has promised to breakfast here at ten on Friday. Will you come?[4]

[1] Robert Bland (1779?–1825: *DNB*) published *Translations, Chiefly from the Greek Anthology*, 1806.

[2] TBM went to Chevening on Tuesday the 15th and returned on Friday the 18th; on this visit he called on Mountstuart Elphinstone in the neighborhood, and dined at Chevening with 'Darwin, a geologist and traveller' (Journal, XI, 21).

[3] George Ticknor (1791–1871), Longfellow's predecessor in the chair of modern languages at Harvard; his major work, which TBM is said to have recommended to Queen Victoria, is his *History of Spanish Literature*, 1849. Ticknor was in Europe buying books for the Boston Public Library, of which he was a founder and trustee.

[4] The party were Robert Mackintosh, Ticknor, Panizzi, Jowett, Milman, Lord Lansdowne, Van de Weyer, and Senior (Journal, XI, 17: 4 July).

TO RICHARD MONCKTON MILNES, 6 JULY 1856

MS: Trinity College.

Holly Lodge July 6. 1856

Dear Milnes,

I shall have great pleasure in breakfasting with you on Friday.[1] Thanks for the Boswelliana.

Very truly yours,
T B Macaulay

TO SELINA MACAULAY, 8 JULY 1856

MS: Trinity College.

Holly Lodge Kensington / July 8. 1856

Dearest Selina,

I have no great reason to complain on the whole. But my wrist has not yet quite recovered from the effects of my accident; and I am not able to write without some inconvenience.

I enjoy my turf and my roses exceedingly. I shall not easily be induced to shut myself up in a town again during the spring and summer. I could willingly remain here all the year. I must however change the air. Next week I go into Kent for a few days, to Lord Stanhope's. I shall then visit Hannah at Oatlands.[2] In August I shall start for the north of Italy, and shall hardly return till the beginning of October. Then I mean to set myself vigorously to work again on my book.[3]

[1] The party at breakfast that day were Lord Lansdowne, George Ticknor, John Palfrey, Lord Stanley, Mr and Mrs Robert Browning, Montagu Butler, and Nathaniel Hawthorne (Journal, XI, 19). Mrs Milnes's notebook adds Lord Goderich, the Comte de Polignac, and Arthur Russell to the guests (Pope-Hennessy, *Monckton Milnes: The Flight of Youth*, p. 39). And from Hawthorne, who describes this party in his *English Notebooks*, we learn that Mrs W. E. Nightingale and her daughter Parthenope were also there. Hawthorne describes TBM at some length on this occasion: 'I had been more and more impressed by the aspect of one of the guests, sitting next to Milnes. He was a man of large presence – a portly personage – gray haired, but scarcely as yet aged. . . . At last – I do not know how the conviction came – but I became aware that it was Macauley, and began to see some slight resemblance to his portraits. But I have never seen any that is not wretchedly unworthy of the original. . . . Well, I am glad to have seen him – a face fit for a scholar, a man of the world, a cultivated intelligence' (Randall Stewart, ed., *The English Notebooks by Nathaniel Hawthorne*, New York, 1941, p. 382).

[2] The Trevelyans went to Oatlands for the summer on 9 July. TBM visited them several times in the next month, e.g., 20 July, when he was much disappointed in the building: 'I had imagined Oatlands a noble country seat, and I expected that even in its decay and partitioned as it is it would be worth seeing. A miserable piece of piecrust – true Wyatt and Walpole Gothic' (Journal, XI, 23).

[3] TBM began the fifth volume on 1 October: Trevelyan, II, 442.

I am truly glad to hear that your Carlsbad waters have agreed with you so well. I hope that the springs will suit my friend Lord Spencer. He is the brother of the Lord Althorpe who led the House of Commons twenty four years ago. The present Lord is an excellent man, but seems rather out of place in his magnificent library amidst rare Greek books of which he cannot read a letter. He owns his deficiencies however so honestly that it is impossible not to respect him.

Kindest love to Fanny.

Ever yours
T B Macaulay

TO MARGARET TREVELYAN, 12 JULY 1856

MS: Trinity College.

British Museum / July 12. 1856

Dearest Baba,

I am at the Board of Trustees, and am writing to you while Panizzi is reading a report on the Lycian marbles.[1] I am pretty well, though my chest still gives me trouble. On Tuesday next I go to Chevening. On Friday I shall return. Early in the following week I hope to be able to run down to you. I miss you sadly; and yet, when you were nearer me, I did not see much of you.

Lord and Lady Holland have just arrived at Holland House; and my Lady has sent me a summons, something in the style of those which the late Lady used to issue. I shall call this afternoon when I return from the Museum. I am a little afraid that they will prove exacting neighbours.

Have you seen the Edinburgh Review? There is a very entertaining article on Rogers, by that blackguard Hayward.[2]

I am glad that your cousin Charles[3] has done so well at the London University. I should like to see something of him. I hardly know him at all. I suppose that he is now at Aldingham for his vacation.

Here is a matter to which I must attend.[4] Love to Mamma and Papa

[1] Brought from Lycia and deposited in the Museum by Sir Charles Fellows, 1842–6.

[2] Abraham Hayward, 'Samuel Rogers,' *ER*, CIV (July 1856), 73–122.

[3] Charles Edward Macaulay (1839–1922), John's second son, entered the Indian army (see 5 May 1857); he was promoted Lieutenant-Colonel in 1883 and retired in 1884.

[4] Perhaps the 'silly vexatious conduct of Hawkins and Madden' that TBM notes in his Journal as the business of the meeting (XI, 19). Sir Frederic Madden, Keeper of the Department of Manuscripts, was notoriously irascible and troublesome. The minutes of the Trustees, however, record nothing involving both of these men at this meeting (information from the late Dr A. N. L. Munby).

and Alice. Poor dear Alice. Did she ever read the fine lines of the judicious poet

> "*One* tolled the church steeple; and blue burned the light,
> And Cora[1] she howled and she trembled with fright;
> And wrapped in a winding sheet in came the Dutchess,
> And carried poor Alice away in her clutches."[2]

Good bye my darling child.

Ever yours
T B Macaulay

TO CHRISTIAN BERNHARD TAUCHNITZ, 18 JULY 1856

Text: Bernhard Tauchnitz, 1837–1887, p. 110.

Holly Lodge, Kensington, July 18, 1856.

I have just received your letter of the 15th, with the inclosures.[3] I am perfectly satisfied with the account, and with the result of our venture. My success here has been very great, I might almost say unprecedented. I have already received twenty thousand pounds from Messrs. Longmans. I am ashamed to think how many better writers have toiled all their lives without making a fifth part of that sum.

TO THOMAS FLOWER ELLIS, 19 JULY 1856

MS: Trinity College. *Extract published:* Trevelyan, II, 390.

Holly Lodge Kensington / July 19. 1856

Dear Ellis,

I shall expect you on Wednesday, and shall be delighted to keep you as long as it suits you to stay. Thanks for the £300[4]. I have received about £500 from Leipsic, – a good deal, you will say, – yet little when it is considered that Tauchnitz has sold near ten thousand copies, – a sale which proves that the number of persons who read English in France and Germany is very great.

1 Alice's dog.
2 See 31 July.
3 'Letter from Tauchnitz with £242.11.6 in addition to the former £250' from the sale of 'nearly ten thousand' of the Tauchnitz edition of the second part of the *History* (Journal, XI, 22: 18 July).
4 A repayment on the £600 that TBM loaned Ellis on 30 June (Journal, XI, 23).

I am much inclined to adopt the route which you suggest. My only difficulty is about the state of the Simplon road, which had, in 1852, been greatly injured by floods, so that travellers were put to much inconvenience. Lord Stanhope is quite confident that the damage has been repaired. Franz will, no doubt, easily learn the truth among his brother couriers.

I think nothing of missing Turin. Turin is merely a well built modern town, a Belgravia or Tyburnia, without antiquities, or great works of art, or historical associations.

Ever yours,
T B Macaulay

TO LORD STANHOPE, [21 JULY 1856][1]

MS: Stanhope Papers, Chevening.

Holly Lodge Kensington

My dear Stanhope,

The little volume came safe, and shall be delivered to Mr. Rawdon Brown,[2] if I find him at Venice.

I should have enjoyed a trip to Hever Castle on so fine a day as Saturday. However, I had so much pleasure at Chevening that it would be very ungrateful in me to repine. Kindest remembrances to Lady Stanhope.

Ever yours truly,
T B Macaulay

TO ADAM BLACK, 24 JULY 1856

MS: Yale University.

Holly Lodge / Kensington / July 24. 1856

My dear Sir,

I am very sorry that I was not at home when you called.

The article on Johnson is nearly finished. It is very long; but I hope not too long for the importance of the subject. You would have had it before now but for an accident which makes it painful to me to use my right

[1] Date added by Stanhope.

[2] Brown (1803–83: *DNB*), an Englishman who went to Venice on a visit in 1833 and stayed until his death, was an expert on the history and antiquities of the city and the editor of an extensive series of Venetian papers connected with English history. He took TBM to the Venetian Archives and to the library of the Ducal Palace (Journal, x, 99; 113).

hand. During three weeks or more I never wrote except in cases of positive necessity. I have no doubt that I shall be able to send you the article before the end of the month.

I must positively have a proof. It would be well indeed if I could have a revise. This is a matter in which you are as much interested as I. Now I leave England for Venice on the 22nd of August, and may not return till the beginning of October. In some way or other therefore I must have the proof sheets before I start.

Ever yours truly
T B Macaulay

When do you go to Edinburgh?

TO THOMAS FLOWER ELLIS, 29 JULY 1856

MS: Trinity College.

Holly Lodge Kensington / July 29. 1856

Dear Ellis,

On Thursday between five and six I am to see the Chancellor.[1] If you chuse, I will call for you at the University Club as soon as I leave him. Let me know.

George has got the Gregory scholarship triumphantly. His letter to his mother on the occasion was touchingly affectionate; and she and the girls, as well as his father, are in raptures.

Ever yours,
T B Macaulay

I have had my first conversation with Pistrucci;[2] and I got on wonderfully. I was quite a marvel to myself.[3] He recommends the Simplon, if we can get a good report of the state of the road.

[1] On some business affecting Ellis; after the interview TBM felt that Lord Cranworth would 'do whatever he properly can' (Journal, XI, 31).

[2] A teacher of Italian whom TBM had engaged in preparation for his Italian tour. TBM later recommended him as Examiner in Italian for the Indian Civil Service examinations, remarking that 'there cannot be a fitter man' (Journal, XI, 443: 28 February 1859).

[3] Trevelyan writes that 'I well remember my uncle's account of the interview. As long as the lessons related to the ordinary colloquialisms of the road, the rail, and the hotel, Macaulay had little to say and much to learn; but, whenever the conversation turned upon politics or literature, his companion was fairly bewildered by the profusion of his somewhat archaic vocabulary. The preceptor could scarcely believe his ears when a pupil, who had to be taught the current expressions required for getting his luggage through the custom-house or his letters from the Poste Restante, suddenly fell to denouncing the French occupation of Rome in a torrent of phrases that might have come straight from the pen of Fra Paolo' (II, 449–50).

TO LORD HOLLAND, 29 JULY 1856

MS: British Museum.

Holly Lodge July 29. 1856

Dear Lord Holland,

I return the papers. I know them well. They are by Horace Walpole. I have in this room a copy of them which was made by Mackintosh.[1]

I am sorry that I shall be out of town on Saturday.

Ever yours truly,
T B Macaulay

TO MARGARET TREVELYAN, 31 JULY 1856

MS: Trinity College.

Holly Lodge July 31. 1856

Dearest Baba,

I hope to be at Weybridge at eleven minutes after three on Saturday afternoon. If you will give me dinner, in opposition to your usual practice, I shall be much obliged to you. I shall go back to town by the train which stops at Weybridge twenty seven minutes after eight, so that I shall have about five pleasant hours with you. I shall be delighted to see George, and to look at his papers. Ellis has written to congratulate me, and to say that he has now no doubt of George's success at Cambridge.

I dined yesterday with Vernon Smith. There was a splendid party – the Duke of Aumale,[2] etc. etc. I was very pleasantly seated, between Lady Dufferin[3] who was a beauty and is a wit, and Lady Morley[4] who never was a beauty, but who is a wit. We talked about Oatlands; and I found that Lady Dufferin and her sister Mrs. Norton were constant visiters there when they were girls of twelve or thirteen. The Duchess of York was very fond of them both. I mentioned the dogs.[5] And then Lady Dufferin

[1] Perhaps the extracts from Horace Walpole's Journal, 1756–8, among the Mackintosh Papers in the British Museum (Add. MS 34,523).

[2] Henri, Duc d'Aumale (1822–97), fifth son of Louis Philippe; he remained in exile in England until 1872. TBM had also dined with him at Holland House on 26 July, when he found the 'party dull as all parties are where there is a prince to be called Sir and Royal Highness. The Duke of Aumale however is sensible and does not want vivacity' (Journal, XI, 27).

[3] Helen Selina (1807–67: *DNB*), eldest of the three beautiful Sheridan daughters, sister of Mrs Norton and of the Duchess of Sutherland; she married Price Blackwood, fourth Baron Dufferin, who died in 1841; on his deathbed in 1862 she married Lord Gifford, heir of the Marquess of Tweeddale.

[4] The dowager Lady Morley was 'one of the most accomplished ladies of the day' (*DNB*).

[5] On a visit to Oatlands TBM had been much struck by a cemetery for the dogs belonging to the Duchess of York containing sixty-four graves and monuments carved with names – 'Presto,' 'Ginger,' 'Poor Devil.' He supposed then that this was the Duchess's folly. But

"did a tale unfold that harrowed up my soul."[1] Oh Baba! Oh Alice! Oh Cora! No wonder that Cora shuddered when she entered that cemetery. Horror of horrors! But I will leave the mystery unrevealed till I see you on Saturday. Indeed I would not miss the sight of the faces of surprise, terror and indignation with which you will hear the true history of Presto and Poor Devil. – Poor Devil indeed! In the meantime I may mention that the epitaphs in verse were the work of Mrs. Norton and Lady Dufferin.

I get on marvellously well with Pistrucci. I am pleased to find that my memory is not at all less quick or retentive than it was thirty years ago. Memory is the first faculty that feels the effect of time and of the infirmities which time brings. I therefore watch my memory anxiously.

Everybody is dying of heat. It is indeed almost as hot as in India on a March morning. My respiration, I am sorry to say, still plagues me. However I slept better yesterday night than I have done for weeks. Love to Mamma and Papa and Alice and George.

Ever yours my darling
T B Macaulay

TO LORD STANHOPE, [JULY?][2] 1856

Text: Basil Williams, *Stanhope*, 1932, p. 271.

[London?]

[. . .] the collection has a unique interest as an example of what were the books of an English gentleman exactly as they stood a century and a half ago.

TO LADY TREVELYAN, 12 AUGUST 1856

MS: Trinity College.

Holly Lodge Kensington / August 12. 1856

Dearest Hannah,

I have to day received a letter from Henry[3] written on Sunday after-

Lady Dufferin told him that 'the Duchess was plagued to death with presents of dogs, which she did not like to refuse, and which would have turned her house into a kennel if she had not poisoned the beasts and sent them to the cemetery. This is quite a new view of her tenderness for four footed animals' (Journal, XI, 30; Trevelyan, II, 405–6n).

1 Cf. *Hamlet*, I, v, 15–16.

2 On his visit to Chevening, TBM was 'very kindly and sensibly' left by Stanhope to 'rummage his library' (Trevelyan, II, 403). Part of that library was the collection of over 1,600 volumes assembled by the first Lord Stanhope (1673–1721).

3 Henry George Macaulay (1836–64), John's eldest son. On 9 August TBM heard from Henry that his father had been seriously injured by a fall into a mine pit (Journal, XI, 35).

noon. The medical men then said that, if John were kept quiet, they apprehended no danger. I shall therefore without hesitation make my arrangements for starting next Wednesday.

Still no news of Franz. I shall engage somebody else on Thursday if he does not make his appearance.

I am as solitary as Robinson Crusoe. It is too hot to go out in the middle of the day. So I lead much the same life that I used to lead at Calcutta when you and Trevelyan were at Hoogley. I [spen][1]d all day in my
[. . . . .]
compound, s[till?][1] reading.

I am pretty well, except that I always wake with a painful difficulty of breathing, which lasts till a violent fit of coughing relieves [me. . . .][1]

TO CHARLES MACAULAY, 12 AUGUST 1856

MS: University of London.

Holly Lodge / Kensington / Aug 12 1856

Dear Charles,

I have a letter from Henry written on Sunday afternoon to the same effect with yours. He seems to think that it would be a comfort to his father that you should go down. But, as John has said nothing on the subject, and as your help is not at all required for any purpose whatever, I should strongly advise you to stay. Indeed I do not see why you should not now return to Margate, if you would like to do so.

Ever yours,
T B Macaulay

TO AUGUSTUS DE MORGAN, 13 AUGUST 1856

MS: University of London. *One sentence published:* Augustus De Morgan, *Newton: His Friend: and His Niece*, 1885, p. 67.

Holly Lodge Kensington / August 13. 1856

My dear Sir,

I am glad that you have found in my book anything to interest you.

I have mentioned the bad state of the coin at the time of the Restoration

[1] The signature on the verso of the last leaf has been cut away, removing parts or all of about four lines on the recto as well.

(page 620). I have said indeed that the mutilation, though general, was as yet slight; and slight no doubt it was, compared with what it afterwards became.

No doubt much gold was coined in the seventeenth century. But the gold coin was merely a commodity like cloth or malt. The silver was the only standard of value and the only legal tender. A man to whom five pounds were due might have refused a ton of gold, and have insisted on being paid in crowns and shillings. The value of the gold, estimated by the money of account, was not the same in any two places or on any two days. In 1695, a hundred guineas would have paid a debt of a hundred and fifty pounds in London, but would not have paid a debt of a hundred and twelve pounds at Lancaster. Three years later a hundred guineas would not, even in London, have paid a debt of a hundred and eight pounds.

By the bye, I think that you are mistaken in supposing that, in that age, the gold coin much exceeded the silver in value. Davenant is perhaps the highest authority on such points; and Davenant confidently affirms that, at the time of the Revolution, there were nine millions in old silver coin, and two millions or more in milled silver coin.[1] The gold coin he estimates at only six million three hundred thousand pounds. I know that political arithmeticians commit great mistakes. But it seems to me incredible that a clever and diligent inquirer should have been fully convinced that the value of the silver was nearly double the value of the gold, if the value of the gold had really been, as you think, very much greater than the value of the silver.

The letter which you mention is curious.[2] I do not altogether reject your hypothesis. Yet I see great difficulties. Why on earth should Lord H[alifax] and Mrs. B[arton] keep their marriage secret? Why above all should the lady keep it secret after Lord H's death? Even had the marriage been avowed, I can hardly think that Newton would have used the words which you quote. Would he not have said "the relationship in which I stood to my Lord," rather than "the circumstances in which I *stand* related to my Lord's *family*." Surely by "my Lord's family" he cannot have meant his own niece. My sister is married to Sir Charles Trevelyan. Should I ever describe my relation to her as "the relation in which I stand to Sir Charles Trevelyan's family"?

[1] Charles Davenant, *Discourses on the Public Revenues, and on the Trade of England*, Part II, in *The Political and Commercial Works of Charles Davenant*, ed. Sir Charles Whitworth, 5 vols., 1771, I, 369.

[2] A letter from Isaac Newton to Sir John Newton, 23 May 1715, that De Morgan took to be decisive evidence in favor of his view of a clandestine marriage between Newton's niece and Lord Halifax (see [28 September 1853]). It is printed in De Morgan's *Newton: His Friend: and His Niece*, p. 49.

Halifax was succeeded in his barony by his nephew George, in whose favour he had, a short time before, resigned the lucrative place of Auditor of the Exchequer. I know of no connection between this younger Halifax and Newton. Perhaps Collins's Peerage may afford some clue.

Ever yours truly,
T B Macaulay

TO SELINA MACAULAY, 15 AUGUST 1856

MS: Trinity College.

Holly Lodge Kensington / August 15. 1856

Dearest Selina,

I start for Italy next Wednesday; and I ought not to go without sending you a line P.P.C.[1] You have of course been kept regularly informed of poor John's state. His recovery is quite wonderful, and seems to have astonished his medical attendants more than anybody else. I am however still anxious to know how he bears his removal. That he should be removed before to morrow seems to be absolutely necessary; and the journey home, though short and performed in the gentlest manner, must try his frame, shattered as it has been. His family seem quite confident that all will be right.

I shall order William to send you the Times as usual, notwithstanding my absence. I hope to be here again before Michaelmas day.

I am just setting out for Oatlands where I shall sleep to night. George's success has made us all very happy. He is both a very good and a very clever fellow.

Ever yours
T B Macaulay

I open my letter to tell you that I have just heard from Aldingham. John has been removed, and has stood it quite well.

TO LORD HOLLAND, 17 AUGUST 1856

MS: British Museum.

August 17. 1856

Dear Lord Holland,

One of my brothers had, on Friday last, a very bad accident. During some time he was in extreme danger; and we are not yet free from

[1] *Pour prendre congé.*

anxiety. But a favourable change has taken place; and we hope for the best. Thanks for your kind solicitude.

Ever yours truly,
T B Macaulay

TO CHARLES MACAULAY, 18 AUGUST 1856

MS: Trinity College.

Holly Lodge Kensington / August 18. 1856

Dear Charles,

Say everything that is proper to Brodie in my name. I am much obliged to him. But I start for Italy early the day after to morrow. The Courier is engaged; the passport visaed; the Napoleons bought; the letters of credit written; and I cannot stop even to enjoy the hospitalities of Broome Park.[1]

If you should have occasion to write to me, direct to the Poste Restante, Turin, till Saturday the 23d inclusive; to Milan till Wednesday the 27th inclusive; to Verona till Saturday the 30th inclusive; and then to Venice where I shall be, I suppose, till the 15th of September.[2]

I was sorry that we did not meet at Oatlands. I do not wonder that your visit was pleasant. I know no house in which there is more goodness or happiness.

Ever yours,
T B Macaulay

Nothing can be better than the news from Aldingham, though it might certainly be communicated in a better style.

TO LADY TREVELYAN, 4 SEPTEMBER 1856

MS: Trinity College. *Address:* Lady Trevelyan / Oatlands / Esher / Inghilterra. *Subscription:* T B M.

Verona September 4. 1856

Dearest Hannah,

I am here,[3] and pretty well, in spite of much fatigue and violent changes

[1] Sir Benjamin Brodie's house in Surrey.

[2] This schedule underwent a good deal of change: see the letters of the next month.

[3] TBM and Ellis left London on 20 August, reached Turin on the 25th and proceeded to Verona by way of Milan, Como, Bergamo, and Brescia, arriving on 3 September (Journal, x, 1–52).

of temperature. The day before yesterday it was so hot that I could not venture to go twenty feet out of the shade without putting up my umbrella. Yesterday all was altered. There was a cold north wind; the hills between Bergamo and Brescia, though not, I should think, much higher than our Cumberland hills, were covered with snow; and I found it necessary to wear my g[reat][1] coat at noon and to put a blanket on my bed at night. To day again the heat is such that I dare not face the sun. I am however much better than when I left London.

I have not found any letter here. Perhaps one may arrive before we depart. Of English news I know nothing. Since last Saturday I have not seen even a number of Galignani; and I am left to gather what information I can from the Milan Gazette which assures its readers that Prince Albert is going to take the command of an Anglo Prussian expedition against the Barbary pirates,[2] and that the Queen of Oude is about to be sent to the Tower of London.[3]

To night we sleep here; to morrow night at Padua; on Saturday at Venice, where we shall stay a week, and then turn homewards. After you receive this, direct to Genoa till Friday the 12th, and then to Marseilles till Tuesday the 16th. If after that there should be any occasion to write, it will be best to direct to the Hotel Bristol, Paris. I hope to be in England on the 25th. Love to my dearest Baba and to her Papa and George if they are with you. I inclose a letter to my little Alice.

Ever yours
T B Macaulay

Your letter has this instant arrived. Thank you for it.

TO ALICE AND MARGARET TREVELYAN,[4] [4?] SEPTEMBER 1856

Text: Trevelyan, II, 408.

[Verona]

You have an amphitheatre which very likely Pliny may have frequented; huge old palaces and towers, the work of princes who were contemporary with our Edward the First; and most charming and graceful architecture

[1] Paper torn away with seal.

[2] On 19 August, the day before TBM left for the Continent, a leader in *The Times* gave an account of the trouble created by the pirates of the Riff and of a skirmish between them and the crew of a Prussian cruiser in which Prince Adalbert had been wounded.

[3] The Queen and Prince of Oudh had come to England to protest against the annexation of their country earlier in 1856.

[4] Trevelyan identifies the recipients thus, but it is likely that this is the letter to Alice mentioned at the end of the preceding letter.

of the time of Michel Angelo and Raphael; and all this within a space not larger than Belgrave Square.[1]

TO MARGARET TREVELYAN, 8 SEPTEMBER 1856

MS: Trinity College. *Address:* Miss Trevelyan / Oatlands / Esher / Inghilterra. *Extracts published:* Trevelyan, II, 247n; 434.

Venice September 8. 1856

Dearest Baba,

We arrived at Venice on Saturday afternoon;[2] and I have hardly recovered, or rather have not recovered from the surprise caused by the first sight of this wonderful city. And yet I had been pretty well prepared by reading and conversation, and, above all, by Stanfield's and Canaletti's pictures for what I was to see. But the real streets and lanes of water, – the lofty mansions rising perpendicular from the brink of the water; – the great doors opening on the green sleeping canals, so that you make but one step from your boat to the marble staircase; – the absolute and entire want of horses, carts, carriages; – the strange silence of a city of a hundred and fifty thousand human beings among whom no wheel is ever heard to rattle; these things, though I knew them, I had never, as the Yankees say, been able to realise; and I have not yet, in forty eight hours, been able to become familiar with them.

The hotel where we are lodged[3] was once the palace of a great Venetian noble. Our rooms are very handsome, and, at this season, pleasant. In December I can imagine that they would be very cold. The musquitoes with which we were threatened have done me little harm. Their buzz is worse than their bite. To be sure we sleep surrounded with curtains of musquito net, which resembles the musquito net of India, except that it is white and not green. My health is still good; and my sleep, which I had never, during some months, enjoyed in England, has during the last fortnight been as deep and sweet as when I was a boy.

I now see Galignani regularly, and am very well pleased with what I see. England seems to be profoundly quiet. God grant that she may long continue so, and that the history of the years which I may yet have to live may be the dullest portion of her history. It is sad work to live in times about which it is amusing to read.

1 So TBM writes in his Journal of this day: 'Here are three quite different kinds of interesting objects. Roman remains – mediaeval remains – fine works of the renaissance, and all crowded thick together' (x, 52–3).

2 They left Verona for Padua on the 5th and reached Venice on the 6th (Journal, x, 61–5).

3 The Albergo d'Europa.

As I was leaving Verona I received a letter from Mamma, for which I had just time to thank her. Pray give me a full account of Mrs. Becher Stowe's visit.[1] There is nothing more pitiable than an ex lion or ex lioness. London, I have often thought, is like the sorceress in the Arabian Nights who, by some mysterious law, can love the same object only forty days. During forty days she is all fon[dness.][2] As soon [as][2] they are over, she [not][2] only discards the poor favourite, but turns hi[m][2] into some wretched shape, a mangy dog or a spavined horse. How many hundreds of victims have undergone this fate since I was born. The strongest instances, I think, have been Betty[3] who was called the Young Roscius, Edward Irving, and Mrs. Becher Stowe. I feel so much pity for the poor woman that I would gladly show her some attention, though she ill deserves it of me.[4] Has she brought her fanatical ass of a husband[5] with her? He has been writing a book against Popery so absurd and abusive as to be a scandal to Protestantism. But I must have done. Lest, by any chance, my letter from Verona should have miscarried, I will repeat my directions, as far as they can now be of any use. From the time when you receive this till Wednesday the 17th inclusive, write to the Poste Restante, Marseilles. If you have occasion to write on the 18th, 19th, 20th or 21st, to the Hotel de Bristol Paris. I shall probably be in town on the 24th. Love to Mamma and Alice and to Papa and George if they are with you.

Ever yours

T B M

TO LADY TREVELYAN, 12 SEPTEMBER 1856

MS: Trinity College. *Address:* Lady Trevelyan / Oatlands / Esher / Inghilterra. *Extract published:* Trevelyan, II, 406–7.

Venice September 12. 1856

Dearest Hannah,

We have been here nearly a week, and have made the most of our time. Yet the place is still as new to us as on the day on which we arrived. I can give you no notion of the strange effect produced by a great, stately, busy, silent city, without a horse or cart or carriage – all consisting of

[1] Mrs Stowe had arrived in England in mid-August on her second European visit.

[2] Paper torn away with seal.

[3] William Betty (1791–1874: *DNB*), the boy actor, a London sensation in 1804–5.

[4] TBM did not appreciate the observations about Gothic cathedrals that Mrs Stowe put in his mouth in her *Sunny Memories*: see 26 July 1854.

[5] Calvin Stowe (1802–86), then Professor of Sacred Literature at Andover Theological Seminary. The book that TBM refers to is perhaps Stowe's *Origin and History of the Books of the Bible*, Hartford, Conn., 1867.

narrow alleys like Cranbourne Alley as you remember it,[1] filled with crowds of walkers, or of canals, up and down which the boats are constantly passing rapidly but quietly. The chief street is the Grand Canal – a noble street as wide as the street between the Treasury and the Banqueting House, or rather wider. The Grand Canal may be a mile and a half or two miles long, and winds like a serpent, thus; and on both sides rises, perpendicular out of the green salt water, a succession of towering palaces, once gay and splendid, now sinking into decay, yet retaining many traces of their ancient magnificence, rich carvings, incrustations of rare marbles, faint remains of gilding and fresco painting. Of these great mansions there is scarcely one so modern as the oldest house in St James's Square. Many were built and crowded with brilliant company in the days of Henry the Eighth and Elizabeth; some as far back as the days of Richard the Second and Henry the Fourth. For Venice then was to London what London now is to Sidney or Toronto. A few of these houses still contain some fine pictures and statues. But the owners are gradually selling the best things in the galleries. We went to the Palace of the Manfrini family, chiefly in the hope of seeing two paintings renowned all over the world, both by Titian, a portrait of Ariosto and a portrait of the Queen of Cyprus. Both had been sold within a few weeks, and the places were vacant on the wall. I was in a bad humour at the disappointment: but my equanimity was restored by learning that the purchaser is an Englishman named Barker,[2] and that the pictures are safe in Piccadilly, so that we may hope to see them next summer at the British Institution. I could tell you a great deal more about what I have seen and what I have thought. But I have not time to write fully. We are going to dinner; and after dinner our Gondola is to be at the door; and we propose to take a row by moonlight, up and down the Grand Canal, which I have already described to you. Our stay here draws fast to a close. When we depart, we shall travel fast homewards, stopping only one day at Genoa and one at Paris. In nine days we expect to get over eleven hundred miles of railway and three hundred miles of posting. I have received a letter from my dear Baba; and glad I

[1] Enlarged from alley to street in 1843.

[2] Alexander Barker (d. 1873: *Boase*), a well-known collector.

The so-called Ariosto is a copy of the 'Portrait of a Man' now in the National Gallery, London; Barker's copy from the Manfrini Gallery (then supposed to be the original) was until recently in the collection of Lord Rosebery at Mentmore House. The 'Queen of Cyprus' may be the 'Caterina Cornaro' from the Manfrini Gallery listed in the catalogue of Mentmore House (privately printed, Edinburgh, 1883); this is not by Titian, but may be related to a lost portrait by him (see H. Wethey, *The Paintings of Titian, II: The Portraits*, 1971, p. 196).

was to receive it. You have all been very good and kind about writing; and you ought to be: for wherever I am my heart is always with you. Love to the dear girls and their Papa. George is of course at school again. I hope for everything good from him.

Ever yours
T B Macaulay

TO LADY TREVELYAN, 16 SEPTEMBER 1856

MS: Trinity College. *Address:* Lady Trevelyan / Oatlands / Esher / Inghilterra. *Extract published*: Trevelyan, II, 408.

Genoa September 16. 1856

Dearest Hannah,

I found your letter and my little Alice's here. I had received my dear Baba's at Venice. You have all been very kind about writing. Our last day at Venice was a very fine one. In the evening the moon was at the full; the water like a sheet of plate glass reflecting the long rows of white palaces with green blinds. We had the gondola after dinner and were rowed the whole length of the Grand Canal and back, with some little deviation, to the Place of St Mark, where we strolled some time listening to the music. The place is strangely fascinating; and I left it with some pain when I thought that I may probably never see it again.

Two days of rapid travelling brought us hither. I am rather knocked up by the run, and must take two days to recruit. The first day of our journey was so cold and rainy that I was forced to wear my great coat. The second day was so hot that I could not walk ten yards in the sun without my umbrella. There have been several great and sudden changes of temperature within the last fortnight. When I posted from Novara to Milan on, I think, the first of September,[1] the Alps, with the exception of Monte Rosa, were dark blue. Yesterday, when we posted from Milan to Novara, the whole ridge was white, Monte Rosa white half way down. These alternations, together with the exertion of travelling from seven in the morning till eight or nine at night, have brought back my difficulty of breathing. In the main however I am the better for my tour. We shall return a little more slowly than I had contemplated. I still expect to sleep at Holly Lodge on Friday the 26th, or, at latest, on Saturday the 27th.[2]

Genoa I had seen before: but I find it prodigiously improved, prospering greatly, and far superior in all that indicates diligence and material

[1] 28 August (Journal, X, 19).

[2] They arrived in London on the 27th (Journal, XI, 40).

wealth to any place in Italy. Yet the change, though doubtless a desirable one, is not altogether agreeable to my taste. A huge old palace, with flights of marble steps, long galleries, halls painted in fresco and gardens of orange trees is a grand sight while it is kept up nobly. It is a pathetic and interesting sight when it is falling into decay and shown by a superannuated family servant who has no wages but what he gets from the bounty of travellers. But the palaces of Genoa are turned into inns, academies, warehouses, manufactories, shops. A tailor is at work cross legged under the scutcheon of an illustrious house and in a court adorned with statues, surrounded by an Ionic arcade, and resounding, all through this hot day, with the noise of a cool fountain. And thus out of the death and corruption of the old and splendid Genoa, a new Genoa is springing which will perhaps surpass the old. In the meantime the process is not altogether pleasing.

I am not sure that I shall have time to write from Marseilles, except to William, to whom I must send a line to announce my return. At any rate, I will write to you from Paris. Love to the dear girls and their Papa. If I had time, I should tell Alice such a story about an adventure that I have had in the railway carriage – the lovely Giuseppa – handsome Englishman – etc. etc.[1] She must not be surprised if I should present her, the week after next, with a Popish aunt, who will be able to assist her in her Italian studies. But perhaps the questions of religion and residence may be as hard to get over in the case of the Chevalier Macaulay as in that of the Chevalier Grandison; and I may be forced to leave the too charming Giuseppa here with a blister on her head and a strait waistcoat on her back.[2]

Ever yours
T B Macaulay

TO HARRIET BEECHER STOWE, [23?][3] OCTOBER 1856

Text: Uncle Tom's Cabin, new edn, 1887, p. xix.

[London]

I have just returned from Italy, where your fame seems to throw that of all other writers into the shade. There is no place where "Uncle Tom"

[1] The Journal for 15 September explains that 'an Italian lady and her daughter, a good looking engaging girl named Giuseppa, were in our company' on the train to Genoa (x, 122); the adventure is not described.

[2] The fate of Clementina della Porretta in *Sir Charles Grandison.*

[3] TBM had received a copy of *Dred* (see next note) from Mrs Stowe on this day: 'Where to direct to her and what to say to her I do not know' (Journal, xi, 51).

(transformed into "Il Zio Tom") is not to be found. By this time I have no doubt he has "Dred"[1] for a companion.

TO JOHN HILL BURTON, 27 OCTOBER 1856

MS: National Library of Scotland.

Holly Lodge Kensington / October 27. 1856

My dear Sir,

May I venture to request your friendly assistance? I am revising my history,[2] and am desirous to be as exact as possible. In a note on my first Volume, page 494, I have said that the Acta of the Scottish Privy Council during almost the whole administration of the Duke of York are wanting. Will you be so kind as to let me know exactly how that is?[3] I shall be most happy to have an opportunity of making any similar researches for you in London.

Very truly yours
T B Macaulay

TO THOMAS FLOWER ELLIS, 28 OCTOBER 1856

MS: Trinity College.

Holly Lodge Kensington / October 28. 1856

Dear Ellis,

I will call at six to morrow – Wednesday – at the University Club, and shall hope to find you there. I want to have your opinion of a long note which I have been writing, and which seems to Hannah and Trevelyan,

1 *Dred: A Tale of the Great Dismal Swamp*, Mrs Stowe's second novel, was published in England at the end of August. TBM read it on 22 October, the day before he received a presentation copy: 'It has merit, but is disfigured by very great blemishes. I do not know however that it is much inferior to Uncle Tom's Cabin' (XI, 51).

2 TBM took great pains over this edition, which is the author's final text of the *History;* he began the work of correcting and revising in May and did not finish it until May 1858. It was published in seven volumes, at 6s. each, at monthly intervals beginning in December 1857.

3 TBM had asked Burton this question before: see 26 September 1848. In the 1857 edition a note added to the original note says that TBM's information has been contradicted but that nevertheless 'the fact is exactly as I have stated it.'

as well as to myself, to prove that the broker in the case of the Taunton girls was no other than William Penn.[1]

Ever yours,
T B Macaulay

TO LORD STANHOPE, 1 NOVEMBER 1856

MS: Stanhope Papers, Chevening. *Published:* Stanhope, *Miscellanies*, pp. 107–8.

Holly Lodge Kensington / November 1. 1856

My dear Stanhope,

I have dated my letter wrongly. I am writing at the table of our board room, while Panizzi is reading the minutes of the last meeting, Hamilton[2] examining vouchers, and the Duke[3] on one side of me and the Dean[4] on the other listening to the Secretary with an attention which puts me to shame. I am very well – for me, and have had a most delightful tour. The passage of Mont Cenis, the Lake of Como, Milan, Verona, Venice, Genoa, and the beautiful and magnificent road along the Mediterranean from Genoa to Nice, have filled my mind with pleasant thoughts and images which will last me my life. I availed myself of your introduction to your friend at Venice.[5] He was as well known to my courier and my Gondolier as the Campanile of St Mark. He proved a most friendly and intelligent Cicerone. We shall have many opportunities of talking over what I have seen. On the whole I think that the finest landscape that I saw was the view on the Italian side of Mont Cenis; the finest building the Cathedral of Milan; the finest relique of antiquity the Amphitheatre at Verona, the finest picture Titian's Assumption of the Virgin, and the finest city Genoa. But Venice, though not exactly the finest, is, beyond all doubt, the most interesting city that I visited.

I am now stationary, and am beginning to work again, though with very little expectation of living to publish anything more. But the employment itself is a pleasure.

[1] See *to* Frances Macaulay, 14 April 1851. TBM's long note – an essay of some 2,000 words added towards the end of ch. 5 in the 1857 edition – replies to Hepworth Dixon's argument and concludes by stating that 'I leave the text, and shall leave it, exactly as it originally stood.'

[2] William Richard Hamilton (1777–1859: *DNB*), a diplomat who, as Lord Elgin's secretary, had supervised the shipment of the Elgin Marbles; he was Under-Secretary of State for Foreign Affairs, 1809–22; Minister at Naples, 1822–5; and a Trustee of the British Museum from 1838. TBM says that Hamilton always supported Panizzi, 'right or wrong' (Journal, II, 159–60: 1 December 1849).

[3] The Duke of Somerset. [4] Milman. [5] Rawdon Brown: see [21 July 1856].

I have read De Tocqueville's book,[1] and agree with you in thinking highly of it.

I have been greatly amused by your Devonshire anecdotes.[2] I was not aware that haunted houses were still to be found in England.

My kindest regards to Lady Stanhope and to my Valentine.

Ever yours truly,
T B Macaulay

TO HENRY STEPHENS RANDALL,[3] 1 NOVEMBER 1856

MS: Historical Society of Pennsylvania.

Holly Lodge Kensington / London / November 1. 1856

Sir,

I am very sensible of your great courtesy and kindness. I have seen at the British Museum the Documentary History of New York,[4] and was much interested by some of the papers which I found there. If you will have the goodness to send me a copy through my booksellers, Messrs. Longmans, I shall be greatly obliged to you.

I am not myself a collector of autographs: but I have many friends who will be delighted to see an undoubted manuscript letter of so great a man as Washington;[5] and it will be a pleasure to me to be able to gratify them. / I have the honor to be, / Sir,

Your faithful Servant,
T B Macaulay

H S Randall Esq / etc. etc. etc.

[1] *L'Ancien Régime et la Révolution*, Paris, 1856; item 868 in the sale catalogue of TBM's library.

[2] Stanhope's note explains that this refers to 'an account which I had given him of a cottage belonging to me in a remote rural parish, which for several years had remained unlet because the neighbours declared it to be haunted.'

[3] Randall (1811–76), an upstate New York squire, school superintendent, journalist, and Democratic politician, was Secretary of State of New York, 1851–3, and is now remembered for his *Life of Thomas Jefferson* (see 18 January 1857).

[4] E. B. O'Callaghan, comp., *The Documentary History of the State of New-York*, 4 vols., Albany, 1849–51. TBM received the work – 'four huge quartos' – on 17 January 1857 (Journal, XI, 77).

[5] Randall sent such a letter: see 18 January 1857.

TO THOMAS FLOWER ELLIS, 24 NOVEMBER 1856

MS: Trinity College.

Holly Lodge Kensington / November 24. 1856

Dear Ellis,

I am sorry that you cannot come to morrow. Wednesday is the only day in the week that would not suit me. Come on Thursday or Friday, or both. Let me know, that the carriage may call for you.

Walter's verses are not very highly finished but there are many excellent lines and truly Ovidian turns.

Lord Campbell and Lady Stratheden,[1] of all people, honored me with a call yesterday. They walked across Kensington Gardens, chatted with me an hour, and then walked home again. He seems as young as when I first saw him thirty years ago. Miss Campbell[2] seems much inclined to be on very friendly terms with Baba; and the Mammas on both sides encourage the acquaintance.

Ever yours,
T B Macaulay

TO WILLIAM WHEWELL, 1 DECEMBER 1856

MS: Trinity College. *Published:* Winstanley, *Early Victorian Cambridge*, pp. 437–8.

Holly Lodge Kensington / December 1. 1856

My dear Whewell,

Lord Lansdowne has shown me the letters which have passed between you, and has done me the honor to ask my opinion.[3] I wish from the bottom of my soul that Milton had been a Trinity man. But, as his parents were so stupid and perverse as to send him to Christ's, I must admit that your arguments against putting up a statue of him in our Chapel are of great weight. I am glad, but not at all surprised, to find that Lord Lans-

[1] Campbell's wife was created Baroness Stratheden in 1836 'in consideration of her husband's legal and political services' (*GEC*). She was a daughter of TBM's old Northern Circuit senior, James Scarlett, Lord Abinger.

[2] Mary, the eldest of Campbell's three unmarried daughters.

[3] Lansdowne wished to present a statue to Trinity to be added to those of Newton and Bacon in the college antechapel. Lansdowne's idea was that it should be of Milton; Whewell (who had given the statue of Bacon) suggested George Herbert, Dryden, John Pearson, Isaac Barrow, or Bentley. Barrow was finally selected. The episode is set forth in Appendix D to Winstanley, *Early Victorian Cambridge*, pp. 436–9. The choice of Barrow seems to have been determined by the arguments of Adam Sedgwick: see J. W. Clark and T. M. Hughes, *Life and Letters of the Reverend Adam Sedgwick*, Cambridge, 1890, II, 330–2.

downe, though not quite convinced, is most amiably and generously desirous to do whatever may be pleasing to the College.

Then comes the question, – Who shall share the honors of Bacon and Newton in our ante chapel? An equal of Bacon and Newton it cannot be. In the registers of all the colleges of Cambridge and Oxford we shall find nobody, Milton excepted, who is worthy to be "terzo tra cotanto senno."[1] We must chuse some second rate man to be the associate of our two first rate men. The choice is difficult. But I think that, if I had a voice, I should give it in favour of Bentley. I told Lord Lansdowne my reasons; and he begged me to write them to you, with whom the decision will rest. They are these.

Bentley is distinguished from all the other candidates mentioned in your letter, by one most important circumstance. He was decidedly the greatest man of his class. This cannot be said of Herbert or Pearson. It cannot be said even of Dryden or Barrow. Dryden's most enthusiastic admirers will hardly put him so high as third among our poets. Barrow did many things well, but nothing, I think, preeminently well. His fame rests chiefly on his sermons; and there are sermons of South, of Taylor, of Robert Hall, which I prefer to Barrow's best. But Bentley is the greatest man in his own department that has appeared in Europe since the revival of letters. That department, it may be said, is not the highest. I grant it. I do not rank the Phalaris or the Epistle to Mill with the Principia or the Novum Organum. Still, great reverence is due to the man who has done best what thousands of able and industrious men have, during four centuries, been trying to do well. And, surely, if there be in the world a place where honor ought to be paid to preeminence in classical learning, that place is our ante chapel. During several generations classical learning has been the peculiar glory of our college. In the sciences of which Bacon and Newton were the great masters we have been equalled, some may perhaps think, surpassed. But, in the studies from which Bentley derives his fame, we are, I believe, unrivalled. And this is to be attributed partly to the influence of his genius. To this day, unless I deceive myself, the scholarship of Trinity men has a peculiar character which may be called Bentleian, and which is not found in the scholarship of men who have gained the highest honors of Oxford. I am far from putting Bentley in the same rank with Newton. But in one respect the two men may fairly be classed together. They were the two intellectual founders of our college. Their minds have left an impress which is still plainly discernible. They may therefore, with peculiar propriety, appear together in our ante chapel.

There is another reason for preferring Bentley to Barrow. Barrow is

[1] Cf. Dante, *Inferno*, IV, 102.

buried in Westminster Abbey, and has a statue there. Bentley lies in our chapel, and has no statue, – not even, to the best of my recollection, a tablet. Now this I think really discreditable to us, – so discreditable that I would gladly subscribe a few guineas towards the removing of such a reproach. I shall be truly glad therefore if Lord Lansdowne's munificence repairs what seems to me a great neglect.

You say, I observe, in your letter to Lord Lansdowne – "Some have a moral blemish, as Bentley and Dryden." I agree with you as to Dryden. But surely you, to whom we owe that fine monument of Bacon, will, on reflection, admit that the faults of Bentley were not such as ought to be punished by permanent exclusion from public honors. Dryden was immoral as a poet, Bacon as a Judge, Bentley as Master of a College. I therefore would not set up any monument to Dryden in his character of poet, to Bacon in his character of Judge, or to Bentley in his character of Master of a College. But Dryden has no claim to a monument except as a poet. His licentiousness taints those very works on which alone his fame depends; and it is impossible to do honor to the writer without doing honor to the libertine. With Bacon and Bentley the case is quite different. You testified your respect for the great philosopher, although you knew that he had been a servile politician and a corrupt Chancellor. And Lord Lansdowne may surely testify in the same way respect for the great scholar, notwithstanding all the bad stories which are to be found in the pamphlets of Professor Colbatch[1] and Serjeant Miller.[2]

This is the substance of what I said to Lord Lansdowne yesterday evening.[3] I shall be anxious to know how you decide. / Ever, my dear Whewell,

Yours very truly,
T B Macaulay

TO SELINA MACAULAY, 5 DECEMBER 1856

MS: Trinity College. *Extract published:* Trevelyan, II, 422.

Holly Lodge / Kensington / Dec 5. 1856

Dearest Selina,

I am not at all angry with Mrs. Crinean, nor unwilling to assist her at

[1] John Colbatch (1664–1748: *DNB*), one of Bentley's stubbornest enemies, was Professor of Moral Philosophy at Cambridge, 1707–44.

[2] Edmund Miller (1670?–1730), Fellow of Trinity, leader of the first phase of opposition to Bentley as Colbatch was of the second.

[3] TBM also gave Lansdowne Monk's *Life of Bentley* to read, though doubting whether that would 'much recommend him to favour' (Journal, XI, 64: 30 November).

a proper time and to a reasonable extent.[1] But as to sending her a hundred pounds as often as she is in difficulties, I really cannot do it without inconvenience to myself or injustice to others. Nor am I at all sure that such liberality would eventually be kindness.

I am at present keeping house. But I am much better than I was last year; and I begin to feel the effect of a purer air and a more commodious disposition of rooms in a way not to be mistaken. You say nothing of your own health. – I am afraid that the last few days must have tried you.

I think, as you do, that Lord Palmerston is taking rather too strongly the Low Church line. Close's was not a good appointment.[2] To be sure he was only made a Dean. Bickersteth[3] is, I believe, merely a ranting preacher. Villiers[4] and Tait[5] are good men, especially Tait. I am truly glad that Vaughan remains for the present at Harrow. After next October,[6] the sooner he is made a Bishop the better. Kindest love to Fanny.

Ever yours,
T B Macaulay

TO SIR CHARLES WOOD, 9 DECEMBER 1856

MS: Victoria Memorial Hall, Calcutta. *Published:* [N. K. Sinha], *Bengal Past and Present*, LXXXIII (1964), 154.

Holly Lodge Kensington / December 9. 1856

Dear Wood,

The time is at hand when the East India College at Hayleybury will cease to exist. I have no doubt that both you and I, in contributing to bring about this result, did our duty to England and to India. Nevertheless, I cannot but feel much pain when I think of the suffering which we have caused to several most respectable families; and I am most desirous to serve those whom I have been the means, not indeed of injuring, but, I am afraid, of ruining. I do hope that your influence will be exerted to

1 TBM had sent her £100 in January; on 25 November he heard from her again, 'begging of me' (Journal, IX, 47–8; XI, 62).

2 Francis Close (see 14 October 1846) had just been appointed Dean of Carlisle. Palmerston's appointments to high ecclesiastical office were notorious: Owen Chadwick says that Palmerston was 'more ignorant about religion and the churches than any other prime minister of the nineteenth century; and enjoyed pretending to be more ignorant than he was' (*The Victorian Church*, 1966, p. 469). He consistently promoted Evangelicals.

3 Robert Bickersteth (1816–84: *DNB*) made a name first at Clapham and then at St Giles-in-the-Fields as an Evangelical preacher; he was now made Bishop of Ripon.

4 Henry Montagu Villiers (1813–61: *DNB*), younger brother of Lord Clarendon; Bishop of Carlisle, 1856; translated to Durham, 1860.

5 Archibald Campbell Tait (see 13 November 1849), Arnold's successor at Rugby; Dean of Carlisle, 1849; Bishop of London, 1856; Archbishop of Canterbury, 1869.

6 When George Trevelyan would leave Harrow.

obtain for the Professors a liberal compensation. I am sure that nothing facilitates reforms so much as liberality in compensating those who suffer by the abolition of abuses. If we really have succeeded in giving to India the inestimable blessing of a good civil service, we may well call on her to bear the charge of the few hundreds of pounds which will make all the difference between comfort and penury to those very deserving persons who have been the victims of our improved policy.

There is one who seems to me to have very peculiar claims, – Heaviside.[1] Personal feeling about him I have none: for I never saw him in my life. But his merits have been strongly represented to me by men of the first distinction in science and literature. He has been nineteen years at the College. For the College he relinquished the fairest prospects at Cambridge. It is a hard thing on such a man, now no longer young, and unfitted by Academical habits for a stirring life, to have to begin the world again. It seems to me that a quiet stall in a Cathedral would be the very place for such a man. I really think that you, who carried through the last India Bill, who introduced the system of competition for civil appointments, and who, by doing so, really destroyed the College, might with peculiar propriety, bring this matter under Lord Palmerston's notice.[2] At all events you will pardon me for writing to you on the subject. Our names will hereafter be mentioned together in connection with a great and beneficial reform; and you, I have no doubt, are as sorry as I am that it was not in our power to do our duty to the public without causing much distress to individuals.

Lefevre agrees with me entirely. I dare say that he will write to you about Heaviside. / Ever, my dear Wood,

Yours most truly,
T B Macaulay

TO NATHANIEL HIBBERT, 13 DECEMBER 1856

MS: The Viscount Knutsford.

Holly Lodge Kensington / December 13. 1856

Dear Hibbert,

Will you breakfast with me at ten next Friday?

You held out to me some hopes that Mrs. Hibbert would do me the

[1] See 16 April 1856.

[2] In his Journal for 12 December TBM writes: 'I am glad that Charles Wood is willing to apply to Palmerston in favour of Heaviside' (XI, 66). Heaviside's appointment to a canonry at Norwich came under Palmerston's administration, but not until 1860.

great honor and pleasure of being my guest. Pray prevail on her to come with you.[1]

Ever yours truly,
T B Macaulay

TO SELINA MACAULAY, 19 DECEMBER 1856

MS: Trinity College.

Holly Lodge Kensington / Dec 19. 1856

Dearest Selina,

I suppose that you told Mrs. Crinean that I was not angry with her.[2] For to day I have a letter from her begging for money most vehemently, and saying that, if I am obdurate, her husband must go to prison. I have sent her twenty pounds – making up what she has had from me within a few months to a hundred and thirty pounds. But I have told her that her husband must take the consequences of his own acts, and that she must expect no further assistance from me. To say the truth, this importunity has provoked me not a little. I have not mentioned this last application to Hannah. But I must say that it goes far to justify Hannah's opinion. I hope that you will take care how you express yourself in writing to Mrs. Crinean. For she seems to have taken up the notion that, if her husband cannot pay his debts, it is my business to pay them. Kindest love to Fanny.

Ever yours,
T B Macaulay

TO SELINA MACAULAY, 22 DECEMBER 1856

MS: Trinity College.

Holly Lodge Kensington / December 22. 1856

Dearest Selina,

Nothing can have been more proper than your conduct about Mrs. Crinean. You quite misunderstood me if you thought that I meant to blame you, even when I supposed that you might, from good nature, have said something which might have encouraged her to apply to me again. I merely wished to give a caution for the future. I now see that no such caution was needed.

1 The party were Hannah, Margaret, Mr and Mrs Hibbert, Henry Reeve, Sir Edward Ryan, Ellis, Dundas, and Lord Carlisle (Journal, XI, 69).

2 See 5 December.

I am getting through the winter much better than I had expected. The air of Campden Hill is beginning to tell on me. I have declined all invitations to country houses, and shall stay by my own fireside through the cold weather. How are you going on? Love and all the good wishes of the season to you and Fanny. It is long since I have heard from her.

There is a most extraordinary volume of Letters by Boswell just published.[1] It well deserves to be read.

Ever yours,
T B Macaulay

P.S. Whenever you write to me direct thus:

Rt Hon T B M
etc.
Holly Lodge
Kensington
London
W.

This W, by a new post office arrangement will much accelerate the delivery of letters.[2]

TO FRANCES MACAULAY, 25 DECEMBER 1856

MS: Trinity College. *Extract published:* Trevelyan, II, 399.

Holly Lodge Kensington / December 25. 1856

Dearest Fanny,

A merry and happy Christmas to you. You, I dare say, have a bright clear sky, and a fine view over a calm blue sea. Here the fog is thick, though without the yellow tinge of London, and I can but just see to the nearest laurels and hollies on my lawn, which is covered with hoar frost. I feel however the benefit of what may by comparison be called rural air, and breathe more freely than during the last two or three winters.

The holiday interrupts my gardening. I have turned gardener – not

[1] *Letters of James Boswell, Addressed to the Rev. W. J. Temple*, just published though dated 1857. These were the letters to Temple accidentally discovered in a shop in Boulogne, the first of the series of discoveries of Boswell's manuscripts. On 19 December TBM writes: 'got Boswell's Letters from Cawthorn's, – an incomparably absurd book – read it at a sitting' (Journal, XI, 69).

[2] Like the penny post, the scheme of dividing London into postal districts was Rowland Hill's.

indeed working gardener, but master gardener. I have just been putting creepers round my windows and forming beds of Rhododendrons round my fountain. In three or four summers, if I live so long, I may expect to see the results of my care.

I trouble myself little about the burglars.[1] They have not been very near me; and they are not very likely to attack a house with four men and a fierce dog, well shut up, and with bells on all the shutters. I have however told my ironmonger to put up a powerful alarm bell on the roof, with bell ropes to the chief bedrooms; so that, if the house should be attacked, all Campden Hill and Kensington will be roused; and people will come running from the Duke of Argyle's and Lord Holland's in three minutes.

I am not surprised to learn that you were pleased with George. He is an excellent young fellow, and gives every promise of being a virtuous honorable and accomplished man. Love to dear Selina.

Ever yours
T B Macaulay

TO HENRY STEPHENS RANDALL, 18 JANUARY 1857

MS: New York Public Library. *Envelope:* H S Randall Esq / etc. etc. etc. / Cortland Village / State of New York / United States. *Subscription:* T B M. *Published: Harper's Magazine*, LIV (February 1877), 460.

Holly Lodge Kensington / January 18. 1857

Sir,

I beg you to accept my thanks for your letter enclosing the autograph of Washington, which reached me three weeks ago, and for the History of the State of New York which I received the day before yesterday.

I shall look forward with curiosity to the appearance of your life of Jefferson.[2] I cannot say that he is one of my Heroes: but it is very probable that you may convince me that I have formed an erroneous estimate of his character.

I am a little surprised to learn from you that Americans generally consider him as a foil to Washington, as the Arimanes of the republic

[1] A leader in *The Times* of 29 September described the failure of police protection in the area of Notting Hill – within the sound of the 'nightingales of Holland Park' – and affirmed that the residents were arming themselves. On reading this article TBM 'talked with William.... I find that there is some real danger. I shall take precautions. It is hardly worth my while to learn the management of fire arms at this time of day. I never loaded a pistol, and scarcely ever fired one. If I had an opportunity, however, I would take a lesson' (Journal, XI, 41).

[2] *The Life of Thomas Jefferson*, 3 vols., New York, 1858.

contending against the Oromasdes.[1] There can, I apprehend, be no doubt that your institutions have, during the whole of the nineteenth century, been constantly becoming more Jeffersonian and less Washingtonian. It is surely strange that, while this process has been going on, Washington should have been exalted into a God, and Jefferson degraded into a Dæmon.

If there were any chance of my living to write the history of your Revolution, I should eagerly and gratefully accept your kind offer of assistance. But I now look to the accession of the House of Hanover as my extreme goal. With repeated thanks I have the honor to be, / Sir,

Your faithful Servant,
T B Macaulay

H S Randall Esq / etc. etc. etc.

TO THOMAS FLOWER ELLIS, 26 JANUARY 1857

MS: Trinity College.

Holly Lodge Kensington / January 26. 1857

Dear Ellis,

I am truly concerned to learn that you are so poorly. You had better take advice. We are getting past the time when fevers and agues are to be trifled with.

The carriage will be at the University Club to morrow (Tuesday) at six. I am much better, quite free from pain, and gradually recovering the use of my right arm.[2] I have not however yet ventured to shave my self. But I think that I shall try to morrow.

Ever yours,
T B Macaulay

TO FRANCES MACAULAY, 27 JANUARY 1857

MS: Trinity College.

Holly Lodge Kensington / January 27. 1857

Dearest Fanny,

Thanks for your letter. Three days ago I should hardly have been able to answer it with my own hand. But my rheumatism is gone, or nearly

[1] Variant spellings of Ahriman and Ormazd, the lords of darkness and light in the Zoroastrian system.

[2] TBM suffered a rheumatic attack in his right shoulder on 19 January and for a week was unable to work (Journal, XI, 78–9: 29 January).

so: I have dismissed my physician; and I leave the completion of my cure to time.

I am sorry for Thackeray.[1] He is a man of real genius, – the best, in my opinion, of living novellists, and quite capable of producing, with care and thought, works which might last as long as the language. But he wants money; and he gets it more rapidly and easily by lecturing than he could get it in any other way. His taste for fame is, I am afraid, not very delicate. He probably prefers it in the coarsest form. Huzzas and claps from crowded rooms give him, I dare say, more pleasure than the esteem of men who are qualified to judge. He should consider that of the sort of applause which he gets by turning mountebank, that wretched Spurgeon[2] gets ten times as much as he.

Kindest love to Selina.

Ever yours,
T B Macaulay

TO FRANCES MACAULAY, 10 FEBRUARY 1857

MS: Trinity College.

Holly Lodge Kensington / Feb 10. 1857

Dearest Fanny,

I do not think that the general feeling is in favour of your plan. Chichester, you know, may be seen in a morning most easily. And then we should have nothing else to see. For, knowing the Duke,[3] I should not like to go to Arundel Castle at a time when he is almost certain to be there. Nor indeed is Arundel Castle worth seeing, except from the road.

Our present plan is to go to Salisbury. It is long since any of us were there. And neither Baba nor George ever saw either the Cathedral or Stonehenge. Then we may possibly go to Longleat and Wells. But these matters require consideration.[4] In any case I count on you as one of the party.

John dined with me yesterday. He looks much older than when I saw him last, so much older that I was seriously apprehensive that his con-

1 Fanny had probably just heard Thackeray, who gave his lectures on *The Four Georges* at Brighton, 21–24 January (Ray, *Letters of Thackeray*, IV, 11).

2 Charles Haddon Spurgeon (1834–92: *DNB*), Baptist preacher, came to London in 1854 and instantly became the town's most popular preacher. 'No actor of the day was half so popular as he' (E. E. Kellett, *As I Remember*, 1936, p. 112).

3 Henry Granville Fitzalan Howard (1815–60: *DNB*), fourteenth Duke of Norfolk; TBM would have known him from the House of Commons, where, as Lord Fitzalan, he sat from 1837 to 1852.

4 For the plan of their trip see 8 April.

stitution had received a severe shock. He has however been overhauled by physicians who pronounce that all is right. I will therefore hope for the best.

I went out to day for the first time after a close imprisonment of twenty four days.[1]

Love to dear Selina.

Ever yours,
T B M

TO THOMAS FLOWER ELLIS, 12 FEBRUARY 1857

MS: Trinity College.

Holly Lodge Kensington / February 12. 1857

Dear Ellis,

I am truly sorry not to have a better account of you. I will call on Saturday, that is if the weather permit; and I hope that I shall then find you better. Is there any book that you would like me to bring you?

Ever yours
T B Macaulay

TO FRANCES MACAULAY, 14 FEBRUARY 1857

MS: Trinity College.

Holly Lodge Kensington / February 14. 1857

Dearest Fanny,

I am glad that you like our plan for Easter. Do not trouble yourself about dear little Alice. Every thing can easily be managed, if her Mamma thinks it right that she should go with us.

I give you joy of the prosperous state of the London and North Western Railway Company.

Love to dear Selina.

Ever yours
T B Macaulay

[1] That is, from 17 January, when TBM 'walked long in the verandah reading pamphlets' (Journal, XI, 77).

TO LORD STANHOPE, 16 FEBRUARY 1857

MS: Stanhope Papers, Chevening.

Holly Lodge Kensington / February 16. 1857

Dear Stanhope,

I suffer so much from the fog and east wind that I dare not leave my fireside to day. I am very sorry that I must miss our first meeting in Great George Street.[1]

I reckon on you for Thursday morning.[2] Thanks for the inscription.

Ever yours truly,

T B Macaulay

If it would not be too presumptuous, I would beg you to persuade Lady Stanhope to come with you on Thursday morning. Pray try what you can do for a prisoner, as I may call myself during this part of the year.

TO LORD STANHOPE, 25 FEBRUARY 1857

MS: Stanhope Papers, Chevening.

Holly Lodge Kensington / February 25. 1857

Dear Stanhope,

Many thanks for the second Volume.[3] I did not lay it down till I had read the whole. It is of great interest.

Yesterday, breakfasting at poor Hallam's, I mentioned the difficulty in which we are about a Secretary. Murray – the Bookseller – was there. He has since written to me to suggest Scharf.[4] I have also heard from Scharf himself. I really think that we could not make a better choice. He is a clever artist, a well read man, and accustomed to good society.

Very truly yours,

T B Macaulay

[1] TBM was among the trustees of the newly-founded National Portrait Gallery, in which Stanhope had a leading part; the Gallery was housed at 29 Great George Street until 1869. TBM speaks of this as the first meeting of the Trustees, and so does Stanhope's endorsement, but the foreword to the *Catalogue of the National Portrait Gallery, 1856–1947*, 1949, p. x, says that the first meeting took place on 9 February. Whether it was the first or second, TBM did, after all, manage to attend the meeting; the weather cleared, he went, and in the discussion about the rules of the new institution 'had everything pretty much my own way' (Journal, XI, 87–8).

[2] The party were Hannah, Margaret, Lord and Lady Stanhope, Senior, and Dundas (Journal, XI, 88).

[3] Of the *Memoirs of Sir Robert Peel*, published on 28 February; Stanhope was joint editor (see 16 May 1856).

[4] See 2 June 1845. Scharf was appointed Director of the Gallery in March, and in the almost forty years of his tenure carried out his duties with indefatigable energy.

TO THOMAS FLOWER ELLIS, 2 MARCH 1857

MS: Trinity College. *Extract published:* Trevelyan, II, 431.

Holly Lodge Kensington / March 2. 1857

Dear Ellis,

I was glad to miss you on Friday, as I inferred from your absence that you were much better. Let me have a line to say what progress you are making.

I have not been able to get out since Saturday. This vile east wind and fog have affected me much. I hope however to be able to dine with the Stanhopes on Wednesday and with the Milmans on Thursday. How soon do you think that you shall be able to come out to me? If you cannot go as far as Bromley, why should you not pass next Sunday here? However, run no risk on any account.

It seems to be generally thought that the ministers will be beaten.[1] It may be very absurd in me, sitting by my fireside, to pretend to judge of the public feeling. But I strongly suspect that the public feeling agrees with mine. I think that Bowring[2] has acted ill, and that the Ministers have shown more generosity than judgment in taking his faults on themselves; but that we must now go through with this China business; that a vote of censure on the government can do nothing but harm;[3] and that the coalition of Peelites, Tories, and Radicals against Palmerston, is highly discreditable to all the three parties. I am glad that I have done with politics. I should not have been able to avoid a pretty sharp encounter with Lord John.[4]

Ever yours,
T B Macaulay

[1] On the matter of the so-called second Chinese war. Hostilities broke out in October; a vote of censure against the government in the House of Lords was defeated, but a similar vote moved by Cobden passed in the Commons on 3 March.

[2] Then Governor of Hong Kong. His action in defending a ship illegally flying the British flag was the immediate *casus belli*, and though TBM approved Palmerston's decision to stand by his agent, he wondered privately 'what could possess them [the ministers] to send that ass and worse than ass Bowring to China?' (Journal, XI, 92: 27 February).

[3] Palmerston came back stronger than before from the elections that followed the dissolution compelled by the vote of censure.

[4] Russell repudiated Bowring's action and thus opposed Palmerston in a speech of 26 February.

TO HENDRIK JACOB KOENEN, 2 MARCH 1857

Text: Copy, University of Amsterdam.

Holly Lodge Kensington / March 2. 1857

My dear Sir,

I beg you to accept my thanks for your very friendly letter. I have no doubt that I shall learn much from your Lectures on the Commercial Policy of Holland.[1] They will be most safely and conveniently transmitted to me through my publishers Messrs. Longman and Co.

I can say with confidence that our archives contain no trace of the Secret Treaty about which you enquired, and I strongly suspect that no such treaty ever existed. I should be glad to know who is said to have signed it on the part of England. That the English Council of State or the English Minister at the Hague, may have encouraged the city of Amsterdam to resist the Prince of Orange, is in the highest degree probable. That hopes may have been held out to the malecontents of the support of an English fleet and army may easily be believed. But that a formal treaty was concluded is quite incredible. I apprehend that, in 1650, no power in this country, except the Parliament, was competent to conclude such a treaty: and a treaty concluded by an Assembly so large would not have been a secret long. / I have the honor to be / My dear Sir

Your faithful Servant

T. B. Macaulay.

TO THOMAS FLOWER ELLIS, 4 MARCH 1857

MS: Trinity College.

Holly Lodge Kensington / March 4. 1857

Dear Ellis,

I have had a miserable time of it since Monday. However starvation, calomel, mustard poultices, and, above all, the change of the wind, have revived me; and I can draw my breath with tolerable ease. But dining out is not at present to be thought of. I have sent excuses to the Stanhopes and Milmans.

I am vexed by the result of the division,[2] more, however, for private than for public reasons. The country will thrive under any government that is likely to be formed.

[1] Koenen's *Voorlezingen over de Geschiedenis des Nederlandschen Handels*, Amsterdam, 1853, is item 399 in the sale catalogue of TBM's library.

[2] The defeat of Palmerston's government the day before.

What a strange thing! Perry[1] – the scholar of Trinity of my year – has published a volume of Miscellanies in prose and verse. There is a poem to me in which he lays claim to a friendship which never existed between us, talks of having reclined by me on mossy banks in high converse while the river gently murmured by.[2] I never reclined on a bank by him in my life, – never, to the best of my belief, ate any meal with him except in hall, never was in his rooms, never saw him in mine.[3] I did not even know him to speak to till our third year; and he never resided after he had taken his degree. The difference between his recollections and mine reminds me irresistibly of a passage, not to be quoted, in the dialogue between Lacon and Comatas in Theocritus.[4] The worst is that the book has been sent me from the author. What am I to say?

A line to tell me how you are? I will write as soon as I am in condition to dine with you.

Ever yours
T B Macaulay

TO THOMAS FLOWER ELLIS, 7 MARCH 1857

MS: Trinity College.

Holly Lodge Kensington / March 7. 1857

Dear Ellis,

After a week of close confinement and rigid observance of Lent – for I have of late eaten no animal food but eggs, – I am convalescent. I have ventured to walk an hour in the Verandah, – and I propose to eat a regular dinner. If I can I shall dine with the Trevelyans on Tuesday,[5] as George will be there, on Exeat. On any later day of the week I will with pleasure

1 Richard Perry (b. 1800?), an equity draftsman and conveyancer, entered Trinity with TBM. He had just published *Contributions to an Amateur Magazine in Prose and Verse*, 1857.

2 The poem is 'To a Distinguished Literary Character, on His Indisposition.' One stanza reads:

'In keen debate, and controversy high,
Then would we join, on mossy bank reclined;
Or, while the river gently murmured by,
With various converse soothe the pensive mind.'

3 A second edition of Perry's book, 1861, contains an appendix of 'Reminiscences of Lord Macaulay' in which, *inter alia*, Perry recalls that 'He was in the habit occasionally of asking a few of us to breakfast with him. When we were at our meal the college servant would come and clean his shoes on his feet, without taking them off, while Macaulay sat quiet under the operation, talking and eating the whole time.'

4 *Idylls*, v, 41–4; even in A. S. F. Gow's recent (1950) scholarly edition the English translation leaves these lines in the decent obscurity of Latin.

5 He did not (Journal, xi, 95).

dine in Bedford Place, unless you are able to come to me, which I should greatly prefer.

Ever yours,
T B Macaulay

TO FRANCES MACAULAY, 8 MARCH 1857

MS: Trinity College.

Holly Lodge Kensington / March 8. 1857

Dearest Fanny,

A student at Cambridge cannot take his first degree, that of Bachelor of Arts, till after a residence of three years and a quarter, that is to say, if I recollect rightly, eleven terms. Thus George, who will go up in October 1857, will take his Bachelor's degree in January 1861, in the eleventh term of his residence.

In general Bishops are unwilling to ordain any person who has not taken a Bachelor's degree. This, however, is not a law of the Church. It is mere matter of discretion. There is probably no Bishop who would not admit that there are excepted cases; and some Bishops are easier than others.

A residence of three terms will do nothing at all for a man, in the way of getting him ordained. I rather think that you or your informant must have confounded two very different things. A person who is in orders, but has never been at College, may, by entering himself at Cambridge and keeping three terms, acquire some Academical privileges. Those who do this are called Ten Year Men.[1] Our old acquaintance, Mr. Bray,[2] was one.

I have had a bad week; but I am now much better. I hope that our April tour will be pleasant. I do not much like the look of public affairs. But I have seen so many changes, and have [. . . .][3]

TO WILLIAM WHEWELL, 14 MARCH 1857

MS: Trinity College.

Holly Lodge Kensington / March 14. 1857

Dear Whewell,

Thanks for your very interesting paper.[4] I must read the Parmenides

[1] Because ten years after their admission they might graduate as Bachelors of Divinity.

[2] Edward Atkyns Bray (1778–1857: *DNB*), bred a lawyer, entered the Church in 1811, and took his degree as a Ten-Year man in 1822; he was Vicar of Tavistock from 1812 until his death. I do not know what link he had with the Macaulay family.

[3] The rest is missing.

[4] 'Of the Platonic Theory of Ideas,' reprinted from the *Transactions of the Cambridge*

again before I give an opinion as to the question of genuineness, or, as old Marsh[1] taught us to call it, authenticity. One thing however occurs to me at the first glance. It is quite true that in this dialogue Parmenides is represented as the superior and Socrates as the inferior. And this, no doubt, is widely different from the relation in which Plato represents Socrates as standing to sophists so eminent as Protagoras, Hippias, and Gorgias. But it seems to me that Plato always makes a wide distinction between the Eleatic philosophers and all others. Are you prepared to pronounce the σοφιστης[2] spurious? Very great scholars have thought that dialogue the masterpiece of Plato, as respects command of language; nor can I conceive that anybody but he could have written it. Now, in the σοφιστης, you will remember, the principal interlocutor is a stranger, ἑταιρος των αμφι Παρμενιδην και Ζηνωνα.[3] Socrates speaks of this person and to him with profound respect, and listens, without putting in a word while the treasures of the Eleatic wisdom are produced. In the πολκοςι,[4] again, which is a continuation of the σοφιστης, Socrates is content to be a learner while the stranger lectures. And these dialogues, as you will see if you look at the beginning of the Theætetus, are supposed to have taken place when Socrates was in the fullest maturity of his powers, indeed a very little before his death. Now if Socrates was represented as paying this sort of respect, at near seventy, to a nameless disciple of Parmenides, is it strange that he should be represented as having, when a very young man, been schooled by Parmenides himself, the greatest of the Eleatic Doctors, full of years and honors? Lord Lansdowne has a very fine Reynolds, – an imaginary Johnson at two years old.[5] Might not Plato have once indulged his imagination in a similar way, and tried to exhibit Socrates, an ardent youth of twenty, eager for truth, but as yet seeing it only by glimpses, not yet a perfect master of dialectical fence, and not yet perfect master of his own temper, – standing, in fact, in the same relation to old Parmenides in which Alcibiades and Theætetus afterwards stood to himself?

I throw out these thoughts at random. I will not plague you with my metaphysical speculations on the Platonic theory of Ideas. To say the truth I am much of the mind of Antiphon, who, when he grew up, left such abstruse matters for the turf, and was busy at a saddler's when his

Philosophical Society, x (1857). To account for what he takes to be the hostile treatment in the 'Parmenides' of the Platonic theory of ideas Whewell suggests that it 'is not a Platonic Dialogue at all' but the work of an Eleatic.

1 The Lady Margaret Professor of Divinity: see 4 November 1813.

2 'Sophist.'

3 'One of the followers of Parmenides and Zeno,' in the first sentence of the 'Sophist.'

4 'Statesman.'

5 1781–2?; reproduced in Ellis K. Waterhouse, *Reynolds*, 1941, plate 228B.

brothers forced him, much against his will, to tell them a long story about ἓν and πολλα, and ὁμοια, and ανομοια.[1]

Ever very truly yours,
T B Macaulay

TO SELINA MACAULAY, 16 MARCH 1857

MS: Trinity College.

Holly Lodge Kensington / March 16. 1857

Dearest Selina,

I have suffered a good deal during the last month. But the spring seems to be coming. My flowers are beginning to show themselves: the lilacs are budding; and I hope that I shall soon draw my breath more freely than I have done of late.

Of politics I know no more than I learn from the Times, and from an occasional chat with an old friend who steals an hour from business to visit my hermitage. Whether the general election will much strengthen the ministry I cannot pretend to guess. But I think that it will give us a much better House of Commons. The last House – this House, I ought to say – was chosen in most unfortunate circumstances. The one point in issue was Protection or Free Trade.[2] The Counties chose any blockhead who was a Protectionist, and the towns any scamp who was a free trader. Many signs lead me to think that the representation, especially the County Representation, will be greatly improved.

I wish that you had told me more about yourself. Kindest love to Fanny.

Ever yours
T B Macaulay

TO WILLIAM WHEWELL, 17 MARCH 1857

MS: Trinity College.

Holly Lodge Kensington / March 17. 1857

Dear Whewell,

I have been much interested by the Three Memoirs.[3] I hope to return

[1] 'One,' 'many,' 'similar,' 'dissimilar.' For Antiphon, see the beginning of the 'Parmenides.'

[2] In the general election of July 1852.

[3] Whewell's articles on Plato's survey of the sciences published in the *Transactions of the Cambridge Philosophical Society*, IX (1855), 582–604, and reprinted in his *The Philosophy of Discovery*, 1860, appendix.

them to you at the Thatched House on the 24th.[1] I really am much inclined to come round to your opinion. Before we meet I will read these Eleatic dialogues again. Speaking from my recollection of them, I should say that they must go together, and that, if any of them be Plato's, they are probably all Plato's.

Will you breakfast with me at ten on Wednesday the 25th – the morning after the Club?

Ever yours truly
T B Macaulay

TO CHARLES MACAULAY, 24 MARCH 1857

MS: University of London.

Holly Lodge Kensington / March 24. 1857

Dear Charles,

I have your note and Sir J R's[2] papers. I really hardly know what to say as to the point which he discusses. My leaning was, I own, different from his; and, though I admit the force of his arguments, I am not quite convinced by them. I ought however to say that the subject is not one on which I think myself entitled to speak with any authority. My knowledge of mediæval history and literature is little more than what every liberally educated gentleman ought to have. My chief attention has been given to other matters.

I have written to Sir William Craig about the Master of the Rolls.[3] Craig will know exactly what can be done and what ought to be done; and his position gives him great influence with all parties. For he is not a candidate; and yet everybody knows that he might be member for the asking.

Ever yours,
T B Macaulay

[1] At a meeting of The Club. TBM did not go, but Whewell was among his breakfast guests on the next day (Journal, XI, 99).

[2] Perhaps Sir John Romilly, Master of the Rolls; I do not know what is referred to.

[3] On 28 March TBM writes: 'Vexed about the Master of the Rolls. Craig writes that the thing might have been managed with the greatest ease if I had only written a few days earlier. I wrote as soon as I heard of Romilly's wishes; and in fact nobody is to blame, though the thing has turned out so ill' (Journal, XI, 100). Probably this refers to the Edinburgh election on 27 March and to the possibility of Romilly's standing (he had been out of Parliament since 1852). The incumbents, Black and Cowan, were returned unopposed but only after the names of a number of potential candidates, including Lord John Russell and Thackeray, had been hopefully suggested.

TO THOMAS FLOWER ELLIS, 30 MARCH 1857

MS: Trinity College. *Partly published:* Trevelyan, II, 430.

Holly Lodge March 30. 1857

Dear Ellis,

I am glad that you bore your journey so well.

I will dine with you on Thursday, nothing unforeseen preventing.

Was there ever anything since the fall of the rebel Angels, like the smash of the Anti Corn Law League[1] – How art thou fallen from Heaven O Lucifer![2] I wish that Bright and Cobden had been returned.

Ever yours,
T B Macaulay

TO MRS CATHERINE GORE, 6 APRIL 1857

MS: Berg Collection, New York Public Library.

Holly Lodge Kensington / April 6. 1857

Dear Mrs. Gore,

Thanks for your constant kindness. Our habits, I find, are very similar. From November to April I keep my nest, and am almost always either by a blazing fire or between warm blankets. Now that the almond trees are in flower and that the thorns and lilacs are green, I begin to enjoy liberty and exercise. I should however scarcely venture so far as Wiltshire even now, but that I do not like to disappoint some young people who have set their hearts on seeing Salisbury Cathedral, Stonehenge, and Longleat, in my company. Our party will fill a railway carriage, and will require all the accommodation that a good inn can afford. You will not expect or wish me to invade your dominions at the head of such a force. Butif ever I wander alone to Southampton and the New Forest, I shall certainly not deny myself the great pleasure of passing a few hours in your society.

I know nothing about Kate Macaulay[3] except what is to be found in books. I learn from the Annual Register that she left an only daughter who married an East India Captain named Gregory. Possibly Mrs. Gregory may have been divorced, and may have resumed the name of

[1] Bright and Milner Gibson were defeated at Manchester, Cobden at Huddersfield.

[2] Isaiah 14: 12.

[3] Mrs Catharine Macaulay (1731–91: *DNB*), wife of a London physician named George Macaulay, and the author of a republican *History of England from the Accession of James I to that of the Brunswick Line*, 8 vols., 1763–83.

Macaulay. In no other way can I account for the circumstances which you mention. Kate, you doubtless know, was a Miss Sawbridge, sister of a stupid, surly, Alderman, who was in the days of our grandfathers what Waithman was in ours.[1] Dr. Macaulay, her husband, was, I suppose, of my clan, but so distant a cousin that no highland Senachie would be able to tell the degree of relationship. Indeed I believe that his branch of the family had long been settled in Ireland.[2]

Ever yours most truly,
T B Macaulay

TO THOMAS FLOWER ELLIS, 8 APRIL 1857

MS: Trinity College. *Mostly published:* Trevelyan, II, 424; G. M. Trevelyan, *Sir George Otto Trevelyan*, pp. 20–1.

Holly Lodge Kensington / April 8. 1857

Dear Ellis,

We start to morrow for Salisbury. On Good Friday, after service, we shall visit Stonehenge and Old Sarum. On Saturday we go to Longleat, for which I have provided myself with a special order from Lord Bath. Easter Sunday we shall pass at Salisbury. On Monday we return.[3]

On what day next week will you come out to me. Will Tuesday suit you? But name your own time; and let me find a line from you here when I return.

George is buried under laurels – first in the examination – Gregory Medal – Peel Medal – every prize that he has contended for without exception. And really he is a good modest boy, not at all boastful or self confident. His home indeed is not one in which a young fellow would be likely to become a coxcomb.

His Latin poem is an account of a tour up the Rhine in imitation of the 5th Satire of Horace's first Book. The close does not please Vaughan, and indeed is not good. I have suggested what I think a happier termination. The travellers get into a scrape at Heidelberg and are taken up. How to extricate them is the question. I advise George to represent himself as saying that he is an Englishman and that there is one who will look to it that an Englishman shall be as much respected as a Roman

1 Her brother John (1732–95) was Lord Mayor of London and an M.P.

2 Dr Macaulay came from Scotland.

3 An echo of this visit is in Trevelyan's account of TBM's virtues as a cicerone: 'to hear him discourse on Monmouth and Bishop Ken beneath the roof of Longleat Hall, or give the rein to all the fancies and reminiscences, political, personal, and historical, which were conjured up by a drive past Old Sarum to Stonehenge, were privileges which a child could appreciate, but which the most learned of scholars might have envied' (II, 214).

citizen. The name of Palmerston at once procures the prisoners their liberty. Palmerston, you remember, is a Harrow man. The following termination has occurred to me: but I have not shown it to George

"Tantum valuit prænobile nomen,
Quod noster collis, nostra hæc sibi vindicat aula,
Quod Scytha, quod torta redimitus tempora mitra
Persa timet, diroque gerens Ser Bella veneno."

Do not mention this. It might lead people to think that I have helped George; and there is not a line in any of his exercises that is not his own.[1]

Ever yours,
T B Macaulay

TO GUILLAUME GROEN VAN PRINSTERER,[2] 15 APRIL 1857

MS: General State Archives, The Hague.

Holly Lodge. Kensington. / April 15. 1857

Sir,

Accept my thanks for your most obliging letter, and for the volume[3] which accompanied it. I shall value that volume as a mark of the favourable opinion of a man of learning and of virtue. / I have the honor to be, / Sir,

Your faithful Servant
T B Macaulay

[1] But on the next day TBM gave these lines to George, who was 'delighted' with them (Journal, XI, 103), and they were read to a 'storm of applause' on the Harrow speech-day. Trevelyan adds this explanation: 'It is necessary . . . to remind the reader that in July 1857 Palmerston's Russian laurels were still fresh; and that he had, within the last few months, brought the Persian difficulty to a successful issue, and commenced a war with China' (II, 424–5 and note).

[2] Groen van Prinsterer (1801–76), was both a historian and a politician. As Royal Archivist he published *Archives ou Correspondance Inédite de la Maison d'Orange-Nassau*, 13 vols., Leiden and Utrecht, 1835–61; in the States-General he was head of the high orthodox and conservative party. Grant Duff reports a conversation with Groen van Prinsterer in 1862 in which he spoke of TBM 'very highly, but wondered at his having used so few new materials' (*Notes from a Diary, 1851–1872*, 1897, I, 215).

[3] Probably the *Handboek der Geschiedenis van het Vaderland*, Leiden, 1846, item 399 in the sale catalogue of TBM's library.

TO HENRY HALLAM, 2 MAY 1857

MS: Harvard University.

Holly Lodge Kensington / May 2. 1857

Dear Hallam,

I shall have very great pleasure in breakfasting with you on Tuesday.[1]

Ever yours,

T B Macaulay

TO JOHN EVELYN DENISON, 3 MAY 1857

MS: University of Nottingham.

Holly Lodge Kensington / May 3. 1857

Dear Denison,

I fully expected to have met you yesterday at the Museum,[2] of which you are now a chief ruler, and to have had the great pleasure of shaking hands with you and giving you joy.[3] As I was disappointed, I must tell you in writing how much your elevation to the first place among English gentlemen has gratified me, and how heartily I wish you many years of health, prosperity, and quiet dignity, before your friends congratulate you on being Lord Ossington. I have so little chance of living to be one of those friends that you must take my congratulations now in advance.[4] –

Ever yours most truly,

T B Macaulay

[1] But when he got there he found that Hallam 'had changed the day. His letter has, by some odd fate, miscarried' (Journal, XI, 113).

[2] On the formal opening of the new reading room before 'not a numerous, but a very illustrious company' assembled there for a breakfast (Journal, XI, 112).

[3] On the opening of Parliament, 30 April, Denison had been chosen Speaker in succession to Charles Shaw-Lefevre.

[4] The prophecy is exact: Denison remained Speaker until 1872, when he was created Viscount Ossington.

TO LORD OVERSTONE,[1] 3 MAY 1857

MS: University of London. *Published:* D. P. O'Brien, ed., *The Correspondence of Lord Overstone*, Cambridge, 1971, II, 737–8.

Holly Lodge Kensington. / May 3. 1857

Dear Lord Overstone,

Thanks for your excellent Queries.[2] I have read them with great pleasure and with entire conviction. My leanings were all to your side of the question; and you have fixed me immovably in my opinion.

I cannot help wishing that we had all been formed like that son of Goliath who is mentioned in the Book of Chronicles as having had twelve fingers and twelve toes.[3] Then we should have had a perfect arithmetical system.

Ever yours truly
T B Macaulay

The / Lord Overstone / etc. etc. etc.

TO LORD BROUGHTON, 5 MAY 1857

MS: British Museum.

Holly Lodge Kensington / May 5. 1857

Dear Lord Broughton,

I have learned, with very great pleasure, that a young relation of mine is indebted to your kindness for a cadetship.[4] This is not the first obligation which you have laid on me. I assure you that I shall not forget it.

Pray come and breakfast with me next Tuesday, the 12th.[5] By that time, I hope, the summer will have begun, and my lilacs will be in all their beauty.

Ever yours truly,
T B Macaulay

[1] Samuel Jones Loyd (1796–1883: *DNB*), head of the London and Westminster Bank and a leading authority on matters of finance; created Baron Overstone in 1850. He was a graduate of Trinity, and a member of The Club.

[2] 'Questions on Decimal Coinage,' 1857, reprinted from evidence given before a Parliamentary commission. TBM calls this 'an excellent paper on the decimal coinage by Lord Overstone. He has disposed for ever of that humbug' (Journal, XI, 113: 4 May).

[3] I Chronicles 20: 6.

[4] John Macaulay's son Charles, just appointed a cadet in the East India Company's service.

[5] He did, together with Hannah, Margaret, the Duke and Duchess of Argyll, Lord Carlisle, Bishop Wilberforce, Dean and Mrs Milman, Dundas, and Denison. 'The turf served for a drawing room' (Journal, XI, 118).

TO LORD GREY, 10 MAY 1857

MS: University of Durham.

Holly Lodge Kensington / May 10. 1857

Dear Lord Grey,

I have read your M.S.[1] with very great interest. Indeed, when once I had begun, I could not stop; and I finished the whole at one sitting. Whether I agree with you or differ from you, you always instruct me and set me thinking. There are passages about which I should much like to talk with you. Lest we should miss each other, I may as well mention that I shall be at home all the Tuesday afternoon. On the Wednesday, I breakfast with the Bishop of Oxford in Pall Mall, and could, with perfect convenience, go straight from him to you, if that suited you.

Ever yours truly,
T B Macaulay

TO LORD GREY, 18 MAY 1857

MS: University of Durham.

Holly Lodge / Kensington / May 18. 1857

Dear Lord Grey,

Àpropos to a matter about which we had some talk the other day,[2] look at the new volume of Lord Campbell's Lives of the Chief Justices, page 144.[3] You will see that he entirely agrees with you. Within the last week I have heard similar sentiments strongly expressed by good lawyers, who look at the question, not as politicians, but merely with a view to the efficiency of the Courts of Westminster Hall.

Ever yours truly,
T B Macaulay

1 'Lord Grey sent me the M.S. of a work on Reform which he thinks of publishing' (Journal, XI, 114: 8 May). This appeared as *Parliamentary Government Considered with Reference to a Reform of Parliament*, 1858.

2 See preceding letter. TBM called on Grey on 13 May (Journal, XI, 118).

3 Where Campbell remarks on how, in the pre-Reform days, the law officers could always be provided with a seat in Parliament, so that political chances did not need to be considered in making the law appointments. Grey regrets the loss of this power in his essay (*Parliamentary Government*, p. 109). Volume 3 of Campbell's book had just been published; TBM got it on the 16th and finished it the next day (Journal, XI, 120).

TO FRANCES MACAULAY, 20 MAY 1857

MS: Trinity College.

Holly Lodge Kensington / May 20. 1857

Dearest Fanny,

I was very sorry to miss you. However, I trust that we shall soon meet again. I must try to arrange a party for Manchester[1] some time in the course of the summer; and I shall count upon you.

Thanks for Rush's[2] last dying speech and confession. I remembered some of the lines, – particularly

"Poor Eliza Calcraft, that much injured girl."

John was delighted with his son's good luck. I only wish that the eldest[3] were as well provided for.

I am glad that you find Brighton so pleasant. It has, no doubt, many attractions. But the want of trees is to me very grievous; and just now, when my lilacs are in full beauty, my thorns and laburnums breaking out, and my thrushes singing, your blue waves and white cliffs seem to me to be but a poor compensation for flowers and leaves and bird's nests. But you, I remember, suffer from hay fever, which must make this season of foliage and blossoms disagreeable to you. I should love it, if it were only for the relief which it brings to my chest. How I run on prating.

Ever yours

T B Macaulay

TO EDWARD PLEYDELL-BOUVERIE, 20 MAY 1857

MS: Osborn Collection, Yale University.

Holly Lodge Kensington / May 20. 1857

My dear Bouverie,

I am out of the question.[4] Of the persons mentioned in your letter, I

[1] See 2 August 1857.

[2] James Blomfield Rush (*DNB*), hanged at Norwich in 1849 for the murder of a Mr Jermy and his son; the case was one of the great sensations of the time.

[3] There was some trouble about John's son, Henry Macaulay. On 27 July 1858 TBM writes that Henry called on him to talk about the examination for an Indian writership that he was then sitting: 'He may possibly succeed next year if not this. Ainsi soit il! – For I heartily wish him any where but near me' (XI, 350). Five years later Lady Trevelyan wrote to her daughter Margaret: 'What a dreadful state of things about H. Macaulay. Oh what a trial compared to *any* we have had, however bitter' (26–30 April 1863: MS, Huntington). I have not penetrated the mystery, though there are several references to Henry's debts in family letters.

[4] As a candidate for membership in the Commission established by the Cambridge University

think Lord Eversley[1] decidedly the best; and I must say that, if to be a Trinity man is not a decisive objection to me, it ought not to be so to him. For I am quite certain that his appointment would be received with more general applause than mine. Either Romilly or George Waddington would do very well. Of the men who are not from Trinity, the best, in my opinion, is Charles Austin. But I much fear that he would not accept the office. The next best, I think, would be Lord Auckland. Pray read his letters in the Peel Memoirs; and judge whether he be fitter to preside over a great University, or to stand in a parish school with a foolscap on his head. The Scotch newspapers are making merry over his bad grammar, and would insult poor Cambridge without mercy, if he were to be made one of her rulers.[2]

One word about Hawtrey.[3] He is an accomplished man, but I think that you had better not take a King's man. King's College is a community apart, and hardly belongs more to Cambridge than Oxford. Of the sciences which are the particular boast of Cambridge, no King's man that I ever knew had even a smattering; and I have no reason to believe Hawtrey to be an exception to this general rule.

Again I say that Lord Eversley seems to me to be the man. No other nomination would be hailed with such unanimous approbation.

Ever yours truly,
T B Macaulay

Act of July 1856 to revise the statutes of the University (see Winstanley, *Early Victorian Cambridge*, pp. 286–8). I cannot explain the occasion of this letter, since so far as I can learn the Commissioners were already appointed, and they included none of the men discussed in it.

[1] Charles Shaw-Lefevre was created Viscount Eversley on his retirement from the Speakership this year.

[2] Another baffling reference. There are no letters from Auckland in the Peel *Memoirs* (see 16 May 1856), and, though the *Scotsman* was running excerpts from the book at this time I have found nothing in it about Auckland – presumably TBM means his old friend Robert Eden, Bishop of Sodor and Man, afterwards of Bath and Wells, who succeeded as third Baron Auckland in 1849.

[3] Edward Craven Hawtrey (1789–1862: *DNB*), Headmaster of Eton, 1834–52, and Provost thereafter.

TO HENRY STEPHENS RANDALL, 23 MAY 1857

MS: New York Public Library. *Envelope:* H. S. Randall Esq / etc. etc. etc. / Cortland Village / Cortland County / New York. *Subscription:* T B M. *Published:*[1] *Harper's Magazine*, LIV (February 1877), 460–1.

Holly Lodge Kensington London / May 23. 1857

Dear Sir,

The four volumes of the Colonial History of New York[2] reached me safely. I assure you that I shall value them highly. They contain much to interest an English as well as an American reader. Pray accept my thanks; and convey them to the Regents of the University.

You are surprised to learn that I have not a high opinion of Mr. Jefferson, and I am a little surprised at your surprise.[3] I am certain that I never wrote a line, and that I never, in Parliament, in conversation, or even on the hustings, – a place where it is the fashion to court the populace, – uttered a word indicating an opinion that the supreme authority in a state ought to be entrusted to the majority of citizens told by the head, in other words, to the poorest and most ignorant part of society. I have long been convinced that institutions purely democratic must, sooner or later, destroy liberty, or civilisation, or both. In Europe, where the population is dense, the effect of such institutions would be almost instantaneous. What happened lately in France is an example. In 1848 a pure democracy was established there. During a short time there was reason to expect a general spoliation, a national bankruptcy, a new partition of the soil, a maximum of prices, a ruinous load of taxation laid on the rich for the purpose of supporting the poor in idleness. Such a system would, in twenty years, have made France as poor and barbarous as the France of the Carlovingians. Happily the danger was averted; and now there is a despotism, a silent tribune, an enslaved press. Liberty is gone: but civilisation has been saved. I have not the smallest doubt that, if we had a purely democratic government here, the effect would be the same. Either the poor would plunder the rich, and civilisation would perish; or order and property would be saved by a strong military

[1] This letter, which naturally aroused great interest in the United States, was published in part as early as 1860 and has frequently been reprinted since, usually in the season of presidential elections or at other times of political crisis; the most recent such reprinting that I know of is in *American Heritage*, February 1974. I give *Harper's Magazine* as the place of first full publication so far as I have been able to determine. For detailed history of the letter to 1925 see H. M. Lydenberg, 'What Did Macaulay Say about America?', *Bulletin of the New York Public Library*, XXIX (July 1925), 459–81.

[2] See *to* Randall, 1 November 1856.

[3] See 18 January 1857. In his Journal for 23 May TBM writes: 'wrote an answer to a Yankeee who is utterly unable to understand on what ground I can possibly dislike Jefferson's politics' (XI, 122–3).

government, and liberty would perish. You may think that your country enjoys an exemption from these evils. I will frankly own to you that I am of a very different opinion. Your fate I believe to be certain, though it is deferred by a physical cause. As long as you have a boundless extent of fertile and unoccupied land, your labouring population will be far more at ease than the labouring population of the old world; and, while that is the case, the Jeffersonian polity may continue to exist without causing any fatal calamity. But the time will come when New England will be as thickly peopled as old England. Wages will be as low, and will fluctuate as much with you as with us. You will have your Manchesters and Birminghams; and, in those Manchesters and Birminghams, hundreds of thousands of artisans will assuredly be sometimes out of work. Then your institutions will be fairly brought to the test. Distress every where makes the labourer mutinous and discontented, and inclines him to listen with eagerness to agitators who tell him that it is a monstrous iniquity that one man should have a million while another cannot get a full meal. In bad years there is plenty of grumbling here, and sometimes a little rioting. But it matters little. For here the sufferers are not the rulers. The supreme power is in the hands of a class, numerous indeed, but select, of an educated class, of a class which is, and knows itself to be, deeply interested in the security of property and the maintenance of order. Accordingly, the malecontents are firmly, yet gently, restrained. The bad time is got over without robbing the wealthy to relieve the indigent. The springs of national prosperity soon begin to flow again: work is plentiful: wages rise; and all is tranquillity and cheerfulness. I have seen England pass three or four times through such critical seasons as I have described. Through such seasons the United States will have to pass, in the course of the next century, if not of this. How will you pass through them. I heartily wish you a good deliverance. But my reason and my wishes are at war; and I cannot help foreboding the worst. It is quite plain that your government will never be able to restrain a distressed and discontented majority. For with you the majority is the government, and has the rich, who are always a minority, absolutely at its mercy. The day will come when, in the State of New York, a multitude of people, none of whom has had more than half a breakfast or expects to have more than half a dinner, will chuse a legislature. Is it possible to doubt what sort of legislature will be chosen? On one side is a statesman preaching patience, respect for vested rights, strict observances of public faith. On the other is a demagogue ranting about the tyranny of capitalists and usurers, and asking why anybody should be permitted to drink Champagne and to ride in a carriage, while thousands of honest folks are in want of necessaries. Which of the two candidates is likely to be preferred by a working man who hears

his children cry for more bread? I seriously apprehend that you will, in some such season of adversity as I have described, do things which will prevent prosperity from returning; that you will act like people who should, in a year of scarcity, devour all the seed corn, and thus make the next year a year, not of scarcity, but of absolute famine. There will be, I fear, spoliation. The spoliation will increase the distress. The distress will produce fresh spoliation. There is nothing to stop you. Your constitution is all sail and no anchor. As I said before, when a society has entered on this downward progress, either civilisation or liberty must perish. Either some Cæsar or Napoleon will seize the reins of government with a strong hand; or your republic will be as fearfully plundered and laid waste by barbarians in the twentieth Century as the Roman Empire was in the fifth; – with this difference, that the Huns and Vandals who ravaged the Roman Empire came from without, and that your Huns and Vandals will have been engendered within your own country by your own institutions.

Thinking thus, of course, I cannot reckon Jefferson among the benefactors of mankind. I readily admit that his intentions were good and his abilities considerable. Odious stories have been circulated about his private life: but I do not know on what evidence those stories rest; and I think it probable that they are false, or monstrously exaggerated. I have no doubt that I shall derive both pleasure and information from your account of him. / I have the honor to be, / Dear Sir,

Your faithful Servant,
T B Macaulay

H. S. Randall Esq / etc. etc. etc.

TO THOMAS FLOWER ELLIS, 2 JUNE 1857

MS: Trinity College.

Holly Lodge / June 2. 1857

Dear Ellis,

I shall be most happy to see you here on Friday. I will call at 1/4 after 6. I can think of no motto for the Insurance Office. The motto which you mentioned is bad, but quite good enough for the purpose.

I have found Collier's book.

Ever yours
T B Macaulay

TO LADY HOLLAND, 15 JUNE 1857

MS: British Museum. *Envelope:* The / Lady Holland. *Subscription:* T B Macaulay.

Holly Lodge / June 15. 1857

Dear Lady Holland,

I shall be most happy to dine with you on Sunday the 28th.[1]

As to the breakfast parties to which you so kindly invite me, there is a difficulty arising from a habit which I have lately contracted, of going to Church on Sundays, when the weather and my chest suffer me to venture out. I promise myself great pleasure from your Wednesdays in July.

Ever yours truly,
T B Macaulay

TO LADY CHARLOTTE DENISON, 23 JUNE 1857

MS: University of Nottingham.

Holly Lodge Kensington / June 23. 1857

Dear Lady Charlotte,

Thanks for your delicious fruit; and still warmer thanks for your kind remembrance of me.

Ever yours truly,
T B Macaulay

TO MONTAGU BUTLER,[2] 23 JUNE 1857

MS: Trinity. *Envelope:* H. M. Butler Esq. / 12 Devonshire Terrace / Craven Hill / W.

Holly Lodge Kensington / June 23. 1857

My dear Sir,

Will you breakfast here on Thursday next at ten?[3]

Ever yours truly,
T B Macaulay

1 The guests were Lord Lansdowne, Lord Lyndhurst, Edward Ellice, Abraham Hayward, Prosper Mérimée, Alexis De Tocqueville, 'and a crowd of people with whom I had little or no acquaintance' (Journal, XI, 138).

2 Butler (1833–1918: *DNB*) had been head of the school at Harrow in the year that George Trevelyan entered; he went on to Trinity, where he was elected Fellow in 1855. In 1859 he was chosen Headmaster of Harrow (see 19 October 1859); after twenty-seven years there, he became Master of Trinity, 1886–1918. He remained one of G. O. Trevelyan's close friends.

3 The party were Butler, Hannah and Margaret, the Duke and Duchess of Argyll, Dundas, and Charles Howard.

TO GEORGE OTTO TREVELYAN, 4 JULY 1857

MS: Massachusetts Historical Society.

Holly Lodge July 4. 1857

Dear George,

I have read your exercises, and am very much pleased with them. I am particularly glad that your Latin prose style is so good and pure, so free from scraps of verse, so redolent of Cicero. I have known many scholars who could write excellent verse in the manner of Horace and Ovid. But I have scarcely known one who had caught the manner of the Epistles to Atticus. Pray, thumb those Epistles to pieces. It is what I should do if I were going to Cambridge next October.

Look at the last line but one of page 37. I presume that the *in* has stolen into the sentence by the fault of the printer.

Are you not a little too fond of the subjunctive mood? Nine people out of ten err on the other side. But you seem to me to carry to an excess your dislike of the Indicative, a very honest, solid, useful, part of every language, whatever you may think. In the last line of page 15, I should have written *possumus* instead of *possimus*. In the last paragraph of page 16, I should have written *fert* and *ostentat* instead of *ferat* and *ostentet*. At the top of the next page I should have written *censent* instead of *censeant*. Remember Horace:

"Sunt quos curriculo pulverem Olympicum
Collegisse *juvat*;"[1]

and a little further on

"Est qui nec veteris pocula Massici,
Nec partem solido demere de die,
Spernit."[2]

So Juvenal, speaking of the barbarous way in which the ladies of his time treated their slaves, says

"Sunt quae tortoribus annua *præstant*."[3]

You may find apparent, but only apparent, instances on the other side. There is a very remarkable passage in Horace's Epistle to Julius Florus.

"gemmas, marmor, ebur, Tyrrhena sigilla, tabellas,
Argentum, vestas Gætulo murice tinctas,
Sunt qui non *habeant*, est qui non *curat* habere."[4]

[1] *Odes*, I, i, 3–4. [2] *Ibid.*, 19–21. [3] *Satires*, VI, 480. [4] *Epistles*, II, ii, 180–2.

Some editors altered *curat* into *curet*, that it might correspond to *habeant*. But Bentley restored the proper reading, which is that of all the best M.S.S. Of his predecessors, who had corrupted *curat* into *curet*, he said; "latuit eos sententiæ energia."[1] "Non habeant," he added, meant "nequeunt habere." "Non curat" does not mean "nequit curare." Its meaning is plainly indicative. The man does not care. I think that Bentley would have corrected your *censeant* into *censent*. Ask Dr. Vaughan, however. I entirely submit my judgment to his.

My old college friend Derwent Coleridge called on me yesterday to congratulate me on your success, and to tell me how much he had been pleased with the speeches.[2] Perhaps some time about the year 1900, Butler or Trotter[3] may congratulate you on the success of some young fellow in whom you are interested, a nephew, or, as I rather hope, a son.

Ever yours,
T B Macaulay

TO CHRISTIAN BERNHARD TAUCHNITZ, 6 JULY 1857

Text: Bernhard Tauchnitz, 1837–1887, p. 110.

Holly Lodge, Kensington, July 6, 1857.

The Third part of my History is hardly begun: and it is not very likely that I shall live to complete it. At all events, it will be a business of six or seven years. You shall be informed, from time to time, of the progress which I make.[4]

TO THOMAS FLOWER ELLIS, 30 JULY [1857]

MS: Trinity College.

Holly Lodge / July 30.

Dear Ellis,

I will dine with you on Monday at 1/2 past 7.

My arrangements as to France[5] are not fixed; and I can easily alter them to suit your convenience.

[1] Bentley's *Horace*, Cambridge, 1711, p. 404.
[2] The Harrow speech day was 2 July.
[3] Coutts Trotter (1837–87: *DNB*), B.A. Trinity, 1859; President of the Union, 1860; Fellow of Trinity, 1861, and successively Junior Dean, Tutor, Senior Dean, and Vice-Master.
[4] TBM received £160 from Tauchnitz on this day (Journal, XI, 140).
[5] See 11 August.

I looked over your papers on the Greek philosophers. They will be of great use to George. But I noticed one or two things which a little surprised me. Why do you put Epimenides[1] on the list of Barbarian philosophers? Diogenes Laertius and St Paul agree in making him a Cretan; and his name is plainly Greek. The names of Calamus and Anacharsis, with whom you have classed him, are not of Greek derivation. I think that you are a little too favourable to the Epicureans. I have no other criticism to make, except that, by a slip of the pen, you have called Aristotle a pupil of Socrates.

The news from India[2] is not bad, on the whole.

Ever yours,
T B Macaulay

TO CHRISTIAN BERNHARD TAUCHNITZ, 1 AUGUST 1857

Text: Bernhard Tauchnitz, 1837–1887, p. 110.

Holly Lodge, Kensington, Aug. 1, 1857.

I readily accede to what you propose as to terms. Give the collection what title you please.[3]

TO SELINA MACAULAY, 2 AUGUST 1857

MS: Trinity College.

Holly Lodge Kensington / August 2. 1857

Dearest Selina,

Your question about Hanover may be very simply answered. None of the Queen's children can reign there, any more than herself. The succession to that crown is through males exclusively.

Yesterday I happened to be in Great Ormond Street, and saw a bill sticking on Number 50. I knocked, asked to see the house, and was let in. How vividly I remembered everything, after the lapse of more than

[1] 'Even his existence is doubted' (*Encyclopaedia Britannica*); he is supposedly the Cretan prophet alluded to in the Epistle to Titus, 1: 12.

[2] The Indian Mutiny broke out on 10 May; the first news of it reached London on 27 June, when TBM wrote: 'Horrible news from India. Massacre of Europeans at Delhi. Mutiny. I have no apprehensions for our Indian Empire. But this is a frightful event' (Journal, XI, 137).

[3] *Biographical Essays*, 1857, volume 405 of Tauchnitz's 'Collection of British Authors,' contains TBM's *ER* essays on Frederic the Great and Barère and his lives of Bunyan, Goldsmith, and Johnson from the *Encyclopaedia Britannica*.

twenty six years. The dining room has never been repainted, or, at any rate, has been repainted of the old colour. It looked exactly as it used to do, only more dingy. The drawing rooms have different paper: but in general everything looks much as it did. The people who are going to leave the place have been there three and twenty years. Francis is the name – Philip Francis[1] – I do not know whether related to Sir Philip or not.

Hannah and the children are on the road to Munich. Trevelyan, to my great sorrow, stays behind. He is so much excited about these Indian events that, though he has no power of doing anything that can be of the smallest use, he will not stir. In the first week of September I shall meet the party at Paris, and pass a day or two with them there. Then I mean to visit Rheims, Bourges, and possibly Bordeaux.

The Manchester exhibition[2] is undoubtedly fine. But I had seen the best things with scarcely an exception. However it was very agreeable to find them all assembled under one roof. The collection of portraits disappointed me, – not that it was not good; – but too much had been said about it; and there were great deficiencies.

I am preparing a cheaper and more convenient edition of my history.[3] I correct the press with much care; and I hope that the printing will be almost faultless. I have retouched the style, and added some notes, particularly about Penn, which are likely, I think, to make a noise.

Ever yours,
T B Macaulay

TO THOMAS FLOWER ELLIS, 6 AUGUST 1857

MS: Trinity College.

Holly Lodge August 6 / 1857

Dear Ellis,

Nothing could be duller than Palmer's[4] speech. The tone too was that

[1] He was a barrister, of the Middle Temple.

[2] The Manchester 'Exhibition of the Art Treasures of the United Kingdom,' organized under the patronage of Prince Albert, opened in May and attracted over a million visitors. TBM, with Hannah and Margaret, went to Manchester to see it on 20 July and returned on the 23rd (Journal, XI, 148–52). The Exhibition, which was the occasion of Ruskin's lectures on 'The Political Economy of Art,' has been called 'the first really great general exhibition of works of art' (Winslow Ames, *Prince Albert and Victorian Taste*, New York, 1968, p. 151).

[3] See 27 October 1856.

[4] Roundell Palmer (1812–95: *DNB*), a leading equity lawyer, afterwards first Earl of Selborne and Lord Chancellor, was appearing for the Duke of Norfolk in the Shrewsbury case. On the death of the 17th Earl of Shrewsbury in 1856, Lord Talbot, a distant cousin

of a man fighting a hopeless battle. I hear only one opinion of the case. Lefevre, Thoms,[1] and two people whose names I did not make out, all said the same. I am afraid that I shall not be able to hear Kelly's[2] reply. When the fight is over to morrow, let me know how it went off. The accounts in the papers are of very little value. Let me know at the same time what your movements are, and how long you expect to be at Liverpool.

Ever yours,
T B Macaulay

TO LADY TREVELYAN, 10 AUGUST 1857

MS: Trinity College. *Partly published:* Trevelyan, II, 434–5.

Holly Lodge Kensington W. / August 10. 1857

Dearest Hannah,

I have just received a letter, half yours and half Baba's, from Frankfort; and glad I was to receive it. The weather at the beginning of last week was as hot here as it could be on the Rhine, as hot as I ever felt it out of the tropics, as hot, I think, as it was last summer at Turin and Milan. Then came a change. We had three days of sullen clouds, heavy showers, and chill breezes. I was forced to draw my blanket about me at night, and once seriously thought of having a fire in the library. Some people, – Lord Overstone among them, – began to fear that the harvest, which had promised so gloriously, would prove a failure. Happily yesterday afternoon the sky cleared. This morning there is not a cloud: the sun is blazing; and, no doubt, hundreds of thousands of acres will be reaped before night. Six or seven such days, and our bread is safe for the year.

No more news from India; that is to say, no later news than we had

successfully claimed the title. Ellis was one of Lord Talbot's counsel in the case, which was heard before the Committee of Privileges of the House of Lords. Talbot's claim was especially opposed by the Duke of Norfolk, to whose infant son the late Lord Shrewsbury had willed his estate. After hearings that began in July 1857 judgment was given in favor of Lord Talbot's claim on 1 June 1858.

1 William John Thoms (1803–85: *DNB*), Clerk of the House of Lords, 1845–63, when he was appointed Deputy-Librarian of the House of Lords; he published much editorial and antiquarian work, and founded *Notes and Queries*. As Clerk of the House of Lords he was able to provide many documents for TBM's use, a help which is acknowledged in ch. 11 of the *History* (III, 90n).

2 Sir Fitzroy Kelly (1796–1880: *DNB*), one of the most successful lawyers of the day, the holder of various law offices under the Tories, and later Chief Baron of the Exchequer, was counsel for Lord Talbot. Ellis had appeared with him before, in Achilli v Newman (see 21 September 1851). TBM went to Westminster Hall on this day hoping to 'hear a good speech from Kelly' but 'heard a bad one from Palmer – tired, went away' (Journal, XI, 160). The speech was Palmer's summing up for the opposition; Kelly replied next day.

before you started: but private letters are appearing daily in the newspapers, and details not found in those letters are reported in conversation. The cruelties of the Sepoys, and, above all, the indignities which English ladies have undergone, have inflamed the nation to a degree unprecedented within my memory. All the philanthropic cant of Peace Societies, and Aborigines Protection Societies, and Societies for the Reformation of Criminals, is silenced. There is one terrible cry for revenge. The account of that dreadful military execution at Peshawar[1] – forty men blown at once from the mouths of cannon, their heads, legs, arms flying in all directions, – was read with delight by people who three weeks ago, were against all capital punishment. Bright himself, Quaker as he is, declares for the vigorous suppression of the mutiny.[2] The almost universal feeling is that not a single Sepoy, within the walls of Delhi, should be spared; and I own that it is a feeling with which I cannot help sympathising.

I am reading Below the Surface.[3] The book has merit. I wish the title were less affected.

I went to the House of Lords on Thursday in the hope of hearing Kelly on the great Shrewsbury case. But I heard only Roundell Palmer; and very dull and feeble his speech was. I was so weary of it that I went away in an hour, and have not ventured on another experiment. London is emptying fast. On Wednesday the 12th, I shall dine with my neighbours the Argylls;[4] and that will probably be the last dinner of the season. Pray let me be accurately informed about your movements. Love to Baba and George, and Alice. I wrote to you last Monday, and to Baba onThursday.

Ever yours

T B M.

1 *The Times*, 4 August.

2 Bright had been invited to stand for Birmingham and had, on the urging of his committee, stated publicly that he would not 'resist' the measures required to suppress the Mutiny. The address is in *The Times*, 10 August.

3 Sir Arthur Hallam Elton, *Below the Surface: A Story of English Country Life*, 3 vols., 1857. TBM explains what he means by affectation in titles in his Journal for 18 July, when he was reading Francis Head's *Bubbles from the Brunnens of Nassau*; this, he writes, was 'one of the first instances of that vile taste in the titles of books of travels which has since become general – Eothen – The Far West – Vines and Oranges – The City of the Sultan – Chow Chow – are instances' (XI, 148).

4 The party were Lord Lansdowne, Sir G. C. Lewis, Labouchere, Sir James Melville, and Lord Granville (Journal, XI, 162).

TO THOMAS FLOWER ELLIS, 11 AUGUST 1857

MS: Trinity College. *Partly published:* Trevelyan, II, 371n.

Holly Lodge Kensington / W / August 11. 1857

Dear Ellis,

I expect that we shall have Franz with us on our short tour. We shall pass the first week of September at Paris, taking out the time necessary for a trip to Bourges and back. Then we shall go to Rheims, thence to Treves, then down the Moselle to Coblentz, – a beautiful voyage, – then down the Rhine to Cologne; and then by railway through Liege and Ghent to Calais. Such, at least, is the plan which occurs to me. Perhaps you may be able to improve it.[1]

Lord Panmure[2] has asked me to write an inscription for a column which is building at Scutari in honor of our sailors and soldiers who died in the East, during the last war.[3] It is no easy task as you may guess. Give me your opinion of what I have written. It is, as you will see, concise and austerely simple. There is not a single adjective. So far I believe that I am right. But whether the execution be in other respects good is a matter about which I feel great misgivings.

What are your plans. No news yet from India. Good news from our travellers in Germany.

Ever yours
T B Macaulay

To the Memory
of the British Soldiers and Sailors
Who
During the years 1854 and 1855
Died far from their Country
In defence of the Liberties of Europe
This monument is erected
By the gratitude
Of Queen Victoria and of her People
1857.

[1] This is substantially the itinerary they followed, though they did not go to Bourges; they left London on 30 August, left Paris for Rheims on 6 September, reached Cologne on the 11th, and were back in London on the 14th (Journal, x, 160–96).

[2] Fox Maule succeeded as second Baron Panmure in 1852 and was now Secretary for War.

[3] Panmure asked TBM, Lord John Russell, and Sir David Dundas each to write an inscription; he then sent their efforts to the Queen, with Palmerston's opinion in favor of Dundas's (Sir George Douglas and Sir George Ramsay, eds., *The Panmure Papers*, 2 vols., 1908, II, 451–2). Apparently none of them was used: see 6 April 1858. A very slightly different MS version of TBM's inscription is at Trinity. See also *to* Russell, 17 August.

TO MARGARET TREVELYAN, 13 AUGUST 1857

MS: Sir William Dugdale, Bt.

Holly Lodge Kensington / August 13. 1857

Dearest Baba,

The Indian news is come. It is not bad: Madras and Bombay are quiet: our troops everywhere victorious in the field: the Punjab safe: the anarchy terrible through the whole region from Benares to the Sutlej: but no regular military resistance except at Delhi. The mutineers have repeatedly made sallies from Delhi, but have always been beaten. Reinforcements are arriving: Calcutta is quiet; and the worst seems to be over. This news is by telegraph.[1] The details we shall not have for two days or so. I write, because you may perhaps not fall in with any newspaper for some time.

Remember to give me full and precise information as to anything that you may wish me to do for you or to order for you at Paris. My present plan is to be there late on the night of the 31st. Shall I take apartments for you; or would you rather trust to Pierotti's[2] management. He will no doubt do the thing well.

Love to Mamma, George and Alice.

Ever yours, my darling,
T B Macaulay

TO FRANCES MACAULAY, 17 AUGUST 1857

MS: Trinity College.

Holly Lodge Kensington / August 17. 1857

Dearest Fanny,

I am glad that you have had so pleasant an excursion. I am, for me, remarkably well. It is long since I have passed a month so comfortably as the last. On the 31st I mean to run to Paris. There I hope to meet Hannah and her children on the 1st of September. I shall visit Rheims, thence proceed to Treves, run down the Moselle to Coblentz and down the Rhine to Cologne, and shall return to England by Calais. I shall be little more than a fortnight away.

Everything will go right in India, I hope and believe; and this storm, like the thunderstorm last week, will clear the air, and give us, I hope, a long calm.

[1] TBM got it at the dinner at Argyll Lodge on the night before (Journal, XI, 162).

[2] The courier on TBM and Ellis's tour in Italy in 1856; he was now accompanying the Trevelyans.

The Speaker called on me yesterday. His wife had just heard from Lady Canning. He gave me a most amusing account of the letter. The King of Oude,[1] you are aware, has been arrested and is confined in Fort William on grave suspicion of having been concerned in the mutiny. The wretched creature imagined that the government was going to retaliate on him all the barbarities which had been committed by the Sepoys at Meerut and Delhi, and implored mercy in the most abject manner. He howled, Lady Canning says, like a jackal. If he is really guilty, I would give him something to howl for. Love to Selina.

Yours ever
T B Macaulay

TO THOMAS FLOWER ELLIS, 17 AUGUST 1857

MS: Trinity College.

Holly Lodge Kensington / August 17. 1857

Dear Ellis,

So your cause is to sleep through the recess, and to wake again in the winter.[2] By all that I can learn, the decision will certainly be in Lord Talbot's favour, unless, within a few months, some other Earl of Shrewsbury is produced, – a most improbable event, and one which your opponents will certainly not assist in bringing about.

I suppose that, by this time, you see your way clear. When shall you be in town? I am glad that my sketch of a tour pleases you. But you will, I am afraid, be less pleased when I tell you that we must positively be at Paris on the evening of the 31st, Monday. Lady Trevelyan will be there the next day; and I must be before her. She will stay only a day or two; but I positively must entertain her at the Frères Provençaux. I have heard from her at Salzburg. They are all well. George, in spectacles, with a pilgrim's staff, and a burden as big as Christian's on his back, is making a pedestrian excursion in the company of Montague Butler.[3]

The Indian news is on the whole good. Barnard[4] had been waiting for

[1] Wazid Ali Shah; his deposition by the British early in 1856 (see *to* Lady Trevelyan, 4 September 1856) was an event contributing to the Mutiny. He was arrested shortly after its outbreak.

[2] After hearing the evidence in the Shrewsbury case (see 6 August) the Committee of Privileges adjourned *sine die*. New hearings began in April 1858.

[3] Trevelyan's own account of this tour is published in G. M. Trevelyan, *Sir George Otto Trevelyan*, pp. 24–7.

[4] Sir Henry William Barnard (1799–1857: *DNB*), commanding the army before Delhi, was already six weeks dead at the time this letter was written, many weeks before the fall of the city.

reinforcements. He meant to try a coup de main; and he had little doubt of succeeding. In health, spirit, and discipline, his army was in the very finest state. The Speaker gave me an account of a very interesting letter which his wife has had from Lady Canning. The King of Oude, when he was brought to Fort William, thought that he was going to be put to some horrible death, and implored mercy in the most piteous manner. He howled, her Ladyship says, like a jackal. By this time I hope that the King of Delhi[1] has howled too, and that he has had something to howl for.

Ever yours
T B Macaulay

TO LORD JOHN RUSSELL, 17 AUGUST 1857

MS: Public Record Office.

Holly Lodge Kensington / August 17. 1857

Dear Lord John,

I will tell you what I think with perfect frankness. For we are, I hope, a good deal above the miserable jealousies and vanities of Vadius and Trissotin.[2]

I think then that your inscription is not an inscription.[3] It is, in some sense, too good, too rich, too eloquent, too much like a fine peroration of a funeral panegyric. Nothing can be better than the carving of Henry the Seventh's Chapel. But I would not carve the Eddystone lighthouse or the piers of London Bridge after that fashion.

I will give you your revenge by sending you what I had written. It is very short, austerely simple, without metaphor, without antithesis, and without a single epithet.

To the Memory
Of the British Soldiers and Sailors
Who
During the Years 1854 and 1855
Died far from their Country

[1] Bahadur Shah (1775–1862), last of the Mogul emperors, exiled in 1858.

[2] In Molière, *Les Femmes Savantes*.

[3] The subject is the inscription for the Scutari monument: see 11 August. A sample will show the style of Russell's inscription: 'To the Memory of the gallant soldiers Who fought at Alma, Inkerman, Balaclava: Who by invincible courage in the field, By fortitude, discipline, and patience, Amid the rigours of an inclement sky, And the labours of a protracted siege, By firmness and intrepidity, By unmurmuring resignation,' etc. (copy, Public Record Office).

In Defence of the Liberties of Europe
This Monument was erected
By Queen Victoria and her People
1857.

The first question to be decided is which of us has formed the more correct notion of what the inscription ought to be. If the decision be in your favour, I will give you all the assistance that I can in details. If a concise and severe style should be preferred, I have no doubt that you will produce, in that style, a composition much superior to that which I have sent you.

The first thing to be done, I think, is to ascertain the opinion of Dundas, who is joined with us in commission. Will you write to him, or shall I? I do not know his address. But I suppose that I can easily learn it. / Ever, dear Lord John,

Very truly yours,
T B Macaulay

TO WILLIAM CHAPPELL,[1] 18 AUGUST 1857

Text: Anderson Galleries Catalogue, 10–11 November 1924, item 594, 4pp. 8vo.: dated Kensington, 18 August 1857.

I never examined into the history of our national hymn. But I have heard, and I believe, that it was first produced soon after the Restoration.[2] . . . I should like to know when "Rule Britannia" became a national favourite.

TO WILLIAM CHAPPELL, 24 AUGUST 1857

Text: Anderson Galleries Catalogue, 10–11 November 1924, item 595, 2pp. 8vo.: dated Kensington, 24 August 1857.

Nature, I grieve to say, has denied me an ear for music. But there is much in your work[3] to interest even a person who is so unfortunate as hardly to perceive the difference between "See, the Conquering Hero comes" and the "Hallelujah Chorus."

[1] Chappell (1809–88: *DNB*), music publisher and historian of music, a pioneer in the study of traditional English music.

[2] Chappell was at this time working on the revision of his *Collection of National English Airs*, published in parts between 1855 and 1859 as *Popular Music of Olden Time*. In that he gives a full treatment of the controversy over the origin of 'God Save the King.'

[3] Probably some parts of Chappell's *Popular Music of Olden Time*, a copy of which is listed in the sale catalogue of TBM's library.

TO FRANCES MACAULAY, 25 AUGUST 1857

MS: Trinity College.

Holly Lodge Kensington / Aug 25. 1857

Dearest Fanny,

I hope to be at the Hotel du Louvre. But possibly I may not be able to find accommodation there. You had better therefore, if you have occasion to write during the six or seven days that I shall pass at Paris, direct to the Poste Restante.

By the last letters from our travellers in Germany I learn that the rain has been more trying than the heat.

It is not impossible that I may visit Brighton for a short time in September or at the beginning of October.

I am very busy with the new edition of my history. It will be, I think, as accurately printed as any book that I know. The form will be commodious, seven volumes of no large size, the type exceedingly good and clear. I have found very few important mistakes to correct. But I have removed many small blemishes, retouched the style, and added some notes, particularly about Penn. The book will be published by volumes monthly, beginning in the winter. Each volume will be six shillings; and the Longmans seem to count on a good sale. Love to dear Selina.

Ever yours,
T B Macaulay

BARON MACAULAY OF ROTHLEY
29 AUGUST 1857–29 DECEMBER 1858

1857 August 28
Receives offer of peerage from Palmerston

– August 30–September 14
Continental tour with Ellis: Paris, Rheims, Trèves, Brussels

– October 22
Elected High Steward of Cambridge

– December 3
Takes seat in House of Lords

1858 April 1–5
Easter tour to Lichfield and Oxford

– May 11
Speech on installation as High Steward of Cambridge

– August 9
Finishes life of Pitt for *Encyclopaedia Britannica*

– August 28–September 14
French tour with Ellis: Paris, Lyons, Avignon, Montpellier, Toulouse, Bordeaux

– November 25
Marriage of Margaret Trevelyan to Henry Holland

TO SELINA AND FRANCES MACAULAY, 29 AUGUST 1857

MS: Trinity College.

Holly Lodge Kensington / August 29. 1857

My dearest sisters,

What I am going to tell you must be for the present a strict secret.

I received yesterday a letter from Lord Palmerston informing me that the Queen had permitted him to offer me a peerage.[1] I was greatly surprised: but I did not hesitate one moment. I notified my respectful and grateful acceptance; and, in a few days, I expect to be Lord Macaulay. I must be Lord Macaulay of some place; and I find it difficult to make a selection. I think I shall be Lord Macaulay of Rothley.[2]

At my time of life and with my habits of mind, I am not likely to be much elated by such distinctions. But it is agreeable to me to think that I have never directly or indirectly solicited anything of the kind. Three years ago I should have doubted whether I could at all support the dignity of a peer. But I am now very far from being the poorest man of the honorable order.

Remember – strict secrecy. I shall write only to our brother Charles and to Trevelyan. Hannah I hope to see at Paris on Tuesday. If you have anything to say, direct to me at the Hotel du Louvre.

Ever yours
T B Macaulay

TO SIR GEORGE CORNEWALL LEWIS, 9 SEPTEMBER 1857

MS: National Library of Wales. *Address:* The Right [Honorable][3] G C Lewis Bart. M.P. / etc. etc. etc. / Downing Street / S.W. / London. *Upper left corner: Private. Subscription:* TBM.

Treves September 9. 1857

Dear Lewis,

Thanks for your most kind letter. I can hardly, in my state of health, hope to appear with distinction on a new stage. But I hope at least to conduct myself in such a way that my friends may not be ashamed of me.

[1] Lord Granville claimed the credit of suggesting this honor. In January 1856 he wrote to Lord Canning: 'I have advised Pam to make an offer of a peerage to Macaulay, who is about to leave the House of Commons – a good idea, eh?'; and, after the event: 'Macaulay's peerage was the result of my teasing for two years. It has been a hit' (Lord Edmond Fitzmaurice, *The Life of Lord Granville, 1815–1891*, 1905, I, 139; 261).

[2] 'I determined to be Baron Macaulay of Rothley. I was born there. I have lived much there. I am named from the family which long had the manor. My uncle was Rector there. Nobody can complain of my taking a designation from a village which is nobody's property now' (Journal, XI, 170: 29 August).

[3] The signature has been cut away; this word on the cover has been taken with it.

I was at Rheims three days ago, admiring the incomparable portal of the Cathedral. To day I have been wandering till my legs sank under me from one Roman monument to another. In no place out of Italy have I seen such magnificent remains of the Cæsars. To be sure I have not seen Nismes. But even Milan and Verona must, as far as Roman antiquities are concerned, give place to Treves. All the interest, however, which I take in baths, basilicas, and ampitheatres is languid when compared with that which I take in Indian affairs. I count the moments till I shall be at Brussels, where I expect to find the London papers, after an interval of a week. God grant that the news may be good!–

Ever yours most truly

[ ][1]

TO LADY TREVELYAN, 14 SEPTEMBER 1857

MS: Sir William Dugdale, Bt.

Holly Lodge Kensington / September 14. 1857

Dearest Hannah,

I wrote to you on Wednesday last from Treves; and I cannot help hoping that you have, by this time, received my letter. I arrived here, in excellent health for me, this afternoon. William frightened me by saying that Baba had been very poorly; but your letter, and a letter from Alice, have reassured me. Pray write without delay; and tell me exactly how she is. I called at the Treasury on my way from the railway station, and learned there that you were at Malvern and Trevelyan with you. Could you secure me a pleasant sitting room and bedroom at the inn there? If you could, I would run down for a couple of days, and have some talk with George, from whose dejection I confidently infer that he will succeed.

I am buried up to the eyes in letters and proof sheets. I have to write to six and thirty people, and to correct more than two hundred pages of the new edition of my book. I must get up at six to morrow, and work three hours before breakfast.

My place is looking lovely. The rain has made the grass as rich and green as it was in April.

I am well pleased with the Indian news which met me at Dover. All will go right. I have told you nothing about my travels. A heavy shower of rain swelled the Moselle, and enabled us to go down to Coblentz by steam on Thursday. Thence we proceeded through Cologne and Aix La Chapelle to Brussels, and thence to London. Both Ellis and I are quite

[1] Signature cut away.

converts to your opinion about Cologne Cathedral. It is the finest of Gothic Churches, except the Duomo at Milan. Ellis will not even make that exception.

Love to both your dear children and their Papa. They tell me at the Treasury that he comes back on Wednesday. I wish that he would dine here quietly on Saturday.

Ever yours –
~~TBM~~

I must sign by my title for the first time. I do assure you that I often forget it hours together. William is a good flapper[1] however. He My Lords me at every other word.

Ever yours
Macaulay

TO LORD JOHN RUSSELL, 15 SEPTEMBER 1857

MS: British Museum; Public Record Office. *Published:* Russell, *Later Correspondence*, II 221–2.

Holly Lodge Kensington / September 15. 1857

Dear Lord John,

I have just returned from a tour of a fortnight, in the course of which I have visited Rheims and Treves, places less known than they deserve to be. I found here your letter of the 2nd. Whether you are still at Minto I have no means of knowing: but I will write at a venture.

I am truly glad that you think I did right in accepting a peerage. I never even hinted to any human being a wish for such an honor, nor had I the least expectation that such an honor, solicited in vain by so many of the opulent and highborn, would be offered to me without the slightest intimation on my part that I desired or that I should accept it. Palmerston's letter took me completely by surprise. In two minutes however I made up my mind; and it gratifies me to find that my decision is generally approved by those whom I love and esteem.

As to the Scutari Monument, I sent the two inscriptions to Dundas; and I received his answer when I was just on the point of starting for the Continent. On the great issues – short or long, – austere or ornamented, – he is strongly on my side. The criticising of details would at present be idle. How is it possible for three people, separated from one another by hundreds of miles, to discuss minute questions touching the choice and

[1] See Part 3 of *Gulliver's Travels*: the savants of Laputa are recalled from their abstraction by servants who strike them with bladders.

arrangement of words. The business must be postponed till we can meet.

My kindest regards to Lady John, and to Lord Minto, if you are still his guests. / Ever, dear Lord John,

Yours very truly
T B Macaulay

TO LORD STANHOPE, 15 SEPTEMBER 1857

MS: Stanhope Papers, Chevening.

Holly Lodge Kensington / September 15. 1857

My dear Stanhope,

I have just arrived here from the Continent. I have been visiting Rheims and Treves, and have been delighted with both. On my table I found your most friendly letter of the 5th. Many thanks for your kind congratulations. Thanks too to Lady Stanhope. I really cannot say how much I feel for her, and for you on her account.[1]

I could write a great deal. But I am so doubtful whether this letter will ever reach you that I think it best to be concise. I have a curious book for you, which you shall have, with explanations, when we meet.

With kindest regards to Lady Stanhope and to the young Lady, if she is of your party, believe me

Ever yours truly
Macaulay

TO LADY HOLLAND,[2] 15 SEPTEMBER 1857

MS: Mr D. C. L. Holland.

Holly Lodge Kensington / September 15. 1857

Dear Lady Holland,

I returned yesterday evening to this place after a short tour of the Continent, and I found a huge pile of letters on my table. They were all written with much kindness, and gave me much pleasure. But none was written with more kindness or gave me more pleasure than yours. Pray accept my thanks.

Ever most truly yours,
Macaulay

[1] The Stanhopes were touring in Switzerland; Lady Stanhope had perhaps broken her arm again (see 19 November 1855).

[2] The wife of Sir Henry, not Lord, Holland.

TO EDMUND BLAKELY,[1] 15 SEPTEMBER 1857

MS: Trinity College.

Holly Lodge Kensington / September 15. 1857

Sir,

On my return from the Continent yesterday evening I found your letter on my table. I am much obliged by the interest which you are good enough to take in my researches. I should much like to see the Norwich papers which you mention.[2] To London papers I have ready access in the British Museum. / I have the honor to be, / Sir,

Your faithful Servant,

Macaulay

E Blakely Esq / etc. etc. etc.

TO UNIDENTIFIED RECIPIENT, 15 SEPTEMBER 1857

MS: Harvard University.

Holly Lodge Kensington / September 15. 1857

My dear Sir,

Thanks for your kind note. I am forced to be concise: for I have just arrived here from the Continent, and have found on my table forty letters which must be answered to day.

Ever yours truly,

Macaulay

TO LADY TREVELYAN, 16 SEPTEMBER 1857

MS: Sir William Dugdale, Bt.

Holly Lodge Kensington / September 16. 1857

Dearest Hannah,

I will go down on Tuesday next, and stay till Friday,[3] if you can procure accommodation for me. I must take William with me. I am delighted to have so good an account of my dear Baba. Thanks to her for her letter.

1 Identified only as a gentleman of Norwich in TBM's Journal.

2 Papers of Queen Anne's time (see *to* Blakely, 28 September). TBM received and read them on 27 September (Journal, XI, 185).

3 At Malvern, where Hannah was staying, apparently for the sake of Margaret's health. TBM was uneasy and could not stay away: he was at Malvern, at the Foley Arms, 22–5 September.

I have all sorts of things to tell you. But they will keep till we meet. I had to write seven and twenty letters at one sitting yesterday. I have paid five hundred pounds for my patent. About my robes I have written to Lord Belper,[1] who has very lately been buying robes for himself, and who is not the man to give an extravagant price for such things.

Love to the dear children.

Ever yours
T B Macaulay

By the bye, though I am called Lord Macaulay since the appearance of the Gazette, the patent is not yet sealed. It bears date to day.

TO ADAM BLACK, 17 SEPTEMBER 1857

MS: National Library of Scotland. *Published:* [Black], *Biographies by Lord Macaulay*, p. liv

Holly Lodge Kensington / September 17. 1857

My dear Sir,

Thanks for your most kind letter. I am truly glad that my old friends at Edinburgh are not displeased with what I have done. I need hardly assure you that I never, directly or indirectly, solicited the honor which has been conferred on me. The letter in which Palmerston informed me that he had received the Queen's permission to offer me a peerage took me altogether by surprise. I was on the point of starting for the continent; and I had nobody to consult. I made up my mind very speedily; but I had, I own, serious apprehensions that both Palmerston and myself would be blamed by a large part of the public. It is therefore most gratifying to me to learn that both the offer and the acceptance are generally approved. / Ever, my dear Sir,

Yours most truly
Macaulay

TO MARGARET TREVELYAN, 18 SEPTEMBER 1857

MS: Sir William Dugdale, Bt.

Holly Lodge Kensington / September 18. 1857

Dearest Baba,

I ought to have written before to you in answer to your two letters. It

[1] Strutt was created Baron Belper in August 1856.

was not because you were not in my thoughts that I omitted to write. For indeed indeed you are very dear to me; and I am even weakly anxious for accounts of your health.

I am overwhelmed with letters of congratulation; and, empty as London is, plenty of people come to shake hands with me. I think I told your Mamma that I had written to Lord Belper for advice about my robes. He informs me that he, in the same situation, took the advice of Lord Overstone, and found it to be good. I have, accordingly, in reliance on the judgment of these very sensible and frugal patricians, sent for a certain Mr Hunter of Maddox Street,[1] who had left a card here, and who is, it seems, robe maker to the Queen. This person, I am assured, will clothe me in scarlet, with the proper quantity of ermine and gold lace for £36.15.0. This I call moderate: for I was afraid that I might have had to pay £100.

On Tuesday I will take down with me to Malvern a heap of letters which I have received since I became a Lord. Some of them will interest you.

Your papa, your uncle Charles and Sir Edward Ryan, are to dine here quietly to day. I wish that I could flatter myself that anything will be talked about but India. The Indian news of to day is unpleasant, but does not at all affect the certainty of the result.[2] Within a month from this time the tide will have completely turned; and another month will bring us news of the turn.

John and his son Charles called on me yesterday morning. Ellis was breakfasting with me. He had never seen either of them before. When they were gone, he said, "A fine young man, that nephew of yours. His mother must be a very handsome woman." A delicate compliment to John's appearance. Charles has been fitted out, and seems impatient for danger and distinction.

Love to Mamma and George.

Ever yours, my darling
TBM

[1] John Hunter, robe maker and tailor to the Queen, 16 Maddox Street (*Post Office London Directory*, 1857).

[2] *The Times* of this day reported that an outbreak of cholera had forced General Havelock's army, after advancing within a day's march of Lucknow, to fall back on Cawnpore and await reinforcements.

TO J. F. MACFARLAN, 18 SEPTEMBER 1857

MS: Berg Collection, New York Public Library. *Envelope:* J F Macfarlan Esq / etc. etc. etc. / Millport / N.B. *Subscription:* M.

Holly Lodge Kensington / September 18. 1857

My dear Sir,

I beg you to accept my thanks for your kind congratulations. It is most gratifying to me to find that my old friends at Edinburgh do not think the Queen's favour ill bestowed, or blame me for accepting it.

Very truly yours,
Macaulay

J F Macfarlan Esq / etc. etc. etc.

TO FRANCES MACAULAY, 26 SEPTEMBER 1857

MS: Trinity College.

Holly Lodge Kensington / September 26. 1857

Dearest Fanny,

I returned yesterday evening from Malvern. I left them all well. Baba is all but perfectly recovered.

I think of going down to Brighton on Monday week, October the 5th. I shall stay there till Thursday the 8th, and shall take Alice back with me to town. Can you get good accommodation for me at the Norfolk? I shall bring William.

I have received no letter from Mrs. Rose. I should not have left a letter from her one post unanswered. Pray let me know her address without delay.

Love to Selina and to my little Alice.

Ever yours
Macaulay

TO THOMAS FLOWER ELLIS, 26 SEPTEMBER 1857

MS: Trinity College.

Holly Lodge / Septr. 26. 1857

Dear Ellis,

I shall call for you at the University Club next Tuesday a little before six. We have dined together on Michaelmas day, these many years. I will order a goose of the geese for you. You had better come again on the

Wednesday to despatch the legs devilled, which I rather prefer to the fillets of the breast.

I had two delightful days at Malvern. My dear Baba is very well. I went with her, her Mamma and her brother over much ground which was familiar to me six years ago, walked to the Wyche, visited the outskirts of the Roman camp, and descended into the plain to look at that beautiful little Popish chapel. I was quartered at the Foley Arms. The floors of the house shake and creak at every step; and I heard sounds which reminded me of the fatal event to which you so feelingly allude.

Ever yours,
Macaulay

TO EDMUND BLAKELY, 28 SEPTEMBER 1857

MS: Trinity College.

Holly Lodge Kensington / September 28. 1857

Sir,

I return with many thanks the Norwich newspapers which you were so good as to send. You will receive them, I hope, safe by the post which takes this letter.

The most interesting number is that which contains the account of Walpole's reception at Lynn after his expulsion and imprisonment.[1] / I have the honor to be, / Sir,

Your obedient servant,
Macaulay

E Blakely Esq / etc. etc. etc.

TO SIR FREDERIC MADDEN, 28 SEPTEMBER 1857

MS: British Museum. *Envelope:* Sir F Madden / etc. etc. etc. / British Museum. W C. *Subscription:* M.

Holly Lodge Kensington / September 28. 1857

Dear Sir Frederic,

I found your letter here on my return from a trip to the country. Thanks for your kind congratulations. It would give me real pleasure to be able to serve you.[2] But I am so situated with respect to Hayter that

[1] TBM summarizes the narrative in his Journal for 27 September, saying 'I note this for future use – possibly' (XI, 186).

[2] Madden was trying to get his son a clerkship in the Audit Office and wanted an introduction from TBM to W. G. Hayter, the patronage secretary of the Treasury (Diary of Sir Frederic Madden, 24–8 September 1857: MS, Bodleian Library).

I cannot with propriety introduce any person to him at present, in his capacity of dispenser of the Treasury patronage.[1]

I am quite willing, however, that, in any application which you may make to him or to any other person in office, you should vouch me as a witness of the able and faithful services which you have rendered to the public. / Believe me, / Dear Sir Frederic,

Very truly yours
Macaulay

Sir F Madden / etc. etc. etc.

TO FRANCES MACAULAY, 2 OCTOBER 1857

MS: Trinity College.

Holly Lodge Kensington / October 2. 1857

Dearest Fanny,

I think that I shall go down to Brighton by the twelve o'clock train on Monday.[2] I shall be at the Norfolk by two or soon after.

I am sorry that Wednesday is the fast day.[3]

I must positively be in town on Thursday afternoon. I have written to Mrs. Rose.

I shall bring you down a heap of letters which I have received since my new dignity was announced. Some of them may amuse you. Love to Selina and Alice.

Ever yours,
Macaulay

TO THOMAS FLOWER ELLIS, 4 OCTOBER 1857

MS: Trinity College.

Holly Lodge Kensington / October 4. 1857

Dear Ellis,

I am sorry that I am under the necessity of being at the British Museum on Saturday afternoon. Panizzi has written to me pressingly. There is to be a meeting of Trustees after a longer interval than usual. There will be much to do. It is not easy in October to muster a Quorum; and I shall

1 What TBM means, I think, is that Trevelyan was on bad terms with Hayter and that TBM necessarily shared his brother-in-law's quarrel.

2 5 October; he returned on Thursday, the 8th.

3 Proclaimed by the Queen on 24 September as a 'Day for Solemn Fast, Humiliation, and Prayer' over the Mutiny.

probably be in the Chair. I may not be able to escape till late; and I should not at all like to keep you waiting at chambers, in utter uncertainty as to the time of my coming.

We must give the plan[1] up for this week; indeed, I fear, for this season. For I am already beginning to feel the approach of winter; and I doubt whether I shall accompany George to Cambridge. I wish to keep myself well in order that I may be able to take my seat on the first day of the Session.

Did you see an article about me in one of the papers of yesterday?[2] I did not think that the splendour of my dress would ever have been a subject of remark in the public journals. It is related that a north country man was lately at a railway station, and that I was pointed out to him. "Look. That is Macaulay, the author." "Hoot man," was the answer; "That an author! Why he's vura weel dressed, that cheeld, and he has a vura gude hat. An author is as ragged as a potatoe bogle." Sir Edward Lytton will envy me this compliment more than any other that I ever received.[3]

Ever yours
Macaulay

TO THOMAS FLOWER ELLIS, 8 OCTOBER 1857

MS: Trinity College.

Brighton October 8. 1857

Dear Ellis,

I write from Brighton, because I do not expect to reach home till after post hours. We must positively give up our Saturday plan. The difficulty which I mentioned to you is now not the chief one. It is probable, though by no means certain, that I may be able, if I attend the Museum on Saturday, to get away before five. But it is now doubtful whether I shall be able to be at the Museum. The change of weather has brought on an attack of my winter complaint; and I have been, during the last forty eight hours, gasping for breath and coughing violently. I have written to beg Panizzi to let me know whether he can get a Quorum without me. I have written also to tell Hannah that I am afraid that I shall not be able to go with her and George to Cambridge next week. The truth is that, when I am in this way, no place suits me but my own house. Long walks are out of the question. Indeed, if the weather continues to be what it is, I shall lose little by not going to Bromley. For more miserable days than

[1] To spend the weekend at Bromley.
[2] I have not been able to find the paper.
[3] Bulwer-Lytton was a notable dandy.

yesterday and to day I never saw; – the sky dark; the wind roaring; the little portion of the sea which can be seen from the cliff all foam. Much higher seas I have seen; but never a sea more wild and dreary.

I went to Church yesterday to please my sisters: but I had better have staid away. For the effects of my compliance were that I was annoyed by hearing a very bad sermon,[1] and the congregation by hearing a very bad cough. I have since passed my time crouching over the fire and reading. The prospect of the journey home is not very pleasant. But the thing must be done.

Ever yours,
Macaulay

TO THOMAS FLOWER ELLIS, 9 OCTOBER 1857

MS: Trinity College.

Holly Lodge Kensington / Oct 9. 1857

Dear Ellis,

Here I am, by my fireside, coughing and wheezing, less however, I think, from the effect of the weather, which, though damp, is mild, than from the effect of a violent draught of wind in the railway carriage in which I went to Brighton. I caught cold; and the cold, as usual, fastened on my chest. I am better to day than I was yesterday: but I have given up all thoughts of Cambridge, and have excused myself to Whewell, who, most kindly, pressed me to be his guest.

If the sky does not clear up to morrow, I shall be consoled, in part at least, for the failure of our plan about Bromley.

I shall be very little, if at all, from home, next week. On any day that suits you, I will call for you, or, if I cannot call, send for you at the University Club.

I send you an incredible specimen of Irish impudence. Read the bill first, and then the letter. I really thought that it would have been the death of Lady Trevelyan.

Ever yours
Macaulay

Bring the inclosed papers with you, whenever you come. I must not lose them.

[1] See *to* Selina Macaulay, 14 October.

TO WILLIAM WHEWELL, 9 OCTOBER 1857

MS: Trinity College. *Mostly published:* Trevelyan, II, 426.

Holly Lodge Kensington / October 9. 1857

My dear Master,

Thanks for your kindness, which is what it has always been. Unhappily I have so bad a cold, and Trevelyan has so much to do, that neither of us will be able to accompany our boy, – for we are equally interested in him, – to Cambridge next week. It is pleasant to me to think that I have now a new tie to Trinity.

Trevelyan and his wife are most sensible of your kindness.

Ever yours,
Macaulay

TO THOMAS FLOWER ELLIS, 12 OCTOBER 1857

MS: Trinity College.

Holly Lodge Oct 12. 1857

Dear Ellis,

Thanks for your letter and Mr. MacDowall's bill.[1] But you do not say when you can come out to dine here. I am disengaged all the week. Come to morrow: but let me have immediate notice. The carriage will be at the University Club at your own hour. I was not in force yesterday, but am much better to day, indeed well. The Indian news has revived me. Trevelyan and the Chairman called yesterday to tell me of it.[2] It is excellent; – better perhaps than appears at the first glance.

Ever yours
Macaulay

TO FRANCES MACAULAY, 13 OCTOBER 1857

MS: Trinity College.

Holly Lodge / Oct 13. 1857

Dearest Fanny,

Let Charles[3] have the inclosed without delay. I am a good deal better

[1] No doubt the specimen of 'Irish impudence' mentioned in *to* Ellis, 9 October.

[2] 'Trevelyan and Mangles called. Good news. Lucknow safe – Delhi hard pressed – reinforcements arriving. Thank God!' (Journal, XI, 192: 11 October). The news of Lucknow was, of course, premature.

[3] Charles was visiting his sisters in Brighton at the same time as TBM (Journal, XI, 189: 6 October).

than when I left you. All here well. George goes to Cambridge to day.[1] His father and mother will be with him. Love to Selina.

Ever yours
Macaulay

TO CHARLES MACAULAY, 13 OCTOBER 1857

MS: Huntington Library.

Holly Lodge Kensington / W / October 13. 1857

Dear Charles,

Be so good as to send me, on a card, a deep, strong, impression of the larger of the two seals which I gave you. I want it to send to Garter King at Arms.[2]

Ever yours,
Macaulay

TO SELINA MACAULAY, 14 OCTOBER 185[7][3]

MS: Trinity College.

Holly Lodge Kensington / October 14. 1856

Dearest Selina,

The High Stewardship of Cambridge[4] has nothing to do with the University; nor must you call it, as Fanny does, the Lord High Stewardship. It is merely an honorary office in the Corporation, which is generally filled by some Peer. The borough of Cambridge has always, since the Reform Bill, affected to pay great respect to literature and science, and boasts that it has chosen better officers and members than the University. I did not wish for this office. But I could not refuse it, when unanimously offered by the town council.

[1] He called on TBM the day before: 'Long and interesting talk. I was much affected – God bless him dear boy' (Journal, XI, 192).

[2] The design of TBM's arms was now being discussed with the Garter King at Arms; on 21 October he proposed 'a wreath round my boot,' to which TBM objected; on the 27th, being asked to choose between three styles of boot, TBM chose 'the simplest' (Journal, XI, 196; 201).

[3] The misdating in the MS is quite clear.

[4] The office, vacant by the death of Lord Fitzwilliam, was offered to TBM on 9 October, when he declined, 'on the ground that my health would prevent me from performing even the ceremonial functions of such an office' (Journal, XI, 191). He seems to say in this letter that he did not refuse the office, but there is no record of his change of mind in the Journal, which merely reports that 'on the 22nd I was elected High Steward of Cambridge' (XI, 199).

What I blamed Vaughan[1] for was not for expressing disapprobation of the conduct of men of a former generation who dismissed Xtn sepoys from the service, but for the wicked and presumptuous folly of saying that the massacre of innocent women and children at Meerut in 1857 was a judgment for the dismissal of a Xtn Sepoy at Meerut in 1819. He ought too to have had the common honesty to say that the dismissed Sepoy continued to draw his full pay. Few soldiers in our army would think it persecution to be permitted to retire from the service on such terms.

I do not at all agree with the construction which you put on the words, "Go ye into all the world, and preach the Gospel to every creature."[2] Those words were addressed to the Eleven, – not to all Xtn men, or to all Xtn Governments. You surely do not hold that every man is bound to leave his home and to wander about the globe preaching, like St Peter or St John. And if those words were addressed only to the Apostles, what argument can you draw from the passage as to the duties of the English government in India?

Love to Fanny. I sent a line to her yesterday.

Ever yours,
Macaulay

TO CHARLES ROGERS,[3] 14 OCTOBER 1857

MS: Trinity College.

Holly Lodge Kensington / October 14. 1857

Sir

I assure you that I am very sensible of the honour done me by the gentlemen in whose name you write. It is from no want of respect for them that I must beg to be excused from becoming a Member of the Scottish Literary Institute. The truth is that their views, as far as I can judge from the papers which you have sent me, differ very widely from mine; and I should not think myself justified in appearing to countenance

[1] James Vaughan (1805–89: *Boase*), Perpetual Curate of Christ Church, Brighton. His sermon on the day of national humiliation, 7 October, greatly offended TBM: 'If the maxims of this fool, and of others like him, are followed, we shall soon have, not the mutiny of an army, but the rebellion of a whole nation, to deal with. He would have the Government plant missionaries everywhere, invite the sepoy to listen to Christian instruction, and turn the government schools into Christian seminaries' (Trevelyan, II, 436).

[2] Mark 16: 15.

[3] Rogers (1825–90: *DNB*), chaplain of the garrison at Stirling Castle, founded in 1855 a 'short-lived Scottish Literary Institute'; in 1863 he went to London and lived thereafter by his pen but continued to found societies. His LL.D. was from Columbia College, New York.

a scheme, which, though well meant, will, if I am not greatly deceived, either do nothing or do harm. / I have the honor to be, / Sir,

Your most obedient Servant,
Macaulay

C Rogers LLD / etc. etc. etc.

TO UNIDENTIFIED RECIPIENT,[1] 14 OCTOBER 1857

MS: Brotherton Library, University of Leeds.

I cannot undertake to examine the table of Contents. I suppose that it has been drawn up with care.

The date in the title page must be altered to 1858. The same change must be made in the title page of Vol. I. Pray let this be looked to.[2]

Macaulay

Holly Lodge Kensington / October 14. 1857

TO EDWARD EVERETT, [27][3] OCTOBER 1857

Text: New York *Ledger*, 25 February 1860, reprinted in S. A. Allibone, 'Life and Writings of Thomas Babington Macaulay,' in *History of England*, Boston, 1861, v, 77: dated October 1857.

[London]

It would be affectation in me to deny that I was gratified at being invited, without the slightest solicitation, direct or indirect, to accept an honor, which many men of great wealth, and of high descent, have been unable to obtain, or have obtained only by unscrupulous service and importunate application.

TO THOMAS FLOWER ELLIS, 28 OCTOBER 1857

MS: Trinity College. *Extract published:* Trevelyan, 2nd edn, II, 442n.

Holly Lodge Kensington / October 28. 1857

Dear Ellis,

I suppose that to day or to morrow you will be in town. I have no

[1] The style is a bit abrupt for a letter to Longman; someone in the printer's office is likely.

[2] Though publication began in December of this year, all the volumes of the new edition of the *History* (see 27 October 1856) are dated 1858.

[3] The printed text is dated only 'October': TBM's Journal for the 27th records that he 'sent off a letter to Everett who had written to me most kindly' (XI, 200–1).

engagement. So let me know when you will come out and drink a glass of claret to the conquerors of Delhi.[1]

That scoundrel Humphreys[2] of Cheltenham, against whom you cautioned me, has played me, or rather tried to play me, the most impudent trick in the world. I have outgeneralled him however, and have sent him such a reprimand as he will not much like. Thank heaven, I have got rid of him.

Ever yours
Macaulay

I received some grapes last week, I suppose from the Miss Telfourds.[3] Let me know that I may make proper acknowledgments.

TO JOHN HILL BURTON, 30 OCTOBER 1857

MS: National Library of Scotland.

Holly Lodge Kensington / W̄. London / October 30. 1857

My dear Sir,

I am very desirous to see Borland's Memoirs of Darien,[4] mentioned in the note at the foot of page 198 of the Darien papers.[5] Longman has in vain tried to procure it for me. If you have a copy, and would be so kind as to lend it me, I should be greatly obliged to you.

Ever yours truly,
Macaulay

J H Burton Esq / etc. etc. etc.

[1] The news of the capture reached London on the 27th.

[2] See [April? 1856]. TBM learned from Longman on this day that Humphreys had drawn up an advertisement stating that his book on India had been revised by TBM: 'Longman will take care that this lying puff does not appear' (Journal, XI, 202). Two days later Longman told TBM that Humphreys 'actually published at Cheltenham, some time ago, his trash about India, as revised by me. Dirty dog!' (XI, 202). The copy of the book that I have seen, published by Longman but printed in Cheltenham, makes no mention of TBM.

[3] That is, the Miss Telfords, Ellis's relatives and neighbors at Bromley: see 21 May 1855.

[4] Francis Borland, *Memoirs of Darien*, Glasgow, 1715. TBM describes this 'curious and interesting narrative' at the end of ch. 24 of the *History*.

[5] A selection of documents edited by Burton for the Bannatyne Club, 1849, and the basis of TBM's account of Darien. The volume is item 300 in the sale catalogue of TBM's library.

TO AUGUSTUS DE MORGAN, 3 NOVEMBER 1857

MS: University of London.

Holly Lodge Nov 3. 1857

My dear Sir,

It is easy to see why Mansuete[1] was indicated only by initials. It was a capital crime to reconcile any person to the Church of Rome. The Duchess of Portsmouth implored Barillon not to mention her name. It was as much, she said, as her life was worth. Huddleston was disguised as a layman, and introduced into the sick room with great precaution. James boasts of having exposed himself to very serious danger in order to save his brother's soul. While a Roman Catholic King was on the throne, it is true, Mansuete and Huddlestone were safe. But the heiress presumptive was a Protestant; and it was by no means impossible that, if she became Queen while the circumstances of Charles's death were fresh in the public mind, those ecclesiastics who had, as it might have been plausibly said, availed themselves of the clouded state of his mind to seduce him from the faith which he had professed while his faculties were entire, might have been called to a severe account.

I think too that you imagine the initials to have been more mysterious than they were. They have puzzled us. But I suspect that they did not in the least puzzle the readers for whom the narrative was drawn up, that is to say, the Roman Catholics of London. They had no more difficulty in making out P.M. than you have in making out Sir R. W. in a political pamphlet of 1740, or the E. of B. and Mr. P. in a political pamphlet of 1761. There was probably not one among them who did not know the name of the Duke's Confessor, – a name now known only to a few curious students of history.

I dare say that you are right about Marlborough and the Duchess of Cleveland.[2]

Very truly yours,
Macaulay

[1] The priest supposed to be indicated by the initials P.M.A.C.F., an actor in the death-bed scene of Charles II: see 4 January 1849.

[2] TBM tells the story of their amour in ch. 4 of the *History*: 'On one occasion he was caught with her by the king, and was forced to leap out of the window. She rewarded this hazardous feat of gallantry with a present of five thousand pounds' (I, 461).

TO ROSS DONNELLY MANGLES, 5 NOVEMBER 1857

MS: Trinity College.

Holly Lodge Kensington / Nov 5. 1857

Dear Mangles,

The precedent most nearly in point is that of the Irish Rebellion of 1798.[1] I cannot tell you much. But I think that I can put you in the right track. The Irish Parliament passed an Act for the relief of suffering loyalists. Under that Act Commissioners were appointed, and claims sent in. Those claims appear from a list printed in November 1799 to have amounted to near £800 000. There my information ends. You had better go to the Library of the House of Commons, and look at the Act in the Irish Statute Book. There may also be something on the subject in the Journals. But, if you wish for fuller information, Larcom[2] is your man. Trevelyan will, I am sure, be glad to put you in communication with him.

I am truly glad to hear that there is so much reason to believe that Grant[3] has been calumniated. Lord Granville's defence of Lord Canning[4] is manly and sensible; and, no doubt, great allowances ought to be made for a man placed in so trying a situation.

Ever yours,
Macaulay

[1] Mangles had written to ask 'about the claims of Indigo planters etc. who have suffered from the war' (Journal, XI, 207: 5 November).

[2] The Permanent Under-Secretary for Ireland: see 2 September 1849.

[3] John Peter Grant; Mangles had expressed hope that 'the story about Grant and the 150 prisoners is unfounded' (Journal, XI, 207). Grant, now a member of Council and acting governor of the Central Provinces, had been sent to Cawnpore, partly in order to enforce the observance of Canning's proclamation of clemency to mutineers who submitted (see next note); for this, Grant was vilified in *The Times* as 'a prim philanthropist from Calcutta' (29 October). On reading the story, TBM wrote in his Journal that 'I begin to be very angry with Lord Canning and with my old friend Grant. I am sorry for Grant – very sorry' (XI, 203). Later, TBM received a letter from Grant 'complaining, with reason enough, God knows, of calumny. Happily the calumny is now so completely refuted that it is unnecessary to say anything about it' (XI, 257–8: 15 February 1858).

[4] Lord Canning's offer of clemency to the mutineers in return for their submission, and his acting to prevent retaliation upon the innocent, made him the target of intense abuse. Granville, his most intimate friend, defended Canning in a speech on 4 November at a dinner following the presentation of the freedom of the City of London to the Duke of Cambridge.

TO JOHN HILL BURTON, 5 NOVEMBER 1857

MS: National Library of Scotland.

Holly Lodge Kensington / November 5. 1857

My dear Sir,

Many thanks for Borland.[1] You shall have him again in the course of next week. He is invaluable.

Ever yours truly,
Macaulay

TO AUGUSTUS DE MORGAN, 7 NOVEMBER 1857

MS: University of London.

Holly Lodge Kensington / November 7. 1857

My dear Sir,

Thanks for your pamphlet.[2] On some points you have undoubtedly answered Lord Overstone. But I will frankly own to you that you seem to me greatly to overrate the advantages and greatly to underrate the inconveniences of the change which you recommend. I have not however time to explain myself fully; and the subject is not one to be treated hastily.[3]

Ever yours truly
Macaulay

TO JOHN HILL BURTON, [10? NOVEMBER 1857][4]

MS: National Library of Scotland.

Holly Lodge / Kensington

My dear Sir,

I send back, by the same post which carries this letter, the very curious little volume which you were so good as to lend me. Many thanks for it.

Very truly yours,
Macaulay

[1] See 30 October.

[2] 'Answers to Questions Communicated by Lord Overstone to the Decimal Coinage Commissioners,' 1857. De Morgan was as much in favor of decimal coinage as Lord Overstone was opposed to it.

[3] As TBM discovered in attempting to answer De Morgan: 'spent a long time in writing to Demorgan about the decimal coinage – dissatisfied however, and sent a short civil answer' (Journal, XI, 208).

[4] Dated on the assumption that it refers to Borland's book, which TBM had promised on Thursday, 5 November, to return 'in the course of next week.'

TO HERMAN MERIVALE, 28 NOVEMBER 1857

MS: Mitchell Library, Sydney.

Holly Lodge Kensington / November 28. 1857

Dear Merivale,

You will find the word *louring* used of the human face, in the second line of the Friar's Prologue in the Canterbury Tales.

You will find the word applied to the sky in our translation of the Gospel of St Matthew, 16. 3. And there it is given as the equivalent for a strongly metaphorical word in the Greek, στυγνάζων.

As far as I have examined into the matter, it seems to me that the human face was said to lour two hundred years before the sky was said to lour. I therefore cannot doubt which was the original and which the metaphorical use of the word.[1]

Ever yours truly,
Macaulay

TO DERWENT COLERIDGE, 7 DECEMBER 1857

MS: University of Texas.

Holly Lodge Dec 7. 1857

Dear Coleridge,

I am just at this moment so situated with respect to Palmerston that I cannot without indelicacy ask any favour of him.[2] I will consider whether I can do anything by means of a third person. I should be truly glad to be of use to you: but, in order to be of use, it is necessary to be careful in choosing times and modes of approach.

Ever yours truly
Macaulay

[1] The *OED* confirms this conclusion. I do not know what prompted Merivale's question; perhaps he was querying TBM's use of the word in the *History*: 'a synod of lowering Supralapsarians' (I, 397: ch. 3).

[2] Perhaps TBM means that as the recipient of a peerage from Palmerston he ought not to ask favors; but I have no evidence of any particular reason for the statement.

TO LORD SHAFTESBURY, 7 DECEMBER 1857

MS: Mr T. S. Blakeney. *Published:* Edwin Hodder, *Life of Shaftesbury*, III, 72.

Holly Lodge Kensington, December 7. 1857

My dear Lord,

I am most deeply sensible of your kindness. But I think it better not to make my first appearance as a speaker in the House of Lords, on an occasion on which there can be no difference of opinion, and on which there would be no room for anything beyond mere rhetorical display.[1] I shall be seldom able to take any part in debate. For my chest suffers severely from continued speaking; and I have been forced entirely to give up reading aloud, of which I was very fond. I therefore wish to reserve myself for occasions on which I have what I think good advice and strong arguments to offer.

As to our officers and soldiers in India, there is no honor or reward which they do not deserve. Thank God, our nation has not degenerated. / Ever, my dear Lord,

Yours very truly,
Macaulay

The Earl of Shaftesbury

TO SELINA MACAULAY, 7 DECEMBER 1857

MS: Trinity College.

Holly Lodge Dec 7. 1857

Dearest Selina,

I am always glad to hear from you. The weather has, as you say, been wonderfully mild and cheerful for December. I am pretty well, but am forced to be careful. I shall go little to the House of Lords during this short Session. There will, I apprehend, be no divisions, and no discussions in which I should wish to take part, till February.

You should see my new coat of arms with the two herons,[2] as it has

[1] Parliament had been summoned for a December meeting in consequence of a severe commercial crisis, and TBM, supported by Lord Campbell and Lord Belper, took his seat in the Lords on the 3rd. Shaftesbury then wrote to TBM asking him to speak on behalf of General Henry Havelock, the hero of Cawnpore and Lucknow (Hodder, *Life of Shaftesbury*, III, 72). Havelock (whose death in November was not yet known in London) was the first popular hero of the Mutiny and was additionally attractive to Evangelicals like Shaftesbury for his intensely religious character.

[2] TBM's arms are described thus in Burke's *General Armory* (1884): 'Gu. two arrows in saltire, points downward ar. surmounted by as many barrulets compony or and az. between

been sent to me blazoned on parchment from the Heralds' College. I have had to pay £115 in fees to Garter King at Arms and his brethren – £480 for my patent, and near £40 for my robes. I have been forced also to get a new court dress, and to have new seals cut. The whole charge to which I have been put on account of my new dignities is between seven and eight hundred pounds. Happily the sale of my books keeps up, and more than enables me to meet these demands.[1]

You ask about Campbell. He was my colleague in the representation of Edinburgh from 1839 to 1841. But we never were elected together.

Kindest love to Fanny,

Ever yours
Macaulay

TO MARGARET TREVELYAN, 14 DECEMBER 1857

MS: Trinity College.

Holly Lodge Dec. 14 / 1857

Dearest Baba,

I will dine with you to morrow.[2]

Ever yours
Macaulay

TO LORD SHAFTESBURY, 31 DECEMBER 1857

MS: Mr T. S. Blakeney.

Holly Lodge Kensington, December 31. 1857

My dear Lord,

Thanks for your kind note; and thanks also for the game which you have been so good as to send me. A happy New Year, and many happy new years, to you and yours.

Ever yours faithfully,
Macaulay

The Earl of Shaftesbury

two buckles in pale of the third, a bordure engrailed also of the third. *Crest* – Upon a rock a boot proper thereon a spur or. *Supporters* – Two herons proper. *Motto* – Dulce periculum.'

1 Longman had just paid TBM £2,300: 'I have paid all the expenses of my new dignity – added more than £200 to my balance at the bankers', and bought 1500£ new 3 per cents' (Journal, XI, 224: 5 December).

2 'Pleasant dinner and evening. All good and happy and affectionate. Talked too much for my chest' (Journal, XI, 228: 15 December).

TO LORD STANHOPE, 31 DECEMBER 1857

MS: Stanhope Papers, Chevening.

Holly Lodge Kensington / December 31. 1857

My dear Stanhope,

Thanks for the letter. It is highly curious. I have locked it up safe, and will give it you when we meet.

A happy new year, and many happy new years to you, and to my Lady, and to my Valentine, and to all yours.

Ever yours faithfully,
Macaulay

TO WILLIAM WHEWELL, 5 JANUARY 1858

MS: Trinity College.

Holly Lodge Kensington / Jany. 5. 1858

Dear Whewell,

Thanks for your pamphlet.[1] I have read it with much interest, sometimes concurring and sometimes dissenting. You are quite right in believing that my affection for our college is undiminished. That feeling will last as long as I live.

Ever yours truly,
Macaulay

TO WILLIAM HAZLITT,[2] 6 JANUARY 1858

MS: Mr F. R. Cowell.

Holly Lodge Kensington / January 6. 1858

Sir,

I have received your note and the books which accompanied it.[3] I beg you to accept my thanks for them. I am afraid that it may be long before I shall be able to find time for a connected perusal of the two volumes. I can however say with confidence, after glancing at a few pages, that the performance is highly creditable to a young man of three and twenty,

[1] Whewell published several pamphlets in 1857 on the new statutes for Trinity College then under discussion; this was probably one of them. See Winstanley, *Early Victorian Cambridge*, ch. 15.

[2] Hazlitt (1811–93), the son of the essayist, was Registrar of the Court of Bankruptcy.

[3] *The History of the Origin and Rise of the Republic of Venice*, 2 vols., 1858, by Hazlitt's son William Carew Hazlitt (1834–1913: *DNB*), later distinguished as a bibliographer, literary historian, editor, and antiquary.

and that I congratulate you on having a son who has so early shown a taste and a capacity for manly studies. I sincerely wish him success. / I have the honour to be, /Sir,

Your obedient Servant,
Macaulay

W Hazlitt Esq / etc. etc. etc.

TO JOHN KENT, 7 JANUARY 1858

MS: Trinity College. *Envelope:* The Reverend J Kent / etc. etc. etc. / The Earl of Carnarvon's / Highclere Castle / Newbury. *Subscription:* M.

Holly Lodge Kensington / January 7. 1858

Sir,

In calling the ancient priest of Mansetter jolly, I treated him with great indulgence.[1] George Fox says of him, "He told my troubles, sorrows, and griefs to his servants, so that it got among the milklasses. It grieved me that I should open my mind to such an one."[2] Surely a clergyman who divulges the religious anxieties and scruples of a penitent to persons who are likely to make game of such things is guilty of a gross breach of the laws of professional honour, to say nothing of higher considerations. I was charitably willing to ascribe the indiscretion of the priest of Mansetter to a cheerful, sanguine, temperament, which made it difficult for him to sympathise with the sufferings of a melancholy and ascetic spirit; and I therefore used the epithet which you seem to think harsh, but which I cannot help considering as very gentle. / I have the honor to be, / Sir,

Your obedient Servant,
Macaulay

The Reverend J Kent / etc. etc. etc.

TO SIR FREDERIC THESIGER, 13 JANUARY 1858

MS: Royal Archives, Windsor Castle.

Holly Lodge / Kensington / January 13. 1858

Dear Sir Frederic,

You will not, I hope, think that I take a liberty, when I venture to tell

[1] In describing the spiritual history of the Quaker George Fox TBM wrote that, in response to Fox's prayers for guidance, 'one jolly old clergyman of the Anglican communion told him to smoke tobacco and sing psalms' (*History*, IV, 24). The statement is paraphrased from Fox's *Journal*, in which the clergyman is identified simply as an 'ancient priest at Mancetter in Warwickshire' (*The Journal of George Fox*, ed. John L. Nickalls, Cambridge, 1952, p. 5).

[2] *Journal*, p. 6, slightly misquoted.

you how sincerely, during many weeks, I have sympathised with your anxiety, and how sincerely, since the arrival of the last Indian mail, I have sympathised with your joy.[1] Our acquaintance, though slight, has always been friendly, and is sufficient, I think, to justify my expressing a feeling which I share with the whole nation.

I hope, indeed I cannot doubt, that Inglis's services will be splendidly rewarded. / Believe me, / Dear Sir Frederic,

Yours very faithfully
Macaulay

Sir F Thesiger M.P. / etc. etc. etc.

TO FRANCES MACAULAY, 22 JANUARY 1858

MS: Trinity College.

Holly Lodge Kensington / January 22. 1858

Dearest Fanny,

I shall be very glad to see the Professor.

I am tolerably well – very well for the time of year. But I shall not go to the concert at the palace on the wedding day,[2] though my attendance has been commanded. To stand without a great coat in a draught at midnight, waiting an hour for my carriage, would not suit me.

Mrs. Crinean is in a hopeful way. From begging she has proceeded to something very like swindling. The other day she wrote to tell me that she and her husband had been raising money on a bill, which she had persuaded a poor old man to indorse as a favour to her. The bill is due. The money is not forthcoming. The poor old man is liable. And she adjures me, for God's sake, to save the poor old man from ruin. I was very angry, and peremptorily refused. If she chuses to raise funds in such ways, she must take the consequences.[3]

Kindest love to Selina.

Ever yours,
Macaulay

1 Thesiger's daughter Julia was the wife of Col. John Inglis, commander of the forces in the residency at Lucknow during a siege of eighty-seven days; she and their three children were present throughout. *The Times* on this day prints Inglis's long report of the siege. Inglis (1814–62: *DNB*) was promoted and knighted for his defence of the residency.

2 The marriage of the Princess Royal, Victoria, to Prince Frederick William of Prussia took place on the 25th, at the Chapel Royal, St James's.

3 TBM vowed that 'if she writes again, I shall return no answer' (Journal, XI, 241: 18 January). But next year he notes: 'Sent the Crineans 10£' (Journal, XI, 577: 14 October 1859).

TO JOHN KENT, 30 JANUARY 1858

MS: Trinity College. *Envelope:* J Kent Esq / etc. etc. etc. / Highclere Castle / Newbury. *Subscription:* M.

Holly Lodge Kensington / January 30. 1858

Sir,

I am much obliged to you for reminding me that you were one of the persons who suggested the explanation, which I believe to be the true one, of that mysterious P.M.A.C.F.[1] I had mislaid your letter, and could not recall the name. I therefore omitted to mention the persons who had, without concert, hit on the same solution. I will now do justice to you and to Lord Stanhope; and I will add that possibly the C may be meant for Capuchin.[2] Mansuete was undoubtedly a Cordelier. But I imagine that all Capuchins are Cordeliers, though all Cordeliers are not Capuchins. / I have the honor to be, / Sir,

Your faithful Servant,
Macaulay

J Kent Esq / etc. etc. etc.

TO LORD BELPER, 2 FEBRUARY 1858

MS: Trinity College.

Holly Lodge Kensington / February 2. 1858

Dear Belper,

Will you breakfast here at ten on Saturday? And will you prevail on Lady Belper to accompany you?[3]

Ever yours,
Macaulay

TO SELINA MACAULAY, 10 FEBRUARY 1858

MS: Trinity College.

Holly Lodge Kensington / Feb 10. 1858

Dearest Selina,

The law which such a blockhead as John Babington[4] picks out of

[1] See 4 January 1849 and 28 January 1851.

[2] Kent had probably written on seeing the note on P.M.A.C.F. in the newly-published edition of 1857–8; it repeats the note originally added in 1856 stating merely that the answer to the riddle had occurred 'almost at the same time, to myself and to several other persons,' and that TBM favored the reading 'Père Mansuete A Cordelier Friar.' TBM did not change the note.

[3] The party were Hannah, Margaret, the Belpers, Dundas, Lord Glenelg, and Thornton (Journal, XI, 251: 6 February).

[4] TBM's cousin, Rector of the family living of Cossington, Leicestershire. His niece Eliza Conybeare remembered him as 'princely-hearted; ingenuous, and with delightful manners.

newspaper reports of trials is not likely to be worth much. You had better write the will[1] again, and sign, for more security, at the bottom of every page as well as at the end. Let every signature be witnessed by two witnesses who are not legatees. This is more than is necessary. But, as you seem to be anxious, I would recommend it for perfect safety. If you will send to the stationer for a large sheet of paper, such as lawyers use, one page will probably hold the whole.

Kindest love to Fanny. I am pretty well, the temperature considered. I was rash enough to go to the House of Lords the day before yesterday when the thanks were voted to the Indian army; and I did not suffer, though it was as cold as it has been this winter.

Ever yours,
Macaulay

TO HENRY HALLAM, 11 FEBRUARY 1858

MS: Trinity College.

Holly Lodge Kensington / February 11. 1858

Dear Hallam,

I am glad that you are in town again. I would call on you to day, but that the weather keeps me at home.

I should be truly glad to serve Mr. Brookfield:[2] but I have already engaged the vote, which I am almost sorry that I possess, to another competitor.[3] It is possible, however, that some candidates may withdraw. Should my man do so, be assured that I will not forget your wishes.

Ever yours affectionately
Macaulay

No movement of meanness ever came in him, but, a prey to women, he carried on with them equally both before and after his marriage; his breast was always a home of excited emotions, generally for many at once. When possible, he always got on to kissing terms, even with those entirely outside the family' ('Aunt Eliza's Story,' 1875).

1 Selina's will is dated 5 January 1858. It gave some trouble later: see 27 September.

2 William Henry Brookfield (1809–74: *DNB*), a clergyman who had been at Trinity with Tennyson and Arthur Hallam. He was well acquainted in literary London but had little success in getting preferment and was now applying for the Preachership of Lincoln's Inn. Mrs Brookfield – Thackeray's Mrs Brookfield – was Hallam's niece. Brookfield himself was the nephew of TBM's old master, Preston.

3 'I am overwhelmed with applications for the Lincoln's Inn Preachership' (Journal, XI, 258: 15 February); it was given to William Thomson, later Archbishop of York.

TO THE DUKE OF ARGYLL, 12 FEBRUARY 1858

MS: Mr F. R. Cowell.

Holly Lodge Feby. 12 / 1858

Dear Duke of Argyll,

I do not like to leave my fireside this bleak gloomy day; or I would have told you in person how much I have been pleased by your speech as it is reported in the Times.[1] I do not think that you could have taken a better line.

Ever yours truly,
Macaulay

TO THOMAS FLOWER ELLIS, 22 FEBRUARY 1858

MS: Trinity College.

Holly Lodge Kensington / February 22. 1858

Dear Ellis,

William is so ill that I am seriously uneasy about him.[2] It would hardly be agreeable to you to dine and sleep here in the state in which my household now is. I have therefore to propose to you a change of plan.

Derwent Coleridge and Moultrie have just called. I could not ask them to dine here. So I have engaged them to dine with me at the Clarendon on Thursday.[3] Dinner on table at seven. I consider you as engaged to meet them. But let me know without delay.

This change of ministry[4] is, on the whole, a happy event for those who are turned out, and for the public. My pity is for those who are coming in. I wish to God Thesiger[5] would make you a Judge.

1 Argyll spoke the day before in reply to Lord Grey, who had presented a petition (drawn up by John Stuart Mill) from the East India Company against the India Bill about to be introduced by the government (*Hansard*, 3rd Series, CXLVIII, 1137–50). The East India Company's power in India was transferred to the Crown by the Government of India Act that passed into law in August of this year.

2 This illness, which persisted for some weeks, is evidently what decided TBM to pension off William and Elizabeth, as he did later this year. The matter was settled by 1 March (Journal, XI, 268).

3 Coleridge fell ill, so only Moultrie and Ellis were there: 'Very good dinner of course and a heavy bill' (Journal, XI, 265–6).

4 Palmerston was defeated on the 19th. The immediate issue was a bill, inspired by Orsini's attempt on Louis Napoleon, to make conspiracy to murder a felony punishable by life imprisonment; behind this was simply general hostility to Palmerston's high-handedness. 'For the public,' TBM wrote, 'I see no reason for sorrow. . . . I feel personally for Palmerston. He should have died last June' (Journal, XI, 262–3).

5 Just made Lord Chancellor in Derby's new ministry.

Crompton[1] spoke of you most warmly and highly to Hannah on Saturday. The tears quite stood in her eyes while she repeated to me what he said.

Ever yours,
Macaulay

I have this moment received your letter of yesterday. I will dine with you on Wednesday.

TO JOHN EVELYN DENISON, 6 MARCH 1858

MS: University of Nottingham.

Holly Lodge Kensington / March 6. 1858

My dear Denison,

The questions which you propose are not to be answered off hand.[2] I should like to consider them well, to consult other people, and to obtain more information about the present state of things than I now possess.

If the whole thing were to do from the beginning, I should very much prefer the plan of having one grand Parliamentary Library for both Houses.

Ever yours truly,
Macaulay

TO ALICE TREVELYAN, 13 MARCH 1858

MS: British Museum.

Holly Lodge Kensington / March 13. 1858

Dearest Alice,

I shall be delighted to see you on Monday.[3] Be here before twelve, that we may see all that is to be seen together. I will take you home at three.

Ever yours,
Macaulay

[1] Sir Charles Crompton (1797–1865: *DNB*), justice of the Court of Queen's Bench, and a veteran of the Northern Circuit.

[2] 'The Speaker has written to me about the different plans for parliamentary libraries' (Journal, XI, 271). It is not clear what they might have been at this period, since the present basis of the libraries had already been determined. There is no reference to plans for the Commons Library in Denison's privately-printed diary (information from Mr D. C. L. Holland, Librarian of the House of Commons).

[3] To see the eclipse on the 15th, which turned out 'a failure. The sun would not show' (Journal, XI, 275).

TO JOHN LEYCESTER ADOLPHUS, 15 MARCH 1858

MS: Berlin State Library, Preussischer Kulturbesitz.

Holly Lodge Kensington / W̄ / March 15. 1858

Dear Adolphus,

I have to thank you for an evening very pleasantly passed by my solitary fireside.[1] I only regret that your travels did not extend to Toledo and Madrid. But perhaps you may make another tour, and give us another volume. So be it.

Ever yours,
Macaulay

TO FRANCES MACAULAY, 19 MARCH 1858

MS: Trinity College.

Holly Lodge Kensington / March 19. 1858

Dearest Fanny,

Our plans for Easter are as follows. On Thursday the 1st of April we propose to go to Lichfield, which we formerly saw to every disadvantage under heavy rain.[2] We shall stay there on Good Friday. On Saturday we shall go to Oxford, and pass Easter Sunday there. Of course we count upon the pleasure of having you with us.[3]

We are all rejoicing in the change of weather. Hannah and Baba, who had been really very unwell, are all but quite recovered. My man William, who has been in very serious danger, and has kept his room more than a fortnight, is about again. And I have been able to dine out thrice in one week, a thing which I have not done, I believe, since 1852.[4] I hope that you and Selina have felt the influence of the spring in so agreeable a manner. Love to her.

Ever yours,
Macaulay

[1] Adolphus had sent his *Letters from Spain in 1856 and 1857*, just published: 'very pleasant light reading' (Journal, XI, 276).

[2] In April 1849 (Journal, I, 566).

[3] They left on 1 April and returned on the 5th (Journal, XI, 284–6).

[4] On 9 March TBM wrote that 'I am altogether better than I have been since 1852' (Journal, XI, 272).

TO RICHARD MONCKTON MILNES, 19 MARCH 1858

MS: Trinity College.

Holly Lodge Kensington / March 19. 1858

Dear Milnes,

I shall be most happy to breakfast with you on Wednesday.[1]

Ever yours truly,

Macaulay

TO THOMAS LONGMAN, 21 MARCH 1858

MS: Trinity College.

Holly Lodge Kensington / March 21. 1858

My dear Sir,

Be so good as to send me Buckle's book – the Introduction to the History of Civilisation.[2]

Ever yours,

Macaulay

TO RICHARD MONCKTON MILNES, 2[4] MARCH 1858

MS: Trinity College.

Holly Lodge / Kensington / March 25. 1858

Dear Milnes,

I am sorry to have missed your party.[3] But you were so good as to ask me conditionally: and, oddly enough, I began to cough as soon as the weather began to improve.

1 TBM forgot the engagement (Journal, XI, 281): see 2[4] March.

2 The first volume of Henry Thomas Buckle's *The History of Civilization in England* appeared in 1857 and was much talked of, though TBM was evidently in no hurry to read it. He may have been driven to send to Longman by the noise that Buckle's lecture of 19 March on 'The Influence of Women on the Progress of Knowledge' was making. On 24 March he read the book, finding it the work of a man who 'wants to make a system before he has got the materials' (Journal, XI, 281).

3 TBM has mistaken the date too. Wednesday, the day of Milnes's breakfast, was the 24th. This was the morning that TBM spent reading Buckle (see the preceding letter): 'I find that he [Buckle] and Froude were both at Milnes's this morning. I am glad to have been away. I hate such parties. And nobody of good taste would make up such parties' (Journal, XI, 281). J. A. Froude had just published the third volume of his *History of England.* On 20 March, when TBM had been invited to dinner at the palace, he reported: 'after dinner the Queen was very gracious. She asked me about Froude's book; and I spoke better of it than I thought, not wishing to lower him or his work in the estimation of his sovereign' (XI, 280). On the 27th, TBM looked at 'Froude's last volumes – poor enough – the partiality is ridiculous' (XI, 282).

Your instances of *its* are in point, with one exception. *Itself*, I suspect, is formed, like *himself* and *themselves*, by the composition of *self* with the accusative of the pronoun.

But it must be admitted that early in the seventeenth century *its* came in, and gradually made *its* way from comic and familiar writing to higher and graver kinds of composition.

Ever yours truly
Macaulay

TO JOHN KENT, 24 MARCH 1858

MS: Trinity College. *Envelope:* J Kent Esq / etc. etc. etc. / High Clere Castle / Newbury. *Subscription:* M.

Holly Lodge Kensington / March 24. 1858

Sir,

I can furnish you with a better instance than any which you have found of the meaning which William was likely to have attached to the word *extirpate*, a word strictly synonymous, as you say, with the phrase to *root out.*[1] He swore, at his Inauguration, as King of Scotland, to root out heresies in that kingdom; and, before he took the oath, he asked whether these words implied that he was to be a persecutor. The Earl of Argyle was authorised by the Estates at Edinburgh to say that the words did not imply persecution.[2] If therefore William saw the same expression in a Scotch despatch, and took the trouble to weigh it, he would naturally have thought that it had not what you call "a remorseless and annihilating meaning attached to it."

I am much obliged to you for the quotation from South. I had forgotten the passage. It is probably the oldest passage in which the words High Church and Low Church are used by a writer entitled to rank among English Classics. Those words had probably been in common use during some years. / I have the honor to be, / Sir

Your faithful Servant,
Macaulay

J Kent Esq / etc. etc. etc.

[1] The reference is to TBM's defense of William for his part in the massacre of Glencoe, a defense which turns on the sense that William assigned to the term 'extirpate' in the official order that led to the massacre (*History*, IV, 205–6).

[2] The episode is given in the *History*, III, 292–3.

TO LADY TREVELYAN, 26 MARCH 1858

MS: Trinity College.

Holly Lodge / March 26. 1858

Dearest Hannah,

How are you going on? This weather makes me a close prisoner.[1]

Ever yours,
Macaulay

TO LORD JOHN RUSSELL, 6 APRIL 1858

Text: Composite from *Later Correspondence of Lord John Russell*, II, 226–8, and copy, Mr F. R. Cowell.

Holly Lodge Kensington / April 6. 1858

Dear Lord John,

Many thanks. I return the resolutions.[2] Your injunctions as to secrecy shall be strictly observed. I will tell you with perfect candour my first thoughts.

I approve of the first two resolutions, except that I think the number of Councillors too large by four at least. The third resolution seems to require some modification. A shorter term than ten years ought to be sufficient for persons who have filled some great offices, for the Governor of a Presidency, for a Legislative Member of the Council of India, for a Judge of the Supreme Court, for a Commander of the Forces, nay, for any General who has held a command in India. The Duke of Wellington was not ten years in India, nor Sir James Mackintosh. Yet either of them would have been an invaluable member of Council.

I do not much like the notion of annexing any privilege to mere

[1] The date seems clear, yet in his Journal for the 26th TBM writes that he called in Grosvenor Crescent, as he did on the day before and the day after (XI, 281).

[2] Russell's 'intended Indian resolutions, which he has sent me, sub sigillo confessionis' (Journal, XI, 288). Two days later TBM writes that 'I have heard from Lord John. To my great delight, he adopts all my amendments' (XI, 289). The Derby ministry had introduced its own India Bill as a rival to that already introduced by Palmerston. To avoid making the question of the government of India a party matter, Russell privately proposed to the ministers to offer resolutions to a committee of the whole House as 'the groundwork of a bill' and was accepted (Spencer Walpole, *The Life of Lord John Russell*, II, 298). On 12 April Russell presented his plan to proceed by resolutions and hinted his willingness to move them himself. 'But this was going rather too far, and there was no answer to "Bear" Ellice's remark that it is "better to have one Government at a time." So Mr. Disraeli undertook to prepare the Resolutions, and prepared so many of them that very few people read them through' (Herbert Paul, *A History of Modern England*, 1904, II, 159–60). TBM's suggestions for an India Bill made in earlier discussions with Russell are reported in Russell to Sir James Graham, 23 and 28 January 1858 (copies, Public Record Office).

residence in India. A man may reside twenty years at Calcutta, as an attorney or a partner in a mercantile house, and may know less about the two hundred millions of natives who live on the other side of the Mahratta ditch than if he had staid in England and read a few good books. The absurd and wicked conduct of the English inhabitants of Calcutta during the last year shows how little mere residence in Asia qualifies an European to govern Asiatics.

The only resolutions to which I am decidedly opposed are the fourth and fifth. I think ten Councillors quite enough. But, whatever the number may be, I am certain that the Crown will name better men than your constituent body will chuse. Even if I agreed to the fourth resolution, I should dissent from the fifth. The fourth resolution creates a constituent body which is quite certain to have a strong class feeling. Your old gentlemen of the Oriental Club are just as little likely to elect an English public man as the Masters of Arts of Oxford to return a Baptist to Parliament. Why should you prohibit your returned Indians from doing what it is only too certain that they will never do?

I cordially approve of all the other resolutions, the tenth excepted, about which I wish to reserve my opinion.

On the whole, I prefer your plan to that of the late Government on every point, your fourth and fifth resolutions excepted. The plan of the present Government is too absurd to be seriously discussed.

I return the inscription.[1] Our commission expired, I presume, with the late Administration; and I am not sorry for it.

As to the Jews, I shall content myself with giving them my vote in silence.[2] You would not, I am sure, advise me to make my *debut* in the House of Lords on a subject long worn out, on a subject which has gone to the debating societies, on a subject on which I made my maiden speech in the Commons twenty-eight years ago, on a subject on which I have harangued and written till I am weary, and on which I have nothing to say but what has long been in print, and has been read, reviewed, quoted, praised and abused both in England and in America. If ever I do strain my voice again in Parliament, it shall be in order to tell the Lords something that I have not told all the world twenty times before. / Ever, dear Lord John,

Yours very truly,
Macaulay

[1] For the Scutari monument: see 11 August 1857.

[2] Russell had introduced an Oaths Bill, intended to provide Jewish relief, in this session. As with earlier bills, it passed the Commons but was mutilated in the Lords (TBM voted with the minority in the division on 27 April); by a compromise arrangement, Baron Rothschild was allowed to take his seat in the Commons in July. For TBM's maiden speech on this subject, see [8 April 1830].

TO JOHN EVELYN DENISON, 6 APRIL 1858

MS: University of Nottingham.

Holly Lodge Kensington / April 6. 1858

Dear Denison,

A thousand thanks. Your letter arrived when I was in the country. I returned yesterday afternoon. I have written to Mr. Glendinning;[1] and I hope to see him in a day or two. Since you are so kind as to take an interest in the operation, I will let you know the result of the consultation.

Ever yours truly,
Macaulay

TO LORD JOHN RUSSELL, 9 APRIL 1858

MS: British Museum.

Holly Lodge Kensington / April 9. 1858

Dear Lord John,

I am truly glad that we agree so well about this Indian question. I have still two suggestions to offer. –

I quite approve of the Resolution which excludes the Councillors from all share in the distribution of the patronage, with one reservation. There is one class of functionaries which, I think, the Council ought to name, subject to the approbation of the Crown. I mean the members of the Indian Councils. The functions of the Indian Councils bear the closest analogy to those of the Home Council. The Governor General is to the Councillors at Calcutta exactly what the Secretary of State will be to the Councillors in London. It seems to me the best arrangement would be to give to the checking and advising body here the appointment of the checking and advising body there. Of course, as I before said, the Crown should have a veto.

The other point is the eligibility of the Councillors to seats in Parliament. I think that it would be better and simpler to let them be eligible without any restraint. It would scarcely ever happen that three of them would sit. But it is just as easy to defend in argument the admission of all as the admission of three; and there would be considerable awkwardness if, by any chance, four of them were returned at a general election. Which of the four is to give place? Are they to draw lots?

[1] A Chiswick nurseryman: 'He tells me that to have a large tree planted will be very difficult and enormously expensive. . . . He proposes to plant some young poplars and horse chesnuts which will grow fast. I am disappointed. But there is no help' (Journal, XI, 290: 9 April).

This difficulty does not arise in the case of Secretaries of State, and Under Secretaries of State. For they, being all members of the government, settle the thing among themselves. But these Councillors will be bound to each other by no such tie. Pray consider this.

Trevelyan likes your plan exceedingly. But on these two points he agrees with me.

Ever yours,
Macaulay

TO THOMAS FLOWER ELLIS, 15 APRIL 1858

MS: Trinity College.

Holly Lodge April 15. / 1858

Dear Ellis,

I am sorry that you are so much overloaded with work. I have no engagement next week except for Saturday.

At what hour do you begin on Tuesday?[1] I have half a mind to be there; and, if that suits you, I will bring you down after the business is over for the day. My lilacs and thorns are in full leaf and promise to be soon in full flower.

Hannah and Margaret have been closely attending Bernard's trial,[2] and are extremely interested. Margaret never was present at a trial before, and is amazed to find that she understands every word that the lawyers say.

I am to be at Cambridge on the eleventh of May, for the purpose of being sworn in High Steward of the Borough.[3]

Ever yours
Macaulay

TO THOMAS FLOWER ELLIS, 19 APRIL 1858

MS: Trinity College.

Holly Lodge / April 19. 1858

Dear Ellis,

I am sorry that I am engaged to the Granvilles on Thursday. I will silently remember the charming Harriet in a glass of claret.

[1] The Shrewsbury case (see 6 August 1857) was resumed before the Committee of Privileges on 20 April. TBM did not go.

[2] Simon Bernard (1817–62: *Boase*), a French doctor living in London, was tried for murder in connection with his part in Orsini's attempt on Louis Napoleon. The law and the evidence were clearly against him, but he was acquitted on 17 April to the applause of the spectators.

[3] His brief speech on this occasion was the last he made in public; it is published in the *Cambridge Independent Press*, 15 May.

I saw Lord Campbell yesterday. He told me – but of course this must not be mentioned – that he had no doubts about the Shrewsbury case, that it was quite proper to allow an interval before deciding, but that unless the Howards have found some new evidence of great weight, Lord Talbot will undoubtedly succeed.

I hope that you will be able to come on Sunday. Here is an invitation which I made just now while loitering among my thorns and lilacs. Let me premise that the Norfolk, or whistling, plover, of the eggs of which you are so fond, has no name in classical Latin.

Huc ades. Ipse suas largus tibi promit Aprilis
Divitias: acino turget tibi prima cucŭmis:
Pubentes horti redolet tibi semita cepas:
Lentam propter aquam, glauci sub fronde salicti,
Guttatum tibi avis tibicina calfacit ovum;
Et vix concretus candet tibi lacte novello
Caseus.[1]

Acinus is used for the grains of the melon, the cucumber, etc. as well as for the stones of the grape. *Guttatus* is, I think, the very epithet for the plover's egg.

Ever yours
Macaulay

TO BISHOP SAMUEL WILBERFORCE, 21 APRIL 1858

MS: Bodleian Library.

Holly Lodge April 21. 1858

Dear Bishop of Oxford,

I shall have great pleasure in breakfasting with you on Wednesday.[2]

Ever yours
Macaulay

[1] 'May you come to this place. Generous April itself promises you its bounty: the first cucumber is swollen with its seed for you: the garden paths are fragrant for you with the ripening onions: near the quiet water, beneath the leaves of a bright willow thicket, the fluting bird warms its speckled egg for you; and a cheese, from fresh milk, scarcely set, is gleaming for you.'

[2] The party were Lord Lansdowne, Van de Weyer and his wife, Whewell, Richard Chenevix Trench, and Sir Alexander Gordon (Journal, XI, 301).

TO BISHOP SAMUEL WILBERFORCE, 4 MAY 1858

MS: Bodleian Library.

Holly Lodge / May 4. 1858

Dear Bishop of Oxford,

On Wednesday the 12th I expect to be at Cambridge.

Ever yours

Macaulay

TO LORD SHAFTESBURY, 4 MAY 1858

MS: Mr T. S. Blakeney.

Holly Lodge, May 4. 1858

Dear Lord Shaftesbury,

I am truly sorry that I am engaged to day. Thanks for the petition.

Ever yours truly,

Macaulay

The Earl of Shaftesbury

TO THOMAS FLOWER ELLIS, 5 MAY 1858

MS: Trinity College.

Holly Lodge May 5. 1858

Dear Ellis,

I was much interested by your speech yesterday.[1] You were rapid, – too rapid, Lord Wensleydale said;[2] but I followed you almost throughout by the help of the papers. Every body that spoke to me about your speech spoke in praise of it. Lord Talbot – but that was before you spoke – talked to me about your wonderful diligence and complete knowledge of the case.

I imagine that there is no doubt about the result. When the Committee adjourned for lunch, Lord Wensleydale said, "If Bethel[3] has no better case than this, he may as well hold his tongue."

Ever yours

Macaulay

[1] Summing up the case for Lord Talbot in the Shrewsbury trial. A brief report of the speech appears in *The Times*, 5 May.

[2] TBM's Northern Circuit colleague, James Parke, was created Baron Wensleydale in 1856.

[3] Richard Bethell (1800–73: *DNB*), leader of the Chancery bar; succeeded Lord Campbell as Lord Chancellor, 1861, when he was created Baron Westbury.

TO LADY STANHOPE, 7 MAY 1858

MS: Stanhope Papers, Chevening.

Holly Lodge / May 7. 1858

Dear Lady Stanhope,

I never was more vexed in my life than when I learned that you had been here this morning to no purpose. It was for Friday the 14th that I asked you; and so, I am glad to find, the Milmans, whom I asked at the same time, understood me. Pray come on the 14th. I purposely put the day so late, because by that time I expect my lilacs to be in full glory, and my thorns in blossom.[1]

Ever yours truly
Macaulay

I shall probably see Lord Stanhope at the Museum to morrow.

TO BISHOP SAMUEL WILBERFORCE, 10 MAY 1858

MS: Bodleian Library.

Holly Lodge May 10. 1858

Dear Bishop of Oxford,

I shall have great pleasure in breakfasting with you on Saturday.[2]

Ever yours
Macaulay

TO EDWARD MATTHEW WARD, 20 MAY 1858

Text: James Dafforne, *Life and Works of Edward Matthew Ward R.A.*, p. 71.

Holly Lodge, Kensington, / May 20, 1858.

My Dear Sir,

I hope you will succeed as well with Charles and Jane Lane as with Alice Lisle.[3] I really have nothing to suggest that would be of use to you. The anecdote about the sign-post I do not remember to have seen. But,

[1] The party were Hannah, Margaret, Dundas, Milnes, Bishop Wilberforce, Lord and Lady Stanhope, the Duke and Duchess of Argyll, and the Milmans: 'The garden looked charming when the sun was out' (Journal, XI, 312).

[2] The other guests were Gladstone, Milman, R. C. Trench, and Thirlwall (Journal, XI, 314).

[3] The reference is to Ward's paintings for the Commons corridor: see *to* Ward, 12 August 1851. The story of Charles's escape after the battle of Worcester with the assistance of Jane Lane is told in Hume.

if you think it a good subject for painting, I would advise you to use it, without troubling yourself to find evidence for it. Whether the thing happened or not, it might have happened.

Very truly yours,
Macaulay.

TO FRANCES MACAULAY, 26 MAY 1858

MS: Trinity College.

Holly Lodge Kensington / May 26. 1858

Dearest Fanny,

The meaning of the words which are the subject of George's Epigram[1] is "He rolls a stone, sweating with his exertions, and does not get on one step." George's lines are very clever. I saw them before they were sent in. Kindest love to Selina. I write in haste.

Ever yours
Macaulay

TO MRS CATHERINE GORE, 2 JUNE 1858

MS: Berg Collection, New York Public Library.

Holly Lodge Kensington / June 2. 1858

Dear Mrs. Gore,

I have just read Heckington,[2] which you were so kind as to send me; and I should be very ungrateful if I did not thank you for the very pleasant hours which I passed over it. They were sad as well as pleasant; for you have mixed more than the usual proportion of tragedy with your comedy; or perhaps some peculiar associations and recollections made the effect of the book more tragic to me than it would be to others.[3]

I direct to your publishers, as the surest way of reaching you, whether you happen to be in town or country, at home or abroad.

Ever yours truly,
Macaulay

[1] He had just won the Browne's Medal for Latin epigrams.

[2] *Heckington: A Novel,* 3 vols., published on 18 May. TBM received it on 17 May and finished it on the 23rd (Journal, XI, 315; 320). He is incidentally mentioned in the book in the company of Froissart, Holinshead, and Clarendon, historians who 'may stir our passions, or aggravate our prejudices' (III, 150).

[3] One of the two brothers with whom the heroine is in love dies in a kind of self-sacrificing exile in the West Indies – did TBM see something of himself in that? The rest of the love story and the complications about possession of an estate have no evident resemblance to TBM's history.

TO JOHN WEALE,[1] 5 JUNE 1858

MS: Mrs Michael Millgate.

Holly Lodge June 5. 1858

Sir,

I am much obliged to you for the scarce volume which you have been so good as to send me: but I will not deprive you of it, as I am already possessed of a copy. I did not see the book till after my history had been printed; and I was glad to find that Parker's testimony[2] was generally in accordance with that of the writers whom I had followed. / I have the honor to be, / Sir,

Your obedient Servant
Macaulay

I return the volume, with many thanks, by this post.

TO RICHARD MONCKTON MILNES, 15 JUNE 1858

MS: Trinity College.

Holly Lodge June 15 / 1858

Dear Milnes,

What is your day? It has escaped my memory.[3]

Ever yours,
Macaulay

TO THOMAS FLOWER ELLIS, 18 JUNE 1858

MS: Trinity College.

Holly Lodge / June 18 1858

Dear Ellis,

Can you come on Monday or Tuesday? They are the only days at my command in the course of next week.

The effect of the intense heat of the day before yesterday has been to give me a bad cold. I coughed yesterday without ceasing. To day I am better.

1 Identified from endorsement on the letter. Weale (1791–1862: *DNB*) was a publisher specializing in works on architecture and engineering.

2 Perhaps Bishop Samuel Parker, *History of His Own Times* (1660–80), translated from the Latin original, 1726. A copy of this is in the shelf-list of TBM's library.

3 It was evidently the 23rd, when TBM writes in his Journal that he had 'excused myself' to Milnes and remained at home (XI, 335).

The Trevelyans have left town for Weybridge. I shall go down to them on Thursday.

I hear that Lord Shrewsbury[1] is going to entertain his counsel magnificently at Greenwich. This was the good old fashion. See the last chapter of Guy Mannering. When Harry Bertram had been served heir, Pleydell and the other lawyers had a grand entertainment – "Macmorlan will stare," says Pleydell, "when he sees the bill." See also the History of John Bull. "After a trial," says John, "I always treated the lawyers; and, when I was drunk, they and their clerks danced round me, whooping and hallooing."[2] I quote from memory; but it is very nearly so.

Ever yours,
Macaulay

TO LORD STANHOPE, 18 JUNE 1858

MS: Mr T. S. Blakeney.

Holly Lodge June 18. 1858

My dear Stanhope,

I willingly submit my judgment to yours and Lord Lansdowne's. I am very sorry that I cannot breakfast with you on Friday. I shall probably be out of town that morning.

Ever yours,
Macaulay

TO [THOMAS LONGMAN], 21 JUNE 1858

MS: National Library of Scotland.

Holly Lodge June 21 / 1858

My dear Sir,

Be so kind as to send my history – the new edition – to E Foster Esq, 21 Market Street, Leicester.[3]

Ever yours truly
Macaulay

[1] Judgment was given in favor of Lord Talbot's claim to the Earldom of Shrewsbury on 1 June.

[2] Arbuthnot, *History of John Bull*, ch. 8: 'The night after a trial I treated the lawyers. . . . I was always hot-headed; then they placed me in the middle, the attorneys and their clerks dancing about me, whooping, and hollowing. . . .' TBM had been reading the book on this day (Journal, XI, 334).

[3] The Leicester directories of this period show no E. Foster at this address, but it is likely that he is the Edward Foster who is listed in the 1863 directory as librarian of the Y.M.C.A.

TO THOMAS LONGMAN, 24 JUNE 1858

MS: Longman Group Ltd.

Holly Lodge June 24. 1858

My dear Sir,

I am sorry that I am engaged on Monday.[1] Indeed whether I shall be able to keep my engagement is a very doubtful question. I caught a cold on Wednesday week, the hottest of days, and have been coughing and pumping for breath ever since. I must try change of air, I think.

Thanks for the account of the sales. It is very satisfactory.[2]

Ever yours truly,
Macaulay

TO THOMAS FLOWER ELLIS, 25 JUNE 1858

MS: Trinity College. *Extract published:* Trevelyan, II, 451n.

Holly Lodge June 25. 1858

Dear Ellis,

I am a little, and but a little, better. I have quite given up all thoughts of speaking to day.[3] I should be forced to sit down in five minutes.

I went yesterday to Weybridge, passed a happy afternoon there, dined, and returned by a late train. We talked about the habit of building castles in the air, a habit in which Lady T and I indulge beyond any people that I ever knew. I mentioned to George what, as far as I know, no critic has observed, that the Greeks called this habit κενη μακαρια.[4] See Lucian's Hermotimus and his πλοιον.[5] Alice, who was some way off and did not hear distinctly, said "Kenneth Macaulay! What did the Greeks say about Kenneth Macaulay?" I shall always call the unreal world in which I pass a large part of my life my Kenneth Macaulay.

They have a very pleasant house, though a little too small, not for their own comfort, but for hospitality; and they are within two minutes'

1 TBM was still ill then and remained at home (Journal, XI, 338).

2 All seven volumes of the 1857–8 edition were now published, each in a printing of 11,000 copies. According to Longman's records, 62,924 volumes had been sold by the end of 1858. TBM's royalties from Longman at the end of this year were £6,276 (Journal, XI, 381: 27 October 1858).

3 TBM had some thought of speaking in the debate this day on the colonization of India. A select committee of the House of Commons had been taking evidence on the matter since March in response to new pressure for colonization against the government's traditional opposition. Among other things attacked were the Black Act and the work of the Law Commission, both dear to TBM.

4 'Empty happiness.'

5 'Hermotimus,' 71; 'The Ship,' 11.

walk of the station, and yet are very little incommoded by the noise of the trains. I expect you on Tuesday.

Ever yours
Macaulay

TO LORD BELPER, 29 JUNE 1858

MS: Fitzwilliam Museum.

Holly Lodge June 29. 1858

Dear Belper,

I am drenched with physic and flayed with mustard poultices. That I should go down to the House this week is out of the question; and I have begged Lord Foley[1] to pair me for the Session, if he can. I have three petitions in favour of the Church rate bill, which ought to be presented, at latest, on Friday before the debate.[2] Could you, without inconvenience, take charge of them?

Ever yours truly,
Macaulay

TO LORD STANHOPE, 29 JUNE 1858

MS: Stanhope Papers, Chevening.

Holly Lodge June 29. 1858

My dear Stanhope,

I give you joy of your speech[3] and of your success. I wish that I could have heard you: but I was swallowing Dr. Bright's prescriptions with a mustard poultice on my breast. I must give up all hope of being able to breakfast with you to morrow; and there is, I am afraid, no chance of my voting either on the Jew question or on the Church Rate Bill. I have desired Lord Foley to pair me for the Session, if he can.

From the report in the Times, I feel satisfied that your speech was excellent. I cannot conceive what can have possessed the Bishop of St Asaph.[4] I thought him a man of sense.

1 Thomas Henry Foley (1808–69: *Boase*), fourth Baron Foley; a Whig.

2 A bill for the abolition of Church rates was defeated in the Lords on its second reading, Friday, 2 July; on the day before some hundreds of petitions were presented for and against.

3 In the House of Lords, successfully moving an address to the Queen to remove from the Prayer Book the so-called state services – for the 5th of November, the martyrdom of Charles I, and the restoration of Charles II.

4 Thomas Vowler Short (1790–1872: *DNB*), Bishop of St Asaph, 1846–70; he was alone among the bishops in opposing Stanhope's motion.

Certainly the coincidence between your Birmingham speech and what I was saying to Dundas the other day is very odd.[1]

Ever yours truly,
Macaulay

TO THE MESSRS PALMER,[2] 29 JUNE 1858

MS: Trinity College.

Lord Macaulay will be obliged to Messrs. Palmer to send him the work which is numbered 199 in their Monthly List for July – Luther–Opera Omnia – 4 vols folio.[3]

Holly Lodge Kensington / June 29. 1858.

TO WILLIAM RAYMOND SAMS,[4] 3 JULY 1858

MS: Huntington Library.

Lord Macaulay will be obliged to Mr. Sams to send five tickets for the Series of Mr. Montgomery Stuart's Lectures on the Influence of Italian Literature.[5] Lord Macaulay incloses a cheque for five guineas.
Holly Lodge July 3. 1858

TO THOMAS FLOWER ELLIS, 4 JULY 1858

MS: Trinity College.

Holly Lodge July 4. 1858

Dear Ellis,

It seems that the last week of August and the first week of September

[1] Stanhope's note states that this 'refers to a line from Dryden
"Once oxen lowed where now the lawyers bawl."
which Macaulay spoke of at the meeting at the British Museum on Saturday last and which I told him I had quoted in my Birmingham Address of 1855; which Address in proof I subsequently sent him.'

[2] Ebenezer Palmer and Son, 'Theological booksellers and publishers,' of 18 Paternoster Row (*Post Office London Directory*, 1858).

[3] Published at Jena, 1578–82 (item 666 in the sale catalogue of TBM's library): 'to day I received in a parcel four huge folio vols of Luther's works. Though called *opera omnia*, they are very far, I find, from being *opera omnia*. I read a good deal with interest, particularly the De Servo Arbitrio' (Journal, XI, 340: 3 July).

[4] 'Bookseller to Her Majesty,' of 1 St James's Street (*Post Office London Directory*, 1858).

[5] Stuart (see 20 January 1854) was now back in London and preparing to deliver a series of lectures at St Martin's Hall. In the first, on 6 July, Stuart mentioned TBM's description of the flight of James II and said that 'he had been surprised at the perfect accuracy of the English historian, who had never had access to the Florentine archives' (*The Times*, 7 July).

would very nearly serve our purpose.[1] If necessary, we can make some change in our plan. As to the particular day, we cannot fix it till we know more both about your engagements and about the time when the packets start.

Lord Wensleydale, whom I met yesterday at Chiswick,[2] strongly advised me to go to Toulouse and Bordeaux. We might, if we liked, return from Avignon by that circuitous route instead of retracing our steps by Lyons. The whole might easily be brought within the fortnight. By the bye there are excellent ortolans at Bordeaux in August and September. What a scolding Lady Trevelyan would give me, if she were looking over my shoulder!

Ever yours,
Macaulay

TO EDWARD EVERETT, 5 JULY 1858

MS: Massachusetts Historical Society.

Holly Lodge July 5. 1858

My dear Everett,

My friend, Sir David Dundas, is about to visit America. You met him in London formerly: but he is sure that you have quite forgotten him, and has asked me to send you a few lines which may prepare you for a call from him. He is a most honorable and excellent man, of very considerable talents and accomplishments. He was, during a short time, Solicitor General. But the state of his health forced him to quit the bar. He has a great social reputation. No man is a more decided favourite in the very best circles of London; and no man is better able to give you full information about all those who enjoyed your society most and who regret it most. Your friends here will miss him much:[3] but they would be content to part with him if they could hope that he will be able to persuade you to accompany him when he returns. Are we never to see you again? Ever, my dear Everett,

Yours truly,
Macaulay

[1] For the outline of this tour see 17 August.

[2] Where TBM dined with Lord Carlisle at Chiswick House (Journal, XI, 340).

[3] It appears that Dundas did not, after all, make the trip. He was to travel with Nassau Senior, but at last refused to do so because of his objection to Senior's inveterate practice of keeping a journal of all his tours and then handing it round on his return to London (Journal, XI, 356; 372: 8 August and 3 October).

TO RICHARD MONCKTON MILNES, 6 JULY 1858

MS: Trinity College.

Holly Lodge July 6 / 1858

Dear Milnes,

I have been advised to breathe sea air for a few days; and I fully expect to be out of town on the 16th.

Ever yours truly,
Macaulay

TO THOMAS FLOWER ELLIS, 12 JULY 1858

MS: Trinity College.

Holly Lodge July 12. 1858

Dear Ellis,

I am quite willing to wait your time. I never expected that we should start before the 25th of August.

I have seen Oberst.[1] He is delighted by the prospect of a fortnight's tour with us. I told him that I would not positively engage him, as it is possible that something better for him may turn up in the course of next month. But I have engaged him conditionally; and, if there should be any hitch, he will let me know in ample time.

Everybody exhorts me to see Bordeaux. Toulouse is not much.

I have at last got rid of my cold: but I am not quite right. On Wednesday[2] I shall run down to Brighton, and shall probably stay there till Monday the 19th. On Tuesday the 20th, I shall expect you to dinner, nothing unforeseen preventing. Let me have a line; and direct to me here. My servants will know my address at Brighton.

The world is perfectly quiet. No road bill ever excited less interest than the India Bill. I am sorry that our friend the Chancellor[3] will persist in making a fool of himself. He brought a great stock of popularity to the woolsack. He wanted it all to cover his professional deficiencies. And he has already talked half of it away over the bottle. Who would have thought it! And yet I do not know why I say so. For I know many people whose characters would, I am confident, be raised in every body's

[1] The courier on their trip to the Continent the year before. 'He is really the very best of Couriers – better, I think, than even Franz' (Journal, x, 198: 13 September 1857). TBM thought equally highly of him this time, too.

[2] The 14th. He stayed, as usual, at the Norfolk Hotel.

[3] Thesiger. *The Times* of this morning contains a sarcastic leader on a self-laudatory speech by Thesiger at a recent public dinner.

estimation by adversity. And I am not quite sure that I know one of whom I feel confident that his mind might not be thrown off the balance by a great and sudden influx of wealth, power, and dignity.

Ever yours
Macaulay

TO THOMAS FLOWER ELLIS, 18 JULY 1858

MS: Trinity College. *Extract published:* Trevelyan, II, 450.

Brighton July 18. 1858

Dear Ellis,

I shall be in town to morrow. If you cannot come on Tuesday, I shall be glad to have you on Wednesday. On Thursday I go to Weybridge.

I am the better for my trip to the sea side. Nothing sets me up like the breeze from the salt water. I have read the speech against Timarchus and the speeches on the Embassy, since I came down. I think Æschines's speech on the Embassy greatly superior to either of his other performances, and not much inferior to the oration to which it is a reply. But what can one believe about the history of those times or the characters of the men. They stand there giving each other the lie about things said and done in public. Each of them calls half a dozen witnesses. Demosthenes, says Æschines, is such a liar that he invents all the minutest circumstances, gives you dates with the utmost particularity, mentions by name people who never existed, and so forth. And Demosthenes says pretty much the same of Æschines. There is one very simple way of settling the matter. I mean Mitford's. Believe everything that Æschines says, and nothing that Demosthenes says. But, though I am inclined to think more favourably of Æschines as a man than of Demosthenes, I cannot quite bring myself to this.[1]

I took up Knight's Magazine the other day, and, after an interval of perhaps thirty years, read a Roman novel which I wrote at Trinity.[2] To be sure, I was a smart lad, but a sadly unripe scholar for such an undertaking. One of the first things which caught my eye was "the mask in which Roscius acted Alecto." What a blunder![3] And yet I am not quite

[1] After putting these questions to himself in his Journal, TBM concludes by saying that 'I must read what Grote says. I will positively read his book through this autumn' (XI, 346: 17 July). Grote concludes that Aeschines was guilty as charged by Demosthenes (*History of Greece*, 2nd edn, XI [1856], 594).

[2] 'Fragments of a Roman Tale,' 1823: see [8? June 1823].

[3] *Knight's Quarterly*, I, 36. According to tradition, Roscius acted without a mask, which may be what TBM means by his 'blunder.'

sure that you will see at the first glance what the blunder is. I leave it till we meet. Write as soon as you come to town.

Ever yours
Macaulay

TO THOMAS FLOWER ELLIS, 22 JULY 1858

MS: Trinity College.

Holly Lodge July 22. 1858

Dear Ellis,

I shall be glad to see you on Tuesday, since it cannot be earlier. We will then settle about Bromley.

Did not I point out to you a most absurd article on Metaphysics in the new edition of the Encyclopædia Britannica? The author is named Mansell.[1] He has now got into a controversy with as great a fool as himself on the highly interesting and important question whether identity can properly be said to be a quality; – whether, for example, one of the qualities of Mr. Thomas Flower Ellis be his being the same person as Mr. Thomas Flower Ellis. Mr. Mansell contends strongly for the negative. He says that your being the same person as Mr. Thomas Flower Ellis is not one of your qualities, but the ground or substratum of your qualities.[2] And these vagabonds pronounce it a desecration of philosophy to call Bacon and Newton philosophers.

I am just setting off for Weybridge. Poor Lady Parker is dead.[3] She had long been hopelessly ill.

Ever yours,
Macaulay

1 Henry Longueville Mansel (1820–71: *DNB*), of St John's College, Oxford. TBM looked at his article on metaphysics in November 1857, and found it 'absolutely incomprehensible. Cur quis non prendent hoc est' (Journal, XI, 211). A few days later he 'read more of the article. . . . What trash! What a waste of the powers of the human mind. I declare that I would rather have written John Gilpin than all the volumes of Fichte, Kant, Schelling and Hegel together' (XI, 213).

2 The reviewer of Mansel's *Encyclopaedia Britannica* article in the *Athenaeum*, 3 July, p. 14, took issue with Mansel's theory of self, arguing that 'personal identity is a quality or attribute' not a ground or basis. Mansel replied that 'unless personal identity be pre-supposed, there is no subject to which the quality or attribute can belong' (*Athenaeum*, 10 July, p. 52).

3 She died on 20 July and is buried in the chapel at Rothley Temple.

TO JOHN THORNTON LESLIE-MELVILLE,[1] 31 JULY 1858

MS: Trinity College.

Holly Lodge / Kensington / July 31. 1858

My dear Sir,

Thanks for your kindness. I find that my servants are not so old as I thought, and that therefore I shall have more to pay.[2] I inclose a note of their ages. Will you be so kind as to let me know what the price of the annuity will be.

Yours ever truly,
Macaulay

The Hon J T Leslie Melville / etc. etc. etc.

TO HENRY THURSTAN HOLLAND,[3] 2 AUGUST 1858

MS: The Viscount Knutsford.

Holly Lodge Kensington August 2 / 1858

My dear Holland,

I have this morning received a note from Lady Trevelyan, in which she tells me that my darling Margaret has consented to be your wife. When I say that this news has given me pleasure, I pay you no common compliment. For Margaret has been very dear to me from the day of her birth: I have watched, year after year, with the most tender interest, the development of her fine understanding and of her noble and amiable character; and it would make me miserable to see her united to any man, however rich and great, of whose principles and whose heart I had not a high opinion.

My pleasure is not without a large mixture of pain. Personally indeed

[1] One of Thornton's partners in the bank: see 1 March 1852. Thornton was out of town – probably with his wife on the Continent – so that TBM turned to Melville.

[2] TBM was buying annuities for William and Elizabeth, who retired from his service in October.

[3] Sir Henry's son; he had just become engaged to TBM's niece Margaret. Henry Thurstan Holland (1825–1914: *DNB*), a graduate of Trinity and a barrister on the Northern Circuit, later entered political life. He was Assistant Undersecretary for the Colonies, 1870–4; Tory M.P., 1874–88; and Secretary of State for the Colonies under Lord Salisbury, 1887–92. He succeeded his father as second Baronet in 1873, was created Baron Knutsford in 1888, and Viscount Knutsford in 1895. Holland's first wife was Emily, daughter of Nathaniel Hibbert and granddaughter of Sydney Smith (his father married Sydney's daughter Saba as his second wife); she died in 1855, leaving three children. Holland had proposed to Margaret in May and been refused, but as TBM wrote then, 'I have little doubt that the thing may be and will be brought to bear if he perseveres; and he will persevere' (Journal, XI, 322–3: 26 May).

I shall lose little by the change. But her father, her sister, and, above all, her mother, have much to suffer. I can wish you nothing better than that she may carry to the home to which she is going as much happiness as she has long diffused through the house which she must leave.

As for myself, the husband who possesses and deserves her affection will always be regarded by me as a most near and dear relation. / Ever, my dear Holland,

Yours very truly,
Macaulay

TO SIR HENRY HOLLAND, 3 AUGUST 1858

MS: The Viscount Knutsford. *Envelope:* Sir H Holland Bart / etc. etc. etc. *Subscription:* Macaulay. *Mostly published:* Sydney Holland, Viscount Knutsford, *In Black and White*, 1926, p. 213.

Holly Lodge Kensington / August 3. 1858

Dear Sir Henry,

One line to thank you for your kind note. I have already written to your son. I hope and believe that my dear child has judged well for her own happiness; and I try to rejoice. But, though the event is gratifying in many lights, and though I have the highest opinion of your son, I cannot but feel sad. It is not on my own account. For I shall lose but little. But she has been so long the darling and the light of the house, that I hardly dare to think how much her father and sister, but above all her mother, have to suffer. But I will look on the bright side. Sooner or later the separation would have come; and it could not have come in a less painful manner. It is a pleasure to me too that the new connections whom this event gives me are dear old friends. I shall be delighted to see you and to talk with you over these matters.

Ever yours,
Macaulay

TO MARGARET TREVELYAN, 7 AUGUST 1858

MS: Trinity College.

Holly Lodge Kensington / August 7. 1858

My dear dear child,

Thanks for your sweet letter. I have read it with tears of pleasure and tenderness. I do indeed love you very much; and it is most gratifying to me to think that you love me, and will remember me kindly many years hence. As to the marks by which I try to show some part of the affection

which I feel for you, you greatly overrate them.[1] What have I to do with this opulence which has come too late for myself, except to employ it in promoting the happiness of others?

I have no doubt that we shall meet quite as often as formerly. And, now that I am going to have a good cook,[2] I shall frequently give family dinners at which I shall hope to see both Mr. and Mrs. Holland. I assure you that I like him more than any young man that I know; and everybody has a good word for him.

By the bye, you cannot think how kindly and warmly Marian Ellis spoke to me about your prospects. She is exceedingly fond of you. Love to all. God bless you my dear Baba. I shall write to you at Calverton.[3]

Yours ever
Macaulay

TO AUGUSTUS DE MORGAN, 12 AUGUST 1858

MS: University of London.

Holly Lodge Kensington / August 12. 1858

My dear Sir,

If there be a matter in the world about which everybody should be at liberty to speak his mind with perfect freedom, it is the meaning of P.M.A.C.F. Pray discuss the point fully; and do not be apprehensive of wounding my feelings.[4]

I do not think it strange that the residuary legatee and Executor of Lord Halifax should have given Mrs. Barton quiet possession of what had been bequeathed to her in an informal manner.[5] Remember that the residuary legatee had been loaded with benefits by the testator, his uncle.

[1] On hearing that Henry Holland would propose to Margaret, TBM wrote that 'I mean to do as much as her parents, at least. I shall charge myself with the trousseau, and allow her a hundred a year for pocket money' (Journal, XI, 322: 25 May). On 4 August he told Hannah that he meant to give Margaret '500£ for outfit' (XI, 354).

[2] Replacing Elizabeth: her name was Mrs Kent. She presented her first dinner on 3 October: 'I perceived at once her immense superiority to poor E, though there could hardly be a plainer dinner. The very apple pie was first rate' (Journal, XI, 372).

[3] In Buckinghamshire. Trevelyan's sister Frances was married to the Rector, Charles Perceval, who had died in late July.

[4] In his *Budget of Paradoxes*, 1872, p. 282, De Morgan suggests that P.M.A.C.F., instead of a 'verbal acrostic' for 'Père Mansuete a Cordelier Friar,' is a 'syllabic acrostic of *PortsMouth and ChifFinch*.' He adds that 'Macaulay adopted the first interpretation, preferring it to the second, which I brought before him as the conjecture of a near relative of my own.'

[5] See [28 September 1853], on the matter of Halifax's relation to Catherine Barton. De Morgan had found that the part of Halifax's will providing for her was not legally binding (*Newton: His Friend: and His Niece*, pp. 97–9). The residuary legatee was George Montagu (d. 1739), Viscount Sunbury and Earl of Halifax, Halifax's nephew.

The last acts of the minister's life were to procure the reversion of a peerage and of the enormously lucrative sinecure of Auditor of the Exchequer for his nephew. The nephew, coming into probably fifteen thousand a year by his kinsman's bounty, could not, for very shame, refuse possession of a single manor to a lady earnestly and pathetically commended to his care by the deceased. I do not think therefore that much is to be inferred from this circumstance.[1]

Very truly yours,
Macaulay

TO AUGUSTUS DE MORGAN, 14 AUGUST 1858

MS: University of London.

Holly Lodge / August 14. 1858

My dear Sir,

One line to mention that, in the last edition of my history, – the small edition, – I propounded my notion about P.M.A.C.F. and said that it had occurred to others as well as to myself. The others were Lord Stanhope and a Mr. Kent,[2] a very respectable man who was tutor, I think, to Lord Caernarvon, and who lives at High Clere with his pupil.[3]

Very truly yours,
Macaulay

TO THOMAS FLOWER ELLIS, 17 AUGUST 1858

MS: Trinity College.

Holly Lodge Kensington / August 17. 1858

Dear Ellis,

We must come to some decision about our arrangements.[4] I propose that we start on Thursday the 26th. We shall reach the Hotel du Louvre by eight in the evening, and we can dine in our own rooms; for it will be too late to be wandering to a Restaurateur's.

[1] De Morgan was still urging his view that Halifax and Mrs Barton were secretly married.

[2] See 28 January 1851.

[3] The fourth Earl of Carnarvon (1831–90: *DNB*) graduated with honors from Oxford in 1852 and was now active in political life. Kent, who served as Carnarvon's secretary after having been his tutor, returned to Canada in 1856.

[4] Their tour, beginning on the 28th, took them from Paris to Avignon, whence they made excursions to the valley of Vaucluse and to Arles. Leaving Avignon on 2 September, they went to Bordeaux via Nîmes, Montpellier, and Toulouse; from Bordeaux, 9 September, they returned to Paris through Orléans and Bourges. They reached London again on the 14th (Journal, x, 204–56).

When shall you be in town? Can you, as you hoped, come to me on Saturday and stay till Monday. On Tuesday the 24th I must go to Weybridge. By that time Hannah and Trevelyan will be at home again. They have been charmed with the Hague and Amsterdam in spite of the heat.

I have been reading Philostratus and Macrobius, bad Greek and bad Latin. I have however found more in Macrobius than I had formerly observed. I turned him over too hastily in India.

Ever yours,
Macaulay

Oberst is not come yet. But I expect him every day. I shall give him grace till the end of the week.

TO THOMAS FLOWER ELLIS, 18 AUGUST 1858

MS: Trinity College.

Holly Lodge Kensington / August 18. 1858

Dear Ellis,

The 28th will suit me perfectly. We shall not be at the Hotel du Louvre till past nine. We must dine at Boulogne.

I have now no doubt that Oberst will be here in time.

The carriage shall be at the University Club by six on Saturday.

I must keep the Addresses[1] till you come. They would do extremely well, as they stand. But that to the Queen might, I think, be improved; and, as you do not mean to be present, you should give them something superfine. On Sunday we will see what we can do, working in the Beaumont and Fletcher way.

Ever yours
Macaulay

TO ADAM BLACK, 23 AUGUST 1858

Text: Copy, Longman Group Ltd.

Holly Lodge Kensington / Augt. 23rd 1858.

My dear Sir,

I send the proofs and the M.S.[2] On Saturday I start for the Continent;

[1] Ellis, as Recorder of Leeds, had been asked to prepare addresses to Victoria and Albert for the opening of the Town Hall, Leeds, on 6 September. The plan of two addresses was then altered to a single joint address. After revising what Ellis had written, TBM decided to write the address himself and did so. It was read on the occasion, and printed in the Leeds *Mercury* the next day. The MSS of Ellis's draft and TBM's final version are in the Leeds City Libraries.

[2] Of the biography of Pitt for the *Encyclopaedia Britannica*, published in February 1859.

and I shall be more than a fortnight absent. Therefore the revise should be sent so that I may get it on Friday morning. Pray be so good as to send a duplicate.[1]

I may as well take this opportunity of saying that I wish to reserve to myself and my executors the right of reprinting my articles in the Encyclopædia in any collection of my Miscellaneous Works which may hereafter appear.

I have no such publication in contemplation; and if it should ever take place it will not be for some years. But you must feel that it would be hard upon me and my family not to be able to publish a complete edition of my works in England while complete editions would be selling in America and Germany.

Very truly yours
Macaulay

TO ADAM BLACK, 27 AUGUST 1858

Text: Copy, Longman Group Ltd.

Holly Lodge Kensington / August 27 1858.

My dear Sir,

Of course you are perfectly at liberty [to use][2] all or any of my articles whenever you think fit and in whatever form. I wish however that before you reprint them you would give me an opportunity of revising them and making some corrections.

I sent back the revise of the paper on Pitt yesterday.

Ever yours truly
Macaulay

A. Black Esqre. M.P.

TO FRANCES MACAULAY, 8 SEPTEMBER 1858

MS: Trinity College.

Bordeaux September 8. 1858

Dearest Fanny,

I have only this moment received your letter of the 31st of August. It

TBM began it in September 1857 and finished it on 9 August 1858: 'What a time to have been dawdling over such a trifle – scarcely ever working at it more than a quarter of an hour at a time' (Journal, XI, 186; 357). It was the last thing that TBM published in his lifetime.

[1] TBM had the revises, one of which he sent to Hannah, by the 26th (Journal, XI, 364); the corrected page proofs, which are now at Trinity, he kept for Ellis to read on their tour.

[2] A phrase has been omitted from the copy.

is now a week since I was informed of dear Selina's death.[1] I was very anxious to know whether she had received the few lines which I wrote to her just before I set out; and I was much affected and much gratified by learning from you that they gave her pleasure.

I find from a letter of our brother Charles that she expressed a wish that the expense of her last illness, of her funeral, and of some little bequests, should be defrayed out of her own money. To this, as matter of form, I have no objection. But my intention is to make good to you whatever may be spent in this way. I wish you to succeed to all that she has left without deduction. I shall therefore take on myself the law expenses, the legacies, and the legacy duty. If Selina has expressed any wish, though not in a legal form, I shall have sincere pleasure in carrying it into effect.

When this is done, I propose to lay out about three thousand six hundred pounds[2] in buying for you a life annuity of two hundred and fifty pounds on the best security. In this way you will be perfectly independent. You will, I hope, be comfortable; and, if you are inclined to sell your railway stock and to sink the proceeds in an additional annuity, you may considerably increase your income.

On Tuesday next I hope to be at Holly Lodge; and I shall hope to find a letter from you there, unless I hear from you at Paris, where I propose to pass the Sunday and Monday. / Ever, my dear Fanny,

Yours affectionately
Macaulay

TO FRANCES MACAULAY, 27 SEPTEMBER 1858

MS: Trinity College.

Holly Lodge Kensington / September 27. 1858

Dearest Fanny,

All is right. I have sent the two lists to my Solicitor; and I anticipate no further difficulty.[3]

You do not quite apprehend the nature of this hitch. Cannot a person, you ask, leave directions of this kind orally, or by letter, or by memorandum, without giving occasion for the expense and trouble of a legal investigation? No doubt that is possible. Dear Selina did give some oral

[1] She died on 29 August; TBM received the news at Avignon.

[2] TBM discovered that it would cost about £900 more than this (Journal, XI, 367: 20 September).

[3] Selina's will mentions a list that she intended to leave regarding different articles to be given as mementos of her to relatives and friends; since this was not part of the will proper, it created a difficulty, as TBM explains in the letter. Selina's will was proved on 28 September.

directions which have been complied with, and with which the Court of Probate has nothing to do. She expressed in her last letter to me a wish with which I mean to comply, and with which the Court of Probate has nothing to do. Nor would the Court of Probate have had anything to do with this list, if she had not referred to it in her will. The reference in the will makes all the difference. It raises the question whether the list ought or ought not to be considered as part of the will. If the list had been attested by two witnesses, it would, I apprehend, have been part of the will, and must have been proved and registered like the rest. Not being attested, it is, in a legal view, mere waste paper; and it is optional with you to comply with the injunction or not. But the Registrar of the Court of Probate, seeing the reference to the list in the will, was quite right in asking how the matter stood.

Ever yours
Macaulay

TO FRANCES MACAULAY, [4 OCTOBER 1858][1]

MS: Trinity College.

[Holly Lodge]

[. . .] course, something still to learn about my ways. But he is most attentive and alert;[2] and I already feel the advantage of having a servant who is not an invalid, and whom I can desire to go to town even on a cold foggy day. Mrs. Kent is immeasurably superior to Elizabeth as a cook.

On Saturday I was at Weybridge. They were all well and happy. On my return in the evening I had from the window of the railway carriage a magnificent view of the Comet.[3] I well remember the great Comets of 1807 and 1811; but this fellow beats them hollow.

Ever yours
Macaulay

TO FRANCES MACAULAY, 7 OCTOBER 1858

MS: Trinity College.

Holly Lodge / October 7. 1858

Dearest Fanny,

Have you the coupons, as they are called, of your stock and Selina's.

[1] TBM's Journal records that he wrote to Fanny on the 4th, and all the internal evidence in this fragment confirms that it is part of the letter of that date.

[2] TBM means his new butler, William's successor, who took up his duties on 2 October. His name was Gray, and he was formerly butler in Sir James Parker's house.

[3] Donati's comet, at its most brilliant in England in this month.

There will be a difficulty in making a sale without them; and there are none at the bank in Birchin Lane. If you have them, pray send them without delay. You know what they are, – papers certifying your right to portions of stock.

Ever yours
Macaulay

TO HENRY STEPHENS RANDALL, 9 OCTOBER 1858

MS: New York Public Library. *Envelope:* H S Randall Esq / etc. etc. etc. / Cortland Village / State of New York / U.S. *Subscription:* M. *Published: Harper's Magazine,* LIV (February 1877), 461–2.

Holly Lodge Kensington / October 9. 1858

Sir,

I beg you to accept my thanks for your volumes which have just reached me,[1] and which, as far as I can judge from the first hasty inspection, will prove both interesting and instructive.

Your book was preceded by a letter, for which I have also to thank you. In that letter you expressed, without the smallest discourtesy, a very decided dissent from some opinions, which I have long held firmly, but which I should never have obtruded on you except at your own earnest request, and which I have no wish to defend against your objections. If you can derive any comfort as to the future destinies of your country from your conviction that a benevolent Creator will never suffer more human beings to be born than can live in plenty, it is a comfort of which I should be sorry to deprive you. By the same process of reasoning one may arrive at many very agreeable conclusions, such as that there is no cholera, no malaria, no yellow fever, no negro slavery, in the world. Unfortunately for me, perhaps, I learned from Lord Bacon a method of investigating truth diametrically opposite to that which you appear to follow. I am perfectly aware of the immense progress which your country has made and is making in population and wealth. I know that the labourer with you has large wages, abundant food, and the means of giving some education to his children. But I see no reason for attributing these things to the policy of Jefferson. I see no reason to believe that your progress would have been less rapid, that your labouring people would have been worse fed, or clothed, or taught, if your government had been conducted on the principles of Washington and Hamilton. Nay, you will,

[1] Randall's *Life of Jefferson* arrived on 7 October; in his Journal TBM dates this reply on the 10th (XI, 374).

I am sure, acknowledge that the progress which you are now making is only a continuation of the progress which you have been making ever since the middle of the seventeenth century, and that the blessings which you now enjoy were enjoyed by your forefathers who were loyal subjects of the Kings of England. The contrast between the labourer of New York and the labourer of Europe is not stronger now than it was when New York was governed by noblemen and gentlemen commissioned under the English Great Seal. And there are at this moment dependencies of the English crown in which all the phænomena which you attribute to purely democratical institutions may be seen in the highest perfection. The colony of Victoria in Australasia was planted only twenty years ago. The population is now, I suppose, near a million. The revenue is enormous, near five millions sterling, and raised without any murmuring. The wages of labour are higher than they are even with you. Immense sums are expended on education. And this is a province governed by the delegate of a hereditary Sovereign. It therefore seems to me quite clear that the facts which you cite to prove the excellence of purely democratic institutions ought to be ascribed, not to those institutions, but to causes which operated in America long before your Declaration of Independence, and which are still operating in many parts of the British empire.

You will perceive therefore that I do not propose, as you thought, to sacrifice the interests of the present generation to those of remote generations. It would indeed be absurd in a nation to part with institutions to which it is indebted for immense present prosperity from an apprehension that, after the lapse of a century, those institutions may be found to produce mischief. But I do not admit that the prosperity which your country enjoys arises from those parts of your polity which may be called, in an especial manner, Jeffersonian. Those parts of your polity already produce bad effects, and will, unless I am greatly mistaken, produce fatal effects, if they shall last till North America has two hundred inhabitants to the square mile.

With repeated thanks for your present I have the honor to be, Sir,

Your faithful Servant

Macaulay

TO [MR LANGLEY?], [10 OCTOBER 1858?][1]

Text: Unidentified newspaper clipping in volume of miscellaneous clippings on TBM at Harvard.

To answer all the cavils of small envious critics would be an endless labor – and, happily, it is a superfluous labor; for such cavils never did the smallest harm to [any] book, which had the principle of life within itself, and they are generally forgotten before the refutation appears. I can with perfect truth declare that they give me no pain at all; that I would not suppress them if I could do so by merely lifting up my hand; and that I should be sorry if persons who, like yourself, think favorably of my works, were to spend time, labor and talents, which might be better employed, in defending me against attacks which can do me no harm.

TO FRANCES MACAULAY, 12 OCTOBER 1858

MS: Trinity College.

Holly Lodge October 12. 1858

Dearest Fanny,

Hannah will take down with her the Certificate for your annuity. Pray keep it carefully. I have some other papers for you, which will show you what you must do every January and July in order to obtain your half yearly payments. But, as these papers require some explanation, I will keep them till we meet. I am glad to find that in January you will be entitled to a half year's income.

Ever yours
Macaulay

TO UNIDENTIFIED RECIPIENT, 13 OCTOBER 1858

Text: Unidentified newspaper clipping in volume of miscellaneous clippings on TBM at Harvard; reprinted from Inverness *Advertiser*: dated Holly Lodge, 13 October 1858.

I have long given up the hope that I shall be able to bring the History of England down to the time of the Porteous mob. I have, therefore, no

[1] The evidence is uncertain, but it is at least possible that this extract is from the letter that TBM wrote to a Mr Langley and recorded in his Journal for 10 October 1858. Langley (whom I have not identified) published a defense of TBM against the *Saturday Review* in the *Literary Gazette*, 9 October 1858, pp. 475–6. The article was published against TBM's wish, for he wrote in his Journal that he had begged Langley to suppress it, no doubt on just such grounds as are stated in this letter. Langley continued to oppress TBM with his services, until, in exasperation, TBM broke off the connection late in 1859 (Journal, XI, 587–9).

motive for investigating minutely the circumstances of that affair, and I should not wish to engage in an enquiry which, however curious and amusing it might be, must divert me from more useful researches.

TO MARGARET TREVELYAN, 14 OCTOBER 1858

MS: Trinity College.

Holly Lodge Kensington / October 14. 1858

My dearest Baba,

I will, as you propose, go down to Brighton on Monday, and bring you back on Tuesday.[1] I should wish to have rooms at the Norfolk. I shall take Gray with me.

I cannot stay one day at the Norfolk without ordering a dinner there. Therefore you and your aunt must dine with me at half past six.[2] If you will let me know that you have secured me the rooms, I will write to the landlord, and order the dinner. I shall go by the Pimlico[3] train which arrives at five. As soon as I have looked in at my inn, I will go to Temple House.

I find that there is a great deal of very vexatious carping and wrangling at the stamp office. My solicitor says that the best course will be to have Selina's effects – as far as can be done – valued by a broker, and that the same broker should, as far as he can, from aunt Fanny's description, put a value on the articles which have been sent away. If your aunt can engage a broker to be at Temple House by ten on Tuesday morning, I will be there; and the thing can be done in the best way.

My dear, dear, child, may God bless you. I believe that you have every chance for happiness. I have the highest opinion of Henry Holland. But I wish you no ill wish, when I wish that he may love you as much as I have done.

Ever yours
Macaulay

Love to Aunt Fanny

1 18 and 19 October.

2 They dined there on a 'very handsome – indeed a luxurious – dinner' on the 18th: 'the bill a heavy one, as I guessed it would be from the larks and grapes' (Journal, XI, 378: 18, 19 October).

3 That is, from the newly-opened Victoria Station.

TO UNIDENTIFIED RECIPIENT, 19 OCTOBER 1858

MS: Fitzwilliam Museum.

Holly Lodge / Kensington / October 19. 1858

Sir,

I am sorry that I can be of no use to you. I am a Trustee of the British Museum. But I have no voice in the disposal of the patronage, which is entirely in the hands of the three Principal Trustees. They are the Archbishop of Canterbury, the Lord Chancellor, and the Speaker of the House of Commons. / I have the honor to be, / Sir,

Your obedient Servant
Macaulay

TO FRANCES MACAULAY, 1 NOVEMBER 1858

MS: Trinity College. *Partly published:* Trevelyan, II, 453.

Holly Lodge Kensington / November 1. 1858

Dearest Fanny,

The fellow who pretends to have a testimonial from me is a lying vagabond. Who he may be I cannot guess and shall not trouble myself to ascertain. Perhaps he may have sent me a pamphlet. I may have written a civil line to acknowledge the receipt of it; and this line he may have the impudence to call a testimonial. A schoolmaster at Cheltenham sent me, two years and a half ago, a wretched pamphlet about British India.[1] In answering him, I pointed out two gross blunders into which he had fallen, and which, as he proposed to publish a small edition for the use of schools, I advised him to correct. My reward was that his book was advertised as "revised and corrected by Lord Macaulay." It is idle to be angry with people of this sort. They do after their kind. One might as well blame a fly for buzzing, or a frog for croaking.

Winter has come, with frost, and fog, and cutting wind. I have fires in my bedroom morning and evening; and scarcely go out at all. As yet I am pretty well.

Ever yours
Macaulay

[1] See [April? 1856].

TO THOMAS FLOWER ELLIS, 4 NOVEMBER 1858

MS: Trinity College. *Partly published:* Trevelyan, II, 401.

Holly Lodge Nov 4. 1858

Dear Ellis,

The coachman is much better; and I should have no scruple about letting him go out in a fine mild morning. But, as his complaint sprang from cold, I do not like sending him out in a raw foggy evening, till he is quite set up. I think therefore that you had better find your own way hither on Saturday.

By the bye, I should be much obliged to you to lend me a bottle or two of that excellent audit ale which you produced the last time that I dined with you. You shall have in return two bottles which still require time to make them perfect. I ask this, because our party on Tuesday will consist exclusively of old fellows and scholars of Trinity;[1] and I should like to give them some of our own nectar. If you can manage this, you had better send the bottles on Saturday with the law papers, that the ale may have time to settle after the journey.

Ever yours
Macaulay

TO [AMELIA MARY LORAINE?],[2] 10 NOVEMBER 1858

MS: Duke University.

Holly Lodge / November 10. 1858

Madam,

I thank you for the volume which you have been so good as to send me. I hope very soon to be able to read it.

1 Ellis, Henry Thornton, Malden, Hampden Gurney, and Henry Parr Hamilton were the guests (there may have been another: the Journal is torn at this point, and a name is perhaps lost). 'I did my best as host. The dinner was well cooked. The audit ale perfect. We had so much to say about auld lang syne that great powers of conversation were not wanted. I have been at parties of men celebrated for wit and eloquence which were much less lively' (Journal, XI, 385: 9 November).

2 Mrs Loraine was not the only woman writer to whom TBM was giving money, but she seems the most likely candidate. She was the author of *Lays of Israel: or Tales of the Temple and the Cross*, 1847 (item 796 in the sale catalogue of TBM's library), and earlier this year had published *Steps on the Mountains, a Tale.* On 26 November TBM wrote again to 'Mrs. Loraine, a most importunate beggar, evading a push that she has made at my purse' (Journal, XI, 391). He sent her £5 on 28 January 1859 (XI, 426); and on 2 April of that year he writes: 'Letter from that Mrs. Loraine again – begging – praying – this the last time – an execution. I will send her 5£ more. That will make up 50£ within a few months given to a bad writer whom I never saw. I shall tell her at the same time that I shall answer no more of her letters' (XI, 463).

Pray do not think of the money which I sent you formerly. I did not consider it as a loan; and I am sorry that your anxiety to repay me should have aggravated your distress.

I enclose a cheque which will, I hope, be of use to you. But I must caution you against expecting similar assistance from me hereafter. The claims on me are numerous and pressing; and I have now done for you as much as I can do without injustice to others. / I have the honor to be, / Madam,

Your obedient servant,
Macaulay

TO CHARLES MACAULAY, 14 NOVEMBER 1858

MS: University of London.

Holly Lodge November 14. 1858

Dear Charles,

I enclose a letter which I received yesterday evening. It is plain that you are the party interested. You had better take this paper with you, and make enquiries at the Unclaimed Dividend Office. How the mistake can have been committed I am at a loss to conceive.

I cannot offer to go with you myself: for an attack of Influenza confines me at present to my fireside.

Ever yours
Macaulay

TO LORD STANHOPE, 26 NOVEMBER 1858

MS: Stanhope Papers, Chevening.

Holly Lodge Kensington / November 26. 1858

Dear Stanhope,

I return Pitt's letters.[1] Many thanks for them. Of course no copy has been taken. But I could not deny myself the pleasure of showing papers so interesting to three or four friends. The opinion of every body who has seen this specimen of the M.S.S. in your possession is that such a mass of valuable and interesting matter ought not to be withheld from the public.[2]

[1] A copy of Stanhope's letter to TBM, 22 November, identifies these as Pitt to his mother, 16 March 1784, and to his brother, 29 May 1799 (MS, Chevening). They are both printed in Stanhope's *Life of William Pitt*, 4 vols., 1861, I, 199; III, 185–6.

[2] Stanhope had just been given access to a large part of Pitt's papers and was evidently considering what use to make of them.

I am delighted to find that you like my sketch,[1] and especially delighted to have my impartiality admitted by one who naturally has a great veneration for Pitt's memory.

The letter to Lady Chatham reminded me of the description of the Close of a Session in one of the Whig Satires of that time.

> "Pitt, in chaste kisses seeking virtuous joy,
> Begs Lady Chatham's blessing on her boy."

Ever yours truly
Macaulay

TO HENRY THURSTAN HOLLAND, 29 NOVEMBER 1858

MS: The Viscount Knutsford.

Holly Lodge November 29 / 1858

My dear Holland,

Your letter has given me great pleasure.[2] Such love as I feel for Margaret can never be unaccompanied by anxiety. But I assure you that there is no man living to whose honor and affection I could, with more confidence, have entrusted the care of her happiness.

And now, my dear Holland, let there be an end of ceremony between us. You are now the son of my dearest sister. How I live with her and hers you have seen, or my dear child can tell you; and on the same footing I wish to live with you.

Ever yours affectionately
Macaulay

TO LORD STANHOPE, 2 DECEMBER 1858

MS: Stanhope Papers, Chevening. *Mostly published:* Earl Stanhope, *Life of the Right Honourable William Pitt*, 1861, I, 161–2.

Holly Lodge December 2. 1858

My dear Stanhope,

I return Burke's paper.[3] It is interesting and very characteristic.

[1] The life of Pitt for the *Encyclopaedia Britannica*; TBM had lent his copy of the proofs to Stanhope on the 18th (Journal, XI, 388).

[2] Holland and Margaret Trevelyan were married on the 25th and were now on their honeymoon.

[3] Stanhope had sent TBM an apologia by Burke dated August 1794 (Stanhope to TBM, 1 December: copy, Chevening). Stanhope does not further identify the paper; perhaps it was the undated memorandum to Pitt on Burke's claims to a pension (printed from the Chatham Papers in *English Historical Review*, XLV [1930], 110–12).

I am afraid that I can find no better authority for the account which I have given of Temple's resignation[1] than that of Wraxall,[2] who tells the story very confidently and circumstantially, but whose unsupported testimony is of little value even when he relates what he himself saw and heard, and of no value when he relates what passed in the secrecy of the Cabinet. After looking at Tomline's narrative[3] and at the Buckingham papers,[4] I am satisfied that I was wrong. Whenever Black reprints the article separately, as he proposes to do, the error shall be corrected.[5] It will be a kindness, if you will note any other passage in which you think that I have been mistaken.

Ever yours truly
Macaulay

TO MRS HENRY THURSTAN HOLLAND, 7 DECEMBER 185[8]

MS: Trinity College.

Holly Lodge / December 7. 1856

Dearest Baba,

I am delighted to hear that you are so well and so happy. From your letter I judge that the weather is much finer at Fox Warren[6] than here. I can hardly see the trees on my lawn; and the City is, no doubt, in Egyptian darkness. I have not stirred out since Thursday; and I had better have staid at home then. However I had the pleasure of seeing the children who are now objects of so much interest to us.[7] Very engaging little things they are. I could with pleasure have spent a much longer time with them.

Lord Lansdowne, who has been in town under the care of a very clever aurist, called here two or three days ago, and talked most kindly about

[1] In his article on Pitt TBM says of Pitt's coming to power in 1783 that he 'wisely determined to give the public feeling time to gather strength. On this point he differed from his kinsman Temple. The consequence was, that Temple, who had been appointed one of the Secretaries of State, resigned his office forty-eight hours after he had accepted it.' In the *Life of Pitt*, Stanhope rejects this account, and concludes that Temple left Pitt in anger over disappointed ambition.

[2] Sir Nathaniel Wraxall, *Historical Memoirs of My Own Time, 1772–1784*, 1815. In his early essay 'On the Athenian Orators,' *Knight's Quarterly*, III (August 1824), 124, TBM cites this as a type of the unreliable, and he mentions, as one of the varieties of lie, the '*Mendacium Wraxallianum*' in the essay on Barère (*ER*, LXXIX, 280).

[3] See 9 July 1844.

[4] The Duke of Buckingham and Chandos, *Memoirs of the Court and Cabinets of George the Third*, 2 vols., 1853.

[5] See 17 February 1859.

[6] The house designed and built by Charles Buxton, near Weybridge, where the Hollands spent their honeymoon.

[7] The daughter and twin sons of Henry Holland by his first marriage.

you and Holland. I really think that my dear old friend is less deaf than he was. He is much pleased by the general approbation which his present to Trinity College has obtained.[1] I mean to see it next Easter; and I hope that you and your honest man, as Lady G. irreverently calls her husband, will be of the party.

Àpropos of Lady G. I applaud you for making poor Holland read Sir Charles Grandison right through. When we meet, your Mamma and I will examine him as severely as if he was a candidate for the Indian Civil Service. "What sum did Sir Charles present to each of the Danby family?" "How did Lord and Lady L. keep their money and draw it out?" "Of what religion was Mr. Bagenhall?" "In what square did Sir Hargrave Pollexfen live?" "In what square Sir Charles Grandison, before his marriage?" "To what square did Sir Charles remove after his marriage?" "Where, and in what manner, did Lord G buy a town house?" "What became of Miss Cantillon?"[2] Make Henry answer these in writing, without letting him see the book, and send me his answers that I may see whether he be worthy of a degree in Richardsonian learning. In the meantime give him my love. I am impatient to see you again, my darling. God bless you.

Ever yours,
Macaulay

TO UNIDENTIFIED RECIPIENT, 7 DECEMBER 1858

Text: Montrose, Arbroath, and Brechin Review, 13 January 1860.

Holly Lodge, Kensington, December 7, 1858.

Sir,

I am much obliged to you for the interest which you are so good as to take in my book. I cannot, however, admit the justice of your criticism. The question is not new to me. Lord Duncan,[3] near three years ago, made the same objection which you now make; and I then succeeded in convincing him that I was right.[4] Dundee certainly had a seat called Glen Ogilvie. To Glen Ogilvie he retired from Dudhope; and from Glen

[1] See 1 December 1856.

[2] The answers are, in order: £5,000; in a locked drawer, all withdrawals being entered in a memorandum book; reared a Protestant, now nominally a Catholic; Cavendish Square; St James's Square; Grosvenor Square; Grosvenor Square, without consulting his wife; she eloped with a penniless captain.

[3] Adam Duncan-Haldane (1812–67), styled Viscount Duncan until 1859, when he succeeded as second Earl of Camperdown; Whig M.P., 1837–59.

[4] In ch. 13 of the *History* TBM wrote that 'Dundee, after his flight from Edinburgh, had retired to his country seat in that valley through which the Glamis descends to the ancient castle of Macbeth' (III, 326). The passage remains unchanged in later editions.

Ogilvie he started for the Highlands. In the Gazetteer of Scotland, I find the following passage under the word Glammis: – "Glammis Burn rises in the hill of Auchterhouse, at the extreme southern boundary, *traverses the whole length of Glen Ogilvie*, cuts its way through the central hilly ridge, and joins the Dean on the demesne of Glammis Castle." I am, therefore, I think, fully warranted in describing Dundee's retreat as situated in the valley through which the Glammis descends, to the ancient Castle of Macbeth.

With repeated thanks, I have the honour to be, sir, your faithful servant,

Macaulay.

TO LORD STANHOPE, 18 DECEMBER 1858

MS: Stanhope Papers, Chevening.

Holly Lodge Kensington / December 18. 1858

My dear Stanhope,

Thanks for the *rifacimento* of the First Book of Paradise Lost.[1] It is indeed a most curious performance. I have another work of the same family, – a translation of the whole poem into prose. It was a present to me from a poor man who was drowned. I hope that the omen may be averted from you.

Ever yours,
Macaulay

TO THOMAS FLOWER ELLIS, 29 DECEMBER 1858

MS: Trinity College.

Holly Lodge December 29 / 1858

Dear Ellis,

Let me know whether I am to send the carriage for you on Saturday, and at what hour.

You must dine here on Thursday the 6th of January, or, as a Puseyite would say, on the Feast of the Holy Epiphany, to meet a few friends.[2] By the bye, there is an odd anachronism in that Ecclesiastical Calendar

[1] In a note accompanying this letter Stanhope states that this was 'an attempt to improve and embellish line by line the poetry of Milton. "New Version of the Paradise Lost" etc. "by a Gentleman of Oxford," Oxford, Printed by W. Jackson 1756.' The author was George Smith Green (d. 1762: *DNB*).

[2] Dundas, Henry Holland, Vaughan Hawkins, Sir William Page Wood, Adolphus, and Charles Buxton (Journal, XI, 413).

which is common to the English, Latin and Greek Churches. Innocents' Day is placed more than a week before the Epiphany. And yet, if you look at St Matthew's narrative, in which alone the Innocents and the Epiphany are mentioned, you will see that the massacre of the children was posterior to the Adoration of the Wise Men, and was the effect of Herod's rage when he found that he was mocked and that those from whom he expected information had stolen away to their own country.[1]

I have been reading Cicero's philosophical works again, and like them exceedingly – the Tusculan disputations always excepted, which are mere anointings for broken bones.

Ever yours,
Macaulay

TO SIR EDWARD BULWER-LYTTON, 29 DECEMBER 1858

MS: Hertfordshire County Council.

Holly Lodge Kensington / December 29. 1858

Dear Sir Edward,

Your new volumes[2] have this moment reached me. They could not have reached me more opportunely. For I have been reading My Novel again with great delight;[3] and at breakfast this morning I was sorry to see how very few pages I had left. I now applaud myself for the resolute self denial with which I abstain from looking at your stories till they are finished. Do not take the trouble to write to me. God knows, you have enough and more than enough to do.[4] With sincere thanks and with all the good wishes which belong to Christmas, believe me

Yours very truly,
Macaulay

[1] Matthew 2: 16.

[2] *What Will He Do with It?* was published in 4 vols., 1859, after being serialized in *Blackwood's*. TBM thought it Bulwer-Lytton's best (Journal, XI, 412: 4 January 1859).

[3] 'Determined to try My Novel again on Hannah's recommendation, – and liked it much, very much better' (Journal, XI, 407: 24 December).

[4] Bulwer-Lytton was Secretary for the Colonies in Derby's government.

THE FINAL YEAR
3 JANUARY–25 DECEMBER 1859

1859 January 6
Learns of offer to Trevelyan of Madras appointment

– February 18
Trevelyan leaves for India

– April 30–May 2
Family party at Cambridge

– May 1
Learns that Hannah, Alice, and George plan to join Trevelyan at Madras in the next year

– July 28–August 17
Northern tour with Hannah: Windermere, Glasgow, Inverary, Stirling, Edinburgh

– October 1–8
Tour of South of England with Ellis: Weymouth, Lyme, Sidmouth, Exeter, Ilfracombe. TBM looking for retirement home

– October 15
Learns that Hannah will leave for India in February

– December 15
Suffers heart attack

– December 28
Death

1860 January 9
Burial in Westminster Abbey

1861 March
History, vol. 5, published

TO HENRY REEVE, 3 JANUARY 185[9]

MS: Mr F. R. Cowell.

Holly Lodge Kensington / Jany. 3. 1858

Dear Reeve,

I send you the two volumes of which you kindly offered to take charge.[1] If you read the Life of Bishop Newton or that of Skelton, you will, I think, be repaid for your trouble. Be so good as to give the enclosed note to Lord Lansdowne.

Ever yours,
Macaulay

TO LORD LANSDOWNE, 3 JANUARY 185[9]

MS: The Marquess of Lansdowne.

Holly Lodge January 3. 1858

Dear Lord Lansdowne,

I send you by Reeve, who has been kind enough to charge himself with my commission, two volumes of biography[2] which I mentioned to you when I was at Bowood in October.[3] I was fortunate enough to pick them up at an old bookshop in Holborn. The first of the four lives, that of Pocock, is the least interesting. The second, that of Bishop Pearce, is not without interest. I ought to tell you that the passages which cement the different parts of the Bishop's narrative were written by Johnson.[4] The Life of Bishop Newton and that of Skelton are, in my opinion, curious and interesting in the highest degree. I shall be most happy to learn that they have afforded you any entertainment.

With all good Christmas wishes for you and yours believe me, / Dear Lord Lansdowne,

Yours affectionately
Macaulay

TO THOMAS FLOWER ELLIS, 8 JANUARY 1859

MS: Trinity College.

Holly Lodge Jany. 8. 1859

Dear Ellis,

I shall be delighted to see you on Tuesday. Harry Holland and Charles

[1] See next letter.

[2] The lives of Bishops Pocock, Pearce, Newton, and Skelton; see *to* Frances Macaulay, 17 March 1853, for full citation.

[3] 23–6 October (Journal, XI, 379–81).

[4] In 1777.

Buxton have been telling their wives that you are a wonderfully agreeable person, the most humorous of men.[1] As I did not happen to hear your *bons môts*, you must tell me them on Tuesday. Otherwise I shall, like a true friend, say to your admirers – "Oh – humour – hmn – good man, Ellis – good lawyer – good scholar – very honorable gentleman – but as for humour –" Of course you are well acquainted with those little delicacies which would furnish out a new Dialogue De Amicitia.

Thanks for the translation. This society is evidently formed on the plan of a Society of clever *Narren* described in the account of Serlo's wanderings. Do you remember the passage in Wilhelm Meister?[2] It is a piece of heavy Teutonic pleasantry; and the authors of it seem to me to be fools; and no mistake. I shall take no notice of it. To send such a diploma, unaccompanied by a graver explanation, is an impertinence. Thanks to the lady who was kind enough to furnish me with a transcript of the hieroglyphics.[3] Kindest remembrances to both your girls.

Ever yours
Macaulay

TO HENRY STEPHENS RANDALL, 8 JANUARY 1859

MS: New York Public Library. *Envelope:* H S Randall Esq / etc. etc. etc. / Cortland Village / State of New York / U.S. *Subscription:* M. *Published: Harper's Magazine*, LIV (February 1877), 462.

Holly Lodge Kensington / January 8. 1859

Sir,

I owe you many thanks for the amusement and information which I have derived from your Life of Jefferson; and I am much more inclined to pay that debt than to trouble you with criticism and controversy. In truth the work of criticism and controversy would be interminable.[4]

I did not know, till I read your book, that the odious imputations which have often been thrown on Jefferson's private character originated with that vile fellow Callender.[5] In the absence of evidence, I supposed

[1] Ellis, Holland, and Buxton were all at TBM's dinner on 6 January (Journal, XI, 413).

[2] *Wilhelm Meister's Apprenticeship*, Book IV, ch. 18. There is no mention in TBM's Journal of the 'diploma' discussed here.

[3] Ellis's daughter Louise: see 17 January.

[4] 'Looked through the Life of Jefferson. A bad book – bad in substance and in style – yet with much curious information. I must answer the writer civilly and yet not insincerely – concisely at all events. His ignorance of England and his hatred of England are of a piece with his hero's' (Journal, XI, 413–14: 7 January).

[5] James Thomson Callender (1758–1803), fled Scotland under indictment for sedition; notable for scandal-mongering and abusiveness in his journalism but patronized by Jefferson, whom he later turned on; drowned while drunk. See Randall's *Life of Jefferson*, III, 16–21.

them, as I told you, to be either wholly false or grossly exaggerated; and I certainly shall not be more disposed to believe them because they rest on Callender's authority.

I again beg you to accept my thanks for much pleasure and much instruction, and to believe me

Your faithful Servant,
Macaulay

H S Randall Esq / etc. etc. etc.

TO WILLIAM HICKLING PRESCOTT, 8 JANUARY 1859

MS: Yale University. *Published:* George Ticknor, *Life of William Hickling Prescott*, Boston, 1864, II, 409–10.

Holly Lodge Kensington / January 8. 1859

My dear Sir,

I have already delayed too long to thank you for your third Volume.[1] It is excellent, and, I think, superior to anything that you have written, part of the History of the Conquest of Mexico excepted. Most of those good judges whose voices I have been able to collect at this dead time of the year agree with me.

This is the season when in this country friends interchange good wishes. I do not know whether that fashion has crossed the Atlantic. Probably not: for your Pilgrim Fathers held it to be a sin to keep Christmas and Twelfth Day. I hope however that you will allow me to express my hope that the year which is beginning may be a happy one to you.[2]

Ever yours truly,
Macaulay

H W Prescott Esq / etc. etc. etc.

TO CHRISTIAN BERNHARD TAUCHNITZ, 10 JANUARY 1859

Text: Bernhard Tauchnitz, 1837–1887, p. 110.

Holly Lodge, Kensington, Jan. 10, 1859.

If I am to bring out any more volumes of my History, I must devote my whole time to that work, and not suffer myself to be seduced from it

[1] Of Prescott's *History of Philip the Second*; TBM read it on 12 December and liked it 'better than the two preceding vols. It relates to matters about which I had more to learn' (Journal, XI, 398).

[2] Prescott died on 27 January, before receiving this letter. 'Prescott dead. Poor fellow – I liked him much, and his writings too. Sixty three – I am not much younger. I may any day go after him' (Journal, XI, 435: 15 February).

by any temptation.[1] A complete and highly finished account of the English literature of the nineteenth century would occupy me many months. A hasty sketch would do me no honour . . . I should not choose to take on myself the business of estimating the merits of my contemporaries. It would be quite impossible for me to speak the truth without inflicting pain and making enemies.

TO FRANCES MACAULAY, 12 JANUARY 1859

MS: Trinity College.

Holly Lodge Jany. 12. 1859

Dearest Fanny,

This is, no doubt, a most unhappy event;[2] and what adds to the bitterness of our feelings is the utter want of sympathy on the part of our friends. Every body out of the inmost domestic circle fancies that we must be in raptures, and pesters us with congratulations.

Trevelyan will not hear of Hannah's going; and there he is quite right. It would be monstrous to deprive the children, and such children, of both parents at the very moment when parental affection is most needed. This is particularly the case as to Alice. I am satisfied however that Trevelyan does not know what a sacrifice he is making in quitting his family. He is now under a delusion. All his virtues and all his faults are brought strongly out; and, between ambition and public spirit, he is as much excited, and as unfit to be reasoned with, as if he had drunk three bottles of Champagne. But his elation, like the elation produced by Champagne, will soon be over. A reaction will come; and he has much, very much to suffer.

In the meantime others are suffering cruelly. I never have seen Hannah so unhappy. Baba has been very miserable. Dear little Alice was terribly shocked. But they are now calm; and, seeing that the thing must be, are making up their minds to it. George, except on their account, is not much distressed. He is sorry to part with his father, but glad to see his father gratified and promoted.

[1] 'Tauchnitz writes to beg me to give him an Essay on Contemporary English literature' (Journal, XI, 417).

[2] Trevelyan had been offered and had accepted the Governorship of Madras; TBM learned of the offer on 6 January, when Trevelyan told him that he meant to go, 'leaving Hannah to keep house here. If she were to go I should die of a broken heart, I think.' Two days later Trevelyan had made up his mind: 'All is over. Go he will. A madman. I can hardly command my indignation. Yet what good can I do by expressing it?' (Journal, XI, 412–13; 415). News of the appointment appeared in *The Times* on the 11th.

In a pecuniary view, no doubt the appointment will be a good thing.[1] But that is a small set off against the happiness of such a family; and I am confident that five times the emolument would not reconcile Hannah and the girls to the separation.

It is satisfactory to find that the appointment is generally approved. I should suppose that Trevelyan will be sworn of the Privy Council before he goes.[2] The Governors of Madras and Bombay have generally been Privy Councillors.

Ever yours,
Macaulay

Let me know whether you have drawn your annuity without difficulty.

TO FRANCES MACAULAY, 14 JANUARY 1859

MS: Trinity College.

Holly Lodge / January 14. 1859

Dearest Fanny,

I return your letter. It seems quite right. There can be no difficulty about the matter, when once we get into the proper course. When do you think of moving?[3] I am anxious about you, and shall be glad to hear that you find yourself comfortable and really independent.

Trevelyan's situation is a very good one, as far as money goes. He is sanguine; and so, I think, is Hannah, as to what he may save. But I really think that, after all expenses in India and here are paid, they ought, during his absence, to lay up between three and four thousand a year.

This is the bright side. As to the rest, the prospect is very sad. However, there is no retreat. His appointment is notified. His place at the Treasury is filled up. Even if he were inclined to change his mind, – and I really think that he has misgivings, – it is now too late.

Ever yours
Macaulay

[1] 'He ought to be able to send home near 6000£ a year during his absence; and of that 6000£ a year Hannah ought to be able to lay 4000£ by' (Journal, XI, 417: 9 January).

[2] He was not.

[3] Fanny moved this spring to 95 Montpelier Road, Brighton. When he was in Montpellier on his French tour in 1858 TBM noted that 'The fashion once was to go thither from England for health; and there is probably not a watering place in our island which has not its Montpelier street or its Montpelier crescent. There are innumerable Montpelier Villas and Montpelier Houses' (X, 227–8).

TO CHARLES HAY CAMERON, 14 JANUARY 1859

MS: Kent County Council.

Holly Lodge Kensington / January 14. 1859

Dear Cameron,

I am sorry that such a gloom has been thrown over your joy. I had heard of the affliction of Lord and Lady Somers from Lord Lansdowne, who was expecting them at Bowood when your niece was taken ill.[1]

I should hardly in any case have been able to join your party on Tuesday.[2] During my hibernation, which began this year early in November, and may probably last till May, I make no engagements, because the chance is much against my being able to keep them. The Christmas visits to the country seats of my friends, which I once used to enjoy, I have long been forced to give up; and, only last Saturday, I was unable to go to the Museum, where my fellow trustees wanted me to make a Quorum. But I assure you that, by my fireside, I shall wish happiness and mutual affection to your young couple as heartily as if I were in the Church at Putney. My kindest regards to Mrs. Cameron.

Ever yours truly,
Macaulay

Trevelyan's appointment is no matter of congratulation to any of his family. But I do not doubt that he will be an excellent Governor.

TO LADY CLARENDON,[3] 14 JANUARY 1859

MS: National Library of Wales.

Holly Lodge Kensington / January 14. 1859

Dear Lady Clarendon,

Your kind invitation is most tempting. But at this season I am forced to lead the life of a dormouse. My hibernation began in November, and will probably last till April. I am truly sorry that I dare not venture: for I retain a most agreeable recollection of days passed at the Grove.

Ever yours truly,
Macaulay

[1] Virginia Pattle, the sister of Mrs Cameron, married Charles, third Earl Somers; their youngest daughter, Virginia, died of diphtheria on 9 January, in her fourth year.

[2] Cameron's only daughter, Julia, was married that day to Charles Loyd Norman, a partner in Baring Brothers. Cameron had invited TBM to the wedding in early November (Journal, XI, 385).

[3] Catherine (1810–74), widow of John Foster Barham, married Lord Clarendon in 1839.

TO THOMAS FLOWER ELLIS, 17 JANUARY 1859

MS: Trinity College.

Holly Lodge January 17 / 1859

Dear Ellis,

I am ashamed to make Louise do the work of a Dragoman for me. But these Germans pester me with letters which may require answers, and which I am as unable to decipher as Rawlinson to read a Ninevite brick. I am forced therefore to trespass again on the kindness of my interpreter.[1] What perverseness it is in a nation to write a different character from all the rest of the world, without a reason or anything that looks like a reason! They can write our character if they chuse. In this very letter *Essays*, *Lays of Ancient Rome*, *Dryden*, are written in the ordinary way.

I expect you on Wednesday.

Ever yours,
Macaulay

TO THOMAS FLOWER ELLIS, 25 JANUARY 1859

MS: Trinity College. *Partly published:* Trevelyan, II, 396n.

Holly Lodge / January 25. 1859

Dear Ellis,

I have a dinner party here on Monday next at seven – Milman, Thackeray, Lord Stanhope, Hibbert, Dundas, Panizzi. Will you make the number up to eight?[2] And will you come any day this week?

Poor Hallam.[3] To be sure he died to me some years ago. I then missed him much and often. Now the loss is hardly felt. I am inclined to think that there is scarcely any separation – even of those separations which break hearts and cause suicides, which might not be made endurable by gradual weaning. In the course of that weaning, there will be much suffering: but it will, at no moment, be very acute.

This is the Burns Centenary. A wonderful man. But if he had been an Englishman he would have had no Centenary.[4]

Ever yours
Macaulay

[1] The letter announced that the writer had sent TBM a translation of Catullus (Journal, XI, 422: 19 January).

[2] Hibbert could not come and was replaced by Arthur Penrhyn Stanley (Journal, XI, 428: 31 January).

[3] He died on the 21st.

[4] TBM had been asked to preside at the celebration in Glasgow to rival the Edinburgh affair, where Brougham was to preside (but in the event did not). 'I refused . . . for fifty

TO LORD CAMPBELL, 26 JANUARY 1859

Text: Life of John, Lord Campbell, Edited by His Daughter the Hon. Mrs Hardcastle, II, 362–3.

Holly Lodge: January 26, 1859.

Dear Lord Campbell,

Thanks for your interesting little volume.[1] I always thought that Shakespeare had, when a young man, been in the lower ranks of the legal profession; and I am now fully convinced of it. It is impossible, I am certain, to mention any writer, not regularly bred to the law, who has made half as many allusions to tenures of land, to forms of action, to modes of procedure, without committing gross blunders. The mistake which you mention about the words "to join issue"[2] was made by no less a man than Lord Castlereagh, when leader of the House of Commons. You may observe that the best writers perpetually use the word "pleading" incorrectly. They think that it means haranguing a jury.[3] I saw the other day a sentence to this effect: "It may be doubted whether Erskine or Curran were the greater pleader." The person who expressed himself thus would have stared if he had been told that Littledale[4] was a far greater pleader than either. Miss Edgeworth's books were carefully revised by her father, a most active magistrate, who ought to have picked up a little law. Yet what monstrous errors there are in every passage which relates to legal proceedings. In a novel of last year a man is taken up and tried in London for a felony committed in the Tyrol. When a writer draws numerous illustrations from legal proceedings, and makes no mistakes, we shall always, if we can learn his history, find that he was of the profession. Fielding is an instance; so is Cowper. In Shakespeare's case the presumption seems to be peculiarly strong. Thanks again and again. Ever, dear Lord Campbell, yours truly,

Macaulay.

good reasons, one of which is that, if I went down in the depth of winter to harangue in Scotland, I should never come back alive' (Journal, XI, 387: 14 November 1858).

[1] *Shakespeare's Legal Acquirements Considered*, just published. TBM is incidentally mentioned as one of those 'men of brilliant intellectual career' who began as students of the law (p. 22).

[2] Campbell says that he had heard the phrase used in the House of Commons to mean 'concur with' (*Shakespeare's Legal Acquirements Considered*, p. 107).

[3] It refers, in English law, to 'the preparation of the statement of the facts on which either party to a criminal prosecution or a civil action founds his claim to a decision in his favour' (*Encyclopaedia Britannica*, 13th edn).

[4] Sir Joseph Littledale (1767–1842: *DNB*), Judge of the Court of King's Bench in the years of TBM's attendance.

TO SAMUEL AUSTIN ALLIBONE,[1] 29 JANUARY 1859

MS: Huntington Library. *Envelope:* S. A. Allibone Esq / Philadelphia / United States. *Extracts published:* S. A. Allibone, *Critical Dictionary of English Literature*, 1858–71, I, 5; Allibone, 'Life and Writings of Thomas Babington Macaulay,' in *History of England*, v, Boston, 1861.

Holly Lodge Kensington / January 29. 1859

Sir,

I have this morning received the first volume of your Dictionary; and I beg you to accept my thanks for it. It cannot fail, I think, to be a valuable addition to English, as well as American, libraries.

Of the article which you propose to publish about myself I do not venture to give any opinion. I will only say that the review of Churchill's Works was not written by me. The author is Mr. Forster; and he has since republished it with his name.[2]

In turning over your pages, I see myself mentioned in a way which is far from agreeable to me. In the article on Dr. Channing I am said to have reviewed his Milton with much severity.[3] I never reviewed his Milton; nor indeed did I ever see his Milton. You will, I am sure, permit me to say that you ought to be very cautious in ascribing anonymous papers to particular persons. A misstatement in such a work as yours may well escape the notice of the person most interested. But in the next generation it will pass for an established truth. Everybody has a right to blame me for what I have written; nor shall I ever complain of the freedom with which that right is exercised. It is only when what I have not written is imputed to me that I am in danger of losing my temper.

I am glad to see that, in the article about myself, the Review of Channing's Milton is not mentioned as mine.

I readily admit that large allowances must be made for a person engaged in such an undertaking as yours, and that a critic who should think himself entitled to sneer at your performance, because he could detect you in some inaccuracy on a subject with which he was peculiarly conversant,

[1] Allibone (1816–89), of Philadelphia, bibliographer and librarian, published as his major work a *Critical Dictionary of English Literature and British and American Authors*, 3 vols., Philadelphia, 1858–71. The volume one of this work containing the page of 'testimonials' in which an extract from this letter appears, though dated 1858, must have been published after the first edition.

[2] Allibone's entry for TBM lists the contents of the Philadelphia edition of his *Essays*, 1849, which mistakenly includes John Forster's 'Charles Churchill,' *ER*, LXXXI (January 1845), 46–88; Allibone adds that 'it is denied that this last-named is properly attributed to Mr. Macaulay.'

[3] The review was in fact by Brougham, *ER*, LXIX (April 1839), 214–30.

would only convict himself of dulness and unfairness. I sincerely wish you success, and have the honor to be

Your faithful Servant
Macaulay

S A Allibone Esq / etc. etc. etc.

TO [MR COCHRANE],[1] 31 JANUARY 1859

MS: Trinity College.

Holly Lodge January 31 / 1859

Sir,

I enclose a cheque for five pounds. It is right that I should distinctly apprise you that I have now done all that I can do for you without injustice to others. / I am, Sir,

Your obedient Servant,
Macaulay

TO LORD BROUGHTON, 6 FEBRUARY 1859

MS: British Museum.

Holly Lodge February 6. 1859

Dear Lord Broughton,

I put off thanking you for your two interesting volumes,[2] in the hope that I might see you in the House, and might be able to tell you there how much pleasure you had given me. But, as I have not been so fortunate as to fall in with you, I will not be guilty of any further delay. I do not know whether I was more gratified by the old or the new parts of your book. I was glad to make acquaintance with what I had never read before, and to renew my acquaintance with what I read more than forty years ago.

Ever yours truly,
Macaulay

[1] TBM calls him 'a ruined bookseller' who has written 'to beg of me the third time' (Journal, XI, 428).

[2] Broughton's *Italy: Remarks Made in Several Visits from the Year 1816 to 1854*, 2 vols., 1859, incorporating his *Historical Illustrations of the Fourth Canto of Childe Harold*, 1818. TBM received the book on 29 January (Journal, XI, 427).

TO BISHOP SAMUEL WILBERFORCE, 14 FEBRUARY 1859

MS: Duke University.

Holly Lodge February 14. 1859

Dear Bishop of Oxford,

I shall be most happy to breakfast with you on Wednesday.[1]

Ever yours,
Macaulay

TO THE STEWARDS AND COMMITTEE OF THE ROYAL ASYLUM OF ST ANNE'S SOCIETY,[2] 16 FEBRUARY 1859

MS: Trinity College.

Lord Macaulay presents his compliments to the Stewards and Committee of the Royal Asylum of St Ann's Society, and is sorry that it will not be in his power to have the honor of dining with them next Tuesday.

Holly Lodge February 16. 1859

TO LORD STANHOPE, 17 FEBRUARY 1859

MS: Stanhope Papers, Chevening.

Holly Lodge February 17 / 1859

My dear Stanhope,

I must admit the validity of your excuses. I think that Friday the 25th was the day on which it was finally settled, after several changes, that I should breakfast with you.[3]

You remember that we exchanged letters about the cause of Lord Temple's resignation in 1783.[4] I could then find no better authority than Wraxall's for my statement that the resignation was caused by a difference of opinion in the Cabinet on the question of dissolution. I now see that Lord Cornwallis believed this to be the true explanation. In a letter of March 3. 1784, he says "I do not believe Lord T. and Mr. P. ever had any quarrel, and think the former resigned because they would not dissolve

[1] The other guests were Lord Lansdowne, Lord Stanhope, Thackeray, Van de Weyer, and Richard Chenevix Trench (Journal, XI, 435: 16 February).

[2] The Society, founded in 1709, maintained a school for needy children at Brixton Hill, Surrey; Wilberforce was once its president.

[3] But TBM breakfasted with Van de Weyer on that day (Journal, XI, 441).

[4] See 2 December 1858.

the Parliament." He adds indeed "I may be mistaken in this."[1] But I think that his opinion, – when his character and position are considered, – must be allowed to have great weight.

Ever yours truly
Macaulay

TO CHARLES ROSS,[2] 24 FEBRUARY 1859

Text: Microfilm in Morgan Library of unlocated MS.

Holly Lodge February 24. 1859

Sir,

I do not know whether the despatch of Sir Henry Clinton which you mention is the same which is now lying before me.[3] Mine bears date the 29th of October 1781. It was brought to England by the Rattlesnake Sloop, and was published in London on Tuesday the 27th of November, the day of the meeting of Parliament. That despatch certainly does not contain the articles of the Capitulation of York Town. But it contains very much more than gloomy anticipations. Indeed a despatch containing nothing worse than gloomy anticipations, even if those anticipations were confirmed by French reports, would hardly have been thought sufficient to justify the King in announcing to his Parliament, as an unquestioned fact, that he had lost an army. Sir Henry's words are "We cannot entertain the least doubt of His Lordship's having capitulated."

Wraxall says that the despatch arrived in Pall Mall about noon on the 25th, – a circumstance which he can have learned only from the report of others. He may have been misinformed; and the endorsement which you mention makes it probable that he was misinformed, and that the news reached Lord George before day break. But surely such a mistake does not justify us in believing that the whole story of the dinner and the conversation is a circumstantial and deliberate lie. In general I think that Wraxall may be trusted as to the substance of what he himself heard and

[1] Charles Ross, ed., *Correspondence of Charles, First Marquis Cornwallis*, 2nd edn, 3 vols. 1859, I, 170. TBM bought this work on the day before (Journal, XI, 436).

[2] Ross (1799–1860: *Boase*) had been a Tory M.P., 1823–37, and served as an assistant whip. TBM calls him 'an ass. What Peel saw in him I never could imagine' (Journal, XI, 436: 16 February). He was the son of General Alexander Ross, Cornwallis's intimate friend, and had just published the *Correspondence* of Cornwallis (see preceding letter); in this, TBM thought, he made 'frightful blunders.'

[3] Clinton (1738?–95: *DNB*) was Commander-in-Chief of the British forces in America. Ross cites Sir Nathaniel Wraxall's account of dining with Lord George Germain on 25 November 1781 and of reading then Sir Henry's despatch of 29 October announcing the surrender of Yorktown; from the evidence of dates, Ross concludes that 'Wraxall's statement is incorrect' (*Correspondence of Cornwallis*, 2nd edn, I, 135–6).

saw. It was when he repeated what others had told him that he was utterly untrustworthy. For my part I have no doubt that he dined with Lord George on this memorable Sunday, and that the table talk was such as is related in the Memoirs. Some inaccuracies there will be in the most veracious and exact account which any man can give, from memory, of events which happened more than thirty years ago. Such inaccuracies there are in this part of Wraxall's narrative, but I really think, only such.

It is from no partiality to Sir Nathaniel that, on this occasion, I take his part. I dislike his politics, his temper, his style. I think ill of his principles; and I despise his understanding. But of the particular charge which you bring against him I must acquit him.

Your book is full of interest. If I should, on a reperusal, observe any mistake such as no care or skill can avoid in a work like that which you have undertaken, I will avail myself of your obliging permission to mention to you what occurs to me. / I have the honor to be, / Sir,

Your most obedient Servant,

Macaulay

C Ross Esq / etc. etc. etc.

TO FRANCES MACAULAY, 9 MARCH 1859

MS: Trinity College.

Holly Lodge March 9 / 1859

Dearest Fanny,

Sir Artegal, the Just Knight, is the hero of the fifth Book of Spenser's Fairy Queen. I have not read that fifth Book since I was twelve years old, and shall never read it again. Of all poets of a high order Spenser is least to my taste. As a critic, I see his merit. But, as a mere courteous reader, I should not much care if every copy of his great work were burned.

I have got wonderfully through the winter. It would perhaps be more correct to say that I have had no winter to get through. At this moment the almond trees round me are in full bloom. My thorns and lilacs are in leaf and all but in flower. I live in constant dread of a frost which will nip the young blossoms.

Trevelyan's expedition has hitherto been most prosperous.[1] His brother[2] will, I am afraid, bore him a good deal when they meet.

[1] He left for India on 18 February.

[2] Henry Willoughby Trevelyan: see 7 December 1834.

I need not, I hope, tell you that I count upon you for our Easter excursion to Cambridge and Ely.[1]

Ever yours,
Macaulay

TO LADY STANHOPE,[2] 10 MARCH 1859

MS: University of California, Los Angeles.

Holly Lodge March 10 / 1859

Dear Lady [Stanhope,]

I shall be most happy to dine with you on Wednesday next.

Ever yours truly,
Macaulay

TO RICHARD MONCKTON MILNES, 11 MARCH 1859

MS: Trinity College.

Holly Lodge March 11 / 1859

Dear Milnes,

I am very sorry that I cannot dine with you on Sunday week.

Ever yours,
Macaulay

TO RICHARD MONCKTON MILNES, 12 MARCH 1859

MS: Trinity College.

Holly Lodge March 12. 1859

Dear Milnes,

Will you breakfast here on Thursday at ten?[3]

Ever yours truly
Macaulay

[1] The plan was first cancelled, and then altered: see 15 and 28 April.

[2] The name in the MS has been overscored. TBM dined at the Stanhopes on 16 March: 'not a very pleasant party; – however I was well placed, next to Lady S., and got on very agreeably with her' (Journal, XI, 452).

[3] He did, with Hannah, Margaret and Henry Holland, Lord Lansdowne, Charles Austin and Mrs Austin, the Milmans, and Dundas. 'Very pleasant – Milnes more than usually absurd' (Journal, XI, 452: 17 March).

TO FRANCES MACAULAY, 15 MARCH 1859

MS: Trinity College.

Holly Lodge March 15. 1859

Dearest Fanny,

I was at my banker's to day, and learned that a sum of £8.6.9 stood there to my credit in my character of Administrator to our father's effects. You are entitled to two sevenths of this money, your own seventh and poor Selina's. I send you a post office order for the amount. –

Ever yours,
Macaulay

TO CHARLES MACAULAY, 15 MARCH 1859

MS: University of London. *Envelope:* C Z Macaulay / 17 Eastbourne Terrace / W̄.

Holly Lodge March 15. 1859

Dear Charles,

I paid a visit to Birchin Lane to day, in consequence of which you are a richer man by about thirty three pounds. I found that two dividends on £1072, which I bought for you in the 3 per Cents when you were abroad, had from some mistake never been drawn, and were lying at the Bank in expectation of a claimant. Thereupon I claimed them, got them, and paid them in to your account at Williams and Deacon's, our mutual bankers, as bad writers say. The amount is thirty one pounds, and some shillings.

I learned also that the sum of £8.6.9 was in the hands of our mutual bankers aforesaid, as part of our father's effects, to which I am administrator. I drew this money out. Your seventh amounts to £1.,3.,10, which I will pay you when we meet next. Poor Selina's share of course goes to Fanny.

Ever yours,
Macaulay

TO FRANCES MACAULAY, 17 MARCH 1859

MS: Trinity College.

Holly Lodge March 17. 1859

Dearest Fanny,

I take great interest in your furnishing operations. I cannot conceive a happier being than a lady going about from upholsterer to upholsterer and cheapening chairs, china, chintzes, and a thousand other things. You

must allow me to contribute to the plenishing, as the Scotch call it, of your new house. Lay out the enclosed in any article which you fancy.[1]

We all count on you for Easter.

Hannah, who is sitting by me, desires me to say that the shawl arrived for the poor woman.

Ever yours,
Macaulay

TO CHARLES AUSTIN, 17 MARCH 1859

MS: Leeds City Libraries.

Holly Lodge March 17. 1859

Dear Austin,

Can you and Mrs. Austin[2] come to breakfast on Wednesday next instead of Thursday.[3] Lady Trevelyan is forced to leave town on Wednesday evening, and would be very sorry not to be here to receive you.

Ever yours,
Macaulay

TO THOMAS FLOWER ELLIS, 19 MARCH 1859

MS: Trinity College.

Holly Lodge Kensington / W / March 19. 1859

Dear Ellis,

By this time, I suppose, you are at Liverpool. Let me hear what your plans are. You will not find my brother at Ulverstone. He is coming up this week to London on business which will detain him some time.

Harry Holland starts for Liverpool to day. Next week his wife, whose health is in a delicate state, will go to St Leonard's with her mother for ten days.

Charles Austin and his wife, a very handsome young woman, breakfasted here last Thursday, and will breakfast here again next Wednesday. I have been eating a round of dinners, with Lord and Ladies, and am not the worse for the fricassees and Champagne. My lilacs are all but in

[1] 'Sent F. 10£ towards her furnishing' (Journal, XI, 453: 17 March).

[2] Austin married Harriet Jane Ingelby in 1856. When TBM called on Austin on 12 March he 'found his wife a very good looking young woman – my godson a sweet boy' (Journal, XI, 450).

[3] The Austins, Lord and Lady Stanhope, Lord and Lady Belper, the Van de Weyers, Hannah, Lord Stanley, Bishop Wilberforce, and Edward Twisleton were the party: 'we were, I think, a little too numerous' (Journal, XI, 456).

flower, my rosebeds in leaf. Everything thrives but my rhododendrons which droop and look miserable. As to politics, they look so ill that anybody less sanguine than myself would be an alarmist. I should be one, if I did not feel sure of two things, first, that the country is wiser than any statesman who is likely to have anything to do with governing it, and secondly that foreign troubles always act on our domestic troubles as a blister acts on an inflammation of the chest, and that the two evils which we are now plagued by will act on each other as counter-irritants.[1]

Ever yours
Macaulay

TO THOMAS FLOWER ELLIS, 24 MARCH 1859

MS: Trinity College.

Holly Lodge Kensington W / March 24. 1859

Dear Ellis,

Thanks for your letter. I have not much to tell you. On Tuesday I went to the House of Lords,[2] and sate there about six hours, hearing those eternal texts about uncovering the nakedness of ladies, and raising up seed to deceased brothers, discussed till I was sick. I heard Philpotts probably for the last time. He was very infirm. It was necessary that a candle should be put close to him to enable him to make out his notes. His lawn sleeves were so near the flame that everybody was nervous. Lord Redesdale repeatedly pulled him back. If the lawn had caught fire it would have blazed like crinoline; and the Right Reverend Prelate would have died the death of Cranmer and Ridley. Your old friend Short[3] spoke; and detestably ill he spoke. I had imagined him a man of more sense. Thirlwall made a strange see saw speech, not of much force or ability, in a tedious style and with a monotonous, mouthing, delivery. Sam of Oxford spoke with great fluency, grace and fire. I had never heard him before. It was no great effort; but it proved him to be an orator. I was heartily glad to be at home again.

The next morning I had a breakfast party – Van De Weyer and his wife, Austin and his wife, Lord and Lady Stanhope, Lord and Lady Belper, Hannah, Lord Stanley, Twisleton, and the Bishop of Oxford. It

[1] The foreign troubles were with France over her interference in Italian affairs, leading to the Franco-Austrian war of this summer. The domestic issue was the Reform Bill introduced by Disraeli on 28 February and defeated on 31 March; Parliament was dissolved on 23 April.

[2] For the debate on the second reading of the Marriage Law Amendment Bill, popularly the Deceased Wife's Sister Bill; TBM voted with the minority for it.

[3] Bishop of St Asaph.

was very pleasant. My dear Margaret was kept at home by influenza. She is somewhat better now; and her mother has taken her to Saint Leonard's.

The political prospect becomes darker and darker. I am not very sorry for it. For I see that nothing but serious danger will lead our party leaders to act honestly. They have all behaved very ill, Palmerston the least so. Lord John is greatly to blame:[1] but I think that he is more likely than any other person to get us out of the scrape. His book about Fox[2] is a wretched thing, made with the scissors rather than with the pen, and better than Tomline's Life of Pitt, only as being shorter.

We have letters from Trevelyan written in the land of Egypt. Whom do you think he met at Cairo? No other than our old friend Pierotti.[3] Pierotti shouted with joy, and has written a most rapturous account of the interview. But it is strange how those couriers go about the world, managing to make themselves understood by everybody. They are like the Ancient Mariner who says

> "I pass like night from land to land
> I have strange power of speech."[4]

Trevelyan has seen the pyramids, but postpones his account of them till he has embarked on the Indian Ocean, and has time to write at large.

Do you begin to see your way to the end of your exile? I wish you would write an elegy in the manner of the Tristia. At any rate let me know when the fatted calf, or rather the grass lamb is to be killed for you, and the delicate infant onions to be brought in with the Stilton cheese. The vegetation proceeds, in spite of blasts from the north. I have never known such a year.

Ever yours
Macaulay

As to the Reform Debate, I hear from various quarters that Lord Stanley's speech was an utter failure[5] – Horsman's very clever, though spiteful and

[1] Russell opposed the Reform Bill on various grounds, among them the contention that the qualifications in the towns should be lowered. The provisions of the Bill and the terms of Russell's resolution condemning it produced contradictory results, some reformers opposing the Bill and some anti-reformers supporting it. TBM disliked what he thought Russell's demagoguery: 'I was sorry to see that Lord John disgraced himself by canting about the poor hardworking honest man who ought to be enfranchised. It is below him to talk that Jacobin jargon' (Journal, XI, 444: 1 March).

[2] The first volume of *The Life and Times of Charles James Fox*, 3 vols., 1859–66.

[3] See 13 August 1857.

[4] Lines 586–7.

[5] On 21 March: 'Hannah and Lord Clarendon tell me that Stanley's speech on Monday was a failure. He is rather losing ground; and I am sorry for it: for I like him personally' (Journal, XI, 456: 23 March).

tending to no good – Bulwer Lytton's very able, notwithstanding a vile delivery, like that of a bad actor.[1] I have not seen anybody who heard the Solicitor General,[2] – at least anybody whom I could ask about such a matter.

TO CHARLES MACAULAY, [30 MARCH 1859][3]

MS: University of London.

Holly Lodge Kensington / W

Dear Charles,

I find that John called here while I was breakfasting out. I do not know where or when I am likely to fall in with him; and I have more engagements than I could wish. But, if you and he could dine with me at seven on Friday, I should be delighted to see you both. If he cannot come then, I will be at home at any hour on Friday that he will fix. To morrow I am engaged morning and afternoon.

I write to you because I think that you said that you expected him to be at your house. At any rate you will know his address. He left no message here.

Ever yours,
Macaulay

Our cousin Kenneth, I hear, spoke like a man of sense yesterday, but not brilliantly.[4]

TO MRS HENRY THURSTAN HOLLAND, 31 MARCH 1859

MS: Trinity College.

Holly Lodge Kensington / March 31. 1859

Dearest Baba,

I received your kind letter yesterday evening. Many thanks for it. I was forced to stay at home and to send an excuse to the Vernon Smiths.

[1] 'Deaf, fantastic, modulating his voice with difficulty, sometimes painful – at first almost an object of ridicule to the superficial – Lytton occasionally reached almost the sublime, and perfectly enchained his audience' (Disraeli to Queen Victoria, 22 March 1859: W. F. Monypenny and G. E. Buckle, *The Life of Benjamin Disraeli*, New York, 1910–20, IV, 206).

[2] Sir Hugh Cairns (1819–85: *DNB*), afterwards Lord Chancellor and first Earl Cairns.

[3] Dated from several points of internal evidence: TBM breakfasted with Lord Stanhope on this date; Kenneth Macaulay's speech was on the day before, the 29th; and John called on Friday, 1 April (Journal, XI, 460–2).

[4] In the Reform Bill debate: *Hansard*, 3rd Series, CLIII, 1089–97.

For the snow was half a foot deep, and was still falling; and it had begun to freeze. To day the thaw is proceeding rapidly. But my trees and flowers have suffered grievously. I breakfasted at the Duke of Argyll's, and met a small, but a very pleasant party.[1] I have invited, for next Wednesday, the Duke, the Duchess, Dundas, Lord Glenelg, Lord Carlisle, Lord Grey, Labouchere, Charles Howard, Lady Trevelyan and Mrs. Holland. Mr. Holland and Lord Macaulay will make the company up to twelve exactly.[2] Lord Grey I met this morning at Argyll Lodge, and found him extremely pleasant.

Whether Alice will come this afternoon I cannot tell. It is fine above, but dreadfully sloppy and dirty below; and the little Buxtons will be unable to have a run in the garden.[3]

I am surprised to hear so bad an account of the St Leonard's circulating Library. You should go to Hastings for books. Love to Mamma.

Ever yours
Macaulay

I open my letter to tell you that your uncle John has just been here. I never was more surprised than by what he told me. I will never again flatter myself that I have the least insight into the character of any human being. What do you think is his reason – his principal reason at least –for running up to town at this season? He has not yet told Charles, and seemed to have some difficulty in telling me. But all the world will know it from the newspapers of next Monday. The people who have been busy of late in providing preachers for great congregations in London had heard, it seems, that a son of the pious and benevolent Z M, a brother of Lord M, and a brother in law of Sir C.E.T. was in the Church. They satisfied themselves that he was not a Puseyite; and they invited him to help them. He, who, I should have thought, would, of all men, have been the least likely to endure the thought of such an exhibition, is to preach in Exeter Hall, next Sunday, to three thousand people. I hardly knew what to say or which way to look. I asked him on what subject he meant to hold forth. He said that he thought that he could not use the opportunity better than by exposing the evils of Auricular Confession. He has chosen for his text "Cease ye from man whose breath is in his nostrils."[4] Those words, he said, would be a good introduction to a discourse on the folly of trusting to the absolution of a frail fellow creature. In truth I hardly

[1] Lord Grey, Lord Carlisle, Labouchere, and Charles Howard (Journal, XI, 460–1).

[2] All of them came (Journal, XI, 465).

[3] 'Then came dear little Alice, bringing two little Buxtons. I gave them ice and cake. The boys were insatiable, and I am afraid will be sick in consequence' (XI, 461).

[4] Isaiah 2:22.

knew him. He seems to be possessed with the notion that now or never is the time for him to signalise himself as a pulpit orator, and that he may rise, nobody can tell how high, in his profession. He mentioned his son: but it was very slightly. Indeed I see that, till after next Sunday, it will be impossible for him to think of anything but the display which he is to make. You and Mamma will be amazed, I think, by all this, unless indeed you happen to remember that this is the first of April – April fools – April fools. Now was not that a good lie, well told? I have not seen John, and do not expect to see him till to morrow. Again ever yours

Macaulay

TO THOMAS FLOWER ELLIS, 1 APRIL 1859

MS: Trinity College. *Partly published:* G. M. Trevelyan, *Sir George Otto Trevelyan*, pp. 38–9.

Holly Lodge April 1, 1859

Dear Ellis,

How are you getting on? Does the case of Lord S——sbury[1] come on or not? And when am I likely to have you here revelling in asparagus and young onions? I hope that last Wednesday has not been fatal to all the nurseries and kitchen gardens hereabouts. But such a change of weather I never saw. Tuesday was like a delicious day in May. Twenty four hours after the snow was falling in such thick large flakes that I could hardly see to the end of my little domain. Some of my trees have lost large boughs, which were unable to bear the double weight of their leaves and of the snow. Lilacs, thorns, willows, violets, wall flowers, almond blossoms, and apple blossoms all disappeared under one dead white covering. It was a most ghastly transformation. I never before saw a landscape in full leaf completely hidden by snow in the space of three hours. However yesterday the sun came out warm; and then the snow caught it. I never saw so rapid a thaw. But my flowerbeds look miserable. My gardener however encourages me to hope that no serious damage has been done. And indeed, as there was frost, it was rather an advantage that there was snow too. A few white patches are still lying on spots covered from the sun and open to the north wind. But, thank heaven, the wind has now changed. Had you anything of the sort? There was no snow at St Leonards as far as I can make out, though much wind and chill

[1] Lord Shrewsbury, having been secured in his title (see 6 August 1857), had now to claim his right to certain estates that belonged to the possessor of the title but which the last Lord Shrewsbury had thought himself competent to will otherwise; the case was argued before the Lord Chief Justice in the Court of Common Pleas and settled in Lord Shrewsbury's favor. See the *Annual Register*, 1859.

rain; and my brother John, who was travelling up from the north fell in with no snow till he got near town.

I hear every day from St Leonards, and sometimes twice a day. My dear child is well again, and expecting her husband, who, I believe, will join her this evening, and will take down little Alice with him. They all return next Monday. We have very good accounts of George from various quarters. He did very well at the University Scholarship examination. No Trinity man of his own year was near him. One man of his own year – a Johnian – was above him; and another – a Kingsman – close upon him. But this looks promising for a high place in the Classical Tripos. The examiners say too that he is very greatly improved. I cannot help feeling pleased that this improvement should have been the effect purely of his own unassisted studies, carried on from real love of ancient literature. He has had no cramming, but has gone in against the pupils of Donaldson[1] and Shilleto[2] with no other training than that which you and I had. I have half a mind to take the responsibility of advising him to go on in the same way during the next twenty months; and he would certainly take my advice: for he has struggled obstinately against the prevailing fashion, and had set his heart, as he owned to his mother, on being a scholar after the pattern of our generation and not after the new mode.[3] His natural feeling about me has done him some harm, with, I hope, some good. His neglect of mathematics is to be ascribed to the bad example which I set him. It is owing to me too, I must say on the other side, that he lives in the very midst of an atmosphere reeking with Carlylism, Ruskinism, Browningism, and other equally noxious isms, without the slightest taint of the morbific virus.[4] How I have run on – pouring out

[1] John William Donaldson (1811–61: *DNB*), philological scholar and, since 1855, a leading private tutor at Cambridge. TBM met him in 1858, at the dinner on his installation as High Steward of Cambridge: 'Donaldson instructed me about the Athenian trireme – a crotchetty conceited man, but learned and acute' (Journal, XI, 310: 11 May). TBM was pleased to find himself respectfully mentioned in Donaldson's *Varronianus*, 1844, which treats the Latin scholarship of England very roughly (Journal, VI, 19: 6 January 1853). See *Varronianus*, 2nd edn, p. 23n; 225.

[2] Richard Shilleto (1809–76: *DNB*), classical scholar and for many years the most sought-after private tutor in Cambridge.

[3] In printing this letter in his memoir of his father, G. M. Trevelyan explains that 'when Macaulay was an undergraduate, the great days of the "private coach" had not begun.' Trevelyan adds: 'In view of this letter . . . I cannot help feeling that Macaulay's death in the following Christmas was not an unmixed catastrophe to his nephew. It set him free from the burden of his own too loyal heart. In 1860 he studied with Shilleto, and won the second place in the Classical Tripos of 1861, being beaten by Abbot of John's alone' (*Sir George Otto Trevelyan*, pp. 38–9).

[4] But after TBM's death, George 'caught the three diseases of Browningism, Ruskinism and Carlylism, and never recovered' (*Sir George Otto Trevelyan*, p. 39). TBM would have been appalled to know that the final text of his nephew's *Life of Macaulay* is prefaced by a letter from Carlyle to the author.

domestic tattle so copiously that I have left myself no room for politics. I could however add but little to what you will see in the papers.

Ever yours
Macaulay

TO SAMUEL AUSTIN ALLIBONE, 9 APRIL 1859

MS: Huntington Library. *Envelope:* S. Austin Allibone Esq / Philadelphia / United States.

Holly Lodge Kensington / April 9. 1859

Sir,

Since I wrote to you last, I have had frequent occasion to consult your Dictionary;[1] and I have scarcely ever failed to find what I sought. I have no hesitation in saying that it is far superior to any other work of the kind in our language. I heartily wish you success proportioned to the labour and cost of your undertaking. / I have the honor to be, / Sir,

Your faithful Servant,
Macaulay

S Austin Allibone Esq / etc. etc. etc.

TO THOMAS FLOWER ELLIS, 12 APRIL 1859

MS: State Library of Victoria.

Holly Lodge April 12 / 1859

Dear Ellis,

I suppose that the Leeds felons cannot keep you beyond to day, and that you will be in town to morrow at the latest. When shall I see you? To morrow I must dine at the palace. On Thursday I am engaged to Lord Lansdowne. On Friday I wish to be at the House, to hear the debate on the state of our foreign relations.[2] On Saturday, I have a dinner party of which I should be very glad if you would make one. There will be Lord Campbell, Lord Cranworth, Lord Kingsdown,[3] Lord Broughton, Lord John Russell, Sir George Lewis, Dundas, and Sir Henry Holland. You know them all, I imagine, and hate none of them except poor Lord John,

[1] See 29 January.

[2] TBM caught cold at the palace and went neither to Lansdowne's nor to the House (Journal, XI, 472).

[3] Thomas Pemberton-Leigh (1793–1867: *DNB*), first Baron Kingsdown, a highly successful barrister, who retired both from practice and from Parliament in 1843 and devoted himself thereafter to the Judicial Committee of the Privy Council. He was a member of The Club with TBM.

whom, however, you can, I suppose, bear to meet.[1] If you come, of course you will stay over Sunday. Let me know as soon as you can whether I may expect you. I am afraid that I shall not be able to send for you. The hour half past seven.

Ever yours,
Macaulay

TO FRANCES MACAULAY, 15 APRIL 1859

MS: Trinity College.

Holly Lodge Kensington / April 15. 1859

Dearest Fanny,

I have given Gray your new address. I am impatient to see your house, and shall contrive to do so before long.

The Cambridge plan[2] is given up for half a dozen good reasons. One is that Easter is the precise time of George's vacation, and that it would be hard to make him keep his holiday at school. Another is that Baba could not go. A third is that the weather is very ill suited at present for such an expedition. Hot days and cold days follow each other in the strangest manner. The reason which made it necessary for us formerly to take our trip in Passion week has ceased to exist.[3] Probably we shall make some expedition later in the year.

I am pretty well, but not the better for having dined at the palace on Wednesday evening, a December evening following a May morning. I caught cold, and had to fast and blister myself yesterday. I am now right again, and expecting to entertain a party of some eight or ten Lords and Privy Councillors to morrow at dinner. Lord John will be of the party.

Ever yours,
Macaulay

TO DERWENT COLERIDGE, 16 APRIL 1859

MS: Cornell University.

Holly Lodge April 16 / 1859

Dear Coleridge,

I am sorry that it will be impossible for me to avail myself of the ticket

[1] Ellis was there: they had 'an excellent dinner excellently served; and pleasant conversation' (Journal, XI, 476).

[2] See 9 March.

[3] TBM means that Trevelyan would not leave his work for a tour unless compelled to by the closing of the public offices.

which you have had the kindness to send me.[1] I therefore return it with many thanks.

Yours ever,
Macaulay

TO WILLIAM BANTING,[2] 18 APRIL 1859

MS: Trinity College.

Holly Lodge April 18. 1859

Sir,

I enclose a cheque for five guineas, as a contribution to the fund for paying the Mortgage Debt of the Kensington Dispensary. / I have the honor to be, / Sir,

Your obedient Servant,
Macaulay

W Banting Esq / etc. etc. etc.

TO CHARLES JOHN DIMOND,[3] 26 APRIL 1859

MS: Library of New South Wales.

Holly Lodge April 26. 1859

Sir,

I am sorry that it will be out of my power to have the honor of waiting on the President and Committee of the Artists' Benevolent Fund to dinner on Saturday week.[4] / I have the honor to be, / Sir,

Your obedient Servant,
Macaulay

C Dimond Esq / etc. etc. etc.

TO SIR EDWARD BULWER-LYTTON, 27 APRIL 1859

MS: Hertfordshire County Council.

Holly Lodge April 27. 1859

Dear Sir Edward,

I am much afraid that it will be out of my power to attend the ballot

[1] Coleridge's endorsement reads: 'returning a ticket for the S. Mark's day celebration.'

[2] Banting lived at 4, The Terrace, Kensington (*Post Office London Directory*, 1859). He is perhaps the Banting noticed in the *DNB*.

[3] Dimond was a solicitor of 10 Henrietta Street, Cavendish Square.

[4] This was the fiftieth anniversary dinner of the Fund.

at the Athenæum on Monday week. But I will with pleasure put my name down as one of Mr. Drummond Wolff's[1] sponsors.

I was very sorry to see in the newspapers an indifferent account of your health.[2] For God's sake take care of yourself. A colonial Secretary, in the House of Commons, should have a constitution of iron.

I wrote to thank you for your last book as soon as I received it.[3] It was ungrateful in me not to write again after I had read it. For it gave me very great pleasure. On the whole, I think it decidedly your best work.

Ever yours truly,
Macaulay

TO SIR CHARLES TREVELYAN, 28 APRIL 1859

MS: University of Newcastle.

Holly Lodge Kensington April 28. 1859

Dear Trevelyan,

Yesterday arrived your letter to Hannah written just as you were reaching Madras; and to day I read at the Athenæum an account of your landing, of the salutes, of the turning out of the bodyguard, and of the ceremony of proclaiming you Captain of Fort St George. I need not tell you how much interest I take in all that befalls you, and how earnestly I wish that, whether I live to welcome you back or not, you may return to a home as happy as that which you left with a public character even higher than that which you carried out.

All the political news that I could send you you will have heard from other quarters, and heard, I am afraid, with very little pleasure. There has scarcely ever been a conjuncture in our history which more required skilful and steady steering; and our steersmen are sad lubbers. The important and alarming event which was announced the day before yesterday,[4]

1 (Sir) Henry Drummond Wolff (1830–1908: *DNB*), son of the missionary and traveller Joseph Wolff (see 20 March 1827), was private secretary to Bulwer-Lytton as Secretary for the Colonies, 1858. He was in Parliament, 1874–85, and held a number of diplomatic appointments and commissions.

2 As early as 10 April TBM noted that 'Lytton is supposed to be, if not deranged, so much overworked as to be quite *hors de combat*' (Journal, XI, 468). Bulwer-Lytton had repeatedly attempted to resign on grounds of health: see Robert Blake, *Disraeli*, New York, 1967, pp. 398–401.

3 See *to* Bulwer-Lytton, 29 December 1858.

4 The news – untrue – of an offensive and defensive alliance between France and Russia appeared not the day before yesterday but in the papers of 27 April. It was officially denied early in May but without entirely persuading the English public. See 16 May.

seems to have taken them quite by surprise. I cannot think so ill of them as to believe that they would have dissolved the Parliament if they had at all foreseen what was coming. Indeed it is inconceivable that Lord Derby would have made such a speech at the Mansion House last Monday evening,[1] if he had at all suspected that an intimate alliance between France and Russia would be proclaimed on the Tuesday morning. The effect on the money market has been frightful. The Times says that the value of the whole property invested in those stocks with which the brokers of the City are conversant has diminished to the extent of fifty millions in a day. And I can well believe this. For if I were to be sold up at this moment, I should be worth about five thousand pounds less than I was worth forty eight hours ago. This matters little to me, who do not want to sell, but must be a great calamity to multitudes. And in the midst of this panic the elections are beginning. What course they will take I do not pretend to foresee. Three days ago the temper of the nation was very far from enthusiastic. The disputes of our domestic factions seemed to have lost their interest. There was little zeal, and a great deal of corruption. What effect this sudden turn in foreign politics may produce remains to be seen. It is not impossible that the passions which have as yet slept may be violently roused. There may be a cry, and with but too much reason, that our rulers have been duped, that the country has, by their fault, been brought into a degrading and even a dangerous situation, that all our defences must be strengthened, that we must make a great display of our naval strength, and that Lord Malmesbury[2] and General Peel[3] are not men equal to such a crisis. A powerful speech from Lord John at Guildhall or from Lord Palmerston at Tiverton would probably, at this conjuncture, be echoed from every part of the country.

If the aspect of public affairs is unpleasant, you may find some consolation in domestic news. All those who are dearest to you are well: they are as happy as they can be [when][4] you are so far from them; and they constantly think and talk of you. My dear Baba is an angel. Her new relations love and prize her almost as much as we who have known her from her birth. George has done finally with his mathematical troubles, and has now a perfectly plain road before him. In Classics, he is one of the three strongest men of the year; and he may, by good training, make himself, during the next twenty months, the strongest of the three. He is now at Cambridge, sitting for a Trinity scholarship, which I have no

[1] 25 April: he said that the government was still hoping to avert war and had just made an eleventh-hour offer of mediation.

[2] Foreign Secretary.

[3] General Jonathan Peel (1799–1879: *DNB*), brother of Sir Robert, was Secretary for War.

[4] TBM has written 'will.'

doubt of his winning.[1] On Saturday next, the 30th, the examination will be over; and, on that day, I shall take down his mother, his two sisters, and his aunt Fanny, to pay him a visit. Harry will join us in the evening.[2] We have secured apartments at the Bull; and I have commissioned George to order the best dinner for ten that is to be had, and have desired him to invite two or three of the best young fellows of his set to make up the party. On the Sunday Harry and I shall dine in hall. We shall hear the sermon in the University Church, I sitting in state among the Dons of Golgotha.[3] We shall attend Trinity Chapel in the evening, and shall probably end the day at the Master's Lodge. On Monday, the 2nd of May, George is to give us all a sumptuous college breakfast, sausages, kidneys, broiled fowls, and I wish there may not be ale.[4] Then we shall return to town. We cannot make a longer trip on account of my sweet Alice's confirmation, a ceremony about which the dear child speaks with such pretty solemnity as brings tears into my eyes.

Marshman,[5] who, by the bye, is trying to get into Parliament, has published a book in two thick Volumes entitled the Life and Times of Carey, Marshman, and Ward, a history in fact of the Baptist Mission. I have found it interesting:[6] Hannah has been still more interested by it; and you would probably be more interested than either of us. I have therefore desired Longman to send you out a copy, which will serve to remind you of me. God bless you, dear Trevelyan, and bring you back to us prosperous and honoured.

Ever yours,
Macaulay

1 He was successful.

2 He was detained by business and could not come (Journal, XI, 483: 30 April).

3 Undergraduate slang for the section of the University Church set apart for the dons. TBM did not go (Journal, XI, 485: 1 May).

4 This did not come to pass.

5 John Clark Marshman (1794–1877: *DNB*), son of the Indian missionary Joshua Marshman, was editor of the *Friend of India* and active in many public affairs and institutions in India. He returned to England in 1852, stood unsuccessfully for Parliament three times, and published a *History of India*. Marshman's paper had been one of the few that treated TBM respectfully during his time in India.

6 TBM read it on 22 April: 'read Marshman's book – 2 volumes – right through at a sitting. . . . Those three Serampore men were certainly very remarkable persons, and, I dare say, quite sincere as to their ends. But it is plain that Marshman was not very scrupulous as to means. His son admits that he preferred crooked to straight roads – a very grave fault' (Journal, XI, 479).

TO CHARLES MACAULAY, 5 MAY 1859

MS: University of London. *Published:* Rae, *Temple Bar*, LXXXVI, 202.

Holly Lodge May 5 1859

Dear Charles,

I am truly glad that the examination has terminated so satisfactorily.[1] Your boy has, I hope, a prosperous and honourable career before him.

Ever yours

Macaulay

TO SIR CHARLES TREVELYAN, 16 MAY 1859

MS: University of Newcastle.

Holly Lodge May 16. 1859

Dear Trevelyan,

I wrote to you last on the 28th of April. It was then universally believed that there was an alliance, offensive and defensive, between France and Russia. The alarm was extreme, and the fall in the value of all sorts of investments immense. Soon the panic subsided; and it became clear that, though there was a closer union between France and Russia than might be wished, that union was by no means so intimate as had been asserted. Whether the report which had caused so much uneasiness was a stock-jobbing lie devised by speculators, or a political lie intended to influence the elections is still a secret. Oddly enough, though the fiction sufficed to send the prices of all sorts of stock down, the discovery of the truth has not sent them up again.

The elections are all but over. Lord Derby has gained, but is still in a minority: and the majority is, as may be supposed, in a much worse temper than before the dissolution. I am satisfied that neither the men who are in or the men who are out can make a government which will stand twelve months. I see no hope except in a coalition on a broad basis. To such a coalition there is no objection on the ground of principle: for on all great questions which press for a speedy decision Lord Derby, Disraeli, Walpole, Henley,[2] Lord Palmerston, Lord John, Lord Granville, Lord Stanley, may be said to be pretty well agreed. They are all for neutrality, but for armed neutrality. They are all for reform, but for

[1] Charles's elder son, Thomas George, had just passed his examination for the Indian army. On 3 July TBM gave Charles '£200 for his boy' (Journal, XI, 522). Thomas Macaulay died of typhoid on the voyage home from India, aged 22, in 1864.

[2] Joseph Warner Henley (1793–1884: *DNB*), President of the Board of Trade, resigned from Derby's cabinet in opposition to the Reform Bill of 1859.

moderate reform. They are all for free trade, some because they think it good, and others because they think that, good or bad, it is inevitable. The Jew question has been disposed of. The India question has been disposed of. There remain only questions of detail, which may easily be compromised, and questions of a personal kind, which ought to be compromised. A coalition cannot take place just at present. For the animosities produced by the general election will continue during some months to be sore. I shall be surprised however if, before the end of 1860, there is not an attempt to form an administration on an extended plan.

We are all quiet and comfortable. George is doing extremely well; nor have I any doubt that he will get a fellowship if he makes that his object, as, I think, he ought to do. He is impatient to be a soldier. That is to say, he, like most of his young friends, will volunteer for the rifle corps which the Lord Lieutenant of Cambridge is about to organize.[1] I mean to consider George as my substitute, and to provide him with his arms and uniform. He will soon, I hope, be able to pick off a French officer at the distance of a quarter of a mile. I took down Hannah, Baba and Alice to Cambridge on Saturday the 30th of April. We gave a handsome dinner on that day to some of George's friends, among whom was Montagu Butler.[2] On the Sunday we went to the University Church[3] and to Trinity Chapel, and, in the evening, were most kindly and hospitably received at the Lodge by the Master and his new wife.[4] The master spoke very handsomely of George, and evidently has his eye on him – a great distinction, – for Whewell pays far too little attention to undergraduates of promise. George will no doubt give you all the details of his examination for the scholarship. His success gave the greatest pleasure to his mother and his sisters. There never was, I believe, more perfect affection in any family; and Harry Holland is quite one of us.

I have read your letters to Hannah with the greatest interest. I well remember your house at Madras. The country house I remember too, but less distinctly. I was there only an hour or so; and I suffered so much

[1] The fear of a French invasion created an eager response to a new National Volunteer Association. The Queen and Prince Consort acted as patrons, and Tennyson contributed his 'Riflemen form!' (published in *The Times* on 9 May). See *to* G. O. Trevelyan, 22 November 1859. Trevelyan later wrote that TBM 'ordered for me a double-barrelled deer-stalking rifle from Mr. Purdey's famous workshop, which was the envy and admiration of all the knowing ones among my Cambridge friends' (*Times Literary Supplement*, 9 May 1916, p. 115).

[2] Another was H. C. Raikes, who provides some recollections of TBM's table-talk on this occasion: see Henry St John Raikes, *Life and Letters of Henry Cecil Raikes*, 1898, p. 22.

[3] There is no mention of TBM's having done so in his Journal for this day.

[4] Mrs Whewell died in 1855; in 1858 Whewell married Everina Frances Ellis, widow of Sir Gilbert Affleck, Bart.; she continued to be called Lady Affleck. She was, TBM wrote, 'apparently an amiable sensible woman' (Journal, XI, 484: 30 April).

from the heat on that day that I could observe little. Your domestic arrangements seem to be excellent.

I do not know whether anybody else will tell you that my brother Charles's boy Tom has passed his examination with credit, and will proceed to Bengal as a cadet in two or three months. He is hard at work, learning Hindostanee, and seems to have a real desire to do well.

Farewell, my dear Trevelyan. Do not trouble yourself to write to me unless you have some particular reason for doing so.

Ever yours affectionately
Macaulay

TO HENRY DRUMMOND, 21 MAY 1859

MS: Mr F. R. Cowell.

Holly Lodge Kensington / W̄. / May 21. 1859

My dear Sir,

Are you thinking of a paper in Number 77 of the Quarterly Review?[1] There you will find something about the severe treatment of schoolboys at Paris, at Eton, and at St Paul's, and specimens of the lamentations of the sufferers. The writer must have been Southey: for, in turning over the pages, I catch sight of the word *worsened*, a bad word, coined by Southey, obstinately used by him in spite of the censure of critics, and never, as far as I know, used by anybody else.[2]

This paper does not, however, in all points agree with your description.

Of course you know Ascham's Schoolmaster. I wonder that Southey did not refer to it.

I can tell you nothing about Bullum and Boatum.

Ever yours truly
Macaulay

[1] TBM heard from Henry Drummond on this day 'wanting to know where he read something about the treatment of schoolboys at the time of the revival of letters. God knows – I suggested an article of Southey's in the Q.R., and Ascham's Schoolmaster' (Journal, XI, 495). The article is Southey's 'Elementary Teaching,' *Quarterly Review*, XXXIX (January 1829), 99–143, in part an attack on the London University.

[2] According to the *OED*, the word, though 'common in dialect,' was 'reintroduced to literature *c.* 1800–1830 (by writers like Southey and De Quincey) as a racy vernacular substitute for *deteriorate* and the like.'

TO LORD STANHOPE, 21 MAY 1859

Text: Sebastian d'Orsai Catalogue, July 1971, item 229: dated Holly Lodge, 21 May 1859.

Dear Stanhope,

I return the Oracles with many thanks. I shall be most happy to breakfast with you next Saturday.[1]

Ever yours truly,
Macaulay

TO THOMAS FLOWER ELLIS, 23 MAY 1859

MS: Trinity College.

Holly Lodge Kensington / May 23. 1859

Dear Ellis,

I am sorry that you are so close a prisoner. Could you not come here to a late dinner, – say eight o'clock, – on Saturday, bring down some of your Shrewsbury papers, and look them over on the Sunday, and go down to Court before ten on the Monday? If not, we must wait, I suppose, till the argument in the Common Pleas is over.

I will mention Mrs. Arnold's house[2] to Hannah. But I do not think that it will suit. And, for my own part, I would as soon have a coffin for a bed and a hearse for a carriage as live under Helm Crag. The cave of Trophonius[3] would have been an exhilarating residence by comparison.

Ever yours,
Macaulay

TO BISHOP SAMUEL WILBERFORCE, 24 MAY 1859

MS: Bodleian Library.

Holly Lodge May 24. 1859

My dear Bishop of Oxford,

I am sorry that I cannot breakfast with you next Saturday. I am engaged

[1] The other guests were Lord Raglan and his wife, Reeve, Wilberforce, and the Comte de Rémusat, his son, and his daughter-in-law (Journal, XI, 499).

[2] Fox Howe, the house in the Lake District belonging to Dr Thomas Arnold's widow. Hannah spent the summer with George and Alice at the Low Wood Hotel on Windermere, only two miles from Fox Howe. TBM joined them there for a week in late July: see 31 July.

[3] The Boetian cave where the oracle could be consulted only under terrifying circumstances and from which all emerged pale and unnerved.

to the Stanhopes. Will you breakfast here at ten on Monday? You will meet Sir John Lawrence;[1] and I will then give you an answer as to your kind invitation to Cuddesdon.[2]

Ever yours truly
Macaulay

TO THOMAS FLOWER ELLIS, 30 MAY 1859

MS: Trinity College.

Holly Lodge May 30. 1859

Dear Ellis,

Here is a specimen of what Lord Malmesbury calls small orthography[3] for you. But when am I to see you? On Friday I dine with Lord Lansdowne, on Saturday with Campbell. On Monday we have a family gathering before a general dispersion for the summer. On Tuesday the 7th of June I must be in the House of Lords, and may possibly be late.[4] On any day except those which I have mentioned I shall be delighted to see you to dinner. If you cannot get to Bromley on Sunday, you had better come here to breakfast. By Wednesday afternoon, I suppose, you will be pretty well able to judge how long the argument in the Shrewsbury case is likely to last. By the bye Lord Wensleydale tells me that, by what he hears, there is nothing at all in the points raised by the bloody Papishes, and that, but for the immense magnitude of the interests at stake, so hopeless a battle never would have been fought.[5]

Write when you see your way clear. Come on Thursday next if you can.

Ever yours
Macaulay

[1] Lawrence (1811–79: *DNB*), Indian administrator and hero of the Mutiny for his part in the capture of Delhi; he was Viceroy of India, 1863–9, and in the latter year was created Baron Lawrence. He had just returned to England after an absence of seventeen years.

[2] Cuddesdon Palace, residence of the Bishops of Oxford.

[3] I have not found where Malmesbury uses the phrase. The letter is written in a small hand on half a sheet of TBM's ordinary writing paper.

[4] The Journal shows that TBM kept all of these engagements.

[5] For the Shrewsbury estates: see 1 April.

TO HENRY REEVE, 1 JUNE [1859]

Text: J. K. Laughton, *Memoirs of the Life and Correspondence of Henry Reeve*, 1898, II, 31.

Holly Lodge, Kensington, June 1st.

Dear Reeve,

Before you determine anything about Dr. T. Campbell's Diary,[1] you had better read it. I have lent my copy,[2] which is probably the only copy in England, and do not expect to get it back till next week. When it comes, I will send it to you, and we will then talk further.

Ever yours truly,
Macaulay.

TO MRS HENRY THURSTAN HOLLAND, 1 JUNE 1859

MS: Trinity College.

Holly Lodge June 1 / 1859

Dearest Baba,

I enclose the ticket for the House of Lords.[3]
Full dress, remember.

Ever yours,
Macaulay

TO MRS HENRY THURSTAN HOLLAND, 1 JUNE 1859

MS: Huntington Library.

Holly Lodge / June 1. 1859

Dearest Baba,

I will call for you at ½ after 11.[4]

Ever yours
Macaulay

[1] Dr Thomas Campbell, *Diary of a Visit to England in 1775*, a work mentioned in Boswell, the MS of which had just been discovered and printed in Sydney; for an account of the circumstances, see the introduction by S. C. Roberts to the edition of the *Diary* by James L. Clifford, Cambridge, 1947. TBM received a copy from Mr Raymond, the editor, on 21 May, and probably mentioned it to Reeve on the 28th, when he met Reeve at Lord Stanhope's breakfast (Journal, XI, 495–6; 499).

[2] To Hannah: see TBM's remark to her in 1831: 'You are – next to myself – the best read Boswellite that I know' (29 June).

[3] For the ceremonies opening the new Parliament. TBM was sworn in on this day.

[4] In answer to Margaret's request that he take her to the studio of the painter George Richmond. They went on the next day (Journal, XI, 503).

TO THOMAS FLOWER ELLIS, 4 JUNE 1859

MS: Trinity College.

Holly Lodge June 4. 1859

Dear Ellis,

I was delighted to see how well you acquitted yourself yesterday.[1] I was afraid that, coming so late, you would have had only the refuse arguments, and a weary and impatient auditory.

The case will end, I suppose, some day or other.

Ever yours,
Macaulay

Your note has just arrived. I shall expect you on Wednesday.

TO THOMAS FLOWER ELLIS, 6 JUNE 1859

MS: Trinity College.

Holly Lodge / June 6. 1859

Dear Ellis,

I cannot go out of town on Saturday next. I have no doubt that the country round you is looking beautiful.

I dined at Campbell's on Saturday. I hope that I may, without any breach of hospitality say that the party was a very stupid one.[2] His son – the eldest – bored Lady Trevelyan more than even John Thornton[3] ever did. She was divided between vexation and laughing; and he went on with a calm imbecility and a perfect self approbation that were quite a study. Creswell[4] was there. He asked after you with much warmth. I told him that I heard that you had done your part well in the Shrewsbury case. He said "Of course, he did. He always does well."

Ever yours,
Macaulay

[1] His speech in the Shrewsbury trial is only summarized in *The Times*, but the Lord Chief Justice Cockburn's remark on it as 'most lucid and able' is quoted (4 June).

[2] 'The parties there are always stupid – the eldest son is the greatest fool in the world. I was seated by Lady Something Pepys. Delane was the best companion there' (Journal, XI, 505: 4 June).

[3] Thornton (1783–1861: *DNB*), of the Clapham Thorntons, was a cousin of TBM's banker Henry Thornton and a Commissioner of the Board of Inland Revenue.

[4] Sir Cresswell Cresswell (1794–1863: *DNB*), a former leader of the Northern Circuit, then a Judge of the Court of Common Pleas, and now Judge in the new Probate and Divorce Court.

TO LADY TREVELYAN, 9 JUNE 1859

MS: Trinity College.

Holly Lodge June 9. 1859

Dearest Hannah,

I do not know whether to give you joy of George's medal or not. He seems to be very ill satisfied. His epigram is certainly a good exercise, but far inferior to the poem which he wrote for the Camden prize.[1]

Macleod was here yesterday, talking about Trevelyan much as he talked to you; and I answered much as you had done.[2]

I am rather anxious to know what arrangement will be made about the Indian department, in the event of a change of ministry. Vernon,[3] thank Heaven, is out of the question. I should prefer Lord Granville to anybody else. Next to Lord Granville I should like Charles Wood. I do not however think it by any means certain that the ministers will be in a minority; and, if they weather this storm, they are safe till 1860.[4]

I have a story for you. Yesterday I breakfasted with the Stanhopes who had asked Mrs. Gaskell[5] to meet me. I walked away, and was crossing the park, when a gentleman who was at some little distance called me by my name, and joined me. I did not know him, but, from the first words he said, I perceived that he had heard the debate in the Lords on the preceding evening. We chatted about it, till he said something which made me doubt whether I could safely continue the conversation. My companion might be a peer. He might be a gentleman of the press; and I might see my careless expressions in the Daily News or the Morning Post of the next day. "May I ask," I said, "with whom I have the honor of conversing?" The answer knocked me down. "The Duke of Cambridge."[6] It was he. As you may suppose my hat was instantly off. "I beg your Royal Highness's pardon. You will not, I hope, suspect me of intentional

[1] He got the medal for the Latin epigram but did not get the Camden prize: 'I shall not easily believe that the successful poem was cleverer than his' (Journal, XI, 508: 8 June). See also 13 June. The subject of Trevelyan's epigram was Baron Hübner; the epigram was, he recalled, 'the best piece of Latin I ever wrote' (G. M. Trevelyan, *Sir George Otto Trevelyan*, p. 169).

[2] Macleod talked about 'some rash unwise things that Trevelyan had said. As Hannah most justly says, Trevelyan has all his life been saying and doing rash things, and yet has always got out of his scrapes' (XI, 508). But Trevelyan was recalled next year for his indiscretions.

[3] Vernon Smith; he had not been a success as President of the Board of Control in Palmerston's recent administration.

[4] The ministers were defeated on 11 June and at once resigned.

[5] Elizabeth Gaskell (1810–65: *DNB*), the novelist. TBM had met her at the Stanhopes in June 1856: 'Mrs. Gaskell, the writer of a book which I have not read and am not likely to read' (Journal, XI, 9).

[6] George William Frederick Charles (1819–1904), second Duke, the Queen's cousin; Commander-in-Chief, 1856–95.

disrespect." And I pleaded that odd infirmity of sight or memory, – I hardly know which to call it, – by which I have been led into so many scrapes. He was as good natured as possible, and we had a long talk about the war and the debate. We agreed very well. By the bye the speech in the debate which was most to my taste was Lord Ellenborough's. I agreed with almost every word of it.[1] Lord Granville spoke well; but he did not, and indeed, situated as he was, could not say all that he thinks. He is, I am confident, of the same opinion with Lord Ellenborough and me.

I had a short walk with Thackeray yesterday and found that the literary world is in quite as unsatisfactory a state as the political worlds. Nothing but jealousies, enmities, cabal, detraction, knavery, ingratitude. Thank God, I have always, even when I was writing for bread, kept quite aloof from the whole race of hackney scribblers. I could hardly believe – even now I can hardly believe – some of Thackeray's anecdotes.[2] I have left myself no room to relate them. Love to my little Alice. Tell me how you are accommodated, and how you spend your days.

Ever yours
Macaulay

TO FRANCES MACAULAY, 13 JUNE 1859

MS: Trinity College.

Holly Lodge June 13. 1859

Dearest Fanny,

George wrote for several prizes, among them for the Chancellor's medal. His best exercise was a copy of Latin hexameters on California, written for the Camden prize. I am surprised that he was beaten, and am much inclined to doubt the justice of the decision. Perhaps his poem was thought too comic for the subject.

The meaning of the words which puzzle you is that, when rulers lose their wits, the punishment of their excesses falls on their subjects, – a truth which is exemplifying[3] at this moment in many parts of the world. [. . .][4]

1 'I see that Lord Ellenborough made a speech exactly expressing all that I thought. A mad world!' (Journal, XI, 506: 8 June). In the debate on the address Ellenborough asserted the need for a strong military and a strong government and called for an end to the rivalries within parties (*Hansard*, 3rd Series, CLIV, 71–4).

2 Thackeray had just quarreled with Edmund Yates in the Garrick Club affair and was now on bad terms with Dickens, Forster, and others.

3 TBM favored this construction: Trevelyan notes his disapproval of 'The tea is being made' in place of 'The tea is a-making' (II, 419).

4 The second leaf of the sheet has been cut away.

TO WILLIAM WHEWELL, 15 JUNE 1859

MS: Trinity College.

Holly Lodge June 15. 1859

Dear Whewell,

A few friends whom you would not dislike to meet will dine with me on Friday the 24th at half past seven.[1] I learn from the Milmans that you will be in town about that time. Could you let me have the pleasure of your company. There will be several ex fellows of Trinity, and some Audit Ale.

Ever yours,
Macaulay

TO FRANCES MACAULAY, 17 JUNE 1859

MS: Trinity College.

Holly Lodge June 17. 1859

Dearest Fanny,

I have heard nothing about Lord Clarendon except that he did not want to be in office – a very probable and natural thing.[2] Of course, if he had wished for a place, he might have had his choice among twenty.

You are mistaken about Lord Cranworth.[3] He was a Chancery Barrister, though, oddly enough, he succeeded better as a Judge of the Common Law than as an Equity Judge.

I do not know why you dislike Charles Wood.[4] He has no fault, that I know of, but a quickness of temper and manner which sometimes amounts to petulance, but which is united with a very extraordinary quickness of intellect.

George starts for Westmoreland[5] to day.

Ever yours,
Macaulay

1 Whewell did not come. The guests were Ellis, Henry Holland, Sir Alexander Cockburn, Lord Broughton, Lord Stanley, Dundas, Lefevre, Bishop Wilberforce, and Horace Waddington. 'All went off well except that Waddington said an improper thing or two' (Journal, XI, 517–18).

2 In the newly-formed ministry, Lord John Russell insisted on the place of Foreign Secretary to the exclusion of Clarendon.

3 Cranworth did not return as Lord Chancellor; the office went instead to Lord Campbell.

4 Secretary for India in the new cabinet. TBM approved of the appointment, but two days before he had noted in his Journal that 'Wood, as Granville said, is unpopular, – particularly with dull men, and dull men are the majority of mankind' (XI, 514).

5 Where his mother and sister Alice were already. TBM joined them late in July.

TO LORD BROUGHTON, 18 JUNE 1859

MS: British Museum.

Holly Lodge Kensington / June 18. 1859

Dear Lord Broughton,

Remember Friday, June 24[1] – Midsummer Day – the Feast of Saint John the Baptist, – at half past seven.

Ever yours,
Macaulay

TO [WILLIAM WILDE?],[2] 18 JUNE 1859

MS: Harvard University.

Holly Lodge Kensington / June 18. 1859

My dear Sir,

The notes and extracts made by Sir James Mackintosh from the Fingall M.S. fill a volume of about 160 quarto pages.[3] That volume has been lent to me by Sir James's family, and is now on my table.

There are scarcely any extracts from the first four or five hundred pages of the Fingall M.S.

Ever yours truly,
Macaulay

TO RICHARD MONCKTON MILNES, 18 JUNE 1859

MS: Trinity College.

Holly Lodge Kensington / June 18. 1859

Dear Milnes,

I am sorry that I have a friend or two coming to me on Friday week,[4] and that it will therefore be impossible for me to dine with you.

Very truly yours,
Macaulay

[1] See 15 June.

[2] According to John T. Gilbert (Historical Manuscripts Commission, *Tenth Report*, Appendix, Part v, 1885, p. 111), the Fingall MS, to which this letter refers, was the subject of a notice sent by William Wilde (see 22 August 1849) to the Royal Irish Academy, Dublin, in 1859. The coincidence of subject and date strongly suggests that Wilde, whom TBM met in Ireland in 1849, was the recipient of this letter.

[3] See 26 June.

[4] The dinner on the 24th: see 15 June.

TO WESTLEYS AND COMPANY,[1] 21 JUNE 1859

MS: Yale University.

Holly Lodge Kensington / June 21. 1859

Gentlemen,

I have some books which require binding. Be so good as to send somebody to take my directions. I shall be at home to morrow afternoon, and all Friday. / I am, Gentlemen,

Your obedient Servant
Macaulay

Messrs. Westleys and Co / etc. etc.

TO [WILLIAM WILDE?],[2] 26 JUNE 1859

MS: Trinity College.

Holly Lodge Kensington / June 26. 1859

My dear Sir,

The M.S. about which you inquire commences thus – "Notes and Extracts from a M.S. work in the possession of Lord Killeen entitled A Light to the Blind, whereby they may see etc. etc. etc."[3] The first extract is from Page 291, and runs thus. "But we suppose His Majesty was pleased to follow the usual custom of speaking in England, which calls the Episcopals the Church of England, as if a Congregation of Hereticks ought to be named a Church." The passage in page 333 which you mention is in the Mackintosh M.S. with the proper number of the page.

I am not aware that Sir James ever made any use of the M.S. Indeed I do not see how he well could have done so. For he did not bring his narrative down to the time to which his extracts, with scarcely an exception, related.

Ever yours truly,
Macaulay

1 Bookbinders, of Friar Street, Doctors' Commons. The day before TBM had been asked to return some borrowed books and had been unable to find them: 'It was now absolutely necessary for me to do what I had a hundred times resolved to do and had not done – a general rummage and clearance could not be delayed. I sent for Gray and the footman, and went vigorously to work' (Journal, XI, 516). The work went on for several days, and brought out some sixty volumes needing binding (XI, 517).

2 See note on the recipient of *to* [Wilde?], 18 June.

3 TBM identifies this in a note to ch. 12 of the *History* thus: 'A Light to the Blind. This last work, a manuscript in the possession of Lord Fingal, is the work of a zealous Roman Catholic and a mortal enemy of England. Large extracts from it are among the Mackintosh MSS. The date in the title-page is 1711' (III, 145). The MS, now in the National Library of Ireland, was partly published in Historical Manuscripts Commission, *Tenth Report*, Appendix, Part v, 1885, pp. 107–200.

TO HENRY REEVE, 27 JUNE [1859]

Text: J. K. Laughton, *Memoirs of Henry Reeve*, II, 32, dated 27 June.

If I were to renew my connexion with the 'Edinburgh Review' after an interval of fifteen years, I should wish my first article to be rather more striking than an article on Campbell's Diary[1] can easily be. You will, no doubt, do the thing as well as it can be done.[2]

TO RICHARD MONCKTON MILNES, 28 JUNE 1859

MS: Trinity College.

Holly Lodge / June 28. 1859

Dear Milnes,

The change of weather has given me a rheumatism and tooth ache which force me to stay at home, and which would make me miserable company if I were to venture out. I am sorry for it.

Ever yours truly,
Macaulay

TO HENRY REEVE, 30 JUNE 1859

MS: Mr F. R. Cowell.

Holly Lodge June 30 / 1859

Dear Reeve,

I send you the Diary. I am sorry that the Volume of Nicholls's Literary Illustrations which contains the correspondence between Bishop Percy and the Campbells is gone to be bound.[3] But it will soon come back; and, as your article is not to appear till October, you will have ample time to consult it in my copy. If you are in a hurry, I will look out the passage the next time that I go to the Athenæum, and will transcribe it for you, as I did for Mr. Raymond.

Ever yours truly,
Macaulay

[1] See 1 June.

[2] Reeve reviewed it in 'A Visit to England in 1775,' *ER*, CX (October 1859), 322–42.

[3] John Bowyer Nichols, *Illustrations of the Literary History of the Eighteenth Century*, 8 vols., 1817–58. The correspondence with Percy (VII, 796) establishes that Campbell's nephew emigrated to Australia and hence provides an explanation for the appearance of the MS in Sydney. On reading the *Diary* TBM looked up this information and sent it to the editor, Samuel Raymond, Prothonotary of the Supreme Court of New South Wales (Journal, XI, 496: 21 May).

TO THOMAS FLOWER ELLIS, 30 JUNE 1859

MS: Trinity College.

Holly Lodge June 30. 1859

Dear Ellis,

You remember that I expect you to morrow. The carriage will be at the U[niversity] C[lub] at 6.

I have had a fit of the gout – the first – short and sharp. I was lame yesterday, and do not walk with perfect ease to day. But on the whole, I am well pleased. It is not, I believe, thought a bad thing for a person approaching sixty to be thus attacked.[1]

Ever yours
Macaulay

TO THE DUCHESS OF ARGYLL, 5 JULY 1859

MS: Mr F. R. Cowell.

Holly Lodge July 5 / 1859

Dear Duchess of Argyll,

Will you do me the honor and pleasure of breakfasting here at ten on Friday?[2] And will you bring the Duke?

Most truly yours
Macaulay

TO FRANCES MACAULAY, 6 JULY 1859

MS: Huntington Library.

Holly Lodge Kensington / July 6. 1859

Dearest Fanny,

I am truly glad to have so good an account of your trip northwards. The weather is glorious here, hot, but not too hot, at least not too hot for those who like me can repose in the shade when the sun is high.

Yesterday poor Lord Ebrington[3] called on me. I was extremely touched by his misfortunes and still more by the courage and cheerfulness with which he endures them. I am ashamed to think that I should ever

[1] 'Everybody knows that a fit of gout clears the constitution of many ailments which have clouded the head and depressed the spirits. . . . as I write this while actually suffering, this may be taken to be my serious judgment' (Journal, XI, 520–1: 29 June).

[2] The party were the Duke and Duchess of Argyll, Lord and Lady Belper, Margaret Holland, Dundas, the Milmans, and Charles Sumner (Journal, XI, 525: 8 July).

[3] Ebrington had visited the Crimean hospitals, where he 'contracted ophthalmia, lost an eye, and seriously injured his health' (*DNB*).

suffer my complaints to make me querulous, when I see how he bears his. I have asked him to breakfast here on Friday where he will meet the Duke and Duchess of Argyle, Lord and Lady Belper, Baba, and, I hope, Dundas and the Milmans. Lord Ebrington gives a delightful account of Madeira. You teetotallers will be delighted to hear that, since the vines perished there, the condition of the common people has greatly improved.[1]

Yesterday I dined at Lord Broughton's and sate next Lord Clarendon. We were talking about the difference between the young fellows of our generation and those of the rising generation. He denied that there had been any moral improvement. "The principal change" he said, "is that I used to call my father the Governor, and that now a youth calls his father the Relieving Officer." This name was quite new to me. Ask George if it is the established word for a father at Cambridge. If Lord Clarendon is right the deterioration is fearful. For the word Governor, irreverent as it is, implies authority. But a Relieving Officer exists merely to disburse money. A lad at home, I suppose, is said to be in the work house, – a lad at Cambridge to be receiving out door relief. By the bye why does not George write either to me or to his sister? "I am sorry to say it: but that young man is not the thing." Where is that?[2]

Alice behaves much better. I had a delightful letter from her this morning which shall be answered in no long time. Love to Hannah, her good girl, and her naughty boy.

Ever yours,
Macaulay

TO THOMAS FLOWER ELLIS, 10 JULY 1859

MS: Trinity College.

Holly Lodge July 10. 1859

Dear Ellis,

By this time I suppose that you are at York. I write chiefly for the purpose of telling you that there is no chance of my leaving town this week or next week. Early in next week you will probably be here. If so, I shall be glad to see you any day except Monday the 18th, on which I am to dine with the Belpers.

Yesterday I dined with Baron Rothschild.[3] What a paradise he lives in.

[1] The vineyards were attacked by *Oidium*, a mildew, in 1852: 'The populations of entire villages emigrated to Brazil or the West Indies' (Rupert Croft-Cooke, *Madeira*, 1961, pp. 91–2).

[2] Jane Austen, *Emma*, ch. 29.

[3] Baron Lionel de Rothschild (1808–79: *DNB*), son of the founder of the English branch of the firm of Rothschild.

I had no notion of the beauty and extent of the gardens behind Kingston House.[1] A palace ought to be built there. It would be the most magnificent and delightful town residence existing. When I said this to the Baron, he acknowledged it, but said that he was only a tenant, and that to purchase the fee simple would be a serious matter. Three hundred thousand pounds had been offered and refused for these eight or ten acres.

The dinner was a curiosity, seeing that pork, in all its forms, was excluded. There was however some compensation as you will see from the bill of fare which I enclose. Send it back to me that I may show it to Lady Trevelyan. Surely this is the land flowing with milk and honey. I do not believe that Solomon in all his glory ever dined on Ortolans farcis à la Talleyrand. I may observe in passing that the little birds were accompanied by some Johannisberg which was beyond all praise. I shall be glad if you enable me to send the Carte to Lowood enriched by notes from your discriminating pen.

I was at the House of Lords on Friday, and tried to get into conversation with the Chancellor.[2] But there were so many interruptions, and the debate went off so soon that I had no opportunity of bringing in your name naturally and easily; and I did not chuse to force it in abruptly. I shall watch for a favourable opportunity.

I shall be glad if, when you have five minutes to spare, you will tell me something more than the Times has told me about Swinfen v. Chelmsford.[3] How did Kennedy[4] reply? There is not a word of his reply in any paper that I have seen. Was his impudence and spite at all quelled by the general disapprobation? I rejoice at his failure. But I cannot think that Lord Chelmsford comes quite clear out of the matter. He acted for the best, no doubt. But he assumed an authority which did not belong to him; and he did so under an erroneous impression as to the true interests of his client.

Ever yours,
Macaulay

[1] Rothschild lived at 147 and 148 Piccadilly, next to the Duke of Wellington at Apsley House, number 149.

[2] TBM hoped that Campbell would do something for Ellis: 'I am certain that Campbell wishes Ellis well, and will do all that he can' (Journal, XI, 514: 16 June). See also *to* Ellis, 5 November.

[3] Lord Chelmsford, when he was still Sir Frederick Thesiger, had appeared for Mrs Patience Swinfen in a suit over a disputed will. Thesiger entered into a compromise agreement without the authority of Mrs Swinfen, who then brought suit for damages against him. The case was heard on 4 and 5 July and was decided in Lord Chelmsford's favor. Ellis was one of his counsel.

[4] Charles Rann Kennedy (1808–67: *DNB*), barrister, counsel for Mrs Swinfen in the trial.

TO THE REVEREND WILLIAM WRIGHT,[1] 11 JULY 1859

MS: Trinity College.

Holly Lodge July 11. 1859

Sir,

It is impossible for me to refuse to comply with the request which you have done me the honor to make.

I only wish that my name were more likely to be of use to the District Visiting Society.[2] / I have the honor to be, / Sir,

Your faithful Servant,
Macaulay

The Reverend W Wright / etc. etc. etc.

TO LORD STANHOPE, 16 JULY 1859

MS: Stanhope Papers, Chevening.

Holly Lodge July 16. 1859

My dear Stanhope,

I return the Fechter.[3] I like it much. I have seen nothing so good in the German language, this long time. Many thanks.

Ever yours truly,
Macaulay

TO CHRISTIAN BERNHARD TAUCHNITZ, 25 JULY 1859

Text: Bernhard Tauchnitz, 1837–1887, pp. 110–11.

Holly Lodge, July 25th, 1859.

It will be long before I shall be able to say with confidence when another portion of my history will be published.... I wrote a few months ago an

[1] Wright (d. 1899?), then curate of Christ Church, Kensington, and of St Mary Abbott, Kensington, was a neighbor of TBM's on Campden Hill.

[2] The General Society for Promoting District Visiting, an Evangelical organization founded in 1828, provided '*a regular system of domiciliary visitation* ... by which *every poor family might be visited at their habitations, from house to house and from room to room, and their temporal and spiritual condition* diligently yet tenderly examined into, and appropriate treatment applied' (*District Visitors' Record for 1832*, quoted in F. K. Brown, *Fathers of the Victorians*, p. 241).

[3] 'Lord Stanhope sent me a German Tragedy – The Gladiator of Ravenna.... I read an act. It has merit, undoubtedly' (Journal, XI, 530: 13 July). The play is Friedrich Halm, *Der Fechter von Ravenna*, Vienna, 1856.

article on *William Pitt*, the younger, for the *Encyclopædia Britannica.* The circulation of the article here has necessarily been small, as very few people care to encumber themselves with a bulky and costly volume for the sake of a few pages. As far however as the circulation has extended, I think that this little sketch has been as popular as anything that I ever wrote. You can consider whether it would be worth your while to reprint it on the old terms.[1]

TO THOMAS FLOWER ELLIS, 31 JULY 1859

MS: Trinity College. *Extract published:* Trevelyan, II, 471.

Lowood Inn Windermere / July 31. 1859

Dear Ellis,

I came hither on Thursday,[2] and have had two delightful days, for a wonder. The Lakes have now reverted to their old bad habits. The wind is blowing: the hills are covered with black clouds: the rain is beating against the windows; and the lake is tossing in waves, not exactly like those of Benacus,[3] but enough to make a delicate lady sea sick. However I have the most pleasant society within doors.

I went with Lady Trevelyan the day before yesterday to Grasmere Churchyard, and saw Wordsworth's tomb. I thought of announcing my intention of going and issuing guinea tickets to people who wished to see me there. For a Yankee who was here a few days ago and heard that I was expected said that he would give the world to see that most sublime of all spectacles, Macaulay standing by the grave of Wordsworth.

I hear the most harrowing accounts of the stern Spartan discipline which Kennedy of Shrewsbury[4] keeps up in his family. He is not now at this Inn: but he was here ten days ago, and kept the whole house in agitation. The passages and stairs were crowded with people admiring the energy with which he performed the duties of a father. "Get out of

[1] The biographies of Pitt and Atterbury were published together in 1860 as volume 507 of the 'Collection of British Authors.'

[2] The 28th. On 5 August TBM, Hannah, and Alice left for Glasgow, travelled to Tarbet, Inverary, and Stirling on 8–11 August, and reached Edinburgh on the 12th. They went to Manchester on the 16th, where TBM parted from them and returned to London on the next day (Journal, XI, 537–50).

[3] Lake Garda: TBM and Ellis presumably saw it on 3 September 1856, on their way from Brescia to Verona (Journal, X, 50).

[4] Benjamin Kennedy (1804–89: *DNB*), brother of Charles (see 10 July), was Headmaster of Shrewsbury School, 1836–66, and Regius Professor of Greek at Cambridge, 1867–89. He was winning prizes at Cambridge and active in the Union during TBM's last year of residence.

my room, you hussies;" he cried to his daughters, who had been interceding for their brother. Out ran the daughters. Then, says Alice, the gruff voice said "How dare you, Sir? What do you mean, Sir?" And then a boy's shrill voice answered "Oh, spare me, spare me." And then – and then. I thought of the far different sounds which you once heard at the same place. Kennedy the schoolmaster seems to be the true brother of Kennedy the barrister.

If you can think of any pleasant plan for a few days between the 17th of August and the beginning of term, I am your man.[1]

Ever yours
Macaulay

TO MRS HENRY THURSTAN HOLLAND, 7 AUGUST 1859

MS: Trinity College. *Extract published:* Trevelyan, II, 478n.

Glasgow August 7. 1859

Dearest Baba,

I was delighted to receive your letter here. We are most comfortably lodged and luxuriously fed at the Royal Hotel. But there was at first one drawback. In all the rooms hung a notice that we were in imminent danger of being robbed; and we were charged to lock our doors at night, or to fasten them with chains. The porter, it was added, was up and about all night, armed, I suppose, to the teeth, and the guests were to communicate, as it was expressed, with him through the opening which the chains permitted. We were startled at finding ourselves in such a den of thieves, and called to mind all the old stories of inns where travellers were plundered and murdered, and where the new comer regularly found his predecessor's corpse in some hole near the bed. I was puzzled to understand who was to rob us – was it the land lord, or the servants, or the other guests? Who else should it be? While I was revolving these thoughts Gray introduced to me Mr. Carrick the land lord, a very civil person who bowed and said; "Everything is perfectly safe, my Lord. Not the least chance of your losing anything. There was a theft two months ago at Glasgow in an inn. But you may be quite easy." I did not reply, as I might have done – "Then why, in heaven's name, do you put up in all the sitting rooms and bedrooms a notice meant to make us uneasy?" In fact everything seems quite safe. We passed yesterday very pleasantly in wandering about Glasgow. Your Mamma is quite a convert, and Alice

[1] TBM and Ellis toured the West of England, from Weymouth to Ilfracombe, 1–8 October (Journal, XI, 569–74).

admires the grandeur of the old, and the neatness of the new town. The gardens at the Western extremity are really very beautiful. We are just going to the Cathedral where Alice will, for the first time in her life, hear the Presbyterian service. I shall leave it to her to describe the impression which it makes upon her.

I greatly fear that my dear old friend Lord Lansdowne and I shall never meet again here.[1] I owe more to him than to any man living; and he never seemed to be sensible that I owed him anything. I shall look anxiously for the next accounts.

I am sorry that Harry's holiday is so much cut up. Love to him. Remember me kindly to your host and hostess.[2] I am much amused by what I hear about the children.

Ever yours my love
Macaulay

TO THOMAS FLOWER ELLIS, 9 AUGUST 1859

MS: Trinity College.

Inverary August 9. 1859

Dear Ellis,

Here I am, with Lady Trevelyan and Alice, enjoying the lakes and mountains in this golden summer weather. I have never seen such fine days in the highlands. Two more such, and we shall have seen Loch Katrine, which I never yet saw except in a smoking rain, and shall be at Edinburgh in the region of hackney coaches, caring little for the showers and sunshine.

On Wednesday the 17th I shall be at Holly Lodge. The sooner after that day that you can come, the better I shall be pleased. If you write on any day to Sunday inclusive, direct to the Post Office Edinburgh – afterwards to London. I am very well; and I hope that you are so. Hannah sends her kind regards.

Ever yours
Macaulay

[1] 'Sorry to hear that Lord Lansdowne has been very ill' (Journal, XI, 539: 4 August). Lansdowne survived TBM by a little more than two years.

[2] Charles Buxton and his wife, at Fox Warren.

TO THOMAS FLOWER ELLIS, 15 AUGUST 1859

MS: Trinity College.

Edinburgh August 15. 1859

Dear Ellis,

To day Mrs. Kemble and Marian called on us at Douglas's Hotel.[1] By ill luck we were then wandering and spouting verses among the woods of Rosslyn. Our visitors left word that they were leaving Edinburgh, but should return on Thursday. On Thursday unfortunately we shall be in England again. We have therefore completely missed them. I find that you were at Lowood on Sunday – a pleasant holiday.

We have had glorious weather except on one day, the day on which we had hoped to see Loch Katrine. The morning was gloomy. But we persisted in going to the very mouth of the Trosachs. There it was raining by pailfulls. No hope of a change before night. After sitting an hour or two in a coffee room crowded by forty or fifty people who had been disappointed like ourselves, we returned to Stirling. This is my third expedition to Loch Katrine. All three have been unhappy. But the mishaps of 1859 exceed those of 1817 and 1833. For this time I did not even get sight of the lake.

I hope to dine at Holly Lodge the day after to morrow. If you come to town this week, you had better take up your quarters with me from Saturday to Monday. At any rate, let me know when you see your way clear. Lady Trevelyan is out shopping, or would send you her kindest regards.

Ever yours,
Macaulay

TO LADY TREVELYAN, 18 AUGUST 1859

MS: Trinity College. *Extract published:* Trevelyan, II, 466.

Holly Lodge August 18. 1859

Dearest Hannah,

When I reached home, after a rapid and quiet journey, I found on my table a letter from Ellis mentioning that he had seen George, who could tell him nothing about our movements. I was in doubt whether your kind host was at the Dingle or not. I therefore wrote to Harry, who has, I suppose, shown you my letter. Probably he had heard of George from Ellis, and had told you all about him. But, as there was a chance that Ellis

[1] There is no reference to this in the Journal. I have not identified Mrs Kemble.

might not have said anything, and as you seemed a little anxious, I thought it best to write without delay.

I found all my repairs completed, and my bedroom so handsomely furnished, so berugged, becarpeted, and bechintzed, that I think of being ill for the mere pleasure of keeping my chamber, and having my friends admitted to see how comfortably and luxuriously I am lodged. The library steps are come; and excellent they are. The books which I had sent to the binder are also come; and Miss Sewards's letters[1] are in condition to bear twenty more reperusals. To morrow the new carriage is to be sent and the old one taken away. Then my arrangements will be complete; and nothing will remain except to pay for them. The figure, as blackguards call it, will be pretty large; but I am rolling in money, notwithstanding fires, income tax, railway quarelling, and the loss of Peninsular and Oriental Steamers.[2]

You are quite right to go down to Margaret on Monday. Let me know when you shall be in Grosvenor Crescent. Love to Alice and Fanny, – to Harry also, if you see him – and kind regards to your host and hostess.

Ever yours
Macaulay

TO D[UNCAN?] STEWART,[3] 18 AUGUST 1859

MS: Mr Walter Leuba.

Holly Lodge August 18 / 1859

Sir,

I was travelling when your letter was sent to me, and did not receive it till long after it was written.

I feel for your distress. But I should not think myself justified in recommending, for a share of the very small sum allotted by the state to the encouragement of letters, a gentleman of whose merits I am quite incompetent to form an opinion. In your case, the only testimony which can have any weight, the only testimony to which Lord Palmerston ought to attend, is that of Orientalists. Such testimony I hope that it may be in your power to obtain. But you must, on reflection, be sensible that I could

[1] Edinburgh, 1811. Selections from TBM's marginalia in his copy of this work, now in the library at Wallington, were published by G. O. Trevelyan in *Marginal Notes by Lord Macaulay*, 1907, pp. 5–9, and reprinted as Appendix IV in the 1908 edition of the *Life*.

[2] 'My income this year will considerably exceed 5000£, and my expenditure will very little exceed 3000£' (Journal, XI, 526: 8 July).

[3] A Duncan Stewart published a *Practical Arabic Grammar*, 1841, printed by the Cambridge University Press; this may be the same person. No one of the name is among the civil list pensioners.

tell Lord Palmerston nothing except what I have been told by yourself. / I have the honor to be, / Sir,

Your obedient Servant,
Macaulay

D Stewart Esq / etc. etc. etc.

TO WESTLEYS AND COMPANY, 24 AUGUST 1859

MS: Mr W. Hugh Peal.

Lord Macaulay will be obliged to Messrs. Westleys to send their bill for binding his books as soon as is convenient.[1]
Holly Lodge Kensington / August 24. 1859

TO FRANCES MACAULAY, 28 AUGUST 1859

MS: Trinity College.

Holly Lodge Kensington / August 28. 1859

Dearest Fanny,

I have been much interested by your account of Toddington.[2] You will, I hope, have been more interested by Woburn than you expected. The house is not much. But the pictures are highly curious. I should have liked to go over them with you. I forget whether you have seen our National Portrait Gallery. If not, you must go when next you visit London.

I am rather out of sorts for several reasons. In the first place I have a toothache – a reason which, you may perhaps think, sufficient, without any other. But secondly Charles and his boy have just been here to take leave. I felt exceedingly for the young fellow, who could not restrain his tears.[3] Lastly, I am beginning to be nervous about Baba. To be sure, she is wonderfully well; and Sir Henry says that he never in all his experience saw a case up to this point so satisfactory.

Pray remember me, not as matter of form, but with very real and earnest kindness, to Lady Inglis. I am constantly reminded of her: for

[1] See 21 June.

[2] Toddington Manor, Bedfordshire, near Milton Bryant, where Fanny was staying with Sir Robert Inglis's widow. Henrietta, Baroness Wentworth of Nettlestede, Monmouth's mistress, is buried in the parish church; her death, funeral, and her name carved on a tree at Toddington 'by the hand of him whom she loved too well' are mentioned in the *History*, I, 629: ch. 5.

[3] See 5 May.

one or more of the folios which I owe to her[1] may be seen at any moment on my table. They are most useful to me; and yet I can truly say that [. . . .][2]

TO BISHOP SAMUEL WILBERFORCE, 29 AUGUST 1859

MS: Bodleian Library.

Holly Lodge Aug 29. 1859

Dear Bishop of Oxford,

I am sorry that I am so engaged that it will be impossible for me to be with you next week.

Yours most truly,
Macaulay

TO THOMAS LONGMAN, [LATE AUGUST 1859][3]

Text: Trevelyan, II, 421n.

There is a great deal about that picture in Mrs. Piozzi's Life of herself. The Lady who is reduced to the last stake was a portrait of her; and the likeness was discernible after the lapse of more than fifty years.

TO FRANCES MACAULAY, 9 SEPTEMBER 1859

MS: Trinity College.

Holly Lodge Sep 9. 1859

Dearest Fanny,

I have written to Thornton about your dividend. All must go right.

I am glad that you and Alice are enjoying Shakspeare together. I remember that, when I was a boy, I was puzzled by the difficulty which

[1] Lady Inglis had presented TBM with a set of the *Commons Journals*.

[2] The rest is missing.

[3] On 20 August 1859 TBM read a collection of Mrs Piozzi's letters and papers 'which have been offered to Longman . . . and about which he asks my advice' (Journal, XI, 553).TBM concluded that a skilful editor could make 'an interesting volume' (XI, 554) out of the material and evidently advised Longman to that effect. Longman engaged Abraham Hayward for the work, which was published as the *Autobiography, Letters and Literary Remains of Mrs. Piozzi*, 2 vols., 1861.

According to Trevelyan, the letter from which this extract is taken is one in which TBM recommends that an engraving of Hogarth's 'The Lady's Last Stake' should be used as the frontispiece to the collection. The picture was used in the edition, where its choice is credited to 'Lord Macaulay's suggestion' (I, 38).

puzzles you. I got over it by supposing, ingeniously enough, that Gertrude was Queen Regnant, and that her husbands merely had the Crown Matrimonial, as Darnley had in Scotland and Philip here in England. But I know better now. In the old northern kingdoms nothing was more usual than for a prince to be succeeded by a brother of mature age in preference to a son of tender age. You will find instances in the history of our Anglo Saxon Kings. Edmund the grandson of Alfred left sons, Edwy and Edgar. But they were very young. Therefore Edmund's brother Edred became King; and after his death his nephews Edwy and Edgar were successively called to the throne. The truth is that, in a rude and simple state of society, people want a King who will really govern them. The notion of having a King in the cradle, whose powers and duties all belong to a Regent, is a refinement of later times. Love to my dear little girl. Her sister is still well; and [. . . .][1]

TO [ALICE TREVELYAN], [14?][2] SEPTEMBER 1859

Text: Trevelyan, 2nd edn, I, 226–7.

I am glad that Mackintosh's Life[3] interests you. I knew him well; and a kind friend he was to me when I was a young fellow, fighting my way uphill.

TO THOMAS FLOWER ELLIS, 16 SEPTEMBER 1859

MS: Trinity College.

Holly Lodge September 16 / 1859

Dear Ellis,

All well. A fine boy.[4] I was at Grosvenor Crescent within an hour after the birth; and then Margaret was doing as well as possible. I shall not see my little grand nephew till to morrow. He already shows a taste for brown sugar, with which he was greeted at his entrance into the world. I expect you on Tuesday.

Ever yours
Macaulay

[1] Most of the last leaf has been cut away. Alice had been sent away to stay with Fanny while Margaret was awaiting the birth of her child at Grosvenor Crescent: see 16 September.

[2] TBM wrote to Alice on the 14th and again on the 17th (Journal, XI, 563–4): this extract could be from either letter.

[3] By Mackintosh's son Robert, 2 vols., 1836.

[4] Margaret's first child, Henry Macaulay Trevelyan Holland (1859–78).

TO FRANCES MACAULAY, 19 SEPTEMBER 1859

MS: Trinity College.

Holly Lodge Kensington / September 19. 1859

Dearest Fanny,

Thanks for your affectionate letter. To day I was permitted to see my dear Margaret. She is doing as well as possible; and nothing can be more charming than her affection for the child.[1] A fine boy he is, and has more hair on his head than his father.

Lucretius says that there is no moment at which the funeral wail for those who are going out of the world does not mingle with the first cries of those who are coming into it.[2] You see that poor Sir James Stephen died[3] within a few hours of the birth of our dear little thing.

I heard to day from George. He was at Brunecken in excellent health and spirits. He purposed to be at Munich this day week, and in town on Friday week at latest.

Love to my little darling Alice.

Ever yours,
Macaulay

TO FRANCES MACAULAY, 24 SEPTEMBER 1859

MS: Trinity College.

Holly Lodge Sep 24 / 1859

Dearest Fanny,

I do not know what is meant by *grains*. The expression *rags of saints* seems to allude to the Roman Catholic custom of putting on the garb of some religious order, to die in.[4] You remember the lines of Milton, Sir Henry's friend and correspondent –

"And they who, to be sure of Paradise,
Dying, put on the weeds of Dominic,
Or in Franciscan think to pass disguised."[5]

[1] 'Saw my dear child again. How amiable she is. And how beautiful it was to see her with the little creature nestling close to her. Certainly the Papists made a great hit when they set up the Madonna as the object of idolatry. The ancient polytheists had no young mother in their Pantheon' (Journal, XI, 565: 20 September).

[2] *De Rerum Natura*, II, 576–80.

[3] 14 September, at Coblenz.

[4] The reference is probably to Sir Henry Wotton, 'A Hymn to My God in a Night of My Late Sickness,' 7–8: 'No hallowed Oyls, no grains I need, / No Rags of Saints, no purging Fire.'

[5] *Paradise Lost*, III, 478–80.

The Annuity Tax[1] is a very oppressive rate levied for the support of the parish ministers of Edinburgh. Of course they are entitled to a maintenance; but there is such a collection of iniquities in the way in which they are now maintained that I do not wonder at the public indignation. In the first place there are many more ministers than are wanted. Some churches with very small congregations have two ministers, both drawing good stipends. In the second place the whole legal profession, Judges, Advocates, writers to the signet, whom we call conveyancers, writers, whom we call attorneys, are exempt from the tax. Now these people are the aristocracy of Edinburgh; and they are very generally members of the Established Church. A poor Dissenter therefore very naturally thinks it hard that, besides paying his own preacher, he is to pay towards a very handsome salary for the minister of the Lord President and the Lord Justice Clerk, and that the Lord President and the Lord Justice Clerk are to pay nothing at all. The people of Edinburgh also complain that while, in other places throughout Scotland, the old ecclesiastical property is charged with the support of the clergy, the ecclesiastical property in Edinburgh has been otherwise disposed of, and a tax substituted for it. You are now, I believe, as well qualified as most people to discuss the question of the Annuity Tax.

Mrs. Edward Cropper must be out of her mind. She wrote to ask me to go down this week and spend some days with her and Edward at Penshurst.[2] I excused myself. She then wrote to insist that I would go on the 18th and stay till the 23d. I again excused myself, – as civilly as possible. She then writes to bid me farewell. She could not do me a greater kindness. I shall take her at her word, and never again, if I can possibly avoid it, have any intercourse but that of the coldest civility with so foolish, exacting, and quarrelsome a person. Edward has not appeared in the matter. She has had a correspondence to much the same effect with Hannah, and is in a rage because Hannah does not chuse to leave Baba.

Ever yours
Macaulay

[1] See *to* William Gibson Craig, 15 July 1852. A bill to abolish the tax passed its second reading this year but the session ended before it could be acted on further. There was then widespread resistance in Edinburgh to the collection of the tax, which was at last abolished in the next year.

[2] Edward Cropper now lived at Swaylands, Kent, near Penshurst.

TO ADAM BLACK, 6 OCTOBER 1859

MS: Mr F. R. Cowell.

Ilfracombe October 6. 1859

My dear Sir,

Your letter has followed me from London, and has overtaken me in Devonshire.[1] I have been looking out for a place where I may hybernate if the cold weather should drive me from London; and I am inclined to think that no spot on this side of the Alps would suit me so well as Sidmouth.[2]

I must beg you to prevent our friends of the University from offering me the Rectorship. It is indeed an honorable office; and I am grateful to them for thinking of me. But the duties, light and merely ceremonial as they may be, would be more than I could undertake. The state of my chest has forced me to give up public speaking. If ever I do harangue again, which is very improbable, it will be in the House of Lords, on some occasion on which I entertain a hope of doing real good. I already hold too many offices of which I am unable to perform the duties. I have repeatedly intreated the members of your Philosophical Institute to chuse another President who may be able really to preside over them. I cannot think of placing myself in a similar relation to so respectable a body as the University.

I am afraid that I can do little or nothing more for the Encyclopædia. Many things remind me that I have no time to spare; and I have set my heart on completing another portion of my history.

I wish that the opposition to the Annuity Tax were conducted with rather more discretion by some of your constituents.[3] However I really hope that the glory of getting rid of it may be reserved for you.

Ever yours truly,
Macaulay

TO WILLIAM WHEWELL, 11 OCTOBER 1859

MS: Trinity College.

Holly Lodge / October 11. 1859

Dear Whewell,

Dr. Latham,[4] I find, is a candidate for the Professorship of Modern

[1] TBM left London with Ellis on 1 October for Weymouth; they then visited Charnmouth, Lyme, Sidmouth, Exeter, and Ilfracombe, returning to London on the 8th.

[2] 'I love Sidmouth. The beauty of the coast and luxurious softness of the air charm me. I shall probably winter there before long, if I live' (Journal, XI, 571: 4 October).

[3] The tax-collectors were meeting with resistance and sometimes violence.

[4] Robert Gordon Latham (1812–88: *DNB*), philologist and ethnologist, who called on TBM

History. I should be glad to serve him, – not from personal regard, – for I have not, in the whole course of my life, passed a quarter of an hour in his company, – but because I believe him to be a learned and able man, and because I am assured that the salary is an object to him, which it would not have been, if he had been content to write superficially on popular topics. I do not know whether you rate his attainments as highly as I am inclined to do; nor do I know whether you are likely to be consulted. But I think it as well to let you know that he is a candidate.

My kind and grateful regards to Lady Affleck.

Ever yours truly,
Macaulay

TO SARAH TELFORD,[1] 14 OCTOBER 1859

MS: Mr F. R. Cowell.

Holly Lodge October 14. 1859

Dear Miss Telford,

I am most grateful to you for remembering me so kindly. I have now been feasting three days on fruit as good as any that Eve gathered in Paradise for Raphael. My best regards and thanks to your sisters.

Most truly yours,
Macaulay

TO THE GOVERNORS OF HARROW SCHOOL, 19 OCTOBER 1859

MS: Trinity. *Extract published:* Edward Graham, *The Harrow Life of Henry Montagu Butler, D.D.*, 1920, p. 124.

Holly Lodge Kensington October 19. 1859

My Lords and Gentlemen,

I understand that Mr. Montagu Butler is a candidate for the Head-mastership of Harrow School;[2] and I sincerely believe that, by electing

on this day to discuss his candidacy. He had first called on TBM on 13 September, when TBM mistakenly supposed that Latham was a medical doctor with bad news about Margaret, but then saw that he was 'a needy man of letters. I was going to give him a Sovereign and send him away, when I discovered that he was the famous philologist, whom I should never have expected to see in such a plight. I felt for him, and gave him a hundred pounds – a hard pull on me, I must say' (Journal, XI, 562). Latham did not receive the Cambridge appointment, vacant by reason of Stephen's death.

[1] Eldest of the three Telford sisters: see 21 May 1855.

[2] Dr Vaughan's love-affair with one of his pupils at Harrow had been revealed to Dr Symonds, TBM's former physician at Clifton (see 8 August 1852). Symonds, whose son was at Harrow, at once compelled Vaughan, under threat of public exposure, to resign

him, you would confer a great benefit on the public. His temper, his principles, his abilities, his attainments, his long connection with Harrow, his love for Harrow, his familiarity with the system which has been so successfully followed at Harrow, seem to me to mark him out as eminently fit for the post which he wishes to obtain. Of the extent of his learning the Fasti of Cambridge afford abundant evidence. Of his talents for business Sir Charles Trevelyan, certainly one of the first men of business of our time, had an opportunity of forming an opinion; and I know that Sir Charles would, if there were time for communication with Madras, bear a strong testimony to Mr. Butler's merits. What I have heard from young men, who looked up to Mr. Butler at school, who have since looked up to him at college, and on whose characters his example and authority have had a most beneficial influence, has convinced me that he possesses in a rare degree the qualities which conciliate the affection and command the respect of youth. I cannot doubt that, under such a head, the distinguished school of which you are the Governors would continue to flourish, to train excellent scholars and honorable gentlemen, and to enjoy the confidence of families. / I have the honor to be, / My Lords and Gentlemen,

Your most obedient Servant,
Macaulay

The / Governors of Harrow School / etc. etc. etc.

TO SIR GEORGE CORNEWALL LEWIS, 23 OCTOBER 1859

MS: National Library of Wales.

Holly Lodge Kensington / October 23. 1859

Dear Lewis,

Thanks for the supplement to Babrius.[1] What a text you have had to

the headmastership, which he did in September. Vaughan was succeeded by Butler, then 26 years old. For the details of this story, see Phyllis Grosskurth, *The Woeful Victorian: A Biography of John Addington Symonds*, New York, 1964, pp. 33–7. To judge from certain entries in his Journal, TBM evidently knew something about the scandal: e.g., 'there are sad stories about Harrow in circulation' (XI, 488: 5 May 1859).

This letter was begun on the day after that on which TBM learned that Hannah would definitely leave for India in February, news that plunged him into deepest grief. His Journal for the next day, the 16th, concludes with this entry: 'even if I should live to see them all again what can compensate for so many happy years taken from a life which must be drawing to its close? I wish I were dead – I hardly know what I write – I will try to frame testimonials for Butler to the Governors of Harrow. That may divert my attention from — I have written the testimonial, but I will keep it a day or two and turn it in my mind' (XI, 578).

[1] *Babrii Fabulæ Æsopæ*, London, J. W. Parker, 1859. An edition of the MS of additional

deal with! It is as corrupt as a Wakefield ten pound householder. Emendatory criticism is out of the question. Bentley could hardly have made such verses better; and Le Clerc[1] could hardly have made them worse. I suppose that what Babrius wrote is intermingled with a great deal that was written after the laws of the old Greek versification had become obsolete.

Pray bear fable 82 in mind, unmetrical as it is. Read it to such of the Cabinet as understand Greek; and translate it to the rest. It contains the quintessence of what I would say to them, if I were one of them.[2]

Ever yours truly,
Macaulay

TO JOHANN HEINRICH KÜNZEL, 2[4?][3] OCTOBER 1859

Text: Copy, Hessische Landes-und-Hochschulbibliothek, Darmstadt. *Published:* Walther Fischer, *Johann Heinrich Künzel*, p. 57.

Holly Lodge Kensington / October 23. 1859

Sir,

I have the honor to acknowledge the receipt of the volume[4] which you have been so obliging as to send me. I promise myself both pleasure and instruction from the perusal of it.

I thank you for mentioning with so much indulgence my review of my friend Lord Stanhope's History of the Spanish war.[5] That review was written very hastily, with very little assistance from books, during the tumult of a contested election at Leeds. I little imagined, when I sent the sheets off to Edinburgh that they would be read in Germany as well as in England, after the lapse of twenty seven years. I am now going over

fables purchased by the British Museum in 1857 and now regarded as the work of the nineteenth-century forger, Minoides Mynas.

1 Jean LeClerc (1657–1736), Swiss scholar resident in Holland; he feuded with Bentley, who exposed LeClerc's ignorance of Greek meters.

2 The fable may be translated thus: 'A wild boar was once standing near to a tree and was sharpening its teeth. A she-goat kept asking, "Why, when you are not in danger nor are you hunting, should you unnecessarily sharpen your teeth?" The boar rejoined: "I would be thoughtless and I would perish wretchedly if I only looked for arms when danger was present. Every man's life is a matter of scheming. It is necessary to be prepared, so that you don't meet a bad end." '

3 This letter, together with those that follow to Ellis and to George Trevelyan, are all entered under 24 October in TBM's Journal; the other letters are also dated the 24th.

4 Künzel's *Das Leben und der Briefwechsel des Landgrafen Georg von Hessen-Darmstadt*, Friedberg and London, 1859.

5 'Auch Lord Macaulay, dem wir die geistreiche übersichtliche Skizze des spanischen Successionskrieges nach Lord Mahons Werk in seinen Essays verdanken, hat den Verfasser mit lebhaftem Interesse zur Herausgabe des Werks angespornt' (p. xi).

the same ground again, but with much more wary steps. With repeated thanks, I have the honor to be, / Sir,

Your faithful servant
Macaulay.

TO THOMAS FLOWER ELLIS, 24 OCTOBER 1859

MS: Trinity College. *Extracts published:* Trevelyan, II, 473; 474.

Holly Lodge Oct 24. 1859

Dear Ellis,

I shall be very glad if you can come here on Saturday or on Sunday morning. I have been very well in body since we parted. But in mind I have suffered much, and the more because I have had to put a force upon myself in order to appear cheerful. It is at last settled that Hannah and Alice are to go to Madras in February. I cannot deny that it is right; and my duty is to avoid whatever can add to the pain which they suffer. But I am very unhappy, so unhappy that I heartily wished when Stephenson's hearse passed through the Park on Friday that I could change places with him.[1] You know what your feelings would be if Marian and Louise were both going to India in February; and you can sympathise with me.

However, I read, and write, and contrive to forget my sorrow during whole hours. But it recurs and will recur. I could almost wish that what is to be were to be immediately. I dread the next four months more than even the months which will follow the separation. This prolonged parting – this slow sipping of the vinegar and the gall – is terrible. It is something that my dear Margaret is left to me, though her grief adds to mine. She is at St Leonard's, getting on very well.

I am pleased to hear from George that he and young Everett[2] are very great friends. Everett seems to be very clever and good hearted, though odd. His scholarship is of a different sort from ours. His composition, of which George sent me a specimen, would be thought very poor here. His quantities are right; and there is meaning and thought; but nothing can

[1] Robert Stephenson (1803–59: *DNB*), the railway engineer, son of the railway engineer George Stephenson; TBM may have known him from the House of Commons, where he sat (as a Tory) 1847–59. By royal permission, Stephenson's hearse was taken in public procession through Hyde Park, a thing unprecedented in a private burial.

[2] William Everett (1839–1910), youngest son of Edward Everett, after graduating from Harvard entered Trinity College; he was President of the Union in 1862 and graduated B.A. in 1863. Earlier TBM had written: 'I am truly sorry to learn [from Sir Henry Holland] that Everett's son whom he thinks a prodigy and is bringing over to Trinity, is an odd, priggish, very Yankeyish youth, certain therefore to be unhappy at Cambridge' (Journal, XI, 514–15: 16 June).

be more tuneless than the verse. On the other hand his reading is very extensive. His knowledge of the Latin authors, George says, is more than thrice that of the best men who go up from Eton and Harrow. This reminds me of the peculiar training which Pitt underwent. I am glad to hear that Everett takes to Cambridge, and still more to hear that he is grateful, warmly and affectionately grateful, for hints as to his deficiencies. George is raving about the seventh Book of Thucydides, and dying to visit Syracuse.

I have been studying Bentley's Horace, often dissenting, often doubting, always admiring. There is a wonderful note on that passage in the pretty hymn to Faunus

> "Ludit herboso pecus omne campo
> Cum tibi Nonæ redeunt Decembres;
> Festus in pratis vacat otiosus
> Cum bove *pagus*.
> Inter audaces lupus errat agnos etc."[1]

I do not know whether you are aware that all the M.S.S. of the greatest celebrity have *pardus* instead of *pagus*. It required, one would think, no great sagacity to see that *pardus* could not be right. For there were no pards in Italy except in the dens under the amphitheatres. But how did the mistake originate? And how did it spread so as to corrupt almost all the M.S.S.? Bentley's solution of this problem is admirable. The transcribers in the middle ages were generally monks. Some good Benedictine had in his head the verse of Isaiah, "Habitabit lupus cum agno; et pardus cum hædo accubabit."[2] He saw that Horace made the wolf live peaceably with the lamb, and was struck by the wonderful coincidence between this profane poem and holy writ. So, knowing nothing about zoology, he brought in the pard too, by the alteration of a letter, and thought, no doubt, that he had done a great feat. This reading, once introduced, was so exactly suited to the taste and the erudition which then flourished in monasteries that it was generally adopted. Does not this strike you as a most ingenious and satisfactory explanation?

But I must stop. Let me know when I shall see you, as soon as you are able to fix a time.

Ever yours
Macaulay

[1] *Odes*, III, xviii, 9–13. [2] Isaiah 11:6.

TO GEORGE OTTO TREVELYAN, 24 OCTOBER 1859

MS: Trinity College. *Published: Times Literary Supplement*, 9 March 1916, p. 115.

Holly Lodge Kensington / October 24. 1859

Dear George,

Thanks for your letters. I am truly glad to find that you are on a friendly footing with Everett. I have a great value for his father. Pray bring the young fellow to call on me when you are next in town, if he should be in town too; and tell him that I should be most happy to be able to serve him in any way.

I hope that you, like him, will be more grateful for good advice than for praise. I therefore take the liberty to point out to you a false spelling of which you are guilty, a false spelling too particularly censurable in a scholar – "to *pander* to the insatiable love of rhetoric." Now you are surely aware that the word *pandar* is simply the proper name of the warrior whom Homer calls Pandarus, and who is prompted by Minerva to break the treaty between the Greeks and Trojans. The poets and romancers of the middle ages, knowing generally that he had been represented by Homer as a faithless and dishonorable man, made him connive, and more than connive, at the gallantries of his niece Cressida. Thence the name of Pandarus and Pandar was given to pimps. When Falstaff wishes Pistol to carry a love letter to a married woman, Pistol exclaims

"Shall I Sir Pandarus of Troy become?"[1]

It is therefore most incorrect to spell the word *pander*. In fact this spelling, like *Syren*, like *Sybil*, like *pigmy*, and some other spellings which might be mentioned, raises a strong presumption that the person who is guilty of it does not know Greek.

I am glad that you are properly interested about the siege of Syracuse. The seventh book of Thucydides is the finest piece of history in the world. Livy, Tacitus, Sallust, Xenophon, vanish before it. It is absolutely perfect. I have often wished to visit Syracuse. But I believe that the coast has undergone considerable changes. The quarries in which the prisoners were confined remain; and, to judge by the pictures which I have seen, must be well worth visiting.

I wonder that you should carry away from the De Natura Deorum no impression but that of the style. Surely the Academic philosopher makes minced meat of the Epicurean. The first book I think the best. But on the whole I prefer the argument against the Epicurean in the De

[1] *Merry Wives of Windsor*, I, iii, 83.

Finibus. The De Fato and the De Divinatione are also, I think, excellently reasoned.

I have of late been reading Bentley's Horace again, with frequent dissent, with frequent doubt, and with constant admiration. I am meditating an attack on Athenæus, of whom I know less than I could wish. I must begin by getting a better edition than the old folio which I now possess.[1]

Mamma came back on Thursday. On Friday she and Alice dined with me; and to morrow I am to dine with them. Yesterday Sir Henry Holland called here. He spoke most kindly about you. In another week, I suppose, Baba will be returning to Chester Square.[2] I am well enough in body – very much otherwise, as you may suppose, in mind – but I put a force on myself, and plague other people with my feelings as little as I can.

Ever yours
Macaulay

TO FRANCES MACAULAY, 26 OCTOBER 1859

MS: Trinity College.

Holly Lodge / October 26. 1859

Dearest Fanny,

Thanks for your affectionate letter.

I have much to make me sad: but it is a great and real pleasure to me to know that you are independent and comfortable. It is kind in you to feel as you do about the share which I have had in placing you above pecuniary anxiety and dependence. But I by no means consider myself as having done more than my strict duty; and I should be very sorry to think that you would have [. . . .][3]

TO LORD STANHOPE, 29 OCTOBER 1859

MS: Stanhope Papers, Chevening.

Holly Lodge Kensington / October 29. 1859

My dear Stanhope,

I am sorry that we missed each other in Devonshire. I did not visit

[1] TBM's copy was a 1607 printing of Casaubon's edition (sale catalogue, item 315). The same phrase about 'meditating an attack' on Athenæus occurs in TBM's letter to Ellis, 25 August 1835.

[2] Margaret and Henry Holland lived at 50 Chester Square.

[3] The last leaf of the sheet has been cut away.

Dartmoor, though I have often meant to do so; and your account of it stimulates my curiosity.

I am afraid that a visit to Chevening in December is out of the question. My hybernation has begun; and I shall scarcely venture more than a few steps from my nest till the trees, which are fast becoming bare, are putting forth new buds. Àpropos of trees, I rejoice to hear that your woods escaped the havock of the late storm.

I am strongly of opinion that the *ludibrium* to which Tacitus alludes was merely *ludibrium fortunæ.*[1] The expression is a very common one. I could give twenty instances from Cicero and Livy. As to the name of Arminius's son, I do not believe that it was Greek, or that it was given him after his captivity. Greek it certainly was not, if my copy of Strabo be correct: for there it is Θουμελικὸς, which is not a Greek name. The boy too was three years old when he fell into the hands of the Romans; and he must have had a name by that time. He was probably named Thumelic, or something of that sort; and the Latins called him Thumelicus, as they called Alaric Alaricus and Theodoric Theodoricus. But, even if you alter Strabo's ου into υ, and make the boy Thymelicus, you are no nearer making a gladiator of him. For no doubt his name was given him while he was a child, and before it was clear for what he would be fit; so that you can no more reason from his name to his calling than you can infer from Nicias's name that he must have been victorious, or from Eusebius's name that he must have been pious. But, if we could infer anything from the name Thymelicus it would surely not be that the person who bore it was a gladiator. The gladiatorial shows were essentially Roman, and were disliked by the Greeks. Θυμελικός meant a choral performer in an exhibition peculiarly Greek. It seems to me just as unlikely that the

[1] Stanhope's memorandum accompanying this letter explains its references: 'I had lent Lord Macaulay the fine play of Halm "Der Fechter von Ravenna" [see 16 July] and in a letter of October 1859 I observed to him how much we may regret that the real fate of the son of Arminius which Tacitus promises to record –

> – educatus Ravennae puer, quo mox ludibrio conflic-
> tatus sit in tempore memorabo (Annal. lib. 1. c. 58) –

– should remain unknown from the loss of that portion of the Annals.

I added that perhaps after all his fate may have been really that which the German poet supposes. Strabo tells us that the boy's name was Thumelicus. Now *Thymele* though the first meaning of that Greek word was the place for the musicians came at last to be applied to any stage; so that Thumelicus might be the Roman form for Thymelicus, and might be given to any public performer and to a Gladiator among the rest. Something also might perhaps be made of the *ludibrium* of Tacitus.

Lord Macaulay in the following letter . . . controverts my supposition. But he has relied too exclusively on Strabo and omitted to consult Tacitus. For he supposes that "the boy was three years old when he fell into the hands of the Romans;" whilst on the contrary Tacitus represents the wife of Arminius as "gravidum uterem intueris" and giving birth to a son in her captivity.'

Romans would give a gladiator an appellation taken from the Attic stage as that our English gentlemen of the fancy would borrow from the Italian opera nicknames for the heroes of the fives' court, and would call Gully or Crib[1] the Soprano or the Contratenor. How I run on. Pray present my kindest regards to Lady Stanhope.

Most truly yours,
Macaulay

TO THOMAS FLOWER ELLIS, 5 NOVEMBER 1859

MS: Trinity College.

Holly Lodge Kensington / November 5. 1859

Dear Ellis,

I have just received the enclosed note from the Chancellor.[2]

I have written to thank him for the frankness and kindness of his communication. I have assured him that you will take no offense. But I have told him that I do not at all expect you to accept his offer. I added that, even if he found it impossible to make you a Judge in Westminster Hall, I trusted that he would have it in his power to serve you, and that I should consider any service which he could do you as an obligation laid on myself.

It strikes me that you may, with perfect propriety, write to him, and tell him that I have shown you his letter. You have an excellent opportunity for explaining your wishes and stating your claims; and I am sure that you will do so without any of the arrogance and querulousness which are often shown on such occasions by men who have less merit and less reason to complain than you. I cannot help thinking that you would do wisely not to press him about a Judgeship in Westminster Hall, but rather to drive the nail that will go, and to hint at some other situation which would suit you. There must be such; and some such must be created, if any extensive law reform is meditated.

I expect you to dinner on Tuesday. But I should like to hear from you before that time.[3]

Ever yours,
Macaulay

[1] John Gully (1783–1863: *DNB*) and Tom Cribb (1781–1848: *DNB*), both champion boxers.

[2] Offering Ellis the County Court Judgeship of Northumberland but expressing fear that the offer will insult Ellis. Campbell admitted that Ellis 'has a right to look higher, but says that he fears that it will be hardly possible to make him a Judge in Westminster Hall' (Journal, XI, 586).

[3] TBM heard from Ellis on the 7th: 'As I foresaw he will not take this place' (Journal, XI, 588).

TO ANTHONY PANIZZI, 5 NOVEMBER 1859

MS: British Museum.

Holly Lodge Kensington / November 5. 1859

Dear Panizzi,

Will you dine with me at half past seven on Saturday the 19th.[1]

Ever yours,

Macaulay

TO WILLIAM WHEWELL, 8 NOVEMBER 1859

MS: Trinity College.

Holly Lodge Kensington / November 8. 1859

Dear Whewell,

I received your Platonic Dialogues[2] yesterday evening, and have already read most of them, – no small compliment, let me tell you. For it is seldom indeed that I read a translation when I can read the original. You have succeeded beyond all expectation in making Plato interesting to the English public; and I hope that you will proceed. I should like to see your version of the Republic.[3]

Much as your volume has pleased me, I sometimes differ from you widely. I never could think the Laches genuine.[4] It is a poor performance. But I grant that from mere inferiority we cannot draw a conclusion with much confidence. Every writer must produce his worst work. But is it possible to believe that Nicias and Socrates were ever on such terms as those on which we find them associating in the Laches? Consider that Nicias was the most important citizen of Athens at the very time when Athens was greatest, and that the strongest light has been thrown on his life, character, and habits. If he had really been intimate with Socrates, if he had really stood talking philosophy by the hour with Socrates in the agora, if he really wished to put his son under the care of Socrates, would circumstances so interesting have escaped the notice of every ancient writer? Would there have been nothing about them in Plutarch? See how Plutarch describes Nicias. Οὔτε κοινολογίαςι οὔτε συνδιημερεύσιν

[1] The guests, besides Panizzi, were Milman, the Duke of Argyll, Sir Charles Wood, Henry Holland, Fitzjames Stephen, Adolphus, Ryan, and Ellis: 'the dinner good – the wine good – the waiting good and the conversation good' (Journal, XI, 593).

[2] The first volume of Whewell's *Platonic Dialogues for English Readers*, 3 vols., Cambridge, 1859–61. The translation is a kind of paraphrase with commentary.

[3] Published in the third volume of Whewell's translation.

[4] With which Whewell's volume begins. The *Laches* is among those dialogues that 'may be confidently accepted as genuine' (*Oxford Classical Dictionary*, 2nd edn, s.v. Plato).

ἐνεβάλλεν ἑαυτὸν, οὐδ᾽ ὅλως ἐσχόλαζε ταῖς τοιαύταις διατριβῖς . . . εἰ δὲ μηδὲν ἐν κοινῷ πράττειν ἔχοι, δυσπρόσοδος ἦν καὶ δυσέντευκτος ἀκουρῶν καὶ κατακεκλεισμένος.[1] Was this a man to submit himself to be publicly catechised by Socrates, like Theaetetus or Menon? Or was Plato so ignorant of the character of Nicias, or so regardless of dramatic propriety, as to turn the reserved, silent, inaccessible general and politician, whom all Athens well remembered, into a noisy disputing sophist? I believe the dialogue to be spurious, and to have been so considered by all the ancient writers: for in no other way can I account for their never mentioning the connection between two men about whom the smallest anecdotes were carefully preserved.

I differ from you also about the date of the Menon.[2] I cannot believe that it was written during the life of Socrates. The episodical introduction of Anytus has always appeared to me one of the happiest things in Plato. We see, in a few short questions and answers, the cause of the death of Socrates, his delight in making great men look small, his delight in putting others out of temper while keeping his own temper unruffled. The muttered menace with which Anytus breaks off the conversation is admirably imagined. You seem to think that, if the dialogue had been written after the death of Socrates, there would have been some more precise prediction. I own that, if the prediction had been more precise, I should have missed the wonderful delicacy of Plato's execution.

Bear with one more criticism – a very slight one. In page 427, you have departed, perhaps intentionally, from the meaning of the original, and have made Socrates appear stern and inhuman when he was really not so. You represent him as speaking with contempt of men who thought it a gain to enjoy a little longer the society of their dearest friends. That, I apprehend, is not his meaning. Ξυγγενομένους γ᾽ ἐνίους ὧυ ἀν τύχωσιν ἐπιθυμοῦντες[3] is an expression on which any Englishman who has been a criminal judge in India is competent to write a comment. In general the last request of a murderer condemned to the gallows in

[1] *Nicias*, v, 1: 'nor indulge in general interchange of views or familiar social intercourse; indeed, he had no leisure for such pastimes. . . . And even if he had no public business to transact, he was inaccessible and hard to come at, keeping close at home with his doors bolted' (Loeb translation).

[2] In a postscript of 'Remarks on the Meno' Whewell argues for a date before the death of Socrates, partly on the grounds that Plato would never have introduced Anytus after the death of Socrates without indicating that Anytus was a main cause of Socrates' death.

[3] This refers to the final phrase in a passage on page 427 of Whewell's translation of the *Phaedo*. Socrates there rejects the suggestion of Crito, who has said: 'I have known persons who have drank the poison late in the evening; who after the announcement was made to them, supped well and drank well, and enjoyed the society of their dearest friends.' The modifying participle expresses the sense 'of being with' and can easily have, as TBM supposes, a sexual meaning.

that country is to be allowed the company of a Nautch girl before his execution. It is of this sort of indulgence, and not of the society of dear friends, that Socrates speaks with disdain. I cannot help thinking that you might, without indelicacy, let this appear when your book is reprinted, as I have no doubt it soon will be.

Pardon my tediousness: remember me most kindly to my Lady; and believe me

Yours ever,
Macaulay

TO HENRY REEVE, 11 NOVEMBER [1859]

Text: J. K. Laughton, *Memoirs of Henry Reeve*, II, 35.

Holly Lodge, November 11th.

My Dear Sir,

I have just received the enclosed letter, which may, perhaps, interest you. It might be worth while to put a short note at the end of the next number of the 'Edinburgh Review.'[1]

Very truly yours,
Macaulay.

TO FRANCES MACAULAY, 15 NOVEMBER 1859

MS: Trinity College.

Holly Lodge November 15 / 1859

Dearest Fanny,

The reports which you mention are quite absurd.[2] Do you imagine that, if Lord Palmerston expected an invasion in a fortnight, the whole nation would not be called to arms? He does not warn the country. He does not, as I think that I can venture to affirm, hint any such apprehension to the Secretaries of State and to the Lord Privy Seal.[3] And am I to believe

[1] The note appears at the end of Reeve's obituary of Macaulay, *ER*, CXI (January 1860), 276; it explains that Mr Raymond of Sydney had found further evidence to confirm that Dr Campbell's Diary (see 1 June and 30 June) reached Australia through Campbell's nephew. The note concludes: 'It will be interesting to our readers to know that the materials for the article on Dr. Campbell's Diary were communicated to us by Lord Macaulay, and that this very note was, in fact, his last contribution to these pages, made within a short time of his death.'

[2] 'Wrote to Fanny who between Louis Napoleon and Dr. Cumming is frightened out of her wits' (Journal, XI, 591: 15 November).

[3] TBM's neighbor the Duke of Argyll.

that he keeps this tremendous secret from his colleagues, only in order to tell it to the gossips of Brighton? These stories are just as idle as the trash of Cumming[1] and Elliot[2] about the prophecies. If you were well acquainted with that subject, you would know that there has never been a generation since the first establishment of Christianity in which it has not been confidently asserted that the prophecies plainly referred to contemporary events, and that the end of the present dispensation was at hand. The taking of Jerusalem in the first Century, the dissolution of the Western Empire in the fifth century, the Crusades in the eleventh Century, the Thirty Years' war, the war of the Spanish Succession, the French Revolution, the conquests of Buonaparte, all have been supposed to indicate the approach of the last scene of the great drama. A hundred and thirty seven years ago Bishop Lloyd[3] of Worcester, a very learned and pious man, not less pious and much more learned than either Elliot or Cumming, proved to Queen Anne out of Daniel and the Revelations that a great and decisive crisis in human affairs was at hand. Lord Treasurer Oxford raised some objections. "Madam," said the Bishop. "I speak according to the word of God, which will be fulfilled, whether your Majesty's Treasurer likes it or not." When I was a boy, no human being doubted that Buonaparte was a principal subject of the prophecies of the old Testament. I was not born when he went to Egypt. But I have heard my father say that the prophets were then wilder than ever he remembered them. They fully expected the battle in the Valley of Jehosaphat and the restoration of the Jews within a year. The truth is that every generation is of more importance to itself than all preceding and all future generations. Every generation therefore imagines that it is of special importance in the great scheme of divine government which goes on slowly unrolling itself through thousands upon thousands of years. Our self love makes us think that visions seen in Assyria two thousand five hundred years ago must have related to us rather than to any of those who have lived before us or who are to come after us. We laugh at Bishop Lloyd who thought that these visions prefigured the French King of his time and the Sultan of his time; and we confidently maintain that they prefigure the troubles

1 Dr John Cumming (1807–81: *DNB*), minister of the National Scottish Church, Crown Court, Covent Garden, since 1832. He was one of the notable popular preachers of London for many years, specializing in anti-Catholicism and the interpretation of biblical prophecy. His latest work was *The Great Tribulation; or, the Things Coming on the Earth*, 1859, developing his contention that the 'Last Vial' was pouring out between 1848 and 1867.

2 Edward Elliott: see 26 July 1822.

3 William Lloyd (1627–1717: *DNB*); TBM describes him as a 'pious, honest, and learned man, but of slender judgment, and half crazed by his persevering endeavours to extract from Daniel and the Revelations some information about the pope and king of France' (*History*, II, 350: ch. 8). The story about Lloyd, the Queen, and Oxford is in Burnet, *History of His Own Times*, 1833, II, 345–6.

of our time. Our grandchildren will laugh at us, and will find in the Bible clear predictions of the wars which will in their time rage between South America and Australasia. Cumming and Elliot are in their calling. But I am sorry that Lord Carlisle should make such a fool of himself.[1]

Ever yours,
Macaulay

TO SIR JOHN ROMILLY, 15 NOVEMBER 1859

MS: Public Record Office.

Holly Lodge / Nov 15. 1859

Dear Romilly,

Will you give me the pleasure of your company to dinner at half past seven next Saturday, the 19th?[2]

Ever yours,
Macaulay

TO MRS HENRY THURSTAN HOLLAND, 22 NOVEMBER 1859

MS: Trinity College.

Holly Lodge Nov 22 / 1859

Dearest Baba,

I have seldom been so much vexed as by finding it impossible to get to you to day.[3] But I cannot see five yards from my window; and I am in some doubt whether this letter will reach you. It is a great disappointment to me. My love to Harry and to the dear little god son.

Ever yours,
Macaulay

TO GEORGE OTTO TREVELYAN, 22 NOVEMBER 1859

MS: Fitzwilliam Museum. *Published: Times Literary Supplement*, 9 March 1916, p. 115.

Holly Lodge Nov 22. 1859

Dear George,

Thanks for your letter. This is the day of the Christening, and the

[1] In the preface to his 'The Second Vision of Daniel,' 1858, a verse paraphrase of the eighth book of Daniel, Carlisle announced that the world was 'in all probability approaching the close of this dispensation.'

[2] Romilly did not come. For the guests, see *to* Panizzi, 5 November.

[3] Margaret's child was christened today.

hour of the Christening; and I am writing to you instead of doing my duty at the font. The reason is that the ninth plague of Egypt is upon us. The fog is such that I cannot see one tree in my garden; and, bad as things are here, the postman reports that they are worse still at Knightsbridge. If I were to venture out, we should probably have a burial in the family, as well as a christening. I therefore stay, very disconsolately, by my fire side, and wait for my footman whom I have sent to Belgravia for news, and who may perhaps find his way back through the darkness in the course of a few hours.

I am glad that you mean to pass the Christmas Vacation at home. But you must read resolutely. There is no chance of my visiting Cambridge at present. The story about my two volumes is a newspaper lie.[1] One Volume may perhaps appear two years hence.

I sympathise with the grievances of your rifle corps.[2] But there is nothing new under the sun. The young volunteers of 1803, of whom few are now left, and those few Law Lords, Archdeacons, and Professors, were treated in just the same way. My old master Preston was one of them, and retained many years a bitter sense of the injustice and incivility which they had to endure. By the bye, one of the most eager and warlike among them was Garratt,[3] the second wrangler and first Smith's prize man of 1804. This always amused me: for Garratt was quite a dwarf, – the very smallest man that I ever saw gratis.

I was delighted by Butler's success;[4] and the more so because it was unexpected. I suppose that he will be made a Doctor of Divinity without delay. My kind regards to him if he is at Cambridge, and my warm congratulations.

Sir Charles Wood, the Secretary of State for India, dined here on Saturday. I was glad to learn from him that your father is going on as well as possible, and giving the highest satisfaction to the home authorities.

Ellis told me that he had heard from you. I am of his mind about the Parmenides and about the two dialogues which cannot be separated from the Parmenides, the Politicus and the Sophista. Here Whewell agrees

[1] I have not found this.

[2] Trevelyan complained in his letter (published in the *Times Literary Supplement* with TBM's) that none of the University, county, or London authorities would pay attention to them.

[3] William Albin Garratt (1782–1858) married a daughter of the elder James Stephen: 'He was a successful barrister and a man of high character, though of diminutive stature. . . . He was for many years on the Committee of the Church Missionary Society, and wrote in defence of Evangelical principles' (Leslie Stephen, *Life of Sir James Fitzjames Stephen*, 1895, p. 29).

[4] His election to the headmastership of Harrow.

with us. But he thinks the Laches genuine; and I am sure that it is spurious. I will give you my reasons at Christmas if you care to hear them.

If you are asked to write the tripos verse of 1860, you may make an excellent eclogue on the Cambridge Rifle Corps. Menalcas, with his bow and quiver, comes to the mouth of a cave overhung with ivy and wild vines, where Daphnis and Alexis are contending in verse, with Damœtas for judge. Menalcas indignantly bids them throw away their pipes, and take to their arms. "Have you not heard that the tyrant who calls himself a Heracleid, threatens Arcadia with invasion and subjugation? All the shepherds are mustering from Cyllene to Phigalia. The beacons are ready to be lighted on the tops of Mænalus and Parthenius. The women and children are taking refuge behind the walls of Tegea and Orchomenus. There are mighty gatherings of archers and spearmen in the valleys of Ladon and Erymanthus. And you sit here disputing the prize of singing (i e the Craven scholarship) as if all were quiet." Perhaps you might bring in a fling at the Lord Lieutenant.

Ever yours,
Macaulay

TO EDWARD WALFORD,[1] 25 NOVEMBER 1859

MS: University of Iowa.

Holly Lodge Kensington / November 25. 1859

Sir,

I assure you that it is from no disrespect to yourself or to the journal of which you are the editor, that I do not comply with your request. I found it necessary, many years ago, to resolve that I would write no more for periodical works. I have pleaded my rule in answer to a multitude of applications. But, if I were now to depart from that rule, I could plead it no longer.

I return the papers which you sent me. / I have the honor to be, / Sir,
Your most obedient Servant
Macaulay

E Walford Esq / etc. etc. etc.

[1] Walford (1823–97: *DNB*), was sub-editor and then editor of *Once a Week*, 1859–65.

TO CHRISTIAN BERNHARD TAUCHNITZ, 26 NOVEMBER 1859

Text: Bernhard Tauchnitz, 1837–1887, p. 111.

Holly Lodge, Kensington, Novbr. 26, 1859.

After much consideration I am unable to suggest any way in which you can make up another volume of my miscellaneous essays.[1] Perhaps I may hereafter write something which you may print with the sketch of Pitt's life. . . . I should be much obliged to you to send me four or five copies of the little volume of my Miscellanies.[2] I have only one copy which I bought in the Palais Royal.

Very truly yours
Macaulay

TO LORD PALMERSTON, 2 DECEMBER 1859

MS: National Register of Archives.

Holly Lodge Kensington December 2. 1859

Dear Lord Palmerston,

I have considered the question which you put to me last Saturday; and I will now tell you my opinion with perfect sincerity.

There may be candidates for the Chair of Modern History at Cambridge of whom I have not heard. Of those whose names have reached me the two of most note are Dr. Latham and Mr. Helps.[3] My acquaintance with those gentlemen is the slightest possible. I have no bias towards either, except that I know Dr. Latham to be very poor, and that, for that reason, I should, if the question were one of mere private feeling, be inclined to give my voice in his favour. But private feeling has nothing to do here; and, as you have done me the honor to ask my advice, I am bound to give it you with a single view to your credit and to the public interest, which are identical.

Both these gentlemen have considerable merit. If I were asked which of them was the superior in abilities and attainments, I should find it difficult to decide. But each of them has his own proper field. If you were looking out for a Professor of Ethnology, I should say that Dr. Latham

[1] See 25 July 1859.

[2] *Biographical Essays*, 1857: see 1 August 1857.

[3] (Sir) Arthur Helps (1813–75: *DNB*), a graduate of Trinity College, had been private secretary to Spring Rice and to Lord Morpeth; he was Clerk of the Privy Council, 1860–75. He published much in many forms, and in history specialized in the Spanish discovery and conquest of the new world. On 30 November TBM bought books by both Latham and Helps 'to enable me to judge of their merits – read some of both. Like Helps's History of the Discovery of America as to substance – not as to style' (Journal, XI, 598). The appointment to the chair went not to Helps or to Latham but to Charles Kingsley.

was your man. But the part of history which has chiefly engaged his attention is so far from being modern history that it is more ancient than what we commonly call ancient history. The Romans and Greeks are to him people of yesterday. His researches go back to times before Nineveh and Memphis were built, nay, before the negro race, and the copper coloured race, and the white race, had branched off from the common stock. He will prove to you that the Magyars and the Laplanders are near of kin, and that the tribes which inhabited the Spanish peninsula, when the first Carthaginian factories were formed there, were not Celtic. As to the history of our own country, he would, I doubt not, have much that would be interesting to say about the early part of it, about the Druidical institutions and monuments, about the fusion of British, Roman, German, and Scandinavian elements in our language and in our blood. But I do not apprehend that he has made a particular study of the events of the last five centuries. Nevertheless, if you should give him this Professorship, I have no doubt that a vigorous mind like his, accustomed to close application and to historical research, would produce much that would be valuable on the subjects to which it would then be his duty to direct his attention. But the attention of Mr. Helps has long been specially directed to some very interesting and important portions of modern history. He has treated those portions of history ably and popularly. Without, therefore, pronouncing him the superior man of the two, I am forced to say that I think him the fitter of the two for the vacant Chair; and all that I hear leads me to think that, if you make choice of him, your choice will be applauded by the public.

Having thus discharged my conscience, at some cost of private feeling, I cannot help adding that I am greatly concerned for poor Latham. His talents and learning are held in high estimation both here and in foreign countries; and yet he is, I am afraid, in extreme penury. I do not wish to see pensions lavished on poets, novellists, and historians. If they write well, they can scarcely fail to find readers in plenty, and will want no other Mæcenas than Longman or Murray. But there are walks of literature and science in which a man may toil long, and diligently, and usefully, and honorably, without earning even a bare subsistence. He may display such powers and make such discoveries that his name shall be mentioned with respect in every Academy from Petersburg[1] to Madrid; and yet he may make less by the labour of his whole life than the booksellers are willing to give for some showy articles in a Review. The case of such a man seems to me to be peculiarly entitled to the attention of such a minister as your friends are proud to believe you to be. Latham seems to me to be exactly

[1] On 30 November TBM had received a diploma from the Imperial Academy of Sciences at St Petersburg (Journal, XI, 598).

the man on whom a pension would be with propriety bestowed.[1] Excuse me for offering this suggestion. I could not help it. Having myself been one of the most fortunate of literary men, one of the very few literary men whom the favour of the public has raised to opulence, I cannot but feel great compassion for writers, who, with perhaps more merit than mine, have had less popularity; and for Dr. Latham I feel peculiar compassion, because I have been compelled by a sense of duty to give, on the present occasion, an opinion adverse to his wishes. / Ever, my dear Lord Palmerston,

Yours most faithfully,
Macaulay

The / Viscount Palmerston / etc. etc. etc.

TO DONALD MACPHERSON,[2] 3 DECEMBER 1859

Text: Rothesay Express, 31 August 1892.

Holly Lodge, Kensington / December 3, 1859.

Sir,

I have just received the herrings which you were so good as to send me. They seem excellent, and remind me very agreeably of the pleasant day which I passed at Inverary in the summer. With many thanks, I remain, your faithful servant,

Macaulay.

TO LADY TREVELYAN, [3 DECEMBER 1859][3]

MS: University of Newcastle.

[Holly Lodge]

Dearest Hannah,

Our host of Inverary has sent me a firkin of Loch Fyne herrings, which seem to be in good condition. I send you a dozen, and another dozen to Chester Square.

Ever yours,
Macaulay

[1] Latham received a pension from Palmerston in 1863.

[2] Identified in the *Rothesay Express* as the proprietor of the Argyle Arms, Argyle; this was the same landlord who attemped, unsuccessfully, to pay for TBM's carriage hire (Trevelyan, II, 472).

[3] TBM notes the present of a gift of herrings from Inverary in his Journal for 4 December; but the 4th was a Sunday, and he had already acknowledged the gift on the 3rd (see preceding letter). Presumably his Journal for that day is misdated.

TO MRS HENRY THURSTAN HOLLAND, [3 DECEMBER 1859][1]

MS: Trinity College.

[Holly Lodge]

Dearest Baba,

I have just received a present of Loch Fyne herrings. As they will not keep even in this weather, I have little merit in giving them away. I send you a dozen. Send a line to say how you and Baby, and Harry are going on.

Ever yours
Macaulay

TO THOMAS FLOWER ELLIS, 17 DECEMBER 1859

MS: Trinity College.

Holly Lodge Dec 17 / 1859

Dear Ellis,

I shall expect you on Tuesday. The carriage shall be at the Club by six.

I have been miserably ill and weak.[2] Something the matter with the heart, I suspect: for I recognise the old symptoms of 1852; the fluttering, and sinking, and tendency to faintness, at the slightest exertion. My pulse, however, which, in 1852, was excessively irregular, now beats quite steadily. I shall soon know what the Doctors say.[3]

Ever yours
Macaulay

TO EDWARD EVERETT, 21 DECEMBER 1859

MS: Massachusetts Historical Society. *Extract published: New York Ledger*, 25 February 1860.

Holly Lodge Kensington / December 21. 1859

My dear Everett,

Last week I received your letter of the 29th of November; and scarcely had I read it, when your son was announced.[4] He found me at a bad time.

[1] See note on date of preceding letter.

[2] The attack began on the evening of 15 December, when TBM entertained Hannah and her children at dinner. From the next morning, as he wrote in his Journal, followed 'some of the least agreeable days of my life' (XI, 605).

[3] His physician pronounced that day that 'there is no organic affection of the heart, but that the heart is weak' (Journal, XI, 605).

[4] 15 December: 'I liked him. Uncouth certainly. . . . In essentials he seems a very good and intelligent young man' (Journal, XI, 604–5).

For a severe frost had just set in. My blood was frozen in my veins; and I could hardly speak for coughing. I was however truly glad to see him; and I hope that, whenever he stays a week or two in London, I shall see much more of him. He was just on the wing for the Speaker's. Thence he meant to go to Lord Hatherton's; and thence to Cambridge. I am assured that he has already made himself liked and esteemed among the undergraduates; and, from the short glimpse which I caught of him, I can well believe it.

There was nothing that the most austere censor could blame in his writing to me. He did not write till I had sent him, through his friend George Trevelyan, a message which it would have been unkind and ungraceful not to acknowledge.

I am truly glad that your son and George are intimate. Originally, I believe, George's motive was to please me. But he very soon found that his new friend, though not, in all points, trained according to the English pattern, was, in parts and character, one of the first young men in the University. [. . .][1]

TO THOMAS FLOWER ELLIS, 25 DECEMBER 1859

MS: Trinity College. *Mostly published:* Trevelyan, II, 477.

Holly Lodge Xmas Day 1859

Dear Ellis,

I send a line, as you desired, though it will tell you only that I am much as I was. The physicians think me better; but there is little change in my sensations. The day before yesterday I had a regular fainting fit, and lay quite insensible. I wish that I had continued to lie so. For if death be no more – Up I got however; and the Doctors agree that the circumstance is altogether unimportant.[2]

I hope that you will be able to come next Saturday. At all events, write from Leeds.

Ever yours
Macaulay

[1] In the article for the *New York Ledger* in which this letter is quoted Everett says that it was not finished but was found in TBM's pocket after his death.

[2] TBM died three days later, on the evening of the 28th, at Holly Lodge.

LETTERS OF UNCERTAIN DATE
1839–1859?

TO SAMUEL ROGERS, [1839–52][1]

MS: Harvard University.

Dear Mr. Rogers,

I am truly sorry to say that on Friday I have asked Miss Berry to breakfast with me. Anybody but a lady I would put off.

Ever yours
T B Macaulay

TO DR J. GRANT [1839–57][2]

MS: Bodleian Library. *Address:* Dr J Grant / etc. etc. etc. *Subscription:* T B Macaulay.

My dear Sir,

I am no Connoisseur in curiosities of this kind. The missal is certainly very prettily written and illustrated. As to its country all that is clear to me is that it must have been in England about three hundred years ago. As to its date, the reference to Philip of France whom I take to be Philip le Bel would fix it early in the fourteenth Century. But I speak quite as one of the unlearned.

Yours truly
T B Macaulay

TO THOMAS FLOWER ELLIS, [1839–57]

MS: Mr F. R. Cowell.

Dear Ellis,

I will dine with you on Thursday, I suppose at seven. Have you company? Will you dine with me on Friday? Heaven confound the beastly iron nails that you use instead of pens.

Ever yours
T B Macaulay

1 TBM gave no breakfasts before his return from India in 1839; the other limit is the death of Miss Berry in 1852. The early or mid-1840s seems the most likely date.

2 I have not identified Grant. TBM is not likely to have received inquiries of the sort that this letter implies before the success of the *History* in 1849, but the date of such a letter as this can only be conjectured within broad limits.

TO [FRANCES MACAULAY?], 23 JUNE [1841–9][1]

MS: Mr W. Hugh Peal.

Albany London / June 23

[ ][2]

I will try to learn in what way the thing can be done with most advantage to you. I shall probably see Edward before the time fixed for payment. If not, I will write to him.

Ever yours
T B Macaulay

TO EDWARD ROMILLY,[3] 24 FEBRUARY [1841–56][4]

MS: University of Texas.

Albany Feb 24

My dear Sir,

I am truly sorry that I have an engagement on Saturday next which will make it impossible for me to have the pleasure of dining with you and Mrs. Edward Romilly.[5]

Ever yours truly
T B Macaulay

TO JOHN LEYCESTER ADOLPHUS, [1841–56]

MS: Columbia University.

Albany – Monday evening

Dear Adolphus,

I have just learned that you are in town. Come and breakfast here at ten to morrow if you can.

Ever yours
T B Macaulay

Ellis breakfasts here. Come with him.

[1] I conjecture that the letter is to Fanny, probably concerning her allowance, part of which, until 1849, was paid by Edward Cropper. The other date is established by TBM's residence in the Albany.

[2] The letter has been mutilated, and though parts of the salutation remain they are illegible.

[3] Romilly (1804–70: *DNB*), third son of Sir Samuel Romilly, was Commissioner of the Board of Audit, 1837–66, and Chairman, 1855–65, when Charles Macaulay was secretary to the Board.

[4] The dates of TBM's residence in the Albany.

[5] Sophia, daughter of TBM's old acquaintance Mrs Marcet (see 10 June 1831).

TO SIR DAVID DUNDAS, [1841–56]

MS: National Library of Scotland.

Albany Saturday

Dear Dundas,

Breakfast here next Thursday at ten.

Ever yours
T B Macaulay

TO WILLIAM WHEWELL, [1841–57][1]

MS: Mr F. R. Cowell.

Dear Whewell,

I shall be delighted to dine with you in Trinity College Lodge.

Ever yours truly
T B Macaulay

TO BISHOP SAMUEL WILBERFORCE, [1845–56][2]

MS: Bodleian Library.

Albany Tuesday

My dear Bishop of Oxford,

I am sorry to say that I am poorly, and must not venture to breakfast with you to morrow.

Ever yours,
T B Macaulay

TO [THOMAS LONGMAN], [1847–57][3]

MS: University of Iowa.

My dear Sir,

I am extremely sorry that I am forced to go to the British Museum this morning, on business of great importance. As soon as the Committee of

[1] The years from the beginning of Whewell's mastership to TBM's peerage, to any one of which this note might belong.

[2] The limiting dates are those of Wilberforce's appointment to the Bishopric of Oxford and the end of TBM's residence in the Albany.

[3] The dates are those of TBM's appointment as one of the trustees of the British Museum and his elevation to the peerage.

which I am a member rises I will go to Paternoster Row, and take my chance of finding you there.

Very truly yours
T B Macaulay

TO MRS GROVE,[1] [*c.* 1849][2]

MS: Mrs Michael Millgate.

Albany Wednesday

Dear Mrs. Grove,

I am extremely sorry that on Thursday evening I must be at a party some miles from London, and shall be unable to have the pleasure of joining your circle.

Very truly yours
T B Macaulay

TO THOMAS FLOWER ELLIS, [1849–59][3]

Text: Trevelyan, II, 418.

[. . .] so vivid that I must tell it. She came to me with a penitential face, and told me that she had a great sin to confess; that Pepys's Diary was all a forgery, and that she had forged it. I was in the greatest dismay. "What! I have been quoting in reviews, and in my History, a forgery of yours as a book of the highest authority. How shall I ever hold my head up again?" I woke with the fright, poor Alice's supplicating voice still in my ears.

TO THOMAS LONGMAN, [1849–59][4]

Text: Trevelyan, II, 413–14.

I have received a rather queer letter, purporting to be from the wife of

[1] Possibly the wife of (Sir) William Robert Grove (1811–96: *DNB*), a barrister, judge, and distinguished physicist.

[2] Dated from watermark.

[3] TBM was reading Pepys in a 'new edition' in November 1848 (Journal, I, 410), but that is hardly evidence for a date. One can say only that the letter is after the publication of the *History* at the end of 1848. Alice is, of course, his niece Alice Trevelyan.

[4] Dated only by the reference to the sham Mary Howitt, described thus in the Journal for 14 November 1849: 'Roused by a letter from Mrs. Howitt whom I never saw in my life, asking for money. She and her husband have ruined themselves by some absurd speculation and have taken to begging. Sent her ten pounds' (II, 146). Two weeks later TBM learned from Longman that the letter was a forgery: 'Strange. I can hardly help doubting' (II, 156).

Mr. D—, the author of —, and dated from Greenwich. Now, I have once or twice received similar letters which have afterwards turned out to be forgeries. I sent ten pounds to a sham Mary Howitt,[1] who complained that an unforeseen misfortune had reduced her to poverty; and I can hardly help suspecting that there may be a sham Mrs. D—. If, however, the author of — is really in distress, I would gladly assist him, though I am no admirer of his poetry. Could you learn from his publishers whether he really lives at Greenwich? If he does, I will send him a few pounds. If he does not, I will set the police to work.

TO GEORGE OTTO TREVELYAN, [1851–7][2]

Text: Trevelyan, II, 422.

It is said, that the best part of a lady's letter is the postscript. The best part of an uncle's is under the seal.[3]

TO SIR CHARLES TREVELYAN, [1852?–6][4]

MS: Trinity College.

Albany

Dear Trevelyan,

I cannot venture out to day.

Ever yours

T B M

TO THOMAS FLOWER ELLIS, [FEBRUARY? 1854?][5]

MS: Trinity College. *Published:* Trevelyan, II, 357.

Dear Ellis,

I send you a treasure. I do believe that it is the autograph of the great Robert Montgomery. Pray let me have it again. I would not lose such a

[1] The real Mary Howitt (1799–1888: *DNB*), with her husband William, was a prolific miscellaneous writer, especially of children's books.

[2] Written during Trevelyan's years at Harrow, i.e., from the Easter term of 1851 to July 1857, and probably in the earlier part of that period.

[3] Trevelyan says that TBM sealed his letters to him at Harrow 'with an amorphous mass of red wax, which, in defiance of post-office regulations, not unfrequently concealed a piece of gold' (II, 422).

[4] Presumably written after the failure of TBM's health in 1852.

[5] Possibly this refers to the 'letters from Montgomery' that TBM sent to Ellis in early 1850 (see 6 April 1850); but it may also refer to Montgomery's protest of late February 1854 (see 4 March 1854). I have preferred the later date, though without clear evidence.

jewel on any account. I have read it, as Mr. Montgomery desires, in the presence of God; and in the presence of God I pronounce it to be incomparable.

Ever yours
T B Macaulay

TO MRS GEORGE ALEXANDER MALCOLM,[1] [1854?][2]

MS: Yale University.

Dear Mrs. Malcolm,

I seldom venture out in the evening. But I would not deny myself the pleasure of joining your party, were it not that I expect a visit which will detain me at home.

Very truly yours,
T B Macaulay

TO WILLIAM WHEWELL, [1855?][3]

MS: Trinity College.

Bull Inn Cambridge

Dear Master,

I shall be delighted to avail myself of your hospitality; and so will my companions be. I will venture to bring to hall my nephew George Trevelyan, who will disappoint us much if he is not entitled to a seat at the fellows' table some eight years hence. My sister and niece will be most happy to join Mrs. Whewell's tea table after chapel.

Ever yours truly,
T B Macaulay

[1] See 28 April 1854.

[2] Conjectured from the fact that her name appears in the Journal only twice, in April and May of 1854.

[3] The reference to George Trevelyan's becoming a fellow 'eight years hence' suggests the date of 1854: Trevelyan entered Trinity in October 1857, took his degree in 1861, and in the normal course of things might have expected election to a fellowship in 1862 – i.e., eight years from 1854. But there is no evidence that TBM travelled to Cambridge with Hannah, Margaret, and George Trevelyan in 1854. He did make such a trip in 1856, but in the Journal account of this there is no mention of dining in hall or of seeing Whewell, nor was there any time in the record of the day that they might have done so. This leaves the spring of 1855 as the compromise date; TBM did not keep his Journal between 24 February and 6 November in that year, so that there is at least no evidence against the choice of a date then.

TO [HARPER AND BROTHERS],[1] [EARLY 1856?][2]

Text: Facsimile in R. H. Stoddart, 'Lord Macaulay and His Friends,' *Harper's*, LIII (1876), 91.

If you should reprint the first two volumes, I hope that you will follow the text of the fourth edition which I have corrected in many places. / I have the honor to be, / Gentlemen,

Your obedient Servant
T B Macaulay

TO NASSAU SENIOR, [BEFORE SEPTEMBER 1857]

MS: Mr Walter Leuba.

Dear Senior,

I am extremely sorry to say that on Wednesday I am engaged.

Ever yours
T B Macaulay

TO UNIDENTIFIED RECIPIENT, [BEFORE SEPTEMBER 1857]

Text: Facsimile in Lawrence B. Phillips, *The Autographic Album*, 1866, p. 158.

I am very sensible of the honor which you have done me. I am sorry that my knowledge of French is not such as to enable me to judge of your diction, [. . .]

T B Macaulay

TO THOMAS LONGMAN, [1857?][3]

Text: Trevelyan, II, 230n.

I have no more corrections to make at present. I am inclined to hope that the book will be as nearly faultless, as to typographical execution, as any work of equal extent that is to be found in the world.

1 Publishers of the authorized American edition of the *History*.

2 The reference to the first two volumes implies the existence of volumes 3 and 4 – i.e., sometime after 1855. TBM probably would not have specified the fourth edition (April 1849) as a copy-text after May 1856, when he began correcting for the revised edition of 1857–8. The probable occasion of this letter is thus a reprinting of the first part of the *History* early in 1856 to meet the interest created by the recent publication of the second part.

3 TBM corrected proofs of the 1857–8 edition of the *History* between 29 May 1856 and 29 May 1858 (Journal, XI, 4–324). The main effort lay in 1857, when he repeatedly wrote of his intention to make the edition as accurate as possible typographically (e.g., 2 and 25 August 1857).

TO HENRY HALLAM, [1857–9][1]

MS: University of Amsterdam.

Dear Hallam,

I will breakfast with you on Thursday with much pleasure.

Ever yours
Macaulay

TO ALICE TREVELYAN, [1858?][2]

Text: Trevelyan, II, 399n.

[Holly Lodge]

My dear little Alice,

I quite forgot my promised letter, but I assure you that you were never out of my mind for three waking hours together. I have, indeed, had little to put you and yours out of my thoughts; for I have been living, these last ten days, like Robinson Crusoe in his desert island. I have had no friends near me, but my books and my flowers, and no enemies but those execrable dandelions. I thought that I was rid of the villains; but the day before yesterday, when I got up and looked out of my window, I could see five or six of their great, impudent, flaring, yellow faces turned up at me. "Only you wait till I come down," I said. How I grubbed them up! How I enjoyed their destruction! Is it Christian like to hate a dandelion so savagely? That is a curious question of casuistry.

[1] This must have been written at some time between TBM's peerage in September 1857 and Hallam's death in January 1859, but I can find no record in the Journal for that period of a Thursday breakfast with Hallam.

[2] TBM's war with the dandelions seems to have intensified in this year, as recorded, for example, in this Journal entry: 'grubbed up dandelions – now a daily pastime' (XI, 304: 5 May 1858). The only letter to Alice at that time of which I have found record is entered in his Journal for 20 August (XI, 362).

ADDITIONAL LETTERS
4 MARCH 1831–16 DECEMBER 1848

TO [RICHARD SHARP?], 4 MARCH 1831

MS: Mrs Michael Millgate.

Gray's Inn March 4. 1831

My dear Sir,

I thank you most heartily for your kind congratulations.[1] I certainly succeeded beyond what I had expected; and I must say, without any mock-modesty, that I am still amazed at the favour with which my speech was received.

I have been solicited by several of our friends to print it. I have not absolutely made up my mind. But I think that I shall do so.

I hope that we shall meet soon. If I should not see you at dinner on Saturday at Sir G Philips's, or on Sunday at Mr. Boddington's, I will call on you.

Ever yours truly
T B Macaulay

TO LADY HOLLAND, [*c.* 15 SEPTEMBER 1831][2]

MS: British Museum. *Address:* The / Lady Holland. *Extract published:* Sonia Keppel, *The Sovereign Lady*, 1974, p. 294.

Dear Lady Holland,

I had not time, in our short conversation, to explain fully my opinions respecting the present crisis; nor have I now time to explain them fully in writing. I will tell you in a few lines what I know and what I think.

The question is this – If the Reform Bill is lost, ought the Ministers to resign? I have conversed on this subject with people of different ranks and of different shades of opinion; and I have heard only one answer. The unanimous sentiment is this – that if the ministers resign they will prove themselves to be men unfit for their station – small men unhappily called to power at a great crisis – that they will act unfairly towards the King, and towards the people who have supported them. A very distinguished Member of the House of Commons, – a County Member, – the heir to a peerage, – said to me a few days ago, "You know my personal attachment to the ministers. You know my public conduct. I have stood by them for twenty years. If they resign in consequence of the decision of the Lords, I have done with them. My confidence in them is at an end for ever."

[1] On TBM's first Reform Bill speech, 2 March.

[2] See TBM's letters of 13 and 15 September 1831, discussing the political crisis of that week. The question was this: if the Lords threw out the Reform Bill, should the Ministers resign? or should they force the King to create new peers in order to secure a majority in the House of Lords?

This is but a single instance. I have heard expressions as strong from at least twenty members for populous places. In fact it is difficult to convince the ministerial Members of the House of Commons that the ministers can possibly think of resigning at such a crisis as this.

The feeling of the Majority in the House of Commons is reasonable. The present Ministers have the confidence of that House; and might, by a very moderate exercise of the undoubted prerogative of the crown, secure a majority in the Lords. A ministry composed of the present opposition would be in a minority in the House of Commons, and could not, I think, obtain a majority by a dissolution. The present ministers have therefore a decided advantage over their opponents. Why then retire? This is what the nation will ask. They may retain their power if they chuse. Why do they not chuse? The answer is obvious. Because they do not wish their bill to be carried. Because they are in their hearts enemies to reform. Because they shrink from the popular measures which they inadvertently introduced. Because they love the present representative system even more than they love place. This is already whispered. It will, if the ministers should now flinch, be loudly proclaimed. They will be accused, – not of weakness, – but of treason. No political party ever fell into such contempt as awaits them. The downfall of Pulteney[1] was nothing to what the downfall of Lord Grey will be. The State may be saved; and I believe will be saved. The House of Commons will save it. But the present ministry and the Whig connection will be lost for ever. If those who are bidden, as the parable says, will not come to the wedding, we must ransack the highways and hedges.[2] Somewhere men will be found, – resolute men, – men, who will not keep the empire in agitation for six or seven months and then run away for fear of their own shadows. I cannot tell you how anxiously I look forward to the events of this week. / Believe me, dear Lady Holland

Yours most faithfully
T B Macaulay

[1] William Pulteney (1684–1764: *DNB*), Whig statesman, whose refusal of office and acceptance of the title of Earl of Bath in 1742 destroyed his political influence.

[2] Luke 14:23.

TO [RICHARD SHARP?], 12 OCTOBER 1831

MS: Mrs Michael Millgate.

[London] Octr. 12. 1831

Dear Sir,

I write a single line to assure you of the pleasure and gratitude with which I have read your kind note.[1] / Ever, Dear Sir,

Yours faithfully
T B Macaulay

TO UNIDENTIFIED RECIPIENT, 28 OCTOBER 1831

MS: Trinity College.

Gray's Inn Octr. 28 / 1831

Dear Sir,

I have franked the three letters which you transmitted to me. My franks for Sunday the 30th I have given to the Anti-slavery Society, so that I fear I can be of no use to you on that day. / Believe me, / Dear Sir,

Yours very truly
T B Macaulay

TO DERWENT COLERIDGE, 27 DECEMBER 1832

MS: University of Texas.

London Decr. 27. 1832

Dear Derwent,

I should be truly glad to be of service to you.[2] But I very much doubt whether the enclosed letter will serve you or injure you. Do what you like with it. I should advise you to burn it. Stamford is all on fire with political fury. The Mayor is, I suspect, in the interest of the Marquess of Exeter.[3] The Marquess is the fiercest and most intolerant of Tories. It is therefore probable that my attestation will do you more harm than good. I have, as you will see, worded my letter in such a way as to exempt you

[1] Probably a note of congratulation on TBM's speech of 10 October, on Lord Ebrington's motion of support for the ministry. This followed just after the Lords had thrown out the Bill and was one of the more threatening of TBM's Reform speeches – 'as inflammatory as possible,' Greville thought (*Memoirs*, II, 207).

[2] Coleridge was a candidate for the mastership of the Stamford grammar school: see the letter of the same date following this.

[3] Brownlow Cecil (1795–1867), third Marquess, Lord Lieutenant of Rutland, 1826–67.

from all suspicion of being a reformer. If I can learn where Tennyson,[1] the late M P for Stamford, is passing his Christmas, I will write to him, and ascertain who the Mayor is, and by what means we are most likely to succeed in that quarter.

I had the pleasure of meeting your brother[2] during my late visit to Leeds. He reminded me strongly of you – no compliment to your person, you will say. He has brought out two or three Numbers of a work entitled "Worthies of Yorkshire," – which I like much. The life of Bentley is capital, – that of Mason not amiss, – that [of][3] Ascham good.[4] The rest I have not yet found time to read.

Remember me kindly to Mrs. Coleridge,[5] and believe me ever, / Dear Derwent,

Yours most truly
T B Macaulay

TO DERWENT COLERIDGE, 27 DECEMBER 1832

MS: University of Texas.

London December 27. 1832

My dear Coleridge,

I have just learned that you are a candidate for the Headmastership of the School at Stamford, and that you think that my good word might be of use to you. I fear that you overrate my power to serve you. But you have a right to command my attestation. I know your talents to be worthy of the name which you bear. I know your temper to be such as cannot fail to make you loved by all who may be placed under your superintendance.

Long as we have been separated, and widely as we differ in our opinions concerning many important and exciting questions, I still remember our early intimacy with the greatest pleasure. I shall always be happy to hear

[1] Charles Tennyson, uncle of the poet; M.P. for Stamford, 1831–2. See 24 June 1831.

[2] Hartley Coleridge (1796–1849: *DNB*), then living in Leeds with the publisher F. E. Bingley. The eccentric and unsuccessful Hartley, noted for his equal brilliance and erraticness, was diminutive, awkward, and prematurely white-haired. He wrote of this meeting with TBM that 'he was very gracious and spoke of his remembrance of Derwent at College. I can't say I was smitten with him at all – he does not seem to be a Liberal of the right, i.e. of the Xtian philanthropic sort. He is not a Clarkson. He is, however, perfectly a Gentleman and this, you Tories will say, is something for a member of the Reformed' (G. E. and E. L. Griggs, eds., *Letters of Hartley Coleridge*, 1936, p. 150).

[3] Paper torn away with seal.

[4] Three numbers of the *Worthies of Yorkshire and Lancashire*, 1832, a series that Hartley undertook for Bingley, appeared before the publisher's bankruptcy put an end to publication. The thirteen biographies included the lives of Richard Bentley, the Reverend William Mason, and Roger Ascham.

[5] Derwent married Mary Pridham in 1827.

of your success, and still more happy to be able to promote it.[1] / Believe me ever, / My dear Coleridge,

Yours most faithfully
T B Macaulay

TO UNIDENTIFIED RECIPIENT, 11 FEBRUARY 1833

MS: Trinity College.

London Feby. 11. 1833

Sir,

I have received your letter and the accompanying volume for which I am greatly obliged to you. I have not had time to read the book. But I see at a glance that it is a book which, if well executed, must be very useful.

I have sent Mr. Auber's[2] parcel. / I have the honor to be, / Sir,

Your most obedient Servant
T B Macaulay

TO ROBERT WILBERFORCE, 15 AUGUST 1833

MS: Bodleian Library. *Address:* Rev R Wilberforce / East Farleigh / Maidstone (in another hand). *Frank:* London August fifteen 1833 / T B Macaulay.

London August 15 1833

Dear Wilberforce,

I shall be most happy to be of any use to your undertaking. I hope that you will avail yourself of my privilege without the least scruple.[3]

The members of parliament who followed the remains of your father to their fit place among the tombs of the great men of England deserve no thanks. They did honor to themselves. They could do none to him. Least of all do I deserve any thanks. For I was bound to him by private as well as by public ties. I felt towards him not only that gratitude which all Englishmen and all human beings were bound to feel, but also the warmest personal affection. I can remember him as early as I can remember any thing: and I can remember nothing of him but the most endearing kindness.

[1] Coleridge remained at Helston grammar school until 1841, when he was appointed principal of St Mark's College.

[2] Peter Auber, the Secretary to the East India Company.

[3] See TBM's letter to Hannah, 15 August 1833. Wilberforce had asked to use TBM's franking privilege in order to assist his work on the biography of his father.

I do not know that I can be of any use to your projected work, except in the very humble way which you point out. But if it occurs to you that, by means of my connections either literary or political, any information could be obtained tending to illustrate your subject, I shall be most happy to give all the assistance in my power.

Remember me in the kindest manner to your mother and believe me ever, / Dear Wilberforce,

Yours most faithfully
T B Macaulay

TO JOHN MOULTRIE, 11 FEBRUARY 1835

Text: Copy, University of Texas. *Extract published:* see vol. III, 135.

Calcutta Feb 11. 1835

Dear Moultrie

Your letter introducing your friend Mr. Dunlop was left at my house when I was in no frame of mind to receive visitors or to answer letters. I had just heard news from England which had broken my heart, and from the effects of which I am recovering only by slow degrees, and many alterations.[1] I was in exile supported in a strange land chiefly by the hope of returning to my country. I had lost that which, more than anything else, made my country dear to me. My sisters have been everything to me. But for them the violence of my passions, and the peculiar circumstances in which I have been placed, would have made me a depraved man, and a mere mixture of libertine and political adventurer. To my two younger sisters I owe it that neither voluptuousness nor ambition have, as I think, impaired the stamina of my character, and that I am, if anything, more open-hearted and more susceptible of the kind affections than I was in our college days. But the affection of brothers for sisters, blameless and amiable as it is beyond almost any human affection, is yet so liable to be interrupted that no man ought to suffer it to become necessary to him. I did not consider this. I permitted my feelings to acquire such a dominion over me that even the separation which was the effect of my youngest sister's marriage was a source of bitter and long continued pain to me. Yet her marriage by no means estranged her affections from me. In England we had plenty of opportunities of meeting. She was the most constant of my correspondents. The hope of seeing her again was the most delightful subject of my thoughts. It is now little more than five weeks since the news of her death reached me. I had

[1] Thus in the text. There are several other doubtful readings in this copy.

never known what it was to be miserable before. I should not go on pouring out private feelings in this way even to so kind and old a friend as you were it not that a letter which I received about a fortnight ago from my father contained some lines of yours about my dear Margaret.[1] You know what I always thought of your poetical powers. I have never relinquished the hope of seeing you establish a lasting literary fame. But of these lines I cannot speak as a critic. I do not know whether they are good or bad. But they have moved me and my sister who is now with me here in a manner which I cannot describe to you. She begs me to thank you for them most warmly. Her society and affection are the greatest comfort to me. She is married most happily. Her husband, a young man of very distinguished talents and of high character, resides with me, and we form a most harmonious family. Your kindness for me will make you rejoice to hear that I have excellent health, that the climate agrees with me, that there is nothing distasteful to me in my public duties or in the tempers of those with whom I have to act, and that my salary enables me to live splendidly, to make my father's old age comfortable, to educate my youngest brother, to support my sisters who remain in England, and to lay by what in a very few years will amount to an independence sufficient for a man of simple tastes and habits.

Whatever I hear of you gives me true pleasure. You might have done and, if you choose, may still do great things. But I cannot blame your choice if you despise greatness and are content with happiness. In less than four years I hope to be again in England, where we shall meet, I trust, and talk over old times and over the adventures of all our Cambridge friends whom the chances of this rough world have scattered through vast countries, professions, and factions. Give my kindest regards and remembrances, I cannot say to Mrs. Moultrie,[2] but to your neighbours my dear cousin, Mrs. Rose,[3] and all her family. You are quite right in saying that there are very few such women. With all kind wishes, / Believe me dear Moultrie

Yours affectionately
T B Macaulay

[1] Moultrie's 'To Margaret in Heaven': see 20 June 1823, note 2.

[2] Moultrie married Harriet Margaret Fergusson in 1825.

[3] TBM's cousin Lydia Babington Rose (see 8 May 1813, note 2). Her daughter, also Lydia, married the Rugby master Bonamy Price in 1834. Moultrie was Rector of Rugby and a friend of Price.

TO UNIDENTIFIED RECIPIENT, 12 JUNE 1840

MS: Osborn Collection, Yale University.

London June 12. 1840

Sir,

Before I can come to any resolution on the subject of your letter I must be fully satisfied that the proposed monument is likely to be a distinguished work of art.[1] The beautiful city which I have the honor to represent is already deformed by some of the most hideous structures in the world. And I am fully resolved not to assist in adding to the number.

Do not imagine that I mean in the least to express an opinion that the proposed monument will not be a very fine one. But not knowing even who the architect is, and never having heard any mention of it from any of my Edinburgh friends on whose taste I can rely, I cannot at once decide.

I have written to Edinburgh for information. / I have the honor to be, / Sir,

Your obedient humble Servant
T B Macaulay

TO UNIDENTIFIED RECIPIENT, 18 NOVEMBER 1840

MS: Mr John Clive.

London Nov 18. 1840

Sir,

I am greatly obliged by your communication. I think that you have acted with very great judgment; and I heartily congratulate you on your well-merited success. / I have the honor to be, / Sir,

Your faithful servant
T B Macaulay

TESTIMONIAL TO DERWENT COLERIDGE, 23 JANUARY 1841[2]

MS: University of Texas.

I had the happiness of being acquainted with the Reverend Derwent Coleridge at the University of Cambridge. Our friendship commenced

[1] The monument to Sir Walter Scott in Edinburgh, to which TBM subscribed 20 guineas (see 12 and 18 June 1840).

[2] Coleridge was the successful candidate for the Principalship of St Mark's College, Chelsea, opened in 1841 by the National Society for Promoting the Education of the Poor. His appointment was announced on 3 February (*The Times*, 8 February 1841). This letter was no doubt part of his official application for the post.

in the year 1820, and during the three following years we lived on terms of brotherly intimacy. Since we left college, we have very seldom met. We adopted different professions, and attached ourselves to hostile political parties. But my regard for Mr. Coleridge continues unabated; and I still remember our early intercourse with great pleasure.

From what I have said it will be readily inferred that his character was such as to inspire attachment and esteem. Indeed I have never known a person who, in the circle in which he was known, was more generally or more justly beloved.

His talents, at the time of which I speak, were considered, not only by myself, but by others of whose approbation he might more justly be proud, as worthy of the distinguished name which he inherits; and I have no hesitation in pronouncing him qualified for posts of far greater dignity and importance than that which he is now seeking.

T B Macaulay

War Office. London / Jan 23. 1841

TO DERWENT COLERIDGE, 11 JULY 1844

MS: University of Texas.

Albany July 11 / 1844

Dear Coleridge,

I do not know why you should call me Sir, though it is now long since we have seen much of each other: and you must at least excuse me if I do not imitate your example. I would with the greatest pleasure join your party if I were not engaged. But I shall be forced to be in less agreeable company than that which you ask me to join.

Ever yours truly
T B Macaulay

TO [HENRY COTTON?][1], 16 DECEMBER 1848

Text: From MS in possession of Mr R. G. E. Sandbach, who furnished transcript.

Albany. Dec 16. 1848

My dear Sir,

I return with many thanks your volume of Quisquiliae. It contains

[1] Cotton (1789–1879: *DNB*), Dean of Linsmore, published a series of Latin squibs on Oxford personalities in 1819 entitled *Eruditis Oxoniae Amantibus Salutem*; this was republished in 1854 or 1855 as *Quisquiliae Volantes*. It may, perhaps, be the work to which this letter refers; but any collection of such material might qualify for TBM's term 'quisquiliae.'

some curious lampoons which I do not remember to have seen elsewhere; but they are of a later date than the part of my history with which I am at present concerned. Perhaps I may on some future occasion ask you to let me look at them again.

Very truly yours,
T B Macaulay

APPENDIXES

ADDITIONS AND CORRECTIONS

Volume I
p. xxi, lines 36-7: the epitaph is not inscribed at Rothley
p. 47, line 13: *for* that that *read* than that
p. 61, note 2: *for* 3 Esdras *read* 1 Esdras
p. 69, note 1, line 5: *for* read *Don Quixote* in the original *read* read *Don Quixote* except in the original
p. 178, note 4: *for* Chauncy *read* Chauncey
p. 196, note 1, line 2: *for* 1783 *read* 1773
p. 221, note 2, line 4: *for* 1850–1 *read* 1846–50
p. 285, note 5: This is not the James Dunn mentioned in the first part of the note, for he later became a clergyman in Ireland and a friend of the Clapham Sect (information from Mr J. A. Scotland).
p. 306, line 26: *for* a *read* at
p. 317, note, line 2: *for* 2 vols., 1837 *read* 3 vols., 1837
p. 323: The proofsheets of TBM's *History of France* were discovered and published by Joseph Hamburger as *Napoleon and the Restoration of the Bourbons*, 1977.

Volume II
p. vii, under June 13: Reform Bill dinner speech is 15 June
p. 4, entries for January 11 and 12 omitted: *cf.* p. vii
p. 39, line 14: *for* women *read* woman
p. 71, line 7: *delete* would
p. 90, note 3: *for* 1775 *read* 1774
p. 114, line 2: *for* Unidentified Recipient *substitute* William Rider; *delete* ? *after* 25?. Rider, a stay-maker, was Secretary of the Radical Reform Union of Leeds. TBM's letter was printed, with a letter from Rider, in *Cobbett's Political Register*, LXX (3 March 1832), 611–12 (information from Mr Philip Hamburger).
p. 114, line 4: *substitute* London, February 25, 1832
p. 157, line 8: TBM is referring to Lady Theresa, née Villiers. See p. 138, note 3.
p. 157, lines 16–17: *after* 'She called him Tom. How delightful!' *insert note 6a*: Jane Austen, *Emma*, ch. 32: 'He called her "Augusta." How delightful!'
p. 261, note 4: *for* August *read* Augusta
p. 275, line 20: for *his* read *this*

Volume III
p. 34, line 1: a comma after 'son' has been suggested and seems a highly likely

conjecture: 'Godson' would then be parallel with 'son,' and not, as I had thought, a proper name. Wellington had numerous godsons, one of whom, Arthur Freese, was in the Indian Civil Service.

p. 149, note 4: *For* The Asiatic Society of Bengal, founded by Warren Hastings *read* The Asiatick Society of Bengal, founded by Sir William Jones and under the patronage of the Governor General

p. 154, note 1: *For* Cicero *read* Demosthenes

Volume IV

p. 102: add numeral before note 3

p. 124, note 3: lower numeral to next line

p. 150: misnumbered 159

p. 159, line 8: *delete hyphen in* D'Au-bigné's

p. 193, letter of 24 May 1844: *correct to* 29 May 1844 (MS, Trinity).

p. 208, note 1: *for* 23 *read* 20

A LIST OF MACAULAY'S PUBLISHED WRITINGS

No full bibliography of Macaulay exists. This is, therefore, a first attempt to provide a complete, authenticated list.

I have extended the term 'published' to include those of Macaulay's speeches that were printed at the time of their delivery, though of course more often than not he had no control over the texts produced, including most of those appearing in *Hansard*.

For a discussion of the evidence in support of the attributions of various unacknowledged writings, see my 'Notes on Macaulay's Unacknowledged and Uncollected Writings,' *Papers of the Bibliographical Society of America*, LXVII (1973), 17–31.

I *Juvenilia*

'A Hymn' [*c.* 1808], *London Scottish Regimental Gazette*, II (June 1897), 92; separately reprinted, ed. Lionel Horton-Smith, Cambridge, Metcalfe and Co., 1902.

[Nature of an Auto-da-Fé], *Christian Observer*, X (March 1811), 161–2. [A collaboration between TBM and his sister Selina].

'Epitaph on Henry Martyn' [1813], *The Miscellaneous Writings of Lord Macaulay*, 2 vols., London, Longman, Green, Longman, and Roberts, 1860, II, 377.

'Lines to the Memory of Pitt' [1814], *Miscellaneous Writings*, II, 378.

'Observations on Novel Reading,' *Christian Observer*, XV (December 1816), 784–7.

'To the Editor of the Christian Observer,' *Christian Observer*, XVI (April 1817), 23–31. [A further contribution on the question of novel reading].

'Paraphrase of the Prophecy of Nahum,' *Christian Observer*, XIX (March 1820), 169–70. [Written *c.* 1818?].

'Venus Crying Cupid whom She Has Lost' [April 1820], Lady Knutsford, *Life and Letters of Zachary Macaulay*, 1900, p. 354.

II *Essays*

'Essay on the Life and Character of King William III' [1822], *Times Literary Supplement*, 1 May 1969, pp. 468–9.

'Fragments of a Roman Tale,' *Knight's Quarterly Magazine*, I (June 1823), 33–44.

'On West Indian Slavery,' *Knight's Quarterly Magazine*, I (June 1823), 85–94.

'On the Royal Society of Literature,' *Knight's Quarterly Magazine*, I (June 1823), 111–17.

'Scenes from "Athenian Revels",' *Knight's Quarterly Magazine*, II (January 1824), 17–33.

'Criticisms on the Principal Italian Writers. No. I. Dante,' *Knight's Quarterly Magazine*, II (January 1824), 207–23.

'Criticisms on the Principal Italian Writers. No. II. Petrarch,' *Knight's Quarterly Magazine*, II (April 1824), 355–68.

'Some Account of the Great Law-Suit Between the Parishes of St. Dennis and St. George in the Water Part I,' *Knight's Quarterly Magazine*, II (April 1824), 404–11.

'A Conversation between Mr. Abraham Cowley, and Mr. John Milton, Touching the Great Civil War. Set Down by a Gentleman of the Middle Temple,' *Knight's Quarterly Magazine*, III (August 1824), 17–33.

'On the Athenian Orators,' *Knight's Quarterly Magazine*, III (August 1824), 117–28.

'On Mitford's History of Greece,' *Knight's Quarterly Magazine*, III (November 1824), 285–304.

'A Prophetic Account of a Grand National Epic Poem, to be Entitled "The Wellingtoniad," and to be Published A.D. 2824,' *Knight's Quarterly Magazine*, III (November 1824), 434–42.

'The West Indies,' *Edinburgh Review*, XLI (January 1825), 464–88.

'Milton,' *Edinburgh Review*, XLII (August 1825), 304–46.

'The London University,' *Edinburgh Review*, XLIII (February 1826), 315–41.

'Machiavelli,' *Edinburgh Review*, XLV (March 1827), 259–95.

'Major Moody's Reports. Social and Industrial Capacities of Negroes,' *Edinburgh Review*, XLV (March 1827), 383–423.

'The Present Administration,' *Edinburgh Review*, XLVI (June 1827), 245–67.

'Dryden,' *Edinburgh Review*, XLVII (January 1828), 1–36.

'History,' *Edinburgh Review*, XLVII (May 1828), 331–67.

'Hallam's Constitutional History,' *Edinburgh Review*, XLVIII (September 1828), 96–169.

'Mill's Essay on Government. Utilitarian Logic and Politics,' *Edinburgh Review*, XLIX (March 1829), 159–89.

'Bentham's Defence of Mill. Utilitarian System of Philosophy,' *Edinburgh Review*, XLIX (June 1829), 273–99.

'Utilitarian Theory of Government, and the "Greatest Happiness Principle,"' *Edinburgh Review*, L (October 1829), 99–125.

'Southey's *Colloquies on Society*,' *Edinburgh Review*, L (January 1830), 528–65.

'Mr. Robert Montgomery's Poems, and the Modern Practice of Puffing,' *Edinburgh Review*, LI (April 1830), 193–210.

'Sadler's Law of Population, and Disproof of Human Superfecundity,' *Edinburgh Review*, LI (July 1830), 297–321.

'Civil Disabilities of the Jews,' *Edinburgh Review*, LII (January 1831), 363–74.

'Sadler's Refutation, Refuted,' *Edinburgh Review*, LII (January 1831), 504–29.

'Moore's *Life of Lord Byron*,' *Edinburgh Review*, LIII (June 1831), 544–72.

'Croker's Edition of Boswell's Life of Johnson,' *Edinburgh Review*, LIV (September 1831), 1–38.

'Southey's Edition of the Pilgrim's Progress,' *Edinburgh Review*, LIV (December 1831), 450–61.

'Lord Nugent's *Memorials of Hampden*,' *Edinburgh Review*, LIV (December 1831), 505–50.

'Nares' Memoirs of Lord Burghley – Political and Religious Aspects of his Age,' *Edinburgh Review*, LV (April 1832), 271–96.

'Dumont's *Recollections of Mirabeau* – The French Revolution,' *Edinburgh Review*, LV (July 1832), 552–76.

'Lord Mahon's *War of the Succession*,' *Edinburgh Review*, LVI (January 1833), 499–542.

'Walpole's *Letters to Sir Horace Mann*,' *Edinburgh Review*, LVIII (October 1833), 227–58.

'Thackeray's *History of the Earl of Chatham*,' *Edinburgh Review*, LVIII (January 1834), 508–44.

'Sir James Mackintosh's *History of the Revolution*,' *Edinburgh Review*, LXI (July 1835), 265–322.

'Lord Bacon,' *Edinburgh Review*, LXV (July 1837), 1–104 [This was separately reprinted in pamphlet form, Edinburgh, 1837 – so far as I know the only one of TBM's *Edinburgh Review* essays to be so treated].

'Life and Writings of Sir William Temple,' *Edinburgh Review*, LXVIII (October 1838), 113–87.

'Church and State,' *Edinburgh Review*, LXIX (April 1839), 231–80.

'Sir John Malcolm's *Life of Lord Clive*,' *Edinburgh Review*, LXX (January 1840), 295–362.

'Ranke's *History of the Popes* – Revolutions of the Papacy,' *Edinburgh Review*, LXXII (October 1840), 227–58.

'Comic Dramatists of the Restoration,' *Edinburgh Review*, LXXII (January 1841), 490–528.

'The late Lord Holland,' *Edinburgh Review*, LXXIII (July 1841), 560–8.

'Warren Hastings,' *Edinburgh Review*, LXXIV (October 1841), 160–255.

'Frederic the Great,' *Edinburgh Review*, LXXV (April 1842), 218–81.

'Madame D'Arblay,' *Edinburgh Review*, LXXVI (January 1843), 523–70.

'Life and Writings of Addison,' *Edinburgh Review*, LXXVIII (July 1843), 193–260.

'Barère's *Memoirs*,' *Edinburgh Review*, LXXIX (April 1844), 275–351.

'The Earl of Chatham,' *Edinburgh Review*, LXXX (October 1844), 526–95.

'Francis Atterbury,' *Encyclopaedia Britannica*, 8th edn, December 1853.

'John Bunyan,' *Encyclopaedia Britannica*, 8th edn, May 1854.

'Oliver Goldsmith,' *Encyclopaedia Britannica*, 8th edn, February 1856.

'Samuel Johnson,' *Encyclopaedia Britannica*, 8th edn, December 1856.

'William Pitt,' *Encyclopaedia Britannica*, 8th edn, January 1859.

III *History*

Napoleon and the Restoration of the Bourbons [1830], ed. Joseph Hamburger,

London, Longman, 1977 [The extant fragment of TBM's projected *History of France, from the Restoration of the Bourbons to the Accession of Louis Philippe*, newly discovered and published by Joseph Hamburger].

The History of England from the Accession of James the Second, London, Longman, Brown, Green, and Longmans [imprint varies], 5 vols., 1848–61. Vols. I, II, 1848; vols. III, IV, 1855; vol. V, 1861.

IV *Speeches*

There are three collections of TBM's speeches: the American piracy published by J. S. Redfield, 2 vols., New York, 1853; the English piracy published by Henry Vizetelly, 2 vols., London, 1853; and the author's selection published by Longman, 1853 (dated 1854). If a speech appears in one of these collections I have added a parenthetical reference to Redfield, Vizetelly, or Authorized. An asterisk means that TBM corrected the speech for publication at the time of its delivery.

One should add that those parliamentary speeches made between 1830 and 1841 were reported in the *Mirror of Parliament* as well as in *Hansard*, and that the *Mirror* report is frequently the fuller.

At the Annual General Meeting of the Anti-Slavery Society, 25 June 1824, *Report* of the Committee of the [London] Society for the Mitigation and Gradual Abolition of Slavery Throughout the British Dominions, London, 1824, pp. 70–9 (Vizetelly).

On Jewish Disabilities, 5 April 1830, *Hansard*, 2nd Series, XXIII, 1308–14 (Vizetelly).

At the Annual General Meeting of the Anti-Slavery Society, 15 May 1830, *Anti-Slavery Monthly Reporter*, III (June 1830), 242–6.

On Punishment for Forgery, 7 June 1830, *Hansard*, 2nd Series, XXV, 58–62.

On Regency Question, 6 July 1830, *Hansard*, 2nd Series, XXV, 1027–32.

In Defense of Lord Brougham, 23 November 1830, *Hansard*, 3rd Series, I, 647–8.

On West India Petition, 13 December 1830, *Hansard*, 3rd Series, I, 1054–6 (Vizetelly).

On the Reform Bill, 2 March 1831, *Hansard*, 3rd Series, II, 1190–1205. Separately reprinted, London, James Ridgway, 1831 (Authorized)*.

On the Reform Bill, 5 July 1831, *Hansard*, 3rd Series, IV, 773–83 (Authorized).

On the Reform Bill, 20 September 1831, *Hansard*, 3rd Series, VII, 297–311 (Authorized)*.

On Lord Ebrington's Motion, 10 October 1831, *Hansard*, 3rd Series, VIII, 390–9 (Authorized)*.

On the Reform Bill, 16 December 1831, *Hansard*, 3rd Series, IX, 378–92. Separately reprinted, London, Hansard, 1831 (Authorized)*.

On Warburton's Anatomy Bill, 27 February 1832, *Hansard*, 3rd Series, X, 842–4. Separately reprinted, n.p. [1832?] (Authorized)*.

On the Reform Bill, 28 February 1832, *Hansard*, 3rd Series, X, 926–33 (Authorized).

On the Reform Bill, 19 March 1832, *Hansard*, 3rd Series, XI, 450–63 (Vizetelly).

On Change of Ministry, 10 May 1832, *Hansard*, 3rd Series, XII, 848–57 (Vizetelly).

On Change of Ministry, 14 May 1832, *Hansard*, 3rd Series, XII, 921–3.

On Slavery, 24 May 1832, *Hansard*, 3rd Series, XIII, 52–5 (Vizetelly).

At Leeds, Coloured Cloth Hall and White Cloth Hall Yard, 15 June 1832, Leeds *Mercury*, 16 June 1832.

On Russian–Dutch Loan, 12 July 1832, *Hansard*, 3rd Series, XIV, 293–300 (Vizetelly).

To the Electors of Leeds, 4 September 1832.
To the Electors of Hunslet, 5 September 1832.
To the Electors of Holbeck Moor, 5 September 1832.
To the Electors of Bramley, 6 September 1832.
To the Electors of Wortley, 6 September 1832.
To the Electors of Armley, 6 September 1832.
To the Electors of Kirkstall, 7 September 1832.
To the Electors of Leeds, 7 September 1832.
At a Public Dinner, Commercial Buildings, Leeds, 7 September 1832.

[All of these campaign speeches in the Leeds election are reported or summarized in the Leeds *Mercury* and other Leeds papers between 6 and 15 September 1832, but the fullest reports are to be found in a pamphlet published immediately following TBM's visit entitled 'The Preliminary Proceedings Relative to the First Election of Representatives for the Borough of Leeds . . .,' Leeds, Baines and Newsome; London, Simpkin and Marshall [September] 1832].

At Leeds election, Music Hall, 29 November 1832, Leeds *Mercury*, 1 December 1832 (Vizetelly).

At Leeds election, Music Hall, 30 November 1832, Leeds *Mercury*, 1 December 1832.

At Leeds election, Music Hall, 3 December 1832, Leeds *Mercury*, 8 December 1832 (Vizetelly).

At Leeds election, Music Hall, 4 December 1832, Leeds *Mercury*, 8 December 1832.

[The preceding four speeches were delivered as 'lectures' to which admission was by ticket and to which the electors belonging to different divisions of the city were invited on successive nights].

To Leeds Electors, Nomination Day, 10 December 1832, Leeds *Mercury*, 11 December 1832 (Vizetelly).

To Leeds Electors, After Declaration of the Poll, 14 December 1832, Leeds *Mercury*, 15 December 1832 (Vizetelly).

To Leeds Electors, at Celebration Dinner, 14 December 1832, Leeds *Mercury*, 22 December 1832 (Vizetelly).

On Irish Union, 6 February 1833, *Hansard*, 3rd Series, XV, 250–64 (Authorized).

On Irish Coercion Bill, 28 February 1833, *Hansard*, 3rd Series, XV, 1326–37 (Vizetelly).

On Irish Tithes Bill, 1 April 1833, *Hansard*, 3rd Series, XVI, 1383–93 (Vizetelly).

On Jewish Disabilities, 17 April 1833, *Hansard*, 3rd Series, XVII, 227–38 (Authorized) [copies reprinted from the *Mirror of Parliament* were circulated by Sir Francis Goldsmid's Jewish Committee].

Against Mr. Hutchinson's Claim Bill, 31 May 1833, *Mirror of Parliament*, 1833, II, 2016–17.

On India Bill, 10 July 1833, *Hansard*, 3rd Series, XIX, 503–36. Separately reprinted, London, Hansard, 1833 (Authorized)*.

On Slavery Bill, 24 July 1833, *Hansard*, 3rd Series, XIX, 1202–9 (Vizetelly).

To Leeds Manufacturers on Corn Laws, 6 November 1833, Leeds *Mercury*, 9 November 1833.

To Leeds Mechanics' Institute, 7 November 1833, Leeds *Mercury*, 16 November 1833.

Reply to Toast by Sir John Grant, 28 November 1834, *Bengal Hurkaru*, 1 December 1834.

Presiding at St Andrew's Day Dinner, 1 December 1834, *Bengal Hurkaru*, 4 December 1834.

To Edinburgh Electors, 29 May 1839, *Caledonian Mercury*, 30 May 1839. Separately reprinted, Edinburgh, Adam and Charles Black, 1839; London, James Ridgway, 1839 (Authorized).

On Nomination Day, Edinburgh, 2 June 1839, *Scotsman*, 4 June 1839.

On Election Day, Edinburgh, 4 June 1839, *Caledonian Mercury*, 6 June 1839 (Vizetelly).

On Election Day, to Electors, to Town Council, and Others, 4 June 1839, *Scotsman*, 5 June 1839.

On the Ballot, 18 June 1839, *Hansard*, 3rd Series, XLVIII, 461–76 (Vizetelly).

At a Public Breakfast, Edinburgh, 30 August 1839, *Scotsman*, 31 August 1839.

At the Edinburgh Mechanics' Library, 2 September 1839, *Scotsman*, 4 September 1839. Separately published, 'Report of a Public Entertainment Held in the Waterloo Rooms on Monday, Sept. 2, by the Edinburgh Mechanics' Library . . .', Edinburgh, A. Murray, 1839.

To Edinburgh Electors, 21 January 1840, *Scotsman*, 22 January 1840.

On the Hustings, Edinburgh, 23 January 1840, *Scotsman*, 25 January 1840.

At a Public Dinner, 23 January 1840, *Scotsman*, 25 January 1840.

Defense of Ministry, 29 January 1840, *Hansard*, 3rd Series, LI, 815–35. Separately reprinted, London, James Ridgway, 1839 (Authorized).

On the Army of the Indus, 6 February 1840, *Hansard*, 3rd Series, LI, 1334–6 (Vizetelly).

On Privileges of the House of Commons (Stockdale vs. Hansard), 6 March 1840, *Hansard*, 3rd Series, LII, 1010–16 (Vizetelly).

On Army Estimates, 9 March 1840, *Hansard*, 3rd Series, LII, 1087–96 (Redfield).

On the War with China, 7 April 1840, *Hansard*, 3rd Series, LIII, 704–20 (Authorized).

On Indian Emigration to the Mauritius, 4 June 1840, *Hansard*, 3rd Series, LIV, 941–4 (Vizetelly).

On Registration of Irish Voters, 19 June 1840, *Hansard*, 3rd Series, LIV, 1349–57 (Vizetelly).

On Copyright, 5 February 1841, *Hansard*, 3rd Series, LVI, 344–57. Separately reprinted, London, Hansard, 1841 (Authorized)*.

On Registration of Irish Voters, 23 February 1841, *Hansard*, 3rd Series, LVI, 926–39 (Vizetelly).

On Army Estimates, 5 March 1841, *Hansard*, 3rd Series, LVI, 1361–71.

On the Earl of Cardigan, 5 March 1841, *Hansard*, 3rd Series, LVI, 1396–9 (Vizetelly).

On Jews' Declaration Bill, 31 March 1841, *Hansard*, 3rd Series, LVII, 761–4 (Vizetelly).

Flogging on the Sabbath – the Earl of Cardigan, 20 April 1841, *Hansard*, 3rd Series, LVII, 956–8 (Redfield).

On Sugar Duties and the Slavery Question, 11 May 1841, *Hansard*, 3rd Series, LVIII, 188–95 (Vizetelly).

On the Earl of Cardigan, 13 May 1841, *Hansard*, 3rd Series, LVIII, 339–42 (Vizetelly).

Defense of Ministry, 27 May 1841, *Hansard*, 3rd Series, LVIII, 877–88 (Vizetelly).

To Edinburgh Electors, 26 June 1841, *The Times*, 29 June 1841 (Vizetelly).

On the Hustings, Edinburgh, 1 July 1841, *Scotsman*, 3 July 1841.

On the Corn Laws, 21 February 1842, *Hansard*, 3rd Series, LX, 746–60 (Vizetelly).

On Copyright, 6 April 1842, *Hansard*, 3rd Series, LXI, 1363–71 (Authorized).

On Right of Petitioning, 7 April 1842, *Hansard*, 3rd Series, LXII, 11–13.

On Income Tax, 11 April 1842, *Hansard*, 3rd Series, LXII, 255–66 (Vizetelly).

On Flogging in the Army, 15 April 1842, *Hansard*, 3rd Series, LXII, 530–1 (Redfield).

On the People's Charter, 3 May 1842, *Hansard*, 3rd Series, LXIII, 43–52 (Vizetelly).

On Sunday Travelling on Railways, 18 June 1842, *Hansard*, 3rd Series, LXIV, 183–5 (Vizetelly).

On the Gates of Somnauth, 9 March 1843, *Hansard*, 3rd Series, LXVII, 612–28 (Authorized).

On the Ashburton Treaty, 21 March 1843, *Hansard*, 3rd Series, LXVII, 1252–67 (Vizetelly).

On the State of Ireland, 7 July 1843, *Hansard*, 3rd Series, LXX, 796–809 (Vizetelly).

On the Extradition of Offenders, 11 August 1843, *Hansard*, 3rd Series, LXXI, 568–72 (Vizetelly).

On Chelsea Out-Pensioners, 15 August 1843, *Hansard*, 3rd Series, LXXI, 745–7.

On Defamation and Libel, 16 August 1843, *Hansard*, 3rd Series, LXXI, 883–5 (Vizetelly).

On the State of Ireland, 19 February 1844, *Hansard*, 3rd Series, LXXII, 1169–94 (Authorized).

On Recall of Lord Ellenborough, 7 May 1844, *Hansard*, 3rd Series, LXXIV, 808–12.

On Dissenters' Chapels Bill, 6 June 1844, *Hansard*, 3rd Series, LXXV, 338–51. Reprinted in *Parliamentary Debates on the Dissenters' Chapels Bill*, London, John Chapman, 1844 (Authorized).

On Opening Letters at the Post Office, 24 June 1844, *Hansard*, 3rd Series, LXXV, 1274–80 (Vizetelly).

On Opening Letters at the Post Office, 2 July 1844, *Hansard*, 3rd Series, LXXVI, 248–51 (Vizetelly).

On Opening Letters at the Post Office, 20 February 1845, *Hansard*, 3rd Series, LXXVII, 840–5 (Vizetelly).

On the Sugar Duties, 26 February 1845, *Hansard*, 3rd Series, LXXVII, 1288–1306. Separately reprinted, London, Hansard, 1845 (Authorized).

On Maynooth, 14 April 1845, *Hansard*, 3rd Series, LXXIX, 646–58 (Authorized).

On the Church of Ireland, 23 April 1845, *Hansard*, 3rd Series, LXXIX, 1180–98 (Authorized).

On Physic and Surgery Bill, 7 May 1845, *Hansard*, 3rd Series, LXXX, 275–7.

On Scottish University Tests, 9 July 1845, *Hansard*, 3rd Series, LXXXII, 227–42. Separately reprinted, Edinburgh, W. P. Kennedy, 1845 (Authorized).

On the Corn Laws, Edinburgh, 2 December 1845, *Scotsman*, 3 December 1845 (Authorized).

On Frost, Williams, and Jones, 10 March 1846, *Hansard*, 3rd Series, LXXXIV, 888–96 (Vizetelly).

On the Ten Hours Bill, 22 May 1846, *Hansard*, 3rd Series, LXXXVI, 1028–44 (Authorized).

To Edinburgh Electors, Music Hall, 9 July 1846, *Scotsman*, 11 July 1846.

On the Hustings, Edinburgh, 10 July 1846, *Scotsman*, 11 July 1846.

On the Hustings, Edinburgh, 13 July 1846, *Scotsman*, 15 July 1846.

On Election Day, Edinburgh, 14 July 1846, *Scotsman*, 15 July 1846.

On Declaration of the Poll, Edinburgh, 15 July 1846, *Scotsman*, 18 July 1846.

On the Literature of Britain, Edinburgh, 4 November 1846, *Scotsman*, 7 November 1846. Reprinted in 'Report of Speeches delivered at the Public Entertainment in Celebration of the Opening of the Philosophical Institution, Edinburgh, 4th November 1846,' Edinburgh, 1847 (Authorized).

At Trinity College Tercentenary Dinner, 22 December 1846, *Illustrated London News*, 2 January 1847, p. 6.

On Catholic Disabilities, 24 February 1847, *Hansard*, 3rd Series, XC, 472–7 (Vizetelly).

Government Plan of Education, 19 April 1847, *Hansard*, 3rd Series, XCI,

1006–26. Separately reprinted, London, Chapman and Hall [1847] (Authorized).

On Affairs of Portugal, 14 June 1847, *Hansard*, 3rd Series, XCIII, 513–26 (Vizetelly).

To Edinburgh Electors, 27 July 1847, *Scotsman*, 28 July 1847.

On Nomination Day, Edinburgh, 29 July 1847, *Scotsman*, 31 July 1847 (Vizetelly).

Remarks to Catholic Electors, Edinburgh, 29 July 1847, *Scotsman*, 31 July 1847.

Remarks following Defeat at Edinburgh, 30 July 1847, *Scotsman*, 31 July 1847.

Response to Toast at Public Dinner for Lord Hardinge, 5 April 1848, *The Times*, 6 April 1848.

Inaugural Address as Lord Rector, University of Glasgow, 21 March 1849, Edinburgh, James Stillie [1849]; London, Longman, Brown, Green and Longmans, 1849 (Authorized)*.

On Presentation of Freedom of the City of Glasgow, 22 March 1849, *Essays, Critical and Miscellaneous*, new and rev. edn, Philadelphia, Carey and Hart, 1849.

To Edinburgh Electors, 2 November 1852, *Scotsman*, 3 November 1852 (Authorized).

On Exclusion of Judges, 1 June 1853, *Hansard*, 3rd Series, CXXVII, 996–1008 (Authorized).

On India, 24 June 1853, *Hansard*, 3rd Series, CXXVIII, 739–59 (Vizetelly).

On Scottish Annuity Tax, 19 July 1853, *Hansard*, 3rd Series, CXXIX, 451–60.

On Installation as High Steward of Borough of Cambridge, 11 May 1858, *Cambridge Independent Press*, 15 May 1858.

V *Minutes and other Official Papers*

1 Indian Legislative Minutes and State Papers

In the form of clerical copies these are to be found in the records of the East India Company, now in the care of the India Office Library. A published collection has been made by C. D. Dharker, *Lord Macaulay's Legislative Minutes: Selected, with a Historical Introduction*, Madras, Oxford University Press, 1946. A few individual items have also found their way into print in various places. One may note, too, the collection of Macaulay's legislative minutes made by George Otto Trevelyan while he was acting as his father's private secretary in India in 1863. For some reason the collection was not published, but the proof sheets, corrected by Trevelyan, are now in the Trinity College Library (Trevelyan made some use of his work on the minutes in his *Life and Letters of Lord Macaulay*). In the list that follows, undated minutes are given the date of the collection of papers to which they belong, as entered in the East India Company's records.

On the Position of the Legislative Member of the Supreme Council of India, 27 June 1834, *Parliamentary Papers*, 1852–3, XXVII, 521–2; 530–1.

On Censorship, 16 April 1835, *Calcutta Gazette*, 29 April 1835, Dharker, pp. 165–7.

Draft of Act Repealing Censorship of the Press in India, 27 April 1835, *Calcutta*

Gazette, 29 April 1835 [This accompanies the minute, above. No doubt many of the legislative acts issuing from the Supreme Council of India and promulgated in the *Gazette* received much of their form from TBM. Here, and in a few other places, it is possible to identify particular instances of this sort of work].

On the Form of Legislative Acts, 11 May 1835, Dharker, pp. 145–50.

On Rules for Legislative Proceedings, 28 May 1835, Dharker, pp. 150–2.

On the Form of Legislative Acts, 31 May 1835, Dharker, p. 152.

On Instructions to Law Commission, 4 June 1835, extract, Trevelyan, *Life of Macaulay*, 1876, I, 412–13. Also in revised form, Calcutta, *Friend of India*, 20 August 1835, as letter of 7 August 1835, from Secretary of Government to Secretary of Law Commission. See also 15 June 1835, below.

On Drafts of Laws, 13 June 1835, *Parliamentary Papers*, 1852–3, XXVII, 533 (Dharker, pp. 153–8).

On the Form of Promulgating Acts, 14 June 1835, Dharker, pp. 158–61.

Official Instructions to Law Commission, 15 June 1835, reprinted from *Calcutta Gazette* in *Bengal Hurkaru*, 13 August 1835, p. 150c.

On the Form of Promulgating Acts, 21 June 1835, Dharker, pp. 161–2.

On Reform of Mofussil Courts, 25 June 1835, Dharker, pp. 203–26.

On Indigo Contracts, 13 November 1835, Dharker, pp. 272–8.

On Prison Discipline, 14 December 1835, Dharker, pp. 278–80.

On the Constitution of Bombay Sadar, 11 January 1836, Dharker, pp. 235–6.

On the Principles of Local Taxation, 16 January 1836, Dharker, pp. 163–4.

On the Office of Government Commissioners, 23 January 1836, Dharker, pp. 280–1.

On Calcutta Court of Requests, 1 February 1836, Dharker, pp. 198–9.

Draft of Act on Jurisdiction of Company Courts ('Black Act'), 1 February 1836, *Bengal Hurkaru*, 4 February 1836, p. 118b.

On Madras Zemindars, 7 March 1836, Dharker, pp. 236–9.

On the Black Act [21] March 1836, *Parliamentary Papers*, 1837–8, XLI, No. 275, 1–3 (Dharker, pp. 175–80).

Reply to Calcutta Petitioners against Black Act, 28 March 1836, *Asiatic Journal*, N.S. XXI (1836), Part 2, 57–9 (Dharker, pp. 168–75).

On the Black Act, 9 May 1836, *Parliamentary Papers*, 1837–8, XLI, No. 275, 6–7 (Dharker, p. 180: misdated March).

On Procedures of Supreme Court, 16 May 1836, Dharker, pp. 199–201.

Against Publication of Interim Civil Code, 6 June 1836, Dharker, pp. 239–40.

On Censorship Act [2] September 1836, Trevelyan, *Life of Macaulay*, 1876, I, 392–4.

On the Black Act [3 October 1836], *Parliamentary Papers*, 1837–8, XLI, No. 275, 15–22 (Dharker, pp. 183–97).

On Bank of Bengal Charter, 14 November 1836, Dharker, pp. 281–5.

On Law Commission [2 January 1837], Trevelyan, *Life of Macaulay*, 1876, I, 413–14 (Dharker, pp. 252–8).

On Salaries of Supreme Court Officers [23 January 1837], Dharker, pp. 201–2.

On Jurisdiction of Sadar Amins, 6 February 1837, Dharker, pp. 226–8.

On Rules of Pleading [3 April 1837], Dharker, pp. 240–3.

On Execution of Decrees, 3 April 1837, Dharker, pp. 243–4.

On Law of Appeal, 3 April 1837, Dharker, pp. 244–6.

On Jurisdiction of Munsiffs [late April? 1837], Dharker, pp. 228–9.

Letter of Transmittal accompanying Indian Penal Code, 2 May 1837, Dharker, pp. 259–71 [in slightly revised form, and dated 14 October 1837, this was printed as the preface to the Indian Penal Code: see below, 1837].

On Jurisdiction of Sadar Amins, 15 May 1837, Dharker, pp. 229–34.

On Qualifications of Witnesses [5 June 1837], Dharker, pp. 246–7.

On Registration of Ships, Bombay [12 June 1837], Dharker, pp. 286–7.

On Separation of Police and Judicial Offices, 10 July 1837, Dharker, pp. 248–51.

On Relation of Governor-General to Governor-General-in-Council, 5 August 1837, Dharker, pp. 287–91.

A Penal Code Prepared by the Indian Law Commissioners, Calcutta, Bengal Military Orphan Press, 1837 [The first printing of this document, for distribution in India]. Also printed in *Parliamentary Papers*, 1837–8, XLI, No. 6 of Accounts and Papers, East India Company, 124pp.

2 Minutes on Education in India

The records of the Committee on Public Instruction are now in the West Bengal State Record Office. Two selections from those minutes that Macaulay wrote for the Committee have been made, the first of which, by Henry Woodrow, appeared in two forms. Woodrow first edited 'Macaulay's Educational Minutes' as Part III of the *Proceedings of the Bethune Society for the Sessions of 1859–60, 1860–61*, Calcutta, 1862, pp. [209]–330. He then reprinted the text of the minutes, with slightly different introductory material, as *Macaulay's Minutes on Education in India, Written in the Years 1835, 1836, and 1837, and now First Collected from Records in the Department of Public Instruction*, Calcutta, Calcutta Baptist Mission Press, 1862. Of this book, only fifty copies were said to have been printed (W. F. B. Laurie, *Some Sketches of Distinguished Anglo Indians*, 2nd Series, London, 1888, p. ix), and, as Woodrow wrote in sending a copy of the book to Sir Charles Trevelyan, it 'has never been sold' (8 August 1865: MS, Mrs Humphry Trevelyan). A second, brief selection of extracts from Macaulay's education minutes not included in Woodrow appears on pp. 342–55 of Laurie's *Sketches*, noted above.

Since the extracts from the education minutes are often quite brief I have not attempted to make an itemized enumeration of those in print; the published selections by Woodrow and Laurie are, as far as I know, all that have been printed, with the exception of the items listed below. I also give an entry for Macaulay's famous education minute of 2 February 1835 as a special case.

Minute on Indian Education, 2 February 1835; found not in the records of the Committee on Public Instruction but in the India Office Records (India Public Proceedings, LXVI: 7 March 1835, no. 15). Extracts from it were first

published by C. E. Trevelyan, *On the Education of the People of India*, London, Longman, 1838, pp. 43–4; 86–7. The first full printing seems to have been in C. H. Cameron, *An Address to Parliament on the Duties of Great Britain to India*, London, 1853, pp. 64–80. It has since been reprinted frequently: by Woodrow, for example; by G. O. Trevelyan in *Macmillan's*, x (May 1864), 2–7; and, most recently, by John Clive and Thomas Pinney, eds., *Thomas Babington Macaulay: Selected Writings*, Chicago, 1972, pp. 237–51.

[Marginal annotations on minute by H. T. Prinsep on Indian education], 15 February 1835, in H. Sharp, ed., *Selections from Educational Records, Part I, 1781–1839*, Calcutta, 1920, pp. 117–30.

Report as Examiner in General Literature and Composition at Hindu College, 1836, James Kerr, *A Review of Public Instruction in the Bengal Presidency, from 1836 to 1851*, Calcutta, 1853, Part 2, pp. 29–30.

3 Political and Parliamentary Papers

[Address to the King], *Hansard*, 3rd Series, XII (10 May 1832), 787–8. Also *Parliamentary Papers*, 1831–2, XLIX, 607–8.

Report on the Indian Civil Service, November 1854, *Parliamentary Papers*, 1854–5, XL, 112–20.

VI *Verses*

'Pompeii. A Poem which Obtained the Chancellor's Medal at the Cambridge Commencement July, 1819' [Cambridge, 1819].

'A Radical War-Song' [1820], *Miscellaneous Writings*, II, 379–81.

'The Lamentation of the Virgins of Israel for the Daughter of Jephthah: A Hebrew Eclogue,' *Christian Observer*, XIX (September 1820), 587–9.

'Evening. A Poem which Obtained the Chancellor's Medal At the Cambridge Commencement, July 1821' [Cambridge, 1821].

'Tears of Sensibility,' *Morning Post*, 16 November 1821, p. 3c.

'Oh Rosamond,' *Knight's Quarterly Magazine*, I (June 1823), 219.

'By thy love, fair girl of France,' *Knight's Quarterly Magazine*, I (June 1823), 219–20.

'Songs of the Huguenots: 1, Moncontour; 2, Ivry,' *Knight's Quarterly Magazine*, II (January 1824), 33–5.

'Songs of the Civil War: The Cavalier's March to London; The Battle of Naseby,' *Knight's Quarterly Magazine*, II (April 1824), 321–5.

'Sermon Written in a Church-Yard' [1825], *Miscellaneous Writings*, II, 388–91.

'Dies Irae' [1825?], *Miscellaneous Writings*, II, 394–5.

'Inscription for a Picture of Voltaire' [30 March 1826], Trevelyan, *Life of Macaulay*, 1876, I, 141.

'Translation of a Poem by Arnauld' [1826], *Miscellaneous Writings*, II, 392.

'Sortes Virgilianae,' *The Times*, 17 April 1827, p. 2e.

'The Country Clergyman's Trip to Cambridge. Part the First,' *The Times*, 14 May 1827, p. 2e.

['O Stay, Madonna, Stay'], [1827], *Miscellaneous Writings*, II, 417.

'The Marriage of Tirzah and Ahirad' [1828], *Miscellaneous Writings*, II, 396–412.

'Political Georgics Book I,' *The Times*, 18 March 1828, p. 2f [with the note 'To be continued.' It was not].

'The Deliverance of Vienna; Translated from Vicenzo da Filicaja,' *Winter's Wreath: A Collection of Original Contributions in Prose and Verse*, London and Liverpool, 1828, pp. 65–71.

'The Battle of Bosworth Field' [*c.* 1828], G. M. Trevelyan, ed., *Macaulay's Lays of Ancient Rome and Other Historical Poems*, London, 1928, pp. 176–82.

'The Armada,' *Friendship's Offering; and Winter's Wreath . . . 1833*, London, 1833, pp. 16–20. [An early MS version of this is published in Trevelyan, ed., *Macaulay's Lays of Ancient Rome*, 1928, pp. 173–5].

'The Last Buccaneer' [1839], *Miscellaneous Writings*, II, 427–8.

The Lays of Ancient Rome, London, Longman, Brown, Green, and Longmans, 1842.

'Valentine' [1847], Trevelyan, *Life of Macaulay*, 1876, II, 208–9.

'Epitaph on a Jacobite' [8 May 1847], *Miscellaneous Writings*, II, 429.

'Lines Written on the Night of the 30th of July, 1847,' *Miscellaneous Writings*, II, 430–3.

'Valentine to the Hon. Mary C. Stanhope, Daughter of Lord and Lady Mahon' [23 January 1851], Lord Stanhope, *Miscellanies*, 1863, pp. 94–5.

'Paraphrase of a Passage in the Chronicle of the Monk of St. Gall' [1856], *Miscellaneous Writings*, II, 437.

VII *Miscellaneous, Including Epitaphs, Inscriptions, and Marginalia*

[Encomium on Wilberforce], [1825], *Second Report* of the Society for the Mitigation and Gradual Abolition of Slavery Throughout the British Dominions, London, 1825, pp. 46–7.

'Fragment of an Ancient Romance' [June 1826], W. T. Lowndes, *The Bibliographer's Manual of English Literature*, ed. H. G. Bohn, Part VI, London, 1861, pp. 1433**–1433***.

'A New Song' [June 1826], printed handbill on the Leicester election (Trinity College).

Latin Asclepiads [1831?], *The Times*, 13 October 1915.

'Inscription on the Statue of Lord William Bentinck at Calcutta' [1835], *Miscellaneous Writings*, II, 438.

'Epitaph on Sir Benjamin Heath Malkin at Calcutta' [December 1837], *Miscellaneous Writings*, II, 439.

'Inscription,' 8 May 1847, Lord Stanhope, *Miscellanies*, 2nd Series, 1872, p. 139.

'Epitaph on Lord Metcalfe' (1847), John William Kaye, *Life of Lord Metcalfe*, new edn, 2 vols., 1858, II, 446.

'Translation from Plautus' [10 September 1850], *Miscellaneous Writings*, II, 435.

Inscription for Scutari Monument [August 1857], Trevelyan, *Life of Macaulay*, 1876, II, 371n.

Address to Queen Victoria and Prince Albert, at Opening of Town Hall, Leeds, 6 September 1858, Leeds *Mercury*, 7 September 1858.

[Marginalia] James Hamilton, 'Marginalia of Lord Macaulay,' *Macmillan's*, VII (April 1863), 489–91.

[Marginalia] Sir G. O. Trevelyan, ed., *The Marginal Notes of Lord Macaulay*, London, Longmans, Green, and Co., London, 1907.

[Marginalia] Hugh Sykes Davies, 'Macaulay's Marginalia to Lucretius,' in Robert Calverly Trevelyan, trans., Lucretius, *De rerum natura*, Cambridge, 1937, pp. 279–90.

[Marginalia] A. N. L. Munby, 'Macaulay's Library' (The David Murray Lectures, 28), Glasgow, 1966.

VIII *Attributed Writings*

Many items have been attributed to Macaulay at one time or another, but of these many only a few, treated here, have much claim to authority or plausibility.

'On the Deceitfulness of the Human Heart,' *Christian Observer*, XV (October 1816), 635. Attributed to TBM in Dorothy Alston, 'Some Personal Recollections of Macaulay,' *London Mercury*, XVIII (May 1928), 59, an article based on the recollections of TBM's friend Henry Thornton. Alston identifies a contribution to the *Christian Observer* signed 'Juvenis' as TBM's; presumably 'On the Deceitfulness of the Human Heart,' which is so signed, is meant. It may in fact be TBM's. Alston's article is indistinct, but contains what appears to be authentic information.

[Note on the Connection between Colonies and the Mother Country], in [W. R. Shepherd], *History of the American Revolution*, London, 1830, p. 64. According to a letter of 13 August 1830 from the Secretary of the Society for the Diffusion of Useful Knowledge, which published this book, 'Mr. Macaulay will add either by way of note or of appendix the little dissertation upon the nature of the connection between Colonies and the Mother Country' (Letter Book, SDUK, University College, London). Such a note does appear in Shepherd's *History*, but it bears no resemblance to anything ever written by TBM. Most likely 'Mr. Macaulay' is Zachary Macaulay, to whom the subject would have been congenial. But since TBM did read and report on several works in MS for the SDUK at this time he cannot be positively ruled out.

[Section on the new East India Company Charter], in [Denis Le Marchant, ed.], 'The Reform Ministry, and the Reformed Parliament,' London, 1833, pp. 43–5. Attributed to TBM in a letter from Le Marchant to James Brougham, [4? September 1833] in the Brougham MSS, cited in Arthur Aspinall, *Politics and the Press, 1780–1850*, 1949, pp. 158–9 and note. As the Secretary to the Board of Control and one of those chiefly responsible both for drawing up the new Charter Act and for steering it through the Commons, TBM would have been the obvious choice to write the section on the charter in this pamphlet. It hardly resembles his work, however, and must have been much altered by the editor, always supposing it to have been TBM's work in the first place.

SOURCES OF TEXT

MANUSCRIPT

American Philosophical Society, VI, 14
Amsterdam, University of, VI, 80, 272
Auckland Public Library, IV, 81

Bavarian Academy of Science, V, 218
Bavarian State Library, IV, 60
Bentham, D. R., V, 78, 481
Bergen, University of, IV, 361
Berlin State Library, VI, 143
Bibliothèque Universitaire, Geneva, III, 328
Blakeney, T. S., IV, 105, 287; V, 142, 431, 470; VI, 134, 135, 151, 155
Bodleian Library, III, 166, 314; IV, 68, 70, 205, 354; V, 7, 110, 111, 119, 166, 278, 364, 398; VI, 40, 45, 150, 151, 152, 216, 236, 265, 267, 279
Bonn University, V, 211
Boston Public Library, IV, 353; V, 36, 479
British Museum, I, 5, 253, 254, 255, 256, 257, 261, 262, 268, 269, 273, 275, 280, 283, 298, 309, 312, 214, 315, 316, 318; II, 7, 14, 40, 96, 107, 108, 109, 110, 111, 113, 115, 119, 120, 121, 135, 149, 190, 200, 201, 212, 222, 227, 264, 305, 306, 311, 316, 320, 333, 335, 341, 351, 366, 370; III, 10, 12, 14, 19, 21, 23, 107, 109, 163, 164, 189, 190, 194, 195, 196, 205, 213, 216, 243, 245, 249, 253, 254, 255, 258, 261, 275, 277, 278, 279, 282, 288, 289, 293, 294, 297, 298, 299, 300, 306, 307, 309, 310, 321, 315, 320, 324, 325, 326, 329, 336, 337, 340, 342, 344, 348, 349, 353, 358, 359, 360, 361, 363, 365, 366, 367, 368, 369, 370, 371, 372, 374, 377, 385, 387; IV, 5, 6, 7, 9, 10, 12, 14, 15, 16, 17, 19, 20, 22, 24, 25, 27, 30, 31, 32, 40, 43, 46, 47, 51, 61, 63, 64, 67, 69, 79, 82, 84, 89, 93, 96, 97, 99, 107, 118, 120, 121, 122, 124, 126, 127, 129, 130, 132, 152, 158, 160, 161, 166, 172, 173, 174, 177, 179, 183, 191, 198, 199, 210, 211, 212, 213, 216, 226, 236, 242, 244, 264, 282, 285, 286, 306, 309, 315, 322, 324, 325, 328, 329, 337, 338, 397; V, 37, 60, 64, 109, 159, 166, 167, 170, 219, 254, 296, 308, 310, 330, 331, 397, 430; VI, 52, 56, 90, 97, 115, 121, 142, 148, 194, 223, 250, 275.
Brotherton Library, University of Leeds, VI, 128
Brumbaugh, Thomas B., IV, 294
Buffalo Public Library, V, 39
Butler, Sir James, VI, 97, 241

California, University of, Berkeley, IV, 372; V, 413, 432
California, University of, Los Angeles, IV, 366; V, 82; VI, 198
Cambridge University Library, III, 307; 319; IV, 353, 392; V, 26, 41, 76
Chicago, University of, V, 464
Christ Church, Oxford, IV, 66, 370
Church Missionary Society, IV, 98
Clive, John, VI, 282
Colby College, V, 466, 473
Columbia University, II, 111; V, 165; VI, 266
Cornell University, V, 335; VI, 15, 44, 208
Corpus Christi College, Cambridge, V, 418
Cowell, F. R., I, 189, 279; II, 376; III, 15, 296, 311, 338; IV, 95, 125, 169, 253; V, 40, 109, 209, 227, 275, 457, 466, 469; VI, 39, 136, 141, 185, 215, 225, 226, 240, 241, 265, 276

Devon County Record Office, III, 360, 362
Dugdale, Sir William, VI, 105, 114, 117, 118
Duke University, II, 202, 232, 285, 333; III, 291; IV, 297; V, 80, 115; VI, 176, 195
Durham, University of, III, 331; IV, 288, 290; VI, 91

Edinburgh Central Public Library, III, 302, 303; IV, 349; VI, 32
Edinburgh, University of, IV, 384, 387
Enoch Pratt Free Library, VI, 17
Errington, Mrs Lancelot, I, 282, 308; II, 184, 203, 205, 226; III, 27, 32, 40, 64, 67, 76, 90, 99, 113, 231; IV, 39

Fitzwilliam Museum, Cambridge, IV, 296; VI, 157, 175, 254
Forster, E. M., Executors of, V, 220
Free Library of Philadelphia, II, 375; IV, 325

General State Archives, The Hague, V, 113, 186; VI, 88
Gennadius Library, American School of Classical Studies, V, 5

Halifax, The Earl of, IV, 364, 384, 385; V, 206, 208, 389, 431, 438, 439, 482
Hamburger, Joseph, V, 35; VI, 26
Hampshire Record Office, V, 133, 134
Harvard University, I, 6, 101, 107, 127, 129, 172, 187, 190; 197; III, 249; IV, 18, 84, 143, 178, 225, 340; V, 128, 144, 287, 316; VI, 89, 117, 223, 265
Haverford College, V, 71, 143; VI, 46
Hertfordshire County Council, III, 343; IV, 42, 62, 65, 83, 106, 182, 323, 329, 368, 393; V, 17, 77, 147, 163, 310, 386; VI, 182, 209
Hessische Landes-und-Hochschulbibliothek, V, 200; VI, 243
Holland, D. C. L., IV, 66, 72, 73; V, 87, 148; VI, 116
Howard, George, III, 24, 386; IV, 334
Huntingdonshire County Record Office, V, 114, 116
Huntington Library, I, 22, 34, 38, 147, 152, 164, 201, 212; II, 131, 161, 237, 290; III, 29, 31, 380; IV, 67, 80, 203, 220, 320, 348, 362, 388, 390; V, 35, 49, 83, 95, 123, 155, 169, 229, 236, 245, 302, 303, 307, 308, 346, 358, 422; VI, 26, 40, 126, 158, 193, 207, 218, 226

India Office Library, II, 364; III, 122, 214, 239
Indiana, University of, V, 98
Iowa, University of, II, 103; IV, 160, 327; VI, 256, 267
Iowa Historical Library, IV, 376

Kansas, University of, IV, 115, 171, 177, 183, 196, 197, 252, 298, 306; V, 221, 326
Kent County Council, VI, 190
King's College, Cambridge, V, 150
Knox College, IV, 265
Knutsford, The Viscount, IV, 385; V, 232; VI, 71, 163, 164, 178

Lansdowne, The Marquess of, I, 311; II, 353; III, 23, 118, 184, 208, 209, 266; IV, 379; V, 163, 370, 372, 481, 483; VI, 21, 185
Leeds City Library, VI, 200
Leuba, Walter, II, 376; VI, 234, 271
Liverpool City Library, IV, 241
London, Corporation of, Records Office, V, 458
London, University College, I, 242, 249; II, 123, 232; III, 13; IV, 124
London, University of, II, 229; III, 203, 214; IV, 355, 382; V, 29, 66, 118, 119, 142, 145, 198, 217, 338, 360, 417; VI, 54, 85, 90, 130, 165, 166, 177, 199, 203, 213
Longman Group Ltd, IV, 251, 260; V, 59, 77, 161, 413; VI, 24, 156, 167, 168

McGill University, V, 23, 329, 350, 474, 483; VI, 10, 37
Manchester Central Library, IV, 112; V, 129, 130, 153, 184, 230
Massachusetts Historical Society, IV, 74, 80, 127, 135, 194, 195, 209, 222, 227, 249, 251, 266, 403; V, 33, 43, 52, 58, 141, 148, 231, 243, 400, 466, 474, 475; VI, 18, 98, 159, 260
Menell, C. S., I, 243; II, 174, 239, 267, 280, 284, 306; III, 26, 171, 192, 198
Michigan, University of, V, 442
Millgate, Mrs Michael, IV, 401; V, 58, 153, 328; VI, 154, 268, 275, 277
Mitchell Library, Sydney, V, 411; VI, 133
Moorman, Mrs Mary, I, 62, 66, 70
Morgan Library, Pierpont, I, 266; II, 85, 123, 130, 132, 135, 139, 141, 144, 149, 151, 154, 158, 160, 172, 193, 208, 214, 222, 224, 225, 227, 231, 233, 234, 236, 237, 272, 360; III, 8, 11, 15, 17, 20, 25, 29, 89, 283; IV, 33, 131, 134, 195, 209, 380; V, 101, 234
Mottahedeh, Roy, IV, 227
Murray, John, Ltd, V, 215

National Library of Australia, IV, 356
National Library of Ireland, III, 224; IV, 178, 259; VI, 45
National Library of Scotland, III, 144, 287, 323, 330; IV, 122, 164, 165, 174, 243, 249, 258, 261, 262, 268 ,283, 300, 303, 359, 368, 374, 375, 378, 380, 387, 389, 390; V, 35, 47, 90, 113, 129, 134, 169, 219, 234, 239, 246, 248, 257, 260, 263, 295, 300, 302, 313, 331, 341, 379, 395, 401, 407, 434, 445, 446, 447, 450, 468; VI, 6, 7, 10, 34, 44, 64, 118, 129, 132, 133, 155, 267
National Library of Wales, IV, 111; V, 293, 317, 354, 443, 477; VI, 20, 42, 113, 190, 242
National Portrait Gallery, V, 29; VI, 33, 41

National Register of Archives, III, 335, 352; IV, 50, 228, 231, 238; VI, 257
New College, Oxford, IV, 327; V, 15, 428, 482
New South Wales, Library of, VI, 209
New York Public Library, II, 287; III, 339, IV, 193, 282, 361, 399; V, 41, 58, 62, 139, 146, 153, 172, 219, 336; VI, 35, 74, 94, 171, 186
Berg Collection, III, 308, 321, 374, 375; IV, 125, 127, 175, 248, 251, 308, 335, 350; V, 102, 175, 287, 392, 393; VI, 6, 86, 120, 153
New York University, V, 111; VI, 11
Newcastle, University of, V, 344; VI, 30, 210, 213, 259
Northumberland Record Office, IV, 325
Nottingham, University of, III, 31, 76, 120, 124, 125, 133, 137, 138, 292; IV, 224, 245, 268, 347, 381, 398; V, 11, 42, 142, 152, 168, 255, 261, 327; VI, 43, 89, 97, 142, 148

Peal, W. Hugh, I, 313; IV, 6, 57, 401, 403; V, 132, 388, 488; VI, 235, 266
Pennsylvania Historical Society, V, 91
Pepys-Whitely, D., IV, 366
Pforzheimer Library, Carl H., IV, 337; V, 384
Pinney, Thomas, IV, 397
Princeton University, V, 10
Public Record Office, IV, 23, 347, 359, 362; V, 7, 50, 61, 154, 155, 235, 260, 433; VI, 107, 115, 254

Ray, Gordon N., I, 18, 23, 28, 30, 48; III, 146
Reading, University of, V, 223
Royal Archives, Windsor, III, 298, 300, 301, 305, 306, 314, 318, 328, 342, 363; IV, 373; V, 150; VI, 137
Royal College of Surgeons, IV, 368
Royal Library, Denmark, III, 347; V, 217
Royal Library, The Hague, V, 229
Rylands Library, John, II, 42, 235, 238; III, 13, 74; IV, 172; V, 55, 126

Sandbach, R. G. E., VI, 283
Scottish Record Office, II, 318; III, 329; IV, 54, 116, 120, 123, 134, 161, 168, 214, 275, 286, 315, 319; V, 104, 231, 242, 243, 246, 247, 252, 256, 259, 262
Seidenstein, Dr Howard R., V, 294, 463
Smith, E. E., V, 437
Spencer, The Earl, V, 85
Stanford University, III, 318
Stanhope Papers, Chevening, II, 171, 238; III, 206, 248, 249; IV, 20, 53, 72, 81, 117, 136, 246, 247, 255, 258, 263, 346, 356, 358, 365, 366, 369, 383; V, 8, 25, 28, 83, 105, 108, 110, 112, 117, 131, 149, 150, 157, 162, 165, 171, 210, 228, 253, 274, 298, 314, 323, 325, 337, 348, 364, 372, 405, 410, 444, 471, 476; VI, 19, 21, 23, 41, 46, 50, 65, 78, 116, 136, 152, 157, 177, 178, 181, 195, 229, 247
Swarthmore College, V, 396

Texas, University of, I, 165, 184, 186, 196, 207, 217, 227, 229, 248; II, 213, 375; IV, 158, 200; V, 102, 413; VI, 132, 266, 277, 278, 280, 282, 283
Trevelyan, Mrs Humphry, I, 145, 148, 154, 274; II, 15, 23, 37, 268, 279, 316
Trinity College, Cambridge, *not listed*
Turnbull Library, Alexander, V, 49, 87, 115

Unidentified source, VI, 196

Victoria, State Library of, II, 377; VI, 207
Victoria Memorial Hall, III, 145; VI, 70

Washington, University of, V, 201, 436
Westminster City Library, V, 108
Williams Library, Dr, VI, 36

Yale University, III, 244; IV, 240, 261; V, 28, 86, 166, 168, 288; VI, 38, 50, 187, 224, 270
Osborn Collection, I, 178; II, 365; III, 263; IV, 96, 211; V, 333, 397, 399, 449, 462, 478; VI, 92, 282

PRINTED

Abbot, W. C., *American Historical Review*, V, 368
'Alfred,' *History of the Factory Movement*, II, 117
American Art Association, Catalogue, IV, 299
Anderson Galleries, Catalogue, I, 8; III, 324; IV, 320, 403; VI, 108
Arnould, Sir Joseph, *Memoir of Lord Denman*, V, 425
L'Autographe, V, 404
Autographic Mirror, V, 445

Bird, Claude Smith, *Sketches from the Life of Charles Smith Bird*, IV, 128

Black, Adam, ed., *Biographies by Lord Macaulay*, III, 346, 384; IV, 100; V, 240, 269, 441

Bovet, Alfred, *Lettres Autographes*, IV, 71

Caledonian Mercury, III, 383

Charnwood, Lady, *An Autograph Collection*, V, 180

Coleridge, Derwent, 'Memoir' in *Poems by John Moultrie*, III, 135

Dafforne, James, *Life of Edward Matthew Ward*, VI, 152

Davey, S. J., Catalogue, V, 172; VI, 45

De Morgan, Augustus, *Newton: His Friend: and His Niece*, V, 355

Devizes and Wiltshire Gazette, II, 8

Dixon, W. H., ed., *Lady Morgan's Memoirs*, IV, 308

D'Orsai, Sebastian, Catalogue, VI, 216

Ellis, S. M., ed., *Unpublished Letters of Lady Bulwer Lytton*, VI, 19

Exeter, Bishop of, *Correspondence between the Bishop of Exeter and T. B. Macaulay*, V, 11, 18

Fagan, Louis, *Life of Panizzi*, I, 229; III, 121

Franz, Sarah Grant, *Wild Flowers*, V, 139

Furniss, Harry, *Paradise in Piccadilly*, IV, 59

Gladstone, William Ewart, *Gleanings of Past Years*, III, 283

Glasgow Constitutional, V, 290

Gordon, Mary Wilson, '*Christopher North*,' V, 252

Hardcastle, Mrs, *Life of Lord Campbell*, III, 381; VI, 192

Hunt, Thornton, ed., *Correspondence of Leigh Hunt*, II, 112

Inverness Courier, V, 117, 120

Laughton, J. K., *Memoirs of Henry Reeve*, VI, 218, 225, 252

Laurie, W. F. B., *Some Sketches of Distinguished Anglo Indians*, V, 114

Leeds Intelligencer, II, 114, 115, 162, 175, 177

Leeds Mercury, II, 92, 115, 120, 132, 162, 175, 177, 198, 211, 212, 221, 235, 236

Macaulay, J. B., *Memoirs of the Clan 'Aulay'*, IV, 34

Mackie, J. B., *Life of Duncan McLaren*, III, 313, 327, 350, 355, 364, 373; IV, 21, 26, 91, 94, 105, 108, 111, 113; V, 319

Maggs Brothers, Catalogues, III, 336, 365, 380; IV, 8, 19, 115, 250, 338, 399, 402; V, 297, 308, 329, 332, 334, 472

Milner, Mary, *Life of Isaac Milner*, IV, 75

Montrose, Arbroath, and Brechin Review, VI, 180

New York Ledger, VI, 128

New York Times, V, 289

Notes and Queries, IV, 193

Parker, Charles Stuart, *Life of Sir James Graham*, V, 445

Phillips, Lawrence B., *Autographic Album*, VI, 271

Pope-Hennessy, James, *Monckton Milnes*, IV, 165

Rendell, Kenneth W., Inc., Catalogue, III, 316

'Report of Philosophical Institution,' V, 464

Roberts, Arthur, *Letters of Hannah More*, I, 55; IV, 116

Ross, Janet, *Three Generations of English Women*, III, 325; IV, 295

Rothesay Express, VI, 259

Sanial, S. C., *Calcutta Review*, III, 126

Sawyer, Charles J., Catalogue, IV, 64

Scotsman, III, 291, 294; IV, 85, 103, 170, 185, 192, 208, 209, 241, 250, 254, 267, 280, 304, 339, 345; V, 237, 238, 289, 325, 329, 377, 399, 408; VI, 13

Sotheby and Co., Catalogues, I, 7, 49; IV, 64; V, 89, 411

Stoddart, R. H., *Harper's*, VI, 271

Stowe, Harriet Beecher, intro. to *Uncle Tom's Cabin*, V, 230; VI, 63

[Tauchnitz], *Fünfzig Jahre der Verlagshandlung Bernhard Tauchnitz*, V, 71, 101, 171, 218, 229, 334, 338, 373, 468, 472; VI, 37, 49, 99, 100, 187, 229, 257

Thomson, D. Cleghorn, *Review of English Literature*, V, 92, 94

The Times, IV, 291, 293

Trevelyan, George Otto, *Life of Macaulay*, I, 252, 264; II, 151; III, 263, 268, 304; IV, 115, 369; V, 38, 88; VI, 58, 236, 237, 268, 269, 271, 272

Unidentified source, V, 360; VI, 173

Williams, Basil, *Stanhope*, VI, 53

Witness, III, 376

GENERAL INDEX

The abbreviations TBM for Macaulay and *ER* for *Edinburgh Review* are used throughout the index. Italicized numbers mean that biographical information will be found at that place. The asterisk indicates that Macaulay is reading, quoting from, or commenting on the work or writer mentioned.

Abbot, Wilbur C., v, 368

Abbotsford, II, 148n, subscription for, 238n

Abdy, Edward Strutt, IV, 50

Abdy, Thomas Neville, IV, 50

Abercorn, James Hamilton, 1st Duke of, his marriage, II, 181

Abercromby, James: *see* Lord Dunfermline

Aberdeen, II, 225

Aberdeen, 3rd Earl of, II, 58n

Aberdeen, George Hamilton Gordon, 4th Earl of, IV, 101, foreign secretary 197n; 231, and Tahiti affair 238; 270, 383n, TBM of his mind v, 156; 181n, hopes for his coalition ministry 303; his arrangements for government 304-5; TBM sends copy of *Paris After Waterloo* to 308; interview with on Annuity Tax 310; 320, 351, resigns 441n

LETTERS TO: v, 308, 310

Aberdeen ministry, v, 435, TBM could not support 442-3

Abinger, James Scarlett, 1st Baron, I, 181, 218n, 229n, *318*, joins Tories II, 33, IV, 89, VI, 67n

Abolition of slavery and slave trade: *see* Anti-Slavery Movement

Abolition Committee, I, 44n

Abolitionists, I, 44, at Allied congress in Paris 45n, 244, government will meet their views II, 239; get changes in anti-slavery bill 281; 289

Abolitionists (Liverpool) II, 246, 259

Aborigines Protection Societies, silenced by Indian Mutiny, VI, 103

Academy, IV, 389n

Accum, Friedrich Christian, *Treatise on Adulterations of Food*, I, 180

Achilles, I, 89; IV, 207

Achilles Tatius, III, 200*

Achilli, Giovanni Giacinto, his suit against Newman, v, *195*, 310n

Achilli v. Newman, v, 371n, VI, 102n

A'Court, William: *see* Baron Heytesbury

Act of Toleration, v, 22

Act of Uniformity, v, 20

Acton Place, Suffolk, I, 45

Actors, Puritan laws against IV, 388; needs different from those of writers v, 164

Acworth, Mrs, v, 357

Acworth, William, v, *357*

Adair, Sir Robert, v, *316*, reprints Fox's pamphlet 316*; gives TBM copy of de Dohna's *Memoires* 316n; 427n

LETTER TO: v, 316

Adair, Robert A. S., 'The Winter of 1846-7,' IV, 332

Adalbert, Prince, of Prussia, VI, 58n

Adam, Admiral Sir Charles, II, *76*

Adam, Sir Frederic, III, *35*, 36, his library 38; 61, 66, 84, 98, 215

Adam, Sir Frederick, II, 191

Adam, William (1751-1839), II, *76*, 170; III, 10

Adam, William (of India), III, *120*, reports on education 120n; 125

Adam & Charles Black, 1807-1957, v, 294n

Addiscombe, East India Company military school, II, 226n

Addison, Joseph, I, 318, II, 190, at Holland House 169; 253, portrait 20; III, 245, his familiar expressions IV, 27, 30; 'know him almost by heart' 98; 129n, and 'Little Dicky' 132; letters by v, 116; Bohn's edn of 472, 481; TBM's attributions to 482

Writings: Cato, I, 81*, *The Drummer*, VI, 25*, *Spectator*, No. 1, I, 63*, II, 216, III, 20, 20n*, 28, 220, IV, 41, Nos.

Addison: *Writings—cont.*
411-21, 130*, No. 530, v, 122*, Nos. 558, 559, vi, 8*, *Tatler*, No. 160, iv, 130*

'Address of the Women of England to the Women of the United States,' v, 298

Adelaide, Queen, at coronation of William IV, ii, 98; iv, 257

Adelaide, South Australia, v, 80

Admiralty, negligence of iv, 238; Keeper of Records at, 391

Adolphus, John, *History of England*, i 51, TBM won't review iv, 53

Adolphus, John Leycester, i, *285*, collaborates with Ellis on *Reports* 285n; ii, 5, on TBM as orator 5n; 308, iii, 146, 155, 160, 179, 183, 212, 323, 'excellent man though a bitter tory' iv, 53; reads MS of *Lays* 57-8; 68, his criticism of *History* v, 31; 58n, 148n, to be at Malvern 190; TBM hears nothing of him 193; 361n, 423, vi, 181n, 250n

Writings: 'The Circuiteers,' i, 285n, *Letters from Spain*, sent to TBM, iv, 143*, *Letters to Richard Heber*, i, 285n

Letters to: iv, 14, 325, v, 10, 58, 130, 330, 396, vi, 143, 266

Adolphus, Mrs John Leycester (Clara Richardson), criticism of *History* v, 10; Hannah to present her at court 395, 396, 398n

Aelius Spartianus, Life of Geta, v, 280*

Aeschines, v, 345, on Demosthenes 161; *Speeches* 181, vi, 161*

Aeschylus, most sublime and magnificent of poets i, 80; 87, 88, fragment translated by TBM 98; 242n, iii, 111*, 118, 159*, compared to Milton v, 344

Writings: Agamemnon, TBM proposes scene altered from to Ellis v, 340, *Choephori*, iii, 111*, *Prometheus Bound*, iii, 140*, 177*, iv, 383*, v, 345*, *Seven Against Thebes*, iv, 240*, *Supplices*, iii, 212

Affleck, Sir Gilbert, vi, 214n

Affleck, Lady: *see* Mrs William Whewell

Afghan War, iv, 99n

Afghanistan, iii, 65n, victory in 360n, 362

African Institution, i, xxv, 60n, 74n, *Report* 127; formation of 127n, 193n, William Evans secretary 198n; 222n, 246n, 319n, ii, 39n, 43n, iv, 207

Africanus and Investigator: *see* Zachary Macaulay

Agapemonites, v, 187

Age, misattributes article by Bulwer to TBM i, 319; ii, 106n, iii, 250, iv, 129

Agnew, Sir Andrew, his Lord's Day Bill ii, *235*; 'Praise God Barebones' defeated 240; 247

Agra, Metcalfe appointed to, ii, 323

Agra College, iii, 139

Agrippina, i, 81

Ahmed, A. F. Salahuddin, *Social Ideas and Social Change in Bengal*, iii, 125

Aikin, Lucy, iv, *118*, angered by TBM's corrections 118; blunders in her *Addison* 126, 128

Writings: Life of Addison, TBM proposes to review iv, 98, 118*, 'Life of Mr. Roscoe,' ii, 335, *Memoirs of the Court of James I*, iv, 118n, *Memoirs, Miscellanies and Letters*, iv, 118n, 266n

Ainsworth, Harrison, 174n

Airy, George Biddle, i, *191*, *Autobiography*, 200n

Aix la Chapelle, congress at, i, 104; TBM at vi, 114

Akatalephia of the second Academy, iv, 381

Akenside, Mark, i, 71*, 'Epistle to Curio,' ii, 321, 'Ode to Curio,' worthless, 321

Aktor, iv, 207

Albany: *see* TBM's residences

Albemarle, Duke of, v, 24

Albemarle, William Charles Keppel, 4th Earl of, ii, 21, iii, 347

Alberoni, Giulio, Cardinal, iv, *232*

Albert, Prince, iii, 316, exults over King of Hanover 347; and Fine Arts Commission iv, 191n; accepts Chancellorship of Cambridge 331; TBM on London committee for 331n; installation at Cambridge 332n; promotes reform at Cambridge 359; consults TBM on Regius professorship 373; and Partridge's 'Fine Arts Commissioners' v, 57, 327; offers TBM chair of history at Cambridge 61n; 137, and Great Exhibition 141n; 265, 378, yelping against 378, 380; 385n, 391, vi, 58, patron to Manchester Exhibition 101n; address to on opening of Leeds Town Hall 167; patron of Rifle Corps 214n

Letter to: iv, 373

Albury, Surrey (Henry Drummond's residence), iv, 197

Alcaics, iii, 202

Alchemy, iii, 123

Alcibiades, vi, 83

Alcock, Rev. Ambrose, v, 226, 283

Alderminster, Warwickshire, John Macaulay appointed to living of I, 314

Alderson, Sir Edward Hall, I, *221*, 266, 267

Aldine editions, at Althorp, V, 345

Aldingham, Lancashire, John Macaulay appointed to living of I, xxvi, V, 50; 62, 421n, TBM visits 426; VI, 48, 56, 57

Aldrich, Henry, 323

Aldus Manutius, I, 90, VI, 22

Alexander the Great, I, 104, 180, IV, 33, V, 178

Alexander I, of Russia, his plan for world peace, I, 104-5

Alexander, Robert, III, 154

Alexander, Sir William John, sends Chandos MS to TBM, V, *104*

LETTER TO: V, 104

Alexander, William Lindsay, III, *350*, 351

Alexandria, III, 183, 184, 353

Alexandrian library, I, 16

Alfieri, Vittorio, I, 73, 73n*, II, 40n, V, 26

Alford, Henry, V, *317*; TBM intends to vote for 318

'Alfred' (Samuel Kydd), *History of the Factory Movement*, II, 117

Algeria, debate on French action in IV, 233; French in 238, 239

Algiers, bombardment of, I, 83

Ali, V, 39, 43

Alice, Princess, V, 112n

Alison, Sir Archibald, TBM gives toast to at Glasgow V, 41n; *133*; candidate for Lord Rectorship at Glasgow 133; elected 134n; 136, *History of Europe* 133n

Allen, H., letter to, VI, 39

Allen, Dr John, II, *21*, 23, 66, 'Atheist in ordinary' to Lady Holland 76; deserves no sympathy 77; 145, 169, 180, provokes Lady Holland 181; TBM not inclined to succeed him 192; 195, 254, 282, his subservience to Lady Holland 336; III, 7, letter to Napier 171n; his death IV, 121; TBM receives volume of Lucan in memory of 296

Writings: Inquiry into the Rise and Growth of the Royal Prerogative in England, I, 279

LETTER TO: III, 310

Allen, Ralph, IV, 394

Allestree Hall, Derbyshire (William Evans's residence), I, 198, 228

Alleyn, Mr, I, 30

Allibone, Samuel Austin, *Critical Dictionary of English Literature,* VI, 193*, 207*, 'Sketch of the Life and Writings of Thomas Babington Macaulay,' V, 143n, VI, 128, 193

LETTERS TO: VI, 193, 207

Alston, Dorothy, 'Some Personal Recollections of Lord Macaulay,' I, 29n, 116n, 141n, 148n, 321, II, 10n, 196n, 302

Althorp, John Charles Spencer, Lord, afterwards 3rd Earl Spencer, II, *6*, 30, 46, invites TBM to presentation of address to King 51; 52, says TBM's 5 July speech best he ever heard 62; 70, only Whig leader in Commons who is not useless 88; TBM describes dinner with 89; no longer timid in speaking 90; TBM's estimate of 90-1; honoured at Reform dinner 101n; on public funeral for Scott 148; 173, threatens to resign 230n; 232, 234; and government plan for abolition 239; 255, advises TBM not to resign 267; compliments TBM on India speech 268; thinks TBM need not resign 268-9, 276; 279, his kind behaviour in slavery crisis 285; 290, succeeds to earldom 315n; III, 10, 23n, 74

Althorp (Earl Spencer's residence), Haydon's sketches of Reformers at, II, 273n; TBM at in 1849 V, 84; library 85; TBM sends O'Meara's book to 85-6; 345

Alvanley, William Arden, 2nd Baron, II, *21*, epilogue to *Follies of Fashion,* 288n

Ambigu, L', I, 54, 55

America, United States of, TBM on the venomous character of I, 78; false story about abolitionist petition to Congress II, 193; contrasting views of Galt and Mrs Trollope 314; III, 50, 332, better described by Mrs Trollope than by Dickens IV, 61; boundary dispute with Canada 105n, 110; president's message and growing dispute 167; War of 1812 207; elections in 224; Canadian boundary question 264-5; Sir Henry Holland reports on favourably 266; TBM says he would like to visit 266; send a stump orator as secretary of legation 296; moderates strengthened in 383; success of *History* there V, viii; spelling in 37; TBM would like to visit without publicity 39; reception of *History* surprising 39, 43, 52; Ireland deserted for 67, 69; sensitive to behaviour of English travellers 81; George Thompson's treatment in 138; and dispute over Canadian fisheries 264, 269n; won't go to war with England 269; TBM rejoices in good will between it and England 287; TBM rumoured there to be

America, United States of—*cont.* opium addict 361; Connecticut twang 426; becoming more Jeffersonian and less Washingtonian VI, 75; TBM's judgement on constitution 94-6; reasons for its prosperity 171-2

American Heritage, and Randall letter, VI, 94n

American Philosophical Society, I, xxxiv

Americans, Mrs Trollope's description II, 136; Yankee captains 136, 146; Yankees ask for biographical information 151, 155; ambassador a specimen Yankee 152; wise to have no established religion 164

Ames, Winslow, *Prince Albert and Victorian Taste*, VI, 101n

Amesbury, Charles Dundas, Baron, II, *145*

Amiens, cathedral, IV, 145

Amiens, treaty of, V, 316n

Ammianus Marcellinus, 'worst written book in ancient Latin,' III, 200*

Amos, Andrew, President of Law Commission III, 213n; *233*, appointed Downing Professor of Law V, 46n

Amsterdam, V, 160, TBM doubts that England could have made secret treaty with VI, 80; Trevelyans at 167

Anacharsis, VI, 100

Ancients and Moderns, III, 217; *see also* Classics, study of

Andalusia, V, 191

Anderson, Sir George William, III, *147*, 210, 217

Anderson, Mrs, TBM stayed with at Clifton in 1811, V, 250

André, Major John, V, 410n

Angell v. *Angell*, I, 208n

Angers, IV, 144, described 150; château 153, 155; 350

Anglesey, Henry William Paget, 1st Marquess of, I, 159, 161, II, 66n, 158, TBM's chambers overlook his London house IV, 318n, V, 224

Anglicists: *see* India, Committee of Public Instruction

Anglo-Indians, their status in England, III, 204

Anglo-Saxon, III, 122, IV, 386, Kemble on V, 61

Annabella, of Scotland, IV, 257

Annaeus Florus, III, 178*

Annan, Presbytery of, condemns Edward Irving, II, 75n

Anne, of Austria, I, 37n, IV, 81n, V, 477

Anne, of Bohemia, IV, 256

Anne, of Denmark, IV, 257

Anne, Queen (of Richard III), IV, 256

Anne, Queen, II, 70, 142, 190, 217, gives Woodstock to Marlborough IV, 148; 257, 386, and Court of St James's V, 112; VI, 253

Annual Register, II, 96, VI, 86

Annuity Tax: *see* Edinburgh

Anson, Mrs Sarah, death of, IV, *310*

Anson, Captain T. V., IV, 310n

Anson, Thomas William: *see* Lord Lichfield

Anster, Dr John, V, *84*

Anti Corn Law League, IV, 22, TBM determines not to join 85; mistaken as to its strength 100-1; 104, has defeated its own ends 107-8; 110, 168, TBM 'will never be their nominee' 172; 188, 193, 274, 346n, defeat of its leaders in 1857 VI, 86

Anti Corn Laws party, a minority, IV, 103-4

Anti-Jacobean, III, 67n

Anti-Slavery Agency Committee, founded by George Stephen I, 163n; agitates for abolition II, 240n; 242, 283, IV, 346n

Anti-Slavery Bill, I, xxv

Anti-Slavery Monthly Reporter, I, xxi, written and edited by Zachary Macaulay 228n; TBM's remarks on October 1828 number 251; 319n

Anti-Slavery Movement, I, ix, xvii, xix, xxi, xxii, iv-xxv, abolition of English slave trade 5; TBM reads Clarkson's book on 44; hopes of Allied congress at Paris 45n; William Smith active in 50n; leaders attacked as pro-slavery 60n; Slave Registration Bill 61n, 74n; TBM has no higher ambition than its success 102; TBM pledges support to 103; Clarkson secures promise of help from Alexander I, 104; African Institution formed to assist 128n; support for from *ER* and *Quarterly* 169; Spain at last joins 173; opposes duties on East Indian sugar 177n; injured by politics of Holy Alliance 179; TBM speaks against colonial system at Cambridge 183-4; implicated in Demerara insurrection 192, 194n; TBM makes speech at Anti-Slavery Society 202; TBM writes article on 'Major Moody's Reports' 212n; Sydney Smith a supporter 245; compulsory manumission clause, order in council 245; movement revived in 1830 281n; orders in council and amelioration policy II, 118; false story about abolition petition to U.S. Congress 193; 'absurd and

malevolent suspicions' of foreigners about IV, 50

Abolition Campaign: plan for general abolition I, 45n; campaign begins, 1823ff 61n, 128n, 196n; provokes attack 192-6; directed by Zachary Macaulay 148n; strong in Commons, not Lords 244; effort to obtain government measure 245n; TBM offers to resign on question II, 14n; made parliamentary issue 14n; TBM supports against ministry 221n; TBM asked to declare position 162n; declares in favour of 163; non-committal report of Commons committee 175; Lords committee makes no report 175; abolition in prospect 226n; hope for decisive government measure 237; TBM remarks on in Commons 237n; TBM's mind made up 238; threatened by Irish Church Bill crisis 258; postponed in Parliament 267; TBM opposed to government plan 267n; accepts alterations 278; saves both honour and place 279; TBM's part generally approved 283, 285; TBM to pay honour to Wilberforce 291; apprenticeship plan to die natural death 307

Abolition, Government Plan for: II, 238n, dispute over compensation 239; laid before Whigs 239n; revised 246; 258, 259-60, introduced in Lords 263n; 267, TBM must oppose 268-9; postponed 271; TBM dislikes it more and more 272; will oppose 274, 275; debate begins 276, 277; altered 278; will pass 279-80; conciliates abolitionists and cows West Indians 281; question of compensation 286; III, 356

Continental Supporters: J. C. L. Simonde de Sismondi, I, 73n, Etienne Dumas, 73n, Auguste de Staël, 176n, Duc de Broglie, 281n, Marquis de La Fayette, 304n, Louis Dumont, 307n

Anti-Slavery Society (Liverpool), first one organised, I, 196n

Anti-Slavery Society (London), I, XXV, second group organised 196n; TBM an original member 196n; speaks at first general meeting 202; *Report*, 1824, 202n; 244n, 246n; 251n, 311n, II, 175n, to be wound up 226n; motto and seal 242n; TBM objects to apprenticeship provision 267n; mission completed 333; IV, 207, 316n, V, 119, VI, 277

Anti-Slavery Society (York), Sydney Smith a speaker there, I, 245

Anti-State Church Association, V, 290

Antiphon, VI, 83

Antwerp, I, 284, fall of II, 217; IV, 8, TBM visits 216; 218, Rubens collection at 219

Anytus, VI, 251

Apollonius Rhodius, III, 152*, 159*

Appalachia, I, 82

Appius, I, 96, 97

Appleby, I, 208n, 227, V, 63

Apreece, Sir Shuckburgh, II, 170n

Aquinas, St Thomas, I, 122

Arabian Nights, VI, 60

Arabic, I, 80, III, 102, as medium of education III, 123, 149, 150

Arabin, William St Julien, *Arabiniana*, IV, *169*

Arbuthnot, Charles, II, *61*, sends Duke of Wellington's compliments on *History* V, 25; his letter 26

Arbuthnot, Mrs Charles, II, 61n

Arbuthnot, John, his attacks on Burnet, V, 145; *History of John Bull*, VI, 155*

Arcesilas, IV, 382

Archaeological Association, IV, 287n

Archaeological Institute, IV, 287

Archbishop of Canterbury, 1856: *see* John Bird Sumner

Archbishop of Dublin: *see* Richard Whately

Arches, Court of, and Gorham Case, V, 96n

Archimedes, I, 131, IV, 39

Archives, V, 458

Arcot, III, 45, 46, 67, 68

Argyle, Argyle Arms, TBM at, VI, 259n

Agyleshire, V, 180

Argyll, Earl of, VI, 145

Argyll, Elizabeth, Duchess of, V, *58*, 337n, VI, 18, 37n, 90n, 97n, 152n, 204, 227

LETTERS TO: V, 58, VI, 226

Argyll, George Douglas Campbell, 8th Duke of, IV, 36n, V, 49n, 58n, 328n, 334n, 337n, TBM's neighbour on Campden Hill VI, x, 10n, *18*; 37n, 74, 90n, 97n, TBM dines with 103; speech on India Bill 141; 152n, 204, 226, 227, 250n, Lord Privy Seal 252

Writings: Autobiography and Memoirs, 1823-1900, I, 109n, IV, 14n, VI, 10n

LETTER TO: VI, 141

Arimanes, VI, 74

Ariosto, III, 62*, IV, 28, alleged portrait by Titian VI, 61; *Orlando Furioso*, I, 65*, III, 9

Aristarchus of Edinburgh, TBM called, I, 284

Aristomenes, I, 250

Aristophanes, I, 83, 242n, III, 118, 160*, 177*, IV, 37n, V, 345, *Comedies,* ed. Holden, 415*; George Trevelyan likes, 421

Writings: The Acharnians, V, 106n*, *The Clouds,* III, 211*, V, 420*, *The Frogs,* V, 387*, *Peace,* V, 420*, *Plutus,* V, 321*, beastly lines in 415*

Aristotle, rules of drama I, 61; 87, 145*, III, 159*, 181, 211*, VI, 100

Writings: Politics, I, 242n, III, 153*, 237*, *Rhetoric,* III, 155*

Arius, V, 333

Arles, TBM at, VI, 166n

Armada, Spanish, V, 409

Arminianism, and articles of Church of England, V, 22

Arminius, VI, 248

Arms, design for TBM's, VI, 126, 134-5

Army, English, organisation of, V, 429-30

Army, foreign troops in, V, 433

Arnold, Frederick, *The Public Life of Lord Macaulay,* I, 203n, II, 137n

Arnold, Matthew, on TBM I, ix; 282n, *On Translating Homer,* IV, 44n, TBM meets V, 79n

Arnold, Dr Thomas, I, 249n, edn of Thucydides, II, 105n, letters to Ellis, III, 63n, IV, *37,* death of 37; TBM's opinion of 37n; 44, V, 26n, 'Arnoldian crotchets' 304; On *Lays of Ancient Rome* IV, 44, urges TBM to complete 66; 68, V, 81n

Arnold, Mrs Thomas, her house in Lake District, VI, 216

Arnold, Thomas Kerchever, I, 143, his death V, *321*

Arnould, Sir Joseph, *Memoir of Thomas, First Lord Denman,* V, 425

Arrian, I, 242n, *Anabasis of Alexander,* III, 200*, *Indica,* IV, 181

Arrowsmith, Aaron, *New General Atlas,* I, 207

Arrowsmith, Thomas, I, 193n

Art Journal, V, 176n

Artaxerxes, I, 32

Arthur, Prince of Wales, IV, 257

Artists' Benevolent Fund, TBM declines invitation from, VI, 209

Arundel Castle, VI, 76

Ascham, Roger, *The Schoolmaster,* VI, 215; his life by Hartley Coleridge, 278*

Ashburton, Alexander Baring, 1st Baron, I, 75n, II, *10,* offered TBM a place in his bank 10n; 16n, 52, tells TBM he should never speak again 64; 159

Ashburton, Harriet, Lady, V, IX, X, *209*
LETTER TO: V, 209

Ashburton, William Bingham Baring, 2nd Baron, II, 16n, unfounded charges against *74*; V, ix, x, 5, 109n, 209n, TBM has been at his Hampshire home 212; on Indian Civil Service Committee 389n

Ashburton Treaty, IV, 110n, 135, 'dastardly' 167

Ashley, Lord: *see* Lord Shaftesbury

Ashton Court, V, 273, 349-50

Asia (ship), choice between it and *Neptune* II, 355-6; passage taken on 361; TBM inspects it 362; III, 11, leaves Gravesend 25n; 28, 31n, 67, 85, 86

Asia, chief mate of, III, 33

Asia, surgeon of, III, 20, 27

Asiatic Journal, III, 31n, 182n

Asiatic Society, III, 149, 150

Aspenden Hall, Hertfordshire, Preston's school removes to I, 50; 53, 54, 64, its isolation 82; 112, 155

Aspinall, Arthur, *Lord Brougham and the Whig Party,* II, 238; *Politics and the Press,* VI, 302; ed., *Three Early Nineteenth Century Diaries,* II, 70n, 239n, 263n, 268n, 279n, 283n, 296n

Assembly of Divines, V, 22

Association for the Repeal of Taxes on Knowledge, V, 430

Association for the Vindication of Scottish Rights, V, 364n

Assyria, VI, 253

Astor, John Jacob, V, 394n

Astrology, preferable to mathematics, I, 122; III, 123

Athanasian Creed, V, 22

Athanasius, III, 237*

Athenaeum, prospectus for Hunt's Poetical Works, II, 112n; III, 326n, IV, 17, 52n, *Lays* advertised in 58n; 75n, 115n, story about TBM and *ER* 242; 337n, 382n, Cooke Taylor reviews *History* for V, 66n; on Byron forgeries 222n; Vizetelly's letter in 370n; review of Mansel on metaphysics VI, 162n

Athenaeum Club, TBM elected to I, 294; II, 49, 50, meets Rogers at 50; dines with Lord Nugent 55; Croker's pamphlet displayed at 110; 158, 161, encounters at 313; 314, 367, IV, 107n, 281, V, 405, VI, 14, TBM sponsors friend of Ellis t 16;

210, sponsors Drummond Wolff for 210; 225
Athenaeus, 'meditating an attack on' III, 154; 159*, planning to read VI, 247; *Deipnosophists* IV, 240*
Athenians, six first-rate ones, V, 345
Athens, I, 88, III, 131, Parthenon 273; Temple of the Winds IV, 28
Atherton, Sir William, V, 361n
Athlone, V, 29, 67
Atkinson, I, lithographic portrait of TBM, II, 206n
Atmospherical railways, IV, 147
Atterbury, Francis, II, 169, his daughter (Mrs Morice) 169; III, 206, and Phalaris controversy V, 317-18; TBM dissents from Mahon's opinion of 323; 'Vindication of Bishop Smallridge, Dr Aldrich, and Himself,' V, 323
Attorney General, 1831: *see* Lord Denman
Attorney General, 1854: *see* Sir Alexander Cockburn
Auber, Peter, II, *364*, VI, 279
LETTER TO: II, 364
Auberoche, IV, 384
Auckland, George Eden, 1st Earl of, II, *224*, behaves admirably about Indian appointments 323; 350n, III, 65n, 119n, 166, 169 170n, TBM describes 172; 185, 'an excellent Governor General' 189; 190, 'lives quietly' 198; 209, 214, 227, 228, ministers save him by refusing to attack Ellenborough IV, 99; 171, 274, 276, to have Admiralty 277; 307n, 390n, 391, death of V, 5
Auckland, Mary Eden, Lady, IV, *390*
Auckland, Bishop Robert John Eden, 3rd Baron, compliments TBM on *History* IV, *390*; succeeds to title V, 5; 7, VI, 38, his letters in Peel *Memoirs* 93
LETTER TO: IV, 390
Audit Office, IV, 388, VI, 121n
Auditor of Exchequer, Lord Halifax's sinecure, VI, 166
Aughrim, V, 67
Augusta, Princess of Wales, IV, 257
Augustan History, III, 181*, 200*, V, 268*, 274*, 280*
Augustine, St, III, viii, *De Civitate Dei*, 'indecent book' 154*; *Confessions*, 'style of a field-preacher' 237*
Aulus Gellius, III, 181*, 237*, *Attic Nights* IV, 49*; V, 416*
Aumale, Henri, Duc d', TBM meets, VI, *52*
Aurelius Victor, III, 178*
Aurungzebe, IV, 389
Austen, Jane, praised to skies by party at Lansdowne House II, 72; third woman of her age 84; TBM visits scenes of her novels at Bath 130-1; in Bentley's Standard Novels 253n; III, 22, TBM re-reads all of her novels V, 416n; went on improving to the last 451; TBM recommends for Alice Trevelyan 465
Writings: Emma, II, 18n, 37, 39*, praised by Mackintosh and Lord and Lady Lansdowne 72; 157* (*see* Additions and Corrections, vol. II); 185*, 245*, IV, 351*, V, 195, 416*, VI, 227*, 287*, *Mansfield Park*, Mackintosh says everybody likes II, 72; 262*, 344*, IV, 351*, V, 195, 271*, *Northanger Abbey*, II, 130, 131, 253*, 278*, V, 451, *Persuasion*, II, 130, 131, 253*, 280*, 'beyond which it seems impossible to go' V, 451; *Pride and Prejudice*, II, 142*, 230*, 243*, 249*, TBM buys in Bentley's Standard Novels 290; *Sense and Sensibility*, V, 451
Austin, Charles, I, xix, at Cambridge Union 183n; 190n, 263n, 295n, III, 325n, IV, 45n, income from railway boom 259n; V, 6n, 42n, would be the very man for Downing Professorship 45; VI, 93, 198n, breakfasts with TBM 200; 201
LETTER TO: VI, 200
Austin, Mrs Charles (Harriet Jane Ingelby), VI, 198n, *200*, breakfasts with TBM 200; 201
Austin, John, I, 263n, III, *325*n, IV, *44*, 'List on German Customs-Union,' IV, 44*, 47*; V, 102n
Austin, Mrs Sarah, 263n, III, 325, IV, 45n, and J. W. Croker 90; edits Sydney Smith's letters V, 15n; a Taylor of Norfolk 40n; 102n
Writings: Characteristics of Goethe, II, 277, translation of Ranke, *History of the Popes*, III, 268n, 325n, 326
LETTERS TO: III, 325, IV, 295, V, 17, 40
Australasia, VI, 254
Australia, gold discovered in, V, 321n
Autographe L', V, 404
Autographic Mirror, V, 445
Avignon, III, 260, 270, 274, VI, 159, TBM at 166n; 169n
Avon, view of, V, 273
Aylesbury, Lord, V, x
Ayr, TBM invited to stand for, IV, 348
Azov, Sea of, V, 476

Baba: *see* Margaret Trevelyan Holland
Babbage, Charles, II, *58*, 'vile temper and strangely twisted understanding' V, 150
Babington, Anthony, his conspiracy, V, 88
Babington, Arthur Thomas, II, *171*
Babington, Charles Roos (1806-26), TBM's cousin, I, *130*, 'a poor creature' III, 99; 101
Babington, Churchill, V, *95*, *Mr. Macaulay's Character of the Clergy*, 95*, ed., *The Oration of Hyperides against Demosthenes*, 95*
LETTER TO: V, 95
Babington, George (1794-1856), TBM's cousin, I, xxii, *170*, 178, 198n, encourages TBM 201; 244, II, 15, 40, 45, 48n, cares for TBM in illness 87; 154n, 161, 185, 192n, 193, 217, opinion about Hannah's health 233; sends Hannah to Liverpool 234; has been ill 234; 236, at Wilberforce's death bed 284; on dark financial prospects of Macaulays and Babingtons 300; has no fears of Indian climate for TBM 301; his advice about Charles 304; 308, 310, 312, 326, 330, cannot speak of Tom Babington with temper 332; 336, 343, 359, 361, inspects *Asia* with TBM 362; 365, writhes at sound of Tom Babington's voice 366; 368, III, 5, 17, 25n, 30, named agent for TBM 22; 25, 26, 28, 30, 31, 40, 72, TBM's banker 73; 89, 90, 97, 98, 99, 101, 106, 116, 117, 140, 182, 213, 'extraordinary conduct' 222-3; behaves in 'unfeeling' way 230-1; 'obstinate silence' 233; TBM dines with 285n; in Italy for his health IV, 198n; returns from Rome but will go back 201; V, 73, 74, 252, 402, death of VI, 5
Babington, Mrs George (Sarah Anne Pearson), I, *170*, 244, II, 66, sees Thames procession with TBM 82; 154n, 158, 161, 185, 192n, getting well 193; 326, fears scene with Tom Babington 332; 362, 366, plagued by sciatica IV, 198; does not want to live in Italy 201; V, 73, 74, 252, 402
Babington, Henry (1803-67), TBM's cousin, I, *76*, at Preston's school 76; II, 294, the cost of his passage to India in 1822 343; III, 80, his standing in India 162; plans American tour V, 80-1
Babington, Mrs Henry (Sarah Disney), III, *80*
Babington, Jean, or Jane (1798?-1839), TBM's cousin, I, *129*, on TBM's reading at Rothley 198; II, 18, 31, her garrulity 49; 85, 193, 303, 361, 364, ill III, 295; 296, her death 311
Babington, John (1791-1885), TBM's cousin, I, *26*, 141n, 308n, VI, 139
Babington, Julia Mary, II, 171
Babington, Lydia: *see* Lydia Babington Rose
Babington, Mary: *see* Lady James Parker
Babington, Matthew (1792-1836), TBM's cousin, I, *48*, in family party at Cambridge 127; 199, 277, II, 75, 85, married a Sykes 86; 192n, III, 33
Babington, Samuel, I, *64*
Babington, Thomas (1758-1837), TBM's uncle, I, *xxi*, xxiv, 30, his house in London 48n; gives TBM *Histories* by Hume and Smollett 51; disapproves debating society at Preston's 76; TBM reassures as to Cambridge morality 111; TBM promises to help Charles Babington 130; 141, on Edward and Henry Elliott 176n; 187n, 199, 201, compared to Jeffrey 238; 267n, 275, 277, 308n, II, 68, 71, 72, 74, 75, 86, 87, 89n, 162, 172, 190, 191, 198, 234, 294, financially helpless 300; 303, scenes with feared 332; III, 99, 157, 280, and Rothley Temple IV, 203; difficulty of his epitaph V, 169-70; epitaph finished 196; on Pitt's speech of 25 March 1801 398
LETTERS TO: I, 111, 129
Babington, Mrs Thomas (Jean Macaulay), TBM's aunt, I, XXI, XXII, XXV, 48, 111, 199, 201, 277, II, 68, 71, 72, 74, 75, abuses Lydia Rose 85; 86, 87, 162, 191, 198, 303
Babington, Thomas Gisborne (1788-1871), TBM's cousin, I, xxii, *115*, partner with Zachary Macaulay 115n; 127, 128, 129, 196n, 252n, forced to sell Rothley Temple 267n; 274n, TBM sees his house in Bath II, 131; absurd malade imaginaire 171; and his wife 263; dishonest but has a claim 336; wants to go to India as TBM's secretary 359; plagues TBM for a place 366; 317n
Babington, Mrs Thomas Gisborne (Augusta Noel), I, *127*, 141n, 145n, dying II, 247; death 262-3
Babington, William, I, *64*, 163, his behaviour evidence of Spoonerism II, 326-7; visits TBM again 328-9
Babington, William, Rector of Cossington, I, 64n
Babington family, I, xxi, 176, household books of III, 286
Babington-Smith, Bernard, I, xxxiv, 115n, 170n

Babrius, *Fables*, from British Museum MS, VI, 242*, 243
Babylon, V, 191
Backhouse, Miss J. M., IV, 236n
Bacon, Francis, 1st Baron Verulam and Viscount St Albans, quoted I, 68; 83, 140, Basil Montagu quotes II, 28; edited by Montagu 28n, III, 163n; formation of TBM's opinion on 194; 202, TBM differs from Napier about 243; IV, 35, his 'knowledge is power' V, 147; statue of in Trinity antechapel VI, 67n; 68, 69, 162, TBM learned investigation of truth from 171
Writings: Advancement of Learning, I, 133n, III 246*, *De Augmentis*, III 62*, V, 147*, *Essays*, III, 197, *Meditationes Sacrae*, V, 147, *Novum Organum*, III, 205, V, 147, VI, 68, 'Of Great Place,' III, 219*
Bacon, Richard M., III, *307*, article defending TBM, 307
LETTERS TO: III, 307, 319
Baildon, Mr, IV, 308
Bain, Alexander, *James Mill*, I, 184n, 263n, II, 366n, IV, 309n
Baines, Edward, elder, II, *103*, 'The Tables Turned,' defense of TBM 202; succeeds TBM as MP for Leeds 361; portrait presented to Mechanics' Institution V, 116n
LETTERS TO: II, 202, 232, 285, 333
Baines, Sir Edward, II, *103*, article on TBM III, 291; IV, 5, 122n
LETTERS TO: II, 202, III, 291, IV, 5, V, 115
Baines, Matthew Talbot, II, *103*n
Baines, William, I, 211, II, 226
Baird, Sir David, anecdote of, II, *224*, 225
Baird, Mrs, mother of Sir David, II, 224
Balearic Islands, III, 353
Ballads, Ellis sends specimens to TBM, III, 383; TBM's collection of 383n; Ellis sends some IV, 48; their style 58
Ballot, TBM undecided on question, I, 313; position explained II, 92-3, 132; best mode of voting 165; III, 150-1, 167, TBM supports 290; will not vote against it IV, 272; opinion has changed 363, V, 232, no longer a question 475
Baltimore, V, 141
Bancroft, George, IV, 323n, *403*, V, 42n, sends TBM American edn of *History* 43; 58
LETTERS TO: IV, 403, V, 43
Bancroft, Mrs George (Elizabeth Davis Bliss), IV, 403, V, *58*
LETTER TO: V, 58
Bandy, W. T., 'Macaulay and His Italian Translator,' V, 404n
Bangalore, described III, 47ff.; 49, 50, 60, 67, 72, 83, attractions of 84; 92
Bangor, TBM at, I, 158, V, 43n
Banim, John, II, *225*
Bank of England, its monopoly II, 162n, 164; charter renewal 192, 194, 258
Bank Charter Bill, IV, 184n
Bankes, William, candidate at Cambridge, I, 212n
Bankes, William John, I, 181n
Banks, Mrs G. L. (Isabella Varley), *Wooers and Winners*, II, 210n
Banks, John H., III, 296
Bannatyne Club, TBM receives Fountainhall's works from, IV, 384, 387; V, 120n, VI, 129n
Bannerman, Alexander, IV, *261*
Banting, William, VI, *209*
LETTER TO: VI, 209
Baptists, V, 88, complain that Bunyan has no monument in Westminster Abbey 426
Barbados, outrages in, I, 195
Barbary pirates, VI, 58
Barbauld, Mrs, and Lucy Aikin, her neice, IV, 128
Barcelona, flood at, V, 135
Barebones, Praise God, V, 176
Barère, Bertrand, *Mémoires*, IV, 163n; his lies 166
Barham, John Foster, VI, 190n
Barham, Lord: *see* Earl of Gainsborough
Barillon d'Amoncourt, Paul, his MS despatches, IV, 313; V, 24, VI, 130
Baring, Alexander: *see* 1st Baron Ashburton
Baring, Sir Francis, afterwards 1st Baron Northbrook, I, 18n, II, 16n, *179*, 327, letter to Trevelyan III, 317n; IV, 271, 272, to be Chancellor of Exchequer 277; 278, TBM applies to for Ellis V, 64; 210n, hurt by Russell's conduct 307
Baring, Sir Thomas, in all-night debate II, 71
Baring, Thomas, II, *16*n
Baring Brothers, VI, 190n
Barker, Alexander, buys Manfrini Titians, VI, *61*
Barley Wood (Hannah More's residence), I, xxix, TBM at 6; 7n, TBM at in 1816 80n; in 1818 112n; in 1819 129n; 132, Macaulay family at 137; 139, Selina Mills Macaulay at 149; 177, TBM's memories of 182; Hannah More leaves 236n; III, 65, V, 265, 270, TBM visits in 1852 V, 273, 275; 349

Barlow, Francis, I, *233*
LETTERS TO: I, 233, 271
Barlow, John, I, *139*, 141, takes low place in Tripos exam 142-3; leaves his Trinity rooms to TBM 143; father dies suddenly 153; Secretary of Royal Institution IV, 366n
LETTER TO: IV, 366
Barlow, Philip, I, *172*
Barlow, Thomas William, death of, I, 153
Barnard, Sir Henry William, commanding at Delhi, VI, *106*
Barnes, James Alexander, I, 143
Barnes, James J., *Free Trade in Books,* V, 224n
Barnes, Thomas, claims credit for TBM's 'Country Clergyman,' II, *57*
Barnett, Mr, V, 90
Baronetage, privileges of, III, 307
Barrackpore, III, 114, 117
Barré, Colonel Isaac, III, *220*, V, 216
[Barrett, Mrs Charlotte Francis], letter to III, 308
Barrett, Eaton Stannard, *The Heroine,* II, 253*
Barron, Arthur, I, *179*
Barron, Captain Richard, III, *36*, 37, 38, 42, 84, 87, 96
Barron, Mrs Richard, III, 37, 38
Barrot, Camille Hyacinthe Odilon, III, *354*
Barrow, Isaac, VI, 67n
Barrow, Sir John, 'Fernando Po – State of the Slave Trade,' I, 169n
Barrow, John Henry, II, 69n
Barry, Sir Charles, III, *367*, on decoration of House of Lords IV, 247-8; V, 72
Barry, Spranger, II, *309*
Barton, Bernard, V, *85*
Barton, Catherine, De Morgan's theory of her marriage to Montagu V, *355n*; VI, 55, and Lord Halifax's will 165
Basle, V, 339, 343, 349, 354, VI, 26
Bassompierre, François de, V, *476*, *Mémoires,* 476n
Bateman, Agnes, Lady, her marriage, V, 372
Bateman, Josiah, *Life of the Rev. Henry Venn Elliott,* I, 219n
Bateman, William Bateman-Hanbury, 2nd Baron, marries Lady Mahon's sister, V, 372n
'Bateman, The Loving Ballad of Lord,' V, 372
Bates, Eli, *Rural Philosophy,* I, 83*
Bath, I, 297, TBM at II, 129; described 130-1; Milsom Street IV, 149; Dr Bright opposes going there V, 109
Bath, 1st Marquess of, IV, *73*
Bath, 3rd Marquess of, VI, 87
Bathie, Captain G. K., of the *Asia,* II, *356*, 361, described 362; III, 11, 27, 30, 33, death of 86
Bathie, Rev. Dr, II, 356n
Bathurst, Henry Bathurst, 3rd Earl, II, *61*
Bavaria, IV, 76
Bavarian Academy of Science, III, xi
Baxter, Richard, IV, *222*
Baxter, W. R., *The Curse of Britain,* III, 297n
Bayonets, called daggers, V, 76
Bayonne, I, 39
Beachy Head, I, 287, IV, 136
Beard, Richard, V, *56*n, daguerreotype of TBM 56n, 57
Beast, Mark of, III, 53, 61
Beatson's Political Index, VI, 41
Beauchamp, Lord, V, 189
Beauclerk, Topham, II, *67*
Beaufort, Louis de, *Dissertation sur l'Incertitude des Cinq Premiers Siècles de l'Histoire Romaine,* II, 142
Beaumarchais, Pierre de, and Goëzman affair V, 315; *Mémoires* 315n 318
Beaumont, Lord, VI, 129n, 234n
Beaumont, Thomas Wentworth, I, 216
Beaumont, Francis, and John Fletcher, *A Wife for a Month,* II, 241*, TBM proposes to work with Ellis in their way VI, 167
Beauvais, V, 419, cathedral, V, 68
Beccaria, Cesare, TBM presented with his works, V, 404n
Bedford, TBM at, I, 156n; Bedford gaol, traditional place of composition of *Pilgrim's Progress,* V, 402
Bedford, 4th Duke of, IV, 7, *72*, 221
Bedford, John Russell, 6th Duke of, II, *65*, 282n, III, 171
Bedford, Francis Russell, 7th Duke of, II, 21, 78, 152n, IV, 272
Bedford, John of Lancaster, Duke of, IV, 246
Bedford, Georgiana, Duchess of, II, 181, *282*, on Lady Cork 283
Begum Samru, III, *169*
Behnes, William, V, *234*
LETTER TO: V, 234
Behr, Camill von, *Genealogie der Europäischen Fürstenhäuser,* V, 373
Belgium, formation of II, 155n; independence of 202n, 217
Bell, Alan, I, xxxiii
Bell, Sir Charles, I, 314n
Bellarmine, Cardinal, V, 332

Bell's Weekly Messenger, ed. F. L. Holt, II, 5n
Belper, Amelia, Lady, VI, 139, 200n, 201, 226n, 227
Belper, Edward Strutt, 1st Baron, II, *35*, 97, at Paris 276, IV, 141; V, 111n, should have been in Aberdeen cabinet 306; 315, TBM consults with about peer's robes, VI, 118; created Baron 118n; 119, supports TBM on taking seat in Lords 134n; TBM asks to take charge of petitions 157; 200, 201, 226n, TBM to dine with 227
LETTERS TO: V, 316, VI, 139, 157
Belsham, William, *History of Great Britain*, V, 279
Belvoir Castle, III, 286
Benares, III, 361, anarchy in Mutiny VI, 105
Benett, John, in all-night debate, II, *71*, 81
Bengal, TBM to arrive in June, II, 342, 343; 357, Bobus Smith Advocate General in 365; 367, III, 66, 87, 118, 173, 191, 193, revenue system 204; 218, 221, 230, IV, 306
Bengal, Bay of, III, 86
Bengal, Council of, proposed act for, III, 312
Bengal, Nabob of, III, 43
Bengal Annual, III, 126n
Bengal Club, III, 90n, 182
Bengal Hurkaru, III, 55n, 79n, 124, 134n, 160n, 177n, 182n, 209, 213n, IV, 218n
Bengalee, II, 198
Benjamin, W. E., catalogue, V, 39n
Benlomond, III, 59
Bennett, Mr, candidate for Cambridge in 1690, V,211
Bennett, William Cox, IV, *369*, sonnet on TBM in *Poems* 369n
LETTER TO: IV, 369
Benson, E. W., V, 228n
Benson, Miss, V, 199
Bentham, Mr D. R., III, xi
Bentham, Jeremy, I, xix, response to TBM's attack on Utilitarians 254n; II, 272n, III, 146, could have wished for nothing better than proceedings in Vizetelly case V, 367
Benthamites, their attack absurd I, 255; 263n, III, 147, 158n, 165, 209n, Cameron an inconsistent one IV, 309: *see also* Utilitarians
Bentinck, Lord George, IV, 299n
Bentinck, Lord William, forbids suttee II, 138; 191, 224n, III, viii, *31n*, 35, 36, 40, 56, 58, TBM received by 59; 60, 61, his household 65; 66, 67, 75, 77, 79, 80, 84, 100, remarks on Trevelyan 101; 102, 106, 110, lends cottage to Trevelyan for honeymoon 114; frightened by TBM's misery 116n; 117, TBM's high opinion of 119; minute on fourth member of Council 119; on Press Regulation Act 124; 134n, 148, permits TBM to settle education question 149; TBM writes to 156; 170, 209n, 244n, death 292n; most liberal of Clive's successors 309; statue of at Calcutta 309n; VI, 38
LETTERS TO: III, 31, 76, 120, 125, 133, 137
Bentinck, Lady William, III, *71*, 72, 88, 95, 97, 106, 110, 114, 116n, 'quite a mother to Nancy' 117; 119, 120, TBM sends sympathy to 292
Bentley, Richard, I, 237n, edn of *Paradise Lost* III, 142; edn of Horace 201*; emendation in Ampelius 202; victory over Oxford confederacy 217; 363n, held that no man written down but by himself IV, 193*; V, 44*, and controversy with Boyle 317; 318, VI, 67n, TBM argues his claim for a statue at Trinity 68-9; immoral as Master of Trinity 69; emendation in his *Horace* 99*; 243, edn of Horace 245*, 247*; his life by Hartley Coleridge 278*
Writings: Dissertation upon the Epistles of Phalaris, III, 183, 201, VI, 68, *Epistle to Mill*, VI, 68
Bentley's Miscellany, publishes Eddis portrait of TBM, V, 55n
Bentley's Standard Novels, Jane Austen in, II, 253n, 290n; Mrs Gore's novels reissued in V, 102n
Berengaria, Queen, IV, 256
Beresford, Lord George, I, *214*
Beresford, James, *The Miseries of Human Life*, I, 46*, 48*, IV, 136
Bergamo, VI, 57, 58
Bergerac, IV, 384
Berlin, IV, 19, 21
Bernal, Ralph, II, *45*, 52
Bernard, Pierre-Joseph, *L'Art d'Aimer*, V 181*
Bernard, Simon, his trial, VI, *149*
Berne, V, 352
Bernese Alps, V, 343, 348, 354
Berni, Francesco, *Rifacimento*, III, 121*, 261
Berri, Duc de, assassination of, IV, 148
Berri, Duchesse de, I, 289
Berry (French province), IV, 143, 146, 152
Berry, Agnes, II, *255*, angered by TBM's 'Walpole' 347; 357, III, 24, IV, 144

Berry, Mary, II, *255*, a favourite of Walpole 317; edits *Letters of the Marquise Du Deffand* 317n, 349; angered by TBM's 'Walpole' 347; her relation to Walpole 348-9; 357, III, 22, TBM's letters to 24n; IV, 60, 119, 236, 265
  LETTERS TO: III, 24, IV, 143
Berthier, General, IV, 148
Bertrand, Count, I, 77n
Bertrand, Mme, subject for examination in Latin verses I, 77
Berwick, V, 243
Berwick Advertiser, II, 375n
Bessborough, John William Ponsonby, 4th Earl of, II, *6*, 10, 66, 80, 365, III, 120n, 298n, IV, 131, in Russell's projected ministry 277
Bethell, Richard, afterwards Baron Westbury, VI, *151*
Betterton, Thomas, II, *309*
Bettws, Wales, I, 158
Betty, William, VI, *60*
Beverley, bull baiting at, III, 384
Bexley, Nicholas Vansittart, 1st Baron, I, 75, speech of 75n; II, *291*
Bible, TBM reads Greek Testament on Sundays at school I, 29; knowledge of essential to a critic of English language II, 22; New Testament, Ram Mohan Roy on 47; story of Joseph 38; allusions in 'Mirabeau' 167; in German III, 194; TBM's means of learning languages 195, 196; Greek Testament given by Ellis To Malkin 228; printing of in Scotland 351, 355-6; rivalled by *History* V, viii; 42, 49, 147, 'Wicked Bible' 471; prophecy in VI, 253-4, Acts, II, 327*, III, 70*, 178, IV, 196*, I Chronicles, VI, 90*, I Corinthians, V, 16*, Daniel, VI, 253, Deuteronomy, II, 72*, Ecclesiastes, I, 159*, II, 287, Exodus, I, 42*, 168*, Genesis, II, 158*, V, 17*, Isaiah, II, 79*, 230, VI, 86*, 204*, 245*, James, IV, 111*, V, 193*, Jeremiah, II, 23*, 141n, Job, II, 36*, 230, V, 297*, I John, I, 161*, Joshua, II, 167n, V, 387, Judges, I, 146*, II, 24*, 188*, V, 217*, I Kings, I, 314*, II Kings, II, 326*, Leviticus, IV, 372, Luke, I, 168*, II, 22*, 88*, 167n, 189*, IV, 41*, 305*, VI, 276*, Mark, II, 185*, 195*, III, 114*, VI, 127*, Matthew, II, 22*, IV, 292, VI, 133*, 182, Proverbs, I, 16*, II, 203*, Psalms, II, 151*, 167n, Revelation, II, 6*, III, 53, IV, 136, VI,;253, Romans, V, 278, Song of Solomon, II, 36*, 332*, Apocrypha, I Esdras, I, 61*
Bible Society, I, xxv, TBM discusses attack on, 41; 43, 104, 176n, 234, IV, 207, 234n
Bible Society, Cambridge, I, 39-40, 72n, meetings 'below par' 135
Bible Society, Edinburgh, disputes over Apocrypha, I, 225n, 235n
Bible Society, Leeds, I, 231n
Bible Society, Llanrwst, TBM refuses to attend, I, 162n
Biblical prophecy, TBM's remarks on, VI, 253-4
Bibliothèque universelle . . . de Genève, publishes TBM's 'Pompeii' in French, I, 150n
Bickersteth, Robert, 'ranting preacher,' VI, 70
Bigelow, John Prescott, letter to, V, 287
Bignon, Louis Pierre Édouard, *Histoire de France sous Napoléon*, III, 340
Bingley, F. E., Leeds publisher, VI, 278n
Biographia Britannia, III, 62*
Birch, Captain Sir Richard James, III, *125*
Birch, Samuel, VI, *23*
Birch, Samuel, pastrycook, II, *319*
Birch, Thomas, *Life of Tillotson*, V, 146
Bird, Charles Smith, I, 156n, heads reading party at Llanrwst *162*; 164, appointed Vicar of Gainsborough IV, 128n
  Writings: A Plea for the Reformed Church, IV, 128*
  LETTERS TO: III, 345, IV, 128
Bird, Claude Smith, *Sketches from the Life of the Rev. Charles Smith Bird*, I, 151n, 157n, 162n, 166n, IV, 128
Birkenhead, fight between Protestants and Catholics at, V, 137
Birmingham, I, 212, 234, TBM at II, 131; 197, VI, 95, 103n
Birmingham Political Union, II, 115n
Bishops Thorpe, Yorkshire, TBM visits with Sydney Smith, I, 245
Bison, in Europe, IV, 73-4
Blache, Comte de la, V, 315n
Black, Adam, III, *287*, 302n, opposed for Lord Provostship 338n; TBM supports 345; 348, opposed by Whigs 350; defeat at Edinburgh 355n; 357, IV, 19n, 108, made Lord Provost 250n; 269, 285, presides at meeting for TBM 301; 315, 320, 335, 348, gives poor account of Edinburgh politics 379; V, xi, on Committee on National Education 90n; worried by TBM's letter to Edinburgh 240n; says TBM's election certain 241; 242, 244, 246, he and Craig alter TBM's letter to electors 253, 256, 257, statement

about election expenses 262; 294, his edition of TBM's biographies 317n; TBM asks him to find a successor 441; TBM consults about Saturday Half Holiday Association 447; TBM repeats request to be relieved 450; TBM consults on announcement of resignation VI, 6; succeeds TBM for Edinburgh 7n; his election opposed 14n; 15, TBM has promised article on Johnson 29; 85n, TBM gives permission to reprint articles 168; 179

Writings: ed., *Biographies by Lord Macaulay*, III, 287, 344n

LETTERS TO: III, 287, 346, 384, IV, 100, 250, 261, 349, V, 239, 240, 243, 269, 289, 373, 377, 379, 434, 441, 446, 447, 450, 466, 468, VI, 6, 7, 50, 118, 167, 168, 240

Black, Adam and Charles, publishers, III, 287

Black, A. and C., *Adam and Charles Black, 1807-1957*, I, 291n

Black, Charles Bertram, V, *294*, 379

LETTER TO: V, 294

Black, Dr John, IV, *181*

Black Act, III, 182n

Black Hole of Calcutta, IV, 202

Blackburn, Hugh, V, *38*

Blackburn, Peter, in Edinburgh election 1847, IV, 341n

Blackburne, John, M.P. for Lancashire, I, 252n

Blackwood, William, I, 203n

Blackwood's Magazine, TBM recommended for by Maginn I, 203n; MacQueen's articles in 222n, 228n; on TBM and Sadler 318-9; insulting description of TBM II, 81; 83, 110, 111, III, 250, Bulwer's *My Novel* in V, 311n; 182n

Blaise Castle (J. S. Harford's residence), I, 175n, II, 16, V, 265, 266, TBM visits 270, 276

Blake, Robert, *Disraeli*, V, 301n, VI, 210n

Blakely, Edmund, offers to send Norwich papers to TBM, VI, 117

LETTERS TO: VI, 117, 121

Blakeney, T. S., III, xi

Blakey, Dorothy, *The Minerva Press*, I, 219n

Bland, Miles, I, *138*, *Algebraical Problems*, 51

Bland, Robert, *Translations, Chiefly from the Greek Anthology*, VI, 46n

Blane, Sir Gilbert, III, *47*

Blenheim, III, 58

Blessington, Lady, II, 156n, *The Repealers*, 260

Blewitt, Octavian, V, *107*

Bligh, Richard, *New Reports of Cases Heard in the House of Lords*, I, 220n

Blois, I, 284, IV, 142, 144, 146, described 148-9; château, 149, 153; 350, V, 417, 419

Blomfield, Charles James, Bishop of London, notes on Euripides I, 77; II, *98*, 290, IV, 323n, TBM dines with V, 110; and Papal aggression 135; 157n, 201, at closing of Great Exhibition 204; second wife of 333

LETTER TO: V, 110

Blomfield, Mrs Charles James (Dorothy Cox Kent), V, *333*

LETTER TO: V, 333

Bloomfield, Sir Benjamin, I, *175*

Bloomsbury gang, IV, 72n

Blount, Martha, V, 356

Blue and Yellow: *see Edinbugh Review*

Blumbo, the, I, 40

Blundell, Benson, defends TBM against Dixon, VI, *45*

LETTER TO: VI, 45

Blundell, Dr, I, 124

Blundell, Major, I, 17n

Blundell, Thomas, at school with TBM I, *17*; head of school 18; 26, 32, 35, 36, TBM will miss him 51; his death described 124-5

Boa Vista, I, xxvi, IV, 312n

Board of Audit, I, xxviii, Charles Macaulay appointed Secretary V, 387; VI, 266n

Board of Control, I, xvi, xx, TBM appointed to II, 122n; its history 122n; no arrangement for business yet made 134; 135, intrigues at 136; 138, conflict between Gordon and other commissioners 139-40; 144, 178, 190n, 191, TBM working at 192; TBM appointed Secretary 209; 214, 228, opposes Mr Hutchinson's claims 247; working on Charter Bill 263, 264; 267, 'worked to an oil' 270; clearing off work at 294; 311, its business neglected 318; TBM as much President as Grant 324; 328, 344, 349, TBM to resign as Secretary 350; 360, Wynn President of 366; III, 22, 150n, 164n, 176n, 184, IV, 124, 166, 184, 218, 277, 316n, 326, V, 221, 392, 439, 442n, Vernon Smith President of VI, 43n; TBM anxious about in event of change of ministry 220

Board of Health, I, xxviii, IV, 253n, V, 118n, Charles Macaulay Secretary to 118n, 119n; Charles Macaulay leaves 387; TBM advises Charles not to return 417

Board of Public Instruction: *see* India, Committee of Public Instruction

Board of Trade, III, 170
Board of Trade, President of, 1833: *see* Lord Auckland
Board of Treasury, IV, 338, 356
Boase, Frederick, ed., *Modern English Biography*, I, xli
Boase, T. S. R., 'The Decoration of the New Palace of Westminster,' IV, 198n
Boccaccio, *Decameron*, I, 65*, II, 54
Boddington, Samual Sidney, II, *21*, 255, dinner with described 365; VI, 275
Bodleian Library Record, III, 166n
Boehme, Jacob, I, 7n
Bohn, Henry, V, 447n, presents edn of Addison to TBM *472*: edn of Addison 481: of Lowndes, *Bibliographer's Manual* 481
  LETTERS TO: V, 472, 481
Boiardo, Mateo, *Orlando Innamorato*, III, 121*
Boileau, Catherine, Lady, II, *157*
Boileau, Sir John Peter, II, 157n, V, 234n
Boileau, Nicolas, *Épitres*, I, 226*, *Le Lutrin*, III, 307
Boleyn, Anne, IV, 257
Bolingbroke, Henry St John, 1st Viscount, II, 190, III, 258, IV, 10
Bolton, described I, 218
Bombay, II, 245, Sir John Keane appointed to 338; III, 184, newspapers of 186; government IV, 307; quiet in Mutiny VI, 105
Bonaparte, Jérôme, TBM meets IV, *314*
Bonaparte, Lucien, *Charlemagne*, I, 56
Bond, Donald F., ed., *The Spectator*, V, 482n
Bonn, V, 220, 349n, 351, 354
Bonnechose, Émile de, calls on TBM V, *384*; *Histoire d'Angleterre*, 384, *Les Quatre Conquêtes d'Angleterre*, 384*
  LETTER TO: V, 384
Bonner, Bishop Edmund, III, 225, IV, *393*, his commission from Henry VIII V, 12, 19
Bonner, William, III, 339
Book of Common Prayer, III, 48*, Stanhope's motion to remove state services from VI, 157n
Book of Jasher, II, 225
Book-Lore, I, 325
Booth, Barton, II, *309*
Bordeaux, VI, 101, 159, 160, TBM at 166n, 168
Bordeaux, Duc de, I, 289
Borland, Francis, *Memoirs of Darien*, VI, 129, 132*, 133n
Borrowdale, III, 46
Bossuet, Jacques, I, 83, *Histoire des Variations des Églises Protestantes*, V, 26*
Boston, Lincolnshire, TBM visits with Ellis, V, 193n, 218n; 233, 267
Boston, Massachusetts, V, 52, 81, 141, George Thompson's treatment at 138; Public Library VI, 46n
Boston Railroad Jubilee, presented to TBM, V, 287n
Boswell, James, Lawrence's sketch of II, 57; Journal 58n; stories about by Lansdowne and Mackintosh 71-2; III, 258, 281n, half the charm of his books their absurdity V, 410; VI, 218n
  Writings: An Account of Corsica, II, 72n, *Letters to Temple*, VI, 73*, *Life of Johnson*, I, 57n, TBM first reads 61n; 84n, 261*, Croker's edn 286n, II, 7; ed. Hill and Powell 58n; 67n, 289n, 309n, IV, 137*, *Tour to the Hebrides*, II, 24*, 57, 193*
Boswelliana, from Milnes, VI, 47
Boulogne, Napoleon at I, 8n; 308, III, 274, V, 69, 70, 70n, 319, 349n, 354, 365, 371, 418, Hotel des Bains 419; VI, 26, discovery of Boswell's letters at 73n; 167
Boundary Commissioners, Ellis one of, II, 105
Bourbon, family of, I, 42, incapable of learning 179; 289
Bourbon, Island of, III, 34
Bourdaloue, Louis, V, *27*
Bourges, described IV, 142-6; 152-3, 157, 350, V, 419, VI, 101, 104, TBM at 166n
Bourke, Lt.-General Sir Richard, his edn of Bourke's Letters, IV, 177n
Bourne, Vincent, 'In Miltonum,' TBM translates, I, 109, 110
Bovet, *Lettres Autographes*, IV, 71
Bovey Tracey, Devon, John Macaulay's living, III, 363n; Frances Macaulay at IV, 316; V, 64
Bowdler, John, Jr, I, *118*, 'A Fragment,' 118*
Bowdler, Thomas, I, 118n
Bowie, Henry, Secretary of Edinburgh Philosophical Institution V, 399
  LETTERS TO: V, 399, 451, 463, 464, VI, 32
Bowood (Lord Lansdowne's seat in Wiltshire), TBM at I, 263; described 264, 265; TBM refuses invitation to II, 213; 355, 356, TBM at 357, 359-60; 361, TBM at III, 341, IV, 84; to spend Christmas there 228; to spend New Year's 1845, 282; just returned from 284; TBM at 353;

palace surrounded by paupers v, 78; TBM at 79, 142n, 144, 212; paradise if in North Lancashire 232; bust of Lansdowne at 234n; 289n, TBM at 290, 308; 366; TBM at 368, 369; 370, 481, TBM forbidden to visit 483; TBM at vi, 185; 190

Bowring, Sir John, iv, *114*, acted ill in China business vi, 79

Boyer, Abel, *History of King William the Third*, v, 279

Boyle, Charles, 4th Earl of Orrery, ii, 201, and controversy with Bentley, v, 317, *Dr. Bentley's Dissertations*, v, 318*

Boyne, The, v, xi, 29, 64n, 65, TBM goes over the battlefield 66; 69, 208

Bracegirdle, Anne, ii, *309*, 310, v, 356

Bradbury and Evans, their bargain with Thackeray, v, 358

Bradford, i, 208n, 213, TBM at for Quarter Sessions 214; 'filthiest and most inconvenient town in the West Riding' 217; 222n, 228, 243n, 253n

Bradgate Park, iii, 81

Bradshaigh, Lady, iv, 126

Bradshaw, John, v, 101n

Braham, John, ii, *36*

Braithwaite, Joseph Bevan, v, 6n

Brantôme, Pierre, 'Charles-Quint, Empereur et Roy d'Espagne,' v, 162*

Braunschweig, v, viii

Bray, Edward Atkyns, vi, *82*

Brazil, revolution in, ii, 40

Breadalbane, John Campbell, 1st Earl of, v, *313*n

Breadalbane, John Campbell, 2nd Marquess of, his papers, v, *313*, 314

Brecknockshire, v, 180

Brescia, vi, 57, 58, 230n

Brest, iv, 155

Bretons, iv, 42

Brewer's Dictionary of Phrase and Fable, iv, 328

Brewster, Sir David, iv, *20*, his malevolence 20-1; iv, 22, 80

Writings: '*The Encyclopaedia Britannica*, 7th Edition,' iv, 47*, 'Harris on Thunderstorms,' 227*, *Life of Sir Isaac Newton*, v, 209-10*, 'Whewell's *Philosophy of the Inductive Sciences*,' iv, 20*

Bridgewater House, iii, 49n

Bright, John, iv, 22n, 168, 170n, *172* elected for Durham iv, 188n; 402, v, 222, TBM agrees with his attack on Palmerston 390; defeated in 1857 vi, 86; on Indian Mutiny 103

Bright, Dr John, called in v, *14*; diagnoses 'suppressed gout' 103; no longer needed 108; opposes cure at Bath 109; Empson to consult 129; has put TBM to rights 211; diagnoses bile 245; prescribes calomel 246, 250; 251, gives TBM stethoscopic examination 257; 258, recommends Clifton 259; 261, his treatment approved by Symonds 270; 279, thinks TBM should not attempt to attend session 283, 284; TBM promises to vote for his candidate 308; 313, 366, 403, forbids TBM to visit Bowood 483; prescribing for TBM vi, 157

Brightfield, Myron F., *John Wilson Croker*, ii, 106n, 108, iv, 89n, 90n

Brighton, i, xxvi, TBM at 48; Lady Huntingdon's Chapel 48; Pavilion 48; The Steyne 48; described 49-50; Jane Macaulay at 154; 169, Selina Mills Macaulay at 170; 172, 174, Royal Chapel opened 175n; court gossip of 175; St Mark's Church 176n; 234, 240, 284, TBM leaves from for France 287; TBM invited to ii, 86; 168, 180, Zachary Macaulay at 328; William IV holds council at 358; iii, 34, Trevelyan family at iv, 38; 134, 154, 219, v, 65, 97, 103, 108, Alice Trevelyan ill at 121n; 155, 161, Margaret and Alice at 202; Hannah at 203; 218, North Street Chapel 224n; Marine Parade 226; TBM thinks of visiting 277; 281, arrangements for visit 282; 283, Ellis plans to see TBM at 284; Pavilion, fancy fair at 286n, 288; TBM plans to visit 298, 302-3; 304, TBM at Norfolk Hotel 305; 346, 354, 355, 361, 364, TBM can't visit 365; 366, Hannah and Margaret at 382, 383; TBM at 385; 386, John Macaulay at 441; sermon preached at on TBM's *History* vi, 5; miserable weather at 123-4; its seaviews don't compensate for flowers and trees 92; 109, TBM at 122; attends sermon at Christ Church 124, 127; 160, TBM at 161; Margaret Trevelyan at 174; invasion fears at 253

Places: Bedford Hotel, v, 282, 284, 367, 383; Bristol Hotel, v, 282; 36 Bedford Square, second home for Macaulay family i, 48n; Montpelier Road, Fanny moves to vi, 189n; New Steyne Hotel, TBM suffers there iv, 136; Norfolk Hotel, v, 284, TBM at 285; 302, 303, 365, 367, TBM at 383n; vi, 120, 122, TBM at 160n, 174; 32 Regency Square, TBM spends week at v, 367; Temple House (residence of Frances

Brighton: *Places—cont.*
and Selina Macaulay), v, 95n, 383, vi, 174; York Hotel, i, 288, Edward Cropper and Margaret honeymoon at ii, 214

Brighton, Poor Boy of: *see* Richard Realf

Brighton College, i, 154n

Brillat-Savarin, Anthelme, i, 296n

Briscoe, John Ivatt, ii, *246*

Bristed, Charles Astor, v, *394*, *Five Years in an English University*, 394

Bristol, i, xvii, Hannah More's school at xxi; xxv, TBM at 7, 156n; 212, burning of 221n; 234, Zachary Macaulay at 236; compared to Rouen 290; iv, 146, 154, 155, TBM visits 216n; TBM a Bristol man v, 35; Selina Macaulay at 63; 185, 277, Brennus and Belinus 283; Crinean's academy 277n; Guildhall 283; Library, Old King Street 275; Museum 275; St Mary Redcliff 65; zoo, TBM visits 280

Bristol, Earl of, i, 181n

Bristol Directory, v, 277n

Bristol Gazette, owned by John Mills ii, 361n; iv, 376n, TBM visits offices v, 272

British Almanac, i, 323

British and Foreign Bible Society: *see* Bible Society

British and Foreign Review, iv, 361n

British Australian Gold Mining Co., v, 411n

British Critic, i, 104n

British Institution, gallery of, i, 216n, ii, 27n; vi, 61

British Museum, i, xiii, TBM's letters in xv; TBM admitted to 215n; Panizzi's career at 227n; Montagu House 300; iii, 348, 350, iv, 15, 68, research at for 'Barère' 170; 236n, 334, 335, TBM refers Ellis to MS in 355; 357, 378, 387, TBM a trustee v, vii; TBM gives tour of to Fanny and the Parkers 54n; TBM receives catalogues from 60; 64, 120, 144, acquires material from Dutch archives 186n; literary forgeries 223; plans for new reading room 299n; 337, papal correspondence at 351; professional copyists at 363-4; 448, to open on Sundays 448n; TBM escorts Mrs Buxton through 449; TBM occupied at 457, 459; 475, Ellis and Hawkins 477-8; collection of tracts at vi, 11; 14, principal librarianship of 19; Owen's candidacy for post at 19-20; TBM's opinion on organisation approved by cabinet 21n; Owen's appointment likely 23; TBM urges gilding of reading room dome 42; reading room opened 89; TBM's source for early London newspapers 117; 152, TBM has no patronage at 175; MS of Babrius 243n
Natural History Department: v, 159n, Owen appointed superintendent vi, 19n; TBM argues for creation of department 19, 20, 22
Royal Commission on, vi, 19n, 20, 22
Trustees: v, 97n, 98n, TBM proposes Milman 118; 120, Trustees' meeting 137, 137n; proposes Milman 149; Lord Northampton's tediousness 149n; man of science needed for trustee 150; dawdling at business 201-2; library sub-committee 296; meet with government on plan for reading room 298-9; 350, Milman appointed 351n; 477, vi, 22, Gladstone appointed 23; meeting 48; TBM must attend 122, 123; 158n, 190, 267

Brittany, iv, 32, 155

Britton, John, *et al.*, *Beauties of England and Wales*, i, 45n

Brixton Hill, Surrey, St Anne's Society Asylum vi, 195n

Broadlands (Palmerston's residence), TBM declines invitation to, iv, 228; to vist briefly 284

Broadstairs, iv, 340, 350, Fanny, George, and Alice spend summer at 351

Broderip, W. J., v, *32*, 33
Letter to: v, 35

Brodie, Sir Benjamin, ii, *26*, iii, 215, iv, 10, TBM consults 366; 376, v, 119, vi, 57

Broglie, Victor, 3rd Duc de, in England, i, 176n; *281*, 289, 297, TBM dines with 300-2; 306, iii, 274, iv, 139

Broglie, Albertine (née de Staël), Duchesse de, i, 297, 300, *301*, 303

Bromley, Kent, Ellis's house at, v, 121, 191, 241, TBM visits 258, 261n; 266, 267, 268, 284, TBM at 286n; 371, 392, 396, 454n, TBM at 467; 470, vi, 79, TBM unable to visit 123; 124, 129n, 162, 217

Brontë, Charlotte, Brocklehurst in *Jane Eyre*, i, 15n

Bronzino, head of Machiavelli, ii, 25

Brooke, Sir James (Rajah), v, 166n

Brookfield, William Henry, TBM can't vote for vi, *140*

Brookfield, Mrs William Henry, vi, 140n

Brooks's Club, TBM elected to, ii, 80n; 326, iii, 23, 289, 322, iv, 107n, 282, 286, v, 90, 246, regret at over Mahon's defeat 253; 300n

Broome Park, Sir Benjamin Brodie's residence, VI, 57

Brougham, Henry Brougham, 1st Baron, I, 75n, and SDUK 122n; *134*, advises on TBM's studies 185, 185n, 186; anti-slavery speech 194n; praises TBM's first speech 202n; link between TBM and *ER* 203n; 221, 223, reports Lansdowne's compliment to TBM 224; 224n, rivalry with Pollock 227-8; TBM's harsh opinion of 230n; helps TBM get Bankrupts appointment 230n; commissions Mackintosh's *Preliminary Discourse* 231n; 238, 242n, recovers from illness 243; 'superficial and uncertain' 245; 252, TBM fears he will domineer over Napier 253n; protests against TBM as editor of *ER* 254n; sworn in with TBM 264n; angered by TBM's getting seat for Calne 265-6; TBM has not spoken to 266; acts with TBM in case at York 266n; 267n, speech on law reform 271n; TBM refuses to review speech 281; returned for Yorkshire 281; speech on colonial slavery 281n; his allusion to 'women of fashion' 283; 'out of his wits' 286; gives TBM letters of introduction for Paris 286n; TBM defends 287n; letter to Napier 298n; domineers over *ER* 298-300; 304, TBM will accept no dictation from 309; reasons for countermanding TBM's article 309n; relation to *ER* 310; TBM defends against Croker 313; appointed Lord Chancellor 313n; '*half knows* everything' 314; gives living to John Macaulay 314; projects edition of Paley 314; 322, founds SDUK 323; and TBM's History of France 323-4; his speeches noticed in *ER* II, 7; 16, TBM shakes hands with 17; promises to serve Zachary Macaulay 70; 71, 78, urges TBM to defend ministers 88; praises Althorp 88n; at coronation of William IV 98; 99, gives place to Zachary Macaulay 101; TBM's violent outburst against 101n; secures position for Henry Macaulay 102, Carlyle's 'Characteristics' attributed to 113; 124n, in great spirits 168; rumoured affair with Mrs Lamb 168–9; 180, spends Christmas with mother 216; engraving of portrait 223; 250, on Lord Campbell and TBM 271-2n; 277n, at Wilberforce's funeral 290; 291, 333n, 343, has influence on Loch 371; III, 100, 170, 174, 177n, criticises TBM's 'Bacon' 243; TBM objects to his abuse of Whigs 243; letter to Napier 243n; designs on *ER* 250; still valuable to *ER*, hates TBM 251, letter to Napier 251n; plagues Napier 255; has done wonders this session 255; letter to *The Times* 255; Lord Rector, University of Aberdeen 255n; persecuting Napier 256; 'a Devil' 257; letter to Napier 257n; 259, will wish he had left Durham alone 262; 278, 279, well managed by Napier 282; 297, 'talks nonsense' 309; wishes to meet TBM 358; objections to TBM's 'Lord Holland' 385; letter to Napier 385n; right about Fox 386; IV, 11, 13, 30, objects to publication of Lord Holland's letter 62; strange praise of TBM 94; abuses Whigs 100; has been making up to TBM 119; compared to Jeffrey 167; suspected of intriguing for office 206n; criticises TBM's 'Chatham' 226; his life of Voltaire 226n; quarrel with Fitzstephen French 263; 'he hath a devil' 348; his friendship more vexing than his enmity 352; would enjoy American publicity V, 39; 89; and TBM's election to Benchership of Lincoln's Inn 89n; embarrasses TBM by offers of help 94-5; TBM returns dry letter to 95n; at Lincoln's Inn ceremony for Campbell 98–9; letter to Southey 131n; 186, 191n, his review of Channing attributed to TBM 193

Writings: A Discourse of Natural Theology, I, 314n, 'Discourse of the Objects . . . of Science,' II, 288n, *Dissertations on Subjects of Science Connected with Natural Theology*, I, 314n, 'Dissolution and General Election,' II, 15n, *Equity Judgments*, IV, 167*, 'Foreign Slave Trade,' I, 169n, 'George the Fourth and Queen Caroline,' III, 243n, 250, *Historical Sketches of Statesmen*, III, 282n, *History of England and France Under the House of Lancaster*, sends to TBM, IV, 352*, *Hydrostatics*, I, 247, II, 288n, IV, 167*, 'Lady Charlotte Bury,' III, 250*, 'The Late Revolution in France,' I, 324, 'Letters on Law Reform,' IV, 159*, 'The Ministry and the State of Parties,' I, 281n, 283*, translator, *Oration of Demosthenes upon the Crown*, IV, 167*, *Political Philosophy*, IV, 159, 167*, 'Practical Observations upon the Education of the People,' II, 288n, 'Reigns of George the Third and Fourth — Political Characters,'

Brougham: *Writings—cont.*
III, 259*, 282n, 'Walpole and His Contemporaries,' III, 325*
Brougham, James, II, *143*, VI, 302
Brougham, William, 2nd Baron, I, *116*, TBM dines with II, 183
Brougham MSS, University College, London, I, 253n
Brougham (carriage), TBM's built by Stocken, V, 160n
Broughton, Sir John Cam Hobhouse, 1st Baron, I, xi, II, *29*, TBM recommends as his successor at Leeds 357; III, 156, President of Board of Control 164n; defends TBM against Praed 164n; 184, supports Anglicist side 214; letter to Lord Auckland 214n; at Campbell's funeral IV, 202; to be at India Board 277; TBM advises on Outram case 306-8; President of Board of Control again 306n; letter to TBM 315n; promises to help Maclagan 319; TBM visits in Wiltshire V, 212; created Lord Broughton 212n; 219n, on the destruction of Byron's diaries 346; appoints John Macaulay's son to cadetship VI, 90; 207, 222n, dinner party 227
Writings: Historical Illustrations of . . . Childe Harold, VI, 194n, *Italy,* sent to TBM, VI, 194*, Journal, IV, 131n, 307n, *Recollections,* on TBM's 3rd Reform speech II, 109n; on TBM at ministerial white-bait dinner 296; 357n, III, 140, 244n, 302n, 282n, IV, 202n, 300n, 362n, V, 254n
LETTERS TO: III, 164, 213, 312, IV, 130, 306, 315, V, 219, 254, VI, 90, 194, 223
Broun, Sir Richard, III, *307*, *Dignity, Precedence, Etc., of the Honourable Baronettesses of the Realm,* 307n
Brown, Ford K., *Fathers of the Victorians,* II, 295n, VI, 229n
Brown, J., engraver, V, 55n
Brown, John, TBM's tutor at Trinity, I, 101n, *113*, 114, 115, his bill for term 122; at Blundell's death bed 124; 137, 144, his bills 151; 181, 182, his bill 182
Brown, Dr John, 'What Ought the Dissenters of Scotland to Do?,' III, 355n
Brown, Rev. Joseph, impudent letter from, V, 421
Brown, Lancelot ('Capability'), II, 197
Brown, Quarter Master, III, 343
Brown, Rawdon, VI, *50*
Browne, James, *A History of the Highlands,* V, 120*
Browning, Oscar, *Memories of Sixty Years,* II, 13n
Browning, Robert, and Shelley letters, V, 223; VI, 47n, 'Browningism' at Cambridge 206
Browning, Mrs Robert, VI, 47n
Brownrigg, John Studholme, II, *349*, 362, advice on Indian outfit 363; III, 6
Broxbornebury (ship), III, 84, 85, voyage on described 86-7
Bruce, James, IV, 143
Bruce, John, V, *166*
LETTER TO: V, 166
Bruce, Robert, of Scotland, IV, 257
Bruce, Thomas, a bore at Clifton V, *265*; absurd behaviour of 272; dies at Clifton 280; fame of his death 281
Bruce, Thomas Charles, standing in polls at Edinburgh V, *245*
Bruce of Kinross, V, 265
Brudenell, James Thomas: *see* Lord Cardigan
Bruges, IV, 220, V, 343
Bruhl, Count, IV, 29
Brumbaugh, Mr Thomas, III, xi
Brunecken, VI, 238
Brunswick, Duchess of, death, I, 24
Brunswick, Duke of, and case against *Satirist,* IV, 129
Brunton, Mrs Mary, *Self-Control,* V, 250
Brussels, IV, 8, 43, 220, V, 39, 347, TBM at VI, 114; Hotel de Bellevue, IV, 8
Brutus, III, 147
Bryant, Sir Jeremiah, III, *273*
Bryce, John, V, 77
Buccleuch, Duke of, II, 170, at Rome IV, 201; 270n
Buchanan, Claudius, III, *56*, lines on (by TBM?) VI, 34
Buchanan, George, V, 332
Buckhurst, IV, 388
Buckingham, George Villiers, Duke of, IV, 45, V, *145*
Buckingham, 2nd Duke of, IV, *103*, 189, 270, 389
Buckingham, James Silk, a teetotaller III, 297n; *America, Historical, Statistic, and Descriptive,* IV, 61; 'mountebank,' *389*; V, 33
Buckingham and Chandos, Duke of, *Memoirs of the Court and Cabinets of George the Third,* VI, 179
Buckinghamshire, 4th Earl of, II, 263n
Buckland, C. E., *Dictionary of Indian Biography,* III, 177n

Buckle, H. T., at Milnes's breakfast, VI, 144n, *History of Civilisation in England,* TBM sends for, 144*, 'The Influence of Women on the Progress of Knowledge,' 144n

Buckner, Richard, portrait of 'The Misses Monk,' V, 282

Buenos Aires, IV, 292

Bulau, Prof. Friedrich, trans. TBM's *History,* V, 71n; VI, 35n

Buller, Charles, III, *294*, contributes to *ER* 295n; his levity 297; speech on colonisation IV, 116; TBM suggests for Irish article 224; and *ER* 226n; offers to take part in debate on Scottish Universities Bill 261; 291

Buller, Sir John Yarde, III, 319n

Bulletin of Friends' Historical Society, V, 6n

Bulletin of the John Rylands Library, V, 55

Bullock, F. W. B., *History of Ridley Hall,* I, 87n

Bullum and Boatum, VI, 215

Bulteel, Miss, V, 144n

Bulteel, Mrs, V, 144n

Bulwer, Emily Elizabeth, IV, 368n

Bulwer, Edward Lytton: *see* Lord Lytton

Bulwer, Sir Henry, afterwards 1st Baron Dalling and Bulwer, III, *343*, 349n, 'France and the East' sent to Napier 359; authorship secret 359; 369, 370, IV, 11, to write article on Spain 322; plan for article disrupted 324; 'France and the East' III, 349n, 358, 359, 360, 361, universally liked 363; 'The Spanish Marriages' IV, 324n

Bunbury, Sir Edward Herbert, VI, *29*

Bunsen, Baron Christian von, V, *158*, 241, 298, 'Bunsenian crotchets' 304; *Hippolytus and His Age,* 424n

Bunsen family, murder threat against, V, 386n

Buntingford, Herts, I, 50n, 53

Bunyan, John, TBM defends his judgment of II, 109; V, 22, has no claim to monument in the Abbey 426

Writings: The Holy City, V, 402, *Pilgrim's Progress,* I, 5n, Part 2, 75*; review of Southey's edition, II, 107; distributed in Italy V, 358n; 359, date of 402; VI, 106, *The Strait Gate,* V, 402

Burdett, Sir Francis, II, *51*, 81, II, 101, in the Tower V, 443

Bürger, Gottfried August, IV, 182

Burgundy, Duke of, IV, 83

Burgundy, Dukes of, III, 41

Burke, *General Armory,* description of TBM's arms, VI, 134n

Burke, Edmund, I, xx, 96, on Henry IV 105*; 318, II, 11, teases Goldsmith 59; TBM compared to 268; speech on Nabob of Carnatic III, 41; 136, should have exchanged politics for literature 159; 220, 258, 281n, 361, IV, vii, his pamphlets 41; and trial of Hastings 62; 69, 177, compared to Russell by TBM 347n; speech on Protestant Dissenters V, 22; 216, apologia by VI, 178*

Writings: 'Essay on the Sublime and Beautiful,' TBM hopes to write a critical examination of IV, 199; *Letters,* IV, 198

Burke, E. P., *History of France,* read by TBM for SDUK, I, 323

Burke, Colonel Sir John, II, *157*

Burleigh, Lord, I, 319

Burleigh (seat), III, 161

Burlington, Earl of, at Rome, IV, 201

Burma, Emperor of, II, 144

Burnet, Bishop Gilbert, V, 6, 91, sources of information about 145; 146

Writings: History of His Own Times, II, 75*, 319–20*; IV, 374*, 388*, V, 7, 279, TBM presents to Edinburgh Philosophical Institution 463; VI, 253n, *History of the Reformation,* IV, 393*, V, 12n, 18, 19n, 172*, TBM presents to Edinburgh Philosophical Institution V, 463, *Lives, Characters, and an Address to Posterity,* III, 108

Burney, Dr Charles, IV, 98

Burney, Rev. Charles Parr, V, 157n

Burney, Fanny: *see* Madame D'Arblay

Burney, Sarah Harriet, IV, 63n, sacrifices her father to her hatred of Croker 97-8

Burns, Robert, V, 226, his centenary VI, 191; TBM asked to preside at Glasgow memorial to 191n

Burton, John Hill, IV, *374*, TBM consults on Scottish history 374; promotes plan for national education in Scotland V, 90n; TBM expects to ask for information 235; on Ferguson the plotter 302; and Breadalbane papers 313; TBM recommends for a place 395; Secretary, Scottish Prison Board 395n, 407; TBM consults about Acta of Scottish Privy Council VI, 64; and Borland's *Darien* 129; editor, *Darien Papers* 129; sends Borland to TBM 132

Writings: History of Scotland, IV, 374n, sends sheets to TBM V, 295, 300-1*; 302n, and Breadalbane papers 313n

Burton, John Hill—*cont.*
LETTERS TO: IV, 374, 374, 375, 375, V, 35, 47, 90, 234, 295, 300, 302, 313, 395, 407, 445, VI, 64, 129, 132, 133
Burton, Richard, IV, 10
Bury, Lady Charlotte, IV, 245n
Bury, J. P. T., ed., *Romilly's Cambridge Diary*, I, xxviii, II, 196n
Bushy Park, V, 406, 412
Bute, Lord, IV, 198, 221
Butler, Sir James, VI, 97, *Passing of the Great Reform Bill*, II, 88n
Butler, Bishop Joseph, V, *426*, *Analogy of Religion*, V, 426n
Butler, Montagu, VI, 47n, *97*, 99, on walking tour with George Trevelyan 106; at TBM's Cambridge dinner 214; TBM recommends for headmastership of Harrow 241; headmaster of Harrow 255
LETTER TO: VI, 97
Butler, Samuel, *Hudibras*, IV, 28, V, 165*
Buttrey, John, II, *236*
LETTER TO: II, 236
Buxton, II, 124, 240
Buxton, Charles, V, 449n, 470n, his house at Fox Warren VI, 179n; 181n, 185, his children 204; 232n
Buxton, Mrs Charles (Emily Mary Holland), TBM escorts through British Museum V, *449*, 470n
LETTER TO: V, 449
Buxton, Priscilla, II, *200*, 'Blue and Yellow' 201; 242, verses on, by TBM 243; her 'Montgomery's *Missionary Voyages and Travels*' sent by TBM to Napier 200
Buxton, Thomas Fowell, in bad health, I, 243n; moves resolutions for abolition II, 14n; Macaulay family stays at his house 17n; 44, *70*, a smoker 81; 101, 193, gives article to TBM for *ER* 200; 201, vindicates TBM's anti-slavery record 221n; shouldn't break with government 239; satisfied with government plan 246; objects to plan of abolition 267n; moves alterations 277; 279, toasted at Leeds 333n; V, 449n
Byng, Frederick Gerald ('Poodle'), II, *195*, 326
Byng, George, V, 144n
Byng, General Sir John: *see* Lord Strafford
Byrd, William, *History of the Dividing Line*, anecdote about Penn, V, 143n; Westover MSS, TBM receives edition of, 165
Byrom, John, 'My Time, Oh Ye Muses,' V, 448
Byron, Lord, compared to Tacitus I, 61; 63, 64, his unmanly conduct 76; 121, 140, 181n, his statue at Trinity 317n; II, 7, *Works*, 1818-20, 26n; sends Stothard illustrations to Lady Holland 26-7; 29, Rogers's anecdotes of 32; made unfavourable impression on men 32-3; TBM will be abused for speaking coldly of 38; occasion of quarrel between Moore and Campbell 56; 112n, his criticism below refutation 321; letter from IV, 34; V, 17, 39, forgeries of his letters 222; *Memoirs*, question of their destruction 346
Writings: 'Bride of Abydos,' I, 45, 47*, *Childe Harold*, I, 47, 'The Corsair,' I, 47*, *Don Juan*, IV, 28, 202n*, its versification V, 18, 'English Bards and Scotch Reviewers,' II, 321n, 'Epistle to Augusta,' 102*, *The Giaour*, IV, 34n, *Hebrew Melodies*, I, 56, 65-6*, 'Fare Thee Well,' I, 76n, *Letters*, ed. Prothero, IV, 34n, *Letters and Journals*, edited Thomas Moore, reviewed by TBM, I, 319, preface to *Marino Faliero*, II, 321n, 'Ode to Napoleon Bonaparte,' I, 43-4*, 46, 'On a Royal Visit to the Vaults,' I, 59*, 'Parisina,' I, 73*, 121, 'Siege of Corinth,' I, 73*, 'A Sketch,' I, 76n
Byron, Major George Gordon, V, *222n*
Byron, Lady, I, 76n, II, 27, defended by Campbell 56; V, 226n

Cabinet, on Eastern question, III, 339
Cabinet Cyclopaedia, I, 311, 317, 319, 324, II, 21n, III, 107n
Cabinet Library, I, 311n, 325
Cade, Jack, VI, 11
Cadell, Robert, IV, *164*, letters to TBM, 164n, 165n
LETTERS TO: IV, 164, 165
Cadogan, Earl of, at Rome, IV, 201
Caesar, Julius, I, 6, 180, assassination of II, 9; *Commentaries*, III, 62*, 147*, 153*, 160*, 196; V, 178, VI, 96
Caffraria, VI, 123
Cairns, Sir Hugh, afterwards 1st Earl Cairns, VI, *203*
Cairo, Trevelyan at, VI, 202
Caithnessshire, VI, 5
Calais, IV, 8, V, 347, 349n, 354, VI, 104, 105
Calamus, VI, 100
Calamus, poem on, V, 227*
Calcutta, cost of living at II, 299; TBM buys views of at print shop 344; 345,

Hannah should prepare for society of 363; preferable with Hannah to London without 370; III, 51, 62, 63, 67, 72, 73, 76, unhealthiness of 84; TBM arrives at 88; described 90ff; 92, 124, 132, 160, modest social style in 161; amusements in 162; 172, lawyers in 'miserable set of fellows' 177; 182, 184, 215, severe hot season 217; sickly season 222; 225, sea voyages from for invalids 226; 230, 246, 312, IV, 306, used to spend all day reading VI, 54; quiet in Mutiny 105; absurd conduct of English in during Mutiny 147

Places: Bishop's College III, 188; cathedral III, 228, 235; Chowringhee IV, 217; Fort William III, 90, 173, 218, VI, 106, 107; College of III, 56n; Garden Reach III, 6, 87; Government House III, 90, 94, 95, 97; picture of Hastings at 362; Hindu College III, 122n, 126, 138; Hooghly College III, 144; La Martinière School III, 160n

Calcutta, Supreme Court of, III, 125n, 158, 165, 176, 182, 186, plan to remodel V, 432

Calcutta Literary Gazette, III, 126n

Calcutta Monthly Journal, III, 126n

Calcutta newspapers, III, 186

Calcutta petitioners against regulation of the press, letter to, III, 124

Calderon de la Barca, Pedro, I, 73, TBM has neglected II, 138; TBM reads a play before breakfast 192*; III, 210*; comedies V, 122

Caledonian Mercury, and 'Anglicanus' letters, I, 235n; 290, III, 317, IV, 269, 348

California, subject for Latin hexameters at Cambridge, VI, 221

Callender, James Thomson, slanders Jefferson, VI, *186*

Callimachus, III, 152*, 159*

Calne, Wiltshire, TBM M.P. for, I, xii; 263, electors at, 265n; TBM at 276; contested election at 276n; 277, TBM at 279; election petition 312; untouched by first Reform Bill II, 6n, 8n; TBM's opponents canvassing in anticipation of Reform 8; impossible to open borough 12; TBM at for re-election 12n; Charles Richard Fox elected with TBM 13; election at 14; 74, subject in Reform Bill debate 84; TBM re-elected at following appointment to office 122n; TBM at for re-election 123, 124; re-elected 129; election day described 130; Lansdowne Arms, dinner at 130n; sworn in for 134; 220n

Calne, electors of, letter to, II, 8

Calverton, Bucks., V, 186n, Margaret Trevelyan at, VI, 165

Calvinism, and articles of Church of England, V, 22

Cambacérès, Jean Jacques, Duc de, II, *72*

Cambridge: Bull Inn, TBM at with family party VI, 212; Deighton Bell's bookshop I, 72n, 143; Round Church, restoration IV, 181

Cambridge, Borough of, TBM made High Steward VI, x, 126; Town Council 126; TBM to be sworn in 149; TBM at 151; his installation 206n

Cambridge, Lord Lieutenant of, VI, 214

Cambridge, Adolphus Frederick, Duke of V, *97*, his death 118n

Cambridge, William Frederick Charles, 2nd Duke of, dinner for VI, 131n; TBM fails to recognise *220*

Cambridge, Richard Owen, anecdote of Pope V, 462n

Cambridge Apostles IV, 361n

Cambridge Chronicle, on TBM reading 'Pompeii' I, 127n; 150n

Cambridge Independent Press, VI, 149n

Cambridge Philosophical Society, *Transactions*, VI, 82n, 84n

Cambridge Union Society, debate on British colonial system I, 183; TBM secretary and treasurer of 183n; its history 183n; TBM and Praed share leadership 190n; 203n, 320n, II, 11n, 35n, 103n, applause there meant more than success in Commons now 271; Everett President of VI, 244n; *Laws and Transactions of the Union Society* I, 183n

Cambridge University I, viii, Evangelicals at xvii, xviii, xxviii, TBM at with his father 14; 15, 25, hesitant about Indian missions 25, 26; 31, its scholarly style 87; TBM enters 101; resides in Jesus Lane 101n; its evils 'must be sought' 102; its monastic life 106; life there irregular 108; decent rather than immoral 111; TBM called 'Beast' Macaulay 114n; examination results 117; TBM reads 'Pompeii' at commencement exercises 127; plans for family party at 127-8, 129; 135, campaign for classical tripos at 137n, 173; contest for university living 138; results of tripos examinations 142; its standards of success not TBM's 143; town and gown fights over Queen Caroline 150; carnival season 151; commencement 156n;

Cambridge University—*cont.*
compared to Oxford 165; fees for graduation 169; takes degree without honours 169; plans to take pupils after graduation 169; plans to reduce expenditures 170; pupils not easy to get 171, 172; plans to read at during long vacation 172; classical tripos established 173n; takes two pupils for 100 guineas 175; does not dislike teaching 177; actors at 178; refuses additional pupil 181; empty at Christmas 182; his pupils his only tie to 186; 234, TBM at 254n; 291, plans to take Hannah to II, 194; visits with Hannah and Margaret 196; III, 112, 270, 286, TBM accompanies Frank Ellis there IV, 59; Henry Fitzmaurce Hallam at 66; illuminated in 1814 77; Latin essay subject 117; value of university distinctions 169; TBM visits 178; Albert made Chancellor 331, 332n; 342, the conditions of fellowships at 360; Jeffrey's treatment of delegates from V, 24; TBM at 50, 51, 54; 136, 188, results in classical examinations odd 228; address to James on his accession 333; TBM advises Charles Macaulay how to see 417; discriminated against by Indian Civil Service examinations 438; Protestant university will interest Montalembert 456; 473, George Trevelyan's chances at VI, 52; TBM explains residence and degrees to Fanny 82; TBM unable to visit 123, 124; George Trevelyan goes to 126; 198, results of university scholarship examinations 206; family party at 214; no chance that TBM can visit 255

Colleges (*see separate entry for* Trinity College): Christ's College, I, 175n, VI, 67, Corpus Christi College, IV, 181, Downing College, I, 177n, King's College, III, xi, IV, 181, a community apart VI, 93; chapel I, 291, IV, 140; Magdalene College, TBM dines at IV, 367, Pembroke College, I, 138, IV, 181, Queens' College, I, xxvi, TBM stays with Dean Milner 27-8; 116, 118, controversy over election of president 152; TBM visits Milner IV, 76; 77, library 378; St John's College, I, 138, 317n, New Court IV, 181; Trinity Hall, I, 320n

Elections: 1822 contest I, 181; for 1826 212; 1827 223; 1831, TBM cannot vote in II, 12-13; meant to vote for Palmerston 14n; 168, TBM at for 1847 election IV, 341n; 346, elections of 1689/90 V, 209; 1856 election VI, 29n

Places: Fitzwilliam Museum I, 170; Pepysian Library, TBM to visit for History IV, 264; 366, 367; Pitt Press IV, 181; University Church V, 317, 'Golgotha' VI, 212; 214; University Library I, 170

Professorships: Regius Professorship of Modern History, candidates for IV, 373; Stephen appointed to V, 65n; TBM recommends Kemble for 61-2; TBM recommends for VI, 240, 257; Downing Professorship of Law V, 45, 46n

Reform: proposals for reform discussed IV, 359-60; commission of inquiry appointed 360n; plans for V, 385n; TBM declines appointment to committee on revising statutes VI, 92; TBM suggests appointments to committee 93

Scholarships and Prizes: Brown's Medal IV, 169, George Trevelyan wins VI, 153n; Camden Prize, George Trevelyan fails to get VI, 220, 221; Chancellor's English Verses Medal, TBM wins with 'Pompeii I, 115n; 150, wins with 'Evening' 151n, 156n, 186; TBM unsuccessful with 'Waterloo' I, 186n; II, 347, V, 228n, George Trevelyan competes for VI, 221; Classical Medal, TBM hopes to compete for I, 168n, 169n; Smith's Prize IV, 78, V, 228; University Scholarship, TBM to compete for I, 108, 114n, 117, 118, 122, does well in competition 126; regulations for 135; competes for 135n; reasons for not competing 136; value of Craven scholarships 136n; 137; TBM takes examination 142; stands high in results 143-4; takes examination 152; wins scholarship 154; III, 111, IV, 66, VI, 256

Studies: classics, advised to devote himself to I, 126; reads for pleasure 136–7; mathematics I, 101, 108, 116n, TBM abominates 122-3; hates and despises 125; insufficient for scholarship 126; 131, resolved to devote himself to 135; principal study 136-7; success in not TBM's idea of success 143; 'very backward' 144; reading at Llanrwst in

preparation for B.A. examination 162; studying over Christmas holiday 168; regrets his neglect of mathematics III, 247

TRINITY COLLEGE: TBM's letters at I, xiv; influence on TBM xix; Master and Fellows of xi; xxviii, Macaulay papers at xliii; 14n, 77n, Commemoration Feast 109, 112; TBM competes for college scholarship 126n; Commemoration 135; TBM not in first class list 1820 136n; Latin declamation 134; English declamation 134, 136; elected to Trinity scholarship 136n, 141n; crowded conditions at 141n; college triumph in tripos 142; on university scholarship examination 144; TBM wins Latin declamation prize 147; unsuccessful in English declamation competition 147; to give public declamation on Dryden 147, 151; college does not pay for his prize 151; 152, troubled by rats 153; Nevile's Court 153; active in campaign for classical tripos 173; college performance on 1831 tripos 317; TBM suggests Trinity friends join in memorial to Malkin III, 247; Frank Ellis enters 59; restoration of Master's Lodge 181; New Court 181; Chelsea Hospital chaplainship suitable for junior fellow 305; TBM accepts invitation to tercentenary of 323, 325; fellow of Trinity TBM's proudest title V, 25; TBM presents *History* to library 37-8; Lodge 45; TBM takes Rutherfurd to visit 48; 104, can't attend Commemoration Feast 299, 300; lay fellowships in 385n; Walter Ellis enters 479n; question of candidate for statue in antechapel VI, 67-9; its scholarship still Bentleian 68; 93, pleasant to have a new tie to 125; TBM's affection for will last as long as he lives 136; new statutes for 136n; TBM gives dinner to old fellows and scholars of 176; Lansdowne's gift to 180; visit to given up 208; TBM visits with family party 212; service in chapel 212, 214; Audit Ale 222; Everett at 244n; TBM dines at Lodge 267

Expenses: I, 122, 144, 151, chandler's bill and vintner's bill 152; 182, 200

Fellowship: examinations I, 131; regulations 170n; TBM eligible 170n; elections 179; TBM's chance small 185; returns to compete when number increased 186n, 190; unsuccessful 191; studying for examination at Rothley Temple 197; another vacated 199; elected fellow 200; his fellowship filled up II, 196n

Graduates and Fellows Contemporary with TBM: Airy, G. B., I, 191n, Alford, Henry, V, 317, Arnold, Thomas Kerchever, V, 321, Baines, Matthew Talbot, II, 103n, Barlow, John, I, 139n, Barron, Arthur, I, 179n, Bird, Charles Smith, I, 162n, Blomfield, C. J., I, 77n, Blundell, Thomas, I, 17n, Bristed, Charles Astor, V, 394, Brookfield, William Henry, VI, 140, Brown, John, I, 113n, Bulwer, Edward Lytton, I, 320n, Bunbury, Sir Edward, VI, 29, Butler, Montagu, VI, 97n, Coddington, Henry, I, 142n, Crowder, Sir Richard, V, 391, Daintry, John, I, 22n, Denman, George, VI, 29, Dicey, Thomas Edward, I, 158n, Drinkwater-Bethune, John, I, 286n, Elliott, Edward Bishop, I, 176n, Elliott, Henry Venn, I, 219n, Ellis, Frank, V, 394, Ellis, T. F., I, xxii, Empson, William, I, 246n, Goode, Francis, I, 179n, Grey, 3rd Earl, II, 52n, Gurney, John Hampden, V, 123, Guthrie, John, I, 264n, Hamilton, Henry Parr, VI, 176n, Hamilton, John William, I, 147n, Hammond, James Lempriere, V, 55, Hawkins, John Heywood, II, 31n, Helps, Sir Arthur, VI, 257, Higman, John Philips, V, 122, Holden, H. A., V, 415n, Holland, Henry Thurstan, VI, 163n, Hume, Joseph Burnley, V, 449, Judgson, W. G., I, 112n, Kindersley, Richard Torin, I, 199n, Lawson, Marmaduke, I, 135, Lister, Thomas Henry, II, 138n, Lockwood, Frederick, II, 142n, Long, George, I, 154n, Lubbock, Sir John, II, 216n, Lyttelton, Lord, VI, 30, Macaulay, John Heyrick, I, 103n, Malden, Henry, I, 57n, Malkin, B. H., I, 122n, Mansel, William Lort, I, 124n, Marriott, William Henry, I, 191n, Monk,

Cambridge University: *Graduates and Fellows—cont.*
J. H., I, 126n, Moultrie, John, I, 190n, Musgrave, Archbishop Thomas, V, 391n, Noel, Baptist, I, 141n, Ollivant, Alfred, I, 117n, Ord, W. H., I, 295n, Overstone, Lord, VI, 90, Parke, Sir James, I, 215, Parker, Sir James, I, 267n, Pashley, Robert, V, 416, Pearson, Edwin, II, 142n, Pearson, William Wilberforce, II, 72n, Perry, Richard, VI, 81, Platt, Thomas Pell, I, 117n, Praed, Winthrop Mackworth, I, 190n, Preston, Matthew Morris, I, 14n, Price, Samuel Grove, II, 11n, Reynolds, Henry Revell, V, 208, Rolfe, Robert, II, 56n, Romilly, John, I, 139n, Scholefield, James, I, 86n, Shaw-Lefevre, John George, I, 122n, Southern, Henry, V, 321, Stainforth, George, I, 18n, Strutt, Edward, II, 35n, Tayler, Thomas, I, 178n, Thornton, Henry, the younger, I, 101n, Tindal, Sir Nicholas, I, 215, Trotter, Coutts, VI, 99, Waddington, George, V, 390, Waddington, Horace, I, 109n, Walker, William Sidney, I, 188n, Warburton, Eliot, V, 49n, Whewell, William, I, 316n, White, Francis, I, 147, Wilberforce, William, Jr, I, 14n, Wood, William Page, V, 305, Wordsworth, Christopher, I, 150n
Rooms: moves into college rooms I, 127; settled in Malden's rooms 129; in Barlow's rooms 141, 143; does not obtain rooms until 1821 141n; expects to get excellent rooms by Christmas 147, 151; takes rooms in Bishop's Hostel 152; moves to Great Court 170; hopes to take up quarters again 317
Cambridge University Act 1856, VI, 92–3n
Cambridge University Bill, TBM thinks should be withdrawn V, 462
Cambridge University Calendar, I, 115n, 117, 126n, 147n, IV, 160, VI, 41
Cambridge University Counselship, TBM asks it for Ellis V, 48
Cambridge University Press, V, 95
Cambridgeshire, IV, 146, 157
Camden, Lord, IV, 206
Camden Society, Cambridge, IV, 181n, V. 166n
Cameron, Dr Archibald, IV, *309*, 312n
Cameron, Charles Hay, III, *125*, arrives in India 146; 147, 149, stays with TBM 152; 162, leaves for Cape 195; 202, at the Cape 209-10; 210n, succeeds TBM as President of Law Commission 213n; defends his Jacobite ancestor IV, 309; 311, President of Committee of Public Instruction 311n; papers from 312; his epitaph for his ancestor 312; V, 111n, leaving for Ceylon 127; on Commission on Laws of India 367n; marriage of his daughter VI, 190
Writings: Address to Parliament on the Duties of Great Britain to India, VI, 300
LETTER TO: VI, 190
Cameron, Mrs Charles Hay (Julia Margaret Pattle), V, 111n, *127*, VI, 190
Cameron, Sir Ewen, of Lochiel, his *Life,* V, 120*
Camoens, *Lusiad,* III, 86*, 181
Campbell, Alexander, bill on Church of Scotland, IV, 36; in Edinburgh election, 1852, V, *245*
Campbell, John, IV, *116*
Campbell, Sir John, III, 291n
Campbell, John of Carbrook, Edinburgh Writer to the Signet, I, 236
Campbell, John, *The Martyr of Erromanga* and TBM, IV, 116n
Campbell, John, 1st Baron, II, *271*, 371, III, 374, 378n, made Lord Chancellor of Ireland 381; his libel bill IV, 136; 209, dared by Ellenborough in Lords 247n; bills on court procedure 248; to be offered Chancellorship of Duchy of Lancaster 277; on Dundas's appointment 305; 315, 363n, V, 35, to succeed Denman as Lord Chief Justice 85, 96; ceremony of leave-taking at Lincoln's Inn 98-9; elated by his elevation 99; too Grandisonian to Miss Sellon 107; and Gorham case 107n; would confirm TBM's judgment of Ellis 206; 207, and dispute over Booksellers' Association 224; on Northern Circuit 255n; 268*, on address from English merchants to Napoleon III 324; what he might say of Robert Montgomery's case 388: Ellis's letter to 470; calls on TBM VI, 67; supports TBM on taking seat in Lords 134n; never elected with TBM at Edinburgh 135; his opinion on Shrewsbury case 150; 207, 217, TBM dines with 219; Lord Chancellor in new ministry 222n; TBM tries to interest

him in Ellis 228; offers Ellis county judgeship 249

Writings: Life, VI, 192, *Life of Lord Eldon*, V, 191*, *Lives of the Chief Justices*, V, 96*, on law appointments before Reform VI, 91*, *Lives of the Lord Chancellors*, II, 271n, IV, 206n, V, 96*, *Shakespeare's Legal Acquirements Considered*, VI, 192*

LETTERS TO: III, 381, VI, 192

Campbell, Mary, VI, *67*

Campbell, Thomas, I, 120, 242n, II, *56*, praises TBM's verses 56; death of IV, 195n; TBM's obituary remarks on 196; his funeral described 202; TBM's criticism of his poems 202n

Writings: Frederick the Great and His Times, IV, 17, *Gertrude of Wyoming*, IV, 196, 'The Last Man,' I, 285

Campbell, Dr Thomas, *Diary of a Visit to England in 1775*, VI, 218*; TBM sends to Reeve 225; how it got to Australia 225n; TBM sends note on to *ER* 252n

Campbell, William Frederick, idiotic behaviour of, V, *99*, bores Hannah VI, 219

Canada, II, 225, and Galt's *Lawrie Todd*, 314n; III, 66, Durham's mission to 262n; 271, proposals for special regiment in 331ff; rebellion in 376, IV, 47; dispute with U.S. over fishing rights V, 269

Canaletto, IV, 234, his pictures of Venice, VI, 59

Canning, Charles John, 2nd Viscount, V, x, 434, 446, appointed Governor-General of India 470; 470n, VI, 113n, defended by Lord Granville 131; his proclamation of clemency 131n

Canning, Lady, V, x, 166n, 470n, her letter about King of Oudh VI, 106; 107

Canning, George, I, 179, death of 224; anecdote of 226; 303, on character of House of Commons 318; II, 6, 33, 66, his joke about Spring Garden gates 82; *Poetical Works* 288; 290, 292, 'The Friend of Humanity' III, 67*; 219, 243n, in Malmesbury's *Diary* IV, 237

Canning, Sir Stratford, afterwards Viscount Stratford de Redcliffe, II, *348*

Cannons (Duke of Chandos's estate), V, 104

Canova, Antonio, his bust of Napoleon at Holland House, II, 27

Canterbury, TBM proposes to meet Ellis there, II, 346, 347, 348; III, 274, TBM at, VI, 29

Canterbury, Archbishop of, 1833: *see* William Howley

Canterbury, Archbishop of, 1848ff: *see* John Bird Sumner

Canterbury, Charles Manners-Sutton, 1st Viscount, I, 181n, II, *6*, Speaker of House of Commons 52; 53, almost fainting after all-night debate 70; at coronation of William IV 97; leads procession of Commons 142; 229, compliments TBM on India speech 268; at Wilberforce's funeral 290; 291

Canton, II, 325

Cape Breton, III, 332

Cape of Good Hope, Pringle's article on, II, 333; stormy seas at III, 33; 140, 212, 219, 222, 229, 232, 233, 234, 235, to stop there briefly 236; 243n, 260

Cape Town, TBM reminded of in Holland, IV, 217

Capefigue, Jean-Baptiste Honoré Raymond, *L'Europe pendant le Consulat et l'Empire de Napoléon*, TBM proposes to review, III, 340

Capel, 1st Baron, V, *62*

Capuchins, VI, 139

Caracalla, V, 278

Caracci, Annibal, 'The Three Maries,' I, 216, III, 61

Caradoc, John Hobart, II, *21*, 23

Cardigan, 7th Earl of, III, *371*, V, 166n

Cardwell, Edward, IV, *336*, defeated at Liverpool V, 233n; 238n, and Oxford election 306; President of Board of Trade 332

Carey and Hart, their edition of TBM's *Essays*, IV, 82

LETTERS TO: III, 374, IV, 18, 194, 209, 225

Carhampton, 2nd Earl of, II, 26n

Carleton, Captain, *Memoirs of an English Officer: see* Daniel Defoe

Carleton, William, *Valentine MacClutchy*, V, 195*

Carlile, Richard, II, *44*, V, 359

Carlisle, I, 208n, 227

Carlisle, 5th Earl of, II, 32n

Carlisle, George Howard, 6th Earl of, I, 216, 240, 254n, III, 61

Carlisle, George William Howard, 7th Earl of, styled Lord Morpeth, I, 61n, II, 209n, 255, 260, TBM dines with 265; 302, Irish Secretary 339n; defeated in West Riding 386n; returns to England IV, 63; West Riding seat open to him 277; 283, speech at opening of Bradford

Carlisle, George William Howard—*cont.* Mechanics' Institution 'trash' 320; invites TBM to Castle Howard 334; v, ix, x, Chancellor of Duchy of Lancaster 100; 109n, 111n, 152n, 157n, presides over court of inquiry 205; 206, 207, 219n, 234n, 299n, hurt by Russell's conduct 307; 311, 314n, vi, 72n, 90n, TBM dines with at Chiswick House 159n; 204, 204n
Writings: Extracts from Journals, iii, 153n, on TBM's quoting odd religious verses v, 398n, 'Second Vision of Daniel,' vi, 254*
Letters to: iii, 339, 386, iv, 334
Carlisle, Georgiana, Countess of, iv, *334*
Carlovingians, vi, 94
Carlyle, Alexander, ed., *New Letters of Thomas Carlyle,* v, 209n
Carlyle, Thomas, on TBM, i, vii; letters of xv; on Thomson's *Reminiscences* 225n; ii, 75n, might as well write in Irving's unknown tongues 113; his judgment of TBM 113n; iii, 196, 294n, 'absurdly overpraised' iv, 11; as writer for *ER* 11n; v, 116n, at Malvern for water cure 182; on TBM at Malvern 182n; appeals to the age which likes the odd and extravagant 194; with TBM at The Grange 209n; Victor Hugo a greater ass than 383; Carlylism at Cambridge vi, 206; prefatory letter to *Life of Macaulay* 206n
Writings: 'Characteristics,' ii, 113*, *Chartism,* TBM considers reviewing, ii, 113n
Carmarthen, i, 46, ii, 105
Carnac, Major Sir James, assures TBM of appointment, ii, *341*; his advice on Indian seasons 342
Carnarvon, 3rd Earl of, at Rome, iv, 201
Carnarvon, 4th Earl of, v 151n, vi, *166*
Carnatic, iii, 41, 44, 48, 84, v, 68
Carnatic, Commander in Chief of, iii, 43
Carnatic, Commission on, iii, 41n
Carnatic, Nabob of, iii, 40, 41, TBM visits 42-3; calls on TBM 43-4; 46, 48, 54, 67
Carnatic, Regent of, iii, 42
Caroline, iv, 47
Caroline, Queen of George II, iv, 257
Caroline, Queen of George IV, question of divorce i, 21; 24n, 144-5, public excitement over her case 148; Cambridge riots over 150; bill of pains and penalties against 148n, 150n; TBM's remarks on her death 158-9; riots attending burial 163n; 266n, 'abominably used' iii, 207; trial of iv, 141; in Malmesbury's *Diary* 237; 257, v, 363
Carpenter, William Benjamin, vi, *35n*
Carpenter, William Hookham, v, *478*
Carr, Robert James, Bishop of Worcester, ii, *145*
Carriage, TBM gets a new one, vi, 234
Carrick, Mr, landlord of Royal Hotel, Glasgow, vi, 231
Carruthers, Robert, v, *117*, TBM asks information of about Highland history 120
Letters to: v, 117, 120
Carte, Thomas, *An History of the Life of James, Duke of Ormonde,* iv, 369*
Carter, Matthew, *A Most True and Exact Relation,* v, 63*
Cartwright, Bishop Thomas, v, 5, *Diary,* 6n
Carus, William, *Memoirs of Charles Simeon,* i, 103n
Cary, Henry Francis, iii, *387*
Casement, Colonel Sir William, iii, *65*, 77
Cass, Lewis, 'odious firebrand,' iv, 383
Cassiobury, papers of Lord Essex at, v, 94
Caste, Ram Mohan Roy predicts its extinction, ii, 47
Castle-building, TBM and Hannah indulge in, vi, 156
Castle Howard, TBM visits with Sydney Smith, i, 216; 241n, TBM declines invitation to iv, 334; TBM at v, 390n
Castlereagh, Lord, suicide, i, 179n; iii, 219, iv, 192
Castor and Pollux, ii, 292
Catherine de Medici, i, 81, iv, 149
Catherine of Aragon, Queen, iv, 256, 257
Catherine of Braganza, Queen, iv, 255, 257, v, 9, 24, 92, 151
Catholic Apostolic Church, i, 232n, 252n, Empson's article on ii, 50; its prophets at the Derby 244
Catholic Association, iii, 253n
Catholic Church, TBM will support 'any well-digested plan for establishing' in Ireland iv, 161; in Ireland 289; TBM's view of in *History* v, 26n; its rule on language of service 428
Catholic disabilities, i, 262n, 311n, iv, 327
Catholic emancipation, i, 21, topic at debating society, Preston's school 23; 109n, issue in Leicester election 211n; at Cambridge 212n; TBM and Sydney Smith discuss 214; Robert Grant must speak out on 223; TBM votes for in Cambridge election 223n; general senti-

ment in favour of 252; enacted 252n; 275n, 281n, 293n, III, 269, IV, 113
Catholic Emancipation Bill, 1825, I, 211
Catholic Emancipation Bill, 1829, Wellington's duel over, V, 295
Catholic Priests, for soldiers in Indian army III, 301; question of payment for IV, 161, 166, 168, 281; payment for chaplains in prisons V, 408
Catholicism, its relation to pagan sensuality I, 171; in Ireland II, 116; fanatical III, 225; in Rome 269; its cultural achievements compared to those of Protestantism V, 27
Catholics, I, 234, in India III, 69; TBM thought unfair to V, 26; their history in England suggested as subject 88; restoration of hierarchy 130n; TBM opposes Guy Fawkes reactions against 135; Miss Cunninghame's effort to make converts 358; in London in 1685 130; and cult of Virgin VI, 238n
Cator, Sir John, V, 314n, *406*
Cator, Mrs John (Julia Hallam), her twins, V, 312, 406n
Catullus, III, 160*, TBM sent German translation of VI, 191n
Caucasus, Mount, V, 476
Causes Célèbres, French, case from cited, I, 244
Cavaignac, Louis Eugène, V, *75*
Cavan, County, I, 219
Cave, Robert Otway-, I, 211n, 223
Cavendish, Charles, V, 427n
Cavendish, Richard, II, *348*
Cavendish, William, afterwards 7th Duke of Devonshire, II, 12n, *13*, 17, 168
Caveri, III, 51
Cawnpore, VI, 119n, 131n, 134n
Cawthorne's, London circulating library, IV, 140, V, 280, VI, 73n
Cecil, Richard, I, *37*
Cellini, Benevenuto, piece by at Great Exhibition, V, 203
Census of 1841, III, 313n
Cervantes, *Don Quixote*, TBM resolved to read in original I, 69, 69n; 'best novel in the world' II, 320*; 329, 359*, III, 9, 62*, 86, 142, 169, IV, 299*, V, 391*
Ceylon, III, 34
Chadwick, Sir Edwin, IV, *253*, his reform of burial practices 253-4; 'a knave' V, 387; 417
Chadwick, Owen, *The Victorian Church*, V, 189n, 297n, VI, 70n
Chaillot MS, V, 9
Chalmers, Alexander, *The British Essayists*, V, 462n, *The Works of the English Poets*, V, 139
Chalmers, Dr Thomas, portrait by Inman, IV, 225n
Chalon, Alfred Edward, offers TBM a dog VI, *19*
LETTER TO: VI, 19
Chalons-sur-Saône, III, 274, V, 343, 349n, 354
Chamberlayne, Edward, *Present State of England*, V, 151
Chambers, Sir Thomas, V, *253*
Chambers, William, V, *424*
Chambers, Dr William Frederick, Macaulay family doctor, II, *48*, 170, 215, III, 98
Chambord, Château of, described IV, 148-9; 153, 159, 350
Chamier, Henry, III, *43*
Chamisso, Adelbert von, *Peter Schlemihl*, II, 29
Champion (London), I, 76n
Chancellor of Duchy of Lancaster, not in Aberdeen cabinet V, 306; office would not add to TBM's standing 255
Chancellor of the Exchequer: *see* Lord Campbell, W. E. Gladstone, Henry Goulburn, Sir George Cornewall Lewis, Sir Charles Wood
Chancery, Court of, Zachary Macaulay's suit heard in I, 149; and Queens' College case 152n; Zachary Macaulay's suit against *John Bull* 220n
Chandos, John, Lord, IV, 247
Chandos, 1st Duke of, V, *104*
Chandos MS, V, 104
Channel Islands, criminal law in, IV, 339n, 355; Ellis on V, 16
Channel Islands Commission, IV, 339, Ellis in V, 206
Channell, Sir W. F., studies law with TBM I, *172n*
Channing, William Ellery, *Milton*, VI, 193; review of by Brougham attributed to TBM 193
Chantrey, Sir Francis, anecdote of him by Rogers II, 55; 365, sculpture at Madras III, 41
Chaplain, House of Commons: *see* Frederick Lockwood
Chapman, Captain Alfred, III, 84, 'not overburdened with brains' 86
Chapman, John, attacks London Booksellers' Association, V, 224n
Chappell, William, VI, *108*; *Collection of*

Chappell, William—*cont.*
National English Airs, 108n; *Popular Music of Olden Time* 108n
LETTER TO: VI, 108
Charlemont, 1st Earl of, V, 93
Charles I, King, I, 59, II, 124, 169, 197, IV, 255, 257, anniversary of execution V, 23; 101n, at Oxford 115; his death a model for TBM's 301; service for martyrdom of VI, 157n
Charles II, King, III, 257, 258, IV, 255, 257, 371, and Nell Gwynn 388; death of and P.M.A.C.F. V, 8n, 9; 24, 50, 433n, 476, his deathbed conversion VI, 130; service for restoration of 157n
Charles II, of Spain, apocryphal story about, IV, 117
Charles V, I, 44, III, 42, V, 26, and his clocks 162
Charles VII, of France, IV, 145
Charles X, of France, I, 289n, 305n, 306
Charles of France, Duke of Guienne, IV, 83
Charleville, Harriet Charlotte Campbell, Lady, IV, *245*
LETTER TO: IV, 245
Charleville, Lord, IV, *245n*
Charlinch, Somerset, V, 187n
Charlotte, Princess, I, 21n, death of 92n; 95-6, 105, 224, IV, 258n
Charlotte, Queen, IV, 257
Charmouth, TBM at, VI, 240n
Charnwood, Lady, *An Autograph Collection,* V, 180
Charterhouse, I, xxvi, xxviii, 130n, III, 99, 111, V, 158n
Charteris, Colonel Francis, IV, *89*
Chartists, nominate Sharman Crawford at Edinburgh III, 290; 291, at Edinburgh 380, IV, 95, refusal of their Charter 113; TBM's opposition to 291-2; TBM defends sentences of Frost, Williams, and Jones 293; monster procession in London 363n; V, 351
Chartres, TBM visits cathedral IV, 139-40; 142, 147, 152, V, 68, 72
Chastelain, M. (French master at Preston's?), I, 60
Chateaubriand, François René, Vicomte de, has genius if not principle I, 183
Writings: Atala, I, 183, *Génie du Christianisme,* I, 183*, 'Shakspere, ou Shakspeare,' I, 183
Chatham, Baroness, IV, 221; Pitt's letter to VI, 177n, 178
Chatham, William Pitt, 1st Earl of, II, 292, 321, IV, 198
Chatham Papers, VI, 178n
Chatmoss, III, 45
Chatsworth, III, 161
Chatterton, Thomas, V, 226
Chaucer, I, 65, II, 54, *Canterbury Tales,* VI, 133*
Cheddar, V, 276, TBM and Malden visit 277
Chelmsford, I, 14
Chelmsford, Sir Frederick Thesiger, 1st Baron, IV, *209*, V, 371, refuses Talfourd's seat 390; TBM congratulates on safety of daughter and son-in-law VI, 137-8; made Lord Chancellor 141; making a fool of himself 160; 175, sued by Mrs Swinfen 228
LETTER TO: VI, 137
Chelsea Asylum, TBM has nothing to do with, IV, 362
Chelsea Hospital, office of physician, III, 320, 324; 363n, chaplainship of, at TBM's disposal IV, 305, 317; patronage of 356; 362
Chelsea Hospital Board, IV, 313, 350, attending it all that TBM does to earn his salary 351; TBM presides at 359
Cheltenham, I, 35, 234, IV, 219, V, 65, 177, 180, 181, 357, Humphreys's book published at VI, 129n
Cheltenham, schoolmaster at: *see* E. R. Humphreys
Cheltenham Grammar School, VI, 38n
Cheltenham Water, III, 204
Cheney, Col. Edward, opposes TBM at Calne, I, 276n, 312n
Chepstow, TBM visits, V, 187, 189, 190, 191
Cherokees, III, 63
Chertsey, V, 409, 441
Chester, TBM less struck by than expected, II, 308; James II and Penn at V, 6n; TBM at V, 43
Chester, diocese of, V, 51
Chester, Elizabeth, II, *310*
Chesterfield, Lord, II, 288, 289, *Letters,* 288*, 321
Chesterton, G. K., *Victorian Age in Literature,* II, 17n
Chetham Society, V, 129n
Chetwood, William Rufus, *A General History of the Stage,* IV, 132*
Chevening (Lord Stanhope's residence), II, 171, IV, 53, TBM hopes to visit 346; pays first visit to V, 171; 172, 254, TBM visits VI, 46n; 48, 50, TBM on library at 53; can't visit 248
'Chevy Chase,' III, 132
Chicago Journal, V, 203n

Chichester, v, 103, vi, 76
Chickasaws, iii, 63
Chief Justice, Supreme Court of Calcutta: *see* Sir John Peter Grant
Child labor, analogy with slave labor, ii, 118
Chile, TBM writes to Black's son in, v, 294; news from 379
Chillianwallah, battle of, v, 31n
Chiltern Hundreds, iii, 384, iv, 363, v, 237, 257, 284, 450, 468, vi, 8, TBM applies for Stewardship of 9
Chilton Priory, Bridgewater (Stradling's residence), iv, 95n
China, free trade with ii, 92; East India Company's monopoly 140; trade with 233, 234, 240, 258; 289, new superintendents to be sent to 324; relations with 358; war with iii, 324; victory in 360n, 362; peace treaty iv, 74; Emperor of, on diplomatic procedure 74-5; 75, conflict in Hong Kong vi, 79; second Chinese war 79n
Chinese, characters of, i, 84
Chinese Exhibition, London, iv, 52, 68
Chippenham, ii, 130
Chipping Norton, ii, 196
Chitapet, pet name for Margaret Macaulay ii, 94, 95
Chivalry, TBM's pronunciation of, v, 466
Cholera, panic on its approach, ii, 48; Lady Holland terrified by 76; TBM has some form of 87, 88, 89n; deaths from 145; reported in London 145n; House of Commons fumigated against 156; 'all humbug' 158; 160, 293, gone from London but raging in Madrid 315; raging in Calcutta iii, 218; in England, 1849, v, 75; outbreak in 1853, 357; 360, in London 1854, 415n
Chouans, iv, 32
Christ, Ram Mohan Roy's ideas of his nature ii, 47
Christian VII, of Denmark, his mad behaviour, ii, 182-3
Christian Observer, i, xxv, review of Norris, i, 41*; 42, TBM contributes to 49; TBM indexes 49n, 56; 74, on Marryat's pamphlet 74n; 118n, novel-reading controversy in 120-1; editorship transferred from Macaulay to Wilks 197n; 198n, criticised by Sydney Smith 214n; general index to be made by TBM 321; TBM's contributions to 321-2; TBM intended as editor 322; disapproves peerage for Col. Fitzclarence 42n; edited J. W. Cunningham ii, 145n; on *Life of Wilberforce* 295n; and Lord Byron iv, 34
Christianity, Ram Mohan Roy's ideas of ii, 47; iii, 193, not a topic for politics 238
Christina, Queen of Spain, her amours, iv, 169-70
Christina, Queen of Sweden, iii, 42
Christison, Robert, iv, *214*, 'Medical Reform,' 214
Christmas, eulogy of, i, 168; most expressive word in England 183
Christmas Eve, TBM's ritual feast on, iv, 279n; v, 87n
Christophe, Madame, widow of Henry Christophe, i, 174n
Christopher, Robert Adam, iv, *110*, 202
'Christopher North': *see* John Wilson
Chrysostom, ed. Bernard de Montfaucon, iii, 237*
Chunam, iii, 37, 41
Chunee, the elephant, i, 240n
Church, Established, principle of discussed, ii, 164, 175-6; 178, iii, 364, TBM will not vote against iv, 161; 334n
Church of England, established in India, i, 25n; behaviour of clergy after Revolution iii, 208; and appointment of school inspectors 356; doctrine of episcopacy v, 8; TBM defends his account of its early doctrine 11-14; doctrine of episcopacy 18-21; convocation 21; articles 22; its prayers compared to Presbyterians' v, 291
Church of Ireland, needs complete reform ii, 114; tithe question 114n; TBM's position on 115-17; vote on Irish Tithe Bill 152; iii, 275, debate on iv, 135; TBM would transfer revenues to Catholics 162, 163; 164, TBM dissents from Senior on 166; 168, 272, v, 290, no longer a question 475: *see also* Irish Church Bill
Church of Scotland, Commission of Assembly, iii, 54; TBM hopes for settlement of intrusion question 321; 327, 344n, TBM's opinion on the establishment 346; seeks parliamentary support of veto 347n; its disputes 357; danger of secession 365; iv, 7, in 1688 16; can't now recede 19; 'hopeless' 36; 'Claim of Right' 36n; TBM fears he must speak 37; 70, question ripe for decision 79; debate expected 98; disruption of 126n; and Poor Relief 252n; disruption 346n; TBM dissents from its claims 400-1; and episcopacy v, 21; provision for in Scottish Universities Bill 325n; vi, 239

Church of Scotland—*cont.*

General Assembly: III, 311n, and veto question 346n; 356, 375, opposes Universities Bill IV, 258n; Claim of Right 400n; protest excites 'universal disgust' 36; V, 14

Intrusion Question: III, 294n, 336, 357, 364-5, 375-6, 378, 379, IV, 400-1

Veto Act: III, 311, declared illegal 311n; 347, 357, 364, IV, 400

Church Rate Bill, petitions for, VI, 157

Churchill, Charles, IV, 198, *Poetical Works*, review of not by TBM but by Forster, 193, 199-200

Churchill, Sir Winston, TBM's mistake about V, 44

Cibber, Colley, II, *309*, III, 308, V, 131; *Memoirs*, II, 309

Cibber, Susannah Maria, II, *310*

Cicero, I, 17*, 66, 90, compared to Demosthenes 91*; his character 96-7; 123, 133, a gift appropriate to any scholar 141; 191, III, 153*, 160*, 178, 197, 200, TBM intends to read entire 211; 237*, and human sacrifice IV, 359*; V, 447n, his letters fatal to his character 460; philosophical works VI, 182*; 248

Writings: Academic Questions, III, 159, *Brutus*, III, 153*, Oration against Cataline, I, 23*, 'De Amicitia,' VI, 186, 'De Divinatione,' IV, 358*, V, 106n*, VI, 247, 'De Fato,' VI, 247, 'De Finibus,' III, 158, V, 484*, VI, 247, 'De Natura Deorum,' V, 484*, VI, 246*, 'De Oratore,' I, 97, 'De Republica,' III, 163, *Epistles*, I, 96*, 97, V, 459*, 460*, TBM recommends as model to George Trevelyan VI, 98, *Letters to Atticus*, III, 147*, 159, 'Pro Domo Sua,' TBM thinks genuine, III, 155, *Tusculan Disputations*, III, 159, V, 484*, anointings for broken bones VI, 182*

Cincinnati, II, 314

Cinderella, IV, 399

Ciphers, in time of Charles II, V, 9

Civil Service, Northcote-Trevelyan report on, V, 387

Civil War, III, 169

Civita Castellana, III, 264

Clanricarde, Harriet (Canning), Marchioness of, II, *66*; TBM describes 66-7; V, 166n

Clanricarde, Ulick John De Burgh, 1st Marquess of, II, *66*, 'poor creature' 67; IV, 99, V, 166n

Clapham, I, viii, described xvii; its influence on TBM xviii; xxiv, xxvii, Macaulay family moves to 6n; TBM leaves for school 14; TBM longs for 16; dreams of it 21; 41n, 50n, 63n, 85, abandoned by Clapham Sect 101n; removal from 115; 124n, TBM spends summer at 129n; school taken over by Elwell 159n; stirred by TBM's failure 169n; Cunningham Vicar of II, 145n; Evangelicals of 363n; III, ix, 51, 93, 336n, Trevelyans take house there IV, 57n; 59, 75, TBM retreats there to avoid Commons 99; TBM walks to 236; 320, 335, 349, to celebrate Michaelmas at 351; 352, TBM at 378; 383, V, 40, 50, 52, 55, 61n, sad to think he will no longer walk to 68; 76, 265, VI, 70n

Places: Battersea Rise (Thornton family residence), I, 55n, 109n, II, 260, TBM dines at 344; III, 304n, IV, 203, 216, TBM dines at V, 47; 220n, Greaves's School at, I, 5n, Grove House (Elliott family residence), I, 176n, II, 24n, Holy Trinity Church, Preachers' Book, I, 19n

Clapham Sect, I, xvii, its influence xvii-xviii; xxiv, 5n, 27n, at Battersea Rise 55n; 56n, remove to London 101n; 138n, second generation 193n; includes John Pearson 198n; and Sykes family II, 86n; III, 103n, title invented by Stephen IV, 200

Claphamites, their achievement, IV, 207

Clapton, III, 56

Clare, County, election in, II, 30

Claremont, Surrey, I, 105, Trevelyans have key to V, 406; TBM visits 406n; 420

Clarence, Duke of, I, 164

Clarendon, 1st Earl of, II, 157n, Lister writing his life 320; VI, 153n

Writings: Correspondence: see S. W. Singer; *History of the Rebellion*, II, 320, III, 63, 135, IV, 386, best edition V, 145; 146, 323, *Life of Edward, Earl of Clarendon*, II, 320*, V, 13*, 20*, TBM presents to Edinburgh Philosophical Institution 463

Clarendon, George William Frederick Villiers, 4th Earl of, II, 31n, 138n, *157*, ambassador to Spain 289; 'most lively and polite of young men' 292; Lord Privy Seal III, 299; 339n, IV, 45, stories about Queen Christina 170; 265, 272, 276, to be President of Board of Trade

277; on Lord Grey 277; invites TBM to The Grove 314; 399n, v, 41n, Lord Lieutenant of Ireland 65; 86, 133, 139n, 290n, 321n, TBM asks for introduction from 418; 419, vi, 190n, 202n, not in new ministry 222; on differences between generations 227
LETTERS TO: v, 66, 418
Clarendon, Catherine, Lady, vi, *190*
LETTER TO: vi, 190
Clark, J. W., and T. M. Hughes, *Life of Adam Sedgwick*, vi, 67n
Clark, William, v, *385n*
Clarke, Edward, i, *138*, death of 174
Clarke, James Freeman, iv, *84*
LETTER TO: iv, 84
Clarke, John, *Paroemiologia*, i, 21n
Clarke, Longueville Loftus, iii, *177*, 182
Clarke, M. L., *George Grote*, iv, 309n
Clarke, Mrs, and J. W. Croker, iv, 89
Clarke, William Stanley, ii, *327*
Clarkson, Edward, *Essay on the Symbolic Evidences of the Temple Church*, iii, 372n, *Robert Montgomery and His Reviewers*, 372n
Clarkson, Thomas, i, *44*, interview with Emperor Alexander 104; toasted at Leeds ii, 333n; iii, 259, made important by Wilberforces' attack on 273
Writings: History of the Abolition of the Slave Trade, i, 44*, *Strictures on a Life of William Wilberforce*, iii, 273n
Classical Museum, iv, 240n
Classics, study of, TBM's doubts about i, 79-80; criticises Cambridge scholarship 87; discussed 88-91, 91-2; Cambridge style not TBM's 107; more exceptionable than modern literature 121; 126, a pleasure when not principal employment 136-7; TBM recommends to Henry Macaulay 165; plan for a course in Greek 242-3
Claude Lorrain, painting of at Rogers's, ii, 82; iv, 41, paintings at Leigh Court, v, 284
Claudet, Antoine, his photograph of TBM, vi, *16n*
Claudian, v, 167n
Claudine, III, 67
Claudius, Emperor, Tyrrhenian history, iii, 179
Clay, Henry, election would assure peace, iv, 224
Clayden, P. W., *Rogers and His Contemporaries*, ii, 28n, 32n
Clayfield, at school with TBM, i, 17
Clayfield, E. R., i, 17n
Clayfield, James Ireland, i, 17n
Clemens, iii, 279*
Clemens Alexandrinus, i, 98
Clement i, Pope, *Clementina*, TBM inquires about vi, 10
Cleon, i, 85, iii, 208
Cleopatra, i, 81
Cleopatra's Needle, ii, 159
Clergy, change in their situation since 17th century v, 83
Clergy List 1844, iii 363
Clerk, TBM's, TBM wishes to take to India ii, 340; offered position 359-60
Clerk, Sir George, iv, *208*
Cleveland, Duchess of, v, 414n, and Duke of Marlborough vi, 130
Cleveland, Duke of, iv, *101*, 110, 189
Clifden, v, 409
Clifford, Charles Cavendish, v, 212n
Clifford, James, L., ed., *Diary* of Thomas Campbell, vi, 218n
Clifton, TBM at i, 7; 58n, TBM at 277; v, 243, 244, TBM at after crisis in health v, 247ff; recollections of in 1811 249-50; misunderstanding with druggist at 251; TBM returns from 256; to go back again 257, 261n; view of 273; pastry cook at 276; 277, 288
Places: 16 Caledonia Place, TBM rents, v, 244n; there August-September 1852 259; Christ Church, TBM attends, v, 274; Royal Hotel, TBM at, v, 244n, 247ff; its splendor in 1811, 249, 250
Clinton, Sir Henry, despatch announcing defeat in Yorktown, vi, *196*
Clinton, Sir William Henry, ii, *61*
Clitheroe, parliamentary seat at, iv, 336
Clive, John, i, xxiii, vi, xii, *Macaulay, the Shaping of the Historian*, iii, viii, 103n, 150n, 185n, 214n
Clive, John, and Thomas Pinney, *Selected Writings of Macaulay*, ii, 5
Clive, Kitty, ii, *309*, 310
Clive, Lord, 'rapacious' i, 70; iii, 43, Henry Fox's protégé 310; iv, 44, on giving good salaries v, 97; 406n
Clodius, iii, 159
Close, Francis, iv, *317*, v, 357, appointed Dean of Carlisle vi, 70
Close, Miss, v, 357
Club, The, ii, 59, iii, 258, 281, TBM first attends 283; improved since departure of Sir Charles Grey iv, 117; 202n, v, ix, 52n, 55n, 59, Col. Mure elected 113;

Club, The—*cont.*
Peel blackballed by 149; meet at Thatched House 157; Richard Owen a member 150n; TBM cuts meetings 226, 401; VI, 85, 90n, 207n
Clumber Park, V, 143n
Coachman, TBM's, ill, VI, 176
Coates, Thomas, secretary of SDUK, I, 322, 323, II, 42n
Cobbett, William, I, 287n, on TBM and Irish Church II, *114n*; 144n, 218n, 231n, 'made a beast of himself' 240; his treatment of TBM 240n; neglects his *Register* 300; IV, 181n, TBM asks Longman to send volumes of V, 129
Writings: Political Register, II, 240n, 300, VI, 287
Cobden, Richard, IV, 22n, *101*, 168, 170n, 190, to be Vice President of Board of Trade 277; 364, 402, V, 222, 316n, moves vote of censure against Palmerston VI, 79n; defeated in 1857 86
Coblentz, V, 351, TBM at VI, 104; 105, TBM at 114
Cochrane, Alexander Cochrane-Baillie, IV, *133*
Cochrane, Mr, TBM sends money to, VI, 194
LETTER TO: VI, 194
Cockburn, Sir Alexander, as attorney general V, 378; on Ellis's speech VI, 219n; 222n
Cockburn, Henry Thomas, Lord, I, 224n, on Napier 237n; letter to Rutherfurd III, 313n; plan for *Life of Jeffrey* V, *92-3*; on Edinburgh electors 259; 260
Writings: Journal, III, 289n, 350n, IV, 125n, 174n, 269n, 301n, V, 92n, 133n, 245n, 263n, on Duke of Argyll VI, 18n, *Life of Jeffrey,* I, 324, II, 7n, IV, 34n, V, 93n, 94n, 221*, TBM declines to review 354, *Memorials of His Time,* V, 92n
LETTER TO: V, 94
Cockerell and Larpent, firm of, II, 349n, 355n, III, 6
Coddington, Henry, I, *142*
Codrington, Admiral Sir Edward, II, *250*
Coeur, Jacques, his house at Bourges IV, 145
Coinage, English, in 17th century, VI, 54-5
Coke, Sir Edward, *Institutes,* TBM wishes to borrow from Ellis, V, 442
Colbatch, John, VI, *69*
Colburn's Standard Novels, IV, 308n
Colby Library Quarterly, V, 473
Colchester, siege of, V, 62-3
Cole, Henry, introduction to catalogue of Great Exhibition, V, 167n
Colebrooke, Sir James Edward, III, *99*, dismissed in disgrace 100; and Trevelyan IV, 218
Coleman, Edward, V, *9*
Coleridge, Derwent, I, *178*, contributes to *Knight's Quarterly* 188n; III, 221, seeks appointment for his son IV, 379; TBM recommends for canonry VI, 15; compliments George Trevelyan 99; TBM can't approach Palmerston for 132; invited to Clarendon dinner 141; TBM recommends for position 277, 278; Principal of St Mark's 279n; testimonial to 282; 282n
Writings: Memoir of Moultrie, I, 190n, III, 135, Memoir of Praed, V, 81n
LETTERS TO: V, 335, VI, 15, 44, 132, 208, 277, 278, 283
Coleridge, Mrs Derwent (Mary Pridham), VI, *278*
Coleridge, Derwent Moultrie (son of Derwent Coleridge), IV, *379*
Coleridge, Hartley, TBM meets, VI, *278*; remarks on TBM 278n; *Worthies of Yorkshire* 278*
Coleridge, Henry Nelson, I, *126*, 143, contributes to *Knight's Quarterly* 188n; 190, III, 221
Coleridge, Sir John Taylor, I, 202n, V, 310n
Coleridge, Samuel Taylor, I, 126, II, 28n, Byron's mistaken judgment of 321; TBM criticises III, 221
Writings: 'The Ancient Mariner,' VI, 202*, *Literary Remains,* III, 221n, *Table Talk,* I, 126n, III, 221n
Collier, Jeremy, controversy with Congreve, III, 340; great public benefactor 342; VI, 96
Collins, Dennis, throws stone at William IV, II, 141n
Collins's Peerage, VI, 56
Colman, III, 185
Colman, Henry, V, *53*, *Fourth Report on Agriculture of Massachusetts,* 53n
Cologne, V, 339, 343, 349n, 351, 354, TBM at VI, 104; 105, TBM at 114; cathedral, finest of Gothic churches except for Milan 115
Colonial Office, I, xxvi, has unfavourable opinion of Henry Macaulay II, 294; V, 29
Colonisation, IV, 116
Colquhoun, John Campbell, II, *307*
Coltman, Lady, IV, 172

Coltman, Sir Thomas, iv, *172*
LETTER TO: iv, 172
Colvin, John Russell, iii, *149*, 162, 171, 177
Combe, George, iv, *303*, papers on capital punishment 304
LETTER TO: iv, 303
Combe Florey, Sydney Smith's living, ii, 33, v, 32
Combermere, 1st Viscount, iii, *94*
Commander-in-Chief, India: *see* Sir Henry Fane
Commines, Philippe de, *Mémoires*, iv, 83*
Commissariat Department, iv, 379; presents portrait to Trevelyan v, 138
Commission on Corporations (*see also* Municipal Corporations Bill), ii, 236; its report iii, 154, 157n, v, 206
Commissioners of Bankrupts, TBM appointed to i, 230, 235; to attend meetings in London 247; meet in Basinghall Street 249; office abolished 272n; work for 314; scene at court ii, 23-4; Basil Montagu at 28; scene at 30; TBM at 37; busied at 54, 55, 62, 64, 82; business slow 86; 89, winding up affairs 110; expiration of commission 111
Common Council, Court of, ii, 251
Common Law Courts, bill on procedure in, iv, 208n, 209
Common Pleas, Court of, v, 96n, vi, 216
Commons Journals, i, 312n, iv, 208n, 300n, presented to TBM vi, 236
Como, Lake, vi, 26, 57n
Conacher, J. B., *The Aberdeen Coalition*, v, 307n, 326n
Congleton, 1st Baron, iii, *85*, 320, 324, commits suicide iv, 37
Congreve, William, his wish to appear a man of the world, i, 239; ii, 82, iii, 340, 358, 365, v, 356
Coningsby, Lord, i, 66
Constance, Council of, v, 88
Constant, Benjamin, i, *179*, 303
Constantinople, iii, 353, 361, Greens and Blues at v, 43
Constitutional Association, iii, 177n
Constitutional (Paris), i, 296
Continental possessions, declamation topic at school, i, 66
Convenor of Catholic Electors, Edinburgh, writes TBM, v, 246
Conversion Society: *see* Incorporated Society for the Conversion and Religious Instruction and Education of the Negro Slaves in the British West Indies
Convocation, v, 278, TBM's mistrust of 297
Conway, Denbighshire, i, 157n
'Conway Morel' (pseudonym of Charles Macaulay), *Authority and Conscience*, i, xxviii
Conybeare, F. A., *Dingle Bank*, i, 282n, ii, 136n, iii, 129n
Conybeare, William John, v, *363*, 'Church Parties,' v, 156n, 362*, 363
Conybeare, Mrs William John (Eliza Rose), v, *362n*, 'Aunt Eliza's Story,' i, xxi, 115n, 170n, 267n, vi, 140n, Recollections of TBM, i, 211n, ii, 15n, 31n, iii, 195n, 253-4n
Conygham, Marchioness, George IV's mistress, ii, *60*
Cook, James, the murderer, ii, 124
Cook, Captain James, scenes from his voyages, ii, 90
Cook, Dr William, v, *24*
Cooke, George Frederick, ii, *309*
Cooke, G. W., ed., Marlyn and Kippis, *Life of the First Earl of Shaftesbury*, iii, 216n
Cooke, Richard Nethercoat, i, 125
Cookesley, John Gifford, ii, *334*
Cookesley, William, ii, *334*
Cookesley, William Gifford, TBM forwards article by ii, *333*; Napier refuses it 335; 367
Cooper, Charles Henry, *Annals of Cambridge*, i, 181n
Cooper, James Fenimore, 'detestable beast,' ii, *314*
Coorg, iii, 52
Coorg, Rajah of, iii, *49*, 'horrible tyrant' 50
Cope, C. W., iv, 198n
Copleston, Edward, Bishop of Llandaff, TBM succeeds in Royal Academy post v, 96n; 97
Copley: *see* Lord Lyndhurst
Coppock, James, v, *222n*
Copyright, convention between France and England on, v, 229; TBM expects no agreement between England and United States 388-9; international treaty for 389n
Copyright Act, iii, 249n, iv, 25n; and TBM's *Essays* 82; 194n
Copyright Bill, TBM modifies iv, 25; 33, TBM's modifications in 82n
[Corbett, the Misses], *Busy-Bodies*, ii, 214
Cordeliers, vi, 139
Corfu, ii, 143, 159
Cork, duties on v, 330
Cork, Ireland, v, 64n, TBM at 66; 68, 69, Irish bull at 70; 208

Cork, 7th Earl of, II, 283n
Cork, Lady (Mary Monckton), II, *283*
Corn Laws, fundamental change required in II, 92, 104; 162n, must be altered 163; 166, 178, TBM speaks on 346, 348; 358, TBM rejoices at attack on III, 275; 321, 373, IV, 19n, TBM inclined to accept compromise 21; 26, TBM opposed to 85; defensible if not protectionist 95; government not ready to take up 101; TBM's opinion 103-4; 105-6, need for compromise 108-10; TBM votes for Villiers's motion 111n; repealers outnumbered 113; ministry must take up question 114; debate on 123; and Edinburgh expectations 164; need for compromise 165; TBM will give no pledge on 168; 170, 172, TBM's position re-stated 185-91; 192, 193, Russell converted to repeal 268; choices of Whigs and Tories 270; 'throws all other questions into the shade' 273; immediate repeal proposed 274n; Whigs divided about 275; TBM certain that repeal 'right and honorable' 275; at ease now repeal determined 277; 280, Peel now forced to settle question 280; 289, fate in Lords unknown 296; passage of repeal 296n; time not ripe for repeal 402
Corn Law Bill, passage of, IV, 300n
Corneille, Pierre, *Dramatic Works*, I, 51
Cornwallis, Lord, III, 49, 76, not attractive subject for TBM IV, 44; on Lord Temple's resignation VI, 195-6; *Correspondence* 196n
Corp, Harriet, *Talents Improved*, V, 271*
Corresponding Society, III, 206, V, 118n
Corrie, George Elwes, on Sir James Stephen V, 85n
Corsicans, taken up by Boswell, II, 72
Corsini Palace, IV, 324
Cortona, III, 264n
Cossington, Leicestershire, I, 64n, 141n, Babington family living VI, 140n
Cotswolds, V, 177
Cottenham, Christopher Pepys, 1st Earl of I, 221n, IV, *272*, to be Lord Chancellor 277; 305, 317, TBM hopes he will resign V, 85; hostility between him and Macaulay family 85n
Cottesloe, 1st Baron: *see* Sir Thomas Francis Fremantle
Cotton, Henry, VI, *283*, *Quisquiliae Volantes* 284n
  LETTER TO: VI, 283
Cotton, J. J., *List of Inscriptions on Tombs or Monuments in Madras*, III, 33n
Cotton, John, III, 33n
Cotton, John Stedman, III, 33
Coulson, Walter, II, *272*, 324
Coulton, David Trevena, on Junius, *Quarterly Review*, V, 215-16*; notes in reply 216n
Counterfeiters, II, 11n
County Coroner's Bill, IV, 180n
Courier, Paul Louis, *Simple Discours de Paul Louis*, IV, 148*
Courier, taken at Aspenden Hall, I, 61; 158 IV, 41
Court Calendar, I, 171
Courtenay, Thomas Peregrine, II, *173*, *Memoirs of Sir William Temple*, reviewed by TBM 173n; III, 216n, IV, 126
Cousin, Victor, IV, *295*, TBM sends information to V, 476
  Writings: 'Discours Prononcé par M. Cousin . . . dans la Discussion Relative aux Cours du Collège de France,' IV, 295*, *Madame de Chevreuse*, V, 476n, 477n
Coutts, James, *History of the University of Glasgow*, IV, 380n, V, 89n
Coutts's Bank, V, 232
Covel, John, V, 338
Coventry, 8th Earl of, II, 337n
Cow Keeper: *see* William Wilberforce the younger
Cowan, Charles, defeats TBM at Edinburgh IV, *341*; disqualified, then re-elected 348; 349, 392, V, 236, campaigning in Edinburgh 240n; standing in poll 245; 246, has not sense enough to be depended on 247; type of the still demagogue 248; 290, 319n, VI, 85n, his *Reminiscences* IV, 341n
Coward, Dr, V, 237n
[Coward, John William Smith], letter to, V, 235
Cowell, F. R., I, xxxiv
Cowley, Abraham, I, 87, V, 409, hermit at Chertsey 441
Cowley, Hannah, I, *82*
Cowley, Henry Richard Charles Wellesley, 1st Earl, V, *419*
Cowper, William, TBM reading his works I, 35-6*; letter to Lady Hesketh II, 38*; III, 245, V, 39, 356, hermit at Olney 441; accuracy of legal points in his writing VI, 192
  Writings: John Gilpin, VI, 162n, *Poems* (posthumous), I, 71*, *The*

Task, I, 63*, drove out Young's *Night Thoughts*, V, 152; translation of Homer, I, 36*, *Iliad*, I, 35*, II, 38
Cowper, 5th Earl, V, 415n
Cowslip Green (Hannah More's residence), I, xxix
Coxe, William, *Memoirs of Marlborough*, V, 44, *Memoirs of Henry Pelham*, III, 108, *Memoirs of Sir Robert Walpole*, III, 275n
Cozens-Hardy, William Hardy, V, 34n
Cozens-Hardy, Mrs William Hardy, V, *34*
LETTER TO: V, 34
Crabbe, George, portrait at Holland House, II, 20
Cradock, Edward, V, *184*
Cradock, Mrs Edward (Harriet Lister), V, *184*
Craig, Sir James Gibson, III, *306*, 378n, 384, advises TBM not to come to Edinburgh IV, 70; 85, and Corn Laws 104n; 161n, 164, 169, 211, TBM calls on 215; 315
LETTER TO: IV, 161
Craig, James Thomson Gibson, TBM dines with, IV, *303*
Craig, Mrs James Thomson Gibson (Jane Grant), IV, *303*
Craig, Sir William Gibson, III, 319, 344, *378*, IV, 36, TBM supports for election to Reform Club 107; and Edinburgh Water Bill 120n, 125n; TBM supposes he will lose election 161, 164; 171, he and TBM regarded differently at Edinburgh 214; TBM advises 215; 243, 261, 284n, 302, 306, appointed Lord of the Treasury 315n; 321, 326, re-elected at Edinburgh 341n; reports reaction in TBM's favour 348; 379, with TBM at Cambridge V, 54; on returning TBM for Edinburgh 231n; 240, 243, 'no man could expect to find twice such a colleague as I had in you' 247; congratulates TBM 249; and TBM's letter to electors 253; his friendship with TBM 253; must consider replacing TBM 257; 258, TBM wishes to pay for expenses 262; 347, may succeed TBM 446, 450, 468; VI, 6, refuses to stand 7n; and Edinburgh election 85
LETTERS TO: IV, 54, 116, 120, 131, 134, 168, 214, 283, 286, 315, 319, V, 242, 243, 246, 247, 252, 256, 256, 259, 262, 331, VI, 14
Craig, Lady, IV, *169*, V, 242, 248, 253, 260, 263, 331
Craigcrook (Francis Jeffrey's residence), I, 233, 235, V, 41n, 73, painful to think of that once happy house 74
Cranbrook, Gathorne Gathorne-Hardy, 1st Earl of, on Elwell's school, I, 159n; 231n
Craniology, subject for examination in Latin verses, I, 77
Cranmer, Archbishop, his character, IV, 175-6; 246, 392-3, his view of episcopacy V, 7; TBM defends his account of 11-14; on Henry VIII's ecclesiastical authority 18; his commission 19; on episcopacy 19*; dishonest 42; his views of episcopacy 172; VI, 201
Cranstoun, George, Lord Corehouse, V, *93*
Cranworth, Robert Monsey Rolfe, 1st Baron, II, *56*, at breakfast IV, 234; TBM hopes he will be Chancellor V, 85; 150, Lord Chancellor V, 304; 305n, 378, TBM will ask for living from 427; 427n, gives Edward Rose living of Weybridge 458; TBM calls on about Ellis VI, 51; 207, better in common law than in equity 222
LETTER TO: V, 150
Cranworth, Lady, V, 427n
Craufurd, E. H. J., his bill on British courts, V, 392
Craufurd, James, IV, *319*
Craven, Augustus, IV, *8*
Craven, Mrs Augustus, IV, *8*
Craven, Lady, V, 228n
Crawford, D. G., *Roll of the Indian Medical Service*, III, 44n
Crawford, William Sharman, III, 290n, IV, *102*
Creevey, Thomas, IV, 245n
Creole affair, IV, 47, 135n
Cresswell, Sir Cresswell, compliments Ellis, VI, *219*
Crewe, Lady, V, 405n
Crewe, Colonel Richard, III, 78, *79*
Cribb, Tom, VI, *249*
Crimean War, V, 390n; day of fast and humiliation proclaimed 396; battle of the Alma 423, 426; interest in as great as in Wellington's campaigns 429; Foreign Enlistment Bill 435; brings overthrow of ministry 441n; committee of inquiry into 445n; reverse will bring in Derby 448; Disraeli moves vote of censure on government's conduct of 455n; Milner Gibson's motion 456; TBM's reasons for supporting war 456; Russell's contradictory conduct 461n; war only subject of talk 475-6; not yet the moment for peace 476

Crimean winter (1855), v, 438n

Crinean, Rev. J., III, 311, his school v, 277; his debts VI, 72

Crinean, Mrs J. (Frances), III, *311*, in Selina Macaulay's will v, 128; calls on TBM 277; not unwilling to assist her VI, 69-70; begging letter from 72; goes from begging to swindling 138; TBM continues to send money 138n

Crisp, Henry, IV, 94

Croft-Cooke, Rupert, *Madeira*, IV, 227n

Croker, John Wilson, I, *286*, parallel with TBM 287n; founds Athenaeum 294n; TBM gives 'dressing' to 312-13; attacks Brougham in Commons 313n; 324, 'most impudent man in the house' II, 6; speech of 4 March 6; TBM detests him 84; mastery of subject of Reform Bill 88n; sarcastic compliment to TBM in Commons 106; furnishes notes for reply to TBM 108n; his pamphlet unanswered 111; dispute over passage in Euripides 111-12n; 154, 155, on Walpole and Miss Berry 349n; review of Madame D'Arblay III, 308; 363, D'Arblay family fight with IV, 63; has 'behaved like Croker' to Mme D'Arblay 64, 70; TBM's remarks on his character and history 89-90; 89n, review of Harriet Martineau 90; article on Soult 90; review of Lady Morgan 90; collecting materials about Johnson 91; will not protest TBM's article 93; remains quiet 96; 98, his behaviour toward women's books 128; v, 53, 55n, TBM edits *ER* reply to 62

Writings: 'Answers to the Edinburgh Reviewer of Croker's Boswell,' II, 110, edition of Boswell, *Life of Johnson*, reviewed by TBM, II, 7n; 'wretchedly ill done' 57; identifies Hannah More in Boswell 57, 58n; 'offensive' 59; 72n, TBM leaves him no leg to stand on 94; has beaten him black and blue 95; 'monstrous blunders' 96; 'smashed' 106; 3rd edn, 112n; 352, 'Memoirs of Thomas Moore,' dirty and spiteful v, 346; review of TBM's *History* v, 31, 44*, 45, 46n, 47*, 52

Croker, Mrs John Wilson, protests passage in Trevelyan's *Life* of TBM, IV, 91n

Croly, Rev. George, III, *320*, *Memoir of Burke*, 320, 325

Crompton, Sir Charles, speaks warmly of Ellis, VI, *142*

Cromwell, Oliver, I, 134, 180, II, 9, 169, III, 118, v, 63, 101n, 359, 409, 433

Cropper, Charles, I, xxviii, birth of, II, 360; 361, 363, III, 8, 11, 12, 15, 17, 20, 28, 29, 40, 89, 107, 116, TBM eager to meet 231; good reports of, 256, 261, 273, 277, mathematics, algebra, or Greek 285; 290, 296, beaten by his father 305; 317, 341, TBM's anxieties about IV, 35; 37, TBM debates with 38; 143, 151, 157, 201, calls on TBM 206; 207, 221, 222, dines with TBM 234; death of 334; TBM had left his library to 335

LETTERS TO: IV, 39, 134

Cropper, Edward, I, xxvi, xxviii, 248n, 282n, engaged to Margaret Macaulay II, *184*; leaves Quakers 184n, 189; 185, 210, does Margaret henpeck him? 215; 216, 222, 223, 226, 227, 230, 231, 232, 233, 234, 237, 239, will do wonders in China trade 240; 241, 243, 244, 246, 249, 251, 252, 254, 257, 259, 261, 263, 266, 269, 271, sends paper to TBM 273; 274, 276, 277, 278, 280, calls on TBM 281; 283, in gallery of House of Commons 287; 291, verses on 292; 293, 294, 296, 302, 304, 310, 312, 317, 320, 322, 324, 327, 329, 330, 332, 335, 337, 341, 344, 349, 350, helps support Zachary Macaulay and daughters 351; John Macaulay borrows from 358-9; 360, 361, 362, 364, 366, 368, 370, III, 9, 11, 12, 15, 17, 20, agent for TBM 22n; 28, 29, 40, 73, 89, 107, TBM repays £600 116; TBM unable to write to 157; 161, 182, 230, TBM too disturbed to write to 231; 233, 255, 265, 273, 277, 281, hopes to hear of his complete recovery 284; 290, 296, in London 305; 341, IV, 37, 38, 46, 134, 143, railways 147; 151, 157, 201, TBM sees 202; 207, railway director 221; 222, 281, director of London and Northwestern Railway 333; TBM writes to for Ellis 334; death of his son 334; marriage (third) to widow of Henry Macaulay 383; v, 41, Margaret Trevelyan with 57; 59, gives allowances to Fanny and Selina 60; death of infant son 61; children by third marriage 61n; 160n, 425, living near Penshurst VI, 239; 266

LETTER TO: III, 231

Cropper, Mrs Edward (Isabella Wakefield, 1st wife of Edward Cropper), I, xli, 248n, fatal illness 283n; death 308n; II, 184

Cropper, Mrs Edward (Margaret Macaulay, 2nd wife of Edward Cropper), TBM's

sister (1812-34), I, ix, and TBM's letters xi-xii; xxvi, xxvii, *xxviii*, 19, TBM sees daily in summer of 1831, London 29n; 31, 39, 40, 66, 68, TBM pleased by her letter 160; Moultrie's poem on her death 190n; 196, 200, TBM's mock quarrel with 238; TBM will escort her from Rothley Temple 246; 247, 248, at Dingle Bank 248n; 271, 279, nurses the dying Mrs Edward Cropper 283; lives at George Babington's II, 17; at James Parker's 18; TBM sees daily 23; 29, 30, 31, 40, 41, 45, TBM takes her to see William IV open Parliament 49; 51, on TBM's 5 July speech 62n; has order for the Ventilator 66; at Golden Square 78; sees Thames procession with TBM 82; leaves London for Rothley Temple 83; 84, TBM's love for her and Hannah his strongest feeling 85; 88, 95, on TBM's fears of revolution 99n; 102, at James Cropper's with Hannah 122n; on Henry's appointment 102n; TBM's pet names for 123; her account of early trip on railroad 124n; 133, turning Quaker 136; 143, travelling in Wales 148; has mumps 152, 180; engaged to Edward Cropper 184; 189, 191, 193, TBM sends farewell letter to on eve of her marriage 203; 207, TBM weeps for 210; 214, sees Mathews act 216; 218, differs from TBM on question of election expenses 225n; TBM offers his portrait as 'funeral relique' 226; affected by TBM's letter 226n; escapes injury in carriage accident 231n; coming to London 237; returns to Liverpool 239; 241, 243, 244, her britchska 244; 246, 248, 249, 251, 252, 254, 257, 259, 261, 263, 266, 267, 269, 271, 274, 276, 277, 278, 280, 283, 287, 288, 290, hopes to go on Scottish tour 291; 293, expecting her child 293n; 294, 296, 299, on TBM and Indian appointment 299n; 301, her advice on Indian appointment to be sought 302; 303, 304, 308, 310, 312, 317, 320, 322, 324, 327, TBM thinks of her during crisis of Indian appointment 328; 329, 330, 332, 335, 337, 338, 341, 344, 347, 351, thought of her makes TBM weak 351; 359, birth of her son 360; doing well 361; 362, 363, 364, TBM will make his parting brief 364; 366, misery of parting from 368; her 'charity' 369; 370, III, vii, ix, TBM's unhappiness over her marriage 8; letter to Hannah 20n; Journal letter 31n; 73, 117, dies of scarlet fever 129n, 136; 219, TBM's grief still bitter 231; 256, her death from scarlet fever v, 380n; effect of her death on TBM VI, 280-1

Recollections of TBM, I, xxvii, xxviii, xli, 58n, 69n, 73n, 80n, 112n, on TBM at Union 183-4n; 230n, on TBM, Brougham, and *ER* 254n; on TBM's maiden speech 272n; 277n, 314n, 318n, 321, II, 5n, 15n, on Marriott 16n; on TBM and Maria Kinnaird 19n; on TBM in summer of 1831 29n; TBM's diatribe against Brougham 101-2n; 108n, on TBM's third Reform Bill speech 109n; discussion of Mirabeau 121n; 122n, on TBM and Charles Grant 137n; 138n, on TBM and Lady Davy 170n; on Charles Grant 204n; like 'reading my love-letters to my first love' 226n; on John Macaulay and his fiancée 358n

LETTERS TO: I, 266, 282, 308, II, 85, 122, 123, 132, 134, 135, 137, 139, 141, 143, 144, 145, 147, 149, 151, 151, 153, 154, 156, 158, 160, 167, 168, 172, 179, 180, 182, 184, 185, 186, 187, 193, 203, 205, 208, 214, 222, 222, 224, 225, 226, 227, 229, 231, 231, 233, 234, 236, 237, 272, III, 8, 11, 11, 15, 17, 17, 20, 25, 27, 29, 32, 40, 64, 67, 76, 89, 89, 90, 99, 113

Cropper, Mrs Edward (Margaret Denman Macaulay, widow of Henry Macaulay and 3rd wife of Edward Cropper), I, xxvi, II, 184n, IV, *34*, 157, 367, marries Edward Cropper 383; V, 41, 199, TBM writes on death of Lord Denman 425; 'must be out of her mind' VI, 239

LETTERS TO: IV, 368, V, 425

Cropper, James, I, xxvi, *196*, 199, 207, 248n, 253n, 282n, Hannah and Margaret spend summer with II, 122n; promoter of Liverpool and Manchester Railway 124n; 135, 136, disputes at Board of Control not for his ears 140; 184n, 265, III, 305

Cropper, John, I, 248n, 282n, II, 243, V, 160n, 199n

Cropper, Mrs John (Anne Wakefield), I, 248n, II, 243, III, 11

Cropper, Mary, her wedding, V, 199

Cropper, Miss, V, 160

Cropper, Sarah, V, 199n

Cropper family, I, 283, V, 55n

Cropper, Benson and Co., I, 196n, 207n, II, 136n, 184n

Crowder, Sir Richard Burden, succeeds Talfourd v, *391*
Crowe, Eyre Evans, I, 324
Crusade, 1st, I, 23n
Crusades, TBM to speak on at school, I, 22, 23; examination question 32; VI, 253
Crystal Palace, 'looks glorious' v, 169
Cuba, IV, 50
Cubbon, Colonel Sir Mark, III, *48*, 49, 50, 53, 66, 83, 102
Cuddesden Palace, residence of Bishops of Oxford VI, 217
Cumberland, III, 58, 61
Cumberland, Ernest Augustus, Duke of, I, *264*, III, 347
Cumin, Patrick, TBM's amanuensis, v, *414n*
Cumming, Dr John, VI, 252n, biblical prophecies *253*; 254, *The Great Tribulation* 253n
Cummins, Mr, II, 30n
Cunningham, Allan, I, *188n*, IV, 388n
Cunningham, John William, I, 152n, II, *145*
Cunningham, Mrs John William, death of, I, 152
Cunningham, Peter, IV, *388*, on TBM's *History* 388-9; *Story of Nell Gwynn* v, 229-30*
LETTERS TO: IV, 388, v, 229
Cunninghame, Margaret, arrested for distributing Bibles in Italy v, 358; wishes to refuse pardon 363
Curioni, Alberico, II, *18*
Curll, Edmund, v, *339*, Pope's treatment of 347; Vizetelly resembles 371
Curran, John Philpot, VI, 192
Currency, state of in 1695, VI, 39; at Restoration 54-5
Currie, Raikes, v, *217*, 312n
LETTER TO: v, 217
Currie, Mrs Raikes, v, 217n
Currie, Mrs Woodhouse, v, *312*
LETTER TO: v, 312
Custom House, III, 243
Cuthbertson, Catherine, *Santo Sebastiano*, II, 51*
Cyrus, I, 32

D-C, Sir John, 'that pest,' III, 326
Dacca, III, 149
Daemonology, preferable to mathematics, I, 122
Dafforne, James, *Life of Edward Matthew Ward*, v, 175, 399
D'Aguesseau, Henri François, v, *100*
Daily News, VI, 220
Daintry, John, I, 22
Dalhousie, 9th Earl of, III, *94*, v, 470n
Dalkeith Palace, IV, 54
Dahl, Curtis, 'Macaulay, Henry Taylor, and Swinburne's Trilogy,' IV, 40n
Dalling and Bulwer, 1st Baron: *see* Sir Henry Bulwer
Dalmeny, Lady, IV, *346*
Dalmeny, Lord, IV, *346*
Dalrymple, Sir John, III, *66*, *Memoirs of Great Britain and Ireland*, 375*
[Dalton, James], *The Invisible Gentleman*, II, 260*
Daly, Henry, I, 5
Damocles, IV, 143
Danby, Lord, IV, 385
Danby, Mr, of Bristol, I, 7
Danby, Mr, murdered, II, 217n
Dandelions, TBM's war with, VI, 272
Daniell, Mrs?, VI, 5
Dante, Brougham's recommendation of, I, 185; trans. Ichabod Charles Wright II, 277; III, 62*, *Divine Comedy* 86; 387, *Inferno* IV, 98*, VI, 68*
Danvers-Butler, George John, II, *49*
D'Arblay, Alexander, III, *308*
D'Arblay, Mme (Fanny Burney), I, 108n, TBM declines to defend her against Croker III, 308; pressed by her family to do so IV, 64; a woman of talents 70; Croker's treatment of 89-90, 93; 97
Writings: Camilla, II, 216, 308, *Diary and Letters*, II, 227n, IV, 30n, 75, *Evelina*, II, 95*, 136n, III, 308, *Memoirs of Doctor Burney*, TBM proposes to review II, 227*, III, 308n
Darien scheme, IV, 15, VI, 129
Darmes, Marius, III, 341n
Darnley, Earl of, III, 207, IV, 40, murder of 71; 257, VI, 237
Dartmoor, IV, 146, VI, 248
Dartmouth, III, 243
Daru, Pierre, IV, *82*, *Histoire de la République de Venise*, III, 108
Darwin, Charles, dines at Chevening with TBM, VI, 46n
Davenant, Charles, v, *356*, *Discourses on the Public Revenue*, VI, 55*
David, v, 34
David II, of Scotland, IV, 255, 257
David, Duke of Rothsay, IV, 257
Davies, Col. Thomas Henry Hastings, II, *32*
Davila, Enrico, *Historia delle Guerre Civili di Francia*, III, 9, 181, IV, 369
Davis, Richard Hart, I, 175n

Davy, Sir Humphry, I, *269*, II, 170n, V, 150n, *Consolations in Travel*, TBM declines to review, I, 269-70
Davy, Lady, I, 269n, II, *170*, dinner with described 250; at Althorp V, 85n; 290n, death of 454
Dawes, Richard, *Miscellanea Critica*, III, 183
(Dawson?, C.), letter to, V, 91
Dawson, George, I, 286, II, 155
De Burgh, Elizabeth, IV, 255, 257
De Burgh, Richard, IV, 246
De la Pryme, Charles, V, *225n*, and Poor Boy of Brighton 226
De Mauley, William Francis Spencer Ponsonby, 1st Baron, death of, V, *454*
De Morgan, Augustus, IV, *355*, intermediary for Guizot V, 145; argues for decimal coinage VI, 132
Writings: 'Answers to Questions Communicated by Lord Overstone,' VI, 132*, *Budget of Paradoxes*, IV, 355n, theory about P.M.A.C.F., VI, 165n, *Formal Logic*, IV, 355*, *Newton: His Friend: and His Niece*, V, 355, VI, 54, 55n, 165n, paper on Mrs Barton and Charles Montagu, V, 355-6*
LETTERS TO: IV, 355, V, 145, 338, 355, 360, VI, 54, 130, 132, 165, 166
De Quincey, Thomas, TBM may succeed to his name of opium eater, V, 361
Deacle, Mr and Mrs, II, 74n
Deal, III, 25n
Dealtry, Emily: *see* Mrs Henry Thornton
Dealtry, William, I, *41*, 42, II, 261, 331
Dealtry, William the younger, V, *220*
Debrett's Peerage 1828, I, 275
Decazes, Elie, Duc, II, *67*
Deceased Wife's Sister question, VI, 201
Decimal coinage, TBM opposed to, VI, 90n, 132
Deffand, Madame du, II, 317, correspondence with Walpole 349; III, 24, *Letters* 21
Defoe, Daniel, I, 271, more original than Pope II, 109
Writings: Memoirs of Captain Carleton, II, 201, *Robinson Crusoe*, I, 5n, 61, 157, II, 313, III, 145, V, 75, 123, 124, 125, 175, VI, 54, 272
Delane, John Thadeus, VI, 219n
Delanoue, M., *La Coquette Corrigée*, V, 81*
Delaune, William, V, *21*
Delcroix and Co., London perfumers, II, 138
Delessert, Benjamin, Baron, I, *306*
Delft, IV, 220
Delhi, VI, 103, in Mutiny 105; 106, siege of 106n; 125n, capture of 129, 217n
Delhi, King of, VI, *107*
Delort, Joseph, *Histoire de l'Homme au Masque de Fer*, IV, 82
Demerara, insurrection in, I, 192n, 194; 'judicial murders' in 195
Democritus, IV, 297
Demosthenes, I, 91*, copy loaned to TBM by Milner 136; 185n, II, 11, III, 137, 160, 180*, 199*, 237*, V, 182*, 345, speeches VI, 161*, on Aeschines 161; 288
Writings: Pro Corona, V, 191*, *Second Philippic*, IV, 170, speech on the Embassy, V, 181*
Denbigh, II, 105
Denham, Sir John, 'News from Colchester,' V, 395*
Denison, George, his letter opposing Gladstone, V, 306
Denison, John Evelyn, afterwards 1st Viscount Ossington, II, *66*, 79, 274, TBM to visit IV, 222n; tour in U.S. 266; sends gift of bread and butter V, 152; 152n, commissions Grant's portrait of TBM 327n; 328n, chosen Speaker of the House VI, 89; created Viscount Ossington 89n; 90n, calls on TBM 106, 107; consults TBM on parliamentary library 142; Diary 142n; 175, 261
LETTERS TO: III, 292, IV, 224, 268, 347, 381, V, 10, 42, 142, 152, 168, 255, 261, 327, VI, 43, 89, 142, 148
Denison, Lady Charlotte, III, 292n, IV, *224*, 347, V, 11, 43, 256, 261, sends gift of fruit VI, 97; 106
LETTER TO: VI 97
Denman, George, TBM asked to contribute to his election expenses, VI, *29*; TBM on his committee 29n; will not give a farthing to 32
Denman, Margaret: *see* Mrs Henry Macaulay, *and* Mrs Edward Cropper
Denman, Richard, IV, *158*
Denman, Thomas Denman, 1st Baron, I, xxvi, *266*, 267, 323, TBM dines with II, 58; 90, 207, IV, 34n, 143, speaking well in Lords 201; to resign at last V, 85; his sad state 90; resigns 96; TBM calls on 99; his death 425; VI, 29n
Denmark, Court of, II, 182-3
Denon, Vivant, *Voyage dans la Basse et la Haute Égypte*, I, 26
Derby, Edward Smith Stanley, 13th Earl of, M.P. for Lancashire, I, 252n; III, 74, 85n, 158

Derby, Edward George Stanley, 14th Earl of, II, *52*, compliments TBM on speech 62; 89, recommends warm negus 90; nervous before speaking 90; 91, 94, 157, 173, moves government plan of abolition 239n; changes in bill 246; TBM dislikes bill 272; sketched by Haydon 272; careless legislation of 274; 276, between Abolitionists and West Indians 281; 290, 312, Colonial Secretary III, 66; 176n, IV, 101, 116, tour in U.S. 266; 270n, 364, V, 98, 162n, his advice to Lord St Leonard's 222; his administration 222; administration doomed 244; weakness of foreign policy 264; 266, 267, 269, 296n, defeat of his government 299n; TBM votes against in division 302; his administration 303; Chancellor of Oxford 350n; 435, 448, forms new ministry VI, 141n; his ministry's India Bill 146, 147; TBM's low opinion of government 211; has gained from elections 213; government defeated 220n

Derby, Edward Henry Stanley, 15th Earl of V, 334n, *448*, TBM's neighbour in the Albany 448n; offers Trevelyan Indian appointment VI, xi; 47n, 200n, 201, speech on Reform Bill a failure 202; 213, 222n

Derby, Countess of (Emma Caroline Wilbraham), II, *229*, V, 226

Derby family, III, 384

Derby (Epsom Downs), a bore II, 244; VI, 43

Derbyshire, III, 49

Dering, IV, 45

Derwentwater, IV, 372

Descartes, René, IV, 295

Devizes, II, 130

Devizes and Wiltshire Gazette, I, 276n, II, 8, 13n, 130n

Devonshire, I, 143, cloth manufacturers from II, 240; III, 53, 64, 81, IV, 43, 100, 104, 109, V, 69, French landing in 96; James Mills in 272; VI, 240, 247

Devonshire, William George Cavendish, 6th Duke of, II, *62*, 98, 288, III, 161n, IV, 149, at Rome 201

Devonshire, Georgiana, Duchess of, 'The Passage of the Saint Gothard,' II, 288n

Dharker, C. D., *Lord Macaulay's Legislative Minutes*, III, 124n, 165n, 176n, 210n, VI, 297

Diaz, Bernal, *Conquest of Mexico*, III, 24

Dibdin, Thomas Frognall, *Bibliographical Tour in the Northern Counties*, I, 216n, III, *13*

LETTER TO: III, 13

Dicey, Thomas Edward, I, *138*

Dick, Thomas, V, *446n*

Dickens, Charles, literary executor of Chauncey Hare Townshend, I, 116n; may have reported TBM's Reform Bill speeches II, 69n; first meeting with TBM IV, 48n; TBM wishes to see in *ER* 61; 63, denies he went to America over copyright 97n; letter to Napier 97n; 174n, acts in Bulwer's *Not So Bad as We Seem* V, 163n; and Guild of Literaure and Art 163n; TBM pleased by his acting 165; 166n, 230n, VI, 221n

Writings: American Notes, IV, 47, 59, 60, a failure 61*; declines to review 63; 'complete failure' 65; 68*, reviewed in *ER* 70; *Dombey and Son*, IV, 314*, *Great Expectations*, I, 116n, *Letters*, I, XV, II, 69n, IV, 48n, V, 415n, *Master Humphrey's Clock*, IV, 61, *Nicholas Nickleby*, I, 101n, III, 247*, 'A Parliamentary Sketch,' mentions TBM II, 69n, *Pickwick Papers*, I, 273n, IV, 25n, more valuable to a publisher than Newton's *Principia* V, 77; VI, 29n*

Dickson, George Claudius, IV, 379

Diderot, Denis, II, 288, *Les Bijoux Indiscrets*, V, 178n, 181

Dieppe, possible site for Preston's school I, 47; 284, TBM at 288; described 289; Charles Grant at II, 318; customs at IV, 137; Inn at 137; 155, Hotel Royal I, 288

Dighton, John, II, 216

Dijon, V, 352

Dillon, Countess, III, 318

Dillon, Major-General Henry, III, 318n

Dillon, Viscount, III, 318n

Dimond, Charles John, VI, *209*

LETTER TO: VI, 209

Dingle Bank, Liverpool (home of the Cropper family), I, 248n, 282, II, 133, Hannah at 234; 236, 237, 243, 255, 273, 288, 291, 293, 295, 302, 303, 304, 312, 315, 351, news from awaited 356; 360, 364, 368, 369, TBM visits III, 15, 17; 261, 313, IV, 399n, VI, 233

Dino, Dorothea, Duchess de, II, *98*

Diodorus, III, 177*, 180*, 200*, V, 318

Diogenes Laertius, *Lives of Eminent Philosophers*, III, 247*, VI, 100

Diomedes, IV, 207

Dionysius of Halicarnassus, III, 163, 211*, IV, 56, *Roman Antiquities*, 358*

Directory, French, III, 206

Disbrowe, Sir Edward Cromwell, IV, *354*, assists TBM's researches 354; V, 186n
LETTER TO: IV, 354

Disney, General F., III, 80n

Disraeli, Benjamin, at Campbell's funeral IV, 202; 364, V, 257, TBM hopes he is strong enough for passage of arms with 261; speech on Peel's government 261*; 299n, detected in plagiarisms 301; speech attacking coalition government 311; motion of censure 455n; resolutions on India VI, 146n; introduces Reform Bill 201n, describes Bulwer Lytton to Queen 203n; 213
Writings: Venetia, V, 301n, *Vivian Grey*, II, 37, Miss Berry in, 349*, *The Young Duke*, II, 29, TBM referred to in 37, 50*

Disraeli, Mrs, V, 222

Dissenters, Baines family, II, 103n; 176, TBM sympathetic to grievances 371; presents petition from 371; and education question III, 327; oppose Factories Education Bill IV, 122n, 334n; at Edinburgh 341; should not support religious equality movement in Ireland V, 290; 379

Dissenters, Calvinistic, V, 22

Dissenters, English, IV, 162

Dissenters, Scottish, III, 313n, 314, 344n, not aggrieved by veto 346; 348, TBM criticises 350-2, 355-8; their preachers excluded from prisons 356; IV, 7, Queen wrongly advised to hear service from 54; 215, oppose TBM 301; VI, 239

Dissenters' Chapels Bill, Whigs saved government on, IV, 200; *see also* TBM's Speeches

Dissenters' Marriages Bill, III, 75

District Visiting Society: *see* General Society for Promoting District Visiting

Dixon, Dr James, V, *76*
LETTER TO: V, 76

[Dixon, W. H.] ed., *Lady Morgan's Memoirs*, IV, 308

Dixon, William Hepworth, V, *158*, charges against TBM VI, 45n
Writings: William Penn, V, 91n; argues against TBM on Penn 158; TBM won't reply to arguments VI, 31

Dodd, Miss Harriett, I, 19

Doddridge, Philip, *Correspondence and Diary*, II, 37*

Dod's Parliamentary Pocket Companion, II, 31n

Dodwell and Miles, *Alphabetical List of Madras Civil Servants*, III, 47n

Dog, TBM must get one VI, 31; has one 74

Dogget, Thomas, II, *309*

Dohna, Christophe, Comte de, *Mémoires Originaux sur le Règne et la Cour de Frédéric I.*, V, 316n

Dolabella, I, 96, 97

Dom Miguel, II, 154n, 250

Dom Pedro, Emperor of Brazil, II, 154, 159, 250

Don Cossack, anecdote of, I, 30

Donaldson, John William, Cambridge private tutor, VI, *206*; *Varronianus*, VI, 206n

Donati's Comet, VI, 170

Doncaster, I, 208n, 230n, TBM at 232; 252n

Donkin, Anna Maria, Lady, II, *153*, 157n

Donkin, General Sir Rufane, II, *153*

Donne, William Bodham, VI, *35*

Dorchester, Lord, IV, 45

Dordrecht, IV, 217

Dorking, II, 59n

D'Orsay, Count, II, 156n

Dorset, 6th Earl of, and Nell Gwynn, IV, 388; V, 356

Dorsetshire, II, 194

Dort, Synod of, V, 8, 13

Dost Mahommed, IV, 232

Douglas, F. Brown, Black's opponent at Edinburgh, VI, 14n

Douglas, Sir George, and Sir George Ramsay, eds., *Panmure Papers*, VI, 104n

Douglas, General Sir Howard, IV, *336*

Douglas, Marjory, of Scotland, IV, 257

Douglas, Mrs Stair, *Life of Whewell*, V, 385n

Douglass, Frederick, V, *138*

Douro, Lord, V, 166n

Dove, Valley of, II, 240

Dover, TBM curious to see, III, 274; 299, IV, 8, 195n, 196, 201, 205, 206, Ellis considers standing for 335; V, 343, 347, 349n, 354, VI, 114

Dover, George Agar-Ellis, 1st Baron, II, 254n, ed., *Letters of Horace Walpole to Sir Horace Mann*, reviewed by TBM 308n

Dover, Georgiana Howard, Lady, II, *254*

Dowden, Edward, ed., *Correspondence of Henry Taylor*, IV, 39

Doyle, Andrew, letter to Longman, IV, 224n

Doyle, Sir Francis, *Reminiscences and Opinions*, V, 366n

Doyle, John (HB), TBM praises his caricatures II, *64*; 139n

Draco, I, 105

Drake, Sir Francis, TBM declines as subject for *ER*, IV, 158

Draper, Sir William, v, 215; his cenotaph *249*
Dreer, F. J., *Catalogue*, v, 91n
Dreyer, F. A., 'The Whigs and the Political Crisis of 1845,' IV, 290n
Drinkwater-Bethune, John, I, *286*, in suttee case II, 138; III, 64, 155, 160, 212, and Medical Bill IV, 242; on church-going 278
Driver, Cecil, *Tory Radical: The Life of Richard Oastler*, II, 369n
Drummond, Edward, IV, 119n
Drummond, Henry, I, *232*, death reported 232n; 252n, II, 31, 75, study of prophecy 75n; verses on 244; IV, 234, speech on Ecclesiastical Titles Bill v, 156; 168n, query about treatment of schoolboys VI, 215
  LETTERS TO: IV, 197, VI, 215
Drummond, Henry (brother of Thomas Drummond), III, *224*, 225
Drummond, Captain Thomas, III, *224*, 224n, 226
Drummond, Mrs Thomas (Maria Kinnaird), I, 279n, II, *19*, III, 224n, TBM dines with IV, 236; v, 321, 322, VI, 43n
  LETTERS TO: III, 224, IV, 125, 178, VI, 40
Dryden, John, I, 63, 140, subject of Latin declamation 147; contract for translation of *Aeneid* II, 82; not a creative mind 109; on Sir George Mackenzie 306; 353, III, 245, contrasted to Scott 246; Lord Holland's copy of 349; IV, 28, 42, TBM presents Scott's edition of to Edinburgh Philosophical Instiution v, 463; VI, 68, immoral as a poet 69; quoted by TBM and Mahon 158n
  Writings: Albion and Albanius, IV, 389, *Conquest of Granada*, IV, 389, 'Discourse of Satire,' II, 306n, *Fables*, 'Theodore and Honoria,' I, 65; 120-1, translation of Virgil, I, 5n, 35, *Georgics*, II, 62
Dublin, typhus epidemic in, II, 48; 52, TBM prefers Calcutta to III, 225; 226, proposal to hold parliaments in IV, 166; v, 64n, TBM at 65; described 65; TBM to make researches in 67; 69, Morrison's Hotel 66; St Patrick's Cathedral, Schomberg buried in VI, 6
Dublin Review, v, 53
Duchêsne, Père: *see* Jacques René Hébert
Dudhope, VI, 180
Dudley, Lord, on TBM and Sharp, *Letters to 'Ivy'*, I, 279n; anecdote of II, *43*; III, 110
Duff, Grant, *Notes from a Diary, 1873-1881*, I, 109n; *Notes from a Diary, 1851-1872*, VI, 88n
Dufferin, Price Blackwood, 4th Baron, VI, 52n
Dufferin, Lady (Helen Selina Sheridan), tells TBM about dogs at Oatlands, VI, *52*; 53
Duffy, Sir Charles Gavan, IV, *259*, TBM sends *Lays* and *Essays* to 260; ed., *The Spirit of the Nation*, sends copy to TBM 259-60*
  LETTER TO: IV, 259
Dugdale, Sir William, I, xxxiv, v, 56n
Dulwich College, Allen warden of II, 21
Dumont, Étienne, I, 73n, *Souvenirs sur Mirabeau*, TBM reviews II, 121
Dumont, Louis, I, *307*, TBM will see in Paris 274; high opinion of TBM 307n; v, 72, 76, 224, becoming a bore 323
Dunbar, Janet, *The Early Victorian Woman*, v, 56n
Duncan, Adam Duncan-Haldane, Lord, afterwards 2nd Earl of Camperdown, VI, *180*
Duncannon, Lord: *see* Lord Bessborough
Duncombe, Thomas, II, *73*, 'odious pert' 159; 181, presents Chartist petition IV, 291; quotes TBM's letter in speech 291n; and Frost, Williams, and Jones 293n; TBM moves into his former chambers in Albany 319n; v, 222, 235n
Dundas, Sir David, III, 322, in high esteem at Brooks's and Holland House 322; Solicitor-General IV, 304; gives legal dinner 331; v, ix, 58n, 110n, 113n, 148, 152n, 157n, 162n, 201, 219n, on Roebuck's drunken speech 222; 234n, 299n, 329n, 364n, 427n, VI, 40n, 72n, 78n, 90n, 97n, to write inscription for Scutari Monument 104n; 108, agrees with TBM about Scutari Monument 115; 139n, 152n, 158, TBM introduces to Everett 159; does not make American tour 159n; 181n, 191, 198n, 204, 207, 222n, 226n, 227
  LETTER TO: VI, 267
Dundee, John Graham, 1st Viscount, IV, 15, v, 117, TBM writing account of his campaign 123; Jacobite life of v, 126; his country seat VI, 180
Dunfermline, James Abercromby, 1st Baron, made Chief Baron of Exchequer, Scotland, I, 263n, elected at Edinburgh II, 200n; III, *85*, 265, retires from Edinburgh seat 276n; accepts peerage 288; his letter of farewell 288; IV, 227

Dungannon, Lord, IV, 188n, *Life and Times of William the Third*, V, 279

Dunkeld, II, 252

Dunlop, Alexander, III, *350*, his bill on reform schools in Scotland V, 411-12n

Dunlop, Mr, in India, VI, 280

Dunn, James, VI, 287

Dunn, Mr, I, 285 (*and see* Additions and Corrections)

Dunning, John, 1st Baron Ashburton, III, *220*

Dunstan, St, IV, 159

Durham, I, 208n, assizes 225; 227, II, 266, TBM at 305; IV, 188, detestable accommodation at V, 387; 390, TBM at 390n; 394n

Durham, Bishop of, V, 132n

Durham, John George Lambton, 1st Earl, II, *65*, 124n, 234, III, 208, attacked by Brougham 262

Durham, Louisa Elizabeth, Countess of, II, 65n

Dutch archives, TBM receives valuable extracts from, IV, 354

Duval, Lewis, TBM studies under I, *172n*

Dyce, Alexander, *Recollections of the Table-Talk of Samuel Rogers*, II, 82n

Dyer, Sir Edward, 'My Mind to Me a Kingdom Is,' I, 64*

East India Bill: *see* East India Company, Charter

East India College, Haileybury: *see* Haileybury College

East India Committee, TBM appointed to II, 136n, 146n

East India Company, I, xxv, xxvii, I, 62n, 63n, 64n, its sins catalogued 70-1; 76n, Zachary Macaulay's motion to 177; Albion Tavern dinners 294n; TBM opposes its monopoly II, 92; and Board of Control 122n; Gordon the Company's creature 140; its monopoly 162n; to lose China monopoly 233; 240, may resist TBM's appointment 302, 322, 323; opposed to Holt Mackenzie 324; revolution in administration 328; willing to cooperate 331; gives dinner to TBM 337; rule about English servants 339-40, 358; III, ix, 13, 18, 55, 60, 83, 92n, 98, 103n, 125n, despatch of 16 July 1834 145n; 165n, 184n, 301, measures regarding Ricketts 218; TBM can't ask favours 252; 347n, salary policy V, 97; TBM has no interest with 221; testimony against it 325n; going to pay off TBM 349, 358; TBM has little influence 413; appropriate age of its appointees 438; and Haileybury VI, 35; its power transferred to Crown 141n

Chairmen: favourable to TBM, II, 334; 337, 338

Charter Act, 1813: 'pious clauses' in I, 25n; 26n, III, 103n

Charter Act, 1833, II, 232-3: 233-4, 245, new rule on servants 340; III, 32n, 63n, 118, 164n, 229, 301, 307, its provisions for Haileybury V, 442-3

Charter Act, 1853: V, 389n, 442n, VI, 71

Charter Renewal: I, 23, 25n, II, 136, 146n, cabinet plan for 207; conference of Commons and Lords 259; V, 315n

Charter Renewal Bill, 1793: III, 361

Charter Renewal Bill, 1833: II, 254, Grant moves resolutions for 255; 258, 263, first reading 264; TBM prepares for debate 266-7; speaks on second reading 268; working on day and night 270; superintends in Committee 271; working on at Grant's 272; in committee till midnight 273; TBM takes pride in 272, 273-4; third reading 279; carried in Commons 279; no trouble expected in Lords 286; provisions for Supreme Council 299; III, 118, 357

Charter Renewal Bill, 1853: V, xi, 315n, TBM speaks on 336; *see also* Government of India Act

Court of Directors: 'foaming' over Grant's absence II, 318; 323, 328, 334, TBM dines with 338-9; 345, 349, approves TBM's appointment 350; 351, 353 formal offer to TBM 364; TBM pays formal calls to 367; III, 100, 145, 150, 210n, provides for priests in India 302n; 312, elections to IV, 54, 115, 127; and Outram case 307; V, 74, report on Indian Civil Service to be submitted to 431; opposed to Civil Service plan 439

East India House, I, 177, III, 11, 184, 204, 233n, 244, elections at IV, 54; 171, 311, V, 104

East India Question, II, 80

East India Register, III, 276n

East Indian Sugar, duties on, I, 177n

East Indies, II, 153, 178, 281
East Retford, III, 19
Eastern Question, III, 339, 349, 352, 353, 359, 360, near crisis V, 357
Eastlake, Sir Charles, V, *457*
LETTER TO: V, 457
Eastnor Castle, Ledbury, V, 193
Ebrington, Hugh Fortescue, Lord, afterwards 2nd Earl Fortescue, II, *79*, 89, resolution of support for ministers 100, 101n; his motion brought about by TBM 106; 139, III, 267, 387, IV, 319, endures his misfortunes cheerfully VI, 226
LETTERS TO: III, 360, 362
Ecbatana, Rawlinson's theories about VI, 25
Economist, V, 332n
Ecclesiastical Courts Bill, IV, 184, given up 200
Ecclesiastical Titles Bill, V, 152, Drummond's speech on 156; not supported by Peelites 156n; TBM's name invoked in debate 156n
Eddis, Eden Upton, V, *56n*, makes three portraits of TBM 55n; 57n, portrait of TBM 1849 59n; portrait of Charles Trevelyan 138
Eddystone lighthouse, VI, 107
Eden, Emily, IV, *202*, TBM meets but does not forgive her insolence to Hannah 202-3; V, 5
LETTER TO: IV, 401
Eden, Frances, V, 5
Eden, Sir Frederick Morton, *The State of the Poor*, III, 286n
Eden, George: *see* 1st Earl of Auckland
Eden, Bishop Robert John: *see* 3rd Baron Auckland
Edenbridge, V, 171
Edgar, King, VI, 237
Edgeworth, Maria, I, 140, second woman of her age II, 84; errors about legal procedure in her books VI, 192
Writings: The Absentee, V, 346*, 363*, *Early Lessons*, III, 89, *Ennui*, I, 50n, II, 194, *Frank*, II, 249*, III, 89, *Harrington*, I, 218, *Letters from England 1813-1844*, ed. Colvin, I, 264n, II, 363n, *Ormond*, V, 346*, *Patronage*, II, 30*
Edgworth, Richard Lovell, VI, 192
Edinburgh, I, viii, xx, dispute over Apocrypha in 225; TBM at 233; visits in 1817 233n; described 233-4; 235, 237, Ellis visits 283; 290, TBM's articles liked at II, 113; Charles Grant at 304; 305, TBM visits with Hannah 306; 308, sorry not to revisit 311; first reformed election at 200; TBM plans visit 252; 266, 'nothing in the East like the view from Castle Rock' III, 109; 257, TBM invited to stand for 287; 289, election of 1839 290-2; TBM strong there 299; 302, TBM vacates seat on accepting office 303; confident there 305; no contest 307, 309; re-election 314n, 315-17; 'most beautiful town in the Empire' 326; re-elected 376-80; opposition threatened 379; election day 380; 383, TBM refuses to subscribe to Race Cup 384; IV, 7, 9, libraries useful for TBM's *History* 15, 16; TBM may visit 45; Queen's visit a 'bad business' 54; won't visit while 'fanatical priests' are sitting 70; anti-corn law meeting at 85; 100, opposition to corn laws 108, 109; TBM wishes to visit privately 159; religious fanaticism in 161; reasons for not visiting 161, 163-5, 168; 'in a foam with all sorts of fanaticism' 164, 168; TBM quite easy about 172; 187, 188, 194, TBM must visit 200; wishes to avoid Sunday there 210; avoids republican ceremony 211; can't enjoy city 213; political visit to 213ff; and medical reform 214; beauty of city 220; 233, sends anti-Maynooth address to TBM 254; anti-Maynooth delegation from calls on TBM 254n; not expedient to visit 264; opposition unlikely 277; opposition at 301-2; anti-Maynooth feeling 302n; patronage at 315; TBM plans to visit 315, 318; speech at 320; free of political excitement 321; meeting at on Ten Hours Bill 325n; TBM visits for election 340; opposition in 341; city 'ashamed' at vote against TBM 348; TBM will never stand for again 349; James II at 374, 376; poor accounts of state of politics at 379; TBM re-elected V, ix; more progressive in century than Catholic countries in two 27; James II at 35-6; TBM at 41n; can't act in any scheme originating there 90-1; TBM at 111n; Privy Council records at 120; TBM wants no part of its public matters 211; movement to return TBM for 231n; can get no respectable candidates 233; plan to nominate TBM 234-5; strange reaction of feeling at 235; TBM explains his relation to 236-7; 238, how to treat electors a problem 240; election certain 241; 242, decides not to visit on election 243; elections 245; religious element in 245n; TBM re-elected for 246; a signal

act of repentance 248-9; elections 250; hopes to speak at soon 252, 254, 255, 256; TBM forbidden to make trip to 257, 258; meeting at postponed 258; plans for visit to 260-1; 279, 289, plans for visit to 290-1; TBM at 291-2; city on Sunday 291, 292; 295, plan for industrial exhibition at 331; Jeffrey's sphere 355; Association for Vindication of Scottish Rights meeting at 364; speech by Bulwer at public dinner 386n; TBM's visit in 1833 387n; reason for re-election of TBM at 400-1; another tie gone with Rutherfurd's death 434; TBM can no longer perform as its delegate 441; 442, 450, new writ to be moved for 483; VI, 6, address to electors on retirement 7; Black to succeed TBM for 7, 14; elections 85n; 118, 120, Campbell represented 135; Burns celebration at 191n; 230n, 232

Places: Assembly Rooms, III, 316, Calton Hill, monument to Muir, Skirving, Gerrald, Palmer, and Margarot, IV, 211; 331, Castle Street (Napier's residence), III, 298, 320, Charlotte Square, IV, 213, Corstorphine Hill, I, 233n, Cousland (Lord Stair's residence), IV, 160, Douglas's Hotel, TBM at, VI, 233, Gibb's Hotel, IV, 322, Heriot Street, I, 236, High Street, I, 241, V, 241, 242, 244, 247, Holyrood, V, 426, Mechanics' Library, III, 298n, Melville Monument, I, 241, Merchants' Hall, V, 247, Music Hall, TBM speaks at, IV, 269n, 320; 340n, V, 242, 252, 262, TBM speaks at, 292, Moray Place, Jeffrey's house, I, 240, Lord Nelson's Monument, Calton Hill, I, 234, Observatory, Calton Hill, I, 241, Oman's Hotel, TBM stays at, II, 305n, III, 290, 315, 378, 380, IV, 214, Prince's Street, V, 291, 292, Queen Street, II, 252, Register House, V, 36n, Royal Hotel, IV, 301, Royal Scottish Institution, I, 241, St George's, I, 225n, Scott Monument, III, 326, TBM subscribes to, 328; IV, 174, proposal for, VI, 282, Waterloo Rooms, III, 378n

Edinburgh, Electors of, TBM will write upon election V, 243; 246, TBM compliments VI, 9; send address on TBM's retirement 13

LETTERS TO: III, 291, 303, 376, 383, IV, 300, 304, 339, 345, V, 246, VI, 9

Edinburgh, Lord Provost: *see* Sir John Melville, Adam Black, Sir James Forrest, Duncan McLaren

Edinburgh, Non-Freeman's Association, IV, 267n

Edinburgh, University of, II, 334, III, 323n, petition from IV, 122; Professorship of Music 179; and medical reform 214; petition on Medical Bill 249; and medical standards 250; 254, TBM can't interfere with appointments 359; Professorship of Greek V, 221; and abolition of tests 341; Associated Societies addressed by Bulwer 386n; 462, TBM cannot accept Rectorship VI, 240

Edinburgh Academy, IV, 379n

Edinburgh and Leith Bank, IV, 399

Edinburgh Annuity Tax, IV, 215, TBM consults Aberdeen on plans about 310; plan for V, 320; 336, TBM explains tax VI, 239; abolished 239n; injustice of 239; opposition to 240

Annuity Tax Bill, V, 319-20, detains TBM in town 336; 337, TBM must support 342

Edinburgh Anti-Corn Law Association, IV, 103n, 104n; TBM attacked at meeting of 113n; TBM declines to attend meeting 170; censures TBM 185; 192, 214n, 215

Edinburgh Cabinet Library, I, 311n

Edinburgh Chamber of Commerce, petition from, IV, 6; letter from TBM 6n; TBM presents petition from 208, 241, 248; wants Heritable Securities Bill 402n; protests on British Courts V, 392n

Edinburgh City Customs Bill, III, 327

Edinburgh College of Physicians, sends delegate to Palmerston V, 397

Edinburgh Evening Post, and TBM's letter about Grey, IV, 283n; 284, 286, 289

Edinburgh Philosophical Institution, TBM speaks at opening IV, 316, 320; 326, TBM elected President V, 399; hopes to speak at 450; unable to speak 451; makes gift of books to 463, 464; library of 463n, 464; its 'Report' 463n, 464; ought not to ask Guizot to lecture VI, 32; TBM wishes to resign 44; 240

Edinburgh Post Office Directory, III, 318n, IV, 308n

Edinburgh Review, I, viii, xi, TBM's connection with xiii, xvi, xvii, xix, xxiii, xxix, xli, 58n, on slave trade 169; TBM's first article for 203n; TBM's early articles

Edinburgh Review—cont.
in 221n; Napier succeeds Jeffrey 253n; delays in publication 254n, 255; TBM offered editorship by Jeffrey 254n; delays in publication 257-8; TBM suggests summary notices 258; possible unidentified articles by TBM 261n; 262, delays in publication 263; 'miserably off' for writers 271; inadequate notice of Niebuhr 280; must avoid puffing and flattering 281; TBM resents Brougham's domination of 298-300; TBM reconciled to 309-10; property of Longmans 320n; TBM does not want his name mentioned in it II, 7; to be published in anticipation of Reform Bill 15; 48, 55, should act during prorogation 107; 134, 144, 148, 158, some gossip about 246, 248; Empson's v. TBM's articles 249; TBM too busy to write for 264; cannot live by writing for and remain public man 299; 311, 320, 322, TBM knows his importance to 351; connection important to TBM while in India 352; bound volumes for India III, 163; 199, 243, 246, prospects good 250; its relation to Brougham 250-1; 252, Brougham threatens to ruin 257; 259, 282, 293, Buller wishes to write for 294; friendly to Melbourne ministry 297; 309, 324, Panizzi annoyed by 329; 354, 372, 385, IV, viii, ix, 7, 10, 13, TBM must choose subjects with reference to *History* 17; TBM hopes Palmerston will write for 51; 53, TBM's name and writings not to be mentioned in 58; 70, and copyright of TBM's articles 71; *Essays* reprinted from 82; and J. W. Croker 90; TBM doubts that he should continue writing for 96; note on Dickens's *American Notes* 97n; extra number 107; 120, 129, too busy with *History* to write for 158; and question of Catholic clergy 163; and Irish question 166; TBM advises against extra number 173, 174-5; 207, almost determined to cease writing for 222; and Irish state trials 224; TBM asks to be excused for several numbers 226; determines not to write for until first part of *History* published 242-3; must go on without TBM 264; and American question 264-5; 283, 285, *History* only reason TBM has ceased to write for 309; 322, Bulwer's article not ready for 324; question of editorship 329-30; no Irish article planned 332; 368, v, xi, TBM supplies notes for reply to Croker 46; 47, TBM edits reply to Croker 62; Empson unfit to edit 74; and marriage question 80; early days of *Review* 93; TBM urges Empson to give up editorship 127; 129, TBM sounds Shaw Lefevre as editor 129n; TBM regrets acrimonious style of his writing in 169; recommends Lewis for editor 300; editorship not settled 303; Lewis accepts 304; 309, 315, does not review Cockburn's *Life of Jeffrey* 354n; TBM cannot ask favours of 388; article on newspaper tax 430; Reeve wishes TBM to write for VI, 225; TBM sends note for 252

Particular Numbers: October 1829, I, 257*, January 1830, I, 269*, 271*, July 1830, I, 280*, June 1831, II, 50*, December 1831, II, 113*, July 1833, II, 277*, October 1833, II, 335*, October 1839, III, 306*, January 1842, not quite satisfied with, IV, 20*, October 1842, IV, 62*, July 1843, IV, 133*, October 1843, IV, 159*, July 1844, IV, 200*, October 1844, IV, 227*, January 1846, 'deficient in entertainment,' IV, 287*, October 1849, V, 79*, July 1856, VI, 48*

Payments: I, 256, 269, 270, 283, II, 108, in arrears 153; 190, 261, summarised 300n; 335, to be in books while TBM in India 352; unsatisfactory payments from III, 281; IV, 30, 31, 32, 227

Edinburgh Select Subscription Library, TBM sends *Essays* to IV, 115

Edinburgh Town Council, IV, 54, petitions against Maynooth and Medical Bill 250; petition in favour of Universities Bill 261; V, 320, against Universities Bill 325; petition on budget 329; plan for industrial exhibition 331n

Edinburgh Water Bill, IV, 120n, 125, 135, committee on 299

Edinburgh Water Company, disputes with city settled IV, 127

Edinburgh Witness, III, 379n

Edinburgh Young Men's Association, V, 335n

Edinburgh Young Men's Protestant Society, protests TBM's failure to oppose Catholic measure V, 408

Edleston, Joseph, V, 24, ed., *Correspondence of Sir Isaac Newton and Professor Cotes*, 25n

LETTER TO: V, 24

Edmonds, Cyrus R., disagreeable corres-

pondence with TBM, v, 447; *Milton*, 447n
LETTER TO: v, 447
Edmonstone, Neil Benjamin, III, *94*
Edmund, King, VI, 237
Edmund Crouchback, IV, 384
Edred, King, VI, 237
Education, TBM's opinion in favour of secular teaching v, 379; Committee on National, in Scotland, v, 90n; debate on, IV, 334, 335
Education Question, debate on, III, 293, IV, 162
Edward I, King, II, 97, IV, 256, VI, 58
Edward II, King, IV, 256
Edward III, King, IV, 256, 284, V, 330
Edward IV, King, IV, 256
Edward V, King, IV, 256
Edward VI, King, IV, 257, insurrection against v, 88
Edward, Prince of Wales (afterwards Edward VII), birth of, IV, 17n; 256, TBM meets at Windsor VI, 10n
Edward the Black Prince, IV, 246, 256
Edwards, Edward, I, *39*
Edwards, Edward, the younger, at Preston's school, I, *39*
Edwy, King, VI, 237
Egenus, advertisement of, IV, 318
Eglinton, Lord, his tournament, V, 364; and Scottish rights movement 364
Eglinton Castle, V, 364n
Eglinton Tournament, V, 201n
Egmont, Lord, 'Faction Detected,' IV, 197
Egypt, III, 140, 339n, 360, victory in 360n, 362; Napoleon in VI, 253
Egypt, Pacha of: *see* Mehemet Ali
Ehrsam, T. G., *Major Byron*, V, 222n
Einhorn, Mr, not specially authorised to translate TBM, VI, 35, 36n
Eldon, Lord, I, 149, rules against Zachary Macaulay 198n; reaffirms decision 220; 221, the butt of TBM's 'Political Georgics' II, 62; 289, defense of Lord Thurlow IV, 206
Eleanor of Aquitaine, Queen, IV, 256
Eleanor of Provence, Queen, IV, 256
Eleatics, VI, 83, 85
Elements of Morality: see C. G. Salzmann
Elgin, Earl of, V, 245n
Eliot, George, IV, 240n; *Scenes of Clerical Life*, I, 15n
Elizabeth, Queen, I, 180, 322, II, 16, 111, 118, III, 207, IV, 71, 257, 386, V, 21, rising of northern earls against 88; VI, 61
Elizabeth, Queen (of Henry IV), IV, 256
Elizabeth, Queen (of Henry VII), IV, 256
Elizabeth, Queen of Bohemia, IV, 255, 257, 258n
Elizabeth of Russia, I, 81
Elizabeth of Scotland, IV, 257
Ellegård, Alvar, *Who Was Junius?*, II, 216n
Ellenborough, Lady, V, 285
Ellenborough, Edward Law, 1st Earl of, II, 61, III, 164n, 165n, *176*, TBM disgusted by vote of thanks to IV, 99; Governor-General of India 99n; debate on in Commons 107n; 'vain, self-willed and insolent' 124; saved by Duke of Wellington 133; TBM intends to move for his recall 180; recall of 180n; TBM's notice for recall 183; 243n, nothing more to be done about 247; 252, his divorce action V, 285n; 435, TBM agrees with his speech VI, 221; *Diary* II, 70n
Ellesmere, Lord, III, 49n
Ellice, Edward, II, *79*, 86, 254, 260, TBM dines with 262; 371, and Palmerston IV, 232n; 274, V, 234n, VI, 97n, 146n
Elliot, Alistair, I, xxxiv
Elliot, Sir Charles, III, *318*
Elliot, Miss, at Clapham, V, 265
Elliott, Charlotte, I, 176n
Elliott, Edward Bishop, I, *176*, and biblical prophecies VI, 253; 254, *Horae Apocalypticae*, I, 176n
Elliott, Henry, I, 176n, 219
Elliott, Mary Sophia, II, *24*, 30
Elliott, Miss, II, 41
Elliott, Mrs and Miss, at Clifton in 1811 V, 250
Elliott family, of Clapham, I, 176n; 'perjured' II, 41; TBM detests IV, 317
Ellis, Arthur Danvers, career in Australia, V, *80*; bad news about 121; TBM pays his bills 182; bill from 240; his head turned by the diggings 320-1
Ellis, Francis (Frank), Ellis's 2nd son, II, *11*; TBM hopes to see him in Trinity College 347; III, 113, 133, 144, 146, 154, 160, 179, 183, 202, 212, bad account of studies 238; enters Cambridge IV, 59; not doing well at Trinity 125; doing better 169; TBM sees at Cambridge 180-1; 191, V, 46, 99, 195, 207, 276, should pursue Miss Harford 285; 292, 394n, VI, 29n
Ellis, Sir Henry (1777-1855), II, *339*, 341
Ellis, Sir Henry (1777-1869), TBM recommends James Stephen to V, *64*; 299, should retire 477; resigns 477n; VI, 19n
LETTERS TO: V, 64, 296

Ellis, Henry (son of T. F. Ellis), IV, 245n, death of *259*

Ellis, Louisa or Louise (daughter of T. F. Ellis), letter to Lady Knutsford III, 322n; V, 80n, 244, 268, Hannah and Margaret praise her acting 307; V, 455, deciphers German for TBM VI, 186, 191, 244

LETTER TO: V, 466

Ellis, Louisa or Marian, Memoir of T. F. Ellis, I, xxii-xxiii, 122n, 218n, III, 63n

Ellis, Margaret (infant daughter of T. F. Ellis), death of, III, 278n

Ellis, Marian (elder daughter of T. F. Ellis), IV, *259*, praised by Hannah 331; finds TBM's *History* entertaining 377; her letter to TBM 'safe in the breast of a man of honor' V, 70; 80n, 100, 111n, asks Hannah to chaperone her at Great Exhibition 159n, 160; 175, 191, 244, skill at trap ball 268; 276, 395, visits Ireland 417; 455, VI, 28, on Margaret's engagement 165; calls on TBM in Edinburgh 233; 244

Ellis, S. M., *Unpublished Letters of Lady Bulwer Lytton*, VI, 19

Ellis, Thomas Flower, the elder (father of T. F. Ellis), death, IV, 179

Ellis, Thomas Flower (1796-1861), TBM's friend, I, xiv, xx, *xxii-xxiii*, on his friendship with TBM xxiii; edits TBM's *Miscellaneous Writings* 50n; friend of Malkin 122n; first meeting with TBM 218n; describes TBM 218n; 242n, and Brougham's *Hydrostatics* 247n; TBM reads article by 249; declines to review Niebuhr 256; proposes to review Mitford 256; residence, 15 Bedford Place 263n; 'Niebuhr-mad' 280; 282, visits Edinburgh 282, 283; collaborates with Adolphus on *Reports* 285n; birth of sixth child 287; letter to Napier 294n; on TBM's History of the Stuarts 322; his work for SDUK 323; II, 23, TBM reads Mrs Thrale with Ellis and wife 34; 46, TBM dines with *en famille* 50; commissioner on boundaries 105; reviews Arnold's Thucydides 105n; parodies TBM 148, 150; 155, at Calais 158; 167, recovering from small-pox 215; Christmas with his family 217; TBM dines with 248; approves Haydon's portrait 280; commissioner on Municipal Corporations 339; TBM tells him of decision to go to India 345-6; 347, letter to TBM 347; 348, 369, III, viii, 9, 'very few . . . so dear to me as you' 110; 154, answers Palgrave 157; professional success 160, 202; 230, death of daughter 278; death of wife 279-80; 281, sends ballads to TBM 383; IV, 37, at Cambridge with TBM 59; and *Lays* 68; 236, illness in family 245; 269, 280, TBM proposes pastoral subject to 331; contributes to Highland relief 332; thinks of standing for Kendal 333-4; for Dover or Oxford 335-6; Liverpool a possibility 336; Clitheroe 336; commissioner on law in Channel Islands 339; Dutch tour with TBM 349n; 355, Recorder of Leeds 370n; French tour with TBM 372n; 377, 381n, 382, V, x, 23n, and Downing Professorship of Law 46; and University counselship, Cambridge 48; 58n, seeks place at Admiralty 64; in Paris with TBM 67; Attorney General, Duchy of Lancaster 68; TBM insists on paying travel expenses of 70; and his son Arthur 80; approves *History*, vol. 3, 83; persuades TBM not to send letter to Brougham 95n; judgeship of Common Pleas his *summum bonum* 99; to work with Lord Carlisle 100; 103, TBM asks him to call in sickroom 105, 106; 110n, 111n, his house at Bromley 121n; 122, reads Greek and Spanish with TBM 125; visits TBM on Isle of Wight 125; 148n, 150n, writing a romance 177; 182, at Worcester Musical Festival with TBM 184; at Chepstow with TBM 187; afflicted by bad Sherry 188; troubles over travel routines 189-90; in Achilli v. Newman 195n, 206; TBM asks solicitorship of the Treasury for 206; 208, 266, 267, visits TBM at Clifton 276n; 277, 280, at Clifton 281n; visits TBM at Brighton 285n; TBM approves his speech 310; 312, supports Alford 317; in low spirits 321; writing a *Troades* 340; visits TBM at Tunbridge Wells 342n; discusses Indian law reform with Wood 366; rheumatism 381; TBM sends Indian Civil Service Report to 411; visits TBM at Thames Ditton 412; 416n, 420n; visits Oxford with TBM 421n; on Commission on Laws of India 424n; 427n, 432, inscription by 452-3; attorney for Royal Mint 460; ill 461; TBM asks to read *History* in proof 463, 465; TBM stays with at Bromley 467; reads proofs of *History* 469; India Law Commission may produce something for VI, 16; commissions Claudet photograph of TBM 16n; in financial difficulties 25n,

27-8; TBM lends money to 28n; 29n, has not had justice but has £2,000 a year 31; repays TBM 49; TBM calls on Lord Chancellor about 51; 52, makes Italian tour with TBM 57ff; TBM wants his opinion on Penn 64; 72n, offers his papers on Greek philosophers for George's use 100; in Shrewsbury case 102n; continental tour with TBM 106, 115; his remark on John Macaulay 119; traditional dinner with TBM on Michaelmas day 120; 141, praised by Crompton 142; Shrewsbury case 149; TBM sends Latin invitation to 150; speech in Shrewsbury case 151; French tour with TBM 167; prepares address to Victoria and Albert 167n; 176n, complimented on his humour 186; TBM suggests he write an elegy 202; Shrewsbury case 216, 219; 222n, TBM hopes to get something for from Lord Campbell 228; counsel for Lord Chelmsford 228n; tours west of England with TBM 231, 240n; offered county court judgeship 249; 250n, on authenticity of Platonic dialogues 255-6

Writings: 'Muller's *History of the Dorians*,' I, 267n; not ready on time 268, 269, *Outline of General History*, I, 249n, 280n, TBM promises to read 284, 323

LETTERS TO: I, 249, 249, 263, 284, II, 5, 9, 12, 104, 345, 346, 369, 377, III, 59, 110, 129, 140, 146, 152, 155, 157, 174, 180, 199, 209, 226, 235, 256, 275, 278, 321, 347, 347, 381, IV, 48, 52, 52, 55, 57, 74, 78, 99, 100, 125, 169, 179, 180, 191, 245, 247, 259, 260, 280, 296, 304, 330, 332, 333, 334, 335, 336, 336, 339, 342, 349, 352, 355, 370, 371, 372, V, 15, 16, 31, 32, 46, 49, 54, 62, 64, 65, 68, 69, 89, 90, 92, 94, 98, 105, 105, 121, 122, 123, 135, 148, 160, 160, 174, 176, 179, 181, 189, 193, 195, 205, 207, 208, 221, 226, 228, 240, 241, 244, 250, 255, 258, 262, 267, 276, 276, 280, 281, 283, 284, 285, 286, 292, 300, 301, 304, 305, 306, 309, 310, 311, 313, 314, 317, 320, 328, 337, 338, 341, 342, 342, 343, 347, 349, 361, 366, 367, 367, 371, 378, 381, 382, 385, 386, 389, 391, 394, 394, 395, 396, 401, 403, 404, 406, 409, 411, 412, 415, 416, 417, 419, 420, 420, 421, 422, 432, 436, 437, 440, 440, 442, 443, 448, 452, 455, 459, 460, 460, 461, 463, 465, 469, 470, VI, 12, 16, 16, 25, 27, 29, 31, 49, 51, 64, 67, 75, 77, 79, 80, 81, 86, 87, 96, 99, 101, 104, 106, 120, 122, 123, 124, 125, 128, 141, 149, 149, 151, 154, 156, 158, 161, 162, 166, 167, 176, 181, 185, 191, 191, 200, 201, 205, 207, 216, 217, 219, 219, 226, 227, 230, 232, 233, 237, 244, 249, 260, 261, 265, 268, 269

Ellis, Thomas Flower, Jr, III, 112n, 179, V, 267, 268

Ellis, Mrs Thomas Flower (Susan McTaggart), I, xxiii, *264*, sends her letters through TBM's frank 267; II, 34, 217, 345, 346, III, 64, 113, 132, 144, 154, 160, 179, 183, 202, 212, 229, 238, 258, 278, death of 279-80

Ellis, Walter, youngest son of T. F. Ellis, V, *190*, at Harrow 190; 207, good accounts of 244, 251; 267, 300, Latin lines by 385; TBM wishes to talk to 415; invited to visit George Trevelyan 415, 419-20; reading Homer 421; TBM talks to 438; verses by 460; TBM sends *History* to 479; enters Trinity College 479n; needs tuition VI, 27; 28n, TBM anxious about 31; his failure and death 31-2n; his verses 67

Elmes, James, *Topographical Dictionary of London*, I, 249n, II, 168

Elphinstone, Lord, V, 212n

Elphinstone, Mountstuart, II, *317*, III, 312, IV, 107, TBM will ask for his influence for Maclagan 171; TBM calls on VI, 46n

Elton, Sir Arthur Hallam, *Below the Surface*, VI, 103*

Elwell, Richard, schoolmaster at Hammersmith, I, *159*, opens pupils' mail 165

Ely, IV, 59, 60, TBM dines there with Peacock 60n, 62; V, 188, VI, 198

Emerson, Ralph Waldo, on TBM V, ix; 182n

Emiliani-Giudici, Paolo, translates TBM's *History* V, *404*; *Storia della Letteratura Italiana*, dedicated to TBM 404n

LETTER TO: V, 404

Empson, William, I, xvi, xix, *246*, correspondence with TBM destroyed 246n; hesitates about *ER* under Napier 253; his relation to Brougham 253n; letter to Napier 254n, 256n; on handling TBM 261n; letter to Napier 270n; TBM tired of defending his writing 271; proposes TBM for Athenaeum 295n; mediates between

Empson, William—*cont.*
TBM and Napier 309; letter to Napier 309n; 318, 324, his fifty loves II, 18; 44, 45, flirting 46; flirts with Charlotte Jeffrey 56; story about Lady Holland 77; party on roof of his chambers 82; flirts with Margaret Macaulay 82; reports TBM vexed by ministers 89n; on TBM's speech 105n; 113, on TBM's plan to review Carlyle 113n; 158, 190, his articles the ruin of the *ER* 249; distressed by TBM's going to India 344; III, 21, 108, letter to Jeffrey 108n; letter to Napier 125n; 126, 154, letter to Napier 163n; TBM's 'best correspondent' 171; 195, letters to Napier 216n; 244, letters to Napier 244n, 245n; marriage to Charlotte Jeffrey 247; lectures on Indian Penal Code 251n; letter to Napier 251n; advises TBM to call police against Wallace 254; 255, TBM discusses Brougham with 255n; letter to Napier 255n; TBM sees in London 256; 257, 259, letter to Napier 275; 280, letters to Napier 300n, 306n, 319n; 337, IV, 7, 15, 18, 37, letters to Napier 37n, 216n, 226n, 247n, 264n; 265, letters to Napier 318n, 319n; on TBM at Trinity Tercentenary 323n; letter to Napier 323n; succeeds Napier as editor of *ER* 329n; letter to Napier V, 32n; TBM sends notes to for reply to Croker 46; 47, 62, very ill 73; congestion on the brain 74; TBM sees in London 108; has had paralytic seizure 127; to consult Bright 129; retains editorship 129n; TBM jokes about 251; 259, hopelessly ill 300; his death 301; TBM a sincere mourner for 302; 303
Writings: 'The Americans and Their Detractors,' II, 172*, 'Character of the Austrian Government,' II, 344, 'Life, Writings, and Character of Mr Malthus,' III, 221*, 'Jefferson's *Memoirs and Correspondence*,' I, 284*, 'Jeremy Bentham,' IV, 159, 'The New Game Laws,' II, 113*, 'Open Questions,' III, 330, 'The Ottoman Empire,' I, 254, 255, 'Political and Vested Rights,' II, 15n, 'Pretended Miracles – Irving, Scott and Erskine,' II, 50*, 'Prior's *Life of Goldsmith*,' IV, 98n, 'Providential and Prophetical Histories,' approved by Zachary Macaulay, I, 270, 'Sewell's *Christian Morals*,' IV, 47n, 'Tour in England, Ireland, and France, by a German Prince,' II, 109, review of Wright's translation of Dante, II, 277
LETTERS TO: II, 375, III, 217, V, 79, 92
Empson, Mrs William (Charlotte Jeffrey), I, 238, 246n, Empson flirts with at Rolfe's II, 56; III, 247, 256, V, 73, 74, 79, 300, child born to recently 301; 302
Encyclopaedia (French), IV, 76
Encyclopaedia Britannica, IV, 10, 47, TBM's biographies for V, XI, 317n; 323, 'Bunyan' 367n, 373n; will pay arrears when *History* finished 446; 'Goldsmith' 459; 466, 'Johnson' VI, X, 29; TBM's biographies in reprinted 100n; absurd article on metaphysics 162; Life of Pitt published in 167n; TBM reserves right of reprinting his articles 168; Life of Pitt 177n, 230; TBM can do little for 240
Encyclopaedia Britannica, TBM's contributions to: *see under* TBM's Writings 'John Bunyan,' 'Frances Atterbury,' 'Oliver Goldsmith,' 'Samuel Johnson,' and 'William Pitt'
Enfield, murder at, II, 217
England, policy towards Greece I, 163; its curse the social ambition of middle class II, 319; quiet in 1848 IV, 383; progress since Reformation V, 26; education obstructed by old Puritan body 54; nobody will be in hurry to invade 429; 'profoundly quiet' VI, 59; state of its colonies 172
English ambassador, at Danish court, II, 183
English language, its literature equal to that of Greek and Latin I, 83, 90; TBM discusses with Lady Holland II, 22; medium of education in India III, 102, 122-3, 138-9, 149, 150, 169
English Reformation, inseparable from continental Reformations V, 88
English slave trade, act abolishing, I, 5
English Catalogue of Books, I, 324
Englishmen, character of, I, 85
Enkvist, Nils Erik, *British and American Literary Letters in Scandinavian Public Collections*, III, 347
Enlistment of Foreigners Bill, V, 433n, 434n, terms of 435
Enmore, Somerset (Mrs Trevelyan's home), III, 96, IV, 313, 373, V, 67, Margaret Trevelyan at V, 125n, 177; 187n, Hannah at 263, 265; Trevelyan family at 358; 381, 390, 391
Epicureanism, II, 275
Epicureans, VI, 100
Epicurus, I, 146

Epimenides, VI, *100*
Epiphany, Feast of, VI, 181, 182
Erasmus, I, 141n, at Queens' College IV, 77
Erastianism, IV, 393
Errington, Mrs Lancelot, I, xv, xxxiv, 244n, II, 223n, V, 85n
Errol, Earl of, IV, 129n
Erskine, Henry, V, *93*
Erskine, Henry David, I, *277*, his boring sermons 278
Erskine, Thomas, Lord, I, *318*
Erskine, Thomas, III, *285*, VI, 192
LETTER TO: III, 285
Erskine, Mrs Thomas, III, 285
Escott, Bickham, V, *233*
Escurial, II, 21
Esher, Sandown Lodge, Trevelyans at, V, 403n, 415, 420
Essex, IV, 100, 148
Essex, 1st Baron, V, 101n
Essex, 1st Earl of, V, 94
Essex, George Capel-Coningsby, 5th Earl of, TBM dines with II, *214*; dinner described 215-16; 217, 282, 'whipping up for a dinner party' 326; 328, 336, 348
Essex, Arthur Capel, 6th Earl of, V, 62n, *63*
Estcourt, Richard, II, *309*
Eton, TBM visits Praed at I, 233n; article on reform of II, 334, 335; V, 136, VI, 215, 245
Eton Latin Grammar, I, 5
Etonian, I, 188n, 190n, Praed's contributions to his best work V, 81
Eu, Chateau d', Victoria visits IV, 151n; 154
Euclid, I, 16, 17, 19, 25, 31, 32, IV, 39
Eugénie, Empress, V, 322
Euripides, I, 61*, 'vilest poet that ever put pen to paper' 77-8; 83, 87, 88, the 'bray' of his ideas 89; II, 111, TBM changes his opinion III, 130*; 137, 153, 159*, 180*, not so philosophical as Aeschylus V, 345
Writings: Alcestis, I, 77n, III, 30, 178, *Bacchae*, III, 30, 178, *Cyclops*, III, 177*, *Hercules Furens*, II, 112n, *Hippolytus*, I, 77n, III, 132-3*, 178, *Iphigenia in Aulis*, III, 178, *Medea*, I, 77-8*, III, 130, 178, *Orestes*, I, 78*, 90*, III, 178, *Phoenissae*, I, 78*, III, 178
Eusden, Laurence, V, 131
Euxine, V, 476
Evangelical Protestant Alliance, V, 195n
Evangelicals, I, viii, at Clapham xvii-xviii; and education in India 26n; disliked at Cambridge 103; taste in poetry 268n; painted by Richmond V, 56n
Evans, William, TBM visits I, 197; *198*, TBM assists in Leicester election 211; spends £22,000 on election 211n; 212, 214, 223, TBM visits 225, 228; returned for Leicester 278, II, 56
Evans, Mrs William (née Gisborne), her freezing manner, I, *198*; wants a place for John Gisborne V, 357; 359
Evelyn, John, IV, 118
Everett, Edward, 'the best article that I have seen from Massachusetts' IV, 74; 204, 213, will be recalled 224; farewells to 263; TBM urges him to write history of U.S. 267; TBM sure he will be president of Harvard 268, 268n; introduces George Hillard 365-6; resigns Harvard presidency V, 33; on sales of *History* in U.S. 49; in bad health 53; TBM introduces Henry Babington to 80; TBM urges him to visit Great Exhibition 141; melancholy letter from 400; failure of his public career 400n; 474n, living in retirement 475; sends American editions of *History* VI, 18; TBM introduces Dundas to 159; his son at Cambridge 244n; 246
Writings: Orations and Speeches on Various Occasions, V, 53n, presented to TBM 141*
LETTERS TO: IV, 74, 80, 127, 135, 194, 195, 209, 227, 227, 249, 251, 266, 403, V, 33, 52, 141, 400, 475, VI, 18, 128, 159, 260
Everett, Miss, IV, 263, 267, V, 34
Everett, Mrs Edward, IV, 263, 267, V, 34
Everett, William, at Cambridge, VI, *244*; his scholarship compared to English standard 244-5; TBM asks to meet him 246; calls on TBM 260-1
Eversley, Charles Shaw-Lefevre, 1st Viscount, III, 381, Trustee of British Museum V, 149; 156, 319, asks TBM to oppose Lord Hotham's bill 328; 386, succeeded by John Evelyn Denison VI, 89n; title conferred 93n; TBM proposes for committee to revise Cambridge statutes 93
Every, Sir Henry Flower, V, 319n
Ewart, J. C., V, 238n
Ewart, William, II, *230*, IV, 114, public libraries and museums act V, 335n
Examiner, I, 258n, 354n, IV, 17, 17n, essays by Fonblanque 41; 330n, 337n, on conflict between MacFarlane and Gladstone V, 181*

Exchequer, Court of, v, 96n
Exclusion Bill, v, 6
Exclusionists, v, 6, 7n
Excubitor, on novel reading I, 120-1
Exeter, III, 243n, IV, 188, 'surplice riots' in 239n; 371, TBM at VI, 240n
Exeter, Bishop of: *see* Henry Phillpotts
Exeter, Brownlow Cecil, 3rd Marquess of, intolerant Tory, VI, *277*
Exeter, Diocese of, v, 16
Exmouth, Lord, at Algiers, I, 83

Faber, F., Paris merchant, I, 192
Fabius, anecdote of, I, 102
Factories Education Bill, IV, 122
Factory Bill: *see* Ten Hours Bill
Factory Commission, II, 312
Faed, James, engraves Watson-Gordon's portrait of TBM, v, 110n
Fagan, Louis, *Life of Panizzi*, I, 229, 230n, VI, 42n; *The Reform Club*, III, 368n
Fagan, Robert, portrait of Lady Holland, II, 25n
Fairfax, Thomas, 3rd Baron, v, 62, 63
Faithfull, George, II, *218*
Falck, Anton Reinhard, Dutch Ambassador, II, 76n
Falmouth, Royal Hotel, III, 29; mayor leads deputation to call on TBM 30
Famianus Strado, *De Bello Belgico*, v, 162*
Famous History of the Lancashire Witches, I, 220n
Fane, General Sir Henry, II, 61, III, *155*, 166, 175, 185, 'dangerously ill' 197
Faraday, Michael, as candidate for British Museum trusteeship v, *150*
Farish, John, I, 104
Farish, William, I, xviii, 104n, 179n
Farneworth, Ellis, translation of Machiavelli, IV, 131
Farnham, 5th Baron, I, 219
Farquhar, George, III, 340, 358, IV, 16, *A Trip to the Jubilee* 132
Farquhar, Sir Robert, III, *45*
Farquharson, Captain, III, 229n, strange life of an East Indiaman captain 230
Faulkner, Thomas, *History and Antiquities of Kensington*, II, 25n, 27n
Fazakerley, John Nicholas, II, *357*
Fearon, Henry Bradshaw, *Sketches of America*, IV, 47
Feilding, Lord, IV, 346n
Fell, Rev. William Henry, v, *426*
Fellows, Sir Charles, VI, 48n
Fénelon, François, *Dialogues des Morts*, I, 28*; *Telemachus*, IV, 134*
Fenestella, IV, 55
Fenwick, Sir John, v, 279n
Ferdinand VII, of Spain, false report of death II, 196
Ferguson, Robert, v, *139*, 302
Ferguson, General Sir Ronald, II, *143*
Ferguson, William, *Scotland: 1689 to the Present*, v, 364n
Fergusson, Robert Cutlar, II, *74*, 371, death of III, 264; 265n
Ferrand, W. B., IV, 325n
Ferrier, Susan, *Destiny*, II, 29, *The Inheritance*, II, 195, *Marriage*, v, 191*
Ferrybridge, IV, 165
Féval, Paul, *Les Bandits de Londres*, VI, 31*
Fichte, Johann Gottlieb, VI, 162n
Ficino, Marsilius, ed., Plato, *Opera Omnia*, III, 142
Fielden, John, IV, *325*, in charge of Ten Hours Bill 325n
Fielding, Henry, III, 142, accuracy of legal points in his books VI, 192
Writings: Joseph Andrews, v, 268*, *Tom Jones*, v, 180*
Fields, James T., v, *39n*
Filmer, Sir Thomas, IV, *47*, v, 34, 332n
Finch, John, *The Millennium*, III, 297n
Findlay, Lt. Col. Alexander, II, *264*, 265
Findlay, James, III, 318
Fine Arts Commission, TBM appointed to IV, 191; Eastlake secretary to v, 457n
Fine Arts Commissioners, IV, 198, TBM submits list of subjects for sculpture to 246-7; plans for decoration of House of Lords 247-8; meet at Gwydir House 255; TBM submits list of subjects for stained glass 255-7; 258, v, 470
Fingall MS, VI, 223, TBM describes in part 224
Finlaison, John, on errors in TBM's *History*, IV, 391
LETTER TO: IV, 391
Finlason, William Francis, *Report on the Trial of Achilli v. Dr. Newman*, 'prodigy of absurdity' v, 310*
Finlay, Frederic, II, 359
Finsbury, TBM asked to stand for v, 235, 237
Fire Box, TBM has one at school I, 34
Firth, Sir Charles, *Commentary on Macaulay's History of England*, III, 252n, IV, 313n, 374n, v, 423n; editor, TBM's *History*, v, 35n
Fischer, Walther, *Johann Heinrich Künzel*, v, 200
Fishmongers' Company, TBM to dine with,

II, 326, 328, 329, less splendid than expected 330
Fitzclarence, Col., raised to peerage II, 42n
Fitzclarence, Lord Adolphus, IV, 129n
Fitzclarence, family of, II, *16*
Fitzgerald, William Vesey-Fitzgerald, Baron, IV, *124*
Fitzmaurice, Lord Edmond, *Life of Lord Granville*, VI, 113n
Fitzwalter, Robert, IV, 246
Fitzwilliam, William Wentworth Fitzwilliam, 2nd Earl, I, 240, entertains Northern Circuit, 251n; 314n, II, *6*
Fitzwilliam, Charles William Wentworth Fitzwilliam, 3rd Earl, II, *78*, offers assistance with TBM's *History* III, 286; IV, 110, TBM succeeds as High Steward of Cambridge VI, 126n; his edition of Burke, IV, 177
Flahault, Auguste, Comte de, V, 212n, 370n
Flahault, Mme de, V, 212n
Flanders, IV, 153
Flavius Vopiscus, V, 278*
Flaxman, John, II, *54*, TBM glad to mark his opinion of Flaxman's genius IV, 263; V, 364
Fleming, Robert, the Younger, *The Blessedness of Those Who Die in the Lord*, VI, 13
Flood, Henry, V, *93n*
Florence, III, 261, Tribune 263; English reading room at 262; 263, 270, Schneiderff's Hotel, IV, 219, V, 380; second only to Athens in arts and letters 404; VI, 19
Florentine Gallery, III, 56
Foley, Thomas Henry Foley, 4th Baron, VI, *157*
Folkestone, V, 70, TBM at 319, 322n; 354, 419n
Follett, Sir William, IV, 189n
Fonblanque, Albany, III, *354*, *England under Seven Administrations*, mistake to publish IV, 41
Fontainebleau, I, 177, 284
Fontenoy, battle of, IV, 148
Foote, Maria, II, *310*, IV, 223
Forbes, Sir William, Croker's error about, II, 96
Forbes (ship), III, 138
Forcellini, Egidio, *Lexicon Totius Latinitatis*, V, 453
Fordyce, James, *Sermons to Young Women* and *The Character and Conduct of the Female*, III, 7
Foreign Office, II, 294, its meanness in Tahiti affair IV, 238
Forfarshire Burghs, I, 314n
Formosa Island, Thames, V, 350
Forrest, Sir James, III, 350, IV, *116*, 120, 'wretched creature' 315; 392
LETTERS TO: IV, 254, 325
Forster, Charles, *Mahomadanism Unveiled*, I, 270n
Forster, E. M., *Marianne Thornton*, I, 14n, 55n, 88n, 169n, 207n, II, 262n, 326n, III, 304n, V, 79n, 220, on Richmond's portrait of Inglis 453n
Forster, John, II, 112n, candidate for editorship of *ER* IV, *330*; review of Churchill mistakenly attributed to TBM VI, 193; 221n
Forster, Josiah, V, 6n
Forster, Thomas, III, 274
Forster, W. E., on Penn, V, 158n
Fortescue, 1st Earl, II, 145n
Fortier, Felix, III, 98
Foscolo, Ugo, I, *230*, III, 107n
Foster, E., TBM sends *History* to, VI, 155
Foster, John, accusations against Sadler, II, *369*
Foster, Joseph, *Alumni Oxonienses*, I, 177n
Foston, TBM visits Sydney Smith at, I, 215; 244
Fountainhall, Sir John Lauder, Lord, *The Decisions of the Lords of Council and Session*, IV, 375n, 376*, *Historical Observes of Memorable Occurents* and *Historical Notices of Scottish Affairs* sent to TBM IV, 384; 387, V, 36
Fox, Caroline, II, *169*, 181, on her brother's temper 195; 282
Fox, Caroline, *Memories of Old Friends*, I, xxvii
Fox, Charles James, and India Bill, I, 226; bust by Nollekens II, 20; 21n, portrait by Lawrence 25; contrasted to Byron 33; as speaker 44; TBM's oratory compared to his 65; duel with William Adam 76; 290, III, 136, 220, 258, 281n, 386, IV, 205, 206, and Barillon's despatches 313n; TBM compares himself to V, 138n; 156, 409
Writings: 'Letter to the Electors of Westminster in 1793,' reprinted by Adair, V, 316, *History of the Early Part of the Reign of James II*, II, 288
Fox, General Charles Richard, II, *13*, anecdote of TBM 13n; elected at Calne 16n; 20, 169, 308, TBM dines with 339; criticises Russell's epitaph for Lord Holland V, 155; at Great Exhibition 203
LETTERS TO: IV, 121, 296

Fox, Mrs Charles Richard (Lady Mary Fitzclarence), II, *339*, V, 203
Fox, George, his encounter with priest of Mansetter, VI, 137; *Journal* 137n
Fox, Henry: *see* 4th Baron Holland
Fox, Mrs Henry Edward: *see* Mary Augusta, Lady Holland
Fox, Lady Mary: *see* Lady Lilford
Fox Howe, Dr Arnold's house, VI, 216n
Fox Warren, Surrey, Henry and Margaret Holland honeymoon at, VI, 179n; 232n
Foxe, John, *Book of Martyrs*, I, 5n, 321
Foy, Maximilian Sébastien, I, *179*
Foyard, Mr, I, 146
France, peace with, I, 42; scheme to reconquer Haiti 54; TBM expects a revolution 179; Chamber of Deputies, TBM attends 303; National Guard 304; disorders in II, 154; Protestant coldness in 266; III, 64, literature of 136; 223, bad roads in 270; and Eastern Question 335n, 339; Chamber of Deputies 352; war party in 353; relations with England IV, 232; and action in Algeria 233; order being restored 383; literary glory derived from struggle against Catholicism V, 27; advanced in taste for Gothic 72; *coup d'état* in 210; state of 211; fears of 308n; existing government as good as it can get 324; alliance with England 423; military cooperation with England 433; importance of friendship with 456; effects of democracy in VI, 194; interference in Italy 201n; supposed alliance with Russia 210n, 211, 213; invasion threat from 214, 252, 256
    Institutions and Organisations: Academy of Sciences, Transactions, V, 338; Bank of, and price of gold V, 468n; Foreign Office, archives, TBM has examined V, 419; Institute V, 350; War Department, archives, TBM seeks access to V, 418-19
    Revolutions: Revolution of 1789, examination subject at Preston's I, 46n; 207, V, 132, VI, 253; Revolution of 1830, I, 280, 298, 299, 305, no Whig manifesto required by 309-10; III, 143; Revolution of 1848, IV, 362, few signs of in Paris V, 72; fighting described 75; 'an earthquake' 210
    Travels in: I, 284, IV, 372n, V, 403n, 418, VI, 99, 101, 104, 159, 166n; *see also separate entry for* Paris
Francis, Clement, I, *108*
Francis, Sir Philip, TBM thinks he wrote Junius letters II, *216*; convinced he is Junius V, 215-16: *see also* Junius
Francis, Philip, barrister, VI, 101
Franck, Richard, *Northern Memoirs*, V, 120*
Franco-Austrian War, VI, 201n
François I, IV, 148
Frankfort, V, 281, 349n, TBM visits 351; 354, Hannah at VI, 102
Franklin, Benjamin, *Poor Richard's Almanack, 1758*, II, 319*
Franklin, Captain Charles Trigance, V, 281n, 292, 312n
Franklin, Sir John, V, 48n
Franklin, Mrs (perhaps Lucy Haywood Franklin), V, 312
Franks, Sir John, III, *75*
Franks, Miss (Trevelyan family governness), IV, 236
Franks, postal, I, 266-7, 278, invalid form II, 206; privilege suspended until reelection 124; privilege expires on dissolution 208; unlimited privilege as Secretary, Board of Control 209; Robert Wilberforce asks for use of 295; parliamentary privilege ending III, 304
Franz, George, superlative courier V, 352, 418, VI, 26, 50, no news of 54; VI, 104, 160n
Franz, Sarah Grant, V, 139, *Wild Flowers* 139
    LETTER TO: V, 139
Fraser, Alexander Campbell, IV, *300*
    LETTER TO: IV, 300
Fraser's, III, 250
Frederic, Prince, III, 207
Frederic, TBM's servant, III, 341
Frederick, Prince of Wales, IV, 257
Frederick the Great, I, 180, III, 53, as subject for TBM IV, 18
Frederick William, Prince, of Prussia, VI, 138n
Free Church of Scotland, its beginning, IV, 126n; and plan for school system 262n; 282, 284, Macfarlan attached to 289; TBM presents petition from 300n
Free Church College, Edinburgh, IV, 300n
Free Churchmen, oppose TBM, IV, 301; at Edinburgh 341
Free Trade, TBM pledges support II, 104; TBM on its limits IV, 91-2; supporters mistake their strength 100; TBM repeats his arguments about 105-6; unattainable 113; TBM supports 165, 192; debate on V, 296, 297; no longer a question 475; issue in 1852 VI, 84; 214

Freemasonry, TBM forwards volumes on to Glasgow University v, 90n
Freese, Arthur, vi, 287
Freetown, Sierra Leone, i, xxiv
Fremantle, Sir Thomas Francis, iv, *131*
French, in India, v, 114; French landing in Devonshire, v, 96; French prisoners, i, 8
French, question of etymology in, iv, 111-12
French, Fitzstephen, and quarrel with Brougham iv, 263; abuses Trevelyan in Commons v, *324*
French, William, i, *138*
French, W. H., and G. D. Saunders, eds., *The Reader's Macaulay*, i, 231n
French Code, iii, 210, 238
Frere, Bartholomew, iv, *67*
Frere, John Hookham, iv, *67*, v, 17
Frere, William, iv, *67*
Fresco painting, iv, 198, 199
Fribourg, v, 349n, 352
Friend of India, vi, 212n
Friendship's Offering, i, 244n
Frith, William Powell, vi, *7*
Froissart, Jean, vi, 153n, *Chronicles*, iv, 17, 384*
Frost, John, iv, *293*
Frost, Williams, and Jones, TBM opposed to addressing Queen in favour of iv, 293
Frothingham, E. R., *Edward Everett*, iv, 74n, 266, v, 475n
Froude, J. A., vi, 144n, *History of England*, TBM recommends to Queen Victoria vi, 144*; *Thomas Carlyle*, ii, 113n
Fry, Herbert, vi, *33*, tries to get biographical information from TBM 41n;
  Letters to: vi, 33, 41
Fryston Hall (Milnes's residence), iv, 165n
Fugitive Slave Law, v, 138
Fuller, Mr, v, 212n
Funchal, Madeira, iii, 6
Furness Abbey, TBM visits v, 426
Furniss, Harry, *Paradise in Piccadilly*, iv, 59
Furruckabad, ii, 245
Fuseli, Henry, v, *194*
Fyfe, Christopher, *History of Sierra Leone*, i, 253n, ii, 264n

GEC, *Complete Peerage*, i, 265n, ii, 21n, 53
Gabrielli: *see* Mrs Mary Meeke
Gainsborough, Charles Noel, 3rd Baron Barham and 1st Earl of, ii, *145*, v, 178
Gainsborough, Lady, v, 188
Gainsborough, Thomas, TBM describes a scene for v, 285
Galiffe, Lt.-Col. John, iii, *328*, 329
Galignani's *Messenger*, v, 352, vi, 58, sees regularly in Venice 59
Gallio, iii, 70, 178
Galloway, Sir Archibald, iii, *92*, iv, 171, 196, 197, death of v, 104
Galt, John, ii, *312*, an odd writer 312
  Writings: Annals of the Parish, ii, 312*, *The Ayrshire Legatee*, ii, 312*, *Autobiography*, ii, 311*, *The Entail*, ii, 310*, 312*, 314, *Lawrie Todd*, ii, 29, 311, 312, 314*, 315, 317, 366*, *Life of Cardinal Wolsey*, ii, 312*, *Life of Lord Byron*, TBM thinks of noticing ii, 14, 312*, *The Provost*, ii, 312*, *Sir Andrew Wylie*, ii, 315*, 317, *Voyages and Travels*, ii, 312*
Gambia, iv, 367
Gambier, Sir Edward John, iii, *112*, 132
Ganges, iii, 87
Ganthony, Richard, watch-maker, ii, 192, 194, 317
Garda, Lake, ii, 230n
Gardiner, Stephen, v, 19
Gardiner, William, on election at Leicester, *Music and Friends*, i, 211n
Gardner, Lord, iv, 129n
Gardner, Richard, v, *233*
Garratt, William Albin, an eager volunteer, vi, *255*
Garrick, David, i, xxix, compared to Jeffrey 238; in Reynolds's painting ii, 147; 227, *309*, iii, 258, v, 164
Garrick, David and George Colman the elder, *The Clandestine Marriage*, ii, 309
Garrick Club, buys Mathews's collection of theatrical portraits ii, 308n; Thackeray's quarrel at vi, 221n
Garrow, Sir William, iv, 305
Garry, v, 126
Garstang, i, 252
Garter King of Arms, and TBM's arms vi, 126; fees 135
Gaskell, Elizabeth, TBM asked to meet vi, *220*
Gassett, Henry, sends volumes on Freemasonry v, 90n
Gathorne-Hardy, A. E., *Gathorne Hardy, First Earl of Cranbrook*, i, 159n, 231n
Gatton, iv, 187, 370
Gauffier, Louis, portrait of Lady Holland, ii, 25n
Gay, John, *The Beggars' Opera*, i, 220, *Fables*, i, 75*
Gazette de Leyde, iv, 354
Geldart, Thomas Charles, v, *384*

General Society for Promoting District Visiting, TBM allows his name to be used by VI, 229
Genest, John, *Some Account of the English Stage,* I, 240n
Geneva, anti-slavery element there I, 73n; III, 156n, 213, V, 337, 339, 343, 349n, TBM at 352; 353, 354
Geneva, Lake of, V, 343, 352, 354
Geneva Public Library, III, xi
Genlis, Mme de, *Petits Romans,* I, 28*, 32
Genoa, and war with Corsica II, 72; III, 260, 270, 274, IV, 220, VI, 26, 58, 61, TBM at 62; described 62-3; Hotel d'Italia III, 261
Gentleman's Magazine, I, 142n, II, 5n, 11n
George, Mr, dancing master for Macaulay family I, 38
George I, King, III, 206, 207, his Queen not part of English sequence IV, 256; 257
George II, King, IV, 257, V, 476
George III, King, II, 256, III, ix, IV, 159, 177, 198, his illness 205; 212, 257
George IV, King (Prince Regent to 1820), letter to Grey and Grenville I, 14; barbarous treatment of his wife 21; Commons send address of condolence to 24; receives Louis XVIII in London 43n; 46, creates Wellington Duke 47; expected at Brighton 48; 59, directs general mourning for Princess Charlotte 92n; succeeds to throne, seeks divorce 145n; popular feeling against 148n; coronation of 157, 159, 161; visit to Ireland 159, 161; TBM defends his criticism of 161; at Brighton 175; sarcastic remarks on his death 273-4; portrait by Lawrence II, 53; 55, 168n, 309, 310, 310n, III, 207, 252, set example of conforming in Scotland IV, 54; 205, first meeting with Princess Caroline 237; 257, acquires Stuart Papers 311n; libelled by Hunt V, 443n
George of Denmark, IV, 257
George Peabody Library, Baltimore, III, xi
Germain, Lord George, VI, 196, 197
German, unintelligible handwriting in, V, 241, VI, 191
Germanic Confederation, II, 159
Germans, TBM born to make game of certain Germans III, 211
Germany, TBM reading theological writers of III, 338; TBM regrets his ignorance of IV, 22; order being restored in 383; TBM's popularity in V, viii; its progress since Reformation 26; its greatness on Protestant side 27; universities 158; 298, Trevelyans travelling in VI, 104, 109
Gettmann, R. A., *A Victorian Publisher,* III, 363n
Ghaus, Chulam Muhammad: *see* Carnatic, Nabob of
Ghent, I, 284, IV, 220, V, 349n, VI, 104
Gibbon, Edward, TBM asks for his copy of to be sent I, 58; 92, 119, III, 9, 159, 178, mistaken about Quintus Curtius 202; 258, 281n, IV, 28, on Hume's criticism of *Decline and Fall* V, 274n
Writings: Autobiography, IV, 15n, 274n, *Decline and Fall,* I, 65*, III, 62*, 220, IV, 369, its indelicacy V, 42*
Gibbons, Grinling, his statue of James II, V, 431
Gibson, Charles Bernard, V, *436*; *The Last Earl of Desmond* 436
LETTER TO: V, 436
Gibson, Milner, his motion on Crimean war, V, 456
Gieseler, J. C. L., *Lehrbuch der Kirchengeschichte,* IV, 356-7*
Gifford, Lord, VI, 52n
Gifford, William, Byron on, II, 321, 334, TBM presents his edition of Ben Jonson to Edinburgh Philosophical Institution V, 463; *The Baviad,* I, 51*
Gilbert, John T., VI, 223n
Gilchrist, Mr, V, 434, 446
Gill, Charles, III, 33
Gillon, William Downe, III, *355*
Gisborne, John, V, *357*, 359
Gisborne, Thomas, I, 198n, II, 191n, 262n, V, 357n, *An Enquiry into the Duties of the Female Sex,* III, 7
Gisborne, Thomas, the younger, II, *262*
Gladstone, William Ewart, I, xv, xvi, his maiden speech II, *250*; TBM will treat him tenderly III, 275; an 'excellent fellow,' 276; 278, letter to TBM 283n; IV, 101, to be at Board of Trade IV, 124; 195, 206, TBM accuses of contradiction on slavery 244; speech on slave question 244n; resigns over Maynooth 250n; V, 141n, 172n, TBM compliments his pamphlets on Naples question 181n; protests about Naples 181n; 228n, in danger in elections 233; offends High Churchmen by taking office with Whigs 306n; difficult struggle at Oxford 307; dines at Westbourne Terrace 319; 320, defends Trevelyan in Commons 324; plans for consolidation of national debt 326; TBM speaks to on points in budget 329; his budget speech

329n; TBM forwards memorials to 330, 331; appoints Charles Macaulay Secretary, Board of Audit 387; and Oxford University Bill 391; speaks well of Charles Macaulay 392; to modify Oxford Bill 394; resigns from ministry 445n; appointed British Museum trustee VI, 23; 152n

Writings: Church Principles Considered in Their Results, III, 340, 344*, 'Giacomo Leopardi,' V, 108, *Gleanings of Past Years*, III, 283, *The State in Its Relations with the Church*, III, 275, 284*, translations with Lord Lyttelton, VI, 30n

LETTERS TO: III, 283, IV, 244, V, 166, V, 167, 170, 330, 331

Gladstone, Mrs William, V, 170

Glamis Castle, VI, 180n, 181

Glammis Burn, VI, 181

Glamorganshire, VI, 5

Glasgow, cholera at II, 76; 266, TBM at 306; 308, anti-corn law feeling at IV, 108, 109; TBM to visit for installation as Rector 380; 390, to speak at V, 31, 38; speech at 40; given freedom of City 40n; speech 41n; TBM at 111n; 116, Palmerston given freedom of 358n; dispute in 379; Burns celebration at VI, 191n; 230n, described 231-2

Glasgow, Royal Hotel, TBM at VI, 231

Glasgow Athenaeum, TBM wanted to speak at IV, 389

Glasgow Cathedral, TBM attends service at VI, 232

Glasgow Constitutional, V, 290

Glasgow Courier, I, 222

Glasgow University, Lord Rectorship, TBM would not refuse IV, 227; proposed 353; declines 354; elected 353n, 380; 381, won't be exhibited at 389-90; plans for inauguration 391-2; inaugural address at 397n; inauguration V, 40n; litigation with railway company 89-90; Watson-Gordon's portrait of TBM for 110; Hunterian Museum 110n; Mrs Money recommends candidate for professorship 116; contest between Palmerston and Alison for Rectorship 133-4; TBM's part in election of successor 133n; TBM gives up his casting vote 134; election 'ridiculous' 136; Rectorship not like English Chancellorship 136-7; 309

Gleig, G. R., III, *363*, IV, 305n, TBM apologises to V, 169; thanks TBM for 'taking him out of pillory' 169n

Writings: 'The Indian Army,' V, 315, *Life of Major-General Sir T. Munro*, III, 362, *Life of Warren Hastings*, III, 344, 359, 361, 'worst book that I ever saw' 363; IV, 42, V, 169n

LETTER TO: V, 169

Glen Ogilvie, Dundee's seat, VI, 180, 181

Glencoe, IV, 15, 16, 392, V, 29, TBM visits 111n; 208, 313n, VI, 145n

Glencorse, Lord: *see* John Inglis

Glendinning, Mr, Chiswick nurseryman, VI, 148

Glenelg, Charles Grant, 1st Baron, I, 223n, 237, II, 33n, 'idle,' 91; 102n, *137*, Gordon quarrels with 140; presents TBM to William IV 142n; astonished by TBM's speed in reading 143; only saint in ministry 145; 179, 194, 204, sends India plan to TBM 207; 208, 240, 243, 244, 245, 246, a languid politician 266; 267, compliments TBM on India speech 268; TBM at his house for consultation 270, 272, 273, 274; advises resignation of ministers 279; 289, at Wilberforce's funeral 290; 291, 301, summoned to Edinburgh 303; 304, 308, TBM impatient for his return 314; at Paris 317; ill at Paris 318; his delays 318-19; on chances of TBM's appointment 322; argues for TBM's appointment 323; TBM in his 'perfect confidence' 324; wishes to appoint James Stephen to China 324; 325, does not know what he will do without TBM 328; 329, 330, out of town 331; more distressed than TBM's father at prospect of separation 331; 332, has spoken to Chairmen of East India Company 334; TBM dines with 336; 337, his kindness to TBM 339; 343, at Brighton 358; 363, 365, has little patronage to give 366; TBM will speak to for Napier 367; has nothing for Napier 370; III, 10, 20n, 22, 166, 220, 243, IV, 202, 234, 387n, V, 58n, 109n, 157n, 299n, 311n, 319, 329n, 427n, VI, 37n, 139n, 204

Globe (London), II, 324, IV, 41, on Disraeli's plagiarism V, 301n; letter in defending TBM VI, 45

Gloucester, V, 177, 181, 189, 268

Gloucester, Bishop of, his palace described V, 282, 283

Gloucester, Duchess of, I, 127n

Gloucester, Duke of, I, 127n, II, *290*, 291

Gloucester assizes, V, 349n

Gloucester Cathedral, V, 180, 183, 185

Gloucestershire, v, 194

Glover, John Hulbert, v, *422*, Selections from Stuart Papers, iv, 311n

LETTER TO: v, 422

Gluck Collection, *Catalogue*, v, 39

Glyn, George Carr, iv, *333*

Glynn, Mr, v, 288

'God Save the King,' origin of, vi, 108

Goderich, Lord: *see* Earl of Ripon

Godfrey, Henry, President of Queens' College, i, *152*

Godolphin, Sydney, Lord, ii, 190, iv, 375

Godwin, William, begging for a place ii, *139*, 260, *Caleb Williams*, ii, 139

Goethe, Johann Wolfgang von, TBM hopes to read his works on voyage from India iii, 234, 236, iv, 35, 182, v, 27, his house at Frankfort 351

Writings: 'Der Edelknabe und die Müllerin,' iii, 236*, *Faust*, ii, 98, *Wilhelm Meister*, iii, 245*, v, 190*, 191*, vi, 186*, *Works*, iii, 194, 196

Goëzmann, Mme, and Beaumarchais, v, 315n

Goëzmann, Valentin, and Beaumarchais, v, 315

Gog and Magog, in Guildhall, ii, 150

Gold, price of, v, 468-9

Goldoni, Comedies, v, 261*, *Le Avventure della Villeggiatura*, v, 409*, *Il Giocatore*, v, 409*, *Le Smanie per la Villeggiatura*, v, 409*

Goldsmid, Sir Francis Henry, ii, *35*, and Jewish Committee 244n; 'Statement of the Civil Disabilities and Privations affecting Jews in England,' reviewed by TBM i, 311n

Goldsmid, Isaac, i, 242n, *311n*, 320, begs TBM to attend fancy-dress ball ii, 24; TBM describes 34-7; 35, 39, 41, iii, 17

LETTERS TO: ii, 123, 232

Goldsmid, Mrs Isaac, ii, 34

Goldsmith, Oliver, ii, 29, anecdote of his vanity 59; 227, 258, 281n, TBM proposes to write an essay on iv, 98; Hallam's predecessor in Royal Academy post v, 97

Writings: 'The Gift,' v, 321-2*, *The Good Natur'd Man*, v, 200* *Grecian History*, i, 250, iv, 9, *She Stoops to Conquer*, v, 110* *Vicar of Wakefield*, i, 219*, iv, 9, 13, 19

Gooch, G. P., ed., *Later Correspondence of Lord John Russell*, iv, 23, 273n

Gooch, Sir Thomas Sherlock, i, *287*, ii, 61n

Goode, Francis, i, *179*

Goodman, Mr, v, 142

Goodrich, Chauncey, v, 36n, 43n

Gordian, iii, 202

Gordon, Sir Alexander Duff, v, *102*, vi, 150n

LETTERS TO: v, 102, 413

Gordon, Lady Duff (Lucie Austin), v, *102n*; TBM takes to Lansdowne's house at Richmond 413-14; embarrasses TBM 414n

Gordon, John Thompson, v, *252*

LETTER TO: v, 252

Gordon, Robert, ii, *139*, his conduct at Board of Control 139-40; on East India Committee 146n; 180, 194, traitor on Board of Control 266; 272, in the country 318; iii, 22n

Gordon, Captain William, ii, *58*, 'ill-natured fellow' 73; 156, 157-8, 160

Gordon, Mrs (Mary Wilson), *'Christopher North': A Memoir of John Wilson*, v, 252

Gorgias, iii, 141, vi, 83

Gore, Mrs Catherine, iii, 371n, v, *102*, TBM dines with 166; 166n, TBM attends wedding of her daughter 336

Writings: The Hamiltons, presented to TBM, v, 102*, *Heckington*, presented to TBM, vi, 153*, *Manners of the Day*, ii, 94*, 95, a favourite v, 102*, *Pinmoney*, ii, 95*, a favourite v, 102*

LETTERS TO: v, 102, 166, 180, vi, 86, 153

Gore, Cecilia Anne Mary, v, *180*, her wedding 336n

Gorham, George Cornelius, i, *128*, v, 96n

Gorham Case, i, 128n, 141n, v, 96, TBM thinks judgment excellent 99-100; Lord Campbell dismissed by Miss Sellon for his part in 107n

Gosford, 1st Earl of, iii, 71n

Gosford, 2nd Earl of, iii, *249*

Gothic architecture, and Cambridge, iv, 181

Gottingen, mistake about in *History*, v, 53

Gough, Sir Hugh, v, *31*

Goulburn, Edward, v, *82n*

Goulburn, Henry, i, 181, candidate at Cambridge 212n, *283*, elected at Cambridge ii, 12n, iii, 293, speech on Sugar Duties iv, 244; 346, v, 185, 201, 319, 384, 402n, vi, 29n

Government of India Act, vi, 141n, plans for 146n

Government of India Bill, vi, 160

Governor-General in Council, letters to, iii, 145, 214

Governor-General of India: *see* Lord William Bentinck; 1st Earl of Auckland

Gow, A. S. F., ed., Theocritus, *Idylls*, VI, 81n

Gower, Lord: *see* Duke of Sutherland

Gowland's Oil, II, 280

Gracchus, I, 85

Grafton, Duke of, IV, 221

Grafton, 4th Duke of, IV, 221n

Graham, Mr, a friend of Henry Macaulay's, II, 320

Graham, Edward, *The Harrow Life of Henry Montagu Butler*, VI, 241

Graham, Sir James, II, *16*, 52, compliments TBM on speech 62; 73, TBM presents dialogue with 73-4; 79, TBM dines with 89; his official house 90; 'afraid or idle' 91; takes abolitionist side 175; 195, plan for abolition 239; 282, 290, tells TBM he will be missed 343-4; TBM learns of his Indian appointment while dining with 350; admires Hannah's behaviour 356; III, 85n, IV, 20, 101, 134, his education clauses 162; Home Secretary 197n; TBM's reply to 201; 206, 209, and Medical Reform Bill 214n; frames new Medical Bill 242n; and Scottish Universities Bill 258; in debate on Scottish Universities Bill 262; 270, his position on Corn Laws 273; 328n, 338n, 364, refers to TBM in speech V, 156; TBM of his mind 156; 185, joins opposition to Lord Derby 253; sends 'fervent' congratulations on TBM's election 255; attacked for indiscreet remarks 390; resigns from ministry 445; VI, 146n

LETTERS TO: IV, 6, V, 445

Graham, John, IV, *361*

Grand Assize, I, 208n

Grand Cross of the Bath, III, 351

'Grand Council, The' pamphlet, V, 216

Grand Coustumier de Normandie, IV, 355

Grand Day: *see* Lincoln's Inn

Grange, The (Lord Ashburton's house), Auckland dies at, V, 5; 209, TBM visits 209n

Grant, Mr, IV, 115

Grant, Sir Alexander, *The Story of the University of Edinburgh*, V, 341n

Grant, Anne, of Laggan, TBM calls on I, *235*; *Essays on the Superstitions of the Highlanders of Scotland*, 235n; *Letters from the Mountains* 235n

Grant, Charles, the elder, I, 62n, *63*, 181n, 223n, IV, 207

Grant, Charles, the younger: *see* Lord Glenelg

Grant, Sir Francis, portrait of TBM, V, *327n*

Grant, Dr J., letter to, VI, 265

Grant, James, *The Bench and the Bar*, I, 215n

Grant, James William, III, *125*

Grant, Sir John Peter (1774-1858), III, *158*, 165, 197, IV, 303n

Grant, Sir John Peter (1807-93), III, *162*, calumniated by English press VI, 131; complains to TBM of his treatment 131n

Grant, Sir Robert, I, 181, *223*, 237, presents petitions against Jewish disabilities 262n; 272n, II, 33n, compliments TBM on speech 63; 137, 213, 232, resolutions on Jewish relief 232n; tedious 244; a twaddle 266; 272, 274, 301, his brother Charles depends on him 328; III, 265

Grant, Mrs Robert, II, *137*, 204, 317

Grant, William, II, *137*, a fool 260

Grant family, I, xvii

Granville, Lady, V, x, 308n

Granville, 1st Earl, III, 359n

Granville, Granville George Leveson-Gower, 2nd Earl, letter to Palmerston III, 335n; V, x, 150n, Greville has rooms in his house 295; 308n, VI, *15*, 103n, claims credit for TBM's peerage 113n; defends Canning 131; 149, 213, TBM would prefer for Board of Control 220; speech 221; on Sir Charles Wood 222n

Grasmere, TBM at, VI, 230

Grattan, Henry, I, 21n, II, 290, 292, III, 136, V, 93

Graves, Algernon, and W. V. Cronin, Catalogue of Sir Joshua Reynolds II, 27n

Gravesend, III, 25

Gray, Mr, or Grey, V, 446

Gray, TBM's butler, VI, *170*, 208, 224n, 231

Gray, Captain Charles, IV, *303*; his *Muckomachy*, 303

LETTER TO: IV, 303

Gray, J. G., on *Knight's Quarterly* contributors I, 188n

Gray, J. H., *The Queens' College*, I, 152n

Gray, John, IV, 214

Gray, Robert, V, 434

Gray, Thomas, I, 140, 'The Bard,' 158*, *Correspondence*, 154*, 'The Progress of Poesy,' 110*

Gray, W. F., 'A Budget of Literary Letters,' III, 144

Great Bedwin, borough of, II, 74

Great Exhibition, V, 141, TBM appointed to committee on medals for 141n; opening 159n; opening week filled with shows and routs 161; fears about disorders 161n; 169, 185, 188, TBM will

Great Exhibition—*cont.*
always remember with affection 192; impatient to revisit 194; last day 202; visits on special ticket 203-4; 321, Marochetti's statue of Richard I a memorial to 334n
Great Exhibition, Committee on Inscriptions, TBM suggests Latin lines v, 167; TBM and Gladstone on 167n; 170-1
Great Exhibition, *Official Descriptive and Illustrated Catalogue,* v, 167n, 203n
Great Northern Railway, accident on, v, 352
Great Western Railway, shares in, iv, 313; v, 309
Greatbach, William, ii, 253n, v, 55n
Greaves, R. W., 'Roman Catholic Relief and the Leicester Election of 1826,' i, 211n
Greaves, William, TBM's first schoolmaster, i, 5n, 16, 21, 42, 61, 169n, his school at Clapham ii, 155n
Greece, our debt to, i, 163
Greek Church, differences from the Roman v, 427-8
Greek Drama, dancing in, iv, 240
Greek Literature, superiority of to Latin iii, 237
Greek War of Independence, i, 163n
Greeley, Horace, TBM suspects of starting opium story V, 361n
Green, George Smith, 'New Version of Paradise Lost,' vi, 181*
Gregory, Barnard, editor of the *Satirist,* iv, *129*
Gregory, Captain, vi, 86
Gregory, Mrs (daughter of Catharine Macaulay), vi, 86-7
Gregory XVI, Pope, iii, 268, 276, spectacle of mass performed by v, 233
Greig, Alexander (1800?-55), TBM's cousin, i, *37*
Greig, David, letter to, iv, 291
Greig, Rev G., i, 37n
Greig, Mrs G. (Catherine Macaulay), i, 37n
Grenada, i, 74n
Grenfell, H., v, 144n
Grenville, William Wyndham, 1st Baron, i, 14, ii, *29*, v, 337, *Nugae Metricae,* 'Oxford and Locke,' 'Dropmore,' ii, 288n
Grenville, George, iv, 198, 221, v, 216
Grenville, George Neville-, iv, *366*
Letter to: iv, 366
Grenville, Thomas, iv, *221*
Greville, Charles, ii, *195*, meets Guizot in exile iv, 362n; v, 41n, Lord Maidstone alludes to in *Times* 295; entrusts his memoirs to Reeve 334n
Memoirs: ed. Strachey and Fulford, i, 69n, 92n, on expenses of George IV's coronation 159n; on Brougham and TBM 185n; on TBM's reading of *Grandison* ii, 15n; 21n, 101n, on TBM at Holland House 180n; 218n, 254n, on TBM's slavery speech 278n; 279n, on Lord Stanley and West Indian Bill 281n; on Walpole and Miss Berry 349n; 357n, iii, 23n, 71n, 322n, 352n, iv, ix, 99n, 163n, 180n, 206n, 265, 266n, 272n, 278n, 291n, 314n, 339n, 362n, 390n, on Lady Ashburton v, 209n; on Sir Robert Adair 316n
Grey, Charles Grey, 2nd Earl, i, 14, praises TBM 185n; 216n, 253n, 271n, ii, 10n, promised Garter by William IV 19; *Correspondence of Earl Grey with King William IV* 19n; portrait at Holland House 25; 62, TBM describes dining with 64-5; treats TBM politely 65; 90, 98, 99, 100, asks TBM to write on Phillpotts 121; has honour of the Reform Bill 124; 124n, 180, appeases Lady Holland 181; gives a rout 248; 253, 255, understands difficult position of Reform ministry 256; commissions Haydon to paint Reformers 273; 276, 290, 296n, 301, says that ministry owes TBM support 322; toasted at Leeds 33n; 343, 357, no patronage at Treasury 377; iii, 10, 264, must remain firm in crisis of Reform Bill vi, 276
Grey, General Charles, i, 216n
Grey, Sir Charles, iv, *117*
Grey, Sir George, iii, *259*, iv, 274, TBM thinks future leader of Whigs in Commons 278; v, 216, possible replacement for TBM at Edinburgh 259; 261, 326, 470n
Letter to: v, 399
Grey, George Henry, v, *216*, 326
Grey, Lady Georgiana, ii, *65*
Grey, Henry, i, *235*
Grey, Mrs Henry, and Anglicanus letters i, 235n
Grey, Henry George Grey, Viscount Howick and 3rd Earl, ii, *52*, invites TBM to dinner 64, 65; married 180; 250, sends article to *ER* through TBM 341; iii, 271, resigns as Secretary-at-War 298; 330, iv, 78n, 187, 189, 261, 270, 271, 274, 'angry and obstinate' over Corn Laws 275; won't take office if Palmerston at Foreign

Office 276; Clarendon prophesies his unpopularity 277; prevents formation of ministry 278, 279, 280; TBM's letter regarding his behaviour published 282, 283; cannot meet again as friends 284; 285, cannot resent TBM's words 286; TBM's apology 288-90; accepted 290n; his letter explaining position 290; letter to TBM 290n; 314n, offers Secretaryship of Mauritius to Charles Macaulay v, 29; on the younger generation in Commons 99; 216, 391, 392, vi, 45n, presents East India Company petition against India Bill 141n; 204, 204n

Writings: Parliamentary Government, TBM reads in MS, vi, 91*, 'Secondary Punishments – Transportations,' ii, 341n, 352

Letters to: iv, 288, 290, vi, 91, 91

Grey, John, of Dilston, 'Letter from J. Grey Esq. in Reply to the Calumnies of the Rev. A. Thomson,' i, 236

Grey, Maria, Countess, ii, *180n*

Grey, Mary, Countess, ii, *64*, 65, TBM at her rout 152, 153; 248, 254, 357, v, 15, 470n

Grey-Egerton, Sir Philip, v, 150n

Griffon (Gennadius Library), v, 5

Griggs, E. L., and G. E., *Letters of Hartley Coleridge,* vi, 278n

Grimblot, Paul, iv, *381*, *Letters of William III. and Louis XIV.,* dedicated to TBM 381n*

Grimm, Baron Friedrich Melchior, *Correspondance,* ii, 288*, iii, 21, 108, v, 261*

Grindal, Edmund, Archbishop of Canterbury, v, 21

Grobel, Monica, 'The Society for the Diffusion of Useful Knowledge, 1826-1846,' i, 314n, 322

Grocers' Company, iii, 83

Groen van Prinsterer, Guillaume, vi, *88*, *Archives ou Correspondance Inédite de la Maison d'Orange-Nassau* 88n; *Handboek der Geschiedenis van het Vaderland* 88n

Letter to: vi, 88

Grosskurth, Phyllis, *The Woeful Victorian,* vi, 242n

Grosvenor, Lord Robert, afterwards 1st Baron Ebury, ii, *276*, bill on Sunday trading v, 461

Grosvenor Gallery, TBM admires, iv, 202

Grote, George, i, 242n, iv, 309n, v, 224n, *History of Greece,* iv, 297*, vi, 161n

Grotius, Hugo, v, 224

Grove, Mrs, letter to, vi, 268

Grove, The (Lord Clarendon's house) TBM at iv, 314n; v, 139, 293, vi, 190

Grove, Sir William Robert, vi, *268n*

Guernsey, Laws of, iv, 355; execution at v, 382n

Guggenheim, John Simon, Memorial Foundation, i, xxxiv

Guicciardini, Francisco, *L'historia d'Italia,* iii, 181

Guido Reni, painting at Rogers's, ii, 82

Guild of Literature and Art, TBM's reasons for not supporting v, 163-4; 163n

Guiscard, Marquis de, iii, 258

Guise, Duc de, iv, 149

Guizot, François Pierre Guillaume, i, *281*, iii, 335n, 340, succeeds as foreign minister 348; his policy that of reason, justice, and public law 354; ministry strong as ever iv, 231; his English policy 231n; and Tahiti affair 238; compared to Thiers 267; flees to London 362; 387n, lends TBM copies of Ronquillo's despatches v, 34n; seeks historical information from TBM 145; 146, commends Ellis's report on Channel Islands 206; TBM sends letter of introduction to 224; proposes TBM for Institute of France 309; 384, introduces Montalembert to TBM 456; unreasonable to ask him to lecture in English vi, 32

Writings: Histoire de la République d'Angleterre et de Cromwell, v, 145n, *Histoire de la Révolution d'Angleterre,* v, 145n, *Monk: Chute de la République et Rétablissement de la Monarchie en Angleterre,* v, 176n

Gulland, George, iv, *267*

Letter to: iv, 267

Gulliver and Lilliputians, figures of at Great Exhibition, v, 203-4

Gully, James Manby, v, *182*

Gully, John, ii, 218n, *249*

Guloseton, Lord, ii, 214

Gunpowder plot, v, 88

Gurney, Baron, ii, 330

Gurney, Sir John, i, *287*

Gurney, John Hampden, TBM recommends to Longman, v, *123*; vi, 176n, *Historical Sketches,* v, 123n

Gurney, Joseph, ii, *146*

Gurney, Samuel, v, 6n, thinks TBM unfair to Quakers *26*

Gurney, William Brodie, ii, *146*

Gurney family, v, 26n

Guthrie, John, i, *264*

Guthrie, Thomas, iii, *364*, and plan for

Guthrie, Thomas—*cont.*
national school system in Scotland IV, 262n; his preaching described V, 291
Gwalior, IV, 183
Gwynn, Nell, II, *309*, her Charles the Second IV, 388; Cunningham's life of V, 229-30

H.B.: *see* John Doyle
Hackney, I, 41n
Haddington, Thomas Hamilton, 9th Earl of, I, *302*, 303, 304, IV, 131n
Haddon House, II, 240
Hadrian's Villa, IV, 331n
Hagley Park, V, 216
Hague, The, IV, 201, 218, 219, 220, Archives V, 186n; Trevelyans at VI, 167
Haiber, J. B., French translation of Von Ranke, III, 268n
Haider Ali, II, 224, III, 48, 51, 52, 60, 71, 361
Haight, Gordon S., I, xxxiii, IV, 240n, ed., *Portable Victorian Reader*, II, 51
Haileybury College, I, 246n, 318n, III, 99, V, 389n, age of entrance to 431n; provisions for in 1833 Charter Act 442; contradictory provisions about 442n; TBM feels responsibility for its closing VI, 35; anxious to serve those injured by closing 70-1; 71
Haiti, ambassadors from I, 54, 55; abolitionists oppose French scheme to reconquer 54
Haitians, I, 84
Halberton, Devon, I, 153n
Halcomb, John, II, *234*, 259
Haldane, Catherine, III, 34
Hale, Sir Matthew, I, *105*
Halévy, Elie, *History of the English People*, III, 349n
Halifax, 1st Marquess of, IV, 118
Halifax, Charles Montagu, 1st Earl of, IV, 118, V, *355n*, his relation to Catherine Barton 355-6, VI, 55, 165
Halifax, Charles Wood, 1st Viscount, II, *10*, IV, 308, 314n, raises private subscription for Highland relief 332; remarks on TBM's *History* 384, 385-6; TBM asks him to make Ellis Solicitor of the Treasury V, 206; 207, 208, defends Trevelyan in Commons 324; TBM discusses Indian plan with 325; 364n, President of Board of Control 366; and Commission on Laws of India 367; appoints Committee on Indian Civil Service 389; TBM dines with 390n; concurs with Committee on Civil Service 416; approves TBM's report 417, 431; TBM protests to about change in examinations 438, 439; 440, succeeds Graham at Admiralty 445; 470n, compliments TBM on *History* 482; VI, 30n, TBM presents Heaviside's case to 71; best for Board of Control after Granville 220; combines quick temper with quick intellect 222; unpopular 222n; 250n, says Trevelyan doing well 255
LETTERS TO: IV, 364, 384, 385, 385, V, 206, 208, 389, 431, 438, 439, 442, 482, VI, 70
Halifax, George Montagu, 2nd Earl of, VI, 55, 56, *165*
Halifax, Viscountess (Mary Grey), II, *10n*, V, 470n, 483
Hall, Sir Benjamin, V, *297*, TBM's opinion of not high 417
Hall, Miss L. A., III, 302n
Hall, Robert, Bishop of Norwich, at Synod of Dort, V, 14n
Hall, Robert, Baptist preacher, VI, 68, 'An Address on the Renewal of the Charter of the East India Company,' I, 23
Hall West and Co, Brighton bankers, VI, 29
Hallam, Arthur, IV, 361n, VI, 140n
Hallam, Henry, I, *244*, praises Malden's *History of Rome* 317; III, 381n, IV, 15n, 60; praises *Lays* 67; on Man in the Iron Mask 82; 191n, 200, 213, at breakfast 234; 287n, 387n, V, ix, x, 23, 42n, 49n, 52, 53, 58n, 94n, TBM's colleague in Royal Academy 97; 108n, 109n, 110n, 111n, death of his son 131; his cruel fate 133; TBM calls on 135; 136, 152n, 157n, 162, 168n, 219n, 228n, 229, 234n, 311n, his grandchild 312; 314n, 328n, 329n, 364n, in great force 365; 370, has paralytic stroke 380; writes illegible letters 406; VI, 40n, 78, death 191
Writings: Constitutional History of England, reviewed by TBM, I, 244n, 322
LETTERS TO: IV, 66, 370, V, 437, VI, 89, 140, 272
Hallam, Henry Fitzmaurice, IV, *66*, 200, death V, 131n; 135n
Halm, Friedrich, *Der Fechter von Ravenna*, VI, 229*, 248n
Hamburger, Joseph, I, xxxiv, ed., *Napoleon and the Restoration of the Bourbons*, VI, 287
Hamburger, Philip, VI, 287
Hamilton, Duke of, IV, 45
Hamilton, Alexander, VI, 171

Hamilton, George, IV, 338n
Hamilton, Henry Pratt, VI, 176n
Hamilton, John William, I, 147n
Hamilton, Penelope Macaulay (TBM's aunt), V, 272n
Hamilton, Sir William, 'Be not Schismatics, Be not Martyrs by Mistake,' IV, 126; suffers stroke 210; IV, 300n
Hamilton, William Gerard, V, *216*
Hammond, V, 49
Hammond, James, 'Love Elegies,' V, 452*
Hammond, James Lempriere, V, *55*
Hampden, John, I, 94, 134, MS concerning in Holland House papers IV, 121
Hampden, Renn Dickson, III, *206*
Hampden Controversy, III, 206n
Hampshire Independent, IV, 195n
Hampshire Record Office, III, xi
Hampson, Sir George Francis, II, *86*
Hampton Court, IV, 191, 375, V, 406, associations of 409; 412, TBM visits with Lansdowne and Lady Duff Gordon 414; Beauties of 409, 412
Handel, George Frederick, 'Hallelujah Chorus,' VI, 108; *Messiah*, at Worcester Music Festival V, 175, 179, 184
Hankey, Thomson, V, *158*
Hankinson, Robert, I, *39*
Hankinson, Robert, the younger, at Preston's school, I, *39*, 62, 65
Hannibal, at Cannae, I, 131
Hanningham, Mr, Jr, III, 6
Hanover, Crown of, VI, 100
Hanover, House of, TBM hopes to reach its accession in *History*, V, 483; VI, 75
Hanover, King of: *see* Duke of Cumberland
Hanoverian family, IV, 255
Hansard, Thomas Curson, II, *376*
Letter to: II, 376
Hansard, *Parliamentary Debates*, I, 211; reporter for finds TBM too rapid 272n; II, 69n, 271n
Haphorstrus, imaginary author, V, 167
Hardcastle, Mrs, *Life of John, Lord Campbell*, III, 381, IV, 363n, V, 96n, 99n, VI, 192
Hardinge, Sir Arthur, *Life of the Fourth Earl of Carnarvon*, V, 151n
Hardinge, Sir Henry, 1st Viscount, VI, 38
Hardwicke, Philip, V, *72*
Hardy, Francis, *Memoirs of the Political and Private Life of Charlemont*, V, 93
Hardy, John, I, *231*, 251, 285n, IV, 135, 228, 231
Hare, Julius Charles, III, 196, *367*, IV, 333n
Letter to: III, 367
Hare, Julius Charles, and Connop Thirlwall, translation of Niebuhr, *History of Rome*, III, 367n
Harewood, Henry Lascelles, 2nd Earl of, I, 232, II, *175*
Harford, Harriet, V, *273*, 285, death 455
Harford, John Scandrett, I, *175*, II, 16, gives TBM admission to Blaise Castle V, 265; 266, visits Barley Wood with TBM 273; gets admission to Park Street Institution for TBM 275; *Memoir of Richard Chapple Whalley*, 275n
Letter to: V, 275
Harford, Mrs John Scandrett (née Hart-Davis), I, 175n, V, 274, 275
Harford, William, V, *273*
Harland, John, V, *129*, edits autobiography of William Stout V, 129n; 153, 184
Letters to: V, 129, 130, 153, 184
Harleian Miscellany, V, 433
Harley, Robert: *see* Earl of Oxford
Harper and Brothers, IV, 380n, buy early proof sheets of *History* 382; on sales of *History* V, viii; spelling in their edition of *History* 36; 43n, commission Beard daguerreotype of TBM 56n; publish American edition of *History*, 3, 4, 467n
Letter to: VI, 271
Harper's Magazine, VI, 94
Harriet, the charming, VI, 149
Harrington, 4th Earl of, II, 152n, 310n
Harris, George Frederick, V, *361*
Harrison, Archdeacon Benjamin, IV, 203n, VI, 29n
Harrison, Mrs Benjamin (Isabella Thornton), letter to Hannah, I, 14n
Harrison, Thomas, V, *62*, 63
Harrow School, Governors of, letter to, VI, 241
Harrow School, Vaughan headmaster of, V, 26n; 137, George Trevelyan enters 188n; Walter Ellis enters 190n; 202, 287, George Trevelyan's success at 415n; 422, Walter Ellis doing badly at 438n; Hannah and Margaret visit 460; George Trevelyan's verses at speech day VI, 88n; Montagu Butler headmaster at 97n; speech day 99; Butler succeeds Vaughan 241n; 245
Harrow School Register, IV, 332n
Harrowby, Dudley Ryder, 2nd Earl of, I, 157, II, *31*, 136, 137, 260, III, 373, IV, 336
Harrowgate, V, 371
Hart, Jennifer, 'Sir Charles Trevelyan at the Treasury,' IV, 310n, 328n
Hart, Major, IV, 388

Harty, Sir Robert, II, *52*
Harvard University, 'Cambridge the Less,' IV, 268; VI, 46n
Harvey, Daniel Whittle, II, *160*
Harwood, Lady, I, 178
Harwood, Sir Busick, I, 178n
Hastings, TBM at IV, 365; 378
Hastings, Sir Charles, candidate in Leicester election, I, 211, 212
Hastings, Warren, 'imperious,' I, 70; II, 129, III, 149n, TBM's remarks on 361-2; portrait of in Government House 362; IV, 44, trial of 61; his character and administration 62; VI, 38
Hatchard, John, V, 469n
Hatchard's, London booksellers, large orders for *History*, V, 469
Hatfield, North Place, Trevelyan family at, V, 343, 344, 346, 348, TBM at 349; 351, 352
Hatfield House, IV, 370
Hatherton, Edward John Littleton, 1st Baron, II, *71*, 75, boasts of his wealth 79; 142, 242n, appointed Secretary for Ireland 258; Diary 268n; 274, Diary 296n; V, 185, 234n, 329n, 334n, VI, 45n, 251
Hatherton, Lady (Hyacinthe Mary), daughter of Lord Wellesley II, *71*; portrait by Lawrence 78; 'loveliest of women' 258, 259; compliments TBM's profile 280; V, 234n, 329n
Havelock, General Henry, VI, 119n, TBM asked to speak on in House of Lords 134n
Havre, IV, 146, 154, 155, 157
Havre de Grace, III, 34
Hawes, Sir Benjamin, IV, *224*, 338n, 368, assists Arthur Ellis V, 80; deputy secretary to War Department 205n; writes about Arthur Ellis 320n; 321
  LETTERS TO: IV, 224, 367, V, 80, 150, 204
Hawes, Benjamin Park, V, *8*
Hawkins, Edward, V, *477*, 477-8, likely to retire from Museum VI, 23; 'vexatious conduct of' 48n
Hawkins, John Abraham Francis, on Commission on Laws of India, V, 367n; *432*, 433
Hawkins, John Heywood, II, *31*, 89, II, 97
Hawkins, Sir John, *Life of Johnson*, II, 57
Hawkins, Vaughan, VI, 181n
Hawthorne, Nathaniel, *English Notebooks*, describes meeting TBM, VI, 47n
Hawtrey, E. C., IV, 333n, VI, *93*
Hay, Miss, V, 265
Hayden, Preston's school may move there, I, 44, 47
Haydn, Joseph, *Book of Dignities*, VI, 41n
Haydon, Benjamin Robert, II, 150n, commissioned to paint Reform Banquet *273*; on TBM 273n; adds TBM to Reform Banquet painting 280; vulgar idea of a man of genius V, 340; *Life* 340*
Hayley, William, I, *239*, IV, 68, *Life of Cowper*, I, 71n
Hayter, Sir George, III, *257*, paints TBM's portrait for House of Commons group 257; TBM suggests subjects for 258
Hayter, William Goodenough, V, *301*, 305, 468, TBM can't apply to him VI, 121-2
Hayward, Abraham, IV, *133*, letters to Napier 221n, 226n; on Impey and TBM 321n; and Plato's character V, 341; 458, VI, 97n
  Writings: ed., *Autobiography of Mrs Piozzi*, VI, 236n, 'Parisian Morals and Manners,' IV, 133*, 'Rio, La Petite Chouannerie,' IV, 41, 'Samuel Rogers,' VI, 48*
  LETTER TO: V, 257
Haywood, Francis, IV, *381*, sends his translation of Kant to TBM 381; V, 175n, 281n, 292, 313n
  LETTER TO: IV, 381
Haywood, Lucy, V, *175*, preparations for her marriage 281; 292n, 312n
Hazlitt, William, likes TBM's 'Southey' I, 271n; *Table-Talk*, III, 245*, 'Wilson's *Life and Times of Defoe*,' I, 271*
Hazlitt, William, the younger, sues Vizetelly V, 367n; VI, *136*, *Life of Louis XVII*, V, 367n
  LETTER TO: VI, 136
Hazlitt, William Carew, VI, *136*, *History of the Origin and Rise of the Republic of Venice*, sent to TBM VI, 136
Head, Francis, *Bubbles from the Brunnens of Nassau*, VI, 103n*
Head, Sir George, IV, *151*
Head, Rev. H. E., IV, *81*
Headley, 2nd Baron, V, *67*
Headley, Lady, V, 67
Heath, John Benjamin, V, 212n, VI, *45n*
Heath, Mrs John Benjamin (Sophia Bland), VI, *45*; sends Robert Bland's *Translations* to TBM 46
  LETTERS TO: VI, 45, 46
Heath House, near Wakefield, I, 231
Heaviside, James, TBM bound to vote for, VI, *35*; TBM asks canonry for 71; appointed canon of Norwich 71n

Heber, Bishop Reginald, III, 41, 69, 70, *Journal* 91n; 161, *Narrative of a Journey through the Upper Provinces of India*, II, 161*, 342*, III, 95n*
Heber, Richard, V *32*
Hébert, Jacques René, 'Almanach du Père Duchêsne,' its indecency, IV, 170
Hebrew Eclogues, TBM's idea of, I, 146
Hebrews, poetry of, I, 110
Hector, I, 89
Hegel, Georg W. F., VI, 162n
Heidelberg, V, 349n, TBM at 351, 354; VI, 87
Heinsius, Grand Pensionary, V, 113, letters from William III, 113n; 118, 186, 187
Heliodorus, III, 200*, *Aethiopica* 211
Heliogabalus, V, 278
Helm Crag, VI, 216
Helps, Sir Arthur, and Chair of Modern History, Cambridge VI, *257*; *The Spanish Conquest in America*, VI, 257*
Helvellyn, III, 81
Hemlow, Joyce, *The History of Fanny Burney*, III, 308
Henderson, Gilbert, II, *5*
Heneage, George Heneage Walker-, canvassing at Calne, II, *8*
Henley, Joseph Warner, VI, *213*
Hennell, Michael, *John Venn and the Clapham Sect*, I, 39n
Henniker, John Minet Henniker-Major, 3rd Baron, II, *159*
Henrietta Maria, Queen, II, 53, III, 258, IV, 255, 257, V, 115, 476n, and 1st Earl Holland 477
Henry I, King, IV, 256
Henry II, King, IV, 256
Henry III, King, IV, 256
Henry IV, King, IV, 256, VI, 61
Henry V, King, IV, 256
Henry VI, King, IV, 256
Henry VII, King, IV, 256
Henry VIII, King, I, 59, IV, 165, 257, and English bishops 392-3; V, 7, his commission to Bonner 12; a kind of Pope 18; insurrections against 88; 359, VI, 61
Henry, Prince of Wales, IV, 255, 257, 258n
Henry III, of France, IV, 149
Henry IV, of France, I, 42, 105, IV, 146
Henry V (son of Duc de Berri), IV, 148
Henry Christophe, King Henry I of Haiti, I, 54
Heraclitus, III, 247
Heraldry, I, 31
Heralds, College of, TBM's arms from, VI, 135
Herbert, George, VI, 67n, 68
Herbert, Sidney, afterwards 1st Baron Herbert of Lea, TBM's opinion of raised V, *435*; resigns from ministry 445n
Herculeaneum, III, 270
Hercules, labours of, II, 148
Herder, Johann Gottfried, V, 27
Hereditary Peerage, argument against, III 167-9: *see also* House of Lords
Hereford, V, 177, 181, 189, 196
Hereford, Bishopric of, III, 206n
Hereford Cathedral, TBM visits IV, 183
Herefordshire, V, 178, 194, William Williams votes in 241; 249, 251
Herefordshire Beacon, V, 193
Heritable Securities Bill, IV, 400, 402
Hermas, III, 279*
Herninius, III, 382
Herod, V, 359, VI, 182
Herodian, III, 237*, TBM asks Hannah to buy edition of V, 271; 274*
Herodotus, I, 53, 172*, 242n, 243*, TBM suggests that Ellis translate III, 63; 111*, 159*, 177*, 211, 382, George Trevelyan to read V, 421-2; 475*
Heron, Sir Robert, V, *159*, *Notes*, 2nd edn, V, 159*
Herries, John Charles, I, 228n, *232*, II, 11, 33, 60, 62, 155
Herschel, Sir John Frederick William, I, *317*, *Preliminary Discourse*, 317*; TBM declines to review 319; II, 58, his translations IV, 333; V, 150
Herschel, Sir William, I, 317n, III, 30
Hertford, Lord Mahon defeated at V, 253n
Hertford, 3rd Marquess of, and J. W. Croker, IV, 89; 118
Hertfordshire, I, 64
Hervey, Lord Frederick, I, 181
Hesiod, IV, 55-6, *Theogony*, III, 129*; *Works and Days* and sabbath V, 303*; 366*
Hettner, Hermann, VI, *26*, *Literaturgeschichte des Achtzehnten Jahrhunderts*, presents to TBM 26
LETTER TO: VI, 26
Hever Castle, VI, 50
Hewett, Dr Cornwallis, I, *170*
Heytesbury, 1st Baron, III, 119n, *148*, 154, 155, 164n
Heyworth, Lawrence, IV, *314*
Heyworth, Lawrencina, marries Richard Potter, IV, 314n
Hibbert, George, I, 245n
Hibbert, Nathaniel, I, 215n, *245*, admires Sydney Smith 247; IV, 383n, VI, 72n, 163n, 191
LETTERS TO: IV, 385, VI, 71

Hibbert, Mrs Nathaniel (Emily Smith), I, *215*, 245n, 'great favourite of mine' II, 193; IV, 383n, VI, 71, 72n
High Church, early instance of term, VI, 145
High Church Party, and Oxford decree of 1683, V, 333
High Churchmen, III, 358, V, 42, 88
High Clere Castle, VI, 166
Highwood Hill (Wilberforce's residence from 1825), I, 225
Higman, John Philips, V, *122*
Hilarion, St, would have been tempted by Miss Monk, V, 284
Hildyard, Robert, III, *275*
Hill, G. B., ed., *Johnsonian Miscellanies*, II, 112n, 260n, 350
Hill, General John, V, 356
Hill, Matthew Davenport, I, *188n*
Hill, Captain Richard, II, 309n
Hill, Rowland, VI, 73n
Hill, Rowland Hill, 1st Viscount, III, 328n, *331*
  LETTER TO: III, 331
Hillard, George S., IV, *365*
Hilman, Mr, III, 34n
Hinds, Miss, TBM's landlady at Malvern, V, 190
Hindu holidays, III, 134
Hinduism, Ram Mohan Roy's notion of, II, 47; III, 193
Hindus and English education, III, 193
Hindustanee, III, 198
Hippias, III, 141, VI, 83
Historians, modern inferior to classic, I, 92
Historical Manuscripts Commission, 8th Report, V, 114n
Historical Memoirs of the House of Bourbon, I, 325
Historical Society of Pennsylvania, V, 91n
History, dignity of, IV, 28
History of the State of New York: see O'Callaghan
History of the Times, I, 37n, IV, 373
Hoadley, Bishop, I, 216n
Hobbema, Meindert, painting at Littleton's, II, 78
Hobbes, Thomas, TBM declines as subject for *ER*, IV, 159; his translation of Thucydides, TBM sends copy to George Trevelyan V, 287*
Hobhouse, Charlotte, afterwards Lady Dorchester, V, *254*
Hobhouse, Sir John: *see* Lord Broughton
Hodder, Edward, *Life and Work of Shaftesbury*, IV, 299n
Hodgkin, John, V, 6n
Hodgson, David, I, *207*, II, 243
Hodson, George, I, *27*, 28, 36, 37
Hodson, Major V. C. P., *List of the Officers of the Bengal Army*, III, 225n
Hodson's Pale Ale, III, 38
Hogarth, William, 'The Lady's Last Stake,' VI, 236n
Hogg, Sir James Weir, IV, *107*; remarks on article misattributed to TBM 107n
Hogg, Thomas Jefferson, I, 281n, 'Niebuhr's History of Rome,' 280*, II, 119, IV, 56*
Hohenems, Count of, IV, 53n
Holden, H. A., V, 415n
Holinshed, Raphael, *Chronicles*, I, 262, VI, 153n
Holland, separation from Belgium, II, 155n, 202, 217; IV, 38, TBM visits 216ff; impressions of 219; Temple and Voltaire on 220; plans for tour in 346; TBM and Ellis tour 349n; States General V, 186; ignominious war with, 433
Holland, D. C. L., VI, 142n
Holland, Earldom of, V, 476
Holland, Elizabeth Vassall Fox, Lady, I, x, xv, II, *16*; introduced to TBM 16-17; on TBM 17n; 21, TBM discusses question of language with 22; portrait at Holland House 25; shows TBM rooms in Holland House 26-7; 28, invites TBM to dinner 58; compliments TBM 65; her treatment of Allen 66; on Talleyrand 68; 74, 75, an '*esprit fort*' yet a coward 76; her treatment of Allen 77; stories of her imperiousness 77-8; praises TBM's 'Mirabeau' 144; frightened by cholera 145; recommends James's *Henry Masterton* 146; 169, wants TBM to continue Mackintosh's history of Holland House 170; apologises for her dinner 180; tantrum 181; TBM forwards her Indian letters 191; wants TBM to make his quarters at Holland House 192; hypochondriac 194, 195; praises TBM's 'War of the Succession' 227; lectures TBM on indecorum of not using 'Miss' 242-3; 254, 276, courteous 282; recommends Lady Morgan's *Dramatic Scenes* 287; 317, angered by TBM's 'Walpole' 335, 336-7; teased for her bad humour 336; distressed by TBM's going to India 344; 347, obtains place for Hensleigh Wedgwood 350; makes scene with TBM III, 6, 7; 349n, wants TBM to write on her husband 372; 385, IV, 42, 46, 60, TBM dines with 63; 106, TBM presents his *Essays* to 124; her gratitude for article on Lord Holland

203; offended by Lord Malmesbury's *Diary* 227; TBM dines with 236; letter to her son 237n; death of 296n; Lord John Russell's epitaph for v, 154n; the style of her invitations vi, 48; TBM lectures on Reform Bill crisis 275-6

Letters to: ii, 190, iii, 19, 283, 286, 374, iv, 16, 67, 122, 124, 152, 211, 397, 397, vi, 275

Holland, Sir Henry, i, xvi, 215n, ii, *282*, praises *Lays* iv, 67; and Madame D'Arblay, 97; tour in U.S. 266; 268, TBM dines with 383; v, ix, sends correction about Penn 5; coming to Malvern 190; his travels 191; 210n, agrees that TBM's trouble is all bile 245; 428n, 449n, vi, 26, 163n, TBM writes on engagement of his son to Margaret 164; 207, his opinion of Margaret 235; 244n, calls on TBM 247

Writings: Recollections of Past Life, i, 295n

Letters to: iv, 66, 73, v, 5, vi, 163, 164

Holland, Henry Fox, 1st Baron, ii, 169, *317*, iii, 310, TBM consults his Diary iv, 213; 221

Holland, Henry Fox, 4th Baron, ii, *181*, his behaviour to Lady Theresa Lister 182; Rogers's remark on 182; 242, his new wife 337; TBM dislikes but admits his power of conversation 339; iv, 362, 369n, vi, x, 48, sends papers by Horace Walpole to TBM 52; 74

Letters to: iii, 263, vi, 52, 56

Holland, Henry Macaulay Trevelyan (Margaret Trevelyan's son), vi, *237*, 238, christened 254, 260

Holland, Henry Rich, 1st Earl of, ii, 169, v, *476*, and Anne of Austria 477

Holland, Henry Thurstan, afterwards 1st Viscount Knutsford, vi, *163*, his engagement to Margaret 163-4, 165; 174, writes TBM on his marriage to Margaret 178; children by first marriage 179; to be examined on *Sir Charles Grandison* 180; 181n, 185, 198n, 200, 204, 206, 212, 'quite one of us' 214; 222n, 232, 233, 234, 250n, 254, 260

Letter to: vi, 178

Holland, Mrs Henry Thurstan (Emily Hibbert, first wife), vi, 163n

Holland, Mrs Henry Thurstan (Margaret Trevelyan, second wife), afterwards Lady Knutsford, called 'Baba' (1835-1906), TBM's niece, i, xii, xx, xxviii, iii, ix, *158*, 161, 172, 173, 175, 179, 183, learning to talk 191; first birthday 192; described 198-9; 212, 219, unwell 222; 227, 230, beguiles TBM of 'many sad thoughts' 231; 261, delighted with her theology 266; 271, 277, song for 281; 285, 290, her strange divinity 295-6; 305, 321, at Brighton iv, 38; 43, 59, 68, dines with TBM 134; 140, 142, 147, 151, 157, 198, 207, her birthday 220; dines with TBM 234; amuses TBM 236; 272, 274, 275, 278, 279, 314, 335, 341, will always call her Baba 351; 353, spends the day with TBM 377; 399, v, 43n, Charles Macaulay delighted with 67; 68, 74, accompanies TBM on Scottish tour 111n; 127, copies Richmond's portrait of TBM 138; saves playbill from Woburn 144; 160, to have an allowance, an 'epoch' 185; 190, her account of Cropper wedding 199; 220, TBM takes to children's service at St Paul's 233; 244, 250, 259, 264, 266, visits TBM at Clifton 267; 268, 270, visits Barley Wood with TBM 274; 276, 286, 292, 295, attends anti-slavery meeting 298n; 307, 313, TBM to show her Paris 315; eager to see the Empress Eugénie 322; 328, 345, 352, 353, going to Brighton 363; 364, breakfasts with TBM 367; dines with TBM 370; safe from scarlet fever 380; out of quarantine soon 381; goes to Brighton 382; 383, TBM visits 386; 390, nursing George Trevelyan 391; 392, presented at court 398n; 425, 427n, 455, sketching 461; 467, vi, 37n, 40n, 43n, 45n, 58, 62, 67, 72n, 76, 78n, 90n, 97n, visits Manchester Exhibition with TBM 101n; writes from Frankfurt 102; 103, unwell 114; at Malvern for her health 117; TBM anxious about 119; well 121; 139n, quite recovered 143; attends Bernard's trial 149; 150n, engagement of 163, 164, 165; TBM's gifts to 165n; TBM gives dinner to at Brighton 174; her marriage 178; unhappy over father's Indian appointment 188; 198n, expecting 200; well 206; 208, an angel 211; TBM takes to Cambridge 212, 214; 226n, 227, Hannah goes to 234; TBM nervous about 235; birth of her son 237; 238, 239, at St Leonards 244; 247, her child christened 254

Writings: Life and Letters of Zachary Macaulay, i, xxv, 6, 13n, 18n, 25n, 39n, 63n, 66n, 104n, 106n, 115n, 192n, 281n, 293n, ii, 44n, 268n, 330n, iii, 156n, iv, 34n, 234n,

Holland, Mrs: *Writings—cont.*
'Recollections of Lord Macaulay' (MS), III, 341n, V, 319n
LETTERS TO: IV, 56, 297, 340, 350, 351, V, 55, 75, 124, 173, 177, 185, 187, 191, 193, 199, 201, 203, 282, 351, 357, VI, 48, 52, 58, 59, 105, 118, 135, 164, 174, 179, 203, 218, 218, 231, 254, 260

Holland, Henry Vassall Fox, 3rd Baron, I, XV, II, 13n, *21*, 22, his friendly manner 23; guides TBM over Holland House 25; story about acoustical trick in library 26; puts up bust of Napoleon 27; inscription for Rogers's seat 27; 28, 29, story about 'Three Consuls' 72; his manner described 76-7; 124n, 181, stories of court of Denmark 182-3; TBM on his character 194-5; lines by 241*; 253, entertaining 282; on Lady Morgan 283; 317, TBM dines with 336; 337, on Dissenters' claims 371; III, 7, 20n, death 342; memorabilia of given to TBM 349; excessively *Gallomane* 353; 371, IV, 46, his letter to Lord Kinnaird 62; 203, lends TBM Barillon's Despatches 313n; Russell's epitaph for criticised V, 154, 155
Writings: The Opinions of Lord Holland, III, 372n
LETTERS TO: III, 23, 320

Holland, Mary Augusta Fox, Lady, II, *337*, 339, inclined to be exacting IV, 313-14; V, 369n, sends invitation in style of her predecessor VI, 48
LETTER TO: VI, 97

Holland, Saba, Lady (Saba Smith, wife of Sir Henry), I, *215*, writes *Memoir* of Sydney Smith V, 15n; compliments TBM on *History* 482; VI, 163n, 204, *Memoir of the Reverend Sydney Smith*, IV, 327, presented to TBM V, 428-9*; VI, 34
LETTERS TO: IV, 72, V, 148, 428, 482, VI, 116

Holland, Sydney, Viscount Knutsford, *In Black and White*, VI, 164

Holland House, I, 279n, II, 16n, TBM to dine at 17; 19, TBM's first visit to 20-3; 24, breakfast at 25-8; TBM dines and sleeps at 66-8; 75, party at 76; TBM dines at 144; dinner described 168-9; history of 169-70; Holland House Papers 169n; 179, weekend at 180-3; 191, 192, weekend at 194-5; Spanish literature appreciated at 227; *dramatics personae* of dinner at 253-4; dinner described 282; 363, III, 322, 377, IV, 203, TBM dines there 313; 314, alterations at 370; V, 316, not the principal seat of Rich family 477; VI, ix, 14, 18, TBM dines at 52n

Holles, Denzil, V, *145*

Hollinshead, Bryan Blundell, II, *5*

Holmes, John, offers corrections for *History*, V, *60*
LETTER TO: V, 60

Holmes, William, Tory Whip, II, *6*, 143

Holroyd, J. B., III, 220n

Holroyd, M., ed., *Memorials of George Elwes Corrie*, V, 85n

Holt, Francis Ludlow, II, *5*

Holtrop, Johannes Willem, IV, *354*

Holy Alliance, damaging to anti-slavery movement, I, 179

Holyrood Park Bill, IV, 131

Home, John, *Douglas*, I, 81*

Home Office, III, 355, 356

Home Secretary: *see* Sir James Graham

Homer, I, 5*, 71, compared with Milton 110; 123, TBM reading at Llanrwst 162-3*; basis of a course in Greek 242-3; III, viii, 9, 111, 132, 153, 237*, 381, 382, IV, 39, 369, TBM changing his mind on authorship question V, 175; now sure that works are mosaic 179; 182*, sabbath in, 303; in Cowper's translation I, 36*, Pope's translation I, 5n, to be read with Selina 69; II, 27, 38
Writings: Iliad and *Odyssey*, III, 62*, *Iliad*, in Cowper's translation, I, 35*; 110*, translations of Pope, Cowper, Sotheby compared II, 38; Sotheby's translation 38*; III, 131, IV, 50*, 294*, Grote's critical remarks on 297; V, 135*, TBM weeps to read 178*; 179*, Walter Ellis reading 421; 422*, VI, 426, *Odyssey*, I, 17*, lines from at Holland House II, 27*; III, 131, 184*, 203, IV, 112*, 294*, V, 179*, Walter Ellis reading 421; 449*

Hong Kong, superintendent at: *see* Lord Napier

Hood: *see* Henry Flood

Hood, Admiral Sir Samuel, II, 338

Hood, Thomas, TBM subscribes for monument to, V, 289; his children 289n

Hoogley River, III, 86, 87, 117, 173, 193, 195, 226, VI, 54

Hook, Theodore, attacks Zachary Macaulay in *John Bull* I, 193n; in Athenaeum 295n; II, 61
Writings: Cousin William, V, 124*, *Gervase Skinner*, V, 124*, *Gurney*

Married, v, 124*, *Love and Pride*, III, 81*, *Maxwell*, II, 256*, *The Parson's Daughter*, II, 254*, 256*, 260

Hook, Dr Walter Farquhar, IV, *370*

Hooke, Nathaniel, *The Roman History from the Building of Rome*, I, 97n

Hoole, John, translator, *Orlando Furioso*, I, 65n

Hope, Lady Frances, v, 144n

Hope, Thomas, v, *284*

Hopkins, Edward, MS of his travels, VI, *15*

Hopkins, MS, TBM makes abridgment of, VI, 15

Hopkinson, Edmund, opposes TBM at Calne, I, 276n; 312n, canvassing at Calne II, 8n; 12

Horace, I, 17*, 21, 23*, 121, III, 9, 62*, 131, Bentley's edition 201*; quoted by Dr Symonds v, 270; VI, 98

Writings: Ars Poetica, I, 10*, III, 111*, *Carmen Seculare*, I, 93, *Epistles*, examination subject, I, 32; v, 270*, 420*, VI, 98*, *Epodes*, III, 143*, IV, 58*, *Odes*, I, 52*, 105*, 127*, 130*, III, 133*, IV, 58*, 112*, v, 268*, 349*, 453*, VI, 27*, 98*, Bentley's note on 245*, *Satires*, I, 88*, IV, 81*, v, 34*, George Trevelyan's imitation of VI, 87

Horatii and Curiatii, IV, 44

Horne, Richard Hengist, *A New Spirit of the Age*, biographical sketch of TBM, IV, 160n

Horne, Thomas Hartwell, IV, *378*

Horne, Sir William, II, 90, III, 75, IV, 305

Horner, Francis, I, 242n, TBM's memory of v, 186

Horner, Leonard, I, 224n, *242*

LETTER TO: I, 242

Hornsey, train accident at v, 353n

Horsley, J. C., IV, 198n

Horsley, Samuel, Bishop of St Asaph, II, *282*

Horsman, Edward, v, *171*, rancorous puppy 172; speech on Reform Bill VI, 202

Hoskins, H. L., *British Routes to India*, III, 184n

Hotham, Beaumont Hotham, 3rd Baron, his bill for excluding Master of the Rolls from Commons, v, *328*; 330n, mistake about in *Speeches* v, 372

Hotten, John Camden, *Macaulay, the Historian, Statesman, and Essayist*, I, 203n, 2nd edn, IV, 44n

Houghton, Richard Monckton Milnes, 1st Baron, I, xv, on Sydney Smith and TBM 216n; on link between Austins, TBM, and Lansdowne 263n; IV, 15n, leaves Tories and joins Whigs 239n; article on TBM 389n; v, 49n, 108n, 152n, and forgeries of Keats 222; 223n, in hopes of being a father 226; says it is 'scandalous' for TBM to enjoy life so 306; 328n, 402n, birth of daughter VI, 37; breakfast with described 47n; TBM disapproves of his selection of guests 144n; 152n, 'more than usually absurd' 198n, *Life, Letters and Literary Remains of John Keats*, v, 222n

LETTERS TO: IV, 8, 132, 165, 239, 398, 400, 402, 402, v, 92, 98, 114, 296, 334, 388, 402, 452, 457, 473, 478, VI, 23, 37, 40, 41, 43, 47, 144, 144, 154, 160, 198, 198, 223, 225

Houghton, Lady, v, 334n, VI, 37

Houghton, Walter, ed., *Wellesley Index to Victorian Periodicals*, I, 267n

Houghton Library, Harvard, III, 210n

House, Madeline, and Graham Storey, eds., *Letters of Charles Dickens*, II, 69n

House of Commons, 'most peculiar audience in the world' I, 317-18; scene at on second reading of Reform Bill II, 9-11; a 'terrible audience' 12; to describe it in detail for Hannah II, 75; assembly at on coronation of William IV 97; presents address to William IV 141-2; curious character of 174; drunken speeches in 232; atmosphere in III, 31n; 61, its noxious climate 118, 132; 168, 180, 182, censures O'Connel 259n; TBM takes seat in 291; 292, reverses itself IV, 195; TBM takes Charles Cropper to 206; in 1660, passage about in *History* v, 101n; bad hours and bad air 249, 257

House of Commons, *Journals*, VI, 131

House of Commons, Library, TBM describes, II, 73; scene in 134; 143, 160, 250, v, 297, VI, 131, 142n

House of Commons, new building for, v, 232; decorations 400n, VI, 152: *see also* Fine Arts Commissioners *and* Houses of Parliament

House of Commons, Smoking Room, TBM describes II, 80-1; 156, 259

House of Commons, Ventilator, I, 264, II, 66

House of Lords, nobody cares what is done there II, 251; TBM thinks the institution doomed 259; 'out of their senses' on Irish Church question 270; frightened 271, 272; 274, 275, 281,

House of Lords—*cont.*
collision with must come 285; III, 74, 118, 151, 'hastening the day of reckoning' 157; 'crisis is at hand' 167-9; TBM foresees its end 187-8; 'must go after Old Sarum and Gatton' 202; TBM must be careful about speaking in VI, 134; TBM takes his seat in 134n; TBM attends 140; gives up plan to speak in 156; TBM attends 201; sworn in 218n; may some day speak in 240
House of Lords, Committee of Privileges, VI, 102n, 106n, 149n, 151
House of Lords, *Journals*, IV, 313
House of Lords, Painted Chamber, described II, 259; IV, 45
Houses of Parliament, burning of, III, 138; 367n, Fine Arts Commission appointed for IV, 191; decorations for 198; 199, list of subjects for statues 246-7; decorations for Lords 247-8; subjects for stained glass 255-7, 258n; V, xi, Ward's pictures for 175n; library VI, 142
Howard, Charles, V, 427n, VI, 45n, 97n, 204, 204n
Howard, George, III, xi
Howard, Henrietta, Lady, II, *32*
Howard, Rev. Henry, II, 32n
Howard, James Kenneth, II, 170n
Howard, Leon, *Herman Melville*, IV, 296n
Howard, Philip Thomas, Cardinal, V, *91*
Howard, Thomas, 2nd Duke of Norfolk, IV, 247
Howard family, II, 254
Howard de Walden, Charles Augustus Ellis, 6th Baron, II, *175*
Howe, Lady, V, 427n
Howe, Lord, V, 427n
Howell, Thomas, ed., *State Trials*, V, 24n, 82n, 92, TBM presents to Edinburgh Philosophical Institution 463
Howell and James, firm, V, 185
Howick, Haydon's Reform Banquet painting at, II, 273n; V, 216
Howick, Lord: *see* 3rd Earl Grey
Howison, John, IV, 214, 215
LETTERS TO: IV, 185, 192
Howitt, Mary, impersonated, VI, 268n; *269*
Howitt, William, VI, 269
Howley, William, Archbishop of Canterbury, II, *98*, 290, 291
Howse, E. M., *Saints in Politics*, I, 25n, 41n, 193n, II, 242n
Howson, J. S., V, *199*
Hübner, Baron, subject of George Trevelyan's epigram, VI, 220n
Huddersfield, Cobden defeated at, VI, 86n
Huddleston, Father, V, 8n, 9, VI, 130
Hudson, [John] C., I, *62*
LETTERS TO: I, 62, 66, 70
Hudson, Derek, *Holland House in Kensington*, II, 27n, IV, 370n; *A Poet in Parliament, The Life of Winthrop Mackworth Praed*, I, 317n
Hudson, John, former servant of Zachary Macaulay, II, 275
Hugo, Victor, letter in *The Times*, V, 382-3
Huguenots, II, 266
Hull, IV, 154
Humber, III, 87
Humboldt, Baron Alexander von, notifies TBM of his nomination to Order of Merit, V, *298*; 301
Hume, David, I, 51, 92, 231n, his criticism of Gibbon, V, 274
Writings: History of England, its skepticism, I, 52-3*; 81*, advertised as introduction to TBM's V, 32; 302n
Hume, Joseph, I, *170*, 242n, II, 178, III, 74, 159, IV, 114, and republican monument at Edinburgh 211; 232, intends motion for recall of Ellenborough 243n, 252; 364, V, 222, pleased by TBM's speech 293; death of 449n; memorial verses by his son 449
Hume, Joseph Burnley, V, *449*, 'Joseph Hume: A Memorial,' 449*
Humphrey, Duke of Gloucester, IV, 246
Humphreys, Edward Rupert, VI, *38*, *Manual of British Government in India*, advertised as revised by TBM 38n; advertisement blocked 129; his fraudulent claim 175
LETTER TO: VI, 38
Humphry, William Gilson, IV, *323*
LETTER TO: IV, 323
Hungary, V, 191
Huns, VI, 96
Hunt, Henry ('Orator'), I, *85*, TBM predicts hanging for 86; speech of 86n; his procession through London 131-2; 133
Hunt, Leigh, I, xv, TBM subscribes for copy of his *Poetical Works*, II, *112*; TBM desires to serve him III, 366; speaks to Melbourne about 367; TBM pities 368; sends money to 368-9; could succeed as laureate 369, 371; pension doubtful 387; offended by Napier letter IV, 10-11; distressed for money 12; letter to Napier 12n; will try less colloquial manner 13; thanks TBM for advice 14; letter to

TBM 14n; 15, letter to Napier 15n; proposes Mme D'Arblay as subject 30, 61; soothing his self-love 62; and Mme D'Arblay review 64; criticises *Lays* and asks for money 70; TBM sends money 120; returns money 121; and loan from TBM 122; receives pension from Sir Percy Shelley 223; TBM will try to get pension for 309; sends repayment 325; and Royal Bounty 328; TBM speaks about to Russell 329; granted pension by Russell 337; TBM sends money to 338; benefit performances for 338n; letter to TBM 338n; break between him and TBM v, 37n; in Newgate 443

Writings: Lord Byron and Some of His Contemporaries, TBM thinks of noticing, II, 14; offends TBM, v, 37n, 'The Colman Family,' III, 366, 368, 370, 371-1, TBM likes 385, *Correspondence*, ed. Thornton Hunt, II, 112, IV, 337n, editor, *Dramatic Works of Wycherly, Congreve, Vanbrugh, and Farquhar*, III, 340, 342, 365, *Imagination and Fancy*, IV, 223*, 'Madame de Sévigné and Her Contemporaries,' IV, 62*, 64, 'Memoirs of the Courts of England,' IV, 64, 120, 'Pepys's *Memoirs and Correspondence*,' IV, 9*, 13, 'To the Queen,' III, 371

LETTERS TO: III, 365, 367, 368, 370, 387, IV, 10, 64, 120, 121, 122, 223, 309, 325, 328, 329, 337, 337, 338, V, 37

Hunter, John, robe maker, VI, 119

Huntingdon, 7th Earl of, TBM defends his judgment of, V, *82*

Huntington, William, I, *92*, V, 22, *The Bank of Faith*, I, 92n

Huntington Library, Macaulay family papers at, I, xv, xli

Hurd, Richard, ed., Addison's *Works*, V, 472n

Huskisson, William, I, *232*, 293, killed by locomotive 303, 304; III, 204

Hutchinson, John Hely-, V, *93*

Hutchinson, Lucy, and *Memoirs of the Life of Colonel Hutchinson*, V, 145-6

Hutchinson, Mr, claims against East India Company opposed, II, 247

Hyde, Anne, IV, 255, 257, 258n

Hyderabad, II, 348

Hyderabad, Nizam of, II, 147

Hyperbolus, III, 208

Hyperides, V, 95*

Idomeneus, IV, 39

Ignatius, III, 279*

Ihne, Wilhelm, *Researches into the History of the Roman Constitution*, V, 313*

Ilchester, Earl of, ed., *Elizabeth Lady Holland to Her Son*, II, 17n, 182n, IV, 202n, 237n, *The Home of the Hollands*, II, 170n

Ilfracombe, TBM at VI, 231n, 240

Illustrated London News, engraving of bust of TBM IV, 321n; report of TBM's speech 323n; photo of TBM VI, 33n

Impey, Sir Elijah, V, 181n

Impey, Elijah Barwell, *Memoirs of Sir Elijah Impey*, unreadable, IV, 321

Income Tax, defeat of I, 75, IV, 26n, VI, 234

Incorporated Society for the Conversion and Religious Instruction and Education of the Negro Slaves in the British West Indies (Conversion Society), criticised by Zachary Macaulay I, 251

Independents, V, 88

India, I, viii, TBM's years in xx; xxvii, 5, British crimes against 70-1; TBM reading its politics II, 129, 134; 144, cabinet committee on 196; strange public indifference to 272; problem of English servants in 340, 349; no more noble field for a statesman 354; expenses of voyage to 356; servant's wages in 358; slavery in III, 36; music 'deplorably bad' 47; precariousness of British rule 50; idolatry in 70; death a common sight 87; medical attention in 98; dialects in 122; Sanscrit College 123; Press Regulation Act, 1823, 124; commercial crash in 161; 'delicious' weather 161; prison discipline 165; heat in 172-3; eating and drinking in 173-4; climate 'destroys all the works of man' 175; act abolishing censorship 184-5; native press 185; idolatry in 193; TBM will leave 'nothing that I shall ever remember with regret' 204; weather violent but faction lukewarm 225; North-western Provinces 227, 229; unfavourable state of exchange in 235-6; press unfit to discuss Penal Code 251-2; legislature 252; English factions in 252; pays her own expenses IV, 29; remarks on government 184; no plan for altering 184; a place of exile to TBM 217; TBM preparing for debate on 243; first Sikh War 296; distances in 306; Secret Committee 307; history of 373; high salaries for officials in V, 97; more interest in than TBM expected 315-16; plan for new charter

India—*cont.*
discussed 325; Lord Grenville's speech on Indian affairs 337; Lord Canning appointed Governor General 470; 479, TBM thinks of speaking on VI, x; Bishops in 38; TBM corrects points about in Humphreys's book 38; 70, all will go right in 105; army in deserves all honour 134; thanks voted to 140; Government of India Act transfers Company's power to Crown 141n; Russell's resolutions on government of 146-7; mere residence in no qualification to govern 147; councils, arrangement for 148; TBM's classical reading in 167; colonisation of, TBM plans to speak on 156n; Baptist mission in 212; question of India disposed of 214; last request of condemned men in 252

India, Black Act, III, 176n, 185-6, petition against 186; 290

India, Catholic priests in, III, 301, 315-16

India, Charter: *see* East India Company, charter renewal

India, Christian missions in, I, ix, 25, 30, Charles Grant's cause 63n; not the government's business VI, 127

India, Commission on the Reform of Laws of India, Ellis appointed to V, 366n; commissioners gazetted 367; has struck a hitch 391-2; 401n, and TBM's Penal Code 424n; plans for Supreme Court 432; may produce something for Ellis VI, 16; its reports 30n

India, Committee of Public Instruction, Anglicists v. Orientalists, III, 102, 103n; 122n, TBM proposes new membership 125; TBM proposes to make its proceedings public 126; 126n, 134n, natives on 137-8; 138-9, oriental publications 139, 150; 144n, 148-50, remodelled 149; 170, 209n, Malkin proposed as president 227; IV, 311n

India, Committee on Prison Discipline, its Report III, 165n; 170

India, Education in, an Evengelical object I, 26n; Trevelyan active in III, 100; 102, survey of 120n; English schools open 149; flourishing 193; TBM will try to learn official plan for IV, 311

India, food, insipid III, 38; 96, 173-4, 197, fruits not worth 'a pottle of Covent Garden strawberries' IV, 217

India, Governor-General in Council, has entire Indian patronage, II, 355; III, 238, sends resolution of thanks to TBM 239

India, Indian Penal Code, III, 152, 193, 212, in press 217: *see also* TBM's Writings

India, Law Commission, III, 125n, 144n, 158, 165, 170, Penal Code 189; illness of Commissioners 195; Commission 'hors-de-combat' 197; 202, 209, Commissioners ill 212; 213, 252, its work to be reviewed V, 367n; its work attacked in Commons VI, 156n

India, Supreme Council, I, xvi, xx, institution of legislative member II, 299n; 345, 351, 353, III, 32n, 35, 60, 66, 70, 76, position of fourth member 118; 124n, 125n, 134n, 144, 145, 148, 164n, 166, 170, 185, 198, 218, 229, TBM succeeded on by Andrew Amos 233; 238-9, its composition 312; Russell's plans for VI, 146, 148

India Board: *see* Board of Control

India House: *see* East India House

India Office Library, III, 118n, 120n

India Register, III, 33n

Indian Civil Service, III, 186, most members content to pass their lives in India 203-4, 223; 252, V, xi, terms of TBM's report on 431n; plan for well-received 443; VI, 71, 180
- *Committee on:* V, 389, 406n, meet to consider TBM's report 409; 416, 424n, terms of its Report 431n
- *Examinations:* TBM defends principle of V, 336n; TBM's plan for 436; TBM protests change in qualifications 438; hitch straightened out 439, 440; VI, 30n, standards for 35n; 43, 51n

Indian Committee 1853, TBM a member V, 315n; 325n

Indian Legislative Council, recommends adoption of TBM's Penal Code V, 424n

Indian Mutiny, VI, xi, first news of 100; Trevelyan's excitement over 101; 'one terrible cry for revenge' 102; 104, news not bad 105, 106; 114, eager for news while on continental tour 114; news bad but event certain 119; day of fast proclaimed 122; good news about 125; TBM's disgust at sermon on 127; capture of Delhi 129; claims of sufferers 131

Ingestre, Lord: *see* 18th Earl of Shrewsbury

Ingham, Sir James Taylor, V, *390*

Ingilby, Sir William Amcotts-, II, *81*

Inglis, John, Lord Advocate, V, *267*, plan for Annuity Tax 310

Inglis, Col. John, commander at Lucknow, VI, *138*

Inglis, Mrs John (Julia Thesiger), VI, *138*

Inglis, Lady, II, *262*, IV, 59, TBM grateful for her gift of *Commons Journals* VI, 235-6

Inglis, Sir Robert, guardian of Thornton children I, 101n; *109*, TBM's verses on 109n; 146, 147, 293, admired Perceval II, 44; 234, 244, 255, 260n, TBM dines with 251-2; 284, TBM consults about India 338; 342, approves TBM's going to India 344; Carnatic Commissioner III, 41; 86, 280, 295, 358, IV, 48, TBM sends *Lays* to 81; 135, 338n, patron of George Richmond V, 56n; may have influence with Lord Ashley 118; presides at British Museum Trustees' meeting 137; 152n, 201, secretary for Mackintosh memorial fund 232; 298, TBM dines with 307n; 328n, retires from Parliament 378; portrait by Richmond 453; death 453; 454

Ingram, T. L., IV, *367*

Ingram, Major T. L., I, 321n

Inland Warehousing Bill, III, 321

Inman, Henry, portrait of TBM, IV, *225*; published in U.S. 225n

Innes, Cosmo, *Memoir of Thomas Thomson*, III, 373n

Innocents' Day, date of, VI, 182

Inns of Court, pre-reform procedures, I, 171n

Institut d'Afrique, Annales, IV, 50

Institute of France, TBM elected to, V, 309

Intrusion question: *see* Church of Scotland

Inverary, I, xxiv, V, 462, VI, 230n, TBM at 232; 259

Inverness, TBM at V, 111n; TBM asks for information about events of 1689 at 117

Inverness Advertiser, VI, 173

Inverness Courier, V, 117n, story about TBM 202n

Inverness-shire, has taste for Indian patronage II, 366; V, 180

Invisible Girl, exposed by Milner, IV, 76

Iona, monastery of, subject for examination in Latin verses I, 77

Ipswich, IV, 144

Ireland, George IV visits, I, 159; Clare election II, 30; typhus epidemic 48n; TBM pledges to support reform in 104; tithes in 154; unrest in 228; III, 46n, 271, agitation in will not subside of itself IV, 133; Wellington in debate on 133; TBM supports established Catholic Church 161; payment of Catholic priests in 161-2, 164; things look blacker than ever 167; debate on state of 175, 178; Lord Lieutenant of 202; TBM thinks of visiting 210; impending famine in 269n; on brink of servile war 273; paying priests in 281; Catholic Church in 284; famine in 310; state of 324; Trevelyan's indiscretions about 328n; reports on relief 329; Trevelyan on relief efforts 331; probably useless to send money to 332; stirred by revolution of 1848 363n; quiet in 1848 383; TBM visits V, 64-70; miserable condition of 67, 69; Pope's policy in 132; religious equality movement in 290n; debate on public debt for famine relief 324n; 417, TBM examines despatches from in Paris 419; rebellion of 1798 VI, 131

Ireland, National Library of, VI, 224n

Ireland, Queen's Colleges, favoured by Indian Civil Service examinations V, 438

Ireland, William Henry, *Vortigern*, V, 223

Ireton, Henry, II, 169

Irish, absurd and profligate as usual, V, 156

Irish Board of Works, IV, 328n, V, 67n

Irish Church Bill, II, 152, 230, crisis on 257, 261, 267, 269, 270; crisis easing 271; 274, 275, 278, government defeated on amendment to 279; passes Lords 280, 285; Bill of 1836, IV, 271

Irish Coercion Bill, II, 228n, 230, TBM supports 238; III, 23n, IV, 300n

Irish Croppies, IV, 52

Irish Evangelical Society, V, 436n

Irish Members, dare not vote for repeal of Corn Laws IV, 101; opposed to free trade 189

Irish Presbyterians, III, 302

Irish Question, cabinet discussion of, IV, 319n

Irish Registration Bill, IV, 184, given up 200

Irish Relief Bill, IV, 328n

Irish Statute Book, VI, 131

Ironside, Edward, III, *81*

Irving, Edward, I, 252n, II, *75*, 113, verses on 244; V, 194, VI, 60

Irving, Washington, at coronation of William IV II, 98

Irvingites: *see* Catholic Apostolic Church

Isabella, Queen, IV, 256

Isabella of Angouleme, Queen, IV, 256

Isla, José de, *Fray Gerundio*, V, 27

Isle of Wight, Preston plans to remove school there I, 46; Ryde, III, 256, IV, 269, TBM at 312; TBM at V, 121-6; Black Gang Chine 122; Undercliff 122; TBM prefers to Malvern 189; 199, 264, described by Mr Bruce 265

Isocrates, III, 199*, 237*, V, 345, 484*
Italian, ease of rhyming in, V, 17-18
Italians, character of, I, 84
Italy, III, 64, literature of 136; good roads in 270; TBM enjoyed 'intensely' 278; its decline since 1600 V, 26; abortive reformation in 88; 187, TBM may winter there 279; revolution in likely 359; TBM hopes to visit again 475; tour planned VI, 26, 27; may have to winter in 44; tour planned 47, 50; 56, TBM and Ellis tour 57ff; Harriet Beecher Stowe's fame in 63-4
'Its', origin of the form, VI, 145

Jack and the Bean Stalk III, 145, V, 194
Jacobites, V, 333; secret toasts in 1694 423
Jacquemont, Victor, *Letters from India*, III, 108, 309*
Jamaica, I, xxi, xxiv, Zachary Macaulay's behaviour in attacked 193n; III, 66
Jamaica Almanacks, attack Zachary Macaulay I, 193n
James, servant, III, 274
James I, King, I, xx, 290, 322, V, 13
James II, King, I, 159, 292n, IV, 255, 257, 354, question of his presence at torture 374; not in Scotland in July 1684 375, 376, 387; and Penn V, 5-6; and death of Charles II, 9; 24, his presence in Edinburgh 36; 76, his treatment of Keppoch 120; 333, and Newton's theories 338; 423, his statue by Gibbons 431; his administration in Scotland VI, 64; 130
James I, of Scotland, IV, 257
James II, of Scotland, IV, 257
James III, of Scotland, IV, 257
James IV, of Scotland, IV, 257
James V, of Scotland, IV, 257
James VI, of Scotland, IV, 257
James, G. P. R., *Henry Masterton*, recommended by Lady Holland II, 146; editor, James Vernon, *Letters Illustrative of the Reign of William III*, III, 326, IV, 18
James, William, II, *90*
Jansenists V, 19, 27
Jaubert, M., III, 353n
J. C—j, 'Report upon the Favourable Disposition of the French Public for the Reception of the Holy Scriptures,' IV, 234n
Jebb, John, ed., Burnet, *Lives, Characters, and an Address to Posterity*, III, 108n
Jefferson, Thomas, article on by Empson, I, 284; contrasted to Washington VI, 75; TBM's dissent from his principles 94; American prosperity not owing to him 171; his hatred of England 186n; and Callender 186, 187
Jeffrey, Charlotte: *see* Mrs William Empson
Jeffrey, Francis, Lord Jeffrey, destruction of TBM's letters to I, xvi; and TBM's first contribution to *ER* 203n; *222*, TBM's *Essays* dedicated to 222n; 224n, 229, wants to compare TBM and Mackintosh on history 231; 235, 236, TBM describes 237-40; compared to Sydney Smith 245; praise of Sydney Smith 247; resigns editorship of *ER* 253n; his pay scale for TBM's articles 256n; 261n, TBM will try to imitate his reviews of bad poets 267; TBM sees in London 273; 276, thinks TBM triumphs too much over Sadler 284; 299, appointed Lord Advocate 312n; 313, to be brought into Parliament 314; defeated at Cupar 316; 317, draws up Scottish Reform Bill 319; TBM anxious about his debut 319; 324, abused by Croker II, 6; TBM praises his speech on Reform Bill 7, 8; elected for Perth 15; TBM calls on 46; his talk compared to Sydney Smith's 56; on Professor Leslie 58; 107, 134, elected at Edinburgh 200n; 250, TBM misses in Edinburgh 306; 311, should write in Napier's favour to TBM 367; 371, III, 109, 164, 244, 245, should review Lockhart's *Scott*, 246; 247, threatened by Brougham 257; 261, 'wonderfully well' 283; 306, 337, 369, refuses to write article on Lord Holland 372; mending fast IV, 7; 18, more remarkable for heart than head 34; on Henry Macaulay 34n; TBM sends *Lays* to 68; TBM knows his articles by heart 119; TBM breakfasts with 120; illness of 126; 127, TBM sums up his achievement 167; poor account of 174; approves 'The Clapham Sect' 203; letter to Napier 264n; 322, on the condition of the *ER* editor 330; 377, on TBM's *History* 382; 'most celebrated critic of our age and country' V, 10; could write about Sydney Smith 16; TBM's last meeting with 41n; bedridden 74; death of 90; TBM hopes some public honour will be paid him 91; TBM's suggestion for a Life of 92-3; revised proofs of TBM's *History* 94; TBM refuses to attend meeting at Brougham's house about monument for 94; thought TBM's *History* 'too rhetorical' 94n; repeats TBM's compliment to Campbell 96n;

186, his *Life* by Cockburn 221; limits of TBM's acquaintance with 354-5
Writings: Contributions to the Edinburgh Review, IV, 119, 167*
Jeffrey, Mrs Francis, I, 238, 239, II, 46, dying V, 108
Jeffreys, George, 1st Baron, TBM defends his account of, V, 24-5; not without excuse in reprimanding Bristol magistrates V, 35
Jehosaphat, Valley of, VI, 253
Jekyll, Joseph, I, *318*
Jemmy Twitcher: *see* 4th Earl of Sandwich
Jennens, William, I, 45n
Jenner, Dr, II, 310
Jennings (Preston's gardener), I, 45, 46
Jephson, Henry, II, *28*, strange theology of 30; Philip calls a quack 39; James Stephen all but worships 50; 54
Jephthah, I, 146
Jephthah's Daughter, TBM's verses on, I, 146; II, 173
Jerdan, William, IV, 174n
Jeremie, Sir John, III, *46n*
Jermy, Mr, murdered by Rush, VI, 92n
Jerome, St, and lost books of Tacitus, V, 63
Jerome, Mr, V, 460
Jersey, Isle of, V, 16
Jerusalem, I, 23, fall of VI, 253
Jervis, Sir John, on Commission on Laws of India, V, 367n
Jesuits, I, 219, II, 21, suppression of IV, 77; V, 27, 88
Jesus Christ, would not have been safe in Edinburgh on a Sunday V, 291, 292
Jewish Disabilities Bill, defeat of I, 273n; dull debate on second reading II, 244; thrown out by Lords 289
Jewry, Frankfort, TBM visits, V, 351
Jews, and idea of future state, I, 146; and Mr Sibthorp 218; apply to TBM for help in campaign for relief 262; intend to reprint TBM's article 320; crowd of at Goldsmid's ball II, 36; 47, reprint TBM's speech of 17 April 244; restoration of VI, 253
Civil Disabilities of: I, 223n, 262, TBM speaks on 272; 311, TBM thinks will end soon 320; II, 232n, IV, 187, TBM declines to speak on VI, 147; TBM's vote on 147n; 157, question disposed of 214
Joan, Countess of Kent, IV, 256
Joanna of England, IV, 255
Joanna of Scotland, IV, 257
Jocelyn, Frances Elizabeth, Lady, Ellis's heroine, V, *415*
Jocelyn, Robert Jocelyn, Lord, death of, V, *415*
Joe Miller, Conybeare perpetrates one, V, 362
Johannisberg, Schloss, V, 351n
John, St, III, 53, 61, VI, 127
John, St, the baptist, VI, 223
John, King, IV, 256
John of Gaunt, IV, 246, 384
John Bull, sued for libel by Zachary Macaulay, I, 193n, 195, suit fails 198, 220; 221, 256n, 278n, 283, 295n, II, 20n, found guilty of libelling a dead woman V, 363
John Murray Ltd, III, xi
Johnson, Edgar, *Sir Walter Scott*, II, 58n, 148n, 224n
Johnson, Esther: *see* Stella
Johnson, Samuel, I, xxix, 83, on the weather 84; 120, TBM orders his works as prize for Latin declamation 151; his rule of revision 261; II, 24, his harsh comment on Hannah More 57-8; 260*, 309, 350, III, 159, 245, 258, 281n, TBM compared to 291n; 308, on Lord Stafford IV, 73n; on a shoulder of mutton 137; TBM's predecessor in Royal Academy post V, 97; portrait of as infant by Reynolds VI, 83
Writings: contribution to *Life of Pearce*, VI, 185, *Dictionary*, authority for 'balderdash,' V, 10, Preface to *Dictionary*, I, 87*, 107*, Prospectus of *Dictionary*, II, 289, Letter to Chesterfield, II, 289, Lines added to Goldsmith's 'Traveller,' I, 57*, *Lives of the Poets*, IV, 132, Life of Akenside, II, 321*, Life of Lyttelton, IV, 79*, Life of Pope, IV, 394*
Johnson, Samuel ('Julian'), V, *146*
Johnston, Andrew, II, 200n
Johnstone, Sir Alexander, II, *146*
Johnstone, Mrs Christian Isobel, *Elizabeth de Bruce*, II, 311*
Johnstone, James, V, 76
Jones and Loyd, bankers, IV, 30
Jones, Col. Sir Harry David, V, *67*
Jones, Inigo, I, 157n, IV, 152, V, 350
Jones, Leslie Grove, III, 33
Jones, Sir William, I, *80*, VI, 288
Jones, William Lloyd, IV, 293n
Jonge, Mr De, of Dutch Archives, IV, 354
Jonson, Ben, I, 81*, 87, II, 5, III, 123, TBM presents Gifford's edition to Edinburgh Philosophical Institution V, 463

Jordan, Mrs, mistress of William IV, II, 16n, 339n
Joseph, compared to Trevelyan, IV, 310
Journal des Débats, IV, 147
Journal of the Asiatic Society, III, 149n
Journal of the Friends' Historical Society, V, 143
Jowett, Benjamin, on Indian Civil Service Committee, V, 389; TBM's early acquaintance with *424*; TBM calls on at Twickenham 424n; recommends Frederick Temple to run Indian Civil Service examination 431; VI, 46n
Joy, Henry Hall, III, *154*
Judas, II, 11
Judge Advocate, TBM offered office of III, 264; not attractive 267; 271, 287
Judgson, William George, Senior Dean of Trinity, I, *112*, 147
'Judicious Poet' (TBM), I, xi, glad that he gives satisfaction II, 155; V, 225, verses at Richmond worthy of 465
Verses by: II, 41, 133, 138, 141, 147, 148, 151, 152, 217, 240, 241, 242, 243, 245, 246, 252, 256, 257, 261, 292, 293, V, 178, VI, 49
Julius Capitolinus, V, 274*
Junius, III, 244*, V, 8, the case for Francis V, 215-16; VI, 7
Jupiter, III, 172
Jupiter Latiaris, feast of, IV, 357, 358
Jura, V, 354
Juvenal, I, 191, V, 171, *Satires*, I, 264*, III, 160, IV, 159*, 166*, V, 167*, VI, 28*, 98*

Kabul, occupied by British, III, 306
Kansas, University, III, xi
Kansas – Nebraska Bill, V, 400n
Kant, Immanuel, *Critick of Pure Reason*, translated Haywood, IV, 381*; 382, VI, 162n
Kay, John, V, *450*
Kaye, J. W., *Life of Lord Metcalfe*, III, 32n
Kaye, John, Bishop of Lincoln, IV, *128*
Kean, Dr, III, 23n
Kean, Dr Archibald, III, *120*
Kean, Mrs Archibald, III, 120
Keane, Sir John, TBM at dinner for, II, *338*; sails for India 342
Keate, George, *An Account of the Pelew Islands*, I, 90n
Keats, John, II, 112n, forgeries of V, 222
Kedgeree, III, 86
Keith, James, pays fee for TBM's portrait, V, 110
Kellett, E. E., on TBM's knowledge of Bible II, 22n; 'The Press,' V, 430n; *As I Remember*, VI, 76n
Kelly, Sir Fitzroy, VI, *102*, 103
Kemble, Charles, thrashes Westmacott, II, 106n; IV, 361n
Kemble, Fanny, II, 106n, *137*
Kemble, John Mitchell, IV, 287n, *361*, candidate for Regius Professorship, Cambridge 361n; TBM recommends him to Prince Albert 373; recommends him to Russell for chair of modern history V, 61-2; supports for post of Principal Librarian, British Museum VI, 20n; 29n, examiner of plays 35n
Writings: ed., *Codex Dilpomaticus Aevi Saxonici*, IV, 361n; *The Saxons in England*, V, 61-2*
LETTER TO: IV, 361
Kemble, John Philip, II, *309*
Kemble, William, III, *188*
Kemble, Mr, letter to, IV, 299
Kemble, Mrs, calls on TBM in Edinburgh, VI, 233
Ken, Bishop Thomas, V, 13, VI, 87n
Kendal, I, 286
Kenmare, 1st Baron, V, *67*
Kennedy, Benjamin, his discipline of his family, VI, *230*; 231
Kennedy, Charles Rann, TBM rejoices at his failure, VI, *228*; 230n, 231
Kennedy, Grace, *Dunallan: or Know What You Judge*, III, 9
Kennedy, John Pendleton, TBM replies to query from VI, *17*; calls on TBM 17n; 'A Legend of Maryland,' 17n
LETTER TO: VI, 17
Kennedy, Thomas Francis, II, *327*
'Kenneth Macaulay,' TBM's term for the unreal world, VI, 156
Kennett, White, *Compleat History of England*, V, 279
Kenney, James, literary chat with, II, *313*; *Sweethearts and Wives*, 313, 314n
Kenrick, William, III, *308*; his attack on Johnson 308n
Kent, Ellis wandering among the corrupt corporations of, II, 347; IV, 109, 149
Kent, the Damsel of: *see* Joan, Countess of Kent
Kent, Victoria, Mary Louisa, Duchess of, II, *252*; TBM dines with 258
Kent, Duke of, IV, 258n
Kent, John, V, *151*, VI, 137, 166
LETTERS TO: V, 151, 151, 332, VI, 137, 139, 145

Kent, Mrs, TBM's new cook, VI, 165n, compared to Elizabeth 170
Kent, Thomas, V, 333n
Keppel, Sonia, *The Sovereign Lady,* III, 286, IV, 152, VI, 275
Keppoch, Colin Macdonald of, V, 117, 120-1
Ker, Charles Henry Bellenden, II, *105*
Kerne, meaning of, VI, 11
Kerr, James, *Review of Public Instruction in the Bengal Presidency,* VI, 300
Kerrison, Edward, V, 308n
Kerrison, General Sir Edward, V, 308n
Kerrison, Mrs, V, 308n
Kerry, William, Earl of, I, *264*, TBM's high opinion of 265; II, 8n, electioneering at Calne 13; 107, at TBM's re-election 130n, 131; marriage III, 120; death 208-9; V, 78, 232
Khitmatgars, III, 174
Khyber Pass, IV, 37
Killarney, V, 64n, 66, 66n, worth the discomforts of travelling 67; described 68-9; 233
Killiecrankie, IV, 16, 392, V, xi, 29, date of battle 126; 208
Kindersley, Sir Richard Torin, I, *199*
King, Frances Elisabeth, *Female Scripture Characters,* III, 7
King, Joshua, I, *116*, succeeds Stainforth as tutor to TBM 116n, 117-18; Senior Wrangler 117; too busy for more pupils 122; tutoring TBM 126; 135, 136n, TBM about to begin new plan of study with 137; gives bond undertaking to put TBM in first class 137; 152
King, Lady (Lady Hester Fortescue), II, *145*
King, Peter, 7th Baron, proposes TBM for Brooks's, II, 80n; *144*, 145, death of 251
King, Tom, II, *309*
King's Bench, Court of, I, xix, Zachary Macaulay's suit in 193n, 198n; passage between Brougham and Lansdowne in robing room 266; where TBM practices 272; Mr Dunn's behaviour before Lord Tenterden 285; Gurney a leading counsel in 287n; III, 63, VI, 192n
King's Lynn, I, 39
King's Speech, debate on, II, 49
Kinglake, A. W., *Eothen,* VI, 103n
Kingsdown, Thomas Pemberton-Leigh, 1st Baron, VI, 10n, *207*
Kingsley, Charles, appointed to Chair of Modern History, Cambridge, VI, 257n
Kingston, V, 403
Kinnaird, Charles, 8th Baron, II, *77*
Kinnaird: *see* Mrs Thomas Drummond
Kistna, III, 84
Kitson Clark, Dr G., I, xxxiv
Kitto, John, *History of Palestine,* V, 34n
Klopstock, Friedrich Gottlieb, *Der Messias,* I, 61*; V, 27
Kloss, courier in 1854, V, 420n
Knaresborough, I, 208n, 229n, 250n
Knatchbull, Sir Edward, and the hanging of his brother, IV, 195
Knatchbull, John, hanged in Australia, IV, 195n
Knight, Arthur, letter to, V, 31
Knight, Charles, I, *188*, *Passages of a Working Life,* 188n; his defects as editor 202; on steam travel 257n; anecdote of Brougham 314n; V, 179n, 181
  LETTER TO: I, 189
Knight, Henry Gally, II, *134*, TBM dines with 139
Knight, John Prescott, V, *31*
Knight-Bruce, Sir James, V, 89n
Knighton, Sir William, II, *60*; his 'absurd' biography III, 297
Knighton, Lady, *Memoirs of W. Knighton Bart.,* III, 297n
Knight's Quarterly Magazine, I, xix, 58n, TBM writing for 186; Zachary Macaulay's opinion of 187n; its history and character 187-9; TBM forced to withdraw from 189; resumes writing for 189n; TBM's judgment of 202; 320n, 374n, TBM looks at after 30 years VI, 161
Kniperdolling, Bernhardt, V, 333
Knole, TBM at, V, 171n, 172
Knowles, Sheridan, *The Hunchback,* II, 137
Knox, Alexander, V, *454*
Knox, John, II, 266, III, 225, V, 88
Knutsford, Margaret, Lady: *see* Margaret Trevelyan Holland
Knutsford, Viscount: *see* Henry Thurstan Holland
Kock, Paul De, IV, 145*, 153*, *Soeur Anne,* IV, 140*
Koenen, Hendrik Jacob, V, *229*, *Voorlezingen over de Geschiedenis des Nederlandschen Handels,* presents to TBM VI, 80
  LETTERS TO: V, 229, VI, 80
Kohinoor, diamond displayed at Great Exhibition, V, 195
Konigsee, Trevelyans visit, V, 275
Kubla Khan, I, 84
Künzel, Johann Heinrich, V, *200*, *Leben des Landgrafen Georg von Hessen-Darmstadt,* sent to TBM, VI, 242, *Leben und Reden Sir Robert Peel's,* V, 201
  LETTERS TO: V, 200, VI, 243

La Fayette, Marquis de, I, 286n; TBM presents letters of introduction to *304*; TBM attends his soirée 305-6; 311
La Fontaine, Jean de, *Tales*, V, 181
La Motte Fouqué, Baron de, *Sintram*, 'trash,' V, 194; 195
Labouchere, Henry, afterwards Baron Taunton, II, *170*, 179, 182, TBM dines with at Somerset House 183; 242, approves TBM's decision to go to India 350; 355, 359, takes TBM to Bowood in his britchska 357, 359; III, 7, 302n, promises to support Scottish Universities Bill IV, 261; 271, 274, 276, to be Irish Secretary 277; agrees with TBM about George Grey 278; V, 41n, 168n, hurt by Russell's conduct, 307; VI, 45n, 103n, 204, 204n
LETTER TO: II, 365
Labouchere, John, V, *220*
Lacaita, Sir James, V, 308n
Lacedaemon, I, 88
Lacedaemonians, I, 276
Lactantius, *Divinae Institutiones*, IV, 357*
Lafitte, Jacques, I *303*
Laidler, III, 39
Laing, David, IV, *384*, assists TBM to settle a point of history 387; V, 36, mistake about date of Killiecrankie 126
LETTERS TO: IV, 383, 387
Lake District, TBM visits, VI, 230
Lamb, Charles, II, 314, III, 249n, IV, 10
Writings: 'A Quaker's Meeting,' II, 252*, 'The Old Actors,' II, 308n, 'On the Artificial Comedy of the Last Century,' III, 348*
Lamb, George, II, *43*, favours prosecutions for blasphemy 44; 78, 79, 80, 168, II, 172, 312
Lamb, Mrs George (Caroline St Jules), II, *168*, 169
Lamb, John, IV, *361*
Lambert, Daniel, III, 57
Lambert, John, V, *359*
Lampridius, V, 268*, 274*, 278*
Lancashire, TBM asks Ellis for political feeling in II, 5; IV, 399, thriving peasantry in V, 78; 232
Lancaster, where TBM joined Northern Circuit, I, 208n; 225, disagrees with TBM 228; 247, 248, IV, 372, County Sessions Hall, I, 252n
Lancaster Assizes, I, 208n, 213, 213n, 217, Wakefield trial 218, 222n, 227-9, extraordinary length of 229n; TBM passes up 233n; 243n, 252, 253, 266, does not attend 277
Lancaster Gazette, II, 11n, 229n
Lancet, IV, 35n, V, 14n
Landen, TBM plans to visit V, 209
Landor, Walter Savage, his poems ascribed to imaginary authors, V, 167; *Pericles and Aspasia*, V, 167n
Landseer, Sir Edwin, V, 166n, 328n
Lane, Jane, Ward's painting of, VI, 152
Lane, Thomas, Steward of Lincoln's Inn, I, 171, *The Student's Guide Through Lincoln's Inn*, 172n
Lane, Thomas Moore, III, *44*
Lang, Andrew, *Life and Letters of John Gibson Lockhart*, IV, 93n
Langley, Mr, publishes defense of TBM's *History*, VI, 173n
LETTER TO: VI, 173
Langton, Bennett, II, 59
Langton, Cardinal Stephen, IV, 246
Lansdowne, Henry Petty, 1st Marquess: *see* Lord Shelburne
Lansdowne, John Henry Petty, 2nd Marquess of, I, *265*
Lansdowne, Henry Petty-Fitzmaurice, 3rd Marquess of, I, xx, 181, *224*, TBM's *Speeches* dedicated to 224n; 232, 242n, offers TBM seat for Calne 263n; associated with Zachary Macaulay's work 263n; 264, 265, expects to put his son in seat for Calne 265n; gives TBM letters of introduction for Paris 286n; 289, 300, II, 8n, his interest at Calne 12-13; refuses TBM's resignation 15n; 16, 62, 66, TBM describes dinner with 71-2; stories about Boswell 71-2; proposes TBM for Brookes's 80n; TBM criticises his timidity on Reform 100; 124n, 155, 161, his villa on Richmond Hill 170; on Irish Church crisis 270; explains Stanley's conduct on West India Bill 281; at Wilberforce's funeral 290; 291, invites TBM to Richmond 292; invites TBM to Bowood before leaving for India 350; TBM explains his reasons for accepting Indian appointment 353-5; TBM acknowledges his indebtedness to 355; 359, III, 85, 171, 220, 271, 281, 288, visits at Bowood 341; wants information on Eastern question 352; 358, 369, IV, 101, and question of Catholic clergy 163; 191n, 195, 204, sensitive about his father's character 221; breakfast for Everett 263; 271, 272, 273, 275, 307n, TBM visits at Bowood 353; TBM recommends Coleridge's son to 379; TBM visits at Bowood V, 79; 98, death of his wife 163, 163n; difficulty

with inscription for monument to Sir William Petty 170; expected at Malvern 182; TBM and Ellis meet at Gloucester 185; 186, older and weaker 189; leaves Malvern 190; 191, Reynolds portrait of Mrs Sheridan in his collection 201; bust of 234; behaviour during formation of coalition ministry 303; 306n, asked to accept dedication by Vizetelly 339; 370, TBM's obligations to 372; 381, 391, TBM wonders at his relation to Lady Gordon 414n; 425, key to grounds of Richmond house 458; TBM dines with 463; invites TBM to Bowood 481; TBM asks to support Owen's appointment VI, 21-2; 46n, 47n, proposes to put up statue of distinguished Trinity graduate 67n; on TBM's argument for Bentley 68; 69, portrait of infant Johnson by Reynolds in his collection 83; 97n, 103n, 150n, 155, pleased by reception of his gift to Trinity 180; TBM sends Lives of Pocock, Pearce, Newton, and Skelton to 185; 190, 195n, 198n, 207, 217, TBM owes more to than to any man living 232; very ill 232

LETTERS TO: I, 311, II, 353, III, 22, 118, 184, 208, 266, IV, 379, V, 163, 370, 481, 483, VI, 21, 185

Lansdowne, 4th Marquess: *see* Lord Shelburne

Lansdowne, Lady, I, 264, 265, II, 170, her birthday rout 230; 359, III, 23, 120, 209

Lansdowne House: *see* London

Laodicea, Church of, IV, 136

Laplanders, VI, 258

Larcom, Captain Thomas, visits the Boyne with TBM, V, 66n; *70*, V, 229n, VI, 131

LETTER TO: V, 84

Lardner, Dionysius, I, 298n, *311*, 317, 319, 324, II, 8, 35, anxious to bring out TBM's History of France 107; 108, his treatment of Mackintosh 353

Larpent, Sir George, II, *355*, 356, 360, makes arrangements for TBM's voyage 361; his honourable conduct 362; 365, III, 6

Lascaris, Constantin, I, 90

Lascelles, William Saunders Sebright, I, *232n*

Latham, Robert Gordon, TBM recommends for Cambridge professorship VI, *240*; TBM's charity to 241n; TBM presents his claims to Palmerston 257-9; receives pension 259n

Latimer, Hugh, V, *123*

Laud, Archbishop William, V, 13, and 'Wicked' Bible 471

Lauder, Sir Thomas Dick, IV, *174*, 215

LETTER TO: IV, 174

Laughton, J. K., *Memoirs of the Life and Correspondence of Henry Reeve*, V, 334n, VI, 218

Laughton Priory, II, 260

Laundress, TBM's, her dying son, II, 331-2

Laurence, French, I, *318*

Laurie, W. F. B., V, *114*, submits MS of book on India to TBM 114; *Some Sketches of Distinguished Anglo-Indians* 114; 2nd Series, VI, 299

LETTER TO: V, 114

Lauriston (Andrew Rutherford's residence), V, 263

Lausanne, V, 339, 343, 349n, 352, 354

Lauzun, Antonine, Comte de, TBM examines his despatches, V, 419

Law, C. E., IV, 346n

Law, Mr, V, 380

Law Journal, I, 193n, 198n

Law List, II, 5n, III, 154n

Law Magazine, I, 218n

Law Reform, TBM supports, II, 104, 163

Lawrence, Frances, in Selina Macaulay's will, V, 128n

Lawrence, Sir John, afterwards 1st Baron, VI, *217*

Lawrence, Sir Thomas, portrait of Fox, II, 25; 53, sketch of Boswell 57; portrait of Duchess of Richmond 66; portrait of Mrs Littleton 78; 155n, portrait of Brougham 223; V, 453

Lawson, Marmaduke, I, *135*

Le Couteur, Sir John, Diaries, II, 11n; on Marian Ellis IV, 259n

Le Marchant, Sir Denis, IV, *335*, Diary, II, 263n, 279n, 283n, *Memoir of Althorp*, II, 139n; IV, 278n, 'The Reform Ministry, and the Reformed Parliament,' VI, 302

LETTER TO: IV, 399

Le Sage, Alain René, *Gil Blas*, I, 65*, III, 68*, TBM reads annually IV, 223

Leach, Sir John, Zachary Macaulay's suit against Thorpe heard by I, 149n; 198n

Leader, Nicholas Philpot, II, *171*

League, organ of the Anti-Corn Law League, IV, 193

Leake, Colonel, V, 157n

Leamington, Zachary, Selina, Fanny, and Hannah at II, 17n; 28n, 30n, TBM asks Hannah to write a description of 45; 50, 56, family leave 68n; 247, III, 106

Lebrun, Charles François, Duc de Plaisance, II, *72*

LeClerc, Jean, VI, *243*

Lee, Dr John, III, *323*, his case 338
  LETTERS TO: IV, 122, 249, V, 341

Lee, Samuel, I, *138*

Leeds, TBM M.P. for, I, viii, xx; 208n, 212, 213, 217, 229n, TBM at 230; 234, proposed as candidate for II, 92n; to be brought in free of expense 94; enthusiastic for TBM 102; formally invited to stand 103; hopes to visit 104; Cobbett lectures in 114n; TBM speaks at Reform Dinner 123; 129, 131, electioneering at 132-3; 134, 135, chances not good 180; wishes to visit 183; endorsed by Political Union, canvassing 188; speeches 188n; 190, 191, results of canvass 193; TBM 'safe' 196; 201, 202, 203, TBM at for election 205-12; Marshall's mills 206; Music Hall, speeches 206n; nominated 209n; fighting 209; poll demanded 210; results at 213; 214, TBM forced to pay election costs 223, 225; Hanover Square (George Rawson's residence), 235; petitions from on corporation reform 236; on abolition 237n; on Sunday observance 235; TBM's conduct on slavery question approved at 283, 285; 302, must visit 312; 317, 328, 329, 332, Hobhouse possible candidate for 357-8; Baines succeeds TBM 361; III, 38, IV, 187, statistics in 17th century 370, 371; TBM cannot speak at V, 116; address on opening of Town Hall VI, 167; Ellis at 207; 243, Ellis at 261; TBM at 278

Leeds, Electors of, TBM compliments, II, 198-200
  LETTERS TO: II, 198, 211, 212, 359, III, 18

Leeds, Queen Street Independent Chapel, II, 371n

Leeds Association for Fit Representatives to Parliament, II, 92, 103, 109n

Leeds Borough Sessions, I, 241n, 243n, 246, 250

Leeds City Libraries, VI, 167n

Leeds Committee for Promoting the Ten Hours Bill, II, 117n

Leeds General Infirmary, II, 238n

Leeds Intelligencer, I, 243n, II, 114, 133n, prints forged letter as TBM's 162n; attacks Macaulay family as place-holders 202n; false story about TBM and anti-slavery question 221

Leeds Mechanics' Institute, opening of, II, 332; TBM speaks at 333; IV, 5, V, 116n

Leeds Mercury, I, 202n, 285n, 324, and Baines family II, 103n; 162n, publishes election pamphlet 188n; reports TBM's speeches 188n, 207, 209; extraordinary election number 211; 291n, 'best and most widely circulated provincial paper in England' 361; 371n, III, 10n, 11, IV, 122n

Leeds Patriot, bankrupt, II, 369n

Leeds Political Union, II, 115, sends resolution of thanks to TBM 120; TBM's replies to questions 162-7; 175n, 177, endorses TBM 186; 214

Leeds Political Union, Secretary: *see* Joseph Lees

Leeds Public Dispensary, II, 238n

Leeds Quarter Sessions, I, 208n

Lees, Joseph, II, *115*, 207
  LETTERS TO: II, 115, 120, 162, 175

Leeves, William, I, *13*

Lefevre: *see* John Shaw-Lefevre

Lefroy, Thomas Langlois, II, *173*

Leggatt, Mr, V, 450

Leghorn, III, 260, 261, 274, V, 359

Leghs, III, 222

Leicester, I, xxi, TBM at for election 211; excitement at 212; election petition defeated in Commons 219; II, 89, 124, 186, 240, III, 57n, elections V, 233; Bell Inn I, 211, 212, Y.M.C.A. VI, 155n

Leicestershire, II, 266, III, 58, 87, V, 83

Leigh Court, V, 282n, 283n, TBM visits V, 284

Leighton, Archbishop Robert, III, *112*, V, 426

Leighton, Sir Thomas, 'Les Lois, coustumes et usages de l'isle de Guernezcy,' IV, 355

Leipzig, III, 236, V, viii, 53

Leleges, III, 63

Lely, Sir Peter, V, 85

Lemon, Sir Charles, II, *157*

Lenclos, Ninon de, III, 216

Lenox, Charlotte Ramsay, *The Female Quixote*, II, 253

Lenthall, Francis Kyffin, V, *100*
  LETTERS TO: V, 100, VI, 15

Lenthall, Sir John, TBM alters reference to in *History*, V, *101n*

Lentulus, Cicero's letter to I, 97

Léo, Dr Frederick, calls on TBM, 'old charlatan,' IV, *234*; 236

Leo X, Pope, V, 26

Leopardi, Giacomo, Gladstone's article on, V, 108

Leopold II: *see* Grand Duke of Tuscany

Leslie, Charles Robert, IV, *297*
Leslie, Eliza, IV, *297*
Leslie, Sir John, TBM meets and dislikes, II, *58*; V, 93
Leslie-Melville, John Thornton, VI, *163*
LETTER TO: VI, 163
Lessing, Gotthold Ephraim, III, 236, V, 27, *Laocoön*, III, 245, V, 175*
Lethbridge, Thomas Prowse, V, *32n*
Lettres Françoises, V, 130
Leven and Melville Papers, ed., W. H. Leslie Melville, IV, 23, 127
Levi, Miss, at Goldsmid's ball, II, 39
Levy, S. Leon, *Nassau W. Senior*, IV, 265n
Lewes, George Henry, IV, *240*, letter to Bulwer-Lytton 240n; 'Was Dancing an Element of the Greek Chorus?' 240n
LETTER TO: IV, 240
Lewin, Sir Gregory, II, *168*, III, 63, 154, his judicial performances 169; *Lewin's Crown Cases*, II, 168n, *A Summary of the Law of Settlement*, III, 152
Lewis, Sir George Cornewall, IV, *111*, 134, marries Lady Theresa Lister 282n; 399n, V, 100, 190, 290n, TBM recommends for editorship of *ER* 300; heavy expenses in election defeats 300; 303, accepts editorship of *ER* 304; 311n, his two defeats in 1852 315; member of senate, University of London 317n; 318, succeeded by Reeve on *ER* 334n; asks TBM to review Cockburn's *Jeffrey* 354; 362, praises Trevelyan - Northcote Report on public offices 369; at Bowood 369; TBM can't ask favours from 388; succeeds as 2nd Baronet 443n; TBM gives opinion on points relating to British Museum 477-8; Chancellor of the Exchequer VI, 9; TBM writes to in support of Owen 20-1; 21, agrees about Owen 22; 23, TBM urges him to allow gilding of British Museum reading room 42; 103n, congratulates TBM on peerage 113; 207
Writings: Essay on the Origin and Formation of the Romance Languages, IV, 111*, editor, *Babrii Fabulae Aesopae*, VI, 242*, *Inquiry into the Credibility of the Early Roman History*, TBM agrees to read MS of, V, 444
LETTERS TO: V, 153, 219, 293, 317, 354, 443, 477, VI, 20, 42, 111, 113, 242
Lewis, Lady Theresa (Theresa Villiers, widow of T. H. Lister, married 2nd Sir G. C. Lewis), II, *138*, 'pretty, witty,' henpecks her husband 153; a pet of her family 157; TBM calls on 161; affair with Henry Fox 182; 242, TBM would put off the King in favour of her invitation 289; 'most accomplished, intelligent, and graceful of women' 292; 320n, marriage to Lewis IV, 282n; forms of her name 399n; asks TBM about Lord Capel V, 62n; about Waller's plot 146; 153, 290n, humiliated by her husband's accepting editorship of *ER* 315; at Bowood speaks well of Margaret Trevelyan 369; TBM reassures her about his health 369; 444
LETTERS TO: II, 287, IV, 282, 399, 399, V, 41, 62, 139, 146, 172, 219, 336, 369
Lewis, William Thomas, II, *309*
Lewis, Wilmarth, ed., *Horace Walpole's Correspondence*, II, 315n
Lexington, Lord, V, 112n
Leyden, IV, 220
L'Hermitage, his letters to States General, V, 186
Libel Law, bill to amend, III, 75; IV, 136n
Licensing Act 1662, V, 474
Lichfield, Bishop of, III, 342
Lichfield, 1st Earl of, III, *296*
LETTERS TO: III, 296, 318
Lichfield, TBM at I, 27n, V, 43n, VI, 143, 143n; Cathedral, II, 186
Liddell, Dean, V, 141n
Lieber, Franz, *Reminiscences of Niebuhr*, III, 178
Liège, IV, 8, VI, 104
Lieven, Dorothea Christophorovna, Princesse de, II, *98*, her fears about Great Exhibition V, 161n
'Light to the Blind, A,' in Fingall MS, VI, 224
Lilburne, Robert, V, *145*
Lilford, 2nd Baron, III, 23
Lilford, Thomas Powys, 3rd Baron, II, 169n, *282*
Lilford, Lady (Lady Mary Fox), II, *169*, 282
Lille, V, 347
'Lillibullero,' VI, 11*
Limerick, V, 64n, 66n, 69, 208, clerk at writes TBM about Indian Civil Service 440
Limerick, 1st Earl of, II, 18n
Limonade, Julien Prévost, Comte de, I, 54
Lin, Commissioner, III, 318
Lincoln, II, 266, IV, 139, TBM at 218n; 233, 267, TBM at 334; Cathedral, II, 186, IV, 334, V, 218
Lincoln, Lord: *see* 5th Duke of Newcastle

Lincolnshire, IV, 104, V, 43, 351
Lincoln's Inn, I, 152, TBM admitted to 171; TBM made Bencher of V, vii, 89; TBM's arms in chapel window 89n; Brougham's behaviour at ceremony for Campbell 98-9; Grand Day at 111; TBM dines with Benchers 161; 443, Preachership of VI, 140n
Lindsay, Lady Charlotte, II, *248*
Lindsay, Sir David, II, 141*
Lindsay, Col. John, II, 248n
Lingard, John, V, *53*, critical remark on TBM 89n; TBM succeeds in Institute of France 309; *History of England*, V, 53n, new volume does not affect TBM's *History* 88-9*
Linthwaite, Yorkshire, III, 273
Linwood, Lyndhurst, Hampshire (Mrs Gore's residence), V, 180n
Lipke, Wilhelm, threatens to murder the Bunsens, V, 386n; 'Lettre sur la Notion de la Monnaie,' 386, 'Notion de la Monnaie,' 386
Lisle, Alice, Ward's painting of, VI, 152
List, I., VI, *35*
LETTER TO: VI, 35
Lister, Miss, V, 144n
Lister, Thomas Henry, II, *138*, nothing in society 153; dinner with described 156-7; 292, TBM thinks he would succeed in history 320; letter to Napier III, 216n; death of IV, 37
Writings: Arlington, a failure, II, 153, *Granby*, II, 138, 277, *Herbert Lacy*, II, 138, *Life and Administration of Edward, first Earl of Clarendon*, II, 320, 'Mr Sheridan Knowles's *Wife of Mantua*,' II, 277
Lister, Mrs Thomas Henry: *see* Lady Theresa Lewis
Liston, John, II, *314*
Literary Gazette, I, 324, defends TBM against Dixon V, 158; 179, Byron forgeries 222n; defense of TBM in VI, 173n
Lithuania, IV, 144
'Little Dicky,' identity of, IV, 132
Little Malvern, V, 190, William Wilberforce at Benedictine house there 196
Little Shelford, Cambridgeshire, TBM at school there, I, 14
Littledale, Sir Joseph, VI, *192*
Littleton, Emily, afterwards Lady Newark, II, *242*
Littleton, George, dinner with described II, 78-80
Liverpool, I, 196n, 212, 217, TBM to see Henry at 227; 229, 234, 248, II, 31, 122n, TBM asks Hannah and Margaret for description of 135; 146, Hannah and Margaret return to 149; 152, 170, 180, 181, 183, 184, 186, 187, election committee 231, 233; 240, merchants of 243; 253, strike at 260; 266, freemen of 281; 283, 293, TBM to arrive at by rail 303; TBM at 305; 335, 343, post office at negligent 359; III, 12, 15n, 91, 255, 266, 273, 313, IV, 154, 155, 156, 189, parliamentary seats at 336; 338n, V, 31, Margaret Trevelyan at 55n; Walker Art Gallery 175n; elections at 238, 242; Ellis at VI, 102, 200, *see also* Dingle Bank
Liverpool, 2nd Earl of, III, 207
Liverpool and Manchester Railway, James Cropper a promoter II, 124; Margaret Macaulay's account of early trip on 124n; 136, Edward Cropper a director 184n; III, 45n
Liverpool County Court, Ramshay's behaviour in, V, 205n
Liverpool Journal, V, 205n
Liverpool Society for Promoting the Abolition of Slavery: *see* Anti-Slavery Society
Livingston, Edward, Louisiana Code, III, 210, 238
Livy, I, 53, III, 142*, 159, 160*, *History of Rome* 211*, 237*, IV, 44, 55, 56, V, 447n, 453, VI, 246, 248
Lizars, John, IV, *359n*, *A System of Anatomical Plates of the Human Body* 359n
Lizars, William Home, IV, *359*
LETTER TO: IV, 359
Llanrwst, Denbighshire, TBM with summer reading party there I, 156ff; described 157-8; expenses at 162, 164; account of fair in 166; town gives farewell party to undergraduates 166n; III, 39, 67
Lloyd, Bishop William, and biblical prophecies, VI, *253*
Lloyd's Register, III, 229n
Loch, John, II, *328*, Brougham's influence with 371; III, 10, IV, 298
Loch Fyne, herrings from, VI, 259, 260
Loch Katrine, II, 262, 266, VI, 232, visits always spoiled by rain 233
Loch Lomond, II, 266
Locke, John, I, 172*, 191, 312n, TBM 'once a disciple of' IV, 381; V, 224, urn dedicated to him at Barley Wood 273n; his attack on innate ideas 313

Lockhart, John Gibson, and TBM's review of Croker, II, *108*; review of Sharp III, 135n; TBM praises his translations IV, 93; V, 31, *Life of Scott*, II, 238n, TBM declines to review III, 245

Lockwood, Frederick, II, *142*

Lodge, John, II, 196n

Loire, described IV, 147-8, 155; not to be compared to Rhine V, 351

London: *see separate entries* for Athenaeum, British Institution, British Museum, Clapham, The Club, East India House, Holland House, Houses of Parliament, Lincoln's Inn, National Gallery, National Portrait Gallery; *for TBM's London residences see under* Macaulay

TBM's praise of I, 63-4; riot in 85; compared to Edinburgh 234; compared to French cities 290; and Paris 294, 296-7; need not fear cholera II, 48; riots of 1780 248; excitement in at coronation III, 246-7; TBM doubts he will continue to live in 253; seat for held by Lord John Russell IV, 277; not good for TBM's health V, 182; darker than TBM ever saw it 309; TBM wants to be out of yet near 475; postal districts created VI, 73

Streets, Districts, and Buildings: Admiralty, Sir James Graham's official residence II, 90; TBM dines at 350; Albany: *see under* TBM's residences; Albert Hall II, 156n; Albion Tavern I, 294, II, 91, provides Reform dinner 101; TBM to dine at 326; dinner with East India Company 337, 338; III, 11; 18 Aldermanbury Street (offices of Anti- Slavery Society), II, 175; Almack's, I, 319n, TBM's pun on II, 284; III, 76; Apsley House, VI, 228n; Argyll Lodge, TBM at VI, 105n; 204; Austin Friars', II, 360; Banqueting House, VI, 61; Basinghall Street, Bankrupt Commissioners meet at I, 249; Battersea, IV, 390n; Bedford Hotel, TBM dines there III, 285n; 15 Bedford Place (Thomas Flower Ellis's residence), I, 263n, II, 345, III, 238, V, 460, 463, VI, 82; Bedford Square (Sir Robert Inglis's residence), IV, 81; Belgrave Square (Lord Essex's residence), II, 215; VI, 59 (*see also* Chesham Place); Belgravia, being developed, II, 301n; V, 418, VI, 50, 255; Berkeley Square, I, 300, III, 71 (*see also* Lansdowne House); 44 Bernard Street (Macaulay family residence), II, 17n, 131, III, 27; 26 Birchin Lane (Zachary Macaulay's office), I, 85, TBM walks to and back V, 159, 232; Birchin Lane, TBM's bank, VI, 171, 199; Bishopsgate Street (London Tavern and City of London Tavern), II, 91n, 252; Blackfriar's Bridge, II, 82; Blackwall, ministerial white-bait dinner at, II, 295-6; TBM presides at white-bait dinner 296n; V, 109n; Blackwall, Lovegrove's Hotel, II, 296n; Bond Street, II, 222; Boodle's, II, 61n; Bow Street, III, 244n; British Institution: *see separate entry*; British Museum: *see separate entry*; Brook Street (Partridge's studio), V, 29; Brunswick Square (James Parker's residence), II, 18, 31, 40, 181; Bruton Street (Greville's rooms in Lord Granville's house), V, 295; I Bryanstone Square (Goldsmid's residence), II, 34; Buckingham Palace, II, 168, TBM dines at V, 391n; TBM at VI, 207, 208; Burlington Arcade, I, 291, 294, 297, II, 280; Burlington Gardens, V, 133; Burlington Hotel, TBM at IV, 325; Burlington Street, I, 20; 19 Cadogan Place, TBM sees the dead Wilberforce at (*see also* TBM's residences) II, 286; Campden Hill, 'El Retiro' (Chalon's residence), VI, 19n; Cannon Row (offices of the Board of Control), II, 122n, III, 184, IV, 316; Carlton House, I, 71; Cavendish Square (Duke of Chandos's residence), V, 104n; where Hope's pictures hung, V, 284; Charing Cross, II, 10, 310, III, 159, IV, 279; Chesham Place (Lord John Russell's residence), IV, 274, 278, 364; 50 Chester Square (Henry Thurstan Holland's residence), VI, 247, 259; Chester Terrace, Regent's Park (James Parker's residence), V, 54; Chiswick House, TBM dines at VI, 159; City of London Tavern, II, 72, 91, III, 11; Clarendon Hotel, III, 382, IV, 331, TBM gives dinner at V, 148, VI, 141; 3 Clarges Street (Zachary Macaulay's residence: *see also* TBM's residences), III, 213n; Cockspur

London: *Streets, Districts, etc.—cont.* St, v, 280; Connaught Terrace, III, 90; Cork Street, II, 97; Cornhill, I, 6n; Covent Garden, I, 291, III, 180; Covent Garden Piazza, I, 294; Covent Garden Theatre, elephant dances there I, 240; II, 106, 171n, 283, IV, 129, 338n; Cranbourne Alley, VI, 61; Crockford's, I, 294; Cross Keys, Wood Street, II, 152, 159, 187; Crystal Palace, v, 157 (*see also* Great Exhibition); Curzon Street, III, 24, 71; Devonshire House, v, 110n, 163n; Downing Street (Lord Grey's official residence), II, 64, Lady Charlotte Lindsay's recollections of 248; 325, III, 159, 188, Russell gives party at v, 37n; delegation of British Museum Trustees to 299; 17 Downing Street (Thomas Babington's town house), I, 49; Draper's Gardens, I, 6n; Drury Lane Theatre, IV, 132, v, 223n; Duke Street Chapel, St James's, I, 139n; East India Docks, II, 362, III, 11; Egyptian Hall, I, 238; Euston Hotel, TBM at v, 172n; Euston Square Station, v, 176; Exeter Hall, I, 197n, IV, 162, 320, Grand Duke would be torn in pieces at v, 359; VI, 204; Farringdon-without, I, 179; The Finish, Covent Garden, I, 294; Finsbury, TBM invited to stand for v, 238; Fishmongers' Hall, II, 326; Fleet Ditch, v, 188; Fleet Prison, II, 300; Rules of the Fleet, III, 159; Fleet Street, v, 32; Freemasons' Hall, I, 197n, TBM speaks at 202n; 219, II, 251; Friar Street, Doctors' Commons, VI, 224n; Fulham (Bulwer's residence), IV, 60; General Post Office, I, 294; George Street (Charles Grant's residence), II, 272; No. 16 George Street (Zachary Macaulay's office), I, 113; 26 Golden Square (George Babington's residence), I, 170n, II, 17n, 40, TBM calls at 78; 192, III, 8, 296; Gough Court, v, 350; Gracechurch Street, II, 252, No. 55 (studios of Maull and Polyblank), VI, 33; Gray's Inn, South Square (offices of the SDUK), I, 323 (*see also* TBM's residences); Great George Street (National Portrait Gallery), VI, 78 (*see also* TBM's residences); Great Ormond Street: *see* TBM's residences; Green Park, Rogers's house looks out on, II, 54; Greenwich, white-bait dinners at, II, 91, 296n; IV, 263, VI, 155, 269; Greenwich Hospital, I, 294, v, 409; Greenwich, Trafalgar Tavern, a favourite place IV, 340; dinner party at, 365; v, ix, TBM entertains party at 46n; TBM gives Northern Circuit dinner at 58; anecdote of TBM there 202n; 203; Grillion's Club, II, 179n; Grillion's Hotel, Albemarle Street, weekly feast at II, 179, 183; 260, 265, IV, 385; 8 Grosvenor Crescent (Trevelyan residence), v, 449n, VI, 39n, 146n, 234, Margaret's child born at 237; Grosvenor Place, Lord Milton's residence in, II, 79; Littleton's residence, II, 78, his servants refuse to live in so 'unheard of part of the world' 79; 41 Grosvenor Place (Mahon's residence), v, 322, 405; Grosvenor Square, I, 240, 300, 301, III, 37; Guildhall, I, 6n, Reform dinner at II, 146, 150, 154; v, 146, 176n, VI, 211; Gwydir House, Fine Arts Commissioners meet at, IV, 255; Hammersmith, Elwell's school, I, 159n; Hampstead, I, 115; 16 Hanover Square (TBM's dentist's office), v, 204n; Hill Street (George Richard Philips's residence), II, 42; 97, 34 Hill Street (John Marshall's town house), II, 17n, 18; Holborn, bookshop in, VI, 185; Holywell Street, v, 182; Horse Guards, II, 52, 213, 248, III, 315, 370; Hyde Park, III, 90, v, 285, VI, 244; Hyde Park Corner, VI, 12, 18; Inner Temple, v, 70n; Harcourt Buildings (Empson's Chambers), II, 82; Islington, Peacock Inn, II, 191; Kensal Green cemetery, monument to Thomas Hood, v, 289n; Kensington, II, 160, 169, 185, Col. Fox's residence 339; 367, VI, ix, 74; Kensington Dispensary, TBM contributes to, VI, 209; Kensington Gardens, III, 90, VI, 67; Kensington Gore, III, 91; Kensington House, v, 282, 283; Kensington, Hyde Park Gate (James Stephen's house), II, 154n; Kensington Palace, II, 169, 252, William III's preference for v, 113; The

Key, Chandos Street, IV, 89; King's Bench Prison, II, 300; King's College, Bookseller, V, 271; Kingston House, a palace, VI, 228; Knightsbridge (Lister's residence), II, 156, 161, 292; VI, 255; Knightsbridge, Gore House (Wilberforce's residence), II, 156n, Knightsbridge, Kent House (Sir George Cornewall Lewis's residence), V, 172; Knightsbridge Barracks, I, 163n; Knightsbridge Road, III, 90; Lambeth, Archbishop's Palace, II, 73; Lamb's Conduit Street, II, 249, 280; Lansdowne House, Berkeley Square, TBM at II, 16; 24, 59, 71, TBM dines at 71-2; 79, 363, V, 52, 232n, 334n; Leadenhall Street, III, 184; Leicester Square, II, 59; Lincoln's Inn Fields, III, 278, IV, 388n; Little Holland House, II, 169n; Lock Hospital, II, 154; Lock Hospital Chapel, II, 79n; Lombard Street, I, 6n; London Bridge, opening of, II, 82; 326, V, 76, VI, 107; London Bridge Station, V, 342; London Library, VI, 35n; Maddox Street, robemaker's shop VI, 119; Mansfield Street (Spring-Rice's residence), II, 152, 215; Mansion House, I, 113n, V, 106, VI, 211; Margaret Street, Cavendish Square (Reynolds's studio), II, 223; Marlborough House, II, 263, V, 282, 283; Marlborough Street Police Station, V, 183, 198; Mayfair, III, 90; Mivart's Hotel (afterwards Claridge's), V, 141n; The Monument, I, 294; Moorfields, I, 6n, IV, 176; Mount Street (Sir George Philips's residence), II, 43; Mount Street (William Brougham's residence), II, 183; Newgate, V, 443; Northumberland House, I, 240; Notting Hill, robberies at, VI, 74n; Nottingham Place (Trevelyan's residence), III, 285; Old Palace Yard, II, 71; Paddington, V, 277, 309; Palace Yard, III, 159, V, 76; Pall Mall, VI, ix, 91; Park Lane, III, 90, 110; Paternoster Row, I, 294, 298, V, 5, 123, VI, 268; Piccadilly, V, 441; Pimlico, II, 168, VI, 174; Portman Square, I, 240, 295, II, 79; Privy Garden, III, 237; Providence Chapel, I, 92n; Putney, Cameron's daughter married at church, VI, 190; Quality Court, Chancery Lane, II, 82n; Queen Street (Marriott's residence), II, 15n; Queen Street, shop where TBM got 'Spiritual Railway Guide,' V, 398; Queen's Bazaar, Oxford Street, II, 308; Ranelagh Gardens, II, 315; Rapp's Hotel, IV, 310; Reform Club, III, 367-8, banquet for Napier at, V, 390n; Regent Street, I, 291, V, 441; Regent's Park, I, 240, III, 91; Regent's Park Zoo, V, 280; Richmond Hill, I, 297; Rotunda, Blackfriar's Road (meeting place of Carlile and Taylor), II, 44; Royal Exchange, I, 85n; Royal Institution, V, 150n; Royal London Homoeopathic Hospital, I, 192n; Royal Opera House Arcade, I, 297; Russell Square, no dancing allowed on upper floors of new houses there, I, 240; 300, II, 247, TBM would prefer modest house there to splendid one in Calcutta 344; III, 97; St Anne's Church, Kensington, TBM attends, V, 396n; St George's, Bloomsbury, Margaret Macaulay's marriage at, II, 210n; V, 336; St George's Hospital, II, 26n, 48n, 225; St Giles's, II, 257; St James's, rats in, I, 153; III, 268, delegation from parish calls on TBM V, 136; St James's, Chapel Royal, VI, 138n; St James's Palace, TBM describes, II, 52-3; 142, IV, 366, court established there by Queen Anne V, 112; St James's Park, II, 49, 64, 90, 248, 263; St James's Place (Samuel Rogers's residence), II, 19n; St James's Square, I, 301; St James's Square, Duke of Chandos's residence, V, 104n; VI, 61; St James's Street, III, 289, IV, 176; St John's Chapel, Bedford Row, attended by Macaulay family, I, 141n; Sibthorp at, 218n; Wilson minister of, II, 33n; Baptist Noel assistant at 33n; 247; St Luke's Hospital, II, 173; St Mark's College, Chelsea, I, 178n, VI, 44, Derwent Coleridge, Principal, 282n St Martin's Hall, VI, 158n; St Martin's Lane, II, 26; St Mary Axe, II, 36; St Paul's, I, 87, 294, 297, IV, 139, Deanery V, 23; 149, children's service at V, 233; St

London: *Streets, Districts, etc.—cont.* Paul's School, VI, 215; Savoy Chapel, IV, 309n; Serjeant's Inn, Campbell admitted to, V, 98n; Sloane Street, II, 80; Smithfield, II, 246, III, 341; Soho Bazaar, I, 291, V, 188; Somerset House, I, 241, 295, II, 82, Labouchere's official residence 183; V, 176, 271, meeting of senate, University of London 308; South Street (Lady Holland's town house), III, 283, 374, IV, 60, 67, 122, 124; Southwark Bridge, II, 82; Spa Fields, I, 85n; Spitalfields, II, 346, 348; Spring Gardens, II, 82; Stafford House, 'most beautiful palace in England,' V, 298; State Paper Office, V, xi, 399; Stationers' Hall, site of Reform dinner, II, 101; Stevens's Hotel, Bond Street, TBM at V, 122; Strand, II, 365, III, 277; Temple, V, 45, 76, 84, 176, 417, 420; Temple, Elm Court, Ellis's chambers, V, 284, 343, 409, 412; Temple Gardens, II, 82; Thames Street, I, 297; Thatched House, III, 283, Club meets at V, 157, 226, VI, 85; Threadneedle Street, III, 14; Throgmorton Street, III, 14; Tower Hamlets, TBM asked to speak at II, 346; 347, 348; Tower Hill, IV, 52, 388; Tower of London, III, 46n, V, 409, 415; Tyburnia, V, 418, VI, 50; University Club, Ellis a member, V, 403, 409, VI, 51, 64, 75, 120, 124, 125, 167, 226, 260; Vauxhall, I, 294; Victoria Station, VI, 174n; Wapping, IV, 153; Waterloo Bridge, I, 294, II, 82; 20 Westbourne Terrace (Trevelyan residence from 1849), V, 56, 68, 76, 121, 125, 127, 138, dinner at 158; 160, 201, 203, 207, 246, 257, TBM spends night at 261n; 266, 318, 321, 337, 366, Christmas dinner at 373; 377, 381, VI, 34; Westminster, I, 179, II, 161, 349, III, 180, 361, electors of V, 266; Westminster Abbey, I, 109, 294, II, 65, coronation of William IV at described 97-9; 263, 284, Wilberforce's burial in 290, 292; III, 138, 208, IV, 30, bust of Zachary Macaulay 112n; Henry VII's Chapel 140; 196, Jerusalem Chamber 202; 232, not a place for monuments to Dissenters 426; TBM buried in VI, xii; 6, 69, Henry VII's Chapel 107; Westminster, Cloisters (Milman's residence) IV, 400n, V, 23; Westminster Hall, rats in, I, 153; coronation of George IV in, 159n; II, 52, 65, 97, 142, Solomon's Porch 243; III, 138, 188, 208, IV, 198, 206, 259, V, 76, reception of General Monk at, 176; 333, VI, 91, TBM attends Shrewsbury trial at 102n; 249; White House, Soho Square, IV, 89; Whitechapel, II, 346, 348; Whitehall, Army Pay Office (Lord John Russell's official residence), II, 152; Whitehall, jammed for judgment in Gorham case V, 100; untouched by Revolution 431; Whitehall Palace, III, 237n, William III on V, 113; White's, II, 288, 289; Willis's Rooms, TBM plans to call meeting at, II, 101n, 106; V, 233n; Wilton Crescent (Hallam's residence), IV, 60

London, Bishop of: *see* Charles James Blomfield

London, Corporation of, gives Reform dinner II, 146, 150; TBM consults its records V, 458

London, Lord Mayor of, at Reform dinner II, 146; Trevelyans attend banquet at Mansion House V, 106n

London, University of, I, xv, examinership in *Materia Medica,* V, 308n; TBM member of Senate 308n; examinership in classics 317n; favoured by Indian Civil Service examinations 438; election of Registrar VI, 35; Charles Edward Macaulay at 48

London and Birmingham Railway, Edward Cropper a director IV, 147n; shares in rise 205; 298, shares 310

London and Northwestern Railway, stock in IV, 316; 333, calls to pay V, 58, 87; dividends 98; calls 168, 212, 238; Fanny does not buy more shares 331; 346, TBM's stock in 358; VI, 77

London and Northwestern Railway Agent, letter to, V, 98

London and Westminster Bank, IV, 30n, VI, 90n

London and Westminster Review, III, 282

London Anti-Slavery Society: *see* Anti-Slavery Society (London)

London Booksellers' Association, V, 224, dissolved 224n

London Catalogue of Books, I, 324

London Debating Society, I, xix, TBM a member 190n; 232n, 282n, II, 52n
London Dock, TBM holds stock in, V, 358
London Gazette, I, 252n, IV, 313, 376, 387, V, 36, 139
London Hibernian Society, II, 156n
London Magazine, V, 321n
London Scottish Regimental Gazette, I, 279n
London Society for Promoting Christianity Amongst the Jews, I, 213, 218n
London Society for the Mitigation and Gradual Abolition of Slavery throughout the British Dominions: *see* Anti-Slavery Society
London University (now University College), I, xix, xxviii, 154n, its founding 242n; TBM attends first Greek lecture at 242n; TBM's sketch of Greek course for 242-3; Macaulay family at inaugural classes of 244n; Charles Macaulay first student of 253n; 273, 311n, its relation to SDUK 323; II, 17n, Zachary Macaulay valuable member of Council 42; 43n, Charles Macaulay first student in medical classes 214n; III, 233n, IV, 129, 309n, VI, 215n
Londonderry, V, 29, 64n, 67, TBM visits 69; 208, defense of 368; VI, 5
Londonderry, Marquess of, *A Steam Voyage to Constantinople*, IV, 49-50*
Long, George, and SDUK, I, 122n; 144, *154*, wins Craven scholarship 154; 185, 191, plan for course at London University 242n; TBM and Zachary Macaulay attend his first lecture 242n; 317n, II, 35
Long Parliament, II, 169
Longfellow, Henry Wadsworth, VI, 46n
Longinus, I, 237*
Longleat, IV, 370, VI, 76, TBM at 86, 87, 87n
Longman, Lady Elizabeth, V, 56n
Longman, Thomas (1804-79), I, xiii, xvi, IV, *52*, his offer for *Lays* 52; 58, 59, 62, 72, urges republication of *Essays* 79; letter to Napier 79n; has joint property in TBM's essays for *ER* 82; 95, 107, 118, 123, 128n, on sale of Jeffrey's book 167; 173, 222, 260, 261, 297, 311, and new editor for *ER* 330; contract with TBM for *History* 365; 377, 381, 382, 403, payments to TBM V, VIII; 38, reports sales of *History* 44-5; 49, commissions Eddis portrait of TBM 55n; 56, thinks Empsom must be replaced 73; 74, tells TBM that Lingard has written against him 88n; TBM recommends Hampden Gurney to 123; payments to TBM 127, 127n, 128; sends book 129; 139n, asks TBM to soften review of Gleig 169n; sends annual accounts 268; anxious about *ER* 300; to publish *Speeches* 338n; payments to TBM 349; 365, delighted by TBM's 'scourging' of Vizetelly 366; Robert Montgomery protests to 387; renews contract for *History* 413n, 414; provides amanuenses for TBM 414n; in ecstasies over proofs of *History* 463; 473, arrangements for publication of *History* 473, 473n; on reprinting *History* 478n; sends reviews to TBM 481, VI, 13; 25, 43n, 78, 128n, 129, and Humphreys's book on India 129n; payments to TBM 135; sends account of sales 156; payments 156n; 212, offered Mrs Piozzi's papers 236n; 258
    LETTERS TO: IV, 57, 59, 60, 68, 69, 75, 81, 96, 115, 115, 208, 251, 260, 265, 369, V, 38, 59, 77, 88, 129, 160, 221, 413, 414, 478, VI, 24, 144, 155, 156, 236, 267, 268, 271
Longman, Mrs Thomas, IV, *377*, V, 59, in ecstasies over proofs of *History* 463
Longman, Thomas Norton (1771-1842), I, *320*, sends TBM Southey's edition of Bunyan II, 107; 111, 190, 201, 227, on sales of *ER* 249; 365, III, 21, 107, 108, 163, sends German books 233; 279, account of payments unsatisfactory 281; accounts with 283; 320, 340, 359, 373, IV, 17, proposes edition of TBM's essays 31; arranges to publish *Lays* 46; 47, his death 52; V, 265
Longman, Thomas Norton (1849-1930), birth of, V, *59*
Longman, William, V, *370*
Longmans, firm of, I, 6n, 257n, 325n, IV, 71, has decision as to *ER* editorship 329; V, 57, 112, 116, in Booksellers' Association 224n; accounts with 346; obtains books for TBM 463; expectations for *History* 467, 469; to pay £20,000 for *History* VI, 24; 28n, 49, 80, expects good sale of new edition of *History* 109
Longus, *Daphnis and Chloe*, III, 200*, 211
Lonsdale, Earl of: *see* William Lowther
Lope de Vega, I, 73
Loppington, Shropshire, III, 342
Loraine, Amelia Mary, VI, *176*, TBM sends money to 176n; *Lays of Israel* 176n, *Steps on the Mountains* 176n
    LETTER TO: VI, 176

Lord Advocate: *see* John Inglis, Francis Jeffrey, Duncan McNeil, James Moncrieff, Andrew Rutherfurd
Lord Chancellor: *see* Lord Brougham, Lord Campbell, Lord Chelmsford, Lord Cottenham, Lord Cranworth, Lord Eldon, Lord Lyndhurst, Lord Thurlow
Lord Chancellor's Secretary of Bankrupts, II, 82n
Lord Hungerford, TBM takes passage in III, 229, famous for luxury 230; 231, arrives Calcutta 232; 236, sails 243n
Lord Lieutenant of Ireland: *see* 4th Earl of Clarendon
Lord Provost, Edinburgh: *see* Adam Black, Sir James Forrest, Duncan McLaren
Lord Steward, II, 45
Lorenzo dei Medici, Michaelangelo's model for statue of, II, 54
Loseley, III, 276
Lothian, Maurice, VI, *44*
LETTER TO: VI, 44
Lothian, Presbytery of, V, 21
Loughborough, Lord, IV, 295
Louis, St, of France, IV, 150
Louis XI, King, IV, 83
Louis XIII, King, I, 37n, V, 477n
Louis XIV, King, II, 190, III, 53, great aqueduct of IV, 139; 148, 152, 159, V, 419, 423
Louis XV, King, IV, 148
Louis XVI, King, II, 124, IV, 152, his death a model for TBM's V, 301
Louis XVIII, King, I, 42, in London on way to France 43; II, 67n, IV, 148
Louis Philippe, I, 295, 296, 311, speech of II, 80; 250, and Eastern Question III, 335; 339n, assassination attempted 341; 353, and Victoria's visit to France IV, 151, 154; 238n, abdicates 362n; his Queen at Claremont V, 406; VI, 52n
Louisiana, III, 210n
'Louring,' original sense of, VI, 133
Louth, V, 69, TBM plans to visit 218
Louvain, IV, 8
Louviers, I, 292
Lovelace, Lady, V, ix
Lovelace, Lord, V, ix
Low, David, 'Condition of the Negroes in Our Colonies,' I, 195n
Low, Sampson, V, 36n, agent for Harpers 467n
Low Church, early instance of term VI, 145
Low Churchmen, V, 42, 88
Lowe, Sir Hudson, I, 180n
Lowe (London circulating library?), II, 260
Lowe, Robert, afterwards 1st Viscount Sherbrooke, on Commission on Laws of India, V, 367n, 388n, VI, *30*
Lowis, John, V, 424n
Lowis, Mrs John (Ellen Mangles), V, 424n
Lowndes, W. T., *Bibliographer's Manual of English Literature,* I, 211n, ed. Bohn V, 472n
Lowood Inn, Windermere, Hannah at VI, 228; TBM at 230; Ellis at 233
Lowther, Henry Cecil, II, *18*
Lowther, John Henry, II, *18*
Lowther, William, II, *18*
Lowther, William, 1st Earl of Lonsdale, II, 18n, *60*
Lowther, William, 2nd Earl of Lonsdale, II, *60*, 143
Lowther, family, V, 118
Lubbock, John, afterwards 3rd Baronet, II, *216*
Lucan, II, 153*, 160*, 'among the most extraordinary men that ever lived' 201, volume of given TBM in memory of John Allen IV, 296, *Pharsalia,* III, 151*, 200-1*, IV, 133*
Lucca, V, 358n
Lucca, Duke of, III, 47
Lucca Collection, IV, 324
Lucian, Hemsterhuis's edition, III, 108; 159*, TBM's praise of 160*, 237, V, 343, TBM gives to George Trevelyan 391, 'Charon,' V, 106*, 'Hermotimus,' VI, 156*, 'The Parasite,' V, 105*, 'The Ship,' VI, 156*
Lucius Ampelius, III, 178*
Lucknow, II, 348, IV, 217, VI, 119n, siege of VI, 125n, 138n; 134n
Lucretius, *De Rerum Natura,* III, 129*, 140*, 159*, VI, 238*
Ludlow, Edmund, V, *145*
Lushington, Stephen, I, *278*, II, 138n, 150, 160, 193, 239, 284, wants TBM to speak at political dinner 346, 347; unpopular with rabble of Tower Hamlets 348; TBM avoids making speech for 357
Luther, Martin, translation of New Testament III, 236*; IV, 77, his psalter for sale 235, 236; V, 333, TBM orders his Opera Omnia VI, 158, 158n*
Luttrell, Henry, II, *26*, *Advice to Julia* 26*; 27, inscription by in garden of Holland House 28; 56, 82, 148, 169, 180, 182, 363, at breakfast IV, 234; V, 41n
Luttrell, Narcissus, TBM consults his diary at All Souls V, 423, 424; VI, 17
Lycian Marbles, VI, 48

Lydenberg, H. M., 'What Did Macaulay Say about America?' VI, 94n

Lyell, Sir Charles, IV, 15n, not of calibre for Museum Trustee V, *150*

Lyme, TBM at VI, 240n

Lyndhurst, John Singleton Copley, 1st Baron, candidate at Cambridge I, 181; at York Assizes *208*; candidate at Cambridge 212n; appoints TBM Commissioner of Bankrupts 230; on his appointment of TBM 230n; 233, TBM attends his levee 233n; undertakes legal reforms 271n; anecdote of with Lord Dudley II, 43; 61, 168, VI, 97n

Lynedoch, 1st Baron, III, 330n

Lynn, Walpole's reception at VI, 121

Lyon, at school with TBM I, 17, 26

Lyon, George, V, *238*

LETTER TO: V 238

Lyons, III, 270, 274, IV, 146, V, 343, 349n, 'interesting city' 353; 354, pleasant day at in 1853 416; VI, 159

Lysias, III, 163, 200*, 237*, V, 484*

Lyttelton, Dowager Lady, at Althorp, V, 85n

Lyttelton, George William Lyttelton, 4th Baron, at Althorp, V, 85n; 141n, VI, *30*, presents his 'A Few Thoughts about Shakspeare' to TBM 30*; *Memoirs and Correspondence*, ed. R. J. Phillimore, IV, 263-4*

LETTER TO: VI, 30

Lyttelton, Spencer, at Althorp, V, 85n

Lyttelton, Thomas, 2nd Baron, identified as Junius, V, *215*

Lytton, Sir Edward Lytton Bulwer-Lytton, 1st Baron, contributes to *Knight's Quarterly*, I, 188n; on the Athenaeum 295n; *320*, conversation with II, 84; edits *New Monthly Magazine* 84; 112n, gives Godwin's letter to TBM 139; his measure on newspaper duties 178; praises TBM in *New Monthly* 289; TBM wonders what he can do to support himself 289; can't combine editing with politics 299-300; IV, 60, praises *Lays* 67, 68; TBM sends *Essays* to 115; inherits Knebworth and changes name 182n; TBM doubts he should have replied to critics 330; death of his daughter 368; TBM objects to his ranking his poetry over his prose V, 17; on TBM's criticism of *The Caxtons* 78n; consults TBM on what Bacon said 147; his Guild of Literature and Art 163n; 230n, sends his Edinburgh speeches to TBM 386*; compliment to TBM 386n; will envy compliment to TBM's dress VI, 123; Secretary for the Colonies 182n; speech on Reform Bill, 1859, 203; described by Disraeli 203n; overworked 210

Writings: The Caxtons, V, 77-8*, *England and the English*, II, 315*, *Eva*, IV, 42*, *Falkland*, II, 22n, *Godolphin*, II, 259, 260, 'Goldsmith,' IV, 368, *Harold, or the Last of the Saxon Kings*, IV, 368*, *King Arthur*, V, 17*, *The Last of the Barons*, historical question in, IV, 83; 106*, 'Letters to John Bull,' V, 163*, 'Lord Lyndhurst's Review of the Last Session,' III, 306*, *Lucretia*, IV, 323-4*, 330n, *My Novel*, V, 147n, TBM's praise of 311*; TBM re-reading VI, 182*, *Night and Morning*, IV, 182*, *Not So Bad as We Seem*, TBM sees at Devonshire House, V, 163; criticises 164-5, 'On the State of Eloquence in England,' II, 289n, *Pelham*, I, 296n, *Poems and Ballads of Schiller*, IV, 182*, *Richelieu*, III, 283n*, 'Spirit of Society in England and France,' I, 320, *What Will He Do with It?* presented to TBM, VI, 182, TBM thinks his best 210*, 'A Word to the Public,' IV, 330*

LETTERS TO: III, 343, IV, 42, 62, 65, 83, 106, 182, 323, 329, 368, 393, V, 17, 77, 147, 163, 310, 386, VI, 182, 209

Lytton, 1st Earl of, *Life of Edward Bulwer*, IV, 42, V, 386

Maberley, Frederick Herbert, 'Melancholy and Awful Death of Lawrence Dundas,' I, *108*

Maberley, William Leader, IV, *36*

Macartney, George, IV, 45

Macbeth, and Glamis Castle, VI, 180, 181

Macaulay, Arthur (TBM's nephew), V, *426*

Macaulay, Aulay (1758-1819), TBM's uncle, I, xxi, 103n, *124*, V, 217n, 462

Macaulay, Mrs Aulay, I, 141

Macaulay, Bell, Zachary Macaulay's cousin, I, 58

Macaulay, Catharine Sawbridge, the historian, VI, *86*, *History of England*, 86n

Macaulay, Charles Zachary (1813-86), TBM's brother, I, xv, *xxviii*, birth and naming 38; bathing at Brighton 48; 66, 113, at London University 253n; at Elwell's school 159n; at Goldsmid's ball II, 34,

Macaulay, Charles Zachary (1813–86)—*cont.* 36, 39; 185, studying surgery 214; sends a place-hunter to TBM 225; 274, recovering from illness 277; 281, 287, TBM will provide for 304; 308, doing very well 310; needs money for his education 314; expenses less than supposed 319; father thinks of sending to Paris 343; TBM will pay for education 345, 354; 360, would gladly have joined Indian army 367; III, 25n, 26, 27, 28, 30, 31, 72, 73, 89, studies medicine in Paris 97; letter to George Babington 97n; 98, TBM responsible for his education 116; 117, 157, 174, education of 176; 198, practising as surgeon 203; 215, 223, 231, 235, 274, appointed TBM's private secretary 301; lecturer at St George's Hospital and reading for Bar 301n; 311, 319n, enters Mauritius Civil Service IV, 9; married 9n; his work in Mauritius 35; 196, 199, well and prosperous 201; remits money 207; his pecuniary affairs 222; on leave in England 310; his fortune 312; going to Liverpool 314; on Mrs Money 316n; returns to England from Mauritius 376n; plans to return to England 382; offered Secretaryship of Mauritius V, 29; plans to send his boy to school 67; celebrates Christmas with TBM and Trevelyan 87n; looking for place on Board of Health 118; appointed Secretary, Board of Health 119; on Eddis portrait of TBM 138n; complimented by Lord Ashley 142; pestered by James Mills 198n; 296, on Grant's portrait of TBM 327n; appointed Secretary to Board of Audit 387; Gladstone recommends him 392; TBM recommends he stay at Board of Audit 417; on Arthur Macaulay 426; on Claudet photo of TBM VI, 16n; need not go down to Aldingham 54; 113, 119, at Brighton 125; 169, TBM sends unclaimed dividends to 199; his boy's success 213, 215; 235, 266n

Letters to: III, 203, IV, 8, 382, V, 29, 118, 119, 142, 198, 217, 417, VI, 54, 57, 85, 126, 177, 199, 203, 213

Macaulay, Mrs Charles (Mary Potter), I, xxviii, IV, 9n, does not return to Mauritius with Charles 310n; 314, 377, TBM hopes to meet soon 383; V, 30, 120, 199, at anti-slavery meeting 298n; 417

Macaulay, Charles Edward (TBM's nephew), has done well at London University VI, *48*; appointed cadet in East India Company 90n; calls on TBM 119

Macaulay, Charles Trevelyan (TBM's nephew), birth of, V, *119*

Macaulay, General Colin (1760-1836), TBM's uncle, I, *xxv*, 5, returns from India 7n; 19, 20, 30, may join army in Peninsula 39; takes Macaulay children to town 45-6; 47, 114, in family party at Cambridge 127; 142, on point of returning to London II, 48; puzzled by Disraeli's remark about TBM 50; imprisoned by Haider Ali 224; discovered rascality of Hutchinson's claim 247; TBM wishes to send him copy of India speech 291; Tom Babington treats dishonestly 336; 338, III, ix, 48, imprisoned at Seringapatam 51; 66, 67, death 182n; leaves TBM £10,000 182; his estate 233; V, viii, ix, entertained TBM at Clifton in 1811 249, 250

Macaulay, Duncan, writes begging letter, II, 225

Macaulay, Frances (1808-88), TBM's sister, called Fanny, I, *xxvii*, has mumps 19; 31, 39, 40, bathing at Brighton 48; 66, 197, 208, 274, 275, on TBM and death of Selina Mills Macaulay II, 14n; 16, love of music 19; 20, 23, 24, 28, 30, 31, 34, 37, 39, intimate with Miss Elliott 41; 45, 46, 48, 50, 53, 55, 58, 62, 63, 66, 69, 72, 74, 129, to stay with George Babington 154, 158; TBM calls on in Kensington 160; 169, 172, 181, guesses Margaret's engagement 185; hurt by something Hannah said 191; 192n, 198, on Leeds portrait of TBM 206n; praises Reynolds portrait 266; on TBM's speech on Irish Coercion Bill 230n; TBM shames her over Baptist Noel 247; 255, 259, 261, 263, at Rothley Temple 294; to Dingle Bank 303; 308, 310, 312, returning to London 320; 327, TBM thinks she should remain in England 330; agrees to remain 332; Zachary Macaulay wishes her to go to India 343; 344, 359, 360, 368, 370, 372, III, 25n, 26, 27, 28, 31n, 72, 193, 199, 215, 243n, 261, 264, 265, 270, 272, 273, 276, 285, 290, to help TBM in housekeeping 305; at Great George Street 313n; shows TBM's *Lays* to Arnold IV, 37n, 66; 57, 134, 141, 147, 151, 156, 157, at Dover with Trevelyan children 201; influenced by her friends the Thorntons 204; 234, 235, with

Trevelyan children at Clapham 236; 272, saw TBM anxious about Corn Laws 277; 281, 'Paymistress of the Forces' 302n; has her own bank account 312; to be housekeeper for TBM 318n; with Trevelyan children at Broadstairs 340; letter from 341; 350, 351, 352, breakfasts with TBM 353; v, 43n, TBM to increase her allowance 60-1; TBM pays call on her railway shares 87; 104, 116, 127, 128, residuary legatee of Selina Macaulay 128n; 144, 157, 161, 184, 204, 220, 226, at John Macaulay's vicarage 232; offers to nurse TBM at Clifton 265; Trevelyan children with her 277; 283, 288, 293, mustn't think that Homer and Hesiod speak of a sabbath 303; 323, 324, TBM instructs her on question of proselytizing 358-9; TBM pays railway call for 362; TBM asks her to find him lodgings in Brighton 366-7; 370, 373, TBM increases her allowance 382; 383, 392, TBM discusses date of *Pilgrim's Progress* with 402; 428, TBM explains army organisation to 429-30; 437, 451, 358, 459, 467, TBM increases her allowance 479; VI, 5, praises TBM's *History* 7; 29, 48, 70, 72, 73, hears Thackeray at Brighton 76n; 84, suffers from hay fever 92; 127, 135, 140, TBM to buy annuity for 169; TBM will pay her for all expenses connected with Selina's death 169; TBM buys annuity for 173; dines with TBM and Margaret at Norfolk Hotel 174; moves to Montpelier Road, Brighton 189n; money for from Zachary Macaulay's estate 199; furnishing her new house 199-200; in her new house 208; TBM takes to Cambridge 212; a teetotaller 227; at Dingle Bank 234; at Milton Bryant 235n; reading Shakespeare with Alice 236; TBM has done no more than his duty to her 247; frightened by invasion rumours 252; her allowance 266n; her Notes on Trevelyan's *Life* of TBM III, 268n, IV, 44n, 282n

LETTERS TO: II, 303, III, 72, 97, 117, 156, 161, 173, 191, 197, 212, 221, 229, 232, 268, 273, 295, 295, 304, 316, 341, 378, 378, 380, IV, 34, 35, 37, 38, 43, 46, 55, 63, 67, 197, 201, 203, 206, 220, 222, 276, 310, 316, 318, 345, 348, 350, 377, V, 14, 46, 47, 51, 54, 58, 72, 73, 73, 76, 80, 81, 83, 84, 87, 95, 103, 107, 109, 121, 123, 125, 132, 136, 137, 152, 155, 157, 158, 168, 169, 171, 182, 188, 217, 224, 232, 236, 238, 251, 272, 277, 279, 281, 290, 295, 297, 302, 303, 304, 307, 308, 318, 319, 326, 330, 336, 346, 353, 358, 361, 362, 363, 365, 366, 377, 377, 380, 381, 382, 383, 398, 402, 426, 429, 435, 453, 454, 465, 468, 472, 479, 480, VI, 5, 7, 10, 13, 34, 39, 74, 75, 76, 77, 82, 92, 105, 109, 113, 120, 122, 125, 138, 143, 153, 168, 169, 170, 170, 173, 175, 188, 189, 197, 199, 199, 208, 221, 222, 226, 235, 236, 238, 238, 247, 252, 266

Macaulay, George, brother of Kenneth Macaulay of Sierra Leone, I, *145*

Macaulay, George, husband of Catharine Macaulay, VI, 86n, 87

Macaulay, Hannah: *see* Mrs Charles Trevelyan

Macaulay, Hector, half-brother of Zachary Macaulay, I, 5n

Macaulay, Henry Denman (TBM's nephew), IV, *158*

Macaulay, Henry George (TBM's nephew), VI, *53*, 54, trouble about 92

Macaulay, Henry William (1806–46), TBM's brother, I, *xxvi*, 5, 7, 15, 19, TBM writes to 31; 39, 40, and bathing women at Brighton 48; 66, TBM watches his diet on travels 156; at Elwell's school 159-60; at home 162; requests private letter from TBM 164; TBM advises on choice of university and profession 165; enters Charterhouse School 182; compiles family magazine 184; TBM can't contribute to 186; joins James Cropper's firm, Liverpool 196n; TBM defends his conduct to parents 199; 201, TBM sends maps to 207; TBM expects to see him 225, 227; self-supporting 253n; sent to Sierra Leone on father's business 293n; 308, his ship-franks expensive II, 39; appointed Commissioner of Mixed Court, Sierra Leone 102; TBM urges to return to England 213; in Africa, 1831-6, 213n; quarrels and duels in Sierra Leone 264-5; TBM will defend him at Colonial Office 294; TBM writes strong letter to 305; has got through his difficulties 307; 310, TBM gets a place for a friend of his 320; 366, III, 20, 30, his judgeship 31n; 98, promoted 157; 174, 192, 198, 223, 'most deplorable man of business' 266; return to England and marriage IV, 34n; crazy letter from 35; 38, in England

Macaulay, Henry William (1806–46)—*cont.* 143; 157, appointed Commissioner at Boa Vista 158n; his situation in Africa 200; 202, 'poor foolish Henry' does not thrive like his brothers and sisters 312; death of 312; absurd letter from 313; 317, TBM's response to his death 323n; 425n

LETTERS TO: I, 165, 184, 186, 196, 207, 217, 227, 229, 248, 248, II, 213, IV, 34, 158, 200

Macaulay, Mrs Henry (Margaret Denman): *see* Mrs Edward Cropper (3rd wife)

Macaulay, Jean: *see* Mrs Thomas Babington

Macaulay, Jean or Jane (1804-30), TBM's sister, I, *xxvi*, 5, 15, 16, 19, 20, TBM will bring gift of rabbits 31; 40, 53, 54, 55, 65, 66, 102, 104, 105, 109, 123, misses letter from her 126; 129n, 137, 139, heart set on seeing TBM at Easter 144; 147, at Brighton 154, 156, TBM frightened by reports of her health 156, 159; recovered 160; 164, TBM uneasy about 167; 173, 176, 179, 186, 'very poorly' 207; death 307

LETTERS TO: I, 38, 43, 68

Macaulay, John (1805-74), TBM's brother, I, *xxvi*, 5, 7, 15, 19, 27, 28, 31, 39, 40, 66, recovers from illness 155; with TBM on tour to Wales 156; at Elwell's school 159n; 160, enters firm of Macaulay and Babington 179; 209, takes B.A. at Cambridge 253n; appointed Rector of Alderminster, Warwickshire 314; Curate of Tilstone, Cheshire 314n; Brougham gives living of Loppington to II, 101n; TBM imagines his *Life* done by 155; performs service of Margaret's marriage 210n; engaged 214; TBM lends money to 261; needs money and ought not to marry 358-9; offended 370; 372, III, 20, 28, 98, 117, 157, 174, 231, TBM asks Melbourne for living for 342; Melbourne gives living of Bovey Tracey to 363; at Bovey Tracey IV, 201; visits TBM at the Albany 206; 207, 317, 318, 378, V, 46, appointed to living of Aldingham 50, 51, 52, one of best livings in gift of crown 54, described 55, 62; on northern peasantry 78; thriving state of his neighbourhood 232; 233, 237, 265, TBM, Hannah and Margaret visit 421n; TBM describes his family 426; 426n, 441, VI, 48n, injured by fall into a mine pit 53-4; makes wonderful recovery 56; dines with TBM 76; 90n, delighted with his son's good luck 92; calls on TBM 119; coming up to London 200, 203; TBM invents April Fool story about 204; 206

LETTERS TO: V, 50, 78

Macaulay, Mrs John (Emma Jane Large), II, 214n, *358*, 372, IV, 317, V, 233, 237

Macaulay, John Heyrick (1799-1840), TBM's cousin, I, *103*; reputation at Cambridge 103; TBM confused with 114; called 'Bear' 114n; 115, 141, 144

[Macaulay, Joseph Babington], *Memoirs of the Clan 'Aulay'*, I, xli, II, 264n, IV, 34, 141n

Macaulay, Kenneth (1780?-1841), of Madras, TBM's cousin, I, *5*, III, 214n, 215

LETTER TO: I, 5

Macaulay, Kenneth (1792?-1829), of Sierra Leone, second cousin of Zachary Macaulay, I, 5, *8*, in England 53; 55, 58, 135, sends a seal to TBM 145; 228n, death of 293n

LETTER TO: I, 8

Macaulay, Kenneth (1815-67), TBM's cousin V, *217*, best for him to be out of Parliament 315; speech on Reform Bill VI, 203

Macaulay, Margaret: *see* Mrs Edward Cropper (2nd wife)

Macaulay, Mary (daughter of Charles Macaulay), III, 25n, birth of IV, 376n; V, 417n

Macaulay, Mary (fictitious), V, 462

Macaulay, Mr (not identified), III, 344

Macaulay, Selina (TBM's niece, daughter of John Macaulay), V, *426*

Macaulay, Selina (1802-58), TBM's sister, I, *xxvi*, xxvii, 5, 7, 15, 16, 19, 24, 30, TBM will bring gift of rabbits 31; 40, reads Byron 45, 47; 53, 54, 55, 66, her poetic efforts 68; 85, to transcribe 'Pompeii' 115; 123, 126, 147, TBM misses arguing with her 156; troubled by TBM's Whiggism 156n; 157, does not write 160; her birthday 173; 179, health not improved 198; TBM reads Mitford's *Greece* to 198n; 199, with TBM at Rothley 201; 224, troubled on account of her head 246; 276, collaborates with TBM 321; II, 19, 23, 24, in the care of Dr Jephson at Leamington 28; improved 30; 31, 34, 39, 45, 46, TBM inquires about her health 48; has confidence in Jephson 50; 53, 54, 55, 58, 62, 63, 66, reports improvement in health 68; 72, 74, 85, 133, going to Rothley Temple 154; 158, not to be told of Margaret's engagement 185; 187, 191, 193, 209, 236, TBM

shames her over Baptist Noel 247; 261, kept ignorant of Henry's duels 265; goes to Rothley Temple 269; 303, her health not reliable 330; 343, 344, 368, 370, III, 26, 27, 28, 72, 193, 199, 215, 243n, 261, 265, 290, retires to Liverpool 311; at Great George Street 313n; 378, 380, IV, 35, 37, 38, 46, 57, 143, 147, 151, 157, 201, too ill to be visited 202; TBM offers to send *Times* to 281; TBM to increase her allowance v, 60-1; TBM pays call on her railway shares 87; 97, in better health 103; 108, must not take a joke too seriously 116; 122, 123, 125, drawing up her will 126, 128; 133, 137, 145, 152, TBM urges to visit Great Exhibition 157; comes to town for Great Exhibition 168; 183, 189 204, 218, with TBM at Clifton in 1811 249, 250; 273, 277, 278, 291, 295, 298, 303, 304, 305, 307, 309, 327, 337, 346, TBM reassures her about public affairs 357; TBM pays railway call for 362; 364, 365, 367, 377, 378, 380, TBM increases her allowance 382; reports on Alice Trevelyan 383; 384, 398, 402, to visit Trevelyans at Esher 403; TBM explains differences between Roman and Greek Churches to 427-8; 430, 465, poorly 480; TBM increases her allowance 480; VI, 8, 11, arrangements for paying allowance 28-9; hopes her health not worse than usual 39; takes Carlsbad waters 48; and Mrs Crinean 69; 72, 74n, 76, 77, 106, 109, 120, 122, 126, 138, writing her will 140; 143, 153, death 169; hitch over her will 169-70; her stock 170; trouble in settling her estate 174; 199

Diary: I, xli, 141n, 190n, on TBM's first meeting with Sydney Smith 214n; on TBM's 'Present Administration' 222n; 223n, on Panizzi 227n; 230n, 233n, on Mrs Anne Grant 235n; on Lydia White 239n; 241n, on first Greek class at London University 242n; 243n, on TBM's meeting Hallam 244n; on Empson 246n; 250n, 251n, 277n, 293n, on Jean Macaulay's death 307n; II, 5n, 39n, on Henry's appointment 102n; 283n

LETTERS TO: I, 20, 38, 43, 68, 72, 109, 270, II, 68, 131, 161, 171, 294, III, 72, 97, 117, 156, 161, 173, 191, 197, 212, 221, 229, 232, 272, 276, 284, 296, 301, 305, 311, 313, 317, IV, 269, 281, 298, 310, 311, 311, 313, 333, 353, 362, 365, 372, V, 40, 51, 59, 60, 63, 103, 116, 126, 128, 144, 157, 160, 168, 169, 184, 196, 211, 212, 225, 264, 288, 293, 322, 323, 335, 355, 357, 362, 370, 373, 383, 392, 403, 425, 427, 434, 437, 441, 450, 458, 467, 480, VI, 5, 28, 47, 56, 69, 72, 72, 84, 100, 113, 126, 134, 139

Macaulay, Selina Mills (1767-1831), TBM's mother, I, *xxv-xxvi*, xxix, 5, on TBM's treatment by the More sisters 6n; 7, 7n, letter to TBM 14n; 19, TBM owes his facility in French to her 26; 30, letter to TBM 34n; birth of her ninth child 38n; 39, 48, 49, invited to Aspenden Hall 50; 51, to visit Aspenden 62; at Aspenden for TBM's declamations 66n; letter to Zacahary Macaulay 80n; 91, 93, 98, 102, 104, 105, 109, 112, 114, 126, 127, distressed by TBM's political opinions 132-3; 141, 142, 147, at Barley Wood 149; 152, 153, 154, TBM's memory of her affection 155; troubled by TBM's Whiggism 156n; 162, at Barley Wood, 164, 166; misses TBM's joke in 'Tears of Sensibility' 167; wishes to know more about TBM's choice of profession 173; 174n, nursing duties 176; annual visit to Barley Wood 177, 180; unwell 186; heard TBM's 'Roman Tale' before publication 188; 196, 201, 209, 210, her eyes recovered 218; 221, 232, troubled by her eyes 246; 247, 252n, 308, dies II, 14; taught TBM to combine ambition with affection 63; 214, on James Mills IV, 141n; V, 35

LETTERS TO: I, 8, 14, 15, 16, 20, 21, 22, 24, 25, 26, 27, 31, 32, 33, 34, 35, 36, 39, 40, 42, 43, 52, 57, 58, 60, 62, 64, 74, 76, 79, 80, 85, 117, 122, 124, 154, 156, 157, 160, 166, 167, 170, 174, 181, 199, 212, 236

Macaulay, Thomas Babington, 1st Baron (1800-59)

see separate entries for: Brighton, Calne, Cambridge, Edinburgh, *Edinburgh Review*, India, Leeds, London, Northern Circuit

SUMMARY: spends summers at Hannah More's I, xxix; enters school at Clapham 5; enters Preston's school, Little Shelford 14; stays with Dean Milner at Cambridge 27-8; spends vacation at Clapham 33n; has room of his own 37; returns to Clapham

Macaulay, Thomas Babington, 1st Baron (1800-59)—SUMMARY, *cont.* for holidays 40; returns to school 40n; sends contribution to *Christian Observer* 49; at Clapham 55; returns to school 64; declamations before parents at Aspenden 66n; ill in summer of 1816 80n; enters Cambridge, 101; spends holidays at Cadogan Place 112; at Barley Wood 112n; wins Chancellor's Medal 115n; spends summer at Clapham reading 129n; defends himself against charge of novel-reading 139; wins Latin Declamation prize 147; takes pupils following graduation 148n; wins Chancellor's Medal 151n; gets rooms in Trinity 152; wins Craven scholarship 154; on reading party at Llanrwst 156ff; studies mathematics for B.A. examination 168; takes degree without honours 169; moves to new rooms, Great Court of Trinity 170; enters Lincoln's Inn 171; called to bar 171n; regularly speaks at Cambridge Union Society 183n; contributes to *Knight's Quarterly* 187-8; leaves Cambridge to study law 186n; at Rothley Temple 187; returns to Cambridge to prepare for fellowship examination 190; joins John Stuart Mill's London Debating Society 190n; unsuccessful in Trinity fellowship examination 191n; elected fellow of Trinity 200; first contribution to *ER* 203n; joins Northern Circuit 208n; appointed Commissioner of Bankrupts 230; becomes responsible for support of family 253n; offered seat for Calne by Lord Lansdowne 263n; must make choice between law and politics 265; maiden speech in Parliament 272; first visit to France 287ff; elected to Athenaeum 294n; makes successful speech on Reform Bill II, 5; offers to resign seat on slavery question II, 14n; in London during summer of Reform Bill debate 15-88; rumoured engaged to Maria Kinnaird 19n; introduced to Holland House 20; sworn in as M.P. in new Parliament 45; at presentation of address from Commons to William IV 51-3; second speech on Reform Bill 62; dines with Prime Minister 64-5; elected to Brooks's 80n; at Rothley Temple 89; formally invited to stand for Leeds 103; appointed to West India Committee 115; re-elected at Calne 122; appointed Commissioner of Board of Control 122n; presented to King on appointment to office 141-3; appointed to East India Committee 146n; at Reform dinner, Guildhall 150; learns of Margaret Macaulay's engagement 184; campaigns at Leeds 188-9; visits Cambridge with Hannah and Margaret 196; elected at Leeds for first reform Parliament 205-12; appointed Secretary, Board of Control 209; offers to resign on abolition question 239; guides East India Charter Bill through Commons 264-79; offers resignation a third time over slavery question 267; speaks against slavery bill 277-8; resignation not accepted 279, 285; offered appointment to Supreme Council of India 299; appointment problematic 322; speech on Corn Laws at Leeds 333, 334; appointed to Supreme Council 350; leaves for India III, 25; at Ootacamund 59ff; at Calcutta 76ff; Hannah engaged 99; receives news of Margaret's death 129; Minute on Education 138n; choice between literature and politics 158-9; avoids Calcutta amusements 162; attacked in Parliament by Praed 164; determined to return to England 175; plans to pass life in quiet study 188; has not acquired habits of the English in India 204; keeps calendar of his life on margins of his books 210; completes Indian Penal Code 213; informs Board of Control of decision to return to England 213; spirits have never recovered from Margaret's death 219; prefers literature to politics 219; may hope to equal Gibbon 220; resigns from Supreme Council 238; receives resolution of thanks from Governor-General in Council 239; arrives in England 243n; in high spirits 244n; plans trip to Rome 252; thinks of leaving London as residence 253; visits nephew in Liverpool

256; catching up on English politics 258; arrives in Italy 260; Florence 261; offered place of Judge Advocate 264; arrives at Rome 266; does not wish to be thought political adventurer 267; to Naples 272n; 'not unwilling' to enter Parliament 278; comforts Ellis on death of wife 280; elected to The Club 281; invited to stand for Edinburgh 287; doubts he will ever hold office again 287; elected at Edinburgh 290-1; takes seat in House of Commons 291; accepts Secretaryship-at-War 298; political visit to Edinburgh 298n; attends cabinet meetings 302; vacates seat on accepting office 303; sworn of Privy Council 303; plans to take a house 305; settles in Great George Street 313; secures Treasury appointment for Trevelyan 317n; presents army estimates 321; became 'too mere a bookworm in India' 321; presents army estimates 331n; anxious over Eastern Question 349; out of touch with contemporary literature 367; hopes for a defeat 372; re-elected at Edinburgh 376-80; thinks Whigs must resign 381; takes chambers in the Albany 382; breaking up household in Great George Street 384; satisfaction with his lot 385; breakfasts at Albany IV, 14n; literature not politics his vocation 23; visits West Country for *History* 44n; accompanies Frank Ellis to Cambridge 59-60; publishes *Lays* 63ff; thinks he should give up writing for *ER* 96; publishes *Essays* 115n; French tour 136ff; subject of biographical inquiry 160; votes for Ten Hours Bill 180; appointed to Fine Arts Commission 191; political visit to Edinburgh 213ff; takes unpopular side on Maynooth 254; political visit to Edinburgh 259; in crisis on Corn Laws 270-1; offered Pay Office by Russell 276; embarrassed by Russell's inability to form a ministry 278; his letter regarding Lord Grey published 282; accepts office of Paymaster General 300; re-elected at Edinburgh 300ff; at Rothley Temple 310; plans to take London house while in office 318n; moves to different rooms in Albany 318n; speaks at opening of Edinburgh Philosophical Institution 320; at Tercentenary Dinner, Trinity College 323n; defeated at Edinburgh 341; thinks it time to retire from public life 341; resigns as Paymaster General 362-4; at cabinet meeting with Duke of Wellington on measures against Chartist demonstration 363n; consulted by Prince Albert on appointment to Regius Professorship 373; offered the Professorship by Albert 373n; elected Lord Rector of Glasgow University 380; publishes *History*, vols. 1 and 2, 382n; trustee of British Museum V, VII; offered Professorship of Modern History at Cambridge by Albert 61n; visits Ireland 64-70; works in French National Archives 73n; elected Bencher of Lincoln's Inn 89; elected Professor of Ancient Literature, Royal Academy 96; Scottish tour 111; at Ventnor 121-6; plans to set up brougham 128; appointed to committee on medals for Great Exhibition 141n; sets up his carriage 160n; at Malvern 172-99; attends *Messiah* 184; offered cabinet post by Russell 211n; elected to Royal Bavarian Academy of Science 218n; acts in case of London Booksellers' Association 224; Edinburgh movement to return him to Parliament 231; TBM accepts plan for his return 234-5; too ill to attend declaration of poll 243; goes to Clifton after crisis in health 244n; re-elected for Edinburgh 246; leaves Clifton for Brighton 285; returns to London after convalescence 287; speech at Edinburgh 291-2; exhausted by late night in House of Commons 297; made Knight of Prussian Order of Merit 298; elected to Institute of France 309; at Tunbridge Wells 338ff; awarded D.C.L. at Oxford 350n; rumoured to be opium addict 360, 361; appointed to Committee on Indian Civil Service 389n; finishes Report on Indian Civil Service 409; French tour with Ellis 419n; examines archives of French War Office 419n; at Richmond Hill 459n; publishes

Macaulay, Thomas Babington, 1st Baron (1800-59)—Summary, *cont.*
History, vols. 3 and 4, 473; public speaking over 474; determines to leave the Albany 475; leaves Albany for Holly Lodge vi, 39n; appointed trustee of National Portrait Gallery 78n; acquires habit of attending church 97; visits Manchester Exhibition 101n; offered peerage by Palmerston 113; appointed High Steward of Borough of Cambridge 126; takes seat in House of Lords 134n; sworn in as High Steward 149; learns of Trevelyan's Indian appointment 188; takes family party to Cambridge 212; visits Lake District and Scotland with Hannah 230-3; makes tour to west of England with Ellis 231n; learns that Hannah will go to India 242n; diploma from Imperial Academy of Sciences, St Petersburg 258n; dies 261n
Appearance: growing fat i, 29; grows fat following illness 80n; caricatured in Blackwood's: 'dumpling of a fellow' ii, 81, 83; hopes illness has made him thinner 87; a 'perfect Lovelace' in court dress 96; described in *New York Observer:* "little man . . . affected utterance' 105n; splendid in new official uniform 222-3; described in New York paper v, 202-3; frail appearance on occasion of India Bill speech 336n; described by Mrs Stowe 412n; described by Hawthorne vi, 47n; newspaper story about his unliterary dress 123
Food and Drink (*see separate entry for Wine*): beer and potatoes at Bowood i, 265; first French meal 288; café style in Paris 296; breakfast at the Duc de Broglie's 302; breakfast at Holland House described ii, 26; breakfast of tea and bread 51; strawberries and cream at Rogers's 55; a feast at Littleton's 79; staple menu at ministerial dinners described 89; a Holland House menu 144; turtle soup at Reform dinner, Guildhall 150; a meal apologised for at Holland House 180; the etiquette of eating melon and macaroni 181; meal of a true English gourmand at Lord Essex's 216; breakfast of eggs, bread, tea 281; dislike of lunch iii, 38, 66; food in India 94-5; drinks only claret, no beer 97; sherry, hock, and soda water in India 173; dinner in India 173; light wines and made dishes of France unsatisfactory iv, 156; Champagne interdicted 366; lobster curry and Champagne for Ellis 372; takes too much wine at Paris v, 72n; fish, turkey and chine, traditional Christmas fare 87n; mountain mutton at Malvern 178; cider cup and perry at Malvern 180; turtle soup for Ellis 262; TBM takes lunch after six months' omission 262; doctor insists on lunch and on wine 271; turtle soup for Malden 276; now lunches regularly 281; orders herring, goose, and game for dinner with Ellis 422; traditional goose for Michaelmas day vi, 120; excellent ortolans at Bordeaux 159; larks and grapes at Brighton 174n; borrows Trinity audit ale from Ellis 176; grass lamb, new onions, and Stilton cheese for Ellis 202; plan of sumptuous college breakfast 212; ortolans farcis à la Talleyrand at Rothschild's 228
Health: illness in 1812 i, 13-14n; illness in 1816 80n; suffers knife wound at Cambridge 102-3; requests nasine lotion 104; touch of hypochondria 112; illness in spring of 1818 112n, 155; troubled by fever and hypochondria 154-5; sprains ankle 158; recovers from fever and other ailments 175; exhausted by fellowship examination 201; swollen eye and face ii, 76; has had touch of 'English cholera' 86-7; laid up with lumbago 113; inflammation of the eye 119, 120; influenza 234; swollen face iii, 12, 14; Adolphus thinks TBM not likely to return alive 14n; lives by strictest rule 17; forbidden to dine out 19; rapidly mending 20; 'as well as ever I was in my life' 73, 88; 'constantly improving since I left England' 118; health 'excellent' 132, 163; unaffected by India 174-5, 186, 197, 218; has had a 'smart touch of fever' 222; plagued with hemicrania 264; always better when forced to make an exertion 274;

treated for gout IV, 366; attack of rheumatism V, 14, 15; 'suppressed gout' diagnosed 103; frequent and serious complaints about health 103n; severe attack of rheumatism 105, 106; better than for many years past 144-5; trouble with teeth 204; rheumatic attacks 211; confined by cold 224; beginning of crisis in health 242n; 'in the midst of my triumphs I am but poorly' 250; suffers relapse 256-7; doubts he will ever make full recovery 269; improved 277; confined to room by cold weather 311ff; became twenty years older in a week of 1852 318; wonderfully well 321; pains in teeth and face 327, 336, 337; better than he ever expected to be again 354; must be valetudinarian in English winters 365; trouble in breathing 366; tormented by cough 369; toothache 394-5; 'fund of life is nearly spent' 403n; confined to chambers 436ff; rheumatic pain 436n; able to venture out after weeks of confinement 446; winter in south may help 450; must give up public speaking 451; might barter some fame for better health VI, 8; sprains ankle 43; in Italy sleep 'as deep and sweet as when I was a boy' 59; beginning to feel good effect of move from London 70; improving at Holly Lodge 73; rheumatic attack 75; 'miserable time of it' 80; remarkably well 105; change of weather disables him 123; dines out thrice in a week 143; a fit of gout 226; well in body but not in mind 244; miserably ill and weak 260

INCOME AND FINANCIAL ARRANGEMENTS: receives £50 for Craven Scholarship I, 154; pays graduation fees from Craven Scholarship 169; 100 guineas as fee for pupils 175; income as Fellow of Trinity 200n; needs money while on circuit 217, 223; income as Commissioner of Bankrupts 230n; combined income in 1829 *c.* £700 253n; income from *ER* 256, 270; £1,200 salary as Commissioner of Board of Control II, 122n; £1,500 salary as Secretary of Board of Control 209; income summarised in verse 261; post on Supreme Council pays £10,000 per annum 299; hopes to accumulate £30,000 in India 299, 345, 354; paid between £60 and £90 for *ER* articles 300n; can pay Charles's expenses and still send Hannah what she wants 315; £1,200 allowance for expense of voyage to India 339; passage costs £450 343; may take 600 guineas 356; £500 for passage 361; expenses of outfit and passage III, 6; borrows £600 from Edward Cropper 17; TBM's private account books at Trinity 27n; expects to save average of £7,000 a year in India 73; money comes in much faster than it goes out 89; to remit £1,500 107, 116; 'money-matters look well' 132; receives 8,000 rupees a month 136; annual expenditure less than £3,000 161; sends £6,000 to England, has £5,000-6,000 in India 161; hopes to save £20,000 170; summary of assets 175; receives £10,000 legacy from Colin Macaulay 182; Indian income summarised 183; 'tolerably at ease as to the future circumstances of our family' 197; will be independent 208; has saved more than he expected 215; will lose from present state of exchanges 231-2, 233, 236; savings worth £17,250 236n; receives £3,200 from settlement of Calcutta property 276; salary £2,500 301; can afford to spend £1,000 a year IV, 12; will save £1,500 a year if he remains in office 318; estimate of his fortune V, viii-ix; £3,002 from Longman for 1850 127, 128; £1,950 from Longman for 1851 127n; has added £10,000 to capital in four years 255; £2,068 for *History* in 1852 268n; $50,000 invested in American securities 269; £3,600 clear in 1853 349; £114 from Tauchnitz 335n; £2,047 for 1853 from Longman 358; £50 for 1854 from Tauchnitz 405n; £1,500 for 1854 from Longman 413n; £300 for American rights to *History* 467; borrows £1,600 to make a favourable purchase 469; now a rich man 480; £20,000 from Longman for *History* VI, 24, 25, 28n, 49; investments guarantee

Macaulay, Thomas Babington, 1st Baron (1800-59)—INCOME, ETC., *cont.*
£3,000 yearly 25; £1,500 a year in addition to fixed income 25n; £67.10 from royalties in colonies 42n; £250 fee from Tauchnitz 49n; £242.11.6 from Tauchnitz edition of *History* 49n; £160 from Tauchnitz in 1857 99n; TBM will not be the poorest peer 113; £500 for patent of nobility 118, 135; £36.15 for peer's robes 119; expenses of peerage between £700 and £800 135; £2,300 from Longman for 1857 135n; £6,276 for 1858 from Longman 156n; buys annuities for William and Elizabeth 163; only use of his opulence to promote happiness of others 165; annuity for Fanny 169; 'rolling in money' 234; income £5,000 in 1859, expenses £3,000 234n
INDIAN CAREER: Indian appointment attractive because domestic career clouded II, 300; doubts whether to accept after Hannah's response 304; appointment beginning to be talked about 331; all but settled 332; plans for outfit 339; Fourth Member of Supreme Council guardian of Indians against Europeans 340; appointment presented to Cabinet 343; appointment certain 345; reasons for accepting 345-6; made official 350; reasons for accepting 353-5; sometimes appalled by responsibility 354; plans for outfit 362-3; formal acceptance of office 364; Macaulay resented by Englishmen in India III, viii; expenses of journey 6; arrives Madras 31; freedom of the press issue 124n, 184-5; proposes committee on prison discipline 165; sits on Supreme Council, Law Commission, Committee of Public Instruction, Committee on Prison Discipline 170; *see also* India
Education: joins Anglicist side III, 102; made president of Committee of Public Instruction 103, 119; defends English instruction 122-3; declaration in favour of 138-9; writes draft of Governor-General's Resolution on Education 138n; summary of conflict of views 148-50; 165, success of English schools 193; Hobhouse sides with Anglicists 214; *see also* India, Committee of Public Instruction; India, Education in
Law Commission: III, 63n; about to bring important reforms before Council 140; TBM accepts presidency of 145; plans 'immense reforms' 146; Indian Penal Code 146-7; 'finest employment' 152; 189, remarks on Penal Code 193; TBM works in illness of others 195; 202, nearly complete 209-10; Code completed 213, 217; *see also* India, Law Commission
Supreme Council: TBM takes oath of office and Council seat III, 59n; begins work 63; proposes reform of civil procedure to 148; question of Fourth Member 164n; 218, TBM resigns from 238-9; remarks on difficulty of position of Fourth Member 239; *see also* India, Supreme Council
LANGUAGES: reads 'insatiably' on *Asia:* Greek, Latin, Spanish, Italian, French, English III, 34; TBM's method for learning 194-5
Dutch: surprised at how easily he makes it out IV, 219; learning 346; a 'smattering' 347; reads with difficulty 464
French: I, 25; in first class 26; 54, TBM talks in to Dutchman at Holland House II, 76; III, 181
German: plans to study II, 29; to be learned on voyage from India III, 194; 195, will write reviews of German books some day 196; 211, plans to study 10 or 11 hours daily on voyage from India 233-4; reading New Testament and Schiller 236; 'indifferently skilled' 235; does not read rapidly VI, 27; requires to have script deciphered 186, 191
Greek: I, 7, 16, 17, 18, wins prize in 22, 23; in third class 26; boys read Greek Testament on Sundays at school 29; intimidated by 31; 32, makes synopsis of notes on Euripides 77; why study it exclusively? 79-80; remarks on its use 88-91; TBM's praise of 145; in 'good condition enough' III, 62; reads 'like a man of the world' 111; has

gone back to Greek literature with 'a passion quite astonishing to myself' 129; suffers from a suppression of 132; 136, 152, 159, reads as 'connected course of study' 163; 180, 199ff; 210, amusing himself with v, 106; reading with Ellis 125; never did so good a day's work in before 179; ought to be studied with aid of translation 287; improvements in means for studying 344-5; understands better than ever before 347; reading with George Trevelyan 411

Hindustani: III, 9, impeded in his progress by Hannah's knowledge of 93

Italian: resolved to attempt seriously I, 69; III, 121, 129, 181, TBM takes lessons in VI, 51; getting on in well 53

Latin: I, 5, 16, 17, 21, 23, in second class 26; writes declamations and hexameters 32; verse exercises in 77; why study exclusively? 79-80; remarks on its use 88-91; reading at Cambridge 108; surprised at winning declamation prize 151; 'in good condition enough' III, 62; 136, 152, 159, reads as 'connected course of study' 163; 'turning over several third-rate and fourth-rate writers' 178; 180, 199ff; 210, amusing himself with v, 106; points of style in VI, 98-9

Persian: TBM seeks books in III, 9; learning 29n

Portuguese: learns on voyage from Madras to Calcutta III, 86; 181, 195

Spanish: may be deferred I, 69; studying 69n; means to carry his conquests 'far and deep into Spanish literature' II, 138; studying 320; III, 129, 181, 195, reading with Ellis 125

LEGAL CAREER *see also* King's Bench, Court of; India, Law Commission; Lancaster Assizes; Leeds Borough Sessions; Lincoln's Inn; Northern Circuit; West Riding Quarter Sessions; York Assizes: enters Lincoln's Inn I, 171n; called to Bar 171n; studies conveyancing 172; wishes to keep terms as quickly as possible 173; 177, decides to begin studies at once 185-6; joins Northern Circuit 208; serves as counsel on election committee at Leicester 211; indiscreet for him to appear as counsel for Zachary Macaulay 221; receives first brief 223; results of first case 225; attendance on circuit and quarter sessions an expense not a source of income 253n; not yet ready to give up 265; counsel for Society of Apothecaries, York Assizes 266n; generally practices in Court of King's Bench 272; Spring 1830 last Northern Circuit attended 277n

LIBRARY: Sale Catalogue, Sotheby's 4 March 1863, I, 51n; shelf-list of made in 1852 III, 108n; has more than 7,000 volumes v, 96; 'near ten thousand volumes' 475; moved to Holly Lodge VI, 16n; sends books for binding 224

Books from (the following titles include only those mentioned in the *Letters* that are also recorded in the sale catalogue or the shelf list or that are in known locations, especially the library at Wallington): Joseph Addison, *Works*, v, 472n; John Adolphus, *History of England*, I, 51n; Athenaeus, ed. Casaubon, VI, 247n; Richard Bentley, *Dissertation upon the Epistles of Phalaris*, III, 183n; James Beresford, *Miseries of Human Life*, I, 46n; *Boston Railroad Jubilee*, v, 287n; James Browne, *A History of the Highlands*, v, 120n; Gilbert Burnet, *History of His Own Times*, II, 75n; *Darien Papers*, ed. John Hill Burton, VI, 129n; Calderon, *Works*, III, 210n; William Chappell, *Popular Music of Olden Time*, VI, 108n; Clement I, *Clementina*, ed. Dressel, VI, 10n; Henry Colman, *Fourth Report on the Agriculture of Massachusetts*, v, 53n; Catherine Cuthbertson, *Santo Sebastiano*, II, 51n; William Hepworth Dixon, *William Penn*, v, 158n; Charles Gavan Duffy, ed., *The Spirit of the Nation*, IV, 259n; Egidio Forcellini, *Lexicon Totius Latinitatis*, v, 453n; Lord Fountainhall, *Historical Observes of Memorable Occurents*, IV, 384n; Charles Bernard Gibson, *The Last Earl of Desmond*, v, 436n; Charles Gray,

Macaulay, Thomas Babington, 1st Baron (1800-59)—LIBRARY, *cont.* *The Muckomachy*, IV, 303n; Guillaume Groen van Prinsterer, *Handboek der Geschiedenis van het Vaderland*, VI, 88n; Hermann Hettner, *Literaturgeschichte des Achtzehnten Jahrhunderts*, VI, 26n; Lady Holland, *Memoir of Sydney Smith*, V, 428n; Wilhelm Ihne, *Researches into the History of the Roman Constitution*, V, 313n; H. J. Koenen, *Voorlezingen over de Geschiedenis des Nederlandschen Handels*, VI, 80n; J. H. Künzel, *Leben und Reden Sir Robert Peel's*, V, 201n; *Lives* of Pococke, Pearce, Newton, and Skelton, V, 319n; Amelia Mary Loraine, *Lays of Israel*, VI, 176n; Martin Luther, *Opera Omnia*, VI, 158n; Lord Lyttelton, 'A Few Thoughts about Shakspeare,' VI, 30n; Henry Manners-Sutton, ed., *The Lexington Papers*, V, 112n; Cornelius Mathews, *Various Writings*, IV, 178n; T. J. Mathias, *The Pursuits of Literature*, III, 137n; Mohan Lal, *Life of Dost Mohammed*, IV, 234n; William Mure, *Selections from the Family Papers Preserved at Caldwell*, V, 401n; Barry O'Meara, *Napoleon in Exile* I, 180n; *Oration of Hyperides against Demosthenes*, V, 95; Josiah Quincy, *Memoir*, V, 231n; Bishop Samuel Parker, *History of His Own Times*, VI, 154n; *Paston Letters*, V, 40n; Photius, ed. Bekker, V, 405n; Plato, ed. Ficino, III, 142n; George Pryme, *Memoirs of Daniel Sykes*, IV, 378n; Grimod de la Reynière, *Almanach des Gourmands*, II, 215n; Schiller, *Works*, III, 194n; Anna Seward, *Letters*, VI, 234n; Alexander Smart, *Rambling Rhymes*, IV, 265n; Percival Stockdale, *Memoirs*, V, 410n; William Stout, *Autobiography*, V, 129n; Thomas Noon Talfourd, *Ion*, III, 249; Georg Willem Vreede, *Correspondence Diplomatique et Militaire*, V, 113n; Eliot Warburton, *Memoirs of Prince Rupert*, V, 49n; *The Westover Manuscripts*, ed. E. C. Ruffin, V, 144n; Bulstrode Whitelocke, *Memorials of the English Affairs*, V, 63n

LITERARY CAREER *see also* TBM's Writings *and* Appendix: A List of Macaulay's Published Writings; early ambition I, ix; sends contribution to *Christian Observer* 49; indexes *Christian Observer* 49n; has offer to write political articles for a newspaper 171; writing for *Knight's Quarterly* 186; adopts 'Tristram Merton' as pseudonym 188n; forced to withdraw from *Knight's* 189; invited to contribute to *ER* 203n; Sydney Smith cautions against 'too much asperity and contempt in controversy' 217; invited to contribute to *Friendship's Offering* 244; doubts whether he should continue with *ER* on Jeffrey's retirement 253-4; offered editorship of *ER* 254n; nearly breaks with *ER* in quarrel with Brougham 298-300, 309-10; his contributions to *Christian Observer* 321-2; pseudonym of 'Malcolm Macgregor, jun.' II, 57n; his contributions the support of *ER* 250; to live as a writer would mean daily writing 300; no wish to mix with popular writers 314; does not want to live by his pen 345; maintains connection with *ER* in Indian years 351-2; won't become a bookseller's hack 353; won't write on education or politics III, 293; office will not interfere with writing for *ER* 299-300; once aspired to be great poet V, 139-40

LITERARY OPINIONS: history should not be cold and incredulous about religion I, 53; pastoral not his mode 64; English literature equal to classic 83; literary merit not dependent on morality 119-20; knowledge of modern literature a grace not a defect 139ff; poetry too sensual for Christianity 171; hates coterie taste 239; on appropriate style for periodical writing 261; critic of English must have Bible at his fingers' ends II, 22; originality not identical with literary skill 109; not successful as a literary critic III, 245; remarks on his own style IV, 27-9; his rule for writing 28; on periodical writings 40; on relation of literary fame to literary criticism 42; indifferent to praise or

blame: 'every book settles its own place' 58; compares himself with Sydney Smith and Jeffrey 167; on diction 385, 386; avoiding the misuse of pronouns 393-4; 'balderdash' a good word v, 10; history must include much of human wickedness and weakness 42; last twenty five years have produced no literature to be remembered 99; pure tragedy need not be oppressive 112; difficulty of inscriptions and epitaphs 170; taste for the odd gives way to that for the true 194-5; criticism does not affect a book that has life vi, 173

Personal Characteristics:

ambition: inseparable from domestic affection ii, 63; overcome by desire for domesticity 85; ambition has palled 271; only *parvenu* who ever despised ambition 276

dislikes: of exhibition – never spoke but with reluctance iv, 389; of games i, 16; of riding i, 146n; of music ii, 18, 34, 35, 41, vi, 108

emotional dependence: i, xi-xii; ii, 203-4, 226

love of books: i, ix, iii, 115, 'what a blessing it is to love books as I love them' 129; 'literature has saved my life and my reason' 158; his reading in India 159-60, 199-202; iv, 56-7

love of home: homesick i, 14; weeps from homesickness 32-3; Zachary Macaulay on TBM's love of home 40n; 'maladie du Clapham' 57; 112, 168, strengthened by exile 182; few have it 'so strongly as I have it' iii, 203; 219, 223, 233

love of sisters: i, viii, 308, ii, 85, 102, 122, 133-4, on Margaret's engagement 184; his farewell to Margaret 203; 211, 271, iii, 106, grief on Hannah's marriage 114; no relief from Margaret's death 156; vi, 280

speaking: acquires 'loud and boisterous tone' at school i, 40n, 42; too-rapid delivery in making speeches 272n, ii, 5n; lacks fervour in speaking 83-4

Political Career: makes maiden speech in Parliament i, 272; sworn in again on accession of William iv 275; Reform Bill speech puts him 'in front rank' ii, 11; resolves to move address to King if Whig leaders fail 100; arranges for resolution of support 100-1; has greatly raised his position in Reform crisis 105; public life not necessary to him 258; cannot continue without independent income 299, 353; sworn of Privy Council 300n; four elections together 'have not cost me 500 pounds' iii, 383; compromise position on free trade and Corn Laws iv, 91, 94, 100-4; will not repeat experience of Melbourne ministry 271; Russell proposes to bring TBM in for Richmond 362; never made a farthing by being cabinet minister v, 255

Calne: offered seat for by Lansdowne i, 263n; elected 264; takes seat in House of Commons 264n; re-elected 276n; petition against TBM's election 276n; return certain 278, 279; election petition decided in TBM's favour 312; rivals canvassing there ii, 8; re-elected 12n, 13n; sworn in for new Parliament 45; re-elected following appointment to Board of Control 122n, 129, 130; sworn in for on re-election 134; *see also* Calne

Edinburgh: TBM invited to stand for iii, 287; cannot spend more than £500 on election 288; elected 290-1; seat vacated on accepting office 303; re-elected 314, 316-17; state of things vexing 344; TBM made no pledges 358; re-elected 1841 376-80; iv, viii, his position on Corn Laws disapproved 104n; TBM supposes he will lose next election 161, 164; TBM no 'representative for fanatics' 164; quite easy about prospect of losing seat 172; avoids republican ceremony at 211; tactics required to meet McLaren's threat 214-15; raises question of Scottish Banking System in Commons 241; conflict over Maynooth 254; helps prepare Scottish Universities Bill 258n; defends Bill 261-3; doubts he will represent Edinburgh again 264; legislation against incorporated trades 267n; seat safe after speech on Corn Laws 269; no difficulty about re-election 275; seat vacated on appointment to Paymaster

Macaulay, Thomas Babington, 1st Baron (1800-59)—POLITICAL CAREER, *cont.*
Generalship 300; re-elected 1846 301-2; spends £500 for re-election 302n, 318; new election on dissolution of Parliament 339; TBM defeated in 1847 341; TBM proud of 'how I risked and how I lost' city's favour 345; farewell address 348, 349; re-elected in 1852 V, ix; plan to return him 231, 234-5; TBM's position 236-7; election certain 241; elected 245, 246; won't be slave to constituents 259-60; offers to pay post-election expenses 262; speech at after election 292; presents petition for museums in Scotland 335; supports Annuity Tax Bill 342; reason for his election 400-1; TBM's convictions on religious questions well known 408; asks for a successor 441; will hold seat until Craig ready 446; asks to be relieved 450; determined to resign 468, VI, 6; addresses electors on retirement 9; *see also* Edinburgh
Leeds: TBM named as candidate for II, 92n; to be brought in free of expense 94; enthusiasm in his favour 102; formally invited to stand for 103; TBM compliments Leeds Political Union 120; speaks at Reform dinner 123n; electioneering at 132-3; declares he will not canvass 162-3; defines his political position 162-7; will give no pledges 165-6, 176, 177-9; endorsed by Political Union 186; campaign speeches at 188; campaigning 190; successful canvass 198-200; elected for 205-12; forced to pay election costs 223, 225; presents Sabbath petition from 235n; petition for corporation reform 236n; petition on abolition 237n; his conduct on slavery question approved at 285; must keep town of 120,000 in good humour 348; TBM thinks he showed unmatched boldness in Corn Law speech at 348; TBM recommends Hobhouse as successor 357; succeeded by Edward Baines 361; resigns seat III, 18; election recalled 115; made no pledges at 358; *see also* Leeds
OFFICES AND APPOINTMENTS (*see separate entry for* Indian Career):
Board of Control: appointed to II, 122n; appointed Secretary to Board of Control 209; offers to resign over abolition question 239n; to resign as Secretary 350; *see also* Board of Control
Commissioner of Bankrupts: appointed I, 230; 271, 272n; *see also* Commissioners of Bankrupts
Paymaster General: III, x, IV, 300; presides at Chelsea Hospital Board 305; doubts he will be a year in office 318; interesting deliberations in cabinet on Ireland 319; ought to resign office on opening of Parliament 350; salary of £2,400 351; retains office at request of Lord John Russell 363n; resigns 362-4; *see also* Chelsea Hospital Board, *and* Pay Office
Secretary at War: III, x, appointed 298-9; 'resolved to be master of the details of the War Office' 302; proposes brevet promotions 314-15; presents army estimates 321, 331; besieged by petitioners 345; defends Lord Cardigan in House 371n; *see also* War Office
POLITICAL OPINIONS: defends his political beliefs to parents apropos of Peterloo I, 132-4; not those of Hunt or Waithman but of Cicero and Milton 133; prefers Tory reaction to popular tumult 163-4; Napoleon one of the great mixed characters of all time 180; on the qualifications of a representative of the university 181; supports Catholic emancipation 211; violent Whigism 211n; opinion on ballot undecided 313; against prosecutions for blasphemy II, 44; supports free trade 92; favours ballot 92-3; fear of revolution 99; pledges to support free trade 104; on ballot 109n; security of property more important than church reform 114; supports ballot 132; reform should have trial before further changes made 132; supports ballot 165; function of representative the pursuit of practical good 166; fear of revolution 257, 270; '*Centre Gauche*' the strongest party III, 74; religion not to be mixed with politics 238; thinks coalition likely 271; opposed

to Corn Laws and Irish Church 275; supports ballot and short Parliaments 290n; makes no distinction between Churchmen and Dissenters on civil matters 346; supports Palmerston on Eastern Question 353; necessity of concession 356; will make no pledges 357-8; State must control Church when the two are connected 364; will not contribute to public amusements for constituents 384; favours free trade IV, 85, 91; determines to oppose sliding scale of corn duties 100; compromise required on free trade question 102, 103-4; always a small class of men who 'have a real veto on all public measures which they agree to oppose' 114; supports education for factory children 122; as much real reform going on under Tories as under Whigs 123; defends his idea of progress 176; on the necessity of compromise 186ff; will not submissively conform 190; does not agree that there should be 'no retrospect in politics' 265; has 'great confidence in the sense, virtue and self-command of the nation' 270; once supported ballot, will not now oppose it 272; Whigs failed to meet responsibility on Peel's resignation 278-9; grounds of opposition to universal suffrage IV, 291-2; holds defensive war to be 'lawful and necessary' 292; defends transportation of Chartist leaders 293; thinks the policies of Guizot 'detestable' 362; further reform made necessary by events of 1848 363; present time (1848) not dangerous 373; events of 1848 have strengthened moderates 383; feelings with Whigs but judgment with Tories in 1851 V, 156; military rule better than chaos in France 210; representatives should have the confidence of their constituencies 236; no longer takes pleasure in contemporary politics 476; democratic institutions opposed to civilisation VI, 94-6; American prosperity not related to democratic institutions 171-2

PORTRAITS: lithographic sketches for Leeds election II, 206n, 207; various 280n; TBM's judgment on V, 56, 57

Richard Beard, daguerreotype by (1848), V, 56; 'hideous caricature' 57

Antoine Claudet, photograph by (1856), VI, 16n; as likeness 16n; engraved for *Miscellaneous Writings* 16n

John Doyle (*H B*), sketches by (1834-47), II, 64n; original sketch of 'Reform Bill Receiving the King's Assent' 64n

Eden Upton Eddis, portraits of TBM (1849), V, 55-6, 57; frontispiece to *Essays*, 1850, 55n; second portrait 55n; third portrait 55n

Sir Francis Grant, portrait (1853), V, 327n

Benjamin Robert Haydon, sketch for painting of Reform Banquet (1833), II, 273, 280

Sir George Hayter, sketch for painting of Reformed House of Commons (1838), III, 257

Henry Inman, portrait (1844), IV, 225

Baron Marochetti, medallion (1848), V, 56

Maull and Polyblank, photograph (1856), VI, 33n; TBM's opinion of 33n; published with biographical sketch 33n, 41n

Patric Park, bust (1846), IV, 321; TBM requests its delivery 361; V, 56

John Partridge, study for group of Fine Arts Commissioners (1849), V, 29; 57

S. W. Reynolds, Sr., oil sketch for 'Reform Bill Receiving the King's Assent' (1832), II, 64n

S. W. Reynolds, Jr., and William Walker, engraving, 'Reform Bill Receiving the King's Assent (1836), II, 64n, 124n

S. W. Reynolds, Jr., portrait (1833), II, 223, 224, offered to Margaret 226; 263, 269, engraving published 273; people think 'very like' 273; TBM approves 277; 278, in Edward Cropper's keeping 290

John N. Rhodes?, lithograph at Leeds (1832), 'hideous hangman-like fellow' II, 214

George Richmond, crayon drawing (1844), V, 56n

George Richmond, crayon drawing (1850), V, 138n; TBM's comment on 138n; engraved for *Works*, 1866, 138n

Macaulay, Thomas Babington, 1st Baron (1800-59)—PORTRAITS, *cont.*
Edward Matthew Ward, portrait (1853), III, 349n, V, xi, 175n, TBM refuses further sitting for 399
Sir John Watson-Gordon, portrait (1850), V, 110; engraved by Faed 110n
Thomas Woolner, statue at Trinity (1863), I, 317n
RELIGIOUS OPINIONS: I, xix; hates all confessors, Protestant or Catholic II, 247; called an infidel 247n; supports sending priests to Catholic soldiers in India III, 301-2; his confession of faith on church matters 346; statement on Church question at Edinburgh 379n; mistrusts Catholic part in Irish movement for religious equality V, 290; does not believe in right to proselytize 358-9; state can teach its own religion to vagrant children 411; missionary command given only to apostles VI, 127; *see also* Catholic and Catholics, Church of England, Church of Ireland, Church of Scotland
RESIDENCES:
Cambridge: Jesus Lane I, 101n; *see also* Trinity College
Clapham: No. 5, The Pavement I, 6n
Clifton: 16 Caledonia Place V, 259
India: Calcutta, 33 Chowringhee Road III, 90; 'best in Calcutta' 93; 97, forced to leave for repairs 172; Ootacamund, Woodcock Hall III, 65
London:
Albany, I, xix; neighbour of Mountstuart Elphinstone II, 137; III, x, ornaments in 349n; 382, 387, IV, vii, 5, rooms furnished as 'very pleasant student's cell' 12; takes new chambers at 318; returns to 328; V, 30, new rooms in 33; 70, 71, F.3, 98; 248, 253, 288, 309, TBM means to leave 475, VI, 8
44 Bernard Street (Macaulay family home) II, 131n; dines at 217; 269, TBM advises keeping 312; 360
Birchin Lane, I, 6n
20 Lower Cadogan Place, I, 101, 109, 115, 126, under repair 131; 142, 150, 156, 161, 182, 187n, family leaves for Great Ormond Street 192n; II, 344, V, 76
3 Clarges Street, III, 213n, 243, 258, 274, 285, IV, 398n
8 South Square, Gray's Inn, I, xix; moves to at beginning of 1830 273n; 323, II, 11, 40, 277
12 Great George Street, III, 313, 317, 320, 336n, servants at 341n; 378, IV, 15n, 57n, 399n, 400
50 Great Ormond Street, I, 141n, 187n, 192, 273n, 284, sold following death of Selina Mills Macaulay II, 17n; how they used to act there 72; 327, period of TBM's residence 375n; III, 95, TBM revisits VI, 100-1
Holly Lodge, Campden Hill, VI, ix, hears of from Milman 10; describes 10n; 12, in treaty for 14; plan for moving to 16; TBM describes 18; furnishing 25; 27, takes possession 29; 34, first breakfast party at 37; TBM occupies 39n; gardening at 73-4; new furnishings for 234
Isle of Wight, Ventnor, Madeira Hall, V, 121
Malvern, The Lodge, V, 174
Richmond Hill, 6 Upper Park Place, V, 458ff
Thames Ditton, Greenwood Lodge, V, 403n, 406, 425
Tunbridge Wells, 1 Wellington Place, V, 338-9
SCHOOL: parent's intention in I, xviii; Greaves's school, Clapham, 5; Preston's school, Little Shelford, studies at 16-17; debating society 16, 18; examinations 18-19; mathematics 19; beaten at 19; determined to apply to mathematics 20, 21; debate topic, Wellington v. Marlborough 21; examinations 22; debate topic, crusades 22; has a little garden of his own 22; mathematics 23; debate topic, Catholic Emancipation 23; speaks on crusade question 23; fagging for examinations 24; mathematics 24; TBM most bashful student 24; examinations 25; TBM stands last in mathematics 25; Sunday routine at 29; examinations in verses, declamation, Greek, Latin, mathematics, history 30-1; 'Burning of Muscow' subject for verses 31;

mathematics 'suit my taste' 31; examination topics 31-2; returns to school after vacation 32; English composition and algebra 46; examinations 46; school moves to Aspenden Hall 50; returns to school 50n; examinations 55; returns to school 57; bullied at 57; has declamation to write 60; declamations 62; examinations 62; 'here it is not the fashion to think' 64; declamation subjects 66; Preston doubtful about debating society 76; declamations at 76; TBM takes pleasure in debating society 77; English verses 77; examinations 77; remarks on the study of Greek and Latin 79-80; Zachary Macaulay approves debating society 81; Mary Queen of Scots debate topic 81; on Greek and Latin 87-91

TRAVELS:

Belgium 1841: IV, 7

Continental tour 1853: Belgium, Germany, Switzerland, France, V, 349n, 351-4

Continental tour 1857: Paris, Rheims, Cologne, VI, 104n

England:

visits Cambridge with Hannah and Margaret 1832, II, 196

Lichfield and Oxford with Hannah and Margaret 1832, II, 186, 187

English provinces 1842, IV, 53

West Country 1842, IV, 95n

Ely and Peterborough with Ellis 1842, IV, 59

West of England with Ellis 1859, VI, 240

Easter tours:

1844: Hereford, IV, 183n

1845: Salisbury and Winchester, IV, 247

1846: Worcester, IV, 268n, 298n, V, 174

1847: Lincoln and York, IV, 334, V, 268n

1849: Chester, Bangor, Lichfield, V, 42n, 43n

1850: Norwich and Ely, V, 97n, 102, 103n

1851: Southampton, Portsmouth, Winchester, V, 159n

1852: Peterborough, Boston, Lincoln, V, 218n, 267

1853: *see main entry for* Paris

1854: York, Castle Howard, Durham V, 390n, 394

1856: Rochester and Canterbury, VI, 25-6, 29

1857: Salisbury, Stonehenge, Longleat, VI, 86

1858: Lichfield and Oxford, VI, 143

France (see also main entry for Paris):

1830: plan of tour, I, 284

1840: III, 336n

1843: Loire valley, IV, 136ff

1854: Boulogne, Paris, Beauvais, Orléans, Blois, Tours, V, 419n

1858: tour with Ellis, VI, 166n

Holland:

1844: IV, 216ff

1847: IV, 339, 346, 347, 349n

India 1834: Madras to Ootacamund, III, 44ff; Ootacamund to Calcutta, 80ff

Ireland 1849: V, 64-70

Italy:

1838-9: III, 259, 260-73; 274; V, 353n

1856:, VI, 57ff

Scotland (see also Edinburgh *and* Glasgow):

1817: I, 233n, II, 306

1828: I, 233-4, 235-41

1833: with Hannah, II, 306-7

1850: V, 111

1859: VI, 230-3

WRITINGS, INCLUDING SPEECHES *see also* Appendix: A List of Macaulay's Published Writings

Essays, Individual: 'Addison,' subject proposed IV, 98; agrees to write 118; 126, TBM partial to it 127; points out Miss Aikin's blunders 128; omissions in reprinting 128n; returns proofs 129; correction in 130; favourable reception 132; note to in *ER* 133n; 194, Cameron welcome to reprint 311; added to collected *Essays* V, 59n; 'The Athenian Orators,' III, 374n, VI, 179n; 'Atterbury,' III, 201n, V, xi, writing 317; 318n, consults Mahon's *History* for 323; published by Tauchnitz VI, 230n; 'Bacon,' Ellis on I, xxiii; II, 28n, III, vii, writing 163; 189, 'prodigiously long article' 190; 191, sent to Napier 194; duplicate copy 195, 196; corrects error in 197; 198, 199, 202, sends correction 205; 216, 217, expects it to be attacked

Macaulay, Thomas Babington, 1st Baron (1800-59)—WRITINGS, *cont.*
234; reprinted in U.S. 263; 281n, 370, IV, 199, criticised by De Morgan 355, 355n; 'Barère,' proposed IV, 163; writing 166; research at British Museum 170; nearly ready 172; sent to Napier 173; returns proofs 174; 'excess of his rascality has spoiled my paper on him' 183; 195, reprinted in Tauchnitz edn VI, 100n; 179n; 'Bentham's Defence of Mill,' I, 254n, TBM thinks of reprinting IV, 96; 'Bunyan' (for *Encyclopaedia Britannica*), V, xi, written at Brighton V, 367n; sent to Black 373; published 373n; 402n, VI, 100n; 'Burghley,' agrees to write II, 111; begins 115; delayed by illness 119, 120, 'strange, rambling performance' 121; sends to Napier 121; praised by Lady Holland 144; not yet paid for 153; payment for 190n; 'Byron,' I, 319, agrees to write II, 7; promised for next number 14; writing will distract TBM from grief over mother's death 14; writing slowly 29; TBM compliments Rogers in 29; 30, 'worst thing I ever wrote in my life' 37; likes neither the book nor its hero 37-8; sends to Napier 40, 41; liked by Napier and Empson 50; Tom Moore pleased by 54; popular 57; liked by Hannah and Zachary Macaulay 58; TBM's criticism of 59-60; plagiarised by Disraeli V, 301n; 'Chatham' (1834), proposed II, 316; TBM agrees to write 335; writing 352; not yet begun 366; 367, scarcely begun 371; III, 6, 9, 10, 11, 12, corrects error in 14; 281n, corrected for Traveller's Library V, 161n; 'Chatham' (1844), suggested IV, 159; decides to write 160; early plans for 177n; 199, writing 210; proposes to salvage from the essay on Burke 212; goes on 'swimmingly' 212; forced to rewrite 213; never took so much trouble as with this paper 216; generally liked 221; criticised by Brougham 226; added to collected *Essays* V, 59n; corrected for Traveller's Library 161n; 'Civil Disabilities of the Jews,' TBM asked to write I, 262; proposed 273; 311, will send next week 312; finished 314; Goldsmid wishes to reprint 320; 'Clive,' II, 107n, III, vii, 125n, agrees to write 216; will begin on return from Italy 259, 262, 276; a grand subject 293; begun 295; proceeding slowly 297; thinks it will take 298; work interrupted 299; TBM wants it reviewed by experts on India 300; will send soon 306; sends to Napier 307; returns corrected 309; Napier's criticism 309; sentence about Bentinck 309n; 310, 310n, generally liked 315; 344, 362, softened in reprinting 363n; 369, IV, ix, 21, V, 97n, plagiarized by MacFarlane 181; 'Comic Dramatists of the Restoration': *see* 'Leigh Hunt'; 'A Conversation between Mr Abraham Cowley and Mr John Milton,' III, 374n, IV, 16; 'Dante', I, 73n, 185n; 'Madame D'Arblay,' II, 227n, III, 308n, agrees to write IV, 30; feels some scruple about 32; not yet ready 44; will write if Hunt does not 61; family has offered assistance 63; TBM explains to Hunt why he has taken the subject 64; will begin at once 70; 79, 82-3, sends to Napier 84; treatment of Croker in 89-90; revisions in 90; and Croker 93; alteration in 94; pleases Burney family 97; 194, added to collected *Essays* V, 59n; 'Dryden,' I, 69n, 167n, nearly finished 229; VI, 191; 'Fragments of a Roman Tale,' I, 188, blunder in VI, 161; 'Frederic the Great,' proposed IV, 17; incomparable subject 19; 21, 'will set to work again' 22; sends to Napier 24; returns proofs 25; amusing enough 26; defends his style against Napier 27-9; 40, reprinted in Tauchnitz edn VI, 100n; 'Gladstone on Church and State,' I, xvi, III, 69n, begins 275-6; will dispose of Gladstone's theory 277; sends to Napier 278; returns proofs 279; praised by Napier 280; returns revises 282; generally liked 284-5; 'Goldsmith,' (for *Encyclopaedia Britannica*) V, xi, 459, sends to Black 466; reprinted VI, 100n; 'Hallam's Constitutional History,' getting on

rapidly I, 244; 258n, IV, 175n; 'Warren Hastings,' II, 216n, III, vii, 32n, proposed 344; 348, 359, sketch of 361; 363, 368, must furnish two articles 369; better as one paper 370; must be delayed 371; a noble subject 385; IV, ix, nearly finished 5; sends to Napier 6; returns revise 7; blunder in 9; praised by Napier 12; 16, 17, blunder in 19; 21, Impey's reply to 321n; in Traveller's Library V, 161n; revised for Traveller's Library and for Gleig's sake 169n; plagiarized by MacFarlane 181; allusion in 201; 'History,' I, xx, 36n, retires to Leeds to write 231; 'Lord Holland,' III, 372n, 374, 377, Brougham's objections to 385; reluctant to write IV, 46; 203; 'Leigh Hunt,' I, 239n, 230n, proposed 340; 342n, 344, 348, collects information at British Museum 350; 353, curtailed in order to meet deadline 358; sent to Napier 358; 'neither profound nor brilliant' 359; TBM values it less than anything written since he was a boy 361; 365n, IV, 18, 43; 'Life of Johnson,' proposed II, 7; agrees to write 57; TBM means to dust Croker's jacket for him 84; has not left Croker a leg to stand on 94; half finished 95; sends first part to Napier 96; effect on Croker 106; abused by *Blackwood's* 108; note added to 111-12n; 'Samuel Johnson' (for *Encyclopaedia Britannica*), V, xi, VI, x, begins 29; composition of 29n; nearly finished 50; reprinted 100n; 'London University,' I, 113n, 242n, allusion to Croker 286n; 'Machiavelli,' I, 221, 'a juvenile essay' IV, 131; 'Sir James Mackintosh,' III, vii, TBM proposes it 21; sent in multiple copies from India 107, 109, 116; approves Napier's alterations 163; 171, 216, 244n, 281n, 374n; 'Lord Mahon's War of the Succession,' proposed II, 190; writing 200; goes slowly 201; to finish at Leeds 205; slowly writing at Leeds 207; slowed by press of official work 213; finished 222; long and dull 223; approved by Napier 227; praised by Lady Holland 227; payment for 261, 300; III, 248n, 283, mentioned by Künzel VI, 243; 'Memorials of Hampden,' I, 105n, tentatively proposed II, 108, 109; writing 109-10; partly narrative, a new form for TBM 110; hastily written 111; 'Mill's Essay on Government,' I, 254n, TBM thinks of reprinting IV, 96; 'Milton,' I, 203n, II, 39n; 'Mirabeau,' proposed II, 121; will finish soon 135; 144, thinks it will be popular 146; sends to Napier 149; praised by Napier 153; scriptural allusions in 167; liked at Rothley Temple 171; payment for 190n; 'Mitford's History of Greece,' I, 36n, III, 374n; 'Robert Montgomery's Poems,' I, 267, proposed 268; will begin soon 269; Napier's alterations in 273; retained in collected *Essays* V, 103n; 'Major Moody's Reports,' I, 221n; 'Pitt' (for *Encyclopaedia Britannica*), IV, 205n, V, xi, corrected for Traveller's Library 161n; slow composition of VI, x; returns proofs 167; returns revise 168; composition of 168n; corrected page proofs at Trinity 168n; read in proof by Stanhope 177; TBM admits mistake about Temple 179; Black intends to reprint separately 179; TBM offers to Tauchnitz 230, 257; 'Present Administration,' attribution of to TBM I, 222n; praised by Lansdowne 224; 263n, 'Ranke,' III, 268n, 325n, 326, 329, nearly finished 336, 337; sent to Napier 337; TBM supposes it will be abused 340; 341, 374n; 'On the Royal Society of Literature,' read to Zachary Macaulay before publication I, 188; V, 163n; 'Sadler's Law of Population,' revisions to I, 275-6; theological question in 276; payment for 283; Jeffrey's opinion 284-5; remarks on in *Sun* 284n; 315n; 'Sadler's Refutation, Refuted,' I, 312, 314, sends to Napier 315; contribution by Napier and changes by TBM 316; its effect 318; 'Southey's *Colloquies*,' proposed I, 256; 258, 261, returns proofs, revisions 262; popular 267; complimented by Hazlitt 271n; payment for 300n; V, 441n; 'Southey's Edition of *Pilgrim's Progress*,' agrees to write II, 107; will finish shortly 108;

Macaulay, Thomas Babington, 1st Baron (1800-59)—WRITINGS, *cont.*
TBM defends his judgment of Bunyan to Napier 109; to be reprinted, a favourite with Dissenters IV, 97; 'Sir William Temple,' II, 173n, 201n, agrees to write III, 216, 243; 249, 254, finished 255; 255n, by no means easy writing 256; 257, 258, 259, 281n, 282n, TBM defends his remarks on Swift in IV, 126; 'Utilitarian Theory of Government,' I, 254n, can write in a week 255; sends off 255; softened by TBM and Napier 255-6; TBM objects to Napier's changes 261; thinks of reprinting IV, 96; 'Walpole,' II, 305, begins 308; going on slowly 311; busy with night and day 315; finished 316; thinks it will be a hit 317; 318, 320, completely re-written 320-1; TBM defends his literary judgments in 321; TBM thinks well of 322; payment for 335; angers Lady Holland 335; 336-7; angers the Miss Berrys 347; resented by Mary Berry 348-9; III, 281n; 'West Indian Slavery,' I, 188n; 'The West Indies,' first contribution to *ER*, I, 203n
Essays, Collected: dedicated to Jeffrey I, 222n, 224n; TBM excludes article on Utilitarians from collection 255n, IV, 96n; first collection published in United States III, 338; revisions in I, 262n, II, 29n, 112n
Essays, 1843, IV, viii, TBM thinks of reprinting 31; determines not to 40; decides to publish 79; new copyright act gives joint property in to TBM and Longman 82; terms with Longman 82, 96n; to include 'Southey's Edition of *Pilgrim's Progress*' 97; published 115n; regrets necessity of republication 119; 160n, TBM sends to Charles Gavan Duffy 260; sales of V, vii; 139, VI, 191
2nd edn, IV, 118, in press 123; 1850 edn, V, 55n, sales of 59n; 59-60; and Robert Montgomery 103n; 7th edn V, 387n; People's edn 1854, V, 387n; in Traveller's Library, TBM's idea for V, 161n
American editions, IV, viii, 25, 40, 71, 'coming over by wholesale' 79; 82, *Critical and Miscellaneous Essays*, Boston, 1840 III, 338n, 374n; *Essays*, Philadelphia, Carey and Hart 1841 III, 374n, IV, 16n; Philadelphia, Carey and Hart, 1841-4 IV, 194n, sent to TBM 209; Philadelphia 1842 III, 375n, IV, 31; Philadelphia 1843 IV, 18n; Philadelphia 1847 IV, 225n; Philadelphia 1849 VI, 193n; Philadelphia 1854 IV, 225n
Essays, Tauchnitz edn, V, viii, 71n, 218; *Biographical Essays*, Tauchnitz edn, V, 71n, VI, 100, TBM requests copies 257; 'Lives of Pitt and Atterbury,' Tauchnitz edn, VI, 230n, 257
Biographies by Lord Macaulay [ed. Adam Black], III, 287; V, 317n, 318n, frontispiece for VI, 33n
History: History of France: *see* Projected Writings
History of England, I, xx, xxi, 122n, on Russell and Sidney II, 332n; begins III, x; thinks of undertaking 'some great historical work' 158; to begin seriously on return from Rome 252; plan for 252; collecting materials 285; begins writing 285n; collecting facts on domestic life in 17th century 286; work suspended by cabinet appointment 299; change of design for 382; IV, viii, ix, 'I have at last begun my historical labours' 15; will not be satisfied unless work 'shall for a few days supersede the last fashionable novel on the tables of young ladies' 15; seriously engaged 17; admitted to State Paper Office for research 20n; must visit line of William's march 43-4; has not written half a volume 47; 95n, ought to devote himself to it exclusively 96; on Penn and Fox 103n; account of Hampden 121n; has got 'into the midst of the stream' 158; will go on faster if he is defeated at Edinburgh 164; thinks of learning Dutch for 219; 'daily literary employment which never presses, and

which never ceases' 222; wants to concentrate on 226; necessary to give up writing for *ER* 242; concentrated work on 264; brings MS to Hannah 266; even in office can give mornings to 276; resumes with pleasure 280; working a little at 287; requires him to give up *ER* 309; consults Stuart Papers 311n; can't be spun out of his own brains but must have materials 313; consults Dutch archives 349n; Dutch archives and Dutch Royal Library 354n; contract for with Longman 365; table covered with despatches not later than 1689 365; visits Pepysian Library 366, 367; title for 369; gathering statistics for third chapter 370-1; expects to begin printing 371, 372; acknowledges Burton in 374n; working without intermission 377, TBM's opinion of 377; publication date 377; finishing last chapter 379; sends sheets to America 380; near the end 381; working twelve hours at a stretch 382; terms of contract 382; published 382n; sales 382n; corrections 388n; defeat at Edinburgh enabled him to bring it out 392; studied the art of arranging pronouns in writing 394n; sales of v, vii, 5, 'enormous' 30; index to 38; sales 41, 45; revisions in 47; transcribed by Snow 48n; mistakes in 53; popularity of 55n; faults in index 60; TBM defends accuracy of details in 76-7; sales 79; TBM defends his judgment of Lord Huntingdon 82-3; on ch. 3 83-4; defends account of Privy Council in 92; proofs revised by Jeffrey 94; on politics of Oxford 332n; Ward's 'Last Sleep of Argyll' based on 400n; contract for renewed with Longman 413n, 414; sales of in original form 414n

History, volumes 3 and 4: TBM's preparation for v, xi; publication of xii; writing of the serious business of TBM's life 34; begins 40n; making preparations 59; at work in earnest 74; writing Irish expedition 74n; 'getting on 79; parts of two chapters written 83; working in unexplored material 96; confined to reign of William III 113; ch. 13 completed 117n, 120n; writes a page or two daily 123; finishes account of Killiecrankie 125; writing ch. 11 137; in great hopes and spirits about 144; stands still 183; TBM defends his slowness in writing 208; account of William's reign will discharge his duty 209; no idea when it will be finished 218; not working on Scotland 235; tries to resume but gives up 263n; begins work again 276; reign of William more than half completed 279; reference to Burton's *History of Scotland* 295n; writing about National Debt 317, 318; hopes to publish in 1854 or '55 355; interrupted by work on Speeches 346; doesn't know when he will finish 360; resumes work 365; hopes to publish early 1855 368; working at daily 370; 371, begins to think volumes will succeed 371; 373, writing about Church of Scotland 378; investigating State Paper Office for 399; expects to be underrated 400; not likely to interest foreigners 404; examining MSS for 406; to resume writing 409; slow work 414; TBM asks for amanuensis 414; examines French War Office records 419n; consults Oxford libraries 421n; consults Stuart Papers 422; concentrated work on completing 427; working on daily 435; effort to finish 443n, 446, 448; consults Corporation of London records 458; commutes into London from Richmond to work on 459, 467; to be out before Christmas 459; Longman and his wife in ecstasies over 463; Ellis reads proofs of 465; vol. 3 in print 465; two-thirds printed 467; subscription for opened 467; out in six weeks 468; working on daily 469; 13,000 advance orders 469; last revise 471; finishes work on 472n, 473; published 473n; does not hope for popularity

Macaulay, Thomas Babington, 1st Baron (1800-59)—WRITINGS, *cont.*
475; reprinting 478n, 479, 480; sometimes regrets having chosen so umpleasing a subject 482-3; index 'worst that I ever saw' VI, 12; William III and Glencoe 145; reprinting 271
History, vol. 5: hopes now to reach accession of House of Hanover V, 483; no longer main occupation VI, ix; begins 47n; accession of Hanovers now extreme goal 75; not likely to live to finish 99; account of Darien 129; can't bring it down to Porteous mob 173; must concentrate on exclusively 187; publication remote 229; hopes to complete 240; retracing ground of Spanish wars 244; may appear in two years 255
History, Editions:
VOLUMES 1 AND 2: 2nd edn, IV, 386, 388, 391, out of print V, 5; revision in 10; sold out 15; 3rd edn, IV, 391, sales of V, 5n; printing 10; revision in 10n; 1250 copies sold 15; correction in 25; 7,000 copies, almost exhausted 37-8; sold 41; revisions in 44n; 4th edn, IV, 388n; revision in V, 6n; stereotyped, 3,000 copies 30n; ready soon, corrected 38; about to appear 44; sold out 44-5; corrected VI, 271; 5th edn, to be put in hand V, 45; 49; 6th edn, V, 60n, corrections in 60n; 79, revision in 101n; 8th edn, V, 268n; 10th edn, V, 414n; 11th edn, V, vii, 479n; 13th edn, V, 414n
Tauchnitz edn, vols. 1 and 2, V, 71n, 101
American edns, vols. 1 and 2, Harpers pay £200 for IV, 382; probably supply the colonies V, 30; question of spelling in 36-7; Boston 1849 43n; frontispiece in Harpers edn 56n; reprinting VI, 271
VOLUMES 3 AND 4: 1st edn, 25,000 copies V, 469; errors in 472; corrected for reprinting 478; 2nd edn, printings VI, 24n; corrections for 24
Tauchnitz edn, vols. 3 and 4, V, 405, 468n, nearly 10,000 sold VI, 49
American edns, vols. 3 and 4, contract for V, 467; copies sent by Everett VI, 18
VOLUMES 1-4, edn of 1857-58: V, 151n, 414n, note added to 423n; careful revision for VI, x-xi; TBM begins revising and correcting for final text 64n; note to 64n; revising for 101; plan for publication 109; working on proofs 114; preliminaries for 128; note on P.M.A.C.F. 139n, 166; TBM presents to E. Foster 155; sales of 156n; TBM hopes it will be nearly faultless 271
History, Income from: V, viii, 127, 127n; from Tauchnitz 171; royalties from 268n; from Tauchnitz 335n; payments in 1853 349; Longman pay £20,000 for vols. 3 and 4 VI, 24; *see also* TBM, Income and Financial Arrangements
History, Reception of:
VOLUMES 1 AND 2: abused by Miss Aikin IV, 128n; Sir Charles Wood on 384, 385-6; Peter Cunningham on 388-9; finds favour among the Episcopal Bench 390; John Finlaison on 391; Bishop Phillpotts on 392-3; Bulwer Lytton on 393-4; success in America V, viii; TBM surprised by American reception of 39; reader wants account of Kirke omitted 41n; spelling controversy in U.S. 43n; outsold only by Bible in America 49; sales of in America 49n; TBM pleased by American success 52
VOLUMES 3 AND 4: early reviews laudatory V, 479, 481, VI, 5; sermon preached on at Brighton 5; much praise and little censure 8, 13; attaches great importance to foreign reviews 18
History, Translations of: V, viii Volumes 1 and 2; German, by F. Bulau V, 71n; Volumes 3 and 4; German by Bessler VI,

36n; by Bulau 35n; by Lemcke 36n; by Paret 36n; by Rodiger and Kretzschmar 36n; by unidentified translator 36n; Italian, v, 404

Inscriptions and Epitaphs: Babington, Thomas, epitaph on, I, xxi, v, 170, text sent to Hannah 196; Bentinck, Lord William, inscription on statue of at Calcutta, III, 31n, 309n; Malkin, Sir Benjamin Heath, epitaph on, III, 235; Metcalfe, Sir Charles, epitaph on, II, 323, v, 170; Scutari monument, inscription for, VI, 104, submitted to Lord John Russell 107; 115-16

Journal: I, xii, at Trinity xiv-xv; xvi, xli, 37n, 58n, 72n, 126, 264n, 267n, II, 253n, deletions in by Hannah III, viii; x, 21n, 24n, 45n, 49n, 56n, 81n, 154n, 234n, 263n, 276n, 283n, 286n, 313n, interrogation of Edward Oxford 326n; 364n, 371n, 381n, IV, 15n, 45n, 69n, 114n, 128n, 141n, 153n, 297n, 324n, 352n, 370n, 372n, 378n, 381n, 382n, 385n, 391n, 392n, gives up Journal in 1855 v, xii; 17n, 18n, 23n, on Wellington's praise of *History* 25n; on *Fray Gerundio* 27n; on Gough 31n; on spelling in American edns of *History* 36n; on Leigh Hunt 37n; on Kirke in *History* 41n; on *ER* review of *History* 46n; on Snow 48n; on Eliot Warburton 49n; on *Dublin Review* and *History* 53n; on service at Trinity 54n; on Trevelyan 56n; on John Holmes 60n; on Edward Cropper's misfortunes 61n; agreements with Tauchnitz 71n; German translation of *History* 71n; meeting Thackeray 72n; Henry Thornton's marriage 79n; on Lord Cottenham 85n; Brougham and Benchership of Lincoln's Inn 89n; his health 103n; Wilberforce and the brothel 110n; Archibald Alison 133n; character of Palmerston 134n; on anti-Papal agitation 135n; Richmond's portrait 138n; on Hannah's portrait 152n; on Lord John Russell 154n; Penn and Penne 158n; Guild of Literature and Art 163n; Carlyle 209n; *coup d'état* in France 210n; Thornton's remarriage 220n; Miss Sellon's pamphlet 227n; on Agnes Strickland 233n; crisis in health 242n; Parker's death 270; once shamed by vulgar relations 272n; on Harriet Beecher Stowe 298n; on Whigs in Aberdeen ministry 305n; Tom Moore's Diary 324n; Miss Gore's wedding 336n; on Abraham Hayward 341n; Robert Montgomery 387n; Bright's attack on Palmerston 390n; failing health 403n; Stuart papers 422n; Benjamin Jowett 424n; ceases to keep Journal March-November 1855 443n; Cambridge University Bill 462n; Prescott's *Philip the Second* 474n; on his peerage VI, x; Ellis's misfortunes 28n; Walter Ellis 32n; on his photograph 33n; Duchess of York's dogs 53n; on arming himself 74n; Indian Mutiny 100n; missions to India 127n; dinner for Trinity men 176n; Trevelyan's Indian appointment 188n; on gout 226n; on the Madonna 238n; on Hannah's going to India 242n

Juvenilia: 'Wake not for Me,' I, x, 93-6; 'Childe Hugh and the Labourer,' 8-13; 'Olaus the Great, or the Conquest of Mona,' 30n; 'The Northern War, a Pindaric Ode,' 31n; 'The Vision,' 45n; 'Lines to the Memory of Pitt,' 50n; 'Inscription for the Column of Waterloo,' 66, 67-8; index making for *Christian Observer*, 'annual employment' 77; 'Moses in monte Pisgâ,' 77; fragment attributed to Aeschylus, 98; 'A Hymn,' 279n, II, 141; 'Nature of an Auto-da-Fé,' I, 321; 'Observations on Novel Reading,' 321; 'Paraphrase of the Prophecy of Nahum,' 321; 'To the Editor of the *Christian Observer*,' 321

Lays of Ancient Rome: their origin III, 381n, IV, 44; prefatory note to III 382n; IV, viii, 'finished at last' 37; TBM proposes their publication 44; to be kept secret until published 45; to be published in November 46; 47, TBM wants Ellis's advice 48; finished 52; contract for 53; sales 53n; hard to keep from being too modern 56; reading proof 57; Adolphus's criticism 57-8; TBM stipulates 'no puffing' 58, 62; finished correcting 59; presentation copies of 60; copy sent to Bulwer 62; Bulwer's criticism 65; well printed 63; publication of 63ff; 64, idea for came in India 65; shown to Arnold 66; reception of 67ff; only a scholar can attack the book 68; sends

Macaulay, Thomas Babington, 1st Baron (1800-59)—WRITINGS, *cont.*
copy to Jeffrey 68; its success in excess of its claims 69; succeeded because everybody predicted failure 70; profits on 78; 79, Everett compliments 80; sends copy to Inglis 81; 'plain chop' rather than 'stale pastry' 83; reprinted in New York paper 84; and *Quarterly Review* 93; praised by Brougham 94; sends copy to William Stradling 95; thanks Napier for not reviewing 97; Preface 142n, 143n; 160n, 191, reprinted in America 194n; 222, sends to Charles Gavan Duffy 260; illustrations for by Scharf 260; sends copy to Alexander Smart 265; sales v, vii; 72n, and Dr Arnold 81n; cited by G. C. Lewis 444n
Individual Lays: 'Battle of the Lake Regillus' III, 381, shortened IV, 48; 55, 56n, 65, 68, 369n; 'Horatius' III, 381n, IV, 49, revisions 52, 58; 65, 68, 80n; 'The Prophecy of Capys' III, 381n, preferred by Arnold 44n; 49, revisions 58; 68, 73n; 'Virginia' III, 381, revisions 58; 65, 68, not the general favorite 84
Editions: 2nd edn expected IV, 72; corrections for 78; 500 copies 79n; corrected copy for 81; 82; Illustrated edn 1847 IV, 261n; Tauchnitz edn v, viii, 71n, payments from 241

Minutes and Official Papers
India Leglislative Minutes and State Papers: on legislative member of Supreme Council 27 June 1834 III, 118n, 164n; draft of act repealing censorship of press 27 April 1835 III, 124n; instructions to Law Commission 4 June 1835 III, 146n; on reform of Mofussil courts 25 June 1835 III, 148n; on prison discipline 14 December 1835 III, 165n; draft of act on jurisdiction of Company courts ('Black Act') 1 February 1836 III, 176, attacked in Commons VI, 156n; on the Black Act 9 May 1836, TBM thinks of reprinting v, 339; on censorship act [2] September 1836 III, 185n; on law commission [2 January 1837] III, 210n; Indian Penal Code III, 146-7, 152, 157-8, 'proceeding very satisfactorily' 164; 165, 'going on slowly' 169, 181-2; delayed by illness 186; commentary on 189; 193, ready for press shortly 195; expects to 'write it all myself' 202; can't tell whether well or ill done 210; slaving to finish 212; completed 213; in press 217; last sheet 'printed off today' 234; to be published next week 237; of great use 'to my own mind' 238; TBM willing to have it reviewed in *ER* 251-2; praised by Baines 291n; pleased to have justice done to it v, 424; enacted 424n; Robert Lowe on VI, 30n
Education Minutes: on Indian education 2 February 1835 III, 100n, 138n, 214n, TBM thinks of reprinting v, 339; resolution on education 7 March 1835 III, 149n; 6 May 1835 III, 144n
Report on the Indian Civil Service, November 1854: v, 389n, working on 406; finished 409; sends to Ellis for correction 411; Charles Macaulay asks to see 417; prepared to see it abused 431; published in *Times* 431n; 438n, 442n
Miscellaneous Writings: index to *Christian Observer*, vol. XIII, I, 56; 'A New Song' I, 211n; 'Fragment of an Ancient Romance' I, 211n; 'Ode to Nancy Notable' II, 138n; verses on Charles Watkin Wynn II, 313n; Valentine verses to Lady Mary Stanhope v, 118n, 149n; a romance 1850 v, 177n; a romance 1851 v, 177, 181; ballad on Vizetelly v, 347-8; verses on Sardanapalus for Alice v, 344; Address to Queen Victoria and Pr. Albert 6 September 1858 VI, 167n
Marginalia: 'Historic doubts touching the battle of the Metaurus' III, 211; G. O. Trevelyan, ed., *Marginal Notes by Lord Macaulay*, III, 142n, 200n, VI, 234n
Miscellaneous Writings (1860), ed. T. F. Ellis, I, 50n; includes articles on Utilitarians 255n; II, 323n, III, 235n, 322n, Claudet photo engraved for VI, 16n
Speeches: a number corrected for *Hansard* 1831-3 II, 376n; reported badly IV, 225; TBM would regret their republication 225

Individual Speeches: At Anti-Slavery Society meeting 25 June 1824 I, 202n, 203n; On Jewish Disabilities 5 April 1830 (maiden speech) I, 266n, success of 272, VI, 147; On Reform Bill 2 March 1831, and Hannah More I, 277n; its reception II, 5n; separately reprinted 5n; does not want noticed in *ER* 7; sends to Napier 8; corrected by TBM IV, 225; asked to print it VI, 275; On Reform Bill 5 July 1831, extravagant compliments for II, 62-3; to correct for *Mirror of Parliament* 62n; did not correct it 69; IV, 225n; On the Reform Bill 20 September 1831 I, 198n, II, 105, corrected for *Mirror of Parliament* 106; IV, 225; At Reform dinner 24 September 1831 II, 101n; On Lord Ebrington's motion 10 October 1831 II, 101n, 105, corrected for *Mirror of Parliament* 106; IV, 225; On the Reform Bill 16 December 1831, published separately II, 109n; impressions of 109n; IV, 225; On slavery 24 May 1832 II, 221n; At Calne election 13 June 1832 II, 130n; At Leeds 15 June 1832 II, 133n; On Russian–Dutch loan 12 July 1832 II, 155n; To electors of Leeds 4 September 1832 II, 188; To electors of Holbeck 5 September 1832 II, 188n; To electors of Hunslet 5 September 1832 II, 188n; To electors of Armley 6 September 1832 II, 188n; To electors of Bramley 6 September 1832 II, 188n; To electors of Wortley 6 September 1832 II, 188n; To electors of Kirkstall 7 September 1832 II, 188n; To the electors of Leeds 7 September 1832 II, 117n, 188n; At public dinner, Leeds, 7 September 1832 II, 188n; At Leeds Music Hall 29 November 1832 II, 206n, 207; At Leeds Music Hall 30 November 1832 II, 206n, 207; At Leeds election 3 December 1832 II, 15n, 206n, 209n; At Leeds Music Hall 4 December 1832 II, 206n, 209n; At Whig county meeting 4 December 1832 II, 209n; At Leeds election, Hunslet, 6 December 1832 II, 209n; At Leeds election, Holbeck, 7 December 1832 II, 209n; At Leeds election, nomination day, 10 December 1832 II, 210n; On Irish Union 6 February 1833 II, 228n; On Irish Coercion Bill 28 February 1833 II, 230n; On Irish Tithes Bill 1 April 1833 II, 230n; On Jewish Disabilities 17 April 1833 II, 232n, 244, reprinted separately, and in pamphlet 244n; 247; Against Mr Hutchinson's Claim Bill 31 May 1833 II, 247; Government plan of education 19 April 1847 II, 248n; Remark on Irish Church Bill 21 June 1833 II, 261; On India Bill 10 July 1833, 'best speech' II, 268; 269, corrected by TBM and separately published 283; corrects proof 287; wishes to send copy to Colin Macaulay 291; 292, sends ill printed copy 294; better printed copy to Selina 294; copy to Fanny 303; IV, 225; Remarks in debate on East India Charter Bill, 12-26 July, 24 August 1833 II, 271n; On Slavery Bill 24 July 1833 II, 267n, 'extremely painful to me' 278; 307n; At Fishmongers' Company dinner 31 October 1833 II, 330; Toasts and responses at Leeds banquet 6 November 1833 II, 333; To Leeds Manufacturers on Corn Laws 6 November 1833 II, 346, 348; To Leeds Mechanics' Institute 7 November 1833 II, 333n; At a public dinner, Calcutta, 1834 II, 137n; To Edinburgh electors 29 May 1839 III, 287n, 290; To Edinburgh electors 1, 2, and 4 June 1839 III, 290n; On the ballot 18 June 1839 III, 330n; At a public breakfast, Edinburgh, 30 August 1839 III, 298n; At Edinburgh Mechanics' Library 2 September 1839 III, 298n; To Edinburgh electors 21 January 1840 III, 316, 317; At a public dinner 23 January 1840 III, 317; On the hustings, Edinburgh, 23 January 1840 III, 317; Defence of ministry 29 January 1840 III, 319n, failure of 319n; 330n; Speeches on Lord Cardigan 5 March, 8 March, 20 April, 22 April, 13 May 1840 III, 371n; On army estimates 9 March 1840 III, 321, 331n; On the war with

Macaulay, Thomas Babington, 1st Baron (1800-59)—WRITINGS, *cont.*
China 7 April 1840 III, 324; On copyright 5 February 1841 IV, 25n, corrected by TBM 225; To Edinburgh electors 26 June 1841 III, 378-9; On the hustings, Edinburgh, 1 July 1841 III, 380; On the Corn Laws 21 February 1842 IV, 21n, 22; On copyright 6 April 1842 IV, 25, 37n; On income tax 11 April 1842 IV, 26n; On the People's Charter 3 May 1842 IV, 291n; On Sunday travelling on railways 18 June 1842 IV, 38n; The Gates of Somnauth 9 March 1843 III, 176n, IV, vii, 99n, 116n; On Ashburton Treaty 21 March 1843 IV, 105n; On the extradition of offenders 11 August 1843 IV, 135n; On the state of Ireland 19 February 1844 IV, 150n, 162n, 175n, 177, 178; On recall of Lord Ellenborough 7 May 1844 III, 176n, IV, 180n; On Dissenters' Chapels Bill 6 June 1844 IV, 194; On opening letters at the Post Office 24 June 1844 IV, 197, 198; On opening letters at the Post Office 2 July 1844 IV, 201; On the sugar duties 26 February 1845 IV, 243, reprinted at Edinburgh 243n; criticizes Gladstone in 244; 248; On Maynooth 14 April 1845 IV, vii, 162, effect of in Edinburgh 250n; revision in text for *Speeches* 250n; attacks Peel in 251n, 265n; On the Church of Ireland 23 April 1845 IV, 163n; On Scottish university tests 9 July 1845 IV, 262n, reprinted in Edinburgh 263n; On the Corn Laws 2 December 1845 IV, 268n, 269; On Frost, Williams, and Jones 10 March 1846 IV, 293n; On the Ten Hours Bill 22 May 1846 IV, vii, regarded by TBM as his best 299n; 325n; To Edinburgh electors 9 July 1846 IV, 301; On the hustings, Edinburgh 10 July 1846 IV, 303n; On the hustings, Edinburgh 13 July 1846 IV, 303n; On election day 14 July 1846 IV, 303; On the declaration of the poll 15 July 1846 IV, 304; On the Literature of Britain 4 November 1846 IV, 316, 'poor debating-society stuff' 320; reprinted at Edinburgh 320n; At Tercentenary dinner, Trinity College, 22 December 1846 IV, 323n; On Government plan of education 19 April 1847 IV, 334n; separately reprinted 334n; To Edinburgh electors 27 July 1847 IV, 340n; Inaugural Address at Glasgow 21 March 1849 IV, 397n, V, 31, 40n, effect of 41; separately reprinted 41n; 53; Toast to Sir Archibald Alison 21 March 1849 V, 41n, 133n; On presentation of Freedom of City of Glasgow 22 March 1849 V, 41n; To Edinburgh electors 2 November 1852 V, xi, 290n, 292, reported in *Times* 293; On exclusion of judges 1 June 1853 V, 328, 330n; On India 24 June 1853 V, 323n, 336; On Scottish Annuity Tax 19 July 1853 V, 319n, TBM goes up to London to deliver 342; On installation as High Steward of Borough of Cambridge 11 May 1858 VI, x, 149
Editions
Speeches 1853 (dated 1854) dedicated to Lansdowne I, 224n; III, 176n, 290n, 316n, 319n, IV, 194n, reconstructed by TBM V, xii; omissions from 41n; 292n, 338n, TBM forced to prepare edition 339; correcting 345; working hard on 346; becoming rather partial to 347; works at daily 348; rather pleased by 350; 354, will not lower his character 359; correcting and revising 360; correcting last proofs 365; preface to 366, 370n; finished 366n; published 372n; Mahon sends corrections to 372; VI, 292
Traveller's Library, 'Speeches on Parliamentary Reform' collected for, V, 161n
Tauchnitz edn, Speeches, V, viii, 71n
Pirated editions: Henry Vizetelly, *Speeches, Parliamentary and Miscellaneous*, V, 339, 371; J. S. Redfield, *Speeches*, New York, V, 339n
Verses: 'The Armada' I, 244n; gives permission to use IV, 222; 'By Thy Love, Fair Girl of France' I, 188;

'Country Clergyman's Trip to Cambridge' I, 223n, Tom Moore wonders who wrote it II, 57; 'Evening' wins Chancellor's Medal I, 151n; TBM sends copies to family 156; 'In Miltonum' I, 109, 110; 'Inscription for a Picture of Voltaire' I, 209; 'Ivry' III, 338n, gives permission to use IV, 222; 'The Lamentations of the Virgins of Israel' I, 146, 321; 'The Last Buccaneer' III, 322-3; 'Lines in Imitation of Lord Byron' I, 138n; 'Ode to Queen Caroline' I, 148n; 'Oh Rosamond' I, 188; On a Button Puller II, 15n; 'Political Georgics' attributed to Moore by Campbell II, 56-7; TBM transcribes for Hannah 60-2; *Times* text 61n; 'Pompeii' wins Chancellor's Medal I, 115; Zachary Macaulay criticizes 117; revised 118; want of moral 119-21; 125, in press 127; TBM reads at university commencement 127n; cuts made in 128; corrected for press 129; translated into French 150; 161n, quoted by Sadler 315n; a schoolboy exercise III, 338; 'Sortes Virgilianae' II, 57; 'Tears of Sensibility' sent in jest to *Morning Post* I, 167; 'Waterloo' unsuccessful entry for Chancellor's Medal I, 186n

Works, Editions

Works, ed. Lady Trevelyan, I, 255n; frontispiece by Richmond V, 138n; IV, 205n; Albany edn, Eddis portrait in V, 56n; American edn of 'works', conjectural II, 151n

Projected Writings: History of the Stuarts I, 249, 322-3; review of Panizzi's Romantic Poetry of the Italians I, 273, postponed 311; History of France (*see* corrections and additions for vol. I) proposed to Napier I, 282; 283, countermanded by Brougham 298; agrees to write for Lardner 311; writing 314; its history 323-5; must concentrate on writing II, 8; sends sheets to Hannah 46; Hannah and Zachary Macaulay pleased by 47; phrase discussed 48; Lardner anxious to publish 107; Lardner asks for 298; published as *Napoleon and the Restoration of the Bourbons* VI, 287; article on plan for reform I, 319; article on slavery debate in House of Commons 1831 II, 14; review of Carlyle, *Chartism* II, 113n; review of Henry Phillpotts on education in Ireland II, 121, 135; review of Mme D'Arblay's *Memoirs of Doctor Burney* II, 227; essay on Voltaire III, 21; essay on Jane Austen's novels III, 22; Panizzi's edn of Boiardo III, 108, 121, 259; impossible to execute 261; Gilbert Burnet, *Lives, Characters, and an Address to Posterity* III, 108; anthology of English prose for Indian schools III, 126n; review of Croly's *Burke* III, 320, 325; review of Romilly's *Letters and Memoirs* III, 325; James's edn of Vernon III, 326; review of Capefigue's *Napoléon* III, 340; essay on Gladstone III, 340, abandoned 344; Vanbrugh and Farquhar III, 363, 366, 372, will hardly do IV, 14; can make nothing of it 16; Tyler's *Henry the Fifth* IV, 17; essay on Alexis Rio IV, 32, decides not to do 41; review of Sewell's *Christian Morals* IV, 46-7; review of Dickens, *American Notes* IV, 48, 'impossible' 61; 65; essay on Goldsmith IV, 98, rejected 107; on Mahon's *Memoir of Condé* IV, 107, 159; Newman's 'Essay on Miracles' IV, 107; review of Walpole's *Letters* IV, 160, revises plan 177; review of Burke's letters IV, 177, 198-9, 210, given up as 'altogether unmanageable' 212

Attributed Writings: 'On the Deceitfulness of the Human Heart' I, 321; 'France and the East' III, 349n; 'Eventide' not by TBM III, 375; 'Joy and Sorrow' not by TBM III, 375n; 'The Shepherd and the Sheep' not by TBM 375; review of Channing's *Milton* VI, 193; 'Charles Churchill' VI, 193

Macaulay, Thomas George (TBM's nephew, son of Charles Macaulay), V, *30*, passes examination for Indian army VI, 213; learning Hindustani 215; pays goodbye visit to TBM 235

Macaulay, Zachary (1768-1838), TBM's father, TBM's relations with I, x; business failure xix; Babington's influence on xxi; xxii, *xxiv-xxv*; agent for Hannah More xxix; meets Selina Mills xxix; 5, 5n, 7n, 14, takes TBM to school at Little Shelford 14n; letters to TBM, 17n, 19n; 20, 25, agitates for Christian missions in India 25n; letters

Macaulay, Zachary (1768–1838)—*cont.*
to TBM 30n, 33n, 34n; at Cheltenham 35; letters to TBM 37n, 38n; 39, 40, letters to TBM 41n; 42; on French surrender 42n; lectures TBM on his manners 40n, 42n; 43, letter to TBM 43n; agent of abolitionists at Paris conference 45n; 46, letters to TBM 46n, 47n; and Brighton 48n; invited to Aspenden Hall 50; 50n, 52, 54, 55, on Henry Thornton 55n; 58, 59, to visit Aspenden 62; offered place in East India Company 63n; laughs at TBM's taste in Byron 65; 66, at Aspenden 66n; corresponds with Sismondi 73n; reply to Marryat 74n; TBM asks his opinion on debating societies 76; 77, 86n, thinks TBM needs discipline of attending to detail 86n; attempts to buy Thornton House 88; 88n, removes to London 101n; accompanies TBM to Cambridge 101n; on John Heyrick Macaulay 103n; on the Emperor Alexander's plans 104n; 106n, TBM invites to Trinity Commemoration 109; 110, moves his City offices 113n; criticizes 'Pompeii' 117; thinks TBM joking about mathematics 125; secretary of African Institution 128n; in Scotland 131; friend of Brougham 134n; distressed by TBM's reputation as 'novel reader' 139; finds house for Stainforths 145n; devotes full time to anti-slavery campaign 148n; accompanies TBM to Wales, annoyed by his carelessness 156n; reproves TBM for remarks on George IV 161; 168n, on TBM's failure to take honors 169n; on TBM's legal studies 172n; and question of TBM's entering church 173n; 174, 179n, TBM asks for arguments against slave system for debate 184; TBM anxious about his health 185; on failure of TBM's 'Waterloo' 186n; on TBM's return to Cambridge 186n; distressed by TBM's contributions to *Knight's Quarterly* 187; compels TBM to withdraw 189; attacked by Port Royal planters 192; in Paris on anti-slavery business 192n; TBM advises against replying to Port Royal charges 192-5; on his conduct as slave driver 194n; founds London Anti-Slavery Society 196n; gives up editorship of *Christian Observer* 197n; his suit against *John Bull* fails 198; furnishes letters of introduction for TBM against rules of Northern Circuit 210; supports campaign of William Evans 211n; *John Bull* suit 220; legal expenses in 220n; 226n, helps Hannah More move to Clifton 236n; on first council of London University 242n; letter to Brougham 243n; in bad health 243n; TBM remarks on his arguments in *Anti-Slavery Monthly Reporter* 251; failure of his business 252-3; carries on without Babington 252-3n; seeks appointment to Poor Law Commission 253n; approves Empson's article on providence 270; 281n, on Guizot 281n; 286n, and TBM's contributions to *Christian Observer* 321-2; intends TBM to edit *Christian Observer* 322; on committee of SDUK 323; severe illness of early 1831 II, 14n; bears up under death of his wife 15; Lord Holland inquires after 23; 24, 28, early visit to Leamington for health 28n; 30, 31, 34, 37, 39, liberals pleased with his conduct on council of London University 42; mistake about in *Morning Chronicle* 42n; eats at Buxton's brewery 44n; 45, 46, 48, 50, 53, 55, 58, 62, 63, assisted financially by John Smith 63n; kind note from on speech of 5 July 1831 66; 68, 69, house-hunting in London 69n; returns to London in excellent health 70; and Edward Irving 75n; in London 78; regards as sinful what pleases others but not himself 81; appointed Commissioner of Public Charities 101n; dispute with TBM over Brougham 101-2n; wishes his daughters to return to London 102; acknowledges Brougham's assistance 102n; in Wales as Charity Commissioner 158, 161; approves Edward Cropper, doesn't keep secret 185; TBM wants his address 193; newspaper lie about 193; congratulates TBM on election 211; 'breaking fast' 214; wants TBM's patronage for his friends 226; 236, has left London 240; mistrusts Anti-Slavery Agency Committee 240n; kept ignorant of Henry's duels 265; TBM cannot fail him in slavery question 267n; TBM asks his advice on slavery bill 268; absent when abolition measure passed 268n; TBM reports to on slavery bill 279; satisfied with TBM's part in slavery question 283; in Wales 285; on Wilberforce's funeral 290n; furnishes materials for *Life of Wilberforce* 295n; financially helpless 300; must not hear of TBM's Indian appointment casually 302; returning to London 308; 309n, wild scheme of going to Sierra Leone 310; receives legacy from Hannah More 310; long conference with on pecuniary affairs 312; affairs worse than ever 314; middling 315; TBM forgives loan to 319; money

matters settled with William Wilberforce 326; gone to Brighton 328; his sight failing 330; pleased rather than distressed at prospect of TBM's going to India 331; not fit to be left alone 332; toasted at Leeds 333n; tries to find place for Pringle 333n; his strange plans for family 343; Indian appointment will enable TBM to maintain 345, 354; urges TBM to speak for Lushington 347, 348; calm at prospect of TBM's departure 351; returns from circuit 369; III, ix, illness 12, 15; 40, 72, 73, 89, 90, 97, 98, 106, 116, 117, leaves England for Paris 156n; 157, 174, in Geneva 192n; returns to London 213n; in bad health 215; 223, 231, 234, TBM hopes to find him in tolerable health 235; death 243n; 251, 341n, IV, 34n, income from his estate 35, 38, 46; bust of for Westminster Abbey 46n, 112; 141n, income from his estate 158; and Stephen's 'Clapham Sect' 204, 207; 234n, 235, income from estate 281; 316n, TBM has some three or four hundred of his books V, 96; 298, and Southey's view of Wesley 454; 462, estate of VI, 199; on Napoleon and biblical prophecies 253

Writings: 'Africanus' in controversy with 'Investigator' over Sierra Leone, in *Times*, I, 144, 'The Colony of Sierra Leone Vindicated,' attributed to, I, 228n, 'A Letter to His Royal Highness the Duke of Gloucester,' I, 60*, 'Negro Slavery,' I, 195n

LETTERS TO: I, 6, 6, 7, 9, 17, 18, 23, 28, 30, 46, 48, 49, 50, 60, 72, 77, 84, 86, 88, 92, 96, 101, 102, 104, 107, 112, 113, 115, 118, 125, 127, 128, 129, 131, 132, 134, 136, 137, 139, 142, 143, 145, 147, 148, 149, 151, 152, 158, 160, 162, 164, 168, 175, 176, 178, 182, 185, 187, 190, 192, 197, 200, 201, 201, 208, 209, 211, 213, 214, 220, 222, 224, 225, 227, 230, 233, 234, 243, 245, 246, 250, 252, 264, 293, 307, 307, II, 174, 239, 267, 269, 274, 279, 280, 284, 290, 294, 305, 306, III, 26, 26, 28, 29, 30, 31, 171, 192, 198

Macaulay, Zachary (b. 1814), TBM's cousin, III, *214*, IV, 317

LETTER TO: III, 214

Macaulay and Babington, firm, I, xxii, 6n, Kenneth Macaulay agent for 53n; in new quarters 113n; financial troubles 148n; assisted by William Evans 198n; failure of, and dissolution of partnership 252n; 293n, receive loan from John Smith II, 63n

Macaulay family, I, xvii, xxi, xxiv, as placeholders II, 202n

MacCann, TBM's struggles with at Malvern V, 190, 192; pasquinades on 193; 251

McCulloch, John Ramsay, I, *237*, 'that bore' IV, 204-5

Writings: Principles of Political Economy, I, 237n, *Treatise on Taxation and the Funding System*, V, 223

LETTER TO: V, 223

Macdonald, Alec, *A Short History of Repton*, I, 103n

Macdonald, Diana Louisa, *Villa Verocchio*, V, 129

Macdonald, Sir James, I, *276*, 312n, joint letter to electors of Calne II, 8-9; 12, elected for Hampshire 13n; 16, 52, 80, dies of cholera 143, 145

Macdonald, John, trial at Lancaster, I, 219

Macdonald, Marshal Jacques Alexandre, II, *52*

Macdonald, Mr, III, 318

MacDowall, Mr, his bill, VI, 125

Macfarlan, Duncan, Principal of University of Glasgow, V, *89*

LETTERS TO: V, 89, 134

Macfarlan, J. F., III, *321*, publishes TBM's letter regarding Lord Grey IV, 282; 283, sends penitent letter to TBM 285; his relation to TBM 289; V, 332n, 393

LETTERS TO: III, 321, 347, 365, 375, IV, 36, 125, 127, 208, 209, 241, 248, 250, 251, 280, 308, 335, 338, 400, 400, 401, 402, V, 392, 393, VI, 120

MacFarlane, Charles, V, *179*, controversy with Gladstone 181; 'The Neapolitan Government and Mr Gladstone' 181n; *Our Indian Empire*, references to TBM's work 181; *Reminiscences* 181n

MacHale, John, IV, *357*

Mackay, Hugh, *Memoirs of the War Carried on in Scotland and Ireland*, V, 120

Mackenzie, Sir George (1630-1714), 1st Earl of Cromarty, II, *306n*

Mackenzie, Sir George (1636-91), II, *306*, *Memoirs of the Affairs of Scotland*, 306n

Mackenzie, Henry, II, 266n

Mackenzie, Holt, II, *266*, 272, 274, 284, TBM wishes he could get Indian appointment 324; 341

Mackenzie, W. F., V, 238n

Mackie, J. B., *Life and Work of Duncan McLaren*, III, 313, 327n

Mackinnon, Sir Frank, *On Circuit*, I, 208n

Mackintosh, Sir James, Sismondi's brother-in-law I, 73n, *231*, 242n, speech on abolition 245n; gives TBM letters of introduc-

Mackintosh, Sir James—*cont.*
tion for Paris 286n; 304, 318, II, 7, 38, TBM usually learns something from him 39; TBM to dine with 44, 47; good stories about Boswell 71-2; death: succeeded by TBM on Board of Control 122n; 124n, 144n, MS account of Holland House 169-70*; 178, 181, sketch of Burke 196; preface to *Encyclopaedia Metropolitana* 196n; 350n, TBM could not bear what Mackintosh bore from Lardner 353; TBM defends against Mill III, 151; his papers in TBM's keeping 252; 254, 265, IV, vii, fell between two stools 23; 69, on Man in the Iron Mask 82; might have done something but did not 96; and Lucy Aikin 128; and Walpole's Memoirs of George III 213; TBM fears to fail as he did 226; his history 'perished in embryo' 242; 'began to build and was not able to finish' 264; 353n, his transcripts from Spanish archives V, 34n; transcripts used by TBM 186; monument to 232; TBM contributes to memorial to 232n; his initials on documents at State Paper Office 399; Walpole papers copied by VI, 52; 146, his extracts from Fingall MS 223, 224; kind to TBM when young 237
Writings: Dissertation on the Progress of Ethical Philosophy, III, 151n, 194, *History of England*, II, 21, III, 21n, 107n, *Preliminary Discourse on History*, I, 231n

Mackintosh, Robert, III, 171n, IV, *353*, VI, 46n, *Life of Sir James Mackintosh*, VI, 237

Mackintosh MSS, V, 113n

Mackintoshes, V, 117

Maclachlan, Daniel, III, 324

Maclagan, Dr David, IV, *115*, TBM tries to find place for his son 252; secures patronage for 306; speech on hustings 306n; TBM reports progress to 319; gets appointment for his son 326
LETTERS TO: IV, 115, 171, 177, 183, 196, 197, 252, 298, 306, 326, V, 221

Maclagan, Douglas, IV, *326*, speech at Edinburgh with TBM 326n

Maclagan, William Dalrymple, IV, *306*, TBM obtains Indian appointment for 306n

MacLane, Louis, IV, 296n

McLaren, Duncan, III, *313*, 'Facts Regarding the Seat-Rents of the City Churches of Edinburgh' 364; attacks TBM on Corn Laws IV, 113, 113n, 114n; 'dirty proceeding' about water bill 120; his morality about private bills 135; reads TBM's letter to Corn Law meeting 170n; TBM won't be his slave 172; and John Bright 172n; his disingenuousness 185; attacks TBM on Corn Laws 190n; 'cunning enemy' 214-15; his intrigues 282; 284, 392, campaigning in Edinburgh V, 240n; standing in poll 245; 246, intriguer but more desirable as colleague than Cowan 247; 319n, opposes Black's election VI, 14n
LETTERS TO: III, 313, 327, 338, 344, 350, 355, 364, 373, IV, 21, 26, 85, 91, 94, 105, 108, 111, 113, 170, V, 319, 325, 329

Macleod, Sir John Macpherson, III, *147*, 162, 'cleverest man I have found in India' 210; 214, 300, 'one of the most distinguished servants of the company' IV, 171; TBM ashamed to see him at Edinburgh meeting 321; reads MS of *History*, ch. 3 377; on TBM's account of Dundee's campaign V, 123; 364n, member of Commission on Laws of India 367n; 391, 427n, alarms TBM about Indian Law Commission 432; dissenting minute on Indian Supreme Court 432n; on Trevelyan's rash behavior VI, 220; *Notes on the Report of the Indian Law Commissioners*, III, 147n

Macleod, Norman (Macleod of Macleod), IV, *332*

Maclise, Daniel, V, 415n

Macmillan, Michael, I, 236n

Macnaghten, Caroline, III, 84n

Macnaghten, Sir Charles, III, 76

Macnaghten, Daniel, IV, 119

Macnaghten, Elliot, V, *158n*

Macnaghten, Sir William Henry, III, *65*, 66, 80, 84, declines to be Law Commissioner 147; 149, 162, IV, 218, V, 158n

McNeile, Hugh, anti-Catholic zealot IV, *162*

McNeill, Duncan, Lord Advocate IV, *208*, 209, assures TBM on Campbell's bill 248; 251, 402

Macpherson, Donald, sends herrings to TBM, VI, 259
LETTER TO: VI, 259

Macpherson, James, IV, 129; *Fingal*, I, 66*

MacQueen, James, attacks Zachary Macaulay I, *222*, 228n, appears before West India Committee, II, 115n

Macready, William, III, 283n

McTaggart, name taken by Frank Ellis, II, 11n

McTaggart, J. M. E., II, 11n

McTaggart, Sir John, V, *368*, 'strange blind story about' 368

Machiavelli, translation of, I, 228*; portrait at Holland House II, 25; III, 181, IV, 130-1

Macrobius, VI, 167*
Madagascar, III, 33
Madan, Martin, *Thelyphthora*, V, 471*
Madden, Sir Frederic, V, *478*, 'vexatious conduct' of VI, 48n; Diary 121n; applies to TBM for place for his son 121
LETTER TO: VI, 121
Maddock, Henry, *Reports of Cases Argued in the Court of the Vice Chancellor*, I, 149n
Madeira, III, 6, 32, VI, 227
Madiai, Francisco and Rosa, their case, V, 290n, 321
Madras, II, 224, Henry Babington at 294; on *Asia's* route 356-7, 361; III, 32, 34, described 36ff; TBM leaves 44; 49, 51, 62, 64, 66, 72, 73, 75, 76, 84, 85, 92, 186, 215, IV, 306, Trevelyan sails for VI, xi; quiet in Mutiny 105; Trevelyan lands at 210; Trevelyan's house at 214; 244
Madresfield Court, TBM visits V, 189
Madrid, Academy of, VI, 258
Madrid, cholera there II, 315; IV, 322, 324, VI, 143
Maestricht, IV, 8
Magee, William, Archbishop of Dublin, II, *158*
Maginn, William, recommends TBM for *Blackwood's*, I, 203n; 'Mr. Thomas Babington Macauley and Mr. Southey' 262n
Magna Carta, barons of, IV, 246
Magyars, VI, 258
Mahomet, the various spellings of, V, 195
Mahometanism, V, 333
Mahometans, I, 23, English education and, III, 193
Mahon, Lord: *see* 5th Earl Stanhope
Mahon, Charles James Patrick, the O'Gorman Mahon, II, *6*, 30n
Mahony, Mr, visits the Boyne with TBM, V, 66n
Mahratta Ditch, VI, 147
Maidstone, II, 347, 348
Maidstone, George James Finch-Hatton, Lord, V, *266*, 267, his foolish letters to *The Times* 293, 294; *Free Trade Hexameters* 293n; TBM ashamed to have attacked him 294; allusion to Charles Greville 295
Maintenon, IV, 139
Mainz: *see* Mayence
Maitland, E. F., V, 319n
Maitland Club, V, 401n
Malabar, III, 50, 57, 60, 67, 72, 76
Malaga, V, 371, 450
Malagrida: *see* Lord Shelburne
Malcolm, General George Alexander, V, 397n
Malcolm, Mrs George Alexander (Georgiana Vernon), TBM inquires after her name V, *397*
LETTER TO: VI, 270
Malcolm, Sir John, II, *107*, 250, III, 83, 312, *Life of Clive*, II, 107n, III, 216n
'Malcolm Macgregor, jun.,' pseudonym of TBM, II, 57
Malden, Henry, new boy at Preston's, I, *57*, he and TBM intimate 58-9; reads Southey with TBM 65; with TBM at Cambridge 103; assisted by Stainforth 108; 122n, TBM occupies his rooms at Trinity 129; 139, 141, has injured his health in study 142; TBM spends two days with in reading novels 142; 144, 147n, 152, wins Craven Scholarship 154; 178, 185, contributes to *Knight's Quarterly* 188n; 190, 191, elected fellow of Trinity 200; hope to have him revise *Knight's Quarterly* 203; reviews Niebuhr 281n; succeeds Long as Professor of Greek 317n; TBM proposes as reviewer of Niebuhr II, 119; TBM will look after the review 121; 369, receives strange letter from Brougham IV, 94; candidate for Rugby headmastership V, 82; his exemplary youth 225; 266, to visit TBM at Clifton 268; visits TBM in Clifton 276; TBM not at ease with 277; VI, 32n, 176n
Writings: History of Rome, will begin forthwith I, 249; MS read by TBM 249n; 317*, 323, 'Jeremie on Colonial Slavery' II, 119*, 'Niebuhr's Roman History' II, 119n
Malet, Sir Alexander, II, 168n
Malkin, Sir Benjamin Heath, I, *122*, 144, on Long's plan for Greek course 242n; 249n, II, 46, 'Brewster's *Life of Sir Isaac Newton*' 201*; TBM recommends for Canton 325; appointed Recorder of Penang III, 64; appointed to Supreme Court, Calcutta 112; 125, 132, 144, 152, arrives in Calcutta 155n; 158, 160, 162, 165, 182, death of 226-9; proposed as President, Committee of Public Instruction 227; his burial 229; TBM a 'sincere mourner' 234; his affairs better than expected 235; memorial to 235; bust of 247; IV, 312
Malkin, Frederick, I, *249*, *History of Greece* 249-50*; 257, read by TBM for SDUK 323
Malkin, Lady, III, 132, 160, 227, her situation 'heart-breaking' 228; returns to England 234; her property 235; 247
Malleray, V, 349n

Malmesbury, James Harris, 1st Earl of, *Diary and Correspondence*, IV, 237*

Malmesbury, James Howard Harris, 3rd Earl, V, *264*, his negotiations 278; VI, 211, and small orthography 217

Malone MS, II, 57n

Malta, IV, 123, Garrison Book Society 123

Malte-Brun, M., I, 54n

Malthus, Thomas Robert, I, 275, pleased by TBM's refutation of Sadler *318*; *Essay on Population* 318n; TBM to meet at Mackintosh's II, 44; 45, compared to Whishaw and Smyth 46; III, 221

Malthus family, II, 46

Malton, Jeffrey elected for, I, 314n

Malvern, I, 87, TBM at IV, 298n, V, 172n, 173-99; 203, TBM hopes to convalesce there 248; 249, 251, 264, VI, 114, Trevelyan family at 114; TBM visits 117; 119, 120, scenes at revisited 121

Places: Abbey Church V, 174, Bellevue Hotel, V, 189, Foley Arms, V, 185, TBM at VI, 117n, 121, Oriel Villa, V, 190, Trafalgar House, V, 190

Man in the Iron Mask, IV, 81-2

Man in the Moon, comic item on TBM, V, 55

Manchester, I, 212, 213, 234, II, 129, 186, 197, 303, IV, 103, 187, 338n, in 17th century 371; Bright defeated at VI, 86n; 92, 95, TBM at 101n, 230n

Manchester, 1st Duke of: *see* Charles Montagu

Manchester, George Montagu, 6th Duke of, at Rome IV, 201; V, *114*, lends Manchester MSS to TBM 116

LETTERS TO: V, 114, 116

Manchester Business: *see* Peterloo

Manchester Exhibition, TBM visits VI, 101

Manchester Free Library, opening ceremonies, V, 230n

Manchester Guardian, V, 129

Manchester MSS, sent to TBM by Duke of Manchester V, 114, 116

Mandell, William, I, *128*, 129, TBM invited to his evening party 151; disappointed in Queens' College election 152n

Manfrini Palace, Venice, VI, 61

Mangles, Ross Donnelly, III, *125*, 162, takes dying Malkin into his house 227; 228, reviews 'Lord Clive' 300n; TBM votes for at India House IV, 54; TBM supports for directorship 115; daughter's marriage V, 424; 470n, calls on TBM with Indian news VI, 125; 'Government of India,' IV, 62*, 'Ministerial Misrepresentations Regarding the East,' IV, 107

LETTERS TO: III, 239, VI, 131

Mangles, Mrs Ross Donnelly, III, 228, V, 470n

Manichean, TBM a, II, 316

Manilius, V, 167n

Mann, Sir Horace, II, 315n

Manners, Lord Charles, I, 287n, III, *382*

Manners-Sutton, Charles: *see* Lord Canterbury

Manners-Sutton, Henry, ed., *The Lexington Papers*, TBM consulted on title, V, 112n

Manning, Anne, *Village Belles*, II, 278, 292

Manning, Henry, Cardinal, V, 96n

Mansel, Henry Longueville, absurd article on metaphysics, VI, 162*

Mansell, William Lort, Master of Trinity and Bishop of Bristol, I, *124*, 126, 150n, 178n

Mansetter, Priest of, TBM defends his description of, VI, 137

Mansfield, William Murray, 1st Earl of, II, 292, *321*, IV, 198, Campbell's *Life* of V, 96; 100

Mansfield, David Murray, 3rd Earl of, II, *16*

Mansfield and Babington, Leicester bank, II, 192

Mansuete, Father, identified as P.M.A.C.F. V, 24, 25n, 151, VI, 130, 139

Marcet, Mrs Jane, II, *39*, *Conversations on Political Economy*, TBM's remarks on 39n; VI, 266n

Marcus Valerius, III, 382

Margaret, Duchess of Burgundy, IV, 83

Margaret, Queen of Scotland, IV, 257

Margaret of Anjou, Queen, IV, 256

Margaret of Denmark, IV, 257

Margate, Charles Macaulay at, VI, 54

Maria, Queen, at Claremont, V, 406

Marie de Medicis, I, 37

Marjoribanks, Campbell, II, *322*, ill 323; resigns as chairman 327; 328, 329

Mark of the Beast Waistcoat, anecdote about V, 155

Market Harborough, II, 191

Markland, Jeremiah, ed., *Euripidis Drama Supplices Mulieres* II, 112; *Remarks on the Epistles of Cicero* III, 155n

Marks, D. W., *Memoir of Sir Francis Henry Goldsmid*, I, 311n

Marlborough, Wiltshire, II, 130

Marlborough, John Churchill, 1st Duke of, I, 21, 66n, 94, II, 190, III, 248, receives Woodstock after Blenheim IV, 148; V, 44n, 84, 118, 433, and Duchess of Cleveland VI, 130

Marmontel, Jean François, *Mémoires*, III, 21
Marochetti, Baron Carlo, V, *56*, his bust of Lansdowne 234; equestrian statue of Richard I 334n
Marriage Act, 1835, V, 79n
Marriage Law Amendment Bill, VI, 201, debate on 201
Marriage Law Reform Association, advertises in *Times*, V, 159
Marriage Question ('deceased wife's sister'), V, 79
Marriott, George, the button-puller, II, *15*, 28
Marriott, Selina, Journal, on TBM at Rothley Temple, V, 268n
Marriott, William Henry, I, 144, *191*
Marryat, Captain Frederick, I, 139n, *A Diary in America*, IV, 47
Marryat, Joseph, I, *74*, 76, 139n, appears before West India Committee II, 115n; 'Thoughts on the Abolition of the Slave Trade,' I, 74, 139, 'More Thoughts,' I, 139, 'More Thoughts Still,' I, 139
Marryat, Samuel, I, *139*
Marseillaise, III, 354
Marseilles, III, 260, English consul at 262; 268, 270, 274, IV, 146, 154, 155, VI, 26, 58, 60, 63
Marsh, Herbert, I, *39*, TBM describes 42-3; VI, 83
Marshall, Beck, IV, 388
Marshall, James, II, 18, preaches a good sermon V, 271; *274*, his sermon described 278
Marshall, John, II, *17*, his wealth 18; TBM dines with 30; described 31-2; at Reform dinner in Leeds 123n; finances Whig campaign at Leeds 135n; TBM visits his flax mills 206; nominates TBM 209n; opposed to Hobhouse 357
Marshall, John, Jr, elected with TBM at Leeds, II, 17n; 115n, 133n, candidate with TBM at Leeds *135n*; 188n, results of canvass for 193; 210n, election expenses 223n; opposed to Hobhouse 357
Marshall, Mrs John, Jr (Mary Spring-Rice), II, *18*
Marshall, William, I, 267n, II, *97*
Marshalls, the Miss, II, 34
Marshman, John Clark, VI, *212*, *History of India*, 212n, *Life and Times of Carey, Marshman, and Ward*, 212*
Marshman, Joshua, VI, 212n
Marston, Edward, *After Work*, on Beard's picture of TBM V, 56n
Martial, II, 313n, 143, IV, 37n, V, 122*
Martin, John, II, *36*
Martineau, Harriet, and Croker, IV, 90; *Society in America*, IV, 47
Martinique, IV, 50
Mary, Queen, IV, 257
Mary, Queen (of William III), IV, 257
Mary de Bohun, Queen, IV, 256
Mary of Guelders, IV, 257
Mary of Guise, IV, 257
Mary of Modena, Queen, IV, 258n, V, 9, 36, 423
Mary Queen of Scots, unjustly glamorised, I, 81; II, 266, 207, subject for tragic drama IV, 40; TBM suggests as subject for Taylor 71; 257, V, 88
Masenius, imaginary author, V, 167
Mason, William (East India cadet) III, 33
Mason, William (poet) II, 57n, his life by Hartley Coleridge VI, 278*
Massachusetts Historical Society, IV, 365n
Master of the Rolls, petition to, on public records V, 166n; bill for excluding from Commons 328
Mathews, Charles, II, *216*, 217, 218, his collection of theatrical portraits 308; 334
Mathews, Charles, the younger, II, 310n
Mathews, Cornelius, IV, *178*, *Various Writings*, 178
LETTER TO: IV, 178
Mathias, Rev. George, Chaplain of Chelsea Hospital, IV, *305*
Mathias, Thomas James, *The Pursuits of Literature*, III, 137, 211
Matilda, Empress, IV, 256
Matilda, Queen, IV, 256
Matilda of Flanders, Queen, IV, 256
Matlock, II, 124, 240
Matthew, Thomas, letter to Napier, IV, 299n
Matthiae, August, ed., *Euripidis Tragoediae*, II, 112
Mattioli, Count Ercole Antonio, man in the iron mask? IV, 82
Maturin, William Henry, and Arthur Ellis, V, *121*
Maude, Francis, entertains TBM, I, 230-1, *231*
Mauguin, François, III, *354*
Maule, Fox: *see* Lord Panmure
Maule, George, V, *206n*, 208
Maull and Polyblank, photographers, portrait of TBM VI, 33n
Maumont, Lt. General, V, 115
Maupertuis, Pierre Louis Moreau de, IV, 18
Mauritius, I, xxviii, III, 45, 46n, 219, IV, 9, 196, 376n, 382, governorship of 392; V, 29
Maxwell, Cole, court martial of, II, 213

Maxwell, Henry, afterwards 7th Baron Farnham, II, *73*

May Meetings, London, I, 197

Mayence, V, 349n, 351, 354

Mayenne, IV, 150

Maynooth, Professor of Ecclesiastical History at, IV, 315n

Maynooth Bill, its terms, IV, 250n; V, 408

Maynooth College, II, 158, III, 301n, TBM's view differs from that of Edinburgh Town Council IV, 250; debate on 251; country disturbed over 252; TBM defends his position on to Edinburgh voters 254; 282, 287, TBM opposed on at Edinburgh 301; feeling against in Edinburgh 302n; V, 232, Scotland mad over the question of 237; 238n, motion concerning by Spooner 408; no longer a question 475

Mazarin, Cardinal, II, 67, IV, 81n

Mazzini, Giuseppe, and opening of letters, IV, 197n

Meadows, John, V, 40

Meath, V, 69

Medical Committee, TBM on, IV, 338

Medical grievances, TBM raises question about IV, 134

Medical Reform, IV, 214

Medical Reform Bill, IV, 184, TBM's remarks in favour of 214n; 215, and Scottish interest 242; 249, postponed 250; supported by Edinburgh Town Council 250; adjourned by Maynooth dispute 252; TBM does not want Chadwick's reforms added to 253; and Scottish education 254n; V, 397n

Medicines, trade in, IV, 338

Meeke, Mrs Mary, TBM's favourite bad novelist, I, *219*, II, 51n, 124, 150n, 154, 216, 270*, 339, TBM making collection of her books for India 358; III, 82, 200n

Writings: Conscience, II, 125, *Laughton Priory*, I, 219, *Stratagems Defeated*, II, 260

Meerut, III, 169n, VI, 106, massacre at 127

Megacles, III, 131

Mehemet Ali, III, 339n, 360, IV, 232

Mehemet Ali, Lord Palmerston, Russia, and France, III, 359n

Meineke, A., *Fragmenta Comicorum Graecorum*, I, 101n

Melancthon, Philip, IV, 77

Melbourne, William Lamb, 2nd Viscount, I, *286*, sketched by Haydon II, 273; 282, 'hard-hearted' 282; 350, 350n, III, 140n, and Mrs Norton 183-4; 244n, 250n, 262n, offers TBM place of Judge Advocate 264; TBM writes 265; letter to TBM 265n; 266, his ministry shaky 271; recalled 289n; TBM defends ministry of 290n; offers TBM Secretaryship-at-War 298; 299, 329, 351, presents living to John Macaulay 363; not a Maecenas 366; 367, will try to do something for Hunt 368; majority against his government 372n; vote of no confidence against 377; and pension for Leigh Hunt 387; IV, 191n, 270, 271, 272

LETTERS TO: III, 298, 300, 301, 305, 306, 314, 316, 318, 328, 342, 363

Melrose Abbey, II, 266, III, 52

Melvill, Henry, V, *389*

Melvill, Sir James Cosmo, II, *329*

Melville, Gansevoort, secretary of legation in London, IV, *296*

Melville, Henry Dundas, 1st Viscount, I, 241, 318, III, 220, IV, 211

Melville, Herman, IV, 296n

Melville, Sir James, VI, 103n

Melville, Sir John, VI, *13*

LETTER TO: VI, 13

Melville, John Thornton Leslie-, V, *220*

Melville, William Henry Leslie-, IV, *127*

Memoirs of the Lord Viscount Dundee, V, 126*

Memorials of Brooks's, II, 80n

Memphis, VI, 258

Menai Bridge, II, 151

Menai Straits, V, 43

Menon, VI, 251

Mentmore House, catalogue of, VI, 61n

Mentor, IV, 39

Mercantile Advertiser, I, 78n

Merchant Tailors' Company, III, 83

Merewether, Henry Alworth, V, *458*

LETTER TO: V, 458

Mérimée, Prosper, VI, 97n

Merivale, Herman, II, *277*, 'must be out of his wits' IV, 31; 80, TBM meets in Switzerland V, 352; 470n

Writings: review of Sarah Austin, *Characteristics of Goethe*, II, 277*, 283*, 'Moore's *Poetical Works*,' IV, 29*, 'Sir Francis Drake,' IV, 158n

LETTER TO: VI, 133

Merivale, Mrs Herman, V, 321, 322, 352

Merle D'Aubigné, Jean Henri, *Histoire de la Réformation du Seizième Siècle*, possible subject for review IV, 159

Meru, Mount, III, 122

Messalina, I, 81

Metastasio, *Guiseppe Riconosciuto*, I, 13*, *Operas*, III, 196

Metcalfe, Charles, 1st Baron, appointed to governship of Agra, II, *323*; III, 133n, 148, favours new educational system 149; 166,

neither reformer nor reactionary 166; 170, not superseded VI, 38
Methodists, V, 454
Methuen, Paul, afterwards 1st Baron Methuen, II, *357*
Metropolitan Water Bill, James Mills concerned about V, 198
Metternich, Prince, II, 67, V, 351
Meurice (of Meurice's Hotel), on duty in National Guard I, 304
Meyer, *Medea*, II, 18n
Mezzofanti, Cardinal, III, 195n
Michaelangelo, terra cotta model by, owned by Rogers, II, 54; III, 268, 368, VI, 59
Michaelmas Day, traditional dinner on, VI, 120
Middleton, Conyers, trans., *Epistles of Cicero*, filled with mistakes V, 460*, *A Free Enquiry into the Miraculous Powers*, IV, 107n
Milan, VI, 26, TBM at 57; 62, 102, 114, Cathedral, finest of Gothic churches 115
Milan Commission, to inquire into conduct of Queen Caroline I, 150
Milan Gazette, VI, 58
Mildmay, Sir Henry, I, 161n
Miles, Charles Popham, I, *277n*
Miles, William, V, *283*, 284
Militia, TBM defends it, IV, 292
Militia Ballot, III, 329
Mill, James, I, 63n, 242n, supposes TBM to write history of Rome for SDUK 249n; attacked by TBM in *ER* 254n; makes no response 255n; II, 272n, advises East India Company to accept TBM 329; TBM finds 'pleasant companion' 365; 366n, 367, attack on TBM attributed to III, 15; TBM regrets using unjust language about 16; writes TBM 146; opposes Anglicizing policy 150n; death 193; would have shuddered at Cameron's piety IV, 309
Writings: 'The Article Colony,' TBM studying for Union debate, I, 184*, essays in *Encyclopaedia Britannica*, III, 16, *A Fragment on Mackintosh*, TBM criticizes, III, 151*, *History of British India*, II, 129n, III, 16, 62*, 362*
LETTER TO: III, 146
Mill, James Bentham, III, *193*
Mill, John Stuart, I, xix, TBM in his London Debating Society 190; on Sir James Stephen 193n; on TBM's attack on Utilitarians 255n; *282*, in France to 'preach up the republic and the physical check' 282; 295n, and *Westminster Review's* praise of Croker II, 106; opposes Anglicizing policy III, 150n; 158, IV, 312, petition against India Act VI, 141n
Mill, William Hodge, III, *188*
Millar, Andrew, III, *302*, 328, IV, 315, characterised 321
Millar, John, *An Historical View of the English Government*, I, 82*
Millbrook Church, Lord Holland's monument in, V, 154n
Miller, Charles, assists TBM to collect colonial royalties VI, *42*
LETTER TO: VI, 42
Miller, Edmund, VI, *69*
Miller, Edward, *Prince of Librarians*, V, 299n, VI, 19n, 20n
Miller, George, *Lectures on the Philosophy of Modern History*, I, 270n
Miller, John, I, 202n
Millgate, Jane, I, xxxiv, 'Father and Son: Macaulay's *Edinburgh* Debut,' 203n; 'History and Politics: Macaulay and Ireland' V, 135
Mills, Hannah (TBM's aunt), dying at Clifton in 1811, V, 250
Mills, Henry James (TBM's cousin), TBM visits his newspaper office V, 272; 277-8
Mills, James (TBM's uncle), at Paris IV, *141*, TBM encounters again at Paris 157-8; TBM determines to take the law against V, 183; 184, continues to pester TBM 189; TBM to have no more to do with 198; sees him again 204; turned away from TBM's house in Clifton 272
Mills, John (TBM's uncle), II, *361*, death IV, 376n; V, 198, 272, 278, VI, 36n
Mills, Selina: *see* Selina Mills Macaulay
Mills, Thomas (1736?-1820), TBM's grandfather, I, XXV, *7*, III, 311n, his MSS of Law, Boehme, and Freher VI, 36
Mills, Virtue (TBM's aunt), I, 14n
Milman, Henry Hart, Dean of St Paul's, I, 230n, II, 5n, reviews *Lays* IV, 93n; Dean of St Paul's *204*; at breakfast 234, 253; TBM dines with before Westminster play 272; 287n, 370, 387n, V, ix, x, 6n, 49n, 52, 58n, 111n, 113n, TBM recommends as trustee of British Museum 118; 141n, 152n, will introduce to All Souls library 155; 157n, 166n, 219n, 224n, 290n, 299n, TBM informs him of sources for history 351; made Trustee of British Museum 351n; 364n, TBM to dine with 365; 402n, recommends Photius to TBM 405n; calls on TBM 484; tells TBM about Holly

Millman, Henry Hart, Dean of St Paul's —*cont.*
Lodge VI, 10; 37, 46n, 79, 80, 90n, 152, 152n, 191, 198n, 222, 226n, 227, 250n
Writings: The Fall of Jerusalem, I, 171*, *History of the Jews*, IV, 204n, *History of Latin Christianity*, V, 351n, new volumes excellent 481*; TBM praises to Milman 484; TBM re-reading VI, 10*, *The Martyr of Antioch*, I, 171*, 'Memoir of Lord Macaulay,' IV, 204n
LETTERS TO: V, 329, 350, 364, 474, 483, VI, 10

Milman, Mrs Henry Hart, IV, *400*, V, 219n, 329, 350, 364, 364n, TBM meets on train 368; 484, VI, 90n, 152n, 198, 226n, 227
LETTERS TO: IV, 400, V, 23, VI, 37

Milman, William Henry, and Mark of the Beast waistcoat, V, *155*

Milner, Charles, I, *285*, II, 5

Milner, Isaac, I, xvii, xviii, *27*, entertains TBM at Queens' College 27-8; his opinion of TBM 27n; continues his brother's *History* 28n; 40n, TBM visits at Cambridge 43; 110, could recommend King as tutor for TBM 118; 123n, 136, 152n, TBM's recollections of IV, 75-8; *The History of the Church of Christ*, IV, 77*

Milner, Joseph, *History of the Church of Christ*, I, 28*

Milner, Mary, IV, *75*, *Life of Isaac Milner* 75
LETTER TO: IV, 75

Milnes, Florence, VI, 37

Milnes, Richard Monckton: *see* Lord Houghton

Milton, John, I, 63, 83, 94, inscription for his statue 109, TBM's estimate of 110*; 133, 140, 202, deed of sale for copyright of *Paradise Lost* II, 82; great creative mind 109n; III, 62, 111, V, 332, 447n, unluckily not a Trinity man VI, 67
Writings: 'Epitaphium Damonis,' III, 121*, 'Epitaph on Hobson the Carrier,' III, 237, 'Il Penseroso,' II, 197*, IV, 140*, 'Lycidas,' I, 69n, II, 33, 'Mansus,' III, 211*, *Paradise Lost*, I, 40*, 110*, 118*, 123*, 131*, TBM intends to learn by heart 158*; 171*, II, 153*, III, 218, IV, 28, TBM recommends as commentary on *Prometheus* V, 344; TBM has prose version of VI, 181; 238*

Milton, Lord: *see* 3rd Earl Fitzwilliam

Milton Bryant, Lady Inglis's residence, VI, 235n

Milverton, Somersetshire, Trevelyan family home III, 243n; TBM visits 295; 296

Mineka, Francis, ed., *Earlier Letters of John Stuart Mill*, I, 193n, 282n

Minerva Press, I, 219n, III, 200

Ministerial White-Bait Dinners, Blackwall and Greenwich, II, 296n

Minto, Gilbert Elliot, 2nd Earl of, 'intriguing,' I, 70; II, 157, *170*, IV, 99, 291, hostility towards 291n; V, 279n, VI, 115, 116
LETTER TO: V, 260

Minto, Mary Brydone, Countess of, II, *170*

Mirabeau, Gabriel, Comte de, TBM and Margaret discuss II, 121n

Mirror of Parliament, TBM to correct 5 July 1831 speech for II, 62n; gives best report 69; account of 69n; TBM corrects speeches for 106; speech on Jewish Disabilities reprinted from 244; 271n, III, 329

Mitford, William, I, 119, 'violent Antijacobin' III, 206; the prejudice of his *History* VI, 161; *History of Greece*, I, 36, TBM borrows 115; reads aloud at Rothley 198*; new edn 256; III, 111, 131, marred by political passions of the age 206

Mivart, James, V, *141*

Moderados, Spanish, III, 335

Mofussil, III, 186

Mohan Lal, calls on TBM in Albany IV, *234*

Mohun, William Charles, 4th Baron, II, *309*, IV, 45

Moira, Lord, 'desperate' I, 70

Molé, Louis Mathieu, Comte, IV, *231*, and Tahiti affair 238-9

Molesworth, Sir William, III, *354*, V, ix, 166n, in coalition cabinet 304; 306, indiscreet remarks at banquet for Napier 390n

Molière, IV, 76
Writings: Comedies, TBM wants to buy with money from Hannah More I, 51, *L'Amour Médecin*, I, 160*, *Le Bourgeois Gentilhomme*, IV, 148, *La Comtesse d'Escarbagnas*, IV, 144, *Les Femmes Savantes*, I, 107*, V, 410, VI, 107, *George Dandin*, IV, 144, 145, 153, *Le Misanthrope*, TBM translates Alceste's song II, 189*, *Monsieur de Pourceaugnac*, IV, 144, *Tartuffe*, III, 72

Molyneux, Emily, II, 145n

Molyneuxes, the Miss, II, 145

Moncrieff, James, V, 314n, 319n, TBM hopes he reviews Cockburn's *Jeffrey* 354, 355; 388n, 407, 'Macaulay's *History of England*,' V, 46n

Money, changes in value of, V, 330

Money, Charles, IV, 317n
Money, James Drummond, IV, *317*
Money, William, V, *359*
Money, Sir William Taylor, IV, *316n*
Money, Mrs William Taylor, IV, *316*, TBM receives 'disgusting' letter from 316-17; joke about her application to TBM V, 116; 359n
  LETTER TO: IV, 317
Money Family, TBM detests, IV, 317; want place for a friend V, 357
Monhur Doss, banker, II, 194
Monk, General George, as subject for painting, V, 176
Monk, James Henry, Bishop of Bristol, his notes on Euripides I, 77; *126*, 138, 144, congratulates TBM on his scholarship exam 144; candidate for president of Queens' College 152; approves TBM's scheme of study 172; made Dean of Peterborough 173; supports foundation of classical tripos 173; attacked by Horsman V, 171n; always generous in money matters 172; TBM dines with 282; compliments Ellis 283
  Writings: 'Documents Respecting the Estate of Horfield Manor,' V, 171n, 'Letter to the Right Reverend John, Lord Bishop of Bristol,' I, 173*, *Life of Bentley*, a favourite book, I, 126n, TBM gives to Lord Lansdowne, VI, 69n, 'Mr. Horsman's Statement Respecting the Horfield Manor Considered,' V, 171-2n
Monk, Mrs James Henry (Jane Hughes), I, 138
Monk, Miss, V, 282, her beauty 284
Monmouth, Duke of, his campaign, IV, 43; scenes of 95n; 385n, V, 143, VI, 87n, and Lady Wentworth 235n
Monmouthshire, V, 177
Monomotapa, V, 178
Monstrelet, Enguerrand de, *Chroniques*, III, 108, IV, 17
Mont Blanc, V, 352, 353
Montagu, Basil, 'a bore of the bores' II, *28*; 35, 36, and his father IV, 221; *Life of Bacon*, reviewed by TBM, II, 28n; III, 163, 189, 198
Montagu, Charles: *see* 1st Earl of Halifax
Montagu, Charles, 1st Duke of Manchester, V, *114n*
Montagu, Elizabeth, *Essay on the Writings and Genius of Shakespear*, I, 65*
Montagu, George: *see* 2nd Earl of Halifax
Montagu, Lady Mary Wortley, II, 310
Montalembert, Charles Forbes, Comte de, TBM introduces to Whewell, V, *456*
Monte Rosa, VI, 62
Monteagle, Thomas Spring-Rice, 1st Baron, I, *271*, 'Mr Sadler's School – Italian Economists' 271*; II, 18, 41, 43, to dine with 44; opposes prosecutions for blasphemy 44; 46, 47, anxious about cholera 48; 52, 79, dinner with, described 152; 170, 179, 213, 215, drunken speech by 231-2; 245, 255, 327, 363, III, 85, 220, 254, 265, 266, IV, 39n, envies TBM his whiskey 99; proposes that TBM write on Burke 177; letter to Napier 177n; admires Stephen's 'Clapham Sect' 207; 323n, V, ix, his place as Comptroller of the Exchequer V, 54; 104, 110n, 300, and Cambridge University Bill 462
  LETTERS TO: III, 74, 166, 244, V, 45
Monteagle, Lady (Lady Theodosia Pery), II, *18*, 43, 171, III, 244, illness 268
Monteagle, Lady (Marianne Marshall, 2nd wife), II, 18n
Montespan, Madame de, V, 60
Montgomery, James, I, *268*
Montgomery, Robert, I, *267*, V, 33, his letters to TBM 103; threatens suit against TBM 387-8; complains to TBM VI, 269
  Writings: The Age Reviewed, attacks TBM and Zachary Macaulay, I, 267n, *Luther*, IV, 42, *The Omnipresence of the Deity*, I, 267n, *Oxford, A Poem*, I, 268n, *The Puffiad*, I, 268n, *Satan, A Poem*, I, 267n
Monthly Review, I, 258, old maid in V, 255
Montmorency, Duc de, resigns, I, 183
Montpellier, TBM at, VI, 166n; fashion for the name in England 189n
Montrose, Duke of, V, 301
Montrose, Arbroath, and Brechin Review, VI, 180
Monypenny, W. F., and G. E. Buckle, *Life of Disraeli*, VI 203n
Moore, Edward, *Fables for the Female Sex*, III, 7
Moore, George, V, 324n
Moore, George Henry, abuses Trevelyan in Commons, V, *324*
Moore, R. J., *Sir Charles Wood's Indian Policy*, V, 367n, 438
Moore, Thomas, I, 61n, 'Little's' poems 187n; *319*, portrait at Holland House II, 20; 29, TBM must speak civilly of his book on Byron 38; 43, favours prosecutions for blasphemy 44; TBM breakfasts with at

Moore, Thomas—*cont.*
Rogers's 54; 56, praises TBM's verses 57; on Canning's wit 82n; impertinent to Lady Holland 336; at Bowood 359; 363, as 'Little' v, 182n; his character 346; affords too good a target to Croker 346
Writings: Journal, III, 154n, *Lalla Rookh*, I, 121, ed., *Letters and Journals of Lord Byron*, reviewed by TBM, I, 319, II, 102n, *Memoirs, Journal, and Correspondence*, ed. Lord John Russell, II, 57n, v, 324*, *Poetical Works of Thomas Little*, I, 188, 'State of Protestantism in Germany,' TBM surprised that Moore should write it, II, 107
Moorman, Mrs Mary, I, xxxiii, xxxiv
Moorshedabad, II, 245
More, Elizabeth, I, 6n
More, Hannah, I, xvii, xxv, xxvi, *xxix*, library a legacy to TBM xxix, TBM with 6; 13, letter to Zachary Macaulay 13n; to visit Cambridge 27; letter to TBM 27n; 29, letter to Zachary Macaulay 31n, 33n, 39n; sends TBM money for book 50n; near fatal accident to 56; TBM read English drama at her house 81; her tragedies criticised 81-2*; sends present of books to TBM 82; 85, TBM hopes to please her by achievement at Cambridge 106; 106n, on TBM's illness 112n; 121*, TBM visits 156; 164n, gives TBM £15 166; 167, informed of TBM's failure to take honors 169n; 175, TBM's memories of 182; 186n, sends money for Henry Macaulay to buy an atlas 207n; reported unwell 232; leaves Barley Wood 236n; her recollections of Garrick 238; her library willed away from TBM 277n; TBM visits for last time 277n; Dr Johnson's remarks about 57-8; death II, 307; leaves nothing to TBM 307; legacy to Zachary Macaulay 310; to Hannah and Zachary Macaulay 334; TBM declines to write critique of III, 216; and Barley Wood IV, 203; memories of at Barley Wood v, 273; 454
Writings: Coelebs, I, 175n, *Essay on the Character of St. Paul*, I, 56, *Poems*, I, 82n, *Sacred Dramas*, I, 5n
LETTERS TO: I, 49, 55, 82, 106
More, Martha (Patty), I, 6n, 83, 107, death 132n
More, Mary, I, 6n, death 29
More, Sarah (Sally), I 6n, 83
Mores, the Miss, I, 6n, 7, 14
Morgan, Sydney, Lady, curious to meet TBM, II, *157*; and her harp 283; and Croker IV, 90
Writings: Book of the Boudoir, II, 283*, *Dramatic Scenes from Real Life*, recommended by Lady Holland, II, 287*, *The Wild Irish Girl*, II, 283n, sends to TBM IV, 308
LETTER TO: IV, 308
Morgan, General Sir Thomas, 'True and Just Relation,' v, 433*
Morier, James Justinian, II, *38*, *Hajji Baba* 38
Morison, Bailie, v, 256
Morison, Colonel Sir William, III, *66*, 84, 197
Morley, Edith J., ed., *Henry Crabb Robinson on Books and Their Writers*, I, 190n, III, 273n
Morley, Lady (Frances Talbot), II, *292*, VI, 52
Morley, John Parker, 1st Earl of, II, *292*
Morning Chronicle, its politics I, 37; prints TBM's Anti-Slavery Society speech 202n; 211, 258n, mistaken about Zachary Macaulay's connection with *Christian Observer* II, 42; praises TBM's speech of 5 July 63n; 101n, Foster's letter in 369n; III, 262, 269, 371n, IV, 75n, 181, 224n, 263n, on Disraeli's plagiarism v, 301n
Morning Herald, bad Greek in I, 286; praises TBM's 5 July speech II, 64; 101n, and articles attacking TBM IV, 226n; on Lord Derby's policy v, 269; parodied by Ellis 281; 401
Morning Post, receptacle for such trash as 'Tears of Sensibility' I, 167; IV, 133, infamous behaviour of 319; v, 226, attacks Prince Albert 378; 380n, VI, 220
Morocco, IV, 239
Morpeth Lord: *see* 7th Earl of Carlisle
Morphia, question of duties on, v, 330; 332
Morris, John, III, 318
Morrison, Adam, v, *248*
Morrison, Angus, I, 60
Morrison, John, v, 21
Morrison Collection, catalogue of, IV, 388
Mortlock, Miss, II, 20
Mortlock, Mr, London merchant, II, *363*
Moselle, VI, 104, 105, TBM travels on by steamer 114
Mottahedeh, Mr Roy, III, xi
Moultrie, John, contributes to *Knight's Quarterly*, I, 188n; *190*, sonnet to TBM in *Poems* 190n; Rector of Rugby III, 135n; plans edition and memoir of Praed v, 81n; at Clarendon dinner VI, 141; TBM affected by his lines on Margaret Macaulay 281

Writings: The Dream of Life, I, 190n, *Poems*, III, 135, 'To Margaret in Heaven,' I, 190n, III, 135n
LETTERS TO: III, 135, VI, 280
Moultrie, Mrs John (Harriet Margaret Fergusson), VI, *281*
Mount Athos, I, 105
Mountain, The, III, 206, 354
Mountfort, William, II, *309*
Moxon, Edward, and Shelley's *Works*, IV, 33n; buys literary forgeries V, *223*
Mozley, Thomas, *Reminiscences*, I, 321
Mudrasa, III, 139
Muffin, Mr, travelling minister, I, 48
Müller, Johannes von, *History of Switzerland*, III, 236
Munby, Dr A. N. L., I, xiv, xv, xxxiii, 230n, II, 5n, III, xi, 'Macaulay's Library' 137n
Muncaster, Lord, IV, 205, 206
Munich, VI, 238
Munich, Royal Academy of, V, 309, 350
Municipal Corporations Act, II, 233n, III, 154n, 157, 179, V, 283
Munro, Sir Thomas, III, *312*
Muntz, George Frederick, IV, *206*
Murchison, Sir Roderick Impey, IV, *236*, not of calibre for Museum trustee V, 150; 150n, TBM dines with 397n; VI, 20
LETTERS TO: V, 109, 397
Mure, Colonel William, TBM defeats for Lord Rectorship of Glasgow, IV, *380*; 390n, elected to The Club and introduced by TBM V, 113; has casting vote in University of Glasgow election 134, 136; 157n, *Selections from the Family Papers Preserved at Caldwell*, presented to TBM 401
LETTERS TO: V, 113, 401
Murillo, V, 284
Murray, Sir Charles Augustus, V, x
Murray, Daniel, Archbishop of Dublin, III, *302*
Murray, Sir George, I, 245n, 'The Duke of Wellington's *Indian Despatches*,' III, 257
Murray, John (1778-1843), and Croker's edition of Boswell, II, *106*, 108
Murray, John (1808-92), V, *215*, buys literary forgeries 223; TBM's letter to reprinted 325n; suggests Scharf for National Portrait Gallery VI, 78; 258
LETTER TO: V, 215
Murray, Sir John Archibald, V, *411*
LETTER TO: V, 411
Murray, Miss, maid of honour, V, 166n
Musgrave, Archbishop Thomas, V, 391n
Mutiny Act, II, 285
Mynas, Minoides, forger, VI, 243n
Mysore, III, 46, 50, 51, 52, 53, 60, 81, 82
Mysore, Rajah of, III, 48, 51, TBM has interview with 53ff; 60, 61, 67, 82, 83

Nabobs, the greatest of bores, II, 129; 231, 311, 318, V, 97
Naevius, epitaph, IV, 49 *; *Hector Proficiscens*, 65 *
Nagpore, Rajahs of, VI, 38
Namur, TBM plans to visit V, 209
Nantes, I, 292, described IV, 154-5; 156, 350, Cathedral 155
Nantua, TBM at IV, 372n; V, 349n
Napier, Admiral Sir Charles, takes Beirut, III, 348; convention with Mehemet Ali 360; IV, *277*, to be one of the Lords of Admiralty 277; V, 390n
Napier, Sir Charles James, and quarrel with Outram IV, 306-8; V, 71n
Napier, Frances Dorothea, Lady, IV, 372n, V, *71*
LETTER TO: V, 71
Napier, Sir George, IV, 372n, V, 72n
Napier, Joseph, 1st Baronet, V, *324*
Napier, Macvey, I, xi, xii, xiii, xv, *237*, 246n, softens 'Utilitarian Theory of Government' 256; TBM objects to his changes in article 261; TBM apologizes to 263; compliments TBM on 'Southey' 270; not to blame for Brougham's behaviour 299; TBM feels no resentment towards 309; provides introduction for reply to Sadler 316; and TBM's History of France 323-4; II, 29, 41, expected in London 48; likes TBM's 'Byron' 50; 58, dissents from TBM's judgment of Bunyan 109; TBM sends condolences 113; TBM anxious to hear about his 'Raleigh' 122; praises 'Mirabeau' but sends no money 153; 222, calls on TBM in London 242; TBM to dine with 248; tells TBM his articles sell the *ER* 249; will guide TBM and Hannah at Edinburgh 252; 277, 306, 317, TBM defends his literary judgments in 'Walpole' to 321; praises 'Walpole' 322; TBM sends articles by Pringle and Cookesley to 333; TBM sends proposal for article by Howick 341; TBM proposes exchange of articles for books while in India 351-2; TBM owes article to 366; TBM will try to do something for his son 366-7; should apply to Loch about his son 371; III, 6, 155, 171, 198, in bad health 216; 221, confuses TBM's request for German books 236; correspondence with Wallace

Napier, Macvey—*cont.*
244; 'sad account of' 256; 257, letter to Brougham 259n; praises 'Gladstone' 280; TBM approves his management of Brougham 282; 287, active on TBM's part in Edinburgh 288; TBM offers paper on Eastern Question to 349; TBM to dine with 378; his ideas of style IV, 10-11; offends Leigh Hunt in letter 10n; on style 30; 58, 64, and *Lays* 69; opposed to republication of TBM's essays 79n; sends TBM whisky (illegally) 99; approves 'The Clapham Sect' 203; TBM dines with in Edinburgh 213; would welcome paper from Buller 224; in ill health 243; TBM to dine with in Edinburgh 302; TBM offers article by Henry Bulwer 322; death of 329n; 384n
Writings: 'Remarks Illustrative of the Scope and Influence of the Philosophical Writings of Lord Bacon,' III, 189n, 194, 'Sir Walter Raleigh,' III, 324, 325*
LETTERS TO: I, 253, 254, 255, 255, 256, 257, 261, 262, 268, 269, 275, 280, 283, 298, 309, 312, 314, 315, 316, 318, II, 7, 8, 14, 14, 40, 96, 107, 108, 108, 109, 110, 111, 113, 115, 119, 120, 121, 121, 135, 149, 190, 200, 201, 212, 222, 227, 264, 305, 306, 311, 316, 320, 333, 335, 341, 351, 366, 370, III, 10, 12, 14, 14, 21, 107, 109, 163, 189, 190, 194, 195, 196, 205, 216, 243, 245, 249, 253, 254, 255, 258, 261, 275, 277, 278, 279, 282, 282, 288, 289, 293, 294, 297, 299, 300, 306, 307, 309, 309, 310, 315, 315, 320, 324, 324, 325, 326, 329, 336, 336, 337, 337, 340, 342, 344, 348, 349, 353, 358, 358, 359, 360, 361, 363, 366, 368, 369, 370, 371, 372, 377, 385, IV, 5, 6, 7, 9, 12, 14, 15, 16, 17, 19, 20, 22, 22, 24, 25, 25, 27, 30, 31, 32, 40, 43, 46, 48, 51, 61, 63, 69, 79, 82, 84, 89, 93, 96, 97, 99, 107, 118, 126, 127, 129, 130, 132, 158, 160, 161, 166, 172, 173, 174, 177, 179, 183, 198, 210, 211, 212, 213, 213, 216, 226, 242, 264, 282, 285, 286, 322, 324

Napier, Macvey, Jr, II, *366*, III, 244, ed., *Selection from the Correspondence of the Late Macvey Napier*, I, xiii, 254, 316n, III, 243n, 250, 251, 257n, 259n, 340n, IV, 130n

Napier, Miss, II, 306, 316, Hannah's opinion of 317; III, 164, 196

Napier, General Sir Thomas, V, *71n*

Napier, Sir William, V, 71n, *Peninsular War*, TBM repeats from without having read it II, 13n; III, 181; *Conquest of Scinde*, and attack on Outram IV, 306n

Napier, William John, 8th Baron, appointed Chief Superintendent at Hong Kong, II, 318n

Naples, III, 268, 270, 272, IV, 220, protests against government of V, 181n; 365, 371

Napoleon, on French coast I, 8; his exile 42; 44, 46, his escape from Elba 59; 72, 77n, his fame compared to Homer's 163; 168, 177, TBM's judgment of his career 180; 297, II, 23, Canova's bust of at Holland House 27; as First Consul 72; III, 53, 56n, 61, 183*, subject for essay 340; IV, 42, abdication of 77; 148, 314, relics of at Althorp V, 86n; as subject for sermon 286; VI, 96, 253, and biblical prophecies 253

Napoleon III, on the whole TBM favours his side V, 210; 211, 217n, 229n, 322n, address to from 'Merchants of London' objectionable 324; 382n, 418, Orisini's attempt on VI, 141n; 149n, and English fears of invasion 252n; in TBM's sketch of an eclogue 256

Nares, Edward, *Memoirs of Lord Burghley*, reviewed by TBM II, 111

Nash, John, II, 168n

Nathan, V, 34

Nation (Dublin), IV, 259n, 260

National, III, 354

National Bank, II, 162n, TBM doubts expediency of 165

National Convention, III, 206

National Education, essential, III, 356

National Gallery, plans for, II, 159; 168, III, 367, IV, 41, 223, TBM takes party of children to 234; statue of James II at V, 431n; bill to open on Sunday 448n; VI, 61n

National Parliamentary Reform Association, IV, 346n

National Portrait Gallery, III, 257n, IV, 260n, V, 29n, 56n, TBM suggests a secretary for VI, 78; founding of 78n; 235, *Catalogue 1856-1947*, 78n

National Portrait Gallery of Scotland, V, 110n

National Society for Promoting the Education of the Poor, VI, 282n

National Volunteer Association, VI, 214n

Naturalists, IV, 382

Naturalisation Act, III, 316

Nauck, Augustus, *Tragicorum Graecorum Fragmenta*, I, 98n

Navarino, Battle of, II, 250n

Neapolitan Ambassador, at Danish court, II, 183

Nearchus, adventure of, IV, 181

Neckar, V, 351

Needobutta, III, 80

Neele, Henry, suicide of, I, 231n; *The Romance of History* 231n

Neilgherries, III, 71, 80, 81, 84, 88, IV, 66

Nelson, Lord, I, 62

Nepal, Rajah of, I, 71

Nepal, war against, I, 71n; envoy from III, 169

Neptune, choice between it and *Asia*, II, 355-6

Nero, I, 119

Nesbitt, George L., *Benthamite Reviewing*, I, 254n

Netherlands: *see* Holland

Netley Abbey, TBM at V, 159n; 188

Neve, Sir Thomas, III, 20n

Neville, Richard, Earl of Warwick, IV, 247

New, Chester, *Life of Henry Brougham to 1830*, I, 243n, 281n

New Bengal Steam Fund Committee, III, 184n

New Brunswick, III, 332

New England, V, 287, its future VI, 95

New Forest, VI, 86

New Holland, III, 63, 123

New Monthly Magazine, edited by Bulwer, I, 320n; II, 84, 289, Bulwer gives up editing 300

New South Wales, IV, 195

New World (New York), publishes entire *Lays*, IV, 84

New York, V, 135, 141, 191

New York, State of, VI, 95, labourer in 172; regents of University VI, 94; *see also* E. B. O'Callaghan

New York Ledger, VI, 261n

New York Observer, report of TBM's Reform Bill speech, II, 105n

New York Tribune, publishes story that TBM an opium addict, V, 360n

New Zealand, scenes of from Cook's voyages, II, 90; TBM can spare nothing for project there V, 119; Walter Ellis dies there VI, 32n

Newark, corrupt elections at II, 211; III, 19

Newark, Lord, II, 242n

Newcastle, I, 208n, 227, V, 243, 244, cholera in 357n

Newcastle, 4th Duke of, I, 275n; ejects tenants for voting against his candidate II, 93; V, 143

Newcastle, 5th Duke of, IV, *131*

Newcastle, University of, I, xxxiv

Newfoundland, III, 332

Newman, Aubrey, *The Stanhopes of Chevening*, III, 206, V, 253n, 471n

Newman, John, coachmaker, IV, 274

Newman, John Henry, Cardinal, I, 170n, II, 286n, 295n, III, 294n, IV, 352, and Achilli trial V, 195, 206, 310n

Writings: translation of Fleury, *Ecclesiastical History*, as subject for review by TBM, IV, 107, *Lectures on the Present Position of Catholics*, V, 195n, editor, *Lives of the Saints*, TBM suggests as subject for review, IV, 159

Newport, Sir John, II, *79*

Newport, Monmouthshire, IV, 293n

Newport Pagnell, I, 156n

Newspaper Stamp Tax, V, 430, abolished 430n

Newton, Sir Charles, VI, *23*

Newton, Sir Isaac, I, 79, 141, TBM reading at Llanrwst 162-3*; III, 179, error about corrected in *History* V, 25; TBM asks Whewell for information about 209; Brewster's Life of 209; and Cambridge election 210-11; his theories doubted in France 338; letter to Covel 338; and his niece Catherine Barton 355n, 356, VI, 55; 56, statue of in Trinity antechapel 67n; 68, 162

Writings: Correspondence, V, 338n, 355n, *Principia*, V, 25n, value to a publisher not that of *Pickwick* 77; VI, 68

Newton, John, II, *81*

Newton, Sir John, VI, 55n

Newton, Bishop Thomas, life of, V, 319; one of TBM's favourite bad books 410; VI, 185

Ney, Marshall, execution of, IV, 62n

Nibelungenlied, IV, 53

Nicene Creed, V, 428

Nichol, John Pringle, IV, *380*

LETTER TO: IV, 380

Nicholas I, Czar, III, 353

Nichols, John Bowyer, *Illustrations of the Literary History of the Eighteenth Century*, VI, 225

Nichols, John Gough, and cabalistic characters V, *444*

Nicias, VI, 248, 250, 251

Nicolas, Sir Harris, *The Chronology of History*, I, 324

Niebuhr, Barthold, Malden's review of, II, 121; III, 178, 179*, IV, 44, his partisan view of Roman history criticized by G. C. Lewis, V, 444n

Writings: History of Rome, TBM asks Ellis to review, I, 256; an 'aera in the intellectual history of Europe' 280*;

Niebuhr, Barthold—*cont.*
TBM proposes Malden as reviewer for II, 119; III, 63n, discussed 142-4*; in English and German 194; English translation by Thirlwall and Hare 196; IV, 56, 294, *Lectures on the History of Rome*, V, 83*
Nightingale, Florence, V, 158n, 435n
Nightingale, Parthenope, VI, 47n
Nightingale, William Edward, V, *158*
Nightingale, Mrs William Edward (née Smith), V, 158n, VI, 47n
Nîmes, VI, 114, TBM at 166n
Nineveh, Rawlinson's theories about VI, 25; 258
'Noctes Ambrosianae,' I, 319n
Noel, Baptist, I, *141*, TBM's opinion of 141n; II, 33, missionary expedition to Ireland 73n; canting about his dying sister 247; grieves over TBM's godlessness 247n; IV, 317n, V, 178n, his daughter Gertrude 319n
Noel, Sir Gerard Noel, I, 127n, 141n
Noel, Gertrude, 'Miss Pert Rude,' V, 319
Noel, Julia Hicks, Tom Babington treats dishonestly, II, *336*
Noel family, IV, 317n
Nollekens, Joseph, bust of Fox, II, 20
Non-Intrusionists, III, 348, 364, 379, *see also* Church of Scotland
Nonnus, III, 153, 'trash' 237*
Norfolk, IV, 53, 109, 139
Norfolk, 4th Duke of, V, 88
Norfolk, 13th Duke of, his conversion, V, 189
Norfolk, 14th Duke of, VI, *76*; and Shrewsbury case 101n
Norfolk, Dukes of, IV, 246
Norman, Charles Loyd, VI, *190*
Norman, Mrs Charles Loyd (Julia Cameron), her marriage, VI, *190n*
Norman-Butler, Belinda, *Victorian Aspirations*, IV, 9n
Norman French, III, 122
Normanby, 1st Marquess of, III, *311*, 360, 385
Norris, Henry, IV, *132*
Norris, Henry Handley, I, *41*, pamphlet on Bible Society 41n
North, Sir Dudley, V, 224, 'Discourses upon Trade,' TBM looking for copy 223
North, Frederick, Lord, compared to Althorp, II, 91; 248n, III, 159, 220, famous speech in 1783 V, 305
North, Roger, V, 224
North American Screw Steamer Ship Company, V, 297
North Midland Railway, shares in, IV, 313
North Wiltshire, Hobhouse to be returned for, II, 357, 358
Northampton, 2nd Marquess of, death of, V, *149*
Northampton Mercury, I, 138n
Northcote, Sir Stafford, afterwards 1st Earl of Iddesleigh, report on public offices with Trevelyan, V, *369*, 387n
Northern Circuit, I, xix, xxiii, described 208n; etiquette of 210; rules of travel 218n; TBM passes up spring assizes 233n; entertained by Lord Fitzwilliam 251n; 253n, 272; spring 1830 final one for TBM 277n; crowd of barristers from at Marshall's II, 18; undignified style of dinners 296n; 377, IV, 172n, entertained by Haywood 381n; TBM gives party for old friends from 385, V, 58n, 148n; 365n, 366n, 390n, Ellis returns from 416; VI, 27n
Lancaster Assizes: March 1826, I, 208, August 1826, I, 213n, March 1827, I, 217, August–September 1827, I, 222, 227, August 1828, I, 243n March 1829, I, 252n, August–September 1829, I, 253, March 1830, I, 266
York Assizes: March–April 1826, I, 208, July 1826, I, 213, March–April 1827, I, 217n, July–August 1827, I, 222-5, July–August 1828, I, 243, March–April 1829, I, 252n, August 1829, I, 253, March–April 1830, I, 266n
Northern Circuit Members: Adolphus, J. L., I, 285n, Alderson, Sir Edward, I, 221n, Baines, Matthew Talbot, II, 103n, Creswell, Sir Creswell, VI, 219, Crompton, Sir Charles, VI, 142, Drinkwater-Bethune, John, I, 286n, Ellis, Thomas Flower, I, 218n, Hardy, John, I, 231, Henderson, Gilbert, II, 5, Hibbert, Nathaniel, I, 245, Holland, Henry Thurstan, VI, 163n, Hollinshead, Bryan Blundell, II, 5, Holt, Francis Ludlow, II, 5, Lewin, Sir Gregory, II, 168, Maude, Francis, I, 231, Milner, Charles, I, 285, Parke, Sir James, Lord Wensleydale, I, 215, Parker, James, I, 267n, Parker, John, V, 148n, Tindal, Sir Nicholas, I, 215, Wood, John, I, 213n
Northey, Edward Richard, sends TBM Hopkins MS, VI, *15*
Northumberland, Hugh Percy, 3rd Duke of, II, *301*, III, 267, his death IV, 331; gift of vase to Cambridge 331
Norton, Andrews, III, *337*, *The Evidences of the Genuineness of the Gospels*, 338n
LETTER TO: III, 337

Norton, Mrs Caroline Sheridan, II, 350n, III, 184, V, 201, VI, 52, 53
Norton, Charles Eliot, III, 337n, ed., *Correspondence of Carlyle and Emerson*, V, 182n
Norton, George, III, 184n
Norwich, early 18th century papers from VI, 117, 121
Norwich Mercury, III, 307n, 319
'Notes and Memorandums of the Six Days Preceding the Death of a Late Right Reverend ------,' V, 145*
Notes and Queries, I, 65n, V, 91, TBM sends query to for Kennedy VI, 17; founding of 102n
Nottingham, I, 212
Nottingham, 2nd Earl of, II, 169
Nottinghamshire, IV, 222
Nova Scotia, III, 332
Novara, VI, 62
Noyes, G. R., ed., *Poetical Works of Dryden*, II, 306n
Nugent, George Nugent Grenville, Baron, II, *55*, going to Ionian Islands 159, *Life of Hampden*, promises TBM a copy, II, 55; TBM can't review 107; 108, offers to mark the good parts 108n; 'dreadfully heavy' 110*
Nugent, Lady, III, 324
Nuncomar, III, 361

Oastler, Richard, II, 133n, *135*, IV, 325n
Oates, Titus, TBM's description of V, 77
Oatlands, TBM visits Hannah at VI, 47; disappoints TBM 47n; dog cemetery at 52n; TBM at 56; Charles Macaulay visits 57, *see also* Weybridge
Oberst, best of couriers, VI, *160*, 167
O'Brien, D. P., ed., *Correspondence of Lord Overstone*, VI, 90
O'Brien, William Smith, V, 65
O'Callaghan, E. B., compiler, *Documentary History of the State of New-York*, Randall sends to TBM, VI, 66, 74, 94
O'Callaghan, Sir Robert, III, *66*
O'Connell, Charles, II, 30n
O'Connell, Daniel, compliments TBM on speech, II, *63*; 81, 158, attacks ministry's Irish policy 228n; 246, compliments TBM on India speech 268; III, 23n, 75, 182, 186, 187, 225, reprimanded by Speaker 258; 259n, 301, his death will not affect Irish agitation IV, 133; 192, rumour that his letters opened 201; his trial 224n; 259n, would enjoy publicity of an American tour V, 39
O'Connell, John, V, 156
O'Connell, Maurice, II, 30n
Ogilby, John, *Itinerarium Angliae*, V, 10n
Okes, Richard, I, 144
Olaides, magazine of Macaulay family, I, 184n, TBM can't contribute to 186; 227n
Olaus Magnus, King, I, 30, 184n
Old Sarum, IV, 103, 187, 370, TBM at VI, 87; 87n
Oldmixon, John, Atterbury's refutation of, V, 323
Oliphant, Major James, IV, *54*
Oliphant, Margaret, *Annals of a Publishing House*, V, 78n
Ollivant, Alfred, I, *117*, wins Craven Scholarship 143; 179, 185, 191
Olney, V, 441
Omar, V, 39, 43
Omar, Caliph, III, 16
O'Meara, Barry, I, *180*, *Napoleon in Exile*, 180*, TBM sends to Lord Spencer V, 85-6; his relics of Napoleon bought by Lord Spencer 86n
Omond, G. W. T., *The Lord Advocates of Scotland, Second Series*, III, 347n
O'Moore, Colonel, II, 59n
Once a Week, TBM declines to write for, VI, 256
O'Neil, Miss, IV, 223
O'Neill, Eliza, II, *310*
Ootacamund, III, 32n, 40, TBM arrives at 59; described 64-5; 'dulness and monotony of life here' 67; 76, 92, 118n, IV, 66
Opium, TBM rumoured to be addicted to, V, 360, 361
Opodeldoc, I, 157
Oporto, II, 154n
Orange, Prince of, VI, 80
Orange, William of: *see* William III
Orange Societies, III, 206, V, 74n
Orangemen, II, 173, III, 225, 271, IV, 162, 202
Ord, W. H., seconds TBM for Athenaeum, I, *295n*
Orders in Council, 1806, IV, 207n
Oregon Question, IV, 232, 264n, 292n
Oriental Club, VI, 147
Orientalists: *see* India, Committee of Public Instruction
Orkney, V, 267
Orkneys, V, 272n
Orléans, IV, 142, 144, described 146-7; 153, 156, V, 419, TBM at VI, 166n; Cathedral, IV, 146, 152
Orleans Collection, I, 216
Ormond, Richard, I, xxxiv, 'John Partridge and the Fine Arts Commissioners,' V, 29n, 57n

Ormonde, Duchess of, IV, 369n
Ormonde, 1st Duke of, II, 169
Ormonde, James, 2nd Duke of, III, 258, IV, 369n, 389
Oromasdes, VI, 75
Orsini, Felice, his attempt on Napoleon III, VI, 141n; 149n
Osborne, Lord Sidney, V, *8*
Osborne House, IV, 269n, V, 265
Oscans, III, 63
Osgood, James R., V, *39n*
Ossington, Nottinghamshire, Denison's residence, TBM visits IV, 224; 347, V, 142, TBM hopes to see again 261
Ossory, Lord, IV, 45
Ostade, Adriaan van, II, 159
Ostend, IV, 8, 350, 351, V, 339, 343, 347
Otaheite (Tahiti), scenes of, from Cook's voyages, II, 90
Ottoman Empire, III, 353
Otway, Thomas, I, *81*
Oude, King of, III, 273n, his behaviour on arrest VI, 106, 107
Oude, Prince of, VI, 58n
Oude, Queen of, VI, 58
Oude, Vizier of, II, 194
Outram, General Sir James, IV, *306*, his quarrel with the Napiers 306-8; *Conquest of Scinde, a Commentary* 306-7n
Overall, Bishop, V, 21
Overstone, Samuel Jones Loyd, 1st Baron, VI, *90*, 'Questions on Decimal Coinage' 90*; 102, his advice about robes 119; De Morgan's reply to 132
  LETTER TO: VI, 90
Ovid, III, 153, V, 167n, 453, VI, 98, *Metamorphoses*, I, 30*, III, 153*, Greek origin of line in V, 106*
Owen, John, V, *22*
Owen, Miss, II, 58n
Owen, Richard, V, *159*, TBM argues his claim for British Museum post VI, 19-20; 21, 22, his appointment likely 23
  LETTER TO: V, 159
Owen, Robert, II, *35*, 36
Oxford, chooses Inglis over Peel, I, 109n; TBM would exchange Cam for Isis 123; excursion to proposed 128; 156n, compared to Cambridge 165; 234, 291, TBM proposes to visit with his sisters II, 186; associates with his sisters 197; young man who wonders what place it is? 197-8; III, 50, 52, High Church party 206n; 270, Tractarian movement 294; observatory at IV, 28; anti-Catholic 162; 181, parliamentary seat at 336; TBM at 362; means to visit libraries V, 7; 136, Gladstone's election struggle at 307n; decree of 1683 332-3; 350, awards D.C.L. to TBM, vii, 350n; degree ceremony at 366n, 424n, 425; plan to visit 388; 409, TBM's visit with Charles Macaulay 417; Angel Inn, TBM at 423; visit to with Ellis 424; discriminated against by Indian Civil Service examination 438; its scholarship distinct from Cambridge's VI, 68; TBM at on Easter Tour 143
  Colleges and Libraries: All Souls, TBM plans to visit library V, 155; at All Souls Library, reads Luttrell's diary at 423, 424; 426, Balliol, I, 156, new court of V, 381, Bodleian Library, TBM at V, 421n, 423, 424, 426, Christ Church, report of its burning IV, 38; 115, 118, Magdalene, V, 115, 417n, Merton, V, 115, New College, chapel, IV, 140, Worcester, TBM calls at V, 424
Oxford, Edward, attack on Queen Victoria, III, 326; interrogated by Privy Council 326n; IV, 119
Oxford, Robert Harley, 1st Earl of, I, 66, II, 190, stabbed by Guiscard III, 258; VI, 253
Oxford and Cambridge boat race, IV, 37
Oxford Convocation, III, 151
Oxford University Bill, 'mischievous' V, 390; its provisions 390n; TBM objects to provision about fellowships 391; to be modified 394
Oxfordshire, TBM invited to stand for IV, 348

P.M.A.C.F., question of identifying, V, 8-9, 24, identification of 25; explained by John Kent 151; identity of VI, 130; Kent's explanation to be acknowledged 139; TBM not proprietary about 165; Stanhope and Kent on 166
Padua, VI, 26, TBM at 58
Paestum, III, 268, 270, 272
Paganini, Nicolo, London reception of II, 34, 41
Paget, John, *Paradoxes and Puzzles*, VI, 6n
Paine, James, *Plans, Elevations and Sections of Noblemen and Gentlemen's Houses*, I, 231n
Paine, Thomas, V, 118, *Age of Reason* 359
Paisley, IV, 213
Pakenham, Thomas, III, *65*, 66
Pakington, John Somerset, 1st Baron, IV, 180
Palace of Westminster: *see* Houses of Parliament
Palermo, V, 365, 371, 450

Palestine, as subject for pastoral poetry, I, 146
Paley, William, *Natural Theology*, I, 314, *View of the Evidences of Christianity*, I, 197*
Palfrey, John, VI, 47n
Palgrave, Sir Francis, III, *157*, V, 458
Palissot de Montenoy, Charles, IV, *43*
Palm Wine, III, 96
Palmer, Charles Fyshe, II, *76*
Palmer, Ebenezer, and Son, TBM orders Luther's works from, VI, *158*
  LETTER TO: VI, 158
Palmer, Sir George Joseph, II, 40n
Palmer, John, the younger, II, *309*
Palmer, Miss, of Wanlip Hall, II, 40
Palmer, Roundell, afterwards 1st Earl of Selborne, speech in Shrewsbury case, VI, *101*, 103
Palmer and Company, II, 147
Palmerston, Lady, V, x
Palmerston, Henry John Temple, 3rd Viscount, I, xxi, candidate at Cambridge 212n; 224n, defeated at Cambridge II, 12n; 46, *91*, 173, 180, 251, compliments TBM on India speech 268; 276, TBM writes to about Henry III, 30; and Eastern Question 335n, 339n, 349, 352; TBM would have resigned with him 353; revises Bulwer's article 358, 359; 'always right' 360; 369, as contributor to *ER* IV, 48; letter to TBM 50n; TBM urges him to write for *ER* 51; he declines 51n; TBM deplores his position on Ellenborough 99; 101, 191n, suspected by his colleagues 206n; TBM on his foreign policy 231-3; on relations with France 231n; letter from gives high idea of his talents 235; speech on naval preparedness 233n; TBM dines with 236; 243, 265, 270, 271, 272, demands Foreign Office in Russell's projected ministry 276; Lord Grey's quarrel with prevents formation of ministry 278; will be scapegoat 279; behaviour 'not altogether creditable' 280; letter to TBM on Macfarlane affair 284n; and Lord Grey 288; 307n, to revise Bulwer's article 322, 324; 346n, 350n, V, x, and rectorship of University of Glasgow 133-4, 136; thinks Papal aggression a 'mare's nest' 136; acquires material from Dutch Archives for British Museum 186n; expresses approval of Napoleon's *coup d'état* 211n; vindicated by Thiers's account of Eastern Question 288; compliments TBM in Glasgow speech 358; his dismissal 378n; Victor Hugo's letter to 382n; letter on university reform 385; attacked for indiscreet remarks on Russia 390; opposes medical bill 397n; 415n, succeeds Aberdeen as Prime Minister 445n; TBM advises on language of a memorial to 445-6; ministry will stay in unless serious reverse in Crimea 448; VI, 22, his low church appointments 70; should hear case for Heaviside 71; supports Bowring in China affair 79; returns stronger than before dissolution 79n; defeat of his government 79n, 80; TBM suggests him as hero for George's Latin verses 88; his triumphs in 1857 88n; favours Dundas's inscription for Scutari monument 104n; offers peerage to TBM 113, 115; 118, TBM can't ask favours of 132; defeat of his ministry 141n; 'should have died last June' 141n; India Bill of 146n, 147; has behaved less ill than others 202; 211, 213, 234, 235, and invasion scare 252; TBM advises on Chair of Modern History at Cambridge 257-9;
  LETTERS TO: III, 335, 352, IV, 50, 228, 231, 231, 238, V, 133, 134, 397, VI, 257
Panckridge, H. R., *A Short History of the Bengal Club*, III, 182n
'Pandar,' proper sense and spelling of, VI, 246
Panic, December 1825, I, 207, 253n, II, 63n
Panizzi, Sir Anthony, I, *227*, 229, sends Foscolo's book to TBM 230; II, 375n, III, 329, TBM refers Leo to IV, 235; 378n, 381n, V, x, 157n, 179, article on government of Naples 181n; assists Gladstone in protests against Neapolitan government 181n; 299, 478, appointed Principal Librarian, British Museum, VI, 19n, 20; reaction to his appointment 20n; 21, 22, plan to gild dome of new reading room 42n; 46n, 48, 122, 123, 191
  Writings: ed., *Orlando Innamorato di Bojardo; Orlando Furioso di Ariosto*, TBM proposes to review, I, 273; III, 108n, 121, 259
  LETTERS TO: I, 229, III, 121, IV, 236, 340, VI, 250
Panmure, Fox Maule, 2nd Baron, III, *288*, to be Secretary-at-War IV, 277; bill on Free Church 300; and movement for national education V, 379n; asks TBM to write inscription for Scutari monument VI, 104; succeeds to title 104n
  LETTER TO: III, 329
Panmure Papers, VI, 104n
Paoli, Pasquale de, II, *72*
Paolo, Fra, 'decidedly at the head' of Italian historians III, 181; 'my favourite historian' V, 26; 'my favourite modern historian'

Paolo, Fra—*cont.* 123*, *History of the Council of Trent*, III, 63, V, 122, 123*, 124*, *Opere*, III, 108
Papal Administration, III, 269
Papal Aggression, V, 130, 132, ballads about 133, 'Guy Faux' proceedings 136; 137, 143, excitement going down 152; 195n
Papists, IV, 162, V, 42
Pardoe, Julia, III, *345*
Pardoe, Major Thomas, III, 345
Pares, Thomas, I, *212*, II, 49
Parini, Giuseppe, V, *26*
Paris, Zachary Macaulay at I, 45n; 283, TBM at 287ff; described 294ff; continued 300-6; 311, III, 261, 270, 273, 274, 298n, 299, short visit to 335n, 336n; 341, 354, IV, 8, 43, TBM writes from 136; 146, TBM's knowledge of 295; 390, TBM at V, 34n; 39, TBM visits with Ellis 65n; plans for tour there 68, 70-2; hardly any change in 75; 208n, plan for Easter Tour to 295; 315, 317, 318, 319, 322, 337, 339, 343, 349n, 352, TBM at 353; 354, 361, TBM examines archives in 418-9; VI, 61, TBM meets Hannah at 101; 104n, 105, 106, TBM at 166n; 169, 215
Places: Café de Paris, V, 70, Café des Mille Colonnes, I, 296, Faubourg St Antoine, V, 75, Faubourg St Germain, III, 90, IV, 153, Galignani's, I, 296, 304, IV, 141, 158, V, 281, Hotel de Bristol, V, 70n, 72, 353, VI, 58, 60, Hotel de Chatham, V, 353, Hotel de Wagram, V, 319, 321, 322, Hotel du Louvre, VI, 109, 113, 166, 167, Luxembourg Gardens, IV, 295, Meurice's Hotel, Rue St Honoré, I, 284, 289, IV, 138, 139, 157, 350, National Archives, TBM visits V, 73, 73n, 208, Palais Royal, I, 284, TBM's interest in 294-6; VI, 257, Rocher de Cancale, IV, 295, St Germain, I, 292, Trois Frères Provençaux, I, 296n, IV, 295, V, 70, TBM gives dinner at for Thackeray 72; VI, 106, Tuileries, V, 321, 322; Tuileries Gardens, IV, 295, Véfour, I, 296, V, 70, Véry's, I, 296, IV, 138, V, 70, 75
Paris, Exhibition of 1854, V, 331
Paris, Parliament of, I, 244
Paris, Treaty of, I, 179n
Park, Sir James Alan, I, *215*
Park, Judge James, his absurdities, I, 266
Park, Mungo, IV, 143
Park, Patric, IV, *321*, his bust of TBM at Edinburgh 321; V, 56
LETTER TO: IV, 361
Parke, Lady Cecilia, II, *18*, V, 427n
Parke, James: *see* Lord Wensleydale
Parker, Annie, IV, 336n
Parker, Charles Stewart, I, 244
Parker, Charles Stuart, *Life of Sir James Graham*, V, 445; *Sir Robert Peel*, III, 140n
Parker, Sir James, I, xxi, 244n, *267*, TBM dines at his house II, 28; an evening with 31; 348, III, 234, 275, IV, 336n, V, 46, 54n, 58n, 'Sketch of the Life of' 85n; 170, death of 270; 458, TBM inherits his butler VI, 170n
Parker, Mrs James (Mary Babington), letter to Henry Macaulay I, 164n; on TBM's failure in Trinity fellowship exam 191n; her marriage obstructed 244n; uses TBM's franks to write fiancé 267; TBM once flirted with 267n; II, 18, her babies 85, 87; afflicted by cook's forgetfulness 180; 359, III, 5, 275, IV, 336n, V, 46, 54n, asks TBM to write her father's epitaph 170; 337, 458n, death VI, 162
Parker, John, V, 148n
Parker, Margaret, II, 31n
Parker, Bishop Samuel, *History of His Own Times*, VI, 154n
Parkhurst, Bishop John, V, *7*
Parliament, TBM describes ceremony of prorogation I, 278-9; duration of, TBM non-committal on question II, 132; 165
Parliamentary Debates on the Dissenters' Chapels Bill, IV, 194n
Parliamentary History, IV, 160, V, 146, VI, 41
Parliamentary Papers, 1830, on Commissioners of Bankrupts, I, 247n, 272n; 1831, I, 230n; 1831-2, on West Indian question, II, 175n; 1831-2, on Bank Charter, II, 192n; 1833, Leeds election expenses, II, 223n; 1843, Chadwick's report, IV, 253n; 1845, Medical Bill, IV, 253n; 1845, Railway Committee Reports, IV, 255; 1845, on Tahiti, IV, 238n; 1847, on Irish relief, IV, 329n; 1847, on medical registration, IV, 338n; 1847, Criminal Law in Channel Islands, IV, 339n; 1847, Laws of Guernsey, IV, 355n; 1849, Annuity Tax, V, 248n; 1852, on public records, V, 166n; 1852-3, on East India Company, V, 325n; 1854, Northcote-Trevelyan report, V, 387n; 1854-5, on Indian Civil Service, V, 389n, 442n; 1856, Report of Commissioners on Laws of India, V, 424n, 432n
Parmenides, VI, 83
Parmenio and Philotas, IV, 33

Parndon House, near Harlow, William Smith's residence, I, 50n
Parnell, Sir Henry: *see* Lord Congleton
Parnell, Thomas, 'The Hermit,' I, 63*, 157*
Parr, Dr, on Akenside, II, 321
Parson, Coleman O., 'Pilgrims of Research,' I, 215n
Parson, W., Leeds publisher, II, 206n
Parson and White, *Leeds Directory*, II, 117n
Parsons, William, II, *309*
Partridge, John, V, *29*, 57n, TBM sitting to 327; 'The Fine Arts Commissioners,' 57, 327n
  LETTER TO: V, 29
Pascal, Blaise, III, 142, *Lettres Provinciales*, II, 110*, IV, 41, *Pensées*, TBM given as school prize, I, 25
Pashley, Robert, TBM forwards Ellis's letter about to Wood, V, *416*
Pasta, Giuditta, II, *18*, 24
Paston Letters, V, 40, 304
Patristic writings, III, 237, 279
Patroclus, I, 89, III, 382
Pattle sisters, V, 127n
[Paul, C. Kegan], *Maria Drummond*, II, 19n, III, 135
Paul, Herbert, *History of Modern England*, VI, 146n
Paul, St, his epistles 'in a geographical point of view' I, 219; V, 284, 424n, VI, 100
Paulet, William, 1st Marquess of Winchester, IV, 247
Pay Office, I, xvi, TBM offered post IV, 276; 316, 354, clerks in 356
Paymaster of the Forces, office would not add to TBM's standing V, 255
Paymaster-General's Office, TBM collects colonial royalties from VI, 42
Payne, George, killed in duel, V, 385n
Payot, Mr, V, 402n
Peace Societies, their cant silenced by Indian Mutiny, V, 103
Peacock, George, IV, *60*, 62, 181, 361
  LETTER TO: IV, 60
Peacock, Thomas Love, V, 212n, *Crotchet Castle*, I, 247n
Peake, R. B., *Memoirs of the Colman Family*, III, 366n
Pearce, Zachary, Life of, V, 319, VI, 185
Pearson, Edwin, II, *142*
Pearson, Henry Hugo, IV, *179*
Pearson, Hugh, I, *37*, sermon on Venn's funeral, I, 37; 175, IV, 179, *Life of Schwartz*, III, 69n, *Memoirs of the Life of Buchanan*, III, 56n
Pearson, John, I, 170n, at Rothley Temple *198*; 210, II, 72n, 142n
Pearson, John, of East India Company, III, *183*
Pearson, John, of Trinity (1613-86), VI, 67n, 68
Pearson, William Wilberforce (Wilber), calls *Emma* a 'vulgar book' II, *72*; IV, 313, and railway shares 317
Pease, Joseph, described, II, *228*; 230, preaches against war at Grillion's dinner 265-6
Peckard, Peter, 'Am I Not a Man and a Brother?' II, 242n
Peckover, P. H., *Thomas Clarkson's Interview with the Emperor of Russia*, I, 104n
Peel, Edmund, I, 286n
Peel, Frederic, V, 49n
Peel, John, V, *185*
Peel, General Sir Jonathan, I, 286, VI, *211*
Peel, Lady, V, 184, 185
Peel, Lawrence, I, 267n
Peel, Miss, V, 184, 185
Peel, Sir Robert, I, 109n, opposes Leicester election petition 219; 232, 252n, TBM describes in Windsor uniform 275; 283, 286, 293, 318, evidently 'trimming' on Reform Bill II, 6; 10, 14n, opposes abolition 15; 61, Lady Clanricarde draws his character 67, civil to TBM in Reform Bill debate 84; 100, 134, 137, 154, 156, answers Cobbett angrily 240; 251, 289, 290, 291, 216, his administration III, 140n; 148n, 271, declines to form government 289n; and Corn Laws IV, 21n; remarks on TBM 23n; new tariff 26; speech on budget 29; 79, 101, 119n, 130, his faction 133; 162, dare not propose paying Catholic priests 166-7; his mistake in sliding-scale policy 168; 191n, his government saved but mortally wounded 195, 200; 231, on Scottish currency 241; in debate on Scottish Universities Bill 262; attacked by TBM for inconsistency 265; his ministry resigning 269; determines to suspend the Corn Laws 269n; his options in Corn Law crisis 270; TBM must support him if he propose repeal 271; will not allow ballot to be open question 272; 273, TBM hopes he will go on with a ministry 274; 279, now forced to settle Corn Law question 280; TBM will not attack until Corn Law question settled 287; 288, 299n, resigns 300n; praises Trevelyan 328; a different opinion of Trevelyan 328n; 364, V, x, blackballed at The Club 149; 184, TBM's

Peel, Sir Robert—*cont.*
feelings on his death 185; TBM's respect for his memory 201; *Memoirs*, ed. Stanhope and Cardwell, presented to TBM VI, 41 *, 78 *, Lord Auckland's letters in 93
LETTER TO: IV, 191
Peel, William, I, 286n, elected at Cambridge II, 12n
Peelites, gap widening between them and Whigs, V, 156; get more than their share of Aberdeen government 305
Peisistratos, V, 78
Pelew Islands, I, ix, 90
Peltier, J. G., I, 54n
Pemberton-Leigh, Thomas: *see* Lord Kingsdown
Pembroke, William Mareschal, Earl of, IV, 246
Penang, III, 112, 132, 160, 182, 227
Pendarves, Edward William Wynne, II, *143*
Peninsular and Oriental Steamers, VI, 234
Penn, William, II, 265, III, 309, Quakers protest TBM's treatment of V, 6; TBM modifies a reference to 6n; Quaker delegation to TBM about 26n; not a Papist 91; TBM has dealt leniently with 143; TBM doubts anecdote about 143; argument between TBM and Dixon about 158; some doubt about TBM's identification of 288, VI, 31; TBM compelled to defend his view of 31n; replies to Dixon's arguments 64-5; adds note about to *History* 101, 109
Pennant, Thomas, *A Tour in Scotland*, V, 120n
Penne, George, V, 158
Pennington, James, II, *272*
Pennington, Col. Jervase, IV, 303n
Pennsylvania, Quakers in, II, 265; bonds IV, 224
Penny Cyclopaedia, I, 154n
Penny Magazine, I, 323
Penny Post, debate on, III, 295n; 304n, inaugurated 318n; 376, VI, 73n
Penshurst, TBM and Ellis to visit, V, 343; VI, 239
Pensions, Civil List, III, 75
Pepys, Christopher: *see* Lord Cottenham
Pepys, Samuel, *Diary*, II, 37, IV, 388 *, on General Monk's reception V, 176 *; and Tom Moore's Memoirs 324n; 414n, TBM dreams that Alice Trevelyan wrote it VI, 268; 268 *
Pepys-Whitely, Mr D., III, xi
Pepysian Library, TBM to visit, IV, 264; TBM at 366, 367; 378
Perceval, Mrs Charles (Frances Trevelyan), VI, *165n*
Perceval, Rev. Charles, VI, 165n
Perceval, Spencer, II, *44*, Sydney Smith's opinion of 44; IV, 207
Perceval, Spencer, the younger, I, 181n, *252n*, II, 173
Percy, Thomas, *Reliques of Ancient English Poetry*, II, 293, 365 *, V, 63n; correspondence with the Campbells VI, 225
Pereira, Manuel, V, 8n, 9
Pereira, Miguel, and P.M.A.C.F., V, 151
Pergolesi, *Arie da Camera*, II, 16
Pericles, I, 286
Périer, Casimir, I, *303*, II, 40, dies 154n
Perizonius, James, III, *142*, IV, 44
Perrin, Louis, II, *52*
Perring, Robert, editor, *Leeds Intelligencer*, II, *221*
Perry, Sir Erskine, his appearance before India Committee, V, *325*
Perry, James, I, 37n
Perry, Richard, claims a friendship with TBM that never existed VI, *81*; reminiscences of TBM 81n; *Contributions to an Amateur Magazine*, I, 126n, 148n, 218n, VI, 81 *
Persian language, I, 80
Persius, satires, III, 62 *, 219 *
Pert Rude, Miss: *see* Gertrude Noel
Perth, Lord, IV, 376
Perth, TBM visits with Jeffrey, I, 238; TBM at V, 111n
Perthshire, IV, 187
Peshawar, execution at, VI, 103
Peter, St, V, 359, VI, 127
Peter the Great, I, 180, III, 53
Peterborough, IV, 59, 60, TBM meets Ellis and Frank there V, 193; Angel Inn 195; TBM at 218n; Lewis defeated at 300n
Peterborough, 3rd Earl of, III, 248, his spelling 249
Peterloo Massacre, I, 131n, TBM's opinion about distresses his mother 132-3; Brougham's response to 134
Petrarch, III, 62 *
Petronius, III, 154
Petty, Sir William, Lord Lansdowne's monument to, V, 170
Petty-Fitzmaurice, Lady Louisa, Lord Lansdowne's daughter, II, *170*
Peyronnet, Charles, Comte de, I, *305*
Phaedrus, III, 178 *, IV, 65 *
Phaeton, V, 106
Phalaris, *Epistles*, III, 132, controversy about III, 217, V, 317-18

Phelps, Naomi, *The Queen's Invalid*, I, 37n
Philadelphia, IV, 43, 52, 141, VI, 19
Philip, Robert, *Life of John Bunyan*, V, 402
Philip II, of Spain, IV, 255, VI, 237
Philip V, of Spain, II, 190
Philip Augustus, of France, IV, 150
Philip le Bel, VI, 265
Philippa, Queen, IV, 256
Philipps, C.S.M., review of Miss Strickland in *ER*, V, 233n
Philips, Sir George, 1st Baronet, I, *213*, 239n, TBM to dine with II, 24, 30; described 38-9; 41, keeps up two London houses 42; dinner with 42-4; 43, 44, TBM dines with 45-6; invites TBM to Weston House 183; 192, 196, 229, 312, wants a place for a brother in law 348; III, 137, 224, VI, 275
Philips, Sir George Richard, 2nd Baronet, II, *24*, TBM dines with 41
Philips, John, '*Blenheim*, a Poem,' IV, 129
Philips, Lady (Sarah Georgiana Cavendish), II, 43
Phillips, Charles, *Recollections of Curran*, V, 410
Phillips, Henry Wyndham, at Bowood, V, *369*
Phillips, Lawrence B., *Autographic Album*, VI, 271
Phillips, Thomas, II, 155n
Phillips, Sampson and Co., Boston, publish English-spelling edition of *History*, V, 43n
Phillpotts, Henry, Bishop of Exeter, TBM asked to review his speech II, *121*; anti-Catholic zealot IV, 162; praises TBM's *History* 390, 392; TBM defends his account of Reformation to V, 11-14; he and TBM courteous adversaries 15, 16; persuades TBM to make slight alterations 18; on TBM's use of Strype 22n; thinks TBM unfair to Church of England 26; and Gorham case 96; TBM certain that he writes Miss Sellon's letters 107; gives up Miss Sellon 227; 'Letter to Miss Sellon' 227n*; TBM hears for last time VI, 201; *Correspondence with TBM*, 2nd edn, IV, 393n, V, 11, 19n
    LETTERS TO: V, 11, 18
Philobiblon Club, IV, 202n
Philological Society, *Proceedings*, V, 100
Philosophes, IV, 144
Philostratus, *Life of Apollonius of Tyana*, III, 211*, 'heap of impudent lies' 237*; VI, 167*
Philpott, Henry, makes proposals for reform at Cambridge IV, *360*
Photius, III, viii, V, 405*, TBM does not get on with 416; finishes 484*
Phrenology, IV, 235, 303n
Pichegru, Charles, IV, 148
Pickering, George, II, 253n
Pickersgill, Henry William, II, *155*
Pierce, E. L., *Memoir and Letters of Charles Sumner*, II, 151n
Piercefield Park, Monmouthshire, I, 156
Pierotti, Italian courier, VI, 105, 202
Pigeons, messages by, III, 341
Pilgrim Fathers, VI, 187
Pindar, I, 5*, 243, II, 2, III, 130*, 131, 133, 152*, 159*
Pinney, Sherrill Ohman, I, xxiii, VI, xii
Pinney, Thomas, 'Notes on Macaulay's Writings,' VI, 289
Piozzi, Mrs, her papers offered to Longman, VI, 236n; TBM advises on publication 326n; in 'The Lady's Last Stake' 236; *Anecdotes of Johnson*, II, 34*, 57, 260*, 350*, *Autobiography, Letters and Literary Remains*, VI, 236n
Pisa, III, 261, IV, 146, Councils of V, 20
Pistrucci, Signor, TBM takes lessons from VI, 51, 53
Pitt, William, the elder, 1st Earl of Chatham, II, 321, III, 159, *Correspondence*, and TBM's 'Earl of Chatham,' IV, 212n; wife's title merged in his 221
Pitt, William, the younger, I, 181, II, 70, 122n, 290, 292, 296n, IV, 206, 211, speech of March 1801 V, 398; Stanhope sends letters of to TBM VI, 177; his papers opened to Stanhope 177; and Temple 179
Pitt Club, III, 151
Pius IX, Pope, and restoration of English hierarchy, V, 130n, 132, 133, 135
Placehunters, TBM plagued by, V, 117
Plantagenet, Henry, Earl of Derby and Duke of Lancaster, IV, 384
Plas Newydd, George IV at I, 159
Plato, I, 145*, 146, 243, III, 132, 141*, his humour 141-2; 146*, 159*, 160, 181, 202, 237*, his poetry the best thing about him IV, 39; V, 343*, 345*, 348*, Whewell's articles on his survey of sciences VI, 84; his dialogues on Eleatics 85; Whewell's translation of 250
    Writings: Opera Omnia, ed. Ficino, III, 142, *Apology*, V, 347*, *Cratylus*, III, 141, *Laches*, TBM thinks not genuine, VI, 250*, 256; *Laws*, III, 153*, *Meno*, date of, VI, 251*, *Parmenides*, question of its authenticity, VI, 82-3, 83*, 255, *Phaedo*, V, 347*, VI, 251*, *Phaedrus*, V, 196, 341*, *Politicus*, VI, 83, 255, *Protagoras*, III, 141, *Republic*,

Plato: *Writings—cont.*
III, 153*, V, 347*, Whewell's version VI, 250; *Sophist*, VI, 83*, 255, *Theaetetus*, V, 347*, VI, 83

Platt, Thomas Pell, I, *117*

Plautus, III, viii, 137*, 159*, V, 122

Playfair, John, V, *93*

Pleydell-Bouverie, Edward, V, *462*
LETTERS TO: V, 462, VI, 92

Pleydell-Bouverie, Philip, V, *158*

Pliny, III, 178, IV, 55, VI, 58, *Natural History*, III, 200*, IV, 56*, 73*

Pliny, the younger, *Epistles*, *Panegyric*, III, 181*; V, 416*

Plumptre, John Pemberton, on Sunday travelling, IV, 38

Plunket, William Conygham, 1st Baron, TBM compared to, II, *63*; TBM and Margaret meet 63n; 71, 78, remark at dinner 79-80; 82, III, 381

Plutarch, III, 177*, 218*, IV, 21, V, 268*
Writings: 'De Adulatore et Amico,' IV, 240*, *Lives*, I, 28*, III, 153*, 159*, 210, 237*, V, 122, 123*, 124*; particular lives: of Eumenes, I, 68, of Julius Caesar, V, 264*, of Nicias, VI, 250-1*

Plymouth, II, 26, Royal Hotel 28; TBM's recollections of sad V, 177; 265

Pocock, Bishop Edward, Life of, V, 319, VI, 185

Poet Laureateship, 'ridiculous,' III, 369; 'most absurd of all distinctions' V, 131

Poles, II, 40

Polignac, Comte de, VI, 47n

Polignac, Jules, Prince de, I, *305*

Polk, James Knox, IV, 224n

Pollock, Sir Frederick, I, 109n, on Writ of Right at York 208n; *Personal Remembrances*, I, 139n; on Brougham's *Hydrostatics* 247n; 285n, on Sir Gregory Lewin II, 168n; IV, 69n, 381n

Pollock, Sir Jonathan Frederick, I, *210*, TBM junior to at York Assizes 223; 225, rivalry with Brougham on circuit 227-8; TBM's dream about II, 26; V, x, 148

Pollok, Robert, 'The Course of Time,' I, xxvii

Poltimore, George Warwick Bampfylde, 1st Baron, II, *144*

Polybius, III, 142, 211*, 237*, IV, 80*

Pomare, Queen, deposed, IV, 238n

Pomona College, I, xxxiv

Pompeii, II, 352, III, 268, 270, 272, V, 417

Ponet, Bishop John, V, *8*

Ponsonby, Augusta, III, 120n

Ponsonby, Richard, Bishop of Derry, II, *158*

Pontefract, I, 208, 208n, 210, TBM at 234

Poole, John, *Turning the Tables*, performed before TBM at Woburn, V, 144n

Poor Law Bill, IV, 184; Whigs saved government on 200

Poor Law Commission, IV, 253

Poor Laws, I, 237; New Poor Law, III, 271

Pope: *see* Gregory XVI and Pius IX

Pope, restoration of, IV, 77; not acknowledged by Greek church V, 427

Pope, Alexander, I, 63, 72, 83, 120, 121, II, 29, bust of by Roubiliac 54; less original than Defoe 109; III, 136, conflict with Cibber 308; IV, 42, 129n, 394, Warton and Roscoe editions of V, 104; 356, pirated by Curll 371; his grotto 409; anecdote of 462; TBM presents Roscoe's edn of to Edinburgh Philosophical Institution 463
Writings: Dunciad, I, 107*, V, 293, 294, *Epistle I*, I, 56*, 'Epistle to Burlington,' V, 104, 'Epistle to Arbuthnot,' II, 74*, V, 131*, 'Essay on Criticism,' II, 172*, *Essay on Man*, IV, 386*, 'A Full and True Account of Mr. Edmund Curll,' V, 347n, *Imitations*, V, 287, 'Messiah,' I, 28*, 'The Rape of the Lock,' I, 147*, III, 307, and Hampton Court V, 409; 'Sober Advice from Horace,' III, 142, translation of Homer, I, 5n, to be read with Selina I, 69; II, 27, 38, *Iliad*, I, 35*, IV, 28

Pope, Willard Bissell, ed., *Diary of Benjamin Robert Haydon*, II, 273n

Pope-Hennessy, James, *Monckton Milnes*, IV, 165, 239n, VI, 47n

Porphyry, *De Abstinentia Carnis*, IV, 358*

Porsena, III, 143

Porson, Richard, his notes on Euripides, I, 77; *Adversaria* 77n; 87n, TBM disputes about with Napier *237*; III, 136, would not have scrupled to use a translation V, 287; 385

Port Royal, France, IV, 139, V, 27

Port Royal, Jamaica, resolutions attacking Zachary Macaulay I, 192n, 195, 196

Porteous, Bishop, urn dedicated to him at Barley Wood, V, 273

Porteous Mob, VI, 173

Porter, Anna Maria, *Honor O'Hara*, II, 94, *The Hungarian Brothers*, II, 197

Porter, Mr, 'an ass,' IV, 43

Porter, Noah, V, *43n*

Portland, 4th Duke of, III, 117

Portsmouth, II, 342, III, 234, IV, 157, TBM visits *Victory* at V, 159n

Portsmouth, Duchess of, V, 8n, 9n, VI, 130

Portugal, and slave trade, I, 173n; II, 152, 153, dynastic struggle in 154; affairs in 181; debate on 250; ministry defeated in Lords on question of 251; affairs in 282; literature of III, 136

Portuguese Minister, V, ix

Post Office, IV, 36, motion for parliamentary committee on IV, 125; government grants committee on 201; appointments 315; 401

Post Office Edinburgh Directory, III, 296n

Post Office London Directory, I, 253n, III, 30n

Potsdam, IV, 19, 21

Potter, Beatrice, IV, 222n

Potter, Sir John, V, *230*

LETTER TO: V, 230

Potter, Richard, IV, 9n, *222*; marries Lawrencina Heyworth 314n

Pottinger, General Sir Henry, TBM wishes to recruit for Whigs IV, *228*

Pottle, Frederick A., *James Boswell, The Earlier Years*, II, 72n

Poussin, Nicholas, 'Massacre of the Innocents,' IV, 324

Power, Mrs, of Sion Hill, Clifton, V, 63

Powis, Lord, IV, 331n

Powys, Charles, III, 23n

Powys, R. Vernon, III, 23n

Praed, Winthrop Mackworth, I, xix, at Union 183n; founds *Knight's Quarterly* 188n; *190*, TBM's letters to 190n; TBM visits at Eton 233n; TBM eager for his parliamentary debut 317; denies that he was elected to oppose TBM 317n; failure of maiden speech II, 12; he and TBM grow colder daily 70; opposes Reform Bill 70n; III, 158, 'paltry attack' on TBM 164; 176, IV, 169, only one of TBM's friends who used him basely V, 81; *Poems*, V, 81n

Pratt, Josiah, *Life of Richard Cecil*, I, 37

Prayer Book and Homily Society, IV, 207

Preaching Price, one of TBM's pet names for Margaret Macaulay, II, 123, 139

PreRaphaelites, at Academy exhibition, V, 328n

Presbyterians, IV, 55, V, 42, 88, TBM attends sacrament service of 291; Alice to hear for first time VI, 232

Prescott, William Hickling, V, *474*, death of VI, 187n

Writings: History of the Conquest of Mexico, TBM declines as subject for review IV, 158; VI, 187, *History of the Reign of Philip the Second*, presented to TBM V, 474*, 475*, VI, 187*, *Works*, sent to TBM IV, 194, 209

LETTERS TO: V, 474, VI, 187

Preston, Ellis at court of inquiry there V, 205, 206

Preston Races, III, 384

Preston, Charles James, VI, 27n

Preston, John, I, 234, 237

Preston, Matthew Morris, I, ix, xviii, TBM's schoolmaster *14*, 15, *Memoranda of Charles Simeon* 15n; lends books to TBM 16; 17, kind to TBM 18; remarks on TBM 18n; 19, 20, 21, to give out prizes 22; 23, 25, hears French lesson 26; 27, 28, gives boys glass of wine on Sundays 29; 34, 'a very despairing politician' 36; gives TBM life of Richard Cecil 37; a 'domestic man' 41; 42, planning to leave Shelford 44n; 45, 47, removes from Shelford to Aspenden Hall 50; 57, 59, 66, doubtful about debating society 76; 77n, absent on account of illness 86; 92, brought to the dying Blundell 124; his remark on his marriage 166; 234n, 237, his gloomy and repressive management V, 437; his language at evening prayer VI, 31; 140n, a volunteer in 1803 255

Preston, Mrs Matthew (Eliza Garratt), I, 124n

Preston, Miss (Matthew Preston's daughter), V, 437

Preston, Miss (Matthew Preston's sister), I, 16, 18, 22, 26, 27, 28, 41, 46, invites TBM's parents to Aspenden Hall 50; 62

Preston, Rebecca, I, 41

Preston, William Thomas, VI, 27n

Preston (of Northern Circuit), his achievements as satyr, VI, 27

Prévost, Abbé, *Mémoires*, III, 310n

Price, Bonamy, IV, 37n, V, *81*, 82, 171, disappointed of *ER* editorship 304; 314n, VI, 281n

Price, Mrs Bonamy (Lydia Rose), II, 85, V, 171n, 172, 314n, 321, taken in by TBM's April fool's letter 323; 337, VI, 281n

Price, Richard, II, *61*

Price, Sir Robert, II, *52*

Price, Samuel Grove, II, *11*, afraid to speak in Commons 12

Prim, Peter, TBM's servant, III, 44-5, illness and death 68-9; 77

Prince, Rev. Henry James, V, 187n

Prince Edward's Island, III, 332

Prince of Wales, V, 423

Pringle, crazy fellow who writes daily, V, 239

Pringle, Thomas, I, *244*, *Ephemerides* II, 333n; 'Kay's *Travels in Caffraria*,' TBM sends to Napier 333
Prinsep, Henry Thoby, III, 124n, *134*, 149, IV, 184
LETTER TO: III, 238
Prior, James, *Life of Goldsmith*, IV, 98*; ed., *Miscellaneous Works of Goldsmith*, IV, 98n
Prior, Matthew, letters, V, 116; *Tales*, V, 18, *Works*, V, 182
Prison Discipline Act, III, 356
Pritchard, Hannah, II, *309*, 310
Pritchard, Mr (British consul at Tahiti), IV, 238n
Privy Council, TBM hears question of suttee argued before II, 138; TBM sworn in III, 300-2; 326n, V, 92, grants for education best scheme in bad system 379; VI, 189
Privy Council, Judicial Committee of, IV, 392n, and Gorham case V, 96n; VI, 207n
Privy Council Committee on Education, III, 293n, 356, IV, 320, proposal to increase grant to 334n; 379, V, 54
Procopius, V, 62n
Proctor, Bryan Waller ('Barry Cornwall'), II, *36*
Propagandists, French, III, 335
Propertius, III, 160*
Property Tax, TBM won't pledge to support II, 132; TBM favours 164
Protagoras, III, 141, VI, 83
Protestants, Bill for uniting, V, 137; *see also* Dissenters, Evangelicals, Puritans
Protheroe, Mr, I, 277n
Protheroe, Edward Davis-, II, *16*, 31, 36
Prout, William, II, *39*
Provis, Thomas, V, 349n
Prussia, King of, appoints TBM to Order of Merit, V, 298
Prussia, Order of Merit, government decides TBM should not accept V, 301; TBM relieved not to accept 303; 309, 350
Prussia, Royal Academy of Sciences, presents TBM for Order of Merit, V, 298
Prussians, Milnes's account of, IV, 239
Pryme, George, IV, 80, *378*, offers to lend TBM collection of historical pamphlets 380; V, 225n, 'old ass at Cambridge' 227; *Autobiographic Recollections*, IV, 378; *Memoirs of the Life of Daniel Sykes*, IV, 378
LETTER TO: IV, 378
Pseudo-Asconius, commentary on Cicero, IV, 49*
Public Charities, Commissioners of, bill for, II, 101
Public Libraries and Museums bill, V, 335n
Public Records, use of by scholars, V, 166n
Publius Decius, IV, 55n, 56
Puffing, TBM's aversion, I, 268; TBM should have his puffers as well as his neighbours II, 84
Pugin, Augustus Welby, IV, 255n
Pulci, Luigi, *Morgante Maggiore*, III, 261
Pulteney, William, VI, *276*
Punch, III, 192
Punch, on opening letters at Post Office, IV, 198n; on TBM and Quakers V, 6n
Punjab, IV, 306, safe in Mutiny VI, 105
Punkahs, III, 92
Purdey, Mr (London gunsmith), TBM gives George Trevelyan rifle from VI, 214n
Puritans, V, 22, TBM thought unfair to V, 26; 54, TBM hates 377
Puseyism, IV, 47, 128, V, 227, charged against Aberdeen ministry 206
Puseyites, IV, 55, 119, 181n, the surplice question 239; Puseyite cant in Lyttelton's *Memoirs* 264; 305, Puseyite hymn (TBM's) 351; V, 100, TBM enjoys their rage and terror 132; their dress 155; at Gladstone's breakfast party 166n; TBM hates 277; VI, 181
Pye, Henry James, V, 131
Pym, John, V, 101n, 146
Pyrenees, I, 39

Quain, Richard, IV, *254*, 'Observations on the Education and Examination for Degrees in Medicine,' IV, 254
Quakers, I, xi, xxv, Thomas Mills's children not brought up as 7n; Cropper family 196; TBM jokes about 197; at Liverpool II, 124, 136 probably burn Hannah and Margaret's novels 138; TBM wishes particular accounts of 144; and novel-reading 146; Edward Cropper leaves 184n, 189; at Leeds 189; their admission to Parliament 288; names for 230; 243, 244, London swarming with 252; verses on 252, 256; will be scandalised by Henry's duelling 265; in Pennsylvania 265; 287, III, 380, delegation of calls on TBM about Penn V, 6; TBM thought unfair to 26; 42, TBM laughs at their outcry over Penn 143; 333, *see also* William Penn *and* William Stout
Quarterly Musical Magazine and Review, III, 307
Quarterly Review, on slave trade, I, 169, 195; criticises TBM's first public speech 202n; a comfort that it is worse than *ER* 271; on Croker's Boswell II, 108n; III, 108, review

of Sharp 135; 250, and Mme D'Arblay 308; IV, 41, 47, 53, and *Lays* 93; 173, 175, 226, and TBM's *History* V, 31; paper on Junius 215-16; article by Southey VI, 215
Quebec, fall of, IV, 77; V, 356
Queen Elizabeth College, University of London, VI, 10n, VI, ix
Queen's Bench, Court of, IV, 307-8, V, 96n, Ellis's speech in Newman trial V, 206
Queensberry, Lord, IV, 376
Quietists, V, 19
Quin, James, II, *309*
Quincy, Eliza Susan, V, *231*
LETTER TO: V, 231
Quincy, Josiah, V, 231n, *Memoir* 231n
Quintilian, III, 178, 200*
Quintus Calaber, III, 159*
Quintus Curtius, III, 200*, 202, TBM gives to George Trevelyan V, 391
Quintus Fabius, IV, 55n, 56
Quintus Smyrnaeus, III, 153
Quisquiliae, VI, 284

Racine, Jean, I, 77, 83
Radcliffe, Ann, *Mysteries of Udolpho*, II, 253
Radicals, TBM's response to their questions at Leeds II, 132; III, 167, 250, 271, 290, support Melbourne 299; at Edinburgh IV, 341
Radnor, William Pleydell-Bouverie, 3rd Earl, II, *144*
Rae, W. Fraser, 'Macaulay at Home,' III, 203
Ragatz, Lowell J., *Guide for the Study of British Caribbean History*, I, 222n
Raglan, Lady, VI, 216n
Raglan, Lord, VI, 216n
Raikes, H. C., at Cambridge dinner with TBM, VI, 214n
Raikes, Henry St John, *Life of Henry Cecil Raikes*, VI, 214n
Railway, II, 124, Margaret Macaulay's account of early trip 124n; 135, 136, TBM has not yet seen 144; Hannah and Margaret see 151; TBM proposes to travel on 186; to travel on with Hannah and Margaret 187; 303, carry *diligence* in France IV, 157; speculation in 239; speculation caught Fanny and Selina V, 362
Railway Bill, TBM worked to death by, IV, 258-9
Railway Committees, IV, 191, TBM on 255, 259, 268n
Railway Shares, Selina's shares in IV, 311-12; shares looking up V, 127; thriving 128; calls on 144
Ralph, James, *History of England*, V, 279
Ram Mohan Roy, Raja, II, *31*, Sydney Smith on 33; described 47-8; 242
Rambouillet, IV, 139
Ramsay, Rev. E. B., IV, 54n
Ramsgate, II, 168, 234, III, 299, IV, 350, 352
Ramshay, William, removed from judgeship, V, *205*
Randall, Henry Stephens, TBM explains his judgment of Jefferson to VI, 94-6; dissents from TBM's prophecy about U.S. 171; *Life of Jefferson*, VI, 74, presented to TBM 171; 186*
LETTERS TO: VI, 74, 94, 171, 186
Ranke, Leopold Von, *History of the Papacy*, III, 268*, 325n, 326*
'Ranke's Italian Narrative and Romantic Poetry,' III, 329n
Raper, Mrs Frances Phillips, III, 308n
Raphael, III, 263, cartoons at Hampton Court V, 409, 412; VI, 59
Rapin Thoyras, Paul de, *Histoire d'Angleterre*, I, 53
Rattlesnake, sloop, VI, 196
Ravaillac, François, III, 326
Rawlinson, Sir Henry, V, x, offers to take TBM's chambers VI, *8*; changes his mind 25; arrangement with 26; 191
LETTERS TO: VI, 8, 26
Rawson, George, II, *92*, 133n, TBM at his house 188n; 205n, 225
LETTERS TO: II, 92, 235, 238
Rawson, George, the younger, II, *238n*
Rawson, Mrs George, II, 207, 235
Ray, Gordon N., ed., *Letters of Thackeray*, V, 72n, 358n, VI, 17n
Raymond, Samuel, sends TBM copy of Campbell's Diary, VI, 218n; 225, 252n
Read, Robert, Jr, *Modern Leicester*, I, 211
Reading, I, 278
Real Property Limitation Act, I, 208n
Realf, Richard ('The Poor Boy of Brighton'), V, *226*, 227, *Guesses at the Beautiful*, 226*
Record, III, 285, laughed at in Athenaeum IV, 281; praises TBM's *History* VI, 13
Recorders, provisions for in Municipal Reform Act V, 283
Records Commission, III, 373n
Red Party, in Paris, V, 75
Redesdale, Lord, I, 220n, 'stupid' edition of Mitford 256, 257; memoir of Mitford 256n; his opinion in *John Bull* case 256n; VI, 201
Redfield, J. S., firm, edition of TBM's speeches, V, 339n, VI, 292

Rees, Dr G. O., v, *308n*
Reeve, Henry, on 'Poodle' Byng, II, 195n; IV, 206n, V, *334*, 337n, points out omission in *History* VI, 6; 72n, 216n, inquires about Campbell's Diary 218; reviews it 225n; obituary of TBM 252n
LETTERS TO: V, 334, VI, 6, 185, 218, 225, 225, 252
Reform Bill (first, 1 March 1831), introduced I, 319n; debate on II, 5, anticipations of at Calne 8; TBM describes scene on second reading 9-11; debate 12; defeated 12n; V, 381
Reform Bill (second, 24 June 1831), introduced II, 15n; 49, arrangements for first reading 54; inspires violence of faction almost unprecedented 70; all night debate 70-1; 73, in committee 80; TBM makes brief remarks in debate 83; 'miserable proceedings' in committee 87; weakness of Whig leaders during debate 88; Althorp has done greatest service for 91; 93, committee stage over 96; defeated in Lords 99n; dinner to celebrate passage through Commons 101; debate has injured health of many members 105; what to do if it is lost VI, 275
Reform Bill (third, 12 December 1831), I, 287n, introduction and second reading II, 109n; passes second reading in Lords 120n; passing of 123n; receives royal assent 124; Guildhall dinner to celebrate 146; further changes should wait until the experiment tried 165; 166, and necessity of compromise 177; 178, 198, III, x, 'absolutely necessary' 150; 168, 188, 356, 357, 'not unexceptionable' IV, 103; 113, not perfect but effective 187; Chandos clause in 187
Reform Bill, 1854, V, 381
Reform Bill, 1859, brought in by Disraeli, VI, 201; opposed by Russell 202n; all parties for 214
Reform Club, III, 273n, TBM elected to 368n; IV, 282, V, 222n
Reform Dinner, II, 101
Reformation of Criminals, societies for silenced by Indian Mutiny VI, 103
Regent, Prince: *see* George IV
Registration of Voters, III, 384
Reid, Sir John Rae, controls seat for Dover, IV, *335*, 336
Reid, Thomas, *Inquiry into the Human Mind*, V, 313*
Reid, T. Wemyss, *Life of Richard Monckton Milnes*, V, 296
Reinhardt, Walter, III, 169n
Religious Equality Association, Ireland, V, 290n
Rémusat, Charles François Marie, Comte de, III, 352, *353*, V, 228n, VI, 216n
Rennell, Thomas, I, *104*, TBM hears him preach 104
Rennell, Thomas, Dean of Winchester, I, 104
Rennes, IV, 155
[Rennie, Eliza], *Traits of Character*, I, 18n, 172n, 321
Renton, Dr Robert, V, *397*
Repton School, I, 103n
Repulse, III, 196
Respirator, TBM gets one, V, 370n
Restoration Stage, decor in, IV, 388-9
Retrospective Review, V, 321n
[Reynière, Alexandre Grimod de la], *Almanach des Gourmands*, II, 215
Reynolds, Henry Revell, V, *208*
Reynolds, Sir Joshua, portrait of Charles James Fox II, 27; portrait of Fox, Lady Sarah Lennox, and Lady Susan Fox-Strangways 27n; 59n, portrait of Garrick 147; II, 258, 281n, V, 195, portrait of Mrs Sheridan as St Cecilia 201; portrait of the infant Johnson VI, 83
Reynolds, Samuel William, Sr, II, 64n, *223n*
Reynolds, Samuel William, Jr, II, 64n, *223n*
Rheims, VI, 101, TBM at 104; 105, TBM at 114; 115, 116, Cathedral IV, 143, 152
Rhine, V, 341, TBM travels up 351; 354, VI, 102, 104, 105
Rhodes, John N., lithographic portrait of TBM, II, 206n; 214n
Rhone, IV, 147, not to be compared to Rhine V, 351
Rib, River, I, 64
Rica, V, 286
Riccarton (Sir William Gibson Craig's residence), IV, 135, 169, TBM visits 215, 302; 319, V, 256, 263, 267
Rich, Henry, afterwards Baronet, II, *216*, IV, 319, 'Mellingen on Duelling,' IV, 45*, 'Recent History of Portugal,' II, 113*, 'What Will the Lords Do?,' II, 216
Rich, Lady Isabella, IV, 369n
Rich Family, papers of, V, 477
Richard I, King, IV, 256; equestrian statue o outside House of Lords V, 334n
Richard II, King, I, 159n, IV, 256, VI, 61
Richard III, King, IV, 256
Richardson, David Lester, III, *126*
LETTER TO: III, 126
Richardson, Rowland, V, 395n
Richardson, Samuel, III, 9, IV, 76, on Swift, 126

Writings: Clarissa, I, 237, II, 96, 136, III, 29, 65n, *Correspondence*, 126n, *Sir Charles Grandison*, I, 237*, II, 15*, TBM thought he could reproduce from memory 15n; 17*, 24*, 67*, 146*, 206*, 215*, III, 76, VI, 63*, examination in 180*
Richelieu, Cardinal, IV, 232
Richmond, Caroline, Duchess of, II, *66*
Richmond, Charles Gordon-Lennox, 5th Duke of, II, *65*, 66, III, 85n, 244n, IV, 270
Richmond, George, V, *56*, portrait of TBM 56; portrait of TBM, 1850, 56n; 2nd portrait of TBM V, 138n; portrait of Hannah for TBM 152; TBM takes Margaret Trevelyan to his studio VI, 218n; portrait of Inglis V, 453; TBM thinks he may aspire to the throne of Lawrence 453
Richmond, Lord Lansdowne's house at, II, 161, 292; Miss Berry's residence, IV, 60; Lord John Russell's residence, TBM at IV, 349; TBM refuses to stand for 363; V, 409, TBM at Lansdowne's house 413; Star and Garter, TBM proposes to dine at 409
Richmond Hill, I, 87, view from II, 170; TBM takes house at 6 Upper Park Place V, 458
Richmond Park, Pembroke Lodge (Lord John Russell's residence), V, 461n
Ricketts, Mordaunt, TBM's encounter with in Holland IV, *217*; pestered by 219-20
Ricks, Mrs, a dwarf, I, 7
Riddick, Mrs (Hannah's servant), III, *27*, 28, 29, 37
Rider, William, VI, *287*, *see* Additions and Corrections, vol. II, p. 114
LETTER TO: II, 114
Ridgway, James, London printer, II, 5n
Ridley, Bishop, II, 241, VI, 201
Rifle Corps, at Cambridge, VI, 214; its troubles 255; TBM suggests eclogue on 256
Riga, cholera in, II, 48
Rigby, Richard, IV, *73*
Rimmer, W. G., *Marshalls of Leeds*, II, 17n
Rio, Alexis François, IV, 32; *La Petite Chouannerie*, 32, 41-2*
Ripon, Frederick John Robinson, Viscount Goderich and 1st Earl of, I, 226n, 228n, resigns 230n; 232, 286, II, 102, and appointment of Henry Macaulay 102n; invites TBM to dinner 230; 255, 260, 263, breaks down in Lords 263; 290, 339, III, 85n, to succeed at Board of Control IV, 124; VI, 47n
Ripon, Sarah, Countess of, II, *263*
Rippen, Joseph, V, 265n
Ritchie, Mrs Margaret Booth, I, xv, xxxiv
Rives, William Cabell, IV, *105*; his speech on Ashburton treaty 105n
LETTER TO: IV, 105
Rizzio, David, III, 207
Robert II, of Scotland, IV, 255, 257
Robert Bruce, IV, 255
Roberts, Arthur, ed., *Letters of Hannah More to Zachary Macaulay*, I, xxix, 31n, 33n, 55, 106n, 112n, 207n, 277n, 321, IV, 116n
Roberts, Charles, III, *47*
Roberts, David, V, 328n
Roberts, S. C., I, viii, VI, 218n
Roberts, William, *Memoirs of Mrs Hannah More*, III, 216n
Robertson, Rev. Mr, describes delegation to TBM on Maynooth, IV, 254n
Robertson, Major-General C. W., *Life of Sir John Beverley Robinson*, IV, 48n
Robertson, Joseph, V, *36*
Robertson, Patrick, II, *226*, TBM pestered about 319, 325-6
Robertson, Roderick, II, 226n
Robertson, William, IV, 10, V, 93
Writings: Disquisition on India, Scotticisms in, IV, 130, *History of England*, II, 38, *History of the Reign of the Emperor Charles V*, I, 17*, IV, 77*, V, 162, 208, *History of Scotland*, I, 81*
Robinson, Archdeacon, III, 85
Robinson, George Richard, II, *73*
Robinson, Henry Crabb, on TBM, Praed, and Austin, I, 190n; *Supplement to Strictures on a Life of William Wilberforce*, III, 273n.
Robinson, Mary, II, *309*, 310
Robinson, Thomas, III, *41*
Robson, Dr R., I, xv, xxxiv, 114n, 200n, IV, 78n, V, 385n, 'Trinity College in the Age of Peel' V, 449n
Rochester, TBM at VI, 29
Rochester, 1st Earl of, IV, 375, V, 323
Rochester, New York, II, 314
Rockingham, Lord, his ministry, IV, 177
Rodd, Thomas, IV, *197*, his shop in Great Newport Street 197; TBM's bookseller for historical works V, 145
Roden, 3rd Earl of, V, 74n, 415n
Roe, Sir Thomas, V, 97
Roebuck, John Arthur, III, *158*, 187, V, 99, drunken speech by 222
Roebuck v. Coppock, V, 222

Roehampton, TBM thinks of spending summer there v, 448
Rogers, Arnold, dentist, v, 204n
Rogers, Charles, vi, *127*
LETTER TO: vi, 127
Rogers, Henry, brother of Samuel, ii, *216*
Rogers, Henry, dentist, v, 204n
Rogers, Henry, writer for *ER*, v, *79*, article on marriage question 79n; review of TBM's *Speeches* 428*; 'few people whom I value more' 428
Writings: The Eclipse of Faith, v, 428, TBM's copy missing 429, 'Puseyism, or the Oxford Tractarian School,' iv, 119*, 128-9*, 'Reason and Faith; Their Claims and Conflicts,' 'very able paper' v, 79*, 'Recent Developments of Puseyism,' iv, 227*
Rogers, Samuel, i, 279n, on Jekyll, i, 318n; ii, *19*, 24, 26, his seat in Holland House garden 27; advises TBM to give up reviewing for more important work 29; TBM's judgment of his poetry 29; in company with Sydney Smith 32; anecdotes of Scott and Byron 32; judgment of Byron 33; contrasted to Sydney Smith 34; breakfast with 50, 51, 54-5; anecdote of Chantrey 55; breakfast with 56-7; 65, his kindness to TBM 80; 81, breakfast with 82, 146, 148; stories about the Listers 153; looking like Lazarus 153; his opinion of Henry Fox 182; 216, 313n, on Byron 321; TBM dines with twice 336; 363, 376, iii, 12, 33, 153n, 281n, should write character of Lord Holland 371; iv, 14n, breakfast 120; presents his *Works* to TBM 124; 191n, at breakfast 234; v, 42n, failing 104; criticises Russell's epitaph for Lord Holland 155; entertaining article on in *ER* vi, 48
Writings: Human Life, TBM quotes and compliments ii, 29, 50, *Italy*, ii, 37, *Poems*, iii, 13*, 137, 'A Wish,' i, 72*
LETTERS TO: iii, 13, iv, 124, vi, 265
Rogers, Thomas, dentist, v, 204n
Rohilla War, iii, 361
Rolfe, Robert: *see* Lord Cranworth
Rollin, Charles, *Ancient History*, i, 69, *Histoire Ancienne des Egyptiens*, i, 5*
Romaine, William, v, *454*
Roman Ballads, iv, 44
Roman Camp, near Malvern, v, 193
Roman Catholics, and authority of General Councils, v, 19-20
Roman Knights, procession of, iv, 55-6
Rome, Niebuhr on, i, 280; early history of iii, 142; 252, 262, 264, TBM delighted by 267; Capitol, Colosseum, St Peter's, Vatican 267; Piazza di Spagna 268; badness of Papal government 269; 270, 278, funerals at iv, 80; St Peter's 139; crowd of English 201; question of human sacrifices at 357, 358-9; English College v, 428; Pantheon vi, 42
Romilly, Charles, ii, 282n
Romilly, Edward, vi, *266*
LETTER TO: vi, 266
Romilly, Mrs Edward (Sophia Marcet), vi, *266*
Romilly, John, 1st Baron, i, *139*, in Cambridge riots 150; ii, 35, 36, 157, iv, 305, v, 88n, v, 166n, on Commission on Laws of India 367n; wished to stand for Edinburgh vi, 85n; 93
LETTER TO: vi, 254
Romilly, Joseph, *Cambridge Diary*, ii, 196n; sends information to TBM v, *210*
Romilly, Sir Samuel, suicide of, i, *105*; 139n, 150, Althorp has his principles ii, 91; *Life*, iii, 325n; not a subject for TBM iv, 44, 46; 72, vi, 266n
Romsey, Hampshire, Abbey Church, v, 170n
Romulus and Remus, iv, 44
Ronquillo, Don Pedro de, despatches, v, 34n
Rosas, General, iv, 292n
Roscius, blunder about in TBM's 'Roman Tale,' vi, 161
Roscoe, William, edition of Pope, v, *104*
Rose, Edward, v, *85*, TBM asks living for 427n; given living of Weybridge 458
Rose, Mrs Edward (Ellen Mary Parker), v, *458n*
Rose, Henry, iii, *33n*
Rose, Rev. Joseph, i, 30, 308n
Rose, Mrs Joseph (Lydia Babington), TBM's cousin, i, *30*, 211n, 308n, ii, 85n, 303, iii, 33n, iv, 37n, v, 82, 84, 85, 168, 170, 427n, 458, vi, 120, 122, 'few such women' 281; Recollections of TBM, i, 27n
Rose, Lydia: *see* Mrs Bonamy Price
Rosebery, Lady, i, 161n
Rosebery, 4th Earl of, i, xvi, 161, iv, 346n, vi, 61n
Rosen, Count, v, 115
Ross, Alexander, iii, 148, 165, 229
Ross, General Alexander, vi, 196n
Ross, Charles, vi, *196*, ed., *Correspondence of Charles, First Marquis Cornwallis*, vi, 196*
LETTER TO: vi, 196
Ross, Janet, *Three Generations of English Women*, new edn, iii, 268n, 325n, iv, 295
Rossini, Gioachino, *Tancredi*, ii, 18n

Rosslyn, TBM at, VI, 233
Rosson, III, 154
Rotch, B., his patent fidd, II, 250
Rotherham, I, 208n, 213, 222n, 243n, 246, 253n
Rothesay Express, VI, 259
Rothley, III, 50
Rothley Grange, II, 84, 85
Rothley Temple, I, xxi, days there 'among the happiest of my life' 130; Macaulay family at 131n, 187; described 197n; TBM at 197, 198n; 200, 201, TBM visits 211; Macaulay family at 214; TBM at 222n, 225, 243n; 244, 246, 247, 248n, 253n, bought by Sir James Parker 267n; TBM at 277n; 278, TBM at 282; 308, II, 20, Zachary Macaulay and daughters at 68n; 78, 80, 81, TBM asks for the gossip of 84: backbiting at 85; 86, 87, 89, 91, 170, 183, 186, TBM to escort Hannah and Margaret there 186; 187, 188, 190, 196, TBM at 198; 234, 266, 233, 294, Babington likely to be turned out of 300; TBM can't pass by without staying 303; 312, 343, 347, 364, 366, 368, 372, III, ix, 15n., 106, 157, 271n, 296, 305, TBM visits 307; 313, TBM at IV, 310, 311; V, 87, 170, TBM awaits its judgment on his epitaph on Babington 196-7; 218, 268n, Parker's death at 270n; 318, 357, VI, 41, TBM chooses for his title 113; Mary Babington Parker buried at 162n
Rothley Vicarage, I, 308, II, 75, 84, 85
Rothschild, firm, II, 60n
Rothschild, Baron Lionel de, first Jewish M.P., I, 320n; takes seat in Parliament VI, 147n; *227*, dinner with described 227-8
Rothschild, Nathan Meyer, II, *60*
Rotterdam, IV, 38, 53, 205, TBM writes from 216; 220
Roubiliac, Louis Francois, bust of Pope, II, *54*
Rouen, I, 284, described 290-1; IV, 137-8, 146, TBM and Ellis visit V, 72; 361, Cathedral, I, 291, V, 68, St Ouen, I, 290, 291, IV, 137, V, 68, Hotel de France, I, 290
Rousseau, Jean Jacques, *Confessions*, III, 21; statue of 349; 'unfeeling disposition' IV, 72; does not attract TBM 223
Routh, Sir Randolph, V, *138*
Rowe, Carpenter, IV, 259n, *268*, 381
Rowe, Nicholas, his plays, I, 81*
Roxburghe Club, III, 13
Royal Academy, II, 159, IV, 41, TBM Professor of Ancient Literature in V, vii; 48, 96, exhibition 97; Professorship 105; anniversary dinner 108, 161; exhibition 382; Grant's portrait of TBM exhibited at 327n; exhibition 328; Ward's 'Last Sleep of Argyll' at 400n; exhibition 453; 457n
Royal Academy, President and Council of, letter to V, 108
Royal Academy of Turin, V, 223
Royal Bavarian Academy of Science, TBM elected to, V, 218n
Royal Blue Book, II, 145n, 156n
Royal Bounty, IV, 328, next grant from promised to Hunt 329
Royal Dutch Academy of Sciences, V, 229n
Royal Humane Society, V, 350
Royal Irish Academy, TBM elected, V, 309n
Royal Institution, TBM joins, I, 139n; IV, 215n, V, 87n
Royal Kalendar, I, 265n
Royal Literary Fund, TBM contributes to, V, 107; TBM a vice-president 107n
Royal Mint, Ellis attorney for, V, 460n
Royal Polytechnic Institution, V, 56n
Royal Scottish Society of Arts, petitions for grant, IV, 243
Royal Society, V, 25n, conversazione at 161; TBM elected 309
Royal Society of Edinburgh, *Transactions*, III, 189n
Royston, Cambridgeshire, V, 473
Royston, Richard, V, *473*
Rubens, Peter Paul, I, 207, IV, 219, V, 143, 'Rape of the Sabines' in National Gallery IV, 234; 'Woman Taken in Adultery' at Leigh Court V, 284
Rubini, Giovanni Battista, II, *18*
Ruffin, Edmund, ed., *The Westover Manuscripts*, V, 144n
Rugby, IV, 37, V, 26n, Fanny at 81n; mastership of 82; 137
'Rule Britannia,' VI, 108
Rumbold, Sir Arthur, V, 415n
Rumbold, Charles Edmund, II, *18*
Rumford, Count, IV, *76*
Rump, The, III, 354
Runciman, Steven, *History of the Crusades*, I, 23n
Runic Superstitions, subject for examination in English verses, I, 77, 80
Rupert, Prince, II, 197, and Magdalene College V, 115
Rush, James Blomfield, last dying speech and confession, VI, *92**
Rushworth, John, *Historical Collections*, V, 146

Ruskin, John, letters of, I, xv; compared with TBM for knowledge of Bible II, 22n; 'Political Economy of Art' delivered at Manchester VI, 101n; *Praeterita* V, 454n; 'Ruskinism' at Cambridge VI, 206

Russel, Alexander, editor of *Scotsman*, V, *430*, 'The Newspaper Stamp' V, 430*

Russell, Arthur, VI, 47n

Russell, Dr Charles William, reviews *History*, V, 53n

Russell, Lord Edward, II, *282*

Russell, Frances Anna Maria Elliot, Lady (2nd wife of Lord John Russell), V, 261, *279*, VI, 10n, 116

Russell, G. W. E., *Collections and Recollections*, I, 264n, IV, 15n

Russell, General Lord George William II, 152n

Russell, Lady Georgiana Elizabeth, II, *282*

Russell, Dr John, III, *99*

Russell, Lord John, afterwards 1st Earl Russell, commissioned by SDUK to write history of England I, 322, 323; II, *6*, 26, moves for leave to bring in Reform Bill 54; 56, remembers TBM's 'Sortes Virgilianae' 57; compliments TBM on speech 62; 67, not worth much in Reform Bill debate 91; honoured at Reform Dinner 101n; 144, an unwilling bachelor 152; dinner with 152; has left off his wig, 159; 169, 229, compliments TBM on India speech 268; 289, III, x, 75, speech on Irish Church 85; 244n, 298n, 299, 335, and Bible-printing question 355; on Corn Laws 272n; IV, 18, defends TBM 23n; on protection 26; 47, declines to write for *ER* 48; plans for history of Europe 38n; letter to TBM 48n; defends 4th Duke of Bedford 73; TBM deplores his position on Ellenborough 99; on Corn Laws 100, 101; TBM supported his sliding scale measure 103; 110, 136, 162, and Ten Hours Bill 180n; and Test Act 186; 189, 261, letter on Corn Laws 'like a shell in a powder-mill' 268; asked to form ministry 269; his options in Corn Law crisis 270; TBM must support 271; 272, his response to invitation to form ministry 272-4; his letter on Corn Laws 273, 274; drawing up a new Corn Law 274; reports decision to Queen 274; appeals to TBM for support 275; and the making of a ministry 276-8; unable to form ministry 278; 283, 288, 288n, supposed to be dominated by his wife 291; and Ten Hours Bill 299n; appoints TBM Paymaster General 300; letter from TBM to, mentioned 302n; TBM does not approve appointment of Dundas 305; on Outram's case 307; and pension for Leigh Hunt 309; 314n, gives cabinet dinner 319n; grants pension to Hunt 337, 338; on TBM's defeat at Edinburgh 347n; 348, TBM sees at Richmond 349; and reform at Cambridge 359n; proposes to bring in TBM for Richmond 362; as Rector of Glasgow University 390; 392, thinks TBM a Trimmer in *History* V, 6; TBM takes Hannah to party of Russell's 37n; gives John Macaulay living of Aldingham 50, 51, 52, 55; TBM recommends Kemble to for Regius Professorship 61-2; 64, his denunciation of Papal aggression imprudent 132; anti-papal bill disappoints people 152; in and out of power 154; TBM criticizes his epitaph for Lord Holland 154, 155; extremely unpopular 156; resigns 156n; long at work on epitaphs for Lord and Lady Holland 170; 184n, offers TBM office 211n; TBM urges national defence on 218n; meeting of M.P.s at his house 222; TBM hopes his election safe 233, 241; 290, TBM advises to join coalition ministry 303n; does not take enough care of Whigs in ministry 305; 306n, has vexed some of his friends 307; plan for Annuity Tax 310; edits Tom Moore's *Memoirs* 324n; gives Croker too good a target 346; plan for education in Scotland 379; different events of his two reform bills 381; TBM speaks to about Oxford Bill 391n; 425, 427n, TBM asks him to see editor of *Scotsman* 430; speech on Enlistment of Foreigners Bill 433n; calls on TBM 461; contradictory behaviour over Crimean War 461; resigns 461, 461n; misunderstanding about Ward's paintings for House of Commons 470; VI, 10n, 40n, TBM supports Palmerston against 79; 85n, 104n, TBM criticizes his inscription for Scutari monument 107; approves TBM's peerage 115; sends his resolutions on India to TBM 146; TBM makes suggestions for India Bill 146n; his inscription for Scutari monument 147; bill for Jewish Relief 147n; TBM's comments on Indian resolutions 148-9; talking 'Jacobin jargon' 202n; has behaved ill 202; 207, 208, 211, 213, Foreign Secretary in new ministry 222n; TBM wishes to consult with 260-1

Writings: editor, *Correspondence of John, Fourth Duke of Bedford*, IV, 72n, 73n,

221n, *Don Carlos*, IV, 69, 'Earls Grey and Spencer,' IV, 283, 287*, *Later Correspondence*, IV, 288n, *Life and Times of Charles James Fox*, made with scissors not pen, VI, 202*, editor, Thomas Moore's *Memoirs*, V, 346n

LETTERS TO: IV, 23, 347, 359, 362, V, 6, 50, 61, 154, 235, 260, 278, 430, 433, 470, VI, 107, 115, 146, 148

Russell, Lady Louisa, afterwards Duchess of Abercorn, II, *181*

Russell, Lady William (1636-1723), V, 470n, 471

Russell, Lady William (Elizabeth Anne Rawdon), II, *152*

Russell, Lord William (1639-83), II, 23, 144, TBM compares himself to 332; his place of execution IV, 388; his last words V, 302; 470n, and Ward's painting 471

Russell, William Russell, Lord, afterwards 8th Duke of Bedford, II, *21*, 254

Russell, family of, II, 181

Russia, the 'Arch-Tartuffe,' I, 163; question of loan to II, 155n; III, 64, 122, education in 125; war against V, 378n; 456, supposed alliance with France VI, 210n, 211, 213

Russian Loan, debate upon, II, 155

Russians, II, 40, V, 426

Rutherfurd, Andrew, III, *288*, 291n, 306, Lord Rector of Glasgow University IV, 227n; in successful trial case 258; introduces Scottish Universities Bill 258n; 261, 262, Lord Advocate under Russell 302; 306, TBM consults about Glasgow inauguration 389-90, 391-2; and Heritable Securities Bill 400n; 402, at Cambridge with TBM V, 48; 54, 242, made Lord of Session 248n; congratulates TBM 249; illness and suffering of 263; TBM calls on in Edinburgh 263n; death 434

LETTERS TO: IV, 258, 261, 262, 262, 378, 380, 389, 391, V, 248, 263

Ruthven, Edward Southwell, II, *73*

Rutland, 4th Duke of, I, 287n, III, 382n

Rutland, 8th Earl of, V, 82

Ryan, Sir Edward, III, *125*, 126n, 144, 152, 158, 162, 165, 183, 227, 228, 229, 235, President of Committee of Public instruction IV, 311n; TBM invites to a breakfast council 312; TBM dines with V, 111n; on Commission on Laws of India 455; VI, 72n, 119, 250n

LETTERS TO: IV, 184, 309, 311, 312, V, 111, 427

Ryde, Isle of Wight, Pier Hotel, V, 124

Rylands Library, John, II, 20n

S.C.E., *New Biographies*, III, 338n

Sabbatarianism, TBM's dislike of V, 291; TBM discusses with Russell 461

Sabbath, observance of not a main issue for abolitionists I, 251

Sabbath Observance, bill on, II, 235; Leeds petition on 235; defeated by shamefully small majority 240; 247

Sabines, III, 179

Sackville, Lord George, V, *216*

Sadleir, Michael, *Bulwer: A Panorama*, I, 295n, II, 112n, *XIX Century Fiction*, V, 102n

Sadler, Michael Thomas, I, *275*, TBM means to show his ignorance 285; personal remarks in his 'Refutation' 315n; effect of TBM's answer to 318; candidate of the Duke of Newcastle II, 93n; 115n, introduces Ten Hours Bill 117; 133n, 135, speech at Leeds 188n; results of canvass for 193; TBM will 'wreak all the bitterness of my heart on' 204; behind in canvass 207; accused of bringing in bludgeon men 209; will be beaten 210; TBM's bitterness towards 211; 211n, 'mad with rage' 213; election expenses 223n; quarrel with John Foster 368-9; making faces 369; IV, 302

Writings: The Law of Population, reviewed by TBM, I, 275, 'Refutation of an Article...,' I, 312, 314, 'A Reply to an Article...,' I, 318n

Sadler, Mrs Michael Thomas, II, 369n

Sadr Diwani, Court of, III, 125n

Sages, The, IV, 37-9

St Anne's Hill, on the Thames, V, 409

St Anne's Society, Stewards and Committee of the Royal Asylum of, letter to, VI, 195

St Antonio, III, 32

St Asaph, Bishopric of, and government minority on, IV, 200

Saint-Aulaire, Louis-Clair de Beaupoil, Comte de, II, *67*

St David's College, Lampeter, I, 175n

St George's, Madras, III, 41

St George's Hill, TBM and Ellis explore, V, 416

St Germains, debate on borough of, II, 78

St Germains, France, TBM and Ellis visit V, 71, 75

St Gothard, VI, 26

St Helena, I, 82, 180n, II, 27, establishment at 312; III, 212, 222, 243n

St James's, Court of, date of the expression, V, 112

St John, Henry: *see* Lord Bolingbroke

St Leger, Francis Barry Boyle, 'The First Love of Henry Quatre,' I, 202*

St Leonards, II, 214n, V, 103, TBM at 467; Margaret Trevelyan goes to VI, 200; 202, Margaret sends bad account of circulating library at 204; 205, TBM hears from daily 206
St Leonards, Lady, V, 222
St Leonards, Edward Burtenshaw Sugden, 1st Baron, I, *221*, III, 204, V, 222
St Lucia, Order in Council for, II, 118
St Mark's College (Chelsea), Derwent Coleridge head of, IV, 379
St Michael, Cornish borough, III, 310
St Paul's, Dean of: *see* Henry Hart Milman
St Petersburg, VI, 19, Imperial Academy of Sciences, TBM receives diploma from, VI, 258n
Saint Réal, César Vichard, Abbé de, *De la Conjuration des Espagnols contre la République de Venise*, III, 108
St Ruth, General, TBM examines his despatches, V, 419
St Vincent, Edward Jervis Ricketts, 2nd Viscount, II, *78*, 175
Sainte-Beuve, Charles Augustin, *Causeries du Lundi*, V, 315n
Salamis, III, 131
Salisbury, VI, 76, TBM at 86, 87, Cathedral 76
Salisbury, Dean of: *see* Hugh Pearson
Salisbury, Lady, V, 226
Salisbury, 2nd Marquess of, his treatment of Mahon, V, *253*; VI, 163n
Salisbury and Winchester Journal, II, 13n
Sallust, III, 153*, 160*, VI, 246
Salvator, 'Prometheus,' IV, 324
Salvin, Anthony, V, 381n
Salzburg, Hannah at VI, 106
Saltzmann, Christian Gotthilf, *The Elements of Morality*, IV, 55*, 57, a 'Socinian' book V, 250
Sams, William Raymond, VI, *158*
Letter to: VI, 158
Sancroft, William, Archbishop of Canterbury, V, 14
Sand, George, *Consuelo*, V, 199, *The Countess of Rudolstadt*, V, 199
Sandbach, R. G. E., VI, 283
Sandes, Maurice, III, *74*
Sandford, Ayshford, V, 144n
Sandon, Lord: *see* Lord Harrowby
Sandwich, 4th Earl of, IV, *73*, 221
Sanford, E. A., VI, 26
Sanial, S. C., 'Captain David Lester Richardson,' III, 126, 'Macaulay in Lower Bengal,' III, 65n
Sanskrit, III, 102, as medium of instruction 123, 149, 150
Sanskrit College, III, 139
Saone, V, 343, TBM travels up 354
Sardanapalus, Alice's letter about and TBM's verses on V, 343-4
Sardhana, III, 169n
Sargent, Epes, V, *36*
Letter to: V, 36
Sarpedon, III, 382
Sarsaparilla, V, 461
Sartain, J., engraver, IV, 225n
Sartine, M. de, his *mot* about Beaumarchais, V, 315n*
Satirist, IV, 129
Sattara, and George Thompson, V, 138
Sattara, Rajah of, IV, 347
Saturday Half Holiday Association, V, 447, TBM contributes to 448
Saturday Review, criticism of TBM, VI, 173n
Saturnian meter, IV, 49
Saugur, III, 86
Saumur, IV, 150
Saville, Sir George, III, *220*
Savonarola, trial of, V, 404n
Sawbridge, John, VI, *87*
Sawyer, Sir Robert, V, 210
Saxe, Marshal, IV, 148
Saxe Weimar, Duke of, III, 47
Scalds, Creed of, I, 77
Scales, Rev. Thomas, II, *371*
Letters to: II, 371, III, 10
Scarborough, V, 371
Scarlett, James: *see* Lord Abinger
Scarron, Pierre, anecdote of, I, 37
Scarsdale, 3rd Earl of, V, 82
Scharf, George, IV, *260*, illustrates *Lays* 260; TBM recommends for secretaryship of National Portrait Gallery VI, 78
Schelling, Friedrich Wilhelm Joseph, VI, 162n
Schiller, Johann Christian Friedrich, II, 138, TBM hopes to read him on return from India III, 234; TBM's opinion of IV, 182; V, 27, TBM orders copy for Margaret Trevelyan 202
Writings: Works, III, 194n, 196, *Bride of Messina*, V, 194*, *Cabal and Love*, V, 194, *Don Carlos*, II, 151, V, 194*, *Fieschi*, V, 194*, *History of the Thirty Years' War*, II, 151, III, 236*, *Maid of Orleans*, V, 194* *Maria Stewart*, IV, 40, V, 194*, *The Robbers*, IV, 182, V, 194*, *Wallenstein*, II, 151, IV, 71, 182, V, 194*, *Wallenstein's Camp*, IV, 324*, *William Tell*, V, 194*
Schmitz, Leonhard, IV, *268*, TBM gives testimonial to 268-9; V, 211n, trans.,

Niebuhr's *Lectures on the History of Rome*, v, 83
Schoell, Gustav Adolf, v, *432*
LETTER TO: v, 432
Scholastic Divinity, preferable to mathematics I, 122
Scholefield, James, I, xvii, xviii, *86*, substitutes for Preston at Aspenden 86-7; 125, 191, used to examine in 'beastly lines' from Aristophanes v, 415
Scholefield, William, IV, *356*
Schomberg, Frederick, Duke of, his place of burial, VI, 6
School Book Society, III, 123
School Inspectors, appointment of, III, 351; 356
Schuler, Frederic, I, 5, III, 98
Schwartz, Christian, III, 55n, *69*, 70
Schwarzenberg, Prince Felix von, v, *285*
Schweighauser, Jean, edition of Polybius, IV, 80
Scinde, IV, 173, conquest of 183
Scinde, Amirs of, IV, 307n, VI, 38
Scindia, Court of, II, 348
Scobell, Henry, *Collection of Acts and Ordinances*, IV, 388*
Scotland, TBM argues for superiority of Scotch over English peasantry I, 30; TBM's visit to in 1828 235-41; II, 97, Charles Grant in 180, 194; TBM plans tour in, 252, 256, 257, 266; Protestant zeal in 266; plans for tour 290, 291, 293, 302, 305; Trossachs 306; improvements in 306-7; Highlands III, 43; 64, 252, pauperism in 385; revolution of 1688 in IV, 15; TBM wants to discuss Scottish history with Napier 159; TBM thinks of visiting Highlands 200; bills affecting 208, 209; and medical reform 214; banking system in 241; privileges of incorporated trades in 248, 251; banking system 251n; new poor law proposed for 252; low standards of medical education in 254n; parochial schools in 262; privileges of incorporated trades 267; famine in western Highlands 310, 332; quiet in 1848 383, Privy Council 287; plans for tour 392; its progress since Reformation v, 26; and John Knox 88; plan for national education in 90n; TBM tours with Hannah and Margaret Trevelyan 111n, 114; distress in Highlands 140n, 180; Maynooth-mad 237; Highlands 267; Board of Customs 272; commercial relations with England after Restoration 295; plan for museums in towns of 335; indifferent to Scottish rights movement 364; resolutions in favour of national education 377; establishment of Presbyterian church in 378; national education in, TBM's opinion 379; its interests adequately guarded in House of Commons 393; bill for reformatory schools in 412n; its universities favoured by Indian Civil Service examinations 438
Scotland, Gazeteer of, VI, 181
Scotland, J. A., VI, 287
Scotsman, III, 257n, 290, 302n, 379n, IV, 6n, 120, 170n, 172n, 174n, 190n, 192n, 208n, 213n, 215n, 251n, 254n, 269, publishes TBM's letter about Lord Grey 282n; 289, 301n, 303n, 304n, description of TBM's bust by Park 321n; 326n, on plan to nominate TBM v, 234n; 237n, on Irish Religious Equality Society 290n; TBM sorry that it opposes plan for national education 379; its high standing 430; affected by stamp tax 430n; prints extracts from Peel *Memoirs* VI, 93n
Scott, George Erving, wins Chancellor's Medal, I, 186
Scott, Hew, *Fasti*, III, 311n
Scott, J. F., ed., *Correspondence of Isaac Newton*, v, 355n
Scott, Sir Walter, his influence on TBM, I, xix-xx; 63, 120, 140, on Moray Place 241; identified by Adolphus 285n; II, 29, anecdote of from Rogers 32; opinion of Prof. Leslie 58n; 108n, dying 148; his financial affairs 148; death of 196; 201n, TBM glad to pay tribute but doubts 'Abbotsford business' 238; III, 41, compared to Virgil 62; TBM's remarks on his character 245-6; 253, monument at Edinburgh 326, TBM subscribes to 328; feebleness of his last works and TBM's dislike of historical novel IV, 106; and Robert Cadell 164n; TBM supports Edinburgh monument to 174; TBM on London committee for Edinburgh monument 174n; founder of Bannatyne Club 384n; none of his novels sold like TBM's *History* v, 30; mistakes about date of Killiecrankie 126; his archaisms and Scotticisms 147; TBM contributes to Edinburgh memorial 282n
Writings: Anne of Geierstein, IV, 106, *The Antiquary*, IV, 235, *Castle Dangerous*, IV, 106, *Count Robert of Paris*, IV, 106, edition of Dryden, II, 306n, TBM presents it to Edinburgh Philosophical Institution, v, 463, *Guy Mannering*, I, 61, III, 49*, IV,

Scott: *Writings—cont.*
33*, VI, 155*, *Journal*, I, 239n, *The Lady of the Lake*, I, 120, *A Legend of Montrose*, III, 157*, *Life of Napoleon*, III, 340, *The Lord of the Isles*, I, 56*, V, 147n, *Marmion*, III, 256*, *Old Mortality*, II, 247*, III, 257*, IV, 168, V, 329*, *Paul's Letters to His Kinfolk*, I, 76, *Peveril of the Peak*, IV, 106, *Redgauntlet*, V, 148n, editor, *Secret History of the Court of King James the First*, I, 65*, 'Song, for the Anniversary Meeting of the Pitt Club of Scotland,' I, 50*, *Tales of a Grandfather*, V, 126, *The Vision of Don Roderick* I, 7, V, 126*, 'Waterloo,' I, 72*, *Waverley*, I, 106*, 121, 235n, *Woodstock*, IV, 106

Scottish Education Bill, V, 379n

Scottish Literary Institute, TBM refuses membership in, VI, 127

Scottish Poor Bill, passage of, IV, 258

Scottish Privy Council, *Acta*, IV, 374, 375, VI, 64

Scottish Reformation Society, V, 238, 239, 240n

Scottish Universities Bill, introduced, IV, 258n; supported by Edinburgh Town Council 261; TBM describes arrangements for second reading 261-2; defeated 262; TBM presents petition on V, 325; 341

Scribe, Eugène, V, ix, *Théâtre Complet*, IV, 352, *Le Nouveau Pourceaugnac*, played before TBM at Woburn V, 144n

Scully, Vincent, abuses Trevelyan in Commons, V, *324*

Scutari Monument, TBM asked to write inscription for, VI, 104; Russell's inscription for 107; inscription for 115-16; inscription by Russell 147

Seaford, Charles Rose Ellis, 1st Baron, II, *78*, 175

Seaforth, Lord, II, 338n

Seal, TBM has new one, II, 192, 194; another 249; 253

Sebastiano del Piombo, 'The Raising of Lazarus,' does not attract TBM IV, 223

Sebastopol, rumoured fall of, V, 423n

Secretary, Anti-State Church Association, letter to, V, 90

Secretary, Committee for Frost, Williams, and Jones, letter to, IV, 293

Secretary, Poor Law Commission: *see* Sir Edwin Chadwick

Secretary of the Treasury, IV, 337

Sedgewick House, near Kendal (Wakefield family residence), I, 248

Sedgwick, Adam, IV, *118*, 323n, VI, 67n

'See, the Conquering Hero Comes,' VI, 108

Seine, compared to the Thames, I, 290; IV, 147, V, 409

Select Committee of the House of Commons on Public Petitions, *Reports*, IV, 249n

Sellon, Priscilla Lydia, her letters to Lord Campbell, V, *107*; her complaint absurd 107; 'Reply to a Tract by the Rev. J. Spurrell' 226-7*

Seneca, III, 178*, 180*

Seneca, the elder, *Controversiae*, III, 178*

Senior, Nassau, II, *169*, IV, 15, essays in *ER* 30*; 99, and Irish Church question 163; letter to Napier 166n; 204, and his American investments 265; letter to Napier 265n; V, 94n, 113n, at Malvern 174; 177, 182, leaves Malvern 190; his practice of keeping a journal 288n; lends TBM pair of spectacles 369; at Bowood 369; VI, 45n, 46n, 78n, Dundas refuses to travel with 159n

Writings: 'Berryer's Autobiographical Recollections,' IV, 62n, 'The Budget of 1842,' IV, 29*, *Conversations with M. Thiers, M. Guizot and other Distinguished Persons*, V, 289n, 'France, America, and Britain,' IV, 29*, 'Free Trade and Retaliation,' IV, 133*, 'Grounds and Objects of the Budget,' III, 385, 'Ireland,' TBM's remarks on the proofs, IV, 166*, 'The Oregon Question,' IV, 264-5*, 'Poor Law Reform,' IV, 9*

LETTERS TO: V, 234, 288, VI, 271

Sentimental System (opposed to Utilitarian), IV, 299

Sentimentalists, IV, 309

Separatists, III, 380

Sepoys, cruelties of, VI, 103, 106; dismissal of Christian 127

Serampore, missionary schools at, II, 340

Seringapatam, taking of, III, 51, 52, 60, 67, 83

Seringapatam, III, 234

Serjeant at Arms, House of Commons, II, 52, 142

Servia, IV, 144

Sesostris, III, 67, 75

Severus, V, 271

Seward, Anna, her abuse of Cowper, I, 71; *239*

Writings: Letters, I, 71n, on Washington and Major André V, 410; the attraction of their badness V, 410*,

rebound VI, 234, marginalia in 234n, *Life of Darwin* V, 410
Sewell, William, *Christian Morals*, IV, 46-7
Seymour, Edward, 1st Duke of Somerset, IV, 247
Seymour, Lord Edward Adolphus: *see* 12th Duke of Somerset
Seymour, Sir George Hamilton, V, 427n
Seymour, Jane, IV, 257
Shackell, Edward, I, 193n, 198n, 220n, 221n
Shackell, William, I, 193n
Shadwell, Sir Lancelot, I, *221*
Shadwell, Thomas, *Lancashire Witches*, I, 220n; V, 131, *The Squire of Alsatia*, V, 84*
Shaftesbury, 1st Earl of, TBM declines as subject for essay, III, 216-17
Shaftesbury, Anthony Ashley Cooper, 7th Earl of, styled Lord Ashley, IV, *180*, and Ten Hours Bill 180n; won't make motion on India 239; and TBM's speech on Ten Hours Bill 299n; and Ten Hours Bill 325n; V, ix, x, 108n, 118, compliments the work of Charles Macaulay 142; 157n, his scheme for petition to women of U.S. 298n; TBM amused by his discomfiture 377; a tool for knaves to work with 387; asks TBM to speak on General Havelock VI, 134; sends present of game to TBM 135
LETTERS TO: V, 142, VI, 134, 135, 151
Shaftesbury, Lady, V, ix, 108n, 157n
Shakespear, Henry, III, *149*, 185
Shakespeare, William, I, 61, 63, 72, the sole merit of English drama 81; 90, compared to Milton 110; 140, 183, II, 54, Stratford Jubilee 72; III, 62, 179, IV, 28, 39, V, 194, TBM wishes to read with Margaret Trevelyan 271; TBM presents Lansdowne edition to Fanny and Hannah 305; his legal learning VI, 192
Writings: All's Well that Ends Well, I, 166-7*, *Antony and Cleopatra*, III, 184, *As You Like It*, I, 123*, *Hamlet*, I, 63*, 207*, II, 259*, 288*, III, 135*, 362*, V, 164, VI, 53*, TBM once puzzled by succession of crown in 237, *1 Henry IV*, I, 41*, 288*, *2 Henry IV*, II, 318*, V, 410, VI, 11*, *Henry VI*, IV, 40*, 71, *King John*, II, 241*, *Macbeth*, V, 67*, 164, 177*, *Merchant of Venice*, I, 128, 219, origin of plot V, 63; 261*, *Merry Wives of Windsor*, VI, 246*, *Much Ado about Nothing*, V, 349*, *Othello*, I, 31*, 38*, II, 133, 223*, 253*, III, 77*, IV, 39, 112*, *Richard III*, I, 135* II, 280*, *The Tempest*, III, 60*, *Troilus and Cressida*, III, 154*, *Twelfth Night*, V, 410
Shanklin, Isle of Wight, V, 124
Shannon, Mr, I, 262
Sharaboji, III, 55
Sharp, Granville, TBM's praise of, I, *44*
Sharp, Henry, ed., *Selections from Educational Records*, III, 138n, VI, 300
Sharp, Miss, III, 137, 226
Sharp, Richard, I, 272n, *279*, 318n, his advice on musical parties II, 18; and Maria Kinnaird 19n; 21, invites TBM to his country place 59; 82, 146, 216, recommends Galt's *Lawrie Todd* 311; long talk with 313; weeps at prospect of TBM's departure 329; 330, more distressed than TBM's father at prospect of separation 331; 332, wishes to entertain Hannah 363; 365, his plan to entertain Hannah 368; III, 5, 9, 22, his death 135, 151; 154, 'owed much to his excellent advice' 224
Writings: Epistles in Verse, I, 279n, *Letters and Essays in Prose and Verse*, I, 279, III, 135
LETTERS TO: I, 279, 313, II, 376, III, 135, VI, 275, 277
Sharp and Boddington, firm, II, 19n
Shaw, Sir Frederick, II, *173*, his absurd conduct in Commons 173-4
Shaw-Lefevre, Charles: *see* Lord Eversley
Shaw-Lefevre, Sir John George, I, *122*, TBM supports at Cambridge IV, 341n; defeated at Cambridge 346; V, 110n, TBM sounds out as candidate for editorship of *ER* 129n; report on Annuity Tax 248n; 319; on Indian Civil Service Committee 389n; will have TBM's report printed privately 409; approves TBM's report 411; 412, TBM visits his house, Sutton Place 418; 438, 439, 440, VI, 43, agrees with TBM about Heaviside 71; 102, 222n
LETTER TO: V, 166
Shaw-Lefevre, Mrs John, V, 321
LETTER TO: V, 166
Shea, Donald F., *The English Ranke: John Lingard*, V, 53n
Shee, Sir Martin Archer, V, 96n
Sheffield, I, 208n, 212, 229n, 234, 250, 251
Sheffield Iris, I, 268n, IV, 348
Sheil, Richard Lalor, II, *11*, speech on Reform Bill 11; gives bad account of Ireland 30; 35, 52, III, 23, 301, ill-advised notice on Algeria IV, 233
Sheil, Mrs Richard Lalor, II, 35
Shelburne, Emily, Lady, V, *370*

Shelburne, Henry Petty, Lord, afterwards 1st Marquess of Lansdowne, 'Malagrida,' IV, *221*

Shelburne, Henry Thomas Petty-Fitzmaurice, Lord, afterwards 4th Marquess of Lansdowne, IV, 221, V, 6n, 370n, *372*

LETTER TO: V, 372

Sheldon, Bishop Gilbert, V, 13

Shelford: *see* Little Shelford

Shelley, Percy Bysshe, I, 178n, II, 112n, forgeries of V, 222

Writings: Works, IV, 33n, *The Cenci*, II, 286*, V, 223, *Letters*, with Introductory Essay by Robert Browning, V, 223n, *The Revolt of Islam*, V, 223

Shelley, Sir Percy, and Leigh Hunt, IV, 223

Shepherd, W. R., *History of the American Revolution*, read in MS by TBM?, I, 323, VI, 302

Shepherd, William, *Paris in Eighteen Hundred and Two and Eighteen Hundred and Fourteen*, I, 282*; II, *111*

Sherbrooke, Lord: *see* Robert Lowe

Sheridan, Richard Brinsley, and 'gentlemanly' II, 22; 248n, 309, III, 184n, 249, Mrs Malaprop V, 10

Sheridan, Mrs Richard Brinsley, V, 201

Sheridan, Thomas (1719-88), II, *309*

Sheridan, Thomas (1775-1817), II, *77*, his daughters 248n

Sherlock, Richard, V, 91

'Shield of Hercules,' not by Hesiod, III, 131

Shilleto, Richard, VI, *206*

Shine, Hill, and Helen, *Quarterly Review under Gifford*, I, 195n

Shipston on Stour, II, 183n

Shirley, James, *Contention of Ulysses and Ajax*, II, 161*

Shore, Charles, *see* 2nd Baron Teignmouth

Shore, Charlotte, V, 103n

Shore, Emily, *Journal of Emily Shore*, I, xxvii, III, 235n

Shore, Frederick John, III, *218*

Shore, Miss, V, 103

Shore family, I, xvii

Short, Thomas Vowler, Bishop of St Asaph, VI, *157*, 201

Shrewsbury, TBM at I, 156; parliamentary seat at IV, 336

Shrewsbury, Mr, minister in Barbados I, 195n

Shrewsbury, John Talbot, 16th Earl of, at Rome IV, 201; and Catholic priests in India *315*; thinks TBM unfair to Catholics V, 26; TBM's reply 27

Shrewsbury, Bertram Arthur Talbot, 17th Earl of, VI, 101n

Shrewsbury, Henry John Chetwynd Talbot, 18th Earl of, TBM meets at Saumur IV, *150*; invites TBM to his house at Dieppe 155; claims title VI, 101-2n; certain to win his case 106; 150, praises Ellis 151; going to entertain his counsel 155; further claims of 205n

Shrewsbury, Countess of (Sarah Elizabeth Beresford), IV, *150*

Shrewsbury, Earls of, IV, 246

Shrewsbury, Lady, IV, 45

Shrewsbury Case, VI, 101n, recessed 106; Lord Campbell's opinion 149; Ellis's speech in 151; judgment in 155; further claims in 205; 216, 217, Ellis's speech in 219

Shrewsbury School, VI, 230n

Sibthorp, Colonel Charles DeLaet Waldo, I, 218n, II, *171*, 'hairy, filthy, blackguard' 174

Sibthorp, Richard Waldo, I, *218*, 219

Sicyon, I, 69

Siddons, Mrs Sarah, death of, II, 39; 309, 310, IV, 223, V, 164

Sidmouth, TBM thinks he may spend winters there, VI, 240

Sidmouth, Lord, I, 157

Sidney, Algernon, I, 94, TBM compares himself to II, 232; V, 23n

Sidney, Sir Philip, I, 106

Sierra Leone, I, xxiv, xxvi, children from at Clapham 5n; transferred to Crown 8n, 44n, 53n, 60, false story about destruction in 78; attacked in *Times* correspondence 144n; 222n, Henry Macaulay in 293n; Mixed Court of Arbitration in I, xxvi, II, 102n; 213n, Henry Macaulay's adventures in 264-5; 265, 295, inhabitants 'wretched ragamuffins' 305; Zachary Macaulay has scheme of going to 310; 320, Tom Babington wants a place at 366; III, 266, IV, 38, 46, 200, 281

Sierra Leone Company, I, xxiv, offices 6n; 8n, 55n, 60n, 128n

Sikh Wars, first and second, V, 31n

Sikhs, V, 31, VI, 38

Silius Italicus, III, 160*

Simancas, Archives of, V, 34

Simeon, Charles, I, xvii, xviii, 14n, dines at Preston's with TBM *15*; 27, 86n, Trinity chapel hours coincide with his services 103; letter to Thomas Thomason, I, 103n; II, 43n, his power greater than that of any primate IV, 207

Simeonites, V, 100

Simon de Montfort, IV, 246

Simon O'Doherty, III, 39

Simond, M., I, 283
Simonides, III, 131
Simplon, VI, 50, 51
Simpson, James, V, *308*, scheme for industrial exhibition at Edinburgh 331; *Paris after Waterloo*, TBM forwards revised edn to Aberdeen 308
Sinai, Mount, III, 272
Sinbad the Sailor, I, 250
Singer, S. W., ed., *Correspondence of Earl of Clarendon and Earl of Rochester*, IV, 375*
[Sinha, N. K.], *Bengal Past and Present*, VI, 70
Sirkin, Gerald and Natalie, 'The Battle of Indian Education,' III, 122
Sismondi, J. C. L. Simonde de, I, ix, his work in anti-slavery movement 73n; TBM admires extremely 78
Writings: De la Littérature du Midi de l'Europe, I, 72-3*, 78-9*, V, 466, *History of France*, III, 9, 62*
Sitwell, William, V, 455n
Sitwell, Mrs: *see* Harriet Harford
Skelton, Philip, Life of, V, 319, VI, 185
Sketch of the Life of Sir James Parker (typescript), I, 244n
Skipton, I, 208n, 213, TBM at for Quarter Sessions 217; 222n, 243n, 253n
Skye, Isle of, IV, 295
Slaney, Robert, II, *79*, 80, IV, 336
Slave Labour, distinguished from hired labour II, 118
Slavery, abolition of: *see* Anti-Slavery Movement
Slavery, in India, abolished by Penal Code III, 193
Slavery and Slave Trade, destroyed by Clapham Sect IV, 207
Slavery Bill: *see* Anti-Slavery Movement, Abolition, Government Plan for
Smalridge, Bishop George, V, 323
Smart, Alexander, IV, *265*, his *Rambling Rhymes* 265n
Smith, new boy at Preston's, I, 57
Smith, Christopher Webb, III, *125*
Smith, Sir Culling Eardley, opposes TBM at Edinburgh IV, 301; TBM defeats 302
Smith, E. E., I, xxxiv
Smith, Emily: *see* Mrs Nathaniel Hibbert
Smith, George, IV, *329*
Smith, Sir Hugh, I, *13*
Smith, John, at Preston's, I, 65
Smith, John, missionary in Demerara, I, *194*
Smith, John (banker, 1767-1842), compliments TBM on speech II, *63*; makes loan to Macaulay and Babington 63n; 87n
Smith, John, the younger, son of the above, II, 63n
Smith, Captain John, III, *45*, 46
Smith, John Abel, IV, *171*
Smith, Judge (at Mauritius), III, 45
Smith, Nowell C., ed., *Letters of Sydney Smith*, I, 213n, 224n
Smith, Robert Percy (Bobus), II, 76n, rude to Lady Holland *336*; his comments on India 365
Smith, Robert Vernon, afterwards 1st Baron Lyveden, II, *76*, 250, 266, III, 293, TBM dines with V, 390n; VI, 40n, President of Board of Control 43n; TBM dines with 52; 203, not fitted for Board of Control 220
LETTER TO: VI, 43
Smith, Mrs Robert Vernon, II, *76*, VI, 40n
Smith, Saba: *see* Saba, Lady Holland
Smith, Samuel, II, *87*
Smith, Sydney, I, xvi, and term 'Clapham Sect' 193n; on Sir George Philips 213n; praises TBM's *ER* articles 216; calls on TBM at York *213*; his mockery of Evangelicals 214n; TBM visits at Foston 215-17; his response to TBM 216n; 224n, on Lord Lansdowne 224n; TBM to visit at Foston 244; TBM's good impression of 245; TBM defends against Zachary Macaulay 247; on Whewell 317n; II, 16, TBM meets at Lansdowne's 17; in company with Samuel Rogers 32; TBM's 'Boswelleana' of 33; judgment of Byron 33; contrasted to Rogers 34; TBM first meets 39n; 43, hostile opinion of Perceval 44; favours prosecutions for blasphemy 44; wittier but less eloquent than Jeffrey 56; 76n, *ER* can't expect anything from 107; at dinner with TBM 139; at Rogers's breakfast 148; 254, teases Lady Holland 336; 363, and his brother Bobus 365; remark on Brougham III, 255; breakfast with IV, 14; compared with Jeffrey 167; TBM breakfasts with 204; on Grenville family and TBM's 'Chatham' 221n; likes TBM's style in 'Chatham' 226n; TBM advises against publication of his sketch of Irish History 327; compared to Swift 327; on Brougham 348; TBM breakfasts with 402; Letters and Memoir V, 15n; TBM reluctant to write about 16; will never see another like him 32; not true that TBM never listened to him 428-9; his opinions of TBM in Lady Holland's *Memoir* 428-9; VI, 163n
Writings: Works, I, 214n, *Elementary Sketches of Moral Philosophy*, sent

Smith, Sydney: *Writings—cont.*
to TBM, v, 87, *Letters*, III, 255n, 265n, 285n, IV, 50n, *Letters of Peter Plymley*, I, 213, II, 44n, his *Life*, VI, 34
Smith, Mrs Sydney, I, 215, IV, 383n, wishes to contribute to Mackintosh memorial v, 232
LETTERS TO: IV, 327, V, 15, 87, 232
Smith, William, I, *50*, 265n, 272n, 278, II, 36, nothing eternal except his great coat 293; 330, V, 158n
Smith, Dr William, ed., *Dictionary of Greek and Roman Antiquities*, IV, 268; V, 317n
Smith Payne and Smith's Bank, VI, 25
Smithies, Jonathan, hanged, II, 154
Smithson, John, II, *177*
LETTER TO: II, 177
Smollett, Tobias, I, 51, *History of England*, I, 52*, V, 279, *Humphry Clinker*, II, 32*
Smyth, Sir Hugh, V, 349n
Smyth, John Henry, I, 181
Smyth, William, I, *128*, makes cuts in 'Pompeii' 128; 193n, 239, described II, 45-6; 146, IV, 361n, death V, 61n
Smyth v. Smyth, V, 349
Smythe, George, and Young England IV, *133*
Sneyd, Lewis, Warden of All Souls, receives TBM kindly, V, *423*
Snody, Andrew, V, *447*
Snow, William Parker, V, *47*, 414n
Snowdon, III, 59
Sobraon, Battle of, IV, 296n
Society for Promoting Christian Knowledge, V, 173n
Society for the Diffusion of Useful Knowledge (SDUK), I, xxiii, group of young Cambridge men writing for 122n; 154n, 188n, 237n, publishes Malkin's *History of Greece*, 249n; Malden's *History of Rome* 249n; Ellis's *Outline of General History* 249n; TBM asked to write History of Rome for 249n; 257, plan to publish Paley's *Natural Theology* 314n; TBM's association with 323; its history 323; Papers, University College 323; TBM's projected History of the Stuarts to be published by 322; II, 43n, 105n, 216n, 272n, III, 181, IV, 355n, TBM to do a history of England for V, 321n
Series Publications: 'Library of Entertaining Knowledge,' I, 323, 'Library of Useful Knowledge,' I, 231, 249n, 280n, 323, 'Natural Philosophy' series, I, 247n, *Quarterly Journal of Education*, II, 105n
Society Islands, IV, 238n
Society of Antiquaries, *Proceedings*, V, 471
Society of Sisters of Mercy of the Holy Trinity, V, 107n
Society of Friends of the People, V, 118n
Society of West India Planters and Merchants of London, subsidize MacQueen, I, 222n
Socinians, II, 47, V, 22
Socinus, V, 333
Socrates, I, 60*, II, 47, his character described III, 141; 247, IV, 39, 297, in *Parmenides* VI, 83; 100, as represented by Plato 250-1; the meaning of his remark in *Phaedo* 251
Solicitor General: *see* Lord Campbell, Lord Chelmsford, Sir William Horne, Lord Lyndhurst
Solomon, V, 34
Solon, IV, 297
Somers, John, Baron, IV, 30, V, 193, 338, 'Discourse Concerning Generosity,' VI, 12
Somers, Charles, 3rd Earl, VI, 190n
Somers, Lady (Virginia Pattle), death of her daughter, VI, 190
Somerset, 11th Duke of, V, x
Somerset, Edward Adolphus Seymour, 12th Duke of, II, 248n, III, *295*, V, 120, 150n, 212n, 298, understands business of British Museum 478
Somerset, Dukes of, IV, 246
Somerset, Duchess of (Jane Sheridan), II, *248*, V, 201, 212n
Somerset Case, I, 44n, 244
Somersetshire, IV, 43, 53, 109, V, 187
Somerville, Thomas, *History of Political Transactions and of Parties*, V, 279
Somerville, William, III, 324n
Sondes, Lord, III, 307
Sophia, Princess, I, 127n, IV, 258n
Sophocles, I, 123, 242n, III, 137, 141*, 159*, IV, 28, his tragedies characterised V, 112; 345
Writings: Philoctetes, III, 140*, 158, *Trachiniae*, III, 178
Sortain, Joseph, Brighton preacher, V, *224*, sermon by 286n
Sotheby, William, I, *239*, TBM dines with II, 38; his translation of *Iliad*, II, 38*; *Orestes*, I, 81*
Sotheby's, I, 325
Sotheran, T. H. S., IV, 188n
Soufflot, Jacques Germain, I, *297*
Soult, Marshall, and J. W. Croker, IV, 90
South, Robert, III, 206, V, 14, never a bishop 50; VI, 68, 145
South America, VI, 254
South Australia, Archivist, V, 80n
South Australia, Arthur Ellis in, V, 80n; 121n, 241n

South Sea House, III, 14
Southampton, TBM at V, 159n; VI, 86
Southern, Henry, death of, V, *321*; to have collaborated with TBM for SDUK 321n
Southern, Thomas, I, 322, 323
Southern Field and Fireside, V, 143n
Southern Literary Messenger, V, 143n
Southey, Charles Cuthbert, *Life and Correspondence of Robert Southey*, V, 131*
Southey, Robert, I, 64, 120, 270, II, 29, TBM reviews his edition of *Pilgrim's Progress* 107; 108, 'cannot live many weeks' III, 369; his best friends must now pray for his death 371; his invention of reviewing style IV, 28; could write twenty works at a time 96; not a competent judge of drama V, 112; remarks on his *Life* 131; 232n, his use of 'worsened' VI, 215
Writings: Book of the Church, IV, 226, *Curse of Kehama*, I, 65*, 'Elementary Teaching,' VI, 215*, *History of Brazil*, IV, 226, *Life of Nelson*, I, 62*, *Life of Wesley*, TBM sends to Selina, V, 441, 441n, misrepresented by Evangelicals 454*, edition of *Pilgrim's Progress*, IV, 97, *Roderick, the Last of the Goths*, I, 56, 121, *Sir Thomas More; or Colloquies on the Progress and Prospects of Society*, reviewed by TBM, I, 256, *Thalaba*, I, 65*
Spagnoletto, V, 286
Spain, and abolition of slave trade I, 173; II, 153, government effort to Christianise Jewish children III, 123; literature of, 136; not threatened by French 335; ministerial crisis in IV, 324; its decline V, 26; abortive reformation in 88
Spalding, Marian Dora, Brougham's step-daughter, II, *168*
Spalding, Mrs Mary Anne, marries Brougham II, 168n
Spanish, ease of rhyming in, V, 17-18
Spanish Succession, War of, VI, 253
Spanish Tract, at Holland House IV, 121
Sparks, Jared, Mahon attacks his editorial practice, V, *274*; ed., *Life and Writings of Washington* 274n
Spartianus, V, 274*, 278*
Speaker of House of Commons: *see* James Abercromby, Lord Dunfermline; John Evelyn Denison, Lord Ossington; Charles Manners-Sutton, Lord Canterbury; Charles Shaw-Lefevre, Lord Eversley
Spear, Percival, *Twilight of the Mughuls*, III, 99n
Spectateur, Le, I, 54n
Spectator, on TBM's letter to Leeds electors II, 167n
Spectator (Addison and Steele), No. 217, II, 265*; III, 20, Nos. 608, 623, V, 482
Spedding, James, 'Dickens's *American Notes*,' IV, 70n
Spelling, earlier English, TBM's interest in, III, 248
Spence, Joseph, III, *136*, Anecdotes 136n
Spence, Mr, torturing of, IV, 375
Spencer, George John, 2nd Earl, his library, II, 20; 315
Spencer, Charles John, 3rd Earl: *see* Lord Althorp
Spencer, Captain Frederick, 4th Earl, II, *89*, invites TBM to examine family papers V, 84; 345, out of place in his library VI, 48
LETTER TO: V, 85
Spencer, Georgiana Elizabeth, Countess, V, *86*
Spencer, Lavinia, Countess, II, 46
Spenser, Edmund, I, 13, 83, 202, TBM's opinion of IV, 223; *Faerie Queene*, II, 267*, IV, 70, TBM indifferent to VI, 197
Spetchley, Worcestershire, TBM's rage at, V, 174, 192
Spirit Licenses Bill, passage of, IV, 308
'Spiritual Banker's Directory,' V, 398
'Spiritual Play Bill,' V, 398
'Spiritual Railway Guide,' V, 398
Spoleto, III, 264n
Spooner, Richard, his anti-Catholic motions, V, 408
Spoonerism, a disease, II, 326
Spottiswoode, Messrs, I, 324, V, vii
Sprat, Bishop Thomas, V, 323
Spring-Rice, Miss, II, 43
Spring-Rice, Stephen, II, *170*, III, 171
Spring-Rice, Thomas: *see* Lord Monteagle
Spurgeon, Charles Haddon, VI, *76*
Spurzheim, Johann Kaspar, IV, 234
Stacey, George, V, 6n
Staël, Baron Auguste de, I, 73n, at Cambridge *176*; should go to Leicester to see excited public feeling 212; *Lettres sur l'Angleterre*, I, 176n, 212n
Staël, Mme de, her opinion of her son, I, 176*; 301n, the first woman of her age II, 84; *De l'Allemagne*, II, 84*
Stafford, 1st Marquess of, IV, *73*
Stafford, Mr, V, 144n
Staffordshire, II, 79
Stainforth, George, at Preston's school, I, *18*, 22, 26, 29, protects TBM 32; 32n, his family expected at Shelford 41; gives

Stainforth, George—*cont.*
Byron's 'Ode to Napoleon' to TBM 43; tutors TBM at Cambridge 101; 101n, 102, 'all attention and kindness' 108; fetches Preston to dying Blundell 124; TBM reads with at Clapham 129n; at Cambridge for fellowship examination 131; 137, 141, hopelessly ill 145; dies 145n; 218n
Stainforth, Georgiana, I, *68*
Stainforth, Maria, I, 18n, on her son's illness 145n
Stainforth, Richard, I, 18n
Stair, 8th Earl of, IV, *160*
Stamford, dominated by Tories, VI, 277
Stamford, 2nd Earl of, IV, *121*
Stamford Grammar School, Derwent Coleridge applies for mastership VI, 277, 278
Stamp Office, and Selina's will VI, 174
Standard (London), I, 286, IV, 41, V, 89
Standing Armies, declamation subject at school, I, 66
Stanfield, Clarkson, IV, *388*, V, 328n, his pictures of Venice VI, 59
Stanhope, Emily, Countess, IV, *53*, 346, V, 118, 149, 168n, 219, 254, 275, 308n, 314, 323, breakfast with TBM 329; 329n, 348, 365, 372, accident to 471; 477, VI, 10n, 37n, 50, 78, 78n, accident to 116; 136, 152n, mistakes date of party 152; 200n, 201, 249
LETTERS TO: VI, 152, 198
Stanhope, Lady Evelyn, V, 337n, 405n
Stanhope, George, V, *24*
Stanhope, James, 1st Earl, his library, VI, *53n*
Stanhope, Lady Mary, V, *118*, 149, 254, 275, 323, 348, 365, 372, 472, 477, VI, 136
Stanhope, Sir Michael, cabalistic inscription on his portrait, V, *444*
Stanhope, Philip Henry Stanhope, styled Lord Mahon, and 5th Earl, II, *21*, he and TBM friends despite politics 70; TBM pairs with 75; 'amusing companion though a bitter Tory' 97; TBM replies to in Commons 109n; 146, 201n, in campaign to aid Scott's family 238n; on TBM and Charles Watkin Wynn 313n; IV, 15n, his copyright bill 25, 82n; 191n, at breakfast 234; 387n, V, ix, on P.M.A.C.F. 24, 25; 42n, 52, 58n, 100, 100n, 137, his explanation of P.M.A.C.F. 151; 166n, 168n, TBM visits at Chevening 171; 185, 216, defeated in 1852 election 253; his criticism of Jared Sparks 274; 299n, 308n, publishes TBM's letter on Junius 325; 328n, 329n, sends sketch from Italy to TBM 364; sends corrections to TBM's *Speeches* 372; 399, 402n, TBM explains the attraction of bad books to 410; submits cabalistic inscription to TBM 444; succeeds as 5th Earl 471n; VI, 10n, TBM enlists to help Owen 19, 21, 22; TBM reports to on Museum affairs 23; 37n, presents his edn of Peel papers to TBM 41; TBM visits at Chevening 46, 47; 50, 78n, and founding of National Portrait Gallery 78n; 79, 80, and P.M.A.C.F. 139; 152, 152n, on removal of state services from Prayer Book 157; address at Birmingham 158; and P.M.A.C.F. 166; reads TBM's life of Pitt in proof 177; sends paper by Burke to TBM 178n; sends improved version of *Paradise Lost* to TBM 181; 191, 195n, 200n, 201, 217, TBM breakfasts with 220; lends TBM Halm's *Fechter* 229; speculates on son of Arminius 248n
Writings: 'Correspondence between Mr. Pitt and the Duke of Rutland,' IV, 53, *Essai sur la Vie du Grand Condé*, IV, 72, 81*, 107, TBM proposes to review 159, *History of England from the Peace of Utrecht to the Peace of Versailles*, II, 21n, III, 206*, IV, 72n, V, 215, 274n, TBM corrects 323; completed 405; on Washington and Major André 410n, *History of the War of the Succession in Spain*, reviewed by TBM II, 190; III, 206, VI, 243, 'Letter to Jared Sparks,' V, 274*, ed., *Letters from the Earl of Peterborough to General Stanhope*, III, 248*, 'Life of Belisarius,' III, 206, *Life of William Pitt*, VI, 177n, 178, 179n, 'Lord John Russell on the Causes of the French Revolution,' I, 324, ed., *Memoirs of Sir Robert Peel*, VI, 78, *Miscellanies*, IV, 356, *Miscellanies*, 2nd Series, V, 8, 83n, *Notices of the Stanhopes as Esquires and Knights*, V, 444n, 'On the Lost Books of Tacitus,' V, 83*, *Spain under Charles the Second*, IV, 117*, 'Were Human Sacrifices in Use Among the Romans?' IV, 356n
LETTERS TO: II, 171, 238, III, 206, 248, 249, IV, 20, 53, 72, 81, 117, 136, 246, 247, 255, 258, 263, 346, 356, 358, 365, 366, 368, 369, 383, 387, 398, 401, V, 8, 25, 26, 28, 49, 83, 105, 108, 110, 112, 117, 131, 149, 150, 157, 162, 162, 165, 171, 210, 219, 228, 253, 274, 298, 314, 322, 325, 337, 348, 364, 372, 405, 410, 444, 471, 476, VI, 19, 21, 23, 41, 46,

50, 53, 78, 78, 116, 136, 155, 157, 177, 178, 181, 195, 216, 229, 247
Stanislaus of Poland, IV, 148
Stanley, Arthur Penrhyn, VI, 191n
Stanley, Edward George: *see* 14th Earl of Derby
Stanley, Edward Henry: *see* 15th Earl of Derby
Stanley, Edward Smith: *see* 13th Earl of Derby
Stanley of Alderley, Lady, VI, 10n
Stanley of Alderley, Lord, VI, 10n
Starkie, Thomas, V, *45n*
State Paper Office, IV, 20n
State Papers, Published under Authority of His Majesty's Commission, II, 22
Stationers' Company, II, 101
Statius, III, 160*, IV, 37n, *Thebais*, III, 200*
Staunton, Sir George, V, 113n
[Stavordale, Lord], *Catalogue of Pictures belonging to the Earl of Ilchester at Holland House*, II, 20n, 27n
Steamships, service between Edinburgh and London I, 257, II, 48
Steele, Sir Richard, IV, 45, and 'Little Dicky' 132n
Steele, Thomas, III, *253*, 254
Steenkirk, TBM plans to visit, V, 208
Stella (Esther Johnson), her spelling, III, 248; 282n, V, 356
Stellard, Samuel, I, 9-13
Stephen, King, IV, 256
Stephen, Anne Mary, I, 138n
Stephen, George, I, *163*, 'mad' II, 240; *Anti-Slavery Recollections*, I, 163n, II, 200n, 240n, III, 45n, IV, 346n
Stephen, George Milner, V, *411*
LETTER TO: V, 411
Stephen, Henry John, I, *194*, TBM meets at Clifton V, 276, 282n, takes TBM to his court in Bristol 283
Stephen, James (1758-1832), I, *74*, 138n, 193n, 'unreasonably timid' 194; 253n, lectures TBM for calling Jephson a quack II, 50; death of 196; 198, IV, 207, VI, 255n, 'Defence of Bill for Registration of Slaves,' I, 74*
Stephen, Sir James (1789-1859), I, *193*, 194, on John Pearson 198n; 295n, on TBM and Maria Kinnaird II, 19n; predicts TBM may be anything but Prime Minister 20n; 154n, lends his house to George Babington 161; TBM calls at his house 181; 284, anticipates the worst for finances of Macaulays and Babingtons 300; TBM dissuades Grant from appointing to China 324-5; TBM recommends for Supreme Council of India 325; TBM hoped he would accept Indian appointment 358; letter to Mill III, 15n; 259, instrumental in Trevelyan's appointment 317n; letter to Napier 324n; 337, pained by TBM's essay on Ranke 340n; IV, 39n, hears TBM has completed vol. of *History* 47n; 159, TBM recommends him to Napier 173-4; and *ER* 174n; 200, TBM's debt to him 204; 210, 227, appointed to Regius Professorship at Cambridge 373n; TBM attempts to get employment for 392; and Regius Professorship V, 61; TBM gets British Museum privilege for 65; attacked for unorthodoxy 85; persecution of abating 104; begins Cambridge lectures 109; 362n, 411n, death VI, 238
Writings: 'The Clapham Sect,' I, xvii, 27n, 50n, 63n, 193n, on Duke of Gloucester II, 290n; IV, 200*, TBM defends 203; TBM praises 207, *Critical and Miscellaneous Essays*, IV, 174, *Essays in Ecclesiastical Biography*, V, 85, 'Ignatius Loyola and His Associates,' IV, 47*, *Lectures on the History of France*, acknowledges TBM in, V, 109n, 'The Port-Royalists,' III, 386, 'Works of the Author of *The Natural History of Enthusiasm*,' III, 325*
LETTERS TO: III, 15, IV, 353, 392, V, 26
Stephen, Mrs James (Jane Catherine Venn), I, 193n, II, *325*, IV, 393
Stephen, Sir James Fitzjames, II, 358, VI, 250n
Stephen, Leslie, on Hannah More I, xxix; life of Henry Thornton 55n; of Whewell 317n; of Sir James Stephen IV, 392n; *Life of Sir James Fitzjames Stephen*, I, 194n, II, 325n, V, 85n, VI, 255n
Stephen family, I, xvii, 27n
Stephenson, George, VI, 244n
Stephenson, Mr, II, 225
Stephenson, Robert, his funeral, VI, *244*
Sterne, Laurence, *Tristam Shandy*, III, 197*; IV, 10
Sternhold and Hopkins, IV, 29
Stevens, Mrs Joan, II, 11n, *Victorian Voices*, IV, 259n
Stevenson, David, letter to, V, 408
Stewart, Dugald, III, *194*, IV, 69, V, 89n, *Account of the Life and Writings of William Robertson*, V, 93, *Dissertation on the Progress of Philosophy*, III, 194n

Stewart, D[uncan?], TBM can't recommend for pension VI, 234; *Practical Arabic Grammar* 234n
LETTER TO: VI, 234
Stewart, Patrick, IV, *261*
Stewart, Randall, ed., *The English Notebooks by Nathaniel Hawthorne*, VI, 47n
Stewart-Mackenzie, James Alexander, II, *146*, 248, 257, 272, 274, 284, 301, consults his wife for information about India 338; 356, III, 22, High Commissioner of Ionian Islands IV, 123n; his death 123n
LETTERS TO: II, 318, IV, 123
Stewart-Mackenzie, Mrs James (Mary Frederica Elizabeth, formerly Lady Hood), II, *338*
Steyning, II, 24, 42
Stillingfleet Manuscript, V, 18, 19
Stirling, TBM invited to speak at, IV, 389; VI, 230n, 233
Stirling, William, of Keir, V, *162n*, 212, *The Cloister Life of Charles V*, 162n
Stockdale, Percival, *Memoirs*, one of TBM's favourite bad books, V, 410
Stocken, firm, V, 160n
Stoddart, brother of John Lawrence Stoddart, I, 177
Stoddart, John Lawrence, TBM's pupil, I, *177*
Stoddart, Lawrence, I, 177n
Stoddart, R. H., 'Lord Macaulay and His Friends,' VI, 271
Stogumber, Somerset, V, 76n
Stoicism, II, 275
Stoics, V, 270
Stokes, Eric, *The English Utilitarians and India*, II, 324n, III, 146, 209n, V, 424n
Stokes, Robert, II, *39*, 226, provision for his maintenance V, 119
Stone of Scone, II, 97
Stonehenge, TBM at IV, 247; VI, 76, TBM at 86, 87; 87n
Stopford, Admiral Sir Robert, III, 360, IV, 29
Stothard, Thomas, II, *26*, decorated Rogers's bookcase 54; III, 13
Stout, William, his autobiography published in *Manchester Guardian*, V, 129n; 130, 153*, presented to TBM 184
Stowe, TBM at I, 156; IV, 152, Junius letter at V, 216
Stowe, Calvin, VI, *60*, *Origin and History of the Books of the Bible* 60n
Stowe, Harriet Beecher, V, *230*, TBM meets V, 298n; anti-slavery petition presented to 298n; TBM's 'gift' to her 321-2; TBM's April Fool letter about 323n; an ex lioness VI, 60; TBM tells her of her fame in Italy 63
Writings: Dred, presents to TBM, VI, 63n; 64, 64n*, *Sunny Memories from Foreign Lands*, I, 282n, remarks on TBM in V, 412*; VI, 60n, *Uncle Tom's Cabin*, V, 230*, 286*, 298n, new edition VI, 63, Italian translation 64
LETTERS TO: V, 230, VI, 63
Strabane, TBM at V, 69n
Strabo, V, 387, VI, 248
Strachey, William, 'Conquest of Scinde,' IV, 173n, 183*
Stradling, William, IV, *95*, *A Description of the Priory of Chilton-super-Polden*, 95n
LETTERS TO: IV, 95, V, 28
Strafford, 1st Earl of, III, 177
Strafford, General Sir John Byng, 1st Baron, III, *253*, resolves quarrel between TBM and Wallace 254
Strangford, Lord, *Poems, from the Portuguese of Camoens*, V, 182*
Strasbourg, IV, 53, V, 339, 343, 349n, 351, 353, 354
Strathbogie Ministers, III, 375, IV, 36
Stratheden, Lady, VI, *67*
Stratford on Avon, Boswell and Jubilee II, 72
Strawberry Hill, V, 409
Streatham, and Dr Johnson, IV, 91; Bedford Priory (Thomas Flower Ellis Senior's residence) IV, 179n
Strickland, Agnes, V, *233*, TBM declines to join attack on her in *ER* 233n, *Historic Scenes*, V, 233n, *Lives of the Queens of Scotland and English Princesses*, V, 233n, *Lives of the Queens of England*, V, 233n
Strickland, Elizabeth, V, 233n
Strickland, George, II, 209n
Strongbow, IV, 246
Strongitharm, John, engraver, II, 194
Strutt, Edward: *see* Lord Belper
Strype, John, *Ecclesiastical Memorials*, V, 18-19*, *Life of Grindal*, V, 21*
Stuart, House of, I, XX, V, 31, 89
Stuart, J. A., letter to Napier, III, 317n
Stuart, James, Earl of Moray, IV, 247
Stuart, James Montgomery, V, *380*, *Reminiscences and Essays*, III, 125n, V, 380n; on Claudet photo of TBM VI, 16n; TBM takes tickets to his lecture series 158; mentions TBM in lecture 158n
Stuart, Sir John, opposes TBM's election as Bencher of Lincoln's Inn, V, *89*
Stuart, Louisa, daughter of Lord Bute, IV, *221*
Stuart Papers, IV, 309, 311, TBM consults V, 422

Studies on Voltaire and the Eighteenth Century, IV, 220n
Stuttgart, V, viii, 286
Styles, Dr John, *Essay on the Stage*, II, 217*
Subscription, editor's term for signature on TBM's letter covers III, 26n
Sudbury, IV, 187
Sue, Eugène, *Martin, ou l'Enfant Trouvé*, V, 175*, *Le Veau d'Or*, V, 409
Suetonius, III, 178*, Life of Julius Caesar V, 264*; 268*, 274*
Suez, III, 138n, 184, 184n
Suffolk, IV, 53, 139
Sugar Duties, and slavery, I, 177n; II, 259-60, III, 373n, IV, 26, debate on 195; 200, 305
Sugden, Edward Burtenshaw: *see* Lord St Leonards
Sumner, Charles, discusses American edition of his works with TBM, II, 151n; IV, 365n, VI, 226n
Sumner, John Bird, Archbishop of Canterbury, Trustee of British Museum V, 149; VI, 20, 21, 22, 175, *The Evidence of Christianity*, TBM asked to review I, 197*
Sun, I, 264, misattributes Hogg's 'Niebuhr' to TBM 284; attributes Carlyle's 'Characteristics' to Brougham II, 113
Sunderland, Robert Spencer, 2nd Earl of, II, 190, IV, 118, V, 24, 84, 288
Sunderland, Charles Spencer, 3rd Earl of, III, 208, IV, 118
Supreme Council: *see* India, *and* Macaulay, Indian Career
Surajah Dowla, VI, 38
Sussex, Augustus Frederick, Duke of, II, *291*
Sutherland, Duchess of, III, *328*, and petition of Women of England V, 298; VI, 52n
LETTER TO: III, 328
Sutherland, George Granville Leveson-Gower, Earl Gower, 2nd Duke of, II, *78*, III, 328n, IV, 149, 174n, at Rome 201; V, 58n
Sutherland, James Charles Colebrooke, III, *144*
LETTER TO: III, 144
Sutlej, and Mutiny, VI, 105
Suttee, TBM hears question discussed before Privy Council II, 138
Sutton Place (John Shaw-Lefevre's residence) TBM visits V, 418
Swayland, Kent (Edward Cropper's residence), VI, 239n
Swift, Jonathan, I, 81*, 131, 'little language' II, 133, 148, 167; 190, 'little language' 258, 259, 325, 358; III, 136, 245, 248, 282, IV, 28, his treatment by Temple 126; 327, note on Burnet V, 7*; his attacks on Burnet 145; and Catherine Barton 355-6; 356
Writings: Gulliver's Travels, III, 145, IV, 263*, VI, 115, *Journal to Stella*, II, 122*, 148*, 258*, V, 355*, 356*, *Polite Conversation*, V, 349*
Swifte, Mr, IV, 126
Swinburne, Sir John, I, 216n
Swinburne, Lady, I, 216n
Swinfen, Mrs Patience, sues Lord Chelmsford, VI, 228
Swinfen v. Chelmsford, VI, 228
Swithland Hall, Leicestershire, near Rothley Temple, II, 49n
Switzerland, III, 223, V, 341, TBM hopes to meet Mahon there V, 348
Sydney, New South Wales, VI, 61, Campbell MSS discovered in 218n
Sykes, William Henry, IV, *171*
Sykes family, of Hull, II, 86
Symmetry, III, 196
Symonds, Dr John Addington, TBM's doctor at Clifton, V, *265*, prescribes for TBM 270; 272, says TBM making progress 277; thinks of sending TBM to Italy 279; thinks TBM should not attempt Session 283; 284, compels Vaughan to resign VI, 241n
Symonds, John Addington (son of the above), V, 265n, VI, 241n
Syracuse, VI, 245, siege of, in Thucydides, 246

Tacitus, I, 61*, life of Agricola 78*; 133, III, 237*, IV, 28, Mahon's theory on lost books V, 83; Niebuhr on *Annals* and *History* 83n; VI, 246, *Annals*, I, 119*, III, 178*, 180-1*, on son of Arminius VI, 248*, *History*, III, 180-1*
Taglioni, Marie, II, *171*
Tagore, Dwarkanath, VI, *38*
Tagore, Rabindranath, VI, 38n
Tahiti Affair, IV, 231n, and English government's behavior 238
Taine, Hippolyte, on TBM, I, x
Tait, Mr, of Edinburgh, III, 318
Tait, Archibald Campbell, V, *82n*, one of Palmerston's good appointments VI, 70
Tait, William, III, 16, 255
Tait's Edinburgh Magazine, III, 15, 250, 255n
Talbot, Fox, I, 144
Talbot, Colonel George, TBM answers query about VI, *17*
Talbot, John, Earl of Shrewsbury, IV, 247
Talbot, Lord: *see* 18th Earl of Shrewsbury
Talbot, Miss, V, x
Talents Improved: see Harriet Corp

Talfourd, Thomas Noon, III, *249*, and copyright IV, 25, 25n; TBM proposes tragic subject to 33-4; TBM meets in Switzerland V, 352; his death 390; 391n
Writings: The Athenian Captive, III, 249n, *Ion*, III, 181*, 249n, *Poems on Various Subjects*, III, 249n, 'Speech for the Defendant,' sends to TBM, IV, 33, *Tragedies*, presented to TBM, IV, 33
LETTERS TO: III, 249, IV, 33
Talleyrand, Charles Maurice de Talleyrand-Perigord, Prince de, TBM meets and describes II, *67;* 80, 98, drawing of III, 349; compared to Cranmer V, 42
Tamerlane, I, 84
Tanjore, Christians in, III, 69-70, 72
Tanjore, King of: *see* Sharaboji
Tarbet, VI, 230n
Tarquinius Superbus, IV, 56
Tarquins, III, 381-2, IV, 55
Tasmania, V, 65
Tasso, Torquato, I, 79, IV, 28, *Jerusalem Delivered* III, 62*
Tate, Nahum, V, 131
Tatler, IV, 130
Tatties, III, 173
Tauchnitz, Christian Bernhard, Baron von, his editions of TBM's writings V, viii, *71*, contract with TBM for *History*, 101; payments to TBM 171; editions privileged in France 229n, payments from 241, 335n; TBM will make no contract with other German publisher 338; presents book to TBM 373; payments from 405; finds errors in *History* 472; has sold near 10,000 copies of *History* VI, 49; payments to TBM 49n, 99n; arranges to publish *Biographical Essays* 100; asks TBM to write essay on modern English literature 186-7; publishes lives of Pitt and Atterbury 230n
LETTERS TO: V, 71, 101, 171, 218, 229, 334, 373, 405, 468, 472, VI, 37, 49, 99, 100, 187, 229, 257
Tauchnitz, C. B., firm, 'Collection of British Authors,' V, viii, 71n, VI, 100n, *Fünfzig Jahre der Verlagshandlung Bernhard Tauchnitz, 1837 bis 1887*, V, 71
Taunton, Lord: *see* Henry Labouchere
Tave, Stuart M., *New Essays of De Quincey*, I, 222n
Tavistock, II, 31
Tavistock, Anna Maria, Lady, II, *152*
Tavistock, Francis, Lord: *see* 7th Duke of Bedford
Taxes on Knowledge (newspaper stamps), II, 162n, TBM opposes 163-4; 178, V, 430n
Tayler, [Thomas], I, *178*
LETTER TO: I, 178
Tayler, Mrs Thomas, I, 178
Taylor, Edgar, *The Suffolk Bartholomeans*, V, 40n
Taylor, Sir Henry, IV, *39*, TBM suggests Mary Queen of Scots to as subject 40, 71; and *Lays* 70; TBM disputes his view of tragedy V, 112
Writings: Autobiography, IV, 392n, *Edwin the Fair*, sends to TBM, IV, 39*, *Philip van Artevelde*, III, 181*, IV, 39*, 43, V, 112*, *The Virgin Widow*, presented to TBM, V, 111-12*
LETTERS TO: IV, 39, 70, V, 111
Taylor, Jeremy, place of publication of his works, V, 473; VI, 68
Taylor, Mr, contributes to *Knight's Quarterly*, I, 188n
Taylor, Ralph, II, *117*
LETTER TO: II, 117
Taylor, Robert, II, *43*, V, 359
Taylor, Tom, V, x, ed., *Life of Benjamin Robert Haydon*, V, 340*, *Still Waters*, TBM sees at Windsor Castle VI, 10n
Taylor, William Cooke, V, *66*, TBM contributes to fund for widow and children of 86
Taylor, Zachary, elected President of U.S., IV, 383
Teague, meaning of, VI, 10-11
Teale, Thomas Pridgin, II, *238*
Tedworth House, Wiltshire (Broughton's residence), TBM at V, 212n
Teetotallers, III, 297
Teignmouth, John Shore, 1st Baron, I, *41*, 80, IV, 207, V, 103n
Teignmouth, Charles Shore, 2nd Baron, I, 181, *Reminiscences*, I, 113n, 124n, 128n, on De Staël, 176n; on TBM's first public speech 202n; 278n, II, 11n, 73n, on TBM and William Grant 137n; on Captain Gordon 156n; on Lady Stewart-Mackenzie 338n; on Mortlock 363n; IV, 323n
Telegraph, Electric, V, 241, 246, 250
Telford, Mary Anne, V, 454n
Telford, Sarah, V, 454n, gift of grapes from VI, 129; gift of fruit from 241
LETTER TO: VI, 241
Telford, Susanne, V, 454n
Telford, the Misses, V, 455
Telford, Thomas, II, 151n
Temple, Frederick, afterwards Archbishop of Canterbury, recommended by Jowett, V, *431*

Temple, Richard, Earl, his resignation from Pitt's ministry VI, 179, 195
Temple, W. J., VI, 73n
Temple, Sir William, III, 217, *Observations upon the Netherlands*, IV, 220*
Ten Hours Bill, sponsored by Sadler, I, 275n; TBM's position on II, 117-18; 133n, 135n, IV, 180n, 184, 200, TBM supports 299n; can't speak on at Edinburgh 325; debate on 330
Ten Year Men, explained, VI, 82
Tennant, Thomas, II, *235*
LETTER TO: II, 235
Tennyson, Alfred, Lord, II, 52n, IV, 361n, succeeds as Poet Laureate V, 131n; 223n, VI, 140n, 'Riflemen Form!,' VI, 214n
Tennyson-d'Eyncourt, Charles, II, *52*, VI, 278
Tenterden, Charles Abbott, 1st Baron, I, *285*
Terence, III, 137*, 159*, *Andria*, IV, 272n, V, 274*, 278*, *Heautontimorumenos*, V, 274*, 278*
Test and Corporations Acts, I, 262n, 311n, III, 284, IV, 186
Test Bill: *see* Scottish Universities Bill
Tewkesbury, V, 177, 180, 181, TBM visits 186; 189
Texas Question, IV, 232
Thackeray, Francis, *History of William Pitt, Earl of Chatham*, reviewed by TBM, II, 316n, 335; IV, 212
Thackeray, William Makepeace, V, ix, x, first meeting with 72n; with TBM and Ellis at Paris 72; proposal for practical joke 72n; his parody of Mrs Gore 102n; 111n, 209n, 230n, his contract for *The Newcomes* 358; forwards query from Kennedy VI, 17; best of living novelists, seduced by lecturing 76; lectures at Brighton 76n; 85n, 140n, 191, 195n, tells TBM about state of literary world 221
Writings: The Four Georges, VI, 76n, *Letters*, V, 358n, *The Newcomes*, TBM buys, V, 358, 368*, *Pendennis*, IV, 89n, V, 304*, *Vanity Fair*, IV, 89n, V, 72n
Thames, procession on, opening of London Bridge II, 82; III, 52, 87, compared to Loire IV, 148; at Thames Ditton V, 406; TBM walks along 409; a subject for poetry 409
Thames Ditton, TBM spends summer of 1854 at, V, 403n
Thatcher, Henry, II, 99n
Thatcher, Mary Mills (d. 1816), TBM's aunt, I, *56*, dies 79n
Theatetus, VI, 83, 251
Theed, William, his bust of Mackintosh, V, 232n
Thelwall, John, V, *118*
Theocritus, I, 57, 145*, TBM thinks of translating 145; 243, III, 159*, 200*, *Idylls*, VI, 81*
Theophrastus, III, 160, *Characters*, III, 160*
Thesiger, Sir Frederick: *see* Lord Chelmsford
Thiebault, Dieudonné, *Mes Souvenirs de vingt ans de séjour à Berlin*, I, 50*
Thiers, Louis Adolphe, III, *335*, 352, 353, IV, 111, 231, visits England to 'make his peace with the Whigs' 266; TBM guides him around London 266, 267; TBM's impressions of 267; TBM can't help laughing at his situation V, 210; on Eastern crisis of 1840 288; speech of plagiarized by Disraeli 301n
Thirlwall, Connop, I, 151n, forced to resign from Trinity tutorship III, *112*; *History of Greece*, 112n; 160, translation of Niebuhr 196; IV, 66, VI, 43, 152n, speech on Marriage Bill 201
Thirty Years' War, VI, 253
Thomas à Becket, Saint, IV, 159
Thomas [Alexandre?], V, 228n; TBM attends lecture by 233n
Thomas, Allen C., 'William Penn, Macaulay, and "Punch",' V, 6n
Thomas, Anne, TBM's servant, III, 341
Thompson, George, IV, *346*, 347, 'mountebank' 389; his speech broken up at Boston V, 138; TBM would gladly exchange him for Everett 141; type of the effervescent demagogue 248; 'Case of Pertaub Shean, the Raja of Sattara,' IV, 347
Thompson, John Reuben, V, *143*, sends Byrd MSS to TBM 165
LETTERS TO: V, 143, 165
Thompson, General T. Perronet, IV, *102*, impossible to make a government out of his kind 114; 'Edinburgh Review and the "Greatest Happiness" Principle' (two articles of this title), I, 254n, ' "Greatest Happiness" Principle,' I, 254n
Thoms, William John, V, 137n, VI, 17n, *102*, TBM acknowledges his assistance 102n
Thomson, Andrew, in Edinburgh Bible Society quarrel, I, *225n*, 235, 236
Thomson, Charles Edward Poulett, afterwards 1st Baron Sydenham, II, *39*, III, 271, 318
Thomson, D. Cleghorn, 'Two Macaulay Letters,' V, 92
Thomson, James, I, 71-2*, his tragedies 81*; 120, 'Hymn,' IV, 386*, *The Seasons*, I, 63*

Thomson, Thomas, II, *306*, III, 328, criminal charge brought against 373
Thomson, William, II, *10*, 160, 362
Thomson, Archbishop William, VI, 140n
Thoresby Society, Leeds, II, 202n, 211n, *Publications*, 212n
Thornhill, IV, 45
Thornton, Henry, the elder, I, xxiv, 14n, on his deathbed *55*; 101n, 109n, married a Sykes II, 86; justice of Stephen's portrait of IV, 203-4; account of debate in 1801 V, 398
Thornton, Henry, the younger, xviii, his bank 6n; 29n, *101*, enters Cambridge with TBM 101n; 103, 107, 116n, 122, on TBM and Baptist Noel 141n; 146, on TBM and Queen Caroline 148n; takes high honors at Cambridge 169n; 182, 196n, in financial panic of 1825 207n; 321, his destined bride II, 261-2; refuses visit from William Wilberforce the younger 326; III, 6, 261, 284, TBM sends *Lays* to IV, 69; on Stephen's article 207; his bank 312; V, 14, remarriage and fight against marriage laws 79n; 'low and taciturn' 159; TBM cannot intervene in his case 220; his behavior 221; the follies of his age after model youth 225; TBM consults about investments VI, 24; 139n, 163n, 176n, 219n, 236, 302
LETTERS TO: VI, 14, 24
Thornton, Mrs Henry (Augusta Harriet Dealtry), II, *261*, 262, 'a pleasing girl' 344; death of V, 79n
Thornton, Mrs Henry (Emily Dealtry, second wife), V, 79n, 220n
Thornton, Isabella, IV, *203*, 204, VI, 29n
Thornton, John, I, 88n, a bore VI, *219*
Thornton, Marianne, on TBM's failure to take honors I, 169n; quotes James Stephen on TBM II, 19-20n; on Mrs William Wilberforce 326n; III, 304, IV, 216n, on TBM's victory at Edinburgh 302n; on TBM's defeat at Edinburgh 341n; on TBM's Irish tour V, 74n
LETTER TO: III, 304
Thornton, Sophia, V, 220n
Thornton family, I, xvii, wards of Inglis 109n; II, 260n, their response to Stephen's article IV, 203
Thornton Papers, Cambridge University Library, I, 14n
Thorp, Thomas, II, 196n, IV, *181*
Thorpe, Anthony, York attorney, I, 210
Thorpe, Robert, opponent of Zachary Macaulay, I, *60*, 60n, 'A Letter to William Wilberforce' 60n; 74n, 76, unsuccessfully sued by Zachary Macaulay 149; attacks Zachary Macaulay 149n; 193n, 221n
Thorpe, Dr William, II, *79*, retires from Lock Chapel 154
Thorwaldsen, Bertel, statue of Byron, I, 317n; his sculptures at Frankfort, V, 351
Thrale, Mrs: *see* Mrs Piozzi
Three Banks Review, 'Henry Sykes Thornton,' V, 220n
Thucydides, I, 61*, 78*, 83*, 85n, 242n, 243, ed. Thomas Arnold, reviewed by Ellis II, 105n; TBM changes his opinion of III, 130*; 'greatest historian that ever lived' 137; 'ne plus ultra of human art' 154; 159*, 177*, 178, 180-1*, model for historians 207; 237*, IV, 28, 37n, 207, V, xii, TBM sends Hobbes's translation to George Trevelyan 287; 345, 475*, George Trevelyan raving about VI, 245; 7th Book 'finest piece of history in the world' 246
Thugs, III, 190
Thurlow, Edward, 1st Baron, I, *71*, 220, IV, 205-6
Thurlow, Edward, 2nd Baron, his poems, I, 61*
[Thursfield, J. R., ed.], Grey and Russell correspondence, *English Historical Review*, IV, 290n
Thymelicus, or Thumelicus, VI, 248
Thynne, Lord Edward, V, 180n, wedding to Miss Gore 336n
Tiber, compared to Thames, V, 409
Tibullus, III, 160*
Tickell, Thomas, II, 169, IV, 129n, *Spectator*, 623 and 608, V, 482n
Ticknor, George, V, 474n, calls on TBM VI, *46*; 46n, 47n, *History of Spanish Literature*, VI, 46n
Tieck, Ludwig, III, 236
Tierney, George, on his terror of House of Commons, II, *12*; 'clearest speaker' 44; always timid before speaking 90
Tilbury Fort, V, 409
Tillotson, John, III, *112*, V, 91n
Tilstone, Cheshire, John Macaulay curate at, I, 314n
Times, on the burning of Washington I, 54-5; 61, received at Preston's school 77; account of destruction of Sierra Leone 78; 'Africanus and Investigator' controversy in 144n; publishes Brougham's letter on TBM 185n; prints Port Royal resolutions 192n; exaggerated idea of its power formed by James Stephen 194; TBM writes reply to for Zachary Macaulay 195; letter to editor 195; on Beaumont's strange

behaviour 216n; 222, TBM's 'Country Clergyman' published in 223n; 258n; on Paganini's London debut II, 34n; TBM summarizes its news 40; eloquence about Paganini 41; TBM reads at breakfast 51; TBM's 'Political Georgics,' 'Country Clergyman,' and 'Sortes Virgilianae' in 56-7; its 'low rancour' 75; describes House of Commons in full dress 141n; false report of abolition petition to U.S. Congress 193n; III, 262, 269, abuse of TBM over Windsor letter 310; IV, 17n, 41, on *Dickens's American Notes* 97n; 129n, 238n, report of TBM's speech 'the best' 263; 263n, TBM subscribes to 281; 301n, 320n, 348, 364n, 373, Miss Sellon's correspondence in V, 107n; TBM reads at dinner, Isle of Wight 124; 125, publishes Russell's letter on Papal aggression 132n; on George Thompson at Boston 138n; advertisement of Marriage Law Reform Assoc. in 159; on charges against Bishop Monk 172n; 179, supplement, sent to Selina 184; forwarded to Ellis 191; reports Ellis's speech 206n; obituaries 280; 281, Greville well known to furnish information to 295; to be sent to Brighton 346; week-old number TBM's only source of information 351; on Scottish Rights movement 364n; publishes TBM's Report on Indian Civil Service 431n; opposes Foreign Enlistment Bill 435n; notices in about Indian Civil Service examinations 436, 438n, 439n; articles on Indian Law Commission VI, 30*; on Dixon and TBM 31n; sent to Selina 56; 84, vilifies John Peter Grant 131n; reports Argyll's speech 141; report of Stanhope's speech 157; leader on Thesiger 160n; on panic in stock market 211; on Shrewsbury Case 219n; 228
Times, New, I, 220
Timodemus, III, 131
Tindal, Charles, V, 449n
Tindal, Sir Nicholas, with TBM at Sydney Smith's, I, *215*; 216n, elected at Cambridge 223n; V, 449n
Tintern Abbey, I, 218, III, 52, TBM at V, 188
Tipu Sultan, II, 224, III, 48, 51, 52, 54, 60, 67, 71
Tithes, should be commuted, II, 163; abolition of 162n
Titian, III, 263, IV, 41, V, 284, and 'Caternina Cornaro' VI, 61n; 'Queen of Cyprus' 61; 'Portrait of a Man' 61n
Tiverton, VI, 211
Tocqueville, Alexis de, VI, 97n
Tod, James, IV, *243*
LETTER TO: IV, 243
Todas, funeral ceremonies of, III, 71
Toddington Manor, Bedfordshire, Fanny visits V, 235
Toledo, VI, 143
Tom Thumb, III, 145
Tom Thumb, General, IV, 389
Tombuctoo, III, 63
Tomkins, Henry George, V, *153*
LETTER TO: V, 153
Tomline, George, *Memoirs of William Pitt*, IV, 205*, VI, 179, 202
Tonson, Jacob, II, *353*
Tony Pasquin, III, 361
Tooke, Horne, III, 136
Tophet, Sons of, I, 69
Toplady, Augustus, V, *454*
Tories, TBM's contempt for, I, 211n; divided after Catholic Emancipation 293n; elections going against II, 217; hope for success on dissolution 269; beaten III, 140; 'must at last give in' 154; 167, 188, mix religion with politics 238; 250, generally liked essay on Gladstone 285; do not oppose TBM at Edinburgh 290; 291, weak in Edinburgh 299; in Scotland 348; opposed to Peel's tariff IV, 26; vote thanks to Ellenborough 99n; strong in Warwickshire 109; and Peel 131; difficulties of their position in 1843 133; won't touch Protestant establishment in Ireland 163; at Edinburgh 341
Toronto, VI, 61
Torquay, IV, 34n, 44
Torrens, Robert, II, *232*
Torrens, Sir Robert Richard, V, *241*
Torrens, W. T. M., *Memoirs of Viscount Melbourne*, III, 74
Torrington, Lord, II, 195n
Tottenham, Col. Charles, V, *93*
Toulouse, battle of, I, 44; VI, 159, 160, TBM at 166n
Tours, I, 284, IV, 144, described 149; 155, 156, 350, V, 417, 419
Townshend, Charles, II, *321*, III, 159, IV, 198
Townshend, Chauncey Hare, I, *116*, TBM's rival for Chancellor's Medal 116; 178, 239, envied Robert Montgomery 268; *Religious Opinions*, I, 116n
Tractarians, IV, 351, V, 130n, *see also* Puseyites
Trades Unions, II, 117n
Trafalgar Tavern: *see* London, Greenwich
Trajan, I, 168
Travancore, Colin Macaulay resident at II, 247; III, 66

Travancore, Rajah of, II, 144
Traveller's Library: *see* Macaulay, Writings, Essays
Travers, Benjamin, II, *330*
Treasury, First Lord of, IV, 317
Treasury, can't use public money for famine relief in Scotland IV, 332; 386, Trevelyan's place at filled up VI, 189; Solicitorship of, TBM asks it for Ellis V, 206, 207; patronage of VI, 122
Treasury Bench, III, 171
Treaty of Amiens, II, 72
Treaty of July, III, 353
Treaty of Paris, I, 45n, 104n
Treaty of Washington, IV, 47n
Trebellius Pollio, V, 274*, 278*
Trench, Major General Sir Frederick, III, *330*
LETTER TO: III, 330
Trench, Richard Chenevix, VI, 150n, 152n, 195n
Treneer, Anne, *The Mercurial Chemist*, I, 269n
Trent, Council of, V, 88, 333
Trevelyan, Alice (1843-1902), TBM's niece, daughter of Hannah and Charles Trevelyan, I, xxviii, IV, *134*, 142, 147, 151, 157, 198, her development 236; 314, 340, 346, 348, 350, 351, 352, her first breakfast out 353; 377, V, 47, 76, ill 121n; 122, 123, 125, her stories about chairmen 127, 161; complains of gout 183; 186, 192, 195, her chairmen 202; 204, 250, 266, 271, 274, 276, 286, her sin of blasphemy 337; letter to TBM about Sardanapalus 343; her parody of Dr Watts 344; 345, 353, 358, has a dog 370, 373; TBM sends books to 381; 'wonderfully delicate' 383; nursing George Trevelyan 391; delighted to be mentioned in Mrs Stowe's *Sunny Memories* 412; TBM hopes Fanny lets her have 'plenty of Miss Austen' 465; her dog VI, 49, 53; 58, 60, 62, a story for about the lovely Giuseppa 63; may go on Easter tour 77; 103, 105n, 114, at Brighton 120, 122; TBM invites her to watch eclipse 142; and 'Kenneth Macaulay' 156; 164, upset by her father's Indian appointment 188; expected at Holly Lodge 204; going to St Leonards 206; TBM takes to Cambridge 212; to be confirmed 212; at Cambridge 214; 221, 222n, writes to TBM 227; with TBM on Northern tour 230n; 231, 232, reading Shakespeare 236; reading *Life of Mackintosh* 237; 238, to go to India 244; dines with TBM 247; and Pepys's *Diary* 268
LETTERS TO: VI, 58, 142, 272
Trevelyan, Sir Charles Edward (1807-86), TBM's brother-in-law, husband of Hannah Macaulay, I, xxvii, xxviii, Assistant Secretary to the Treasury III, ix; 48n, engaged to Hannah *99*; described 99ff; income 102; report on internal transit duties 102; better financier than wooer 105; agrees to live in TBM's house 105; 109, 'man of real genius' 110; 'insatiable thirst for knowledge' 111; 113, resides with TBM in Calcutta 114; salary £1800 a year 116; described 117; letter to Bentinck 125n; 129n, 132, 136, 147n, 149, studies Sanskrit 149n; 161, 170, 172, 173, 175, TBM enables to pay his debts 176; 183, 191, to take furlough 204; 215, 218, in bad health 222; expenses of return to England 230; 234, at Milverton vicarage 243n; 261, 265, 266, 271, 277, 281, residence in Nottingham Place 285; 290, 300, lives with TBM at Great George Street 313n; 316, appointed Assistant Secretary to the Treasury 317; letter to Walter Trevelyan 317n; will aid TBM with Hastings essay 362; 380, IV, 38, TBM reluctant to ask political favours from 54; and *Lays* 68; 141, 142, in Ireland 147; 151, 157, tour to Holland 197, 201; Treasury appointment 204n; and Sir Edward Colebrook 218; with Hannah in Somerset 233n, 235; 238, 272, 274, used to official secret-keeping 276; worked like Joseph in Egypt 310; his letter books 328n; praised by Peel 328; Peel calls him a fool 328; letter to Peel 328n; his part in Irish relief safe from criticism 329; on suitable charity for Irish relief 331; raises private funds for Highland relief 332; 350, made a K.C.B. 365n; deer hunting 372; 376, letter to Charles Macaulay 376n; has no patronage in Commissariat Department 379; 382, 384, thinks Charles should take Mauritius offer V, 30; 43n, portrait by Eddis 56n; TBM counsels him on behaviour in London 56n; his reputation for hard work 68; 74, 76, assists Arthur Ellis 80n; TBM reads Irish narrative of *History* to 83; unjustly treated by Lord Cottenham 85n; at work on question of official salaries 97; 119, 120, has no news of Arthur Ellis 121; German tour 125n; his portrait presented to Hannah 138; his reply on presentation of portrait corrected by TBM 138n; 140, 186, his hunting 187; 192, his odd ways of spelling Oriental words 195; 199, agrees with TBM about Ellis for Solicitorship of Treasury 206; 207, 208, and plan to return

TBM for Edinburgh 231n; 232, 250, on American dispute 264; 266, to visit Tyrol 268; his affairs have spoiled pleasure of Easter tours 268; 271, 274, 276, his emigration scheme 286n; 295, calls on TBM 313; taken in by TBM's April fool letter 323n; subject of debate in Commons 324; defends his policy on Irish famine debt 324n; his recall from Madras 332n; 345, escapes from train accident 352; 353, at Enmore 358; report on public offices with Northcote 369; summoned to mother's deathbed 381; looks ill 382; time not ripe for his civil service plans 387; TBM consults about Indian Civil Service 389; to take George and Walter Ellis shooting 419; writes TBM 424; alarmed by plans of Indian Law Commission 432; TBM not quite easy about 465; 467, Indian appointment VI, xi; 48, and George's success 51; 53, 54, 55, 58, 60, 62, 63, approves TBM's note on Penn 64; refuses to leave London during Indian Mutiny 101; 113, at Malvern 114; TBM wishes him to dine 115, 119; on bad terms with Hayter 122n; unable to accompany George to Cambridge 125; calls on TBM with Indian news 125; accompanies George to Cambridge 126; 131, likes Russell's Indian plan 149; 164, in Holland 167; accepts Governorship of Madras 188; income from Indian appointment 189n; 190, on his way to India 197; writes from Egypt 202; refused to leave his work 208n; lands at Madras 210; rash behaviour and recall 220n; high opinion of Montagu Butler 242; well spoken of by Wood 255; part of TBM's family 281

Writings: The Application of the Roman Alphabet to All the Oriental Languages, III, 100n, *On the Education of the People of India*, III, 100n, VI, 300, and Sir Stafford Northcote, 'On the Organisation of the Permanent Civil Service,' V, 387n, *A Report upon the Inland Customs and Town-Duties of the Bengal Presidency*, III, 100n, 'The Thugs; or Secret Murderers of India,' III, 190, 216, *A Treatise on the Means of Communicating the Learning and Civilization of Europe to India*, III, 100n

LETTERS TO: V, 97, VI, 210, 213, 269

Trevelyan, Mrs Charles (Hannah More Macaulay), afterwards Lady Trevelyan (1810-73), TBM's sister, I, viii, and TBM's letters xi-xii; *xxvii-xxviii*, xxix, 19, 31, 39, 40, 66, TBM pleased by her letter 160; 'Hannah More the lesser' 167; 197, on TBM's first contribution to *ER* 203n; 208, 221, 224, 227, TBM's mock quarrel with 238; 247, 266, 271, on TBM's maiden speech 272n; her idolatry of TBM 274n; 308, TBM prefers her company to that of Lord and Lady Holland II, 28; studies German 29; best-read Boswellite next to TBM 57; has maid servant at Leamington 58; criticizes TBM's 'Byron' 59; TBM pines for her society 69; TBM's love for her and Margaret his strongest feeling 85; on Murray and Croker's book 106n; at James Cropper's 122n; TBM's pet names for 123; her pertness 136; her Sunday reading 138; TBM would rather kiss her lips than William IV's hand 143; travelling in Wales 148; German studies 151; would make a queer Quaker 155; her Sunday reading 160; 173, tooth ache 180; her loss will leave TBM nothing but ambition 203; 209, not to see TBM's farewell letter to Margaret 204; TBM has no one but her 210-11; with Edward and Margaret at Brighton 214; praises Reynolds portrait 226; Margaret cautions about leaving TBM 226n; 229, unwell 233; to Dingle Bank for her health 234; some mystery about plans for 236; improved 237; leaves for Dingle Bank 239-40; TBM prefers her company to that of lords and ladies 255; health recovered 259; 273, TBM's decision on Indian offer depends on her 301, 302; urges TBM to give up appointment 303n; receives small legacy from Hannah More 307; and Miss Napier 317; TBM anxious that uncertainty of Indian business should not trouble her 324; TBM thinks only of her 328; praised to Sharp 330; going to India must not look like matrimonial speculation 332; must choose a maid 339-40; advice on Indian outfit 343; to preside over 'seventy or eighty Hindoos and Mahometans' 352; her behaviour praised by TBM's friends 356; on Captain Bathie 356n; her Indian outfit 358; negotiations for servant 358; Sharp wishes to entertain 363; her maid 364; her happiness TBM's chief object 368; does not wish to be shown London society 368; TBM prefers Calcutta with her to London without 370; TBM weeps at thought of separating her from Margaret 372; marriage III, vii; ix, TBM's love for 5; 8, 11,

Trevelyan, Mrs Charles (Hannah More Macaulay)—*cont.*
12, 15, 17, 20, behaviour on leaving England 25; letter to Margaret 25n; 26, 27, letter to Fanny 27n; seasick but recovered 28; 29, letter to Fanny 29n; 31, extremely social on the *Asia* 34; letter to Fanny 34n; stays with Bishop of Calcutta 35; 38, 40, 60, 66, 67, safe and well at Calcutta 71, 73, 80, 86, in excellent health 88; 89, TBM reunited with 90; 92, her routine in India 95; 97, discourages Trevelyan 102; grows in love with Trevelyan 103; TBM's despair on losing 104; frightened at thought of marriage 105; 109, 110, 113, TBM's grief upon her marriage 114; dreads moral more than physical separation from 115; marriage 117; 136, 144, expects to be confined shortly 156; 161, 164, 170, 172, 173, 175, 183, 196, death of child 214; 215, 217, 222, 227, assists Lady Malkin 228; 230, 234, 244, letter to quoted 253n; 275, returns to London 281; 285, gratitude to Lady William Bentinck 292; 295, kept in England by TBM's efforts 317n; 321, accompanies TBM to Paris 336n; 380, IV, vii, near-fatal accident? 34-5; 'remarkably well' 38; returns from Brighton 43; 55, and the *Lays* 68; tour to Holland 197, 201; her presence in England owing to James Stephen 204; TBM anxious about her health 233; TBM brings MS of *History* to 266; 276, 310, at Enmore 313; praises Marian Ellis 331; delighted to see again 350; more desirous than TBM that he should remain in Parliament 350; at Enmore, 372; predicts success for *History* 377; returns from Hastings 378; 382, health improved 383; 390, V, 14, 30, TBM takes to party at Downing Street 37n; approves Eddis's portrait of TBM 55; 59, on TBM's response to Irish tour 74n; 76, moves to Westbourne Terrace 76n; TBM reads *History* to 83; 95, unwell 105, 106; accompanies TBM on Scottish tour 111n; 116, German tour 125; makes speech on presentation of Trevelyan's portrait 138; commissions Eddis portrait of TBM 138n; her portrait by Richmond for TBM 152; asked to chaperone Marian Ellis at Great Exhibition 159, 160; 186, 188, 192, 195, TBM sends his epitaph on Babington to 196; reading George Sand's wicked books 199; at Cropper wedding 200; at Brighton 203; 204, and plan to return TBM for Edinburgh 231n; TBM takes to children's service at St Paul's 233; visits Harrow 251; TBM asks her to make his excuses to Edinburgh 258; calls on Dr Bright about TBM 259; accompanies TBM to Clifton 261n; on gluttony 262; TBM sees her at Bristol station 263n; at Enmore 265; visits TBM at Clifton 267n; back in town 268; to visit Tyrol 268, 276; TBM keeps comic verses for 281; 286, 287, 295, compelled to sign Lord Shaftesbury's petition 298; praises Louise Ellis's acting 307; 313, 314n, eager to see the Empress Eugenie 322; TBM takes to Royal Academy exhibition 328; 329n, to stay with TBM at Tunbridge Wells 339; 341, at Tunbridge Wells 342; enjoying summer at Hatfield 344; 345, 358, 361, going to Brighton 363; 364, 364n, breakfasts with TBM 367; 370, 371, gets scarlet fever 380; looks like new court of Balliol 381; goes to Brighton 382; 383, TBM visits in Brighton 386; at Enmore dividing up Mrs Trevelyan's estate 390; 391, 392, to present Mrs Adolphus at court 395, 396; 411, 416, takes Ellis and TBM for drive 420; visits John Macaulay with TBM 421; 425, 427n, admired Sydney Smith 429; should return Preston's advice to him 437; 455, 460, TBM invites to to Richmond 461; 465, has proof sheets of *History* 467; 472, TBM must be near her and her family 475; contributes to allowance for Fanny and Selina 479, 480; TBM's dread of her leaving for India VI, xi; chooses carpets for Holly Lodge 25; 37n, moving to Grosvenor Crescent 39; 40n, 43n, 45n, at Oatlands 47; 48, and George's success 51; 53, 60, approves TBM's note on Penn 64-5; her opinion of Mrs Crinean 72; 78n, 79, 90n, on misbehavior of her nephew Henry 92n; 97n, on way to Munich 101; visits Manchester exhibition with TBM 101n; TBM to meet at Paris 105, 106, 113; 119, 121, to accompany George to Cambridge 123; 124, 126, 139n, reports compliment to Ellis 142; quite recovered 143; attends Bernard's trial 149; 150n, would scold TBM about ortolans 159; will suffer loss of Margaret 164; in Holland 167; 173, will examine Holland on *Sir Charles Grandison* 180; won't accompany Trevelyan to India 188; 198n, to go to St Leonards with Margaret 200; 201, on Stanley's Reform Bill speech 202n; 204, TBM takes to Cambridge 212, 214; spends summer in Lake District 216n; TBM lends Campbell's Diary to 218n; bored by Lord

Campbell's son 219; in Lake District 222n; 227, with TBM at Wordsworth's tomb 230; admires Glasgow 231; 232, Mrs Edward Cropper in a rage at 239; to go to India 242n, 244; returns from St Leonards 247; moved by Moultrie's lines on Margaret 281

Memoir of TBM, I, xli, 7n, 15n, 156n, 192n, 218n, 264, on TBM and Whewell 317n; II, 233n, on Indian appointment 303n; 307n, III, viii, 31n, 65n, 116n, 129n, 158n, IV, 342n, on his dislike of society V, x; 437n, on TBM's peerage VI, x

LETTERS TO: I, 217, 274, 274, 277, 278, II, 15, 17, 20, 23, 24, 28, 30, 31, 34, 37, 40, 42, 45, 47, 49, 51, 54, 56, 59, 62, 64, 66, 69, 70, 71, 73, 74, 76, 78, 80, 81, 83, 86, 86, 87, 88, 89, 94, 95, 99, 100, 122, 123, 132, 134, 135, 137, 139, 141, 143, 144, 145, 147, 149, 149, 151, 151, 153, 154, 156, 158, 160, 167, 168, 172, 179, 180, 182, 185, 186, 187, 188, 191, 192, 194, 194, 197, 205, 206, 207, 208, 209, 210, 215, 217, 239, 242, 243, 245, 246, 251, 253, 255, 257, 259, 261, 263, 264, 266, 268, 270, 270, 273, 275, 276, 277, 279, 281, 285, 288, 291, 293, 295, 299, 303, 307, 308, 311, 315, 316, 318, 322, 323, 324, 328, 329, 331, 334, 336, 337, 338, 341, 347, 349, 350, 355, 357, 359, 360, 360, 361, 362, 365, 367, 369, 372, III, 5, 5, 9, 260, 263, 264, 270, 279, 290, IV, 59, 136, 139, 144, 147, 154, 195, 216, 219, 233, 236, 266, 269, 272, 274, 276, 278, 301, 302, 313, 320, 328, 341, 365, 376, V, 5, 44, 51, 66, 74, 106, 127, 159, 220, 231, 245, 245, 249, 258, 263, 266, 266, 270, 273, 275, 291, 292, 324, 328, 352, 353, 368, 423, 461, 467, VI, 53, 57, 60, 62, 102, 114, 117, 146, 220, 233, 259

Trevelyan, Frances: *see* Mrs Charles Perceval

Trevelyan, George Macaulay (1876-1962), TBM's great-nephew, I, xiv, xxxiii, *Sir George Otto Trevelyan*, III, 99, VI, 106n, 206n

Trevelyan, Sir George Otto (1838-1928), TBM's nephew, I, xvi, III, 129n, *271*, 281, 290, 295, and Brighton bathing machine IV, 43; nearly well 55; 57, to enter Cambridge in fourteen years 59; dines with TBM 134; 142, 147, 151, 157, 198, 207, on seeing the sights 234; 236, 335, 340, 346, 348, 350, 352, V, 43n, 140n, 186, 188, enters Harrow 188n; queer object in stickups 190; 192, ill at Harrow 202; denies truth of anecdote about TBM 203n; a good boy, competed for Latin prize 228; 266, at Bromley 266, 267, 268; can buy edition of Herodian for TBM 271; 274, 276, TBM advises him to use a translation 287; to have his first sight of Paris 295; success in examinations 300; returns to school 307; excited by prospect of Paris visit 315; 353, doing well at school 361; dines with TBM 370; confined to his room with a sprain 390, 391, 392; invites Walter Ellis to Esher 415; a hunter 419; Greek studies 421-2; his Harrow successes promise well for Cambridge 434; doing well 437; Matthew Preston shocked by his easy ways 437; his success 451; on TBM's death VI, xi; wins Gregory scholarship 51; Ellis sure of his success at Cambridge 52; 53, 56, 58, 60, TBM's hopes of 62; to leave Harrow in October 70n; his promise 74; 76, 81, to enter Cambridge 82; wins Gregory and Peel medals 87; imitation of Horace 87; TBM contributes to his Latin verses 88n; and Montagu Butler 97n; TBM discusses his Latin composition 98; 103, 105, on walking tour with Butler in Austria 106; 114, 119, at Malvern 121; TBM cannot accompany to Cambridge 123; goes to Cambridge 126; his epigram for Browne's Medal 153; wins Browne's Medal 153n; 156, pleased by father's Indian appointment 188; studies without a coach 206; did well in scholarship examinations 206; infected by Carlylism, Browningism, and Ruskinism 206n; 208, wins Trinity scholarship 211-12; to entertain family at Cambridge 212; doing extremely well 214; TBM gives rifle to 214n; gets Latin prize, misses Camden prize 220; writes for several Cambridge prizes 221; joins family in Lake country 222; does not write 227; 233, in Germany 238; friendly with young Everett 244; raving about Thucydides 245; and William Everett 261; to enter Trinity 270; makes collection of TBM's minutes 297

Writings: Life of TBM, I, vii, viii, ix, xi, composition of xii-xiii; xiv, xvi, xx, xxi, xxii, xxiv, xxv, xxvii, xxviii, xliii, 1908 edn xliii, 2nd edn xliii; 61n, 101n, 146n, 147n, 170n, on TBM on Jeffrey 222n; on TBM and Brougham 266n; on proofs of History of France 324; II, 15n, 41n, 155n, 215n, 256n,

Trevelyan, Sir George Otto—*cont.*
on slavery question 267n; 283n, 317n, 349n, 363n, 373n, IV, 51n, revision in 91n; 180n, 193n, 234n, 279n, 297n, 316n, 351n, 373n, V, 388n, 405n, 406n, on Italian lessons VI, 51n; 87n, prefatory letter by Carlyle 206n; 1908 edn 234n, *Marginal Notes by Lord Macaulay*, III, 142
LETTERS TO: V, 287, 344, VI, 98, 246, 254, 269
Trevelyan, Harriet Louisa (sister of Charles Trevelyan), IV, *314*
Trevelyan, Harriet Selina, birth and death III, 210; 212, 214, 218-19, 278
Trevelyan, Henry Willoughby (brother of Charles Trevelyan), III, *100*, marriage 234; will bore his brother VI, 197
Trevelyan, Mrs Henry Willoughby (Emilia Anne Greig), III, 234
Trevelyan, Humphrey, *The India We Left*, III, 48n, 113
Trevelyan, Mrs Humphry, I, xv, xxxiv, III, 317n
Trevelyan, John (brother of Charles Trevelyan), III, 243n
Trevelyan, Sir John, 5th Baronet, III, *110*, 113
Trevelyan, Margaret: *see* Mrs Henry Thurstan Holland
Trevelyan, Mrs (mother of Charles Trevelyan), IV, 134, to be in London 238; 314, V, 74, 76, 125, 186, 264, 358, her death 381; her estate 390, 391
Trevelyan, Otto (brother of Charles Trevelyan), V, *76*
Trevelyan, Sir Walter, VI, xi
Trevelyan, William (brother of Charles Trevelyan), V, 158n, *186*, 358
Trevelyan, Mrs William (Maria Pleydell-Bouverie), V, 158n
Trevelyan family, III, 235, 296, takes house in Clapham IV, 57n; Dutch tour 205; not yet returned 206; accompany TBM on Easter tour 334; return to Clapham 349; move to Westbourne Terrace V, 56n, 74; Christmas with TBM and Charles Macaulay's family 87n; with TBM at Ryan's 111n; at Frankfurt 281; return to London 361; at Esher for summer 403n, 406; plan to entertain Walter Ellis 419; 440, dinner party at 470; make Easter tour with TBM VI, 25, 29; 81, at Weybridge 155, *see also* Clapham, and London: Grosvenor Crescent and Westbourne Terrace
Trevelyan Papers, I, xxxiv, V, 138n
Trèves, TBM at VI, 104; 105, TBM at 113; Roman monuments at 114; 115, 116
Trevor, Arthur Hill-, *Life and Times of William the Third*, IV, 18
Trichinopoly, II, 245, III, 72
Triennial Parliaments, V, 232
Trimmer, TBM identified as, V, 6
Trinidad, I, 74n
Trinity College, Dublin, III, 160
Tristram Merton, TBM's pseudonym in *Knight's Quarterly*, I, 188n, 203n
Trollope, Mrs Frances, II, 136, 172, *Domestic Manners* contrasted to Galt's *Lawrie Todd* 314; her description of United States IV, 61
Trophonius, Cave of, VI, 216
Trossachs, VI, 233
Trotter, Coutts, VI, *99*
Truro, Thomas Wilde, 1st Baron, IV, *125*, appointed Chief Justice, Common Pleas 305; V, 85n, Trustee of British Museum 149; 207
Tucker, Henry St George, II, *328*
Tufnell, Henry, IV, *334*, V, x, calls with TBM on Aberdeen 310; 319n, has patronage of Commissariat Department IV, 379
Tuke, Samuel Hack, I, *245*
Tulchan Bishops, V, 21
Tullia, Cicero's daughter, I, 97
Tummel, V, 126
Tunbridge Ware, III, 54
Tunbridge Wells, TBM wishes to see again before leaving England II, 347; III, 67, V, xii, 336, 337, TBM takes house there 338-9
Tunis, IV, 239
Turberville, A. S. and Frank Beckwith, 'Leeds and Parliamentary Reform' II, 212n
Turenne, Marshal, V, 433
Turin, VI, 50, TBM at 57; 102, Royal Academy of, TBM a member V, 309, 350
Turkey, TBM hopes for defeat in Greece I, 163; 254, and Eastern Question III, 335n; 339n, 349n, IV, 228
Turnbull, H. W., ed., *Correspondence of Isaac Newton*, V, 338n
Turner, Charles, V, 238n
Turner, Ellen, I, 218n
Turner, J. M. W., II, 49, 159, III, 13
Turner, John, III, *65*
Turner, Mr, TBM's landlord in Cambridge, I, 113; room for family party 127, 129; TBM pays on leaving for rooms in college 144
Turner, T. Hudson, IV, *287n*
Turton, Sir Thomas, III, *177*, 186, and Mordaunt Ricketts IV, 218

Tuscany, v, 358, Madiai case 290, 321n
Tuscany, Leopold II, Grand Duke of, III, 61, 263, and the Madiai v, 321n; 358n, and case of Miss Cunninghame 359; expelled 359n; 363n
Tussaud, Mme, TBM not yet in her wax works v, 32
Tweeddale, Marquess of, VI, 52n
Twickenham, v, 424n, Kneller Hall, TBM meets Frederick Temple at 431n
Twisleton, Edward, TBM meets but cannot identify v, *173*; VI, 200n, 201
Twisleton, Mrs Edward (Ellen Dwight), v, 173n
Twiss, Horace, II, *10*, 33, political adventurer III, 267, *Life of Eldon*, IV, 202*, TBM's remarks on 205-6*
LETTER TO: IV, 205
Tyler, Endell, *Henry of Monmouth*, TBM thinks of reviewing IV, 17
Tyler, Wat, I, 85
Tyrer, III, 90, 97
Tyrol, Trevelyans visit v, 268; 305
Tytler, John, III, *122*
LETTER TO: III, 122
Tzetzes, John, translation from v, 62

Ulverston, Lancashire, v, 421, 425, VI, 200
Unclaimed Dividend Office, VI, 177
Unidentified Recipients, letters to: I, 272, II, 42, 111, 112, 147, 231, 237, 375, III, 294, 311, 319, 323, 328, 336, 349, 374, 380, IV, 19, 19, 71, 80, 160, 175, 193, 193, 222, 241, 242, 253, 268, 287, 294, 320, 327, 338, 353, 356, 397, 403, V, 23, 28, 35, 39, 41, 57, 57, 82, 86, 101, 126, 128, 129, 132, 140, 144, 148, 153, 172, 173, 201, 211, 227, 237, 294, 297, 306, 308, 312, 329, 332, 360, 368, 388, 413, 431, 442, 445, 445, 448, 452, 456, 464, 466, 473, 479, VI, 7, 11, 11, 35, 117, 128, 173, 175, 180, 271, 277, 279, 282, 282
University College, London, I, 323: *see also* London University
University of London: *see* London University *and* London, University of
University Reform, v, xi, Palmerston's letter on 385; TBM opposed to requirement of orders 385; Oxford bill 390, 391, 394; Cambridge bill 462; Cambridge committee VI, 92
Unwin, Mary, v, 356
Unwin, William, I, 71n
Upper Ossory, 2nd Earl of, II, 76n
Urquhart, David, IV, *346*
[Usher, T.], letter to, v, 335
Utilitarian System, IV, 299
Utilitarianism, I, xix, attacked by TBM 254n; 263n, and *Westminster Review* II, 106
Utilitarians, IV, 309
Utrecht, Historical Society of, TBM a member v, 309; 350
Utrecht, Peace of, I, 66n

Vail, Aaron, II, *152*
Vaizey, John, v, *296*
LETTER TO: V, 296
Valentine, TBM's: *see* Lady Mary Stanhope
Valerius Maximus, III, 178*, IV, 55, 56
Valletort, Lord, v, 144n
Van Citters, Arnold, his despatch to States General, v, 333
Van Der Heim, Hendrik Jacob, *Het Archief van der Raadpensionaris Antonie Heinsius*, v, *187*
Van de Weyer, Sylvain, Belgian minister, IV, *202*, 204, v, ix, x, 11n, 405n, VI, 43, 46n, 150n, 195n, 200n, 201
LETTER TO: VI, 40
Van de Weyer, Mrs Sylvain, VI, 40, 43, 150n, 201
Van Dieman's Land, III, 63
Van Dyck, Sir Anthony, portrait of Henrietta Maria, II, 53; 214, III, 258
Vanbrugh, Sir John, I, 216, III, 358, IV, 16, letters in Manchester MSS v, 116
Vandals, VI, 96
Vandamme, General, defeat of, I, 36
Vandenhoff, J. M., III, 370
Vane, Lord Henry, v, 337n
Vansittart, Nicholas: *see* Lord Bexley
Vatican, III, 56
Vatinius, III, 159
Vaucluse, Valley of, TBM at VI, 166n
Vaughan, Dr Charles James, corrects references in TBM's *Life* IV, 49n; thinks TBM unfair to Puritans v, *26*; 422, TBM glad he remains at Harrow VI, 70; 87, TBM defers to his authority in Latin 99; compelled to resign 241n
Vaughan, James, TBM offended by his sermon on Indian Mutiny VI, *127*
Vedas, II, 33
Veitch, Dr William, v, *211n*
Velleius Paterculus, III, 160*
Vellore, III, 50
Vendean War, IV, 32, 42, 151
Venice, power of the name St Mark in, I, 183; VI, 26, TBM at 50n; 51, 57, 58, TBM describes 59; Albergo d'Europa 59n; 60-1, last day at 62
Venn, Emilia, on TBM's failure to take honors I, 169n

Venn, Henry, I, *15*, 108n, 145n, 196n, married a Sykes II, 86
LETTER TO: IV, 98
Venn, J. A., *Alumni Cantabrigienses*, I, 22n, 177n, II, 5n
Venn, John, Rector of Clapham, I, 15n, *29*, 37n, 39n, 41n, 169n, 176, 193n, II, 179n, 325n, 327
Venn family, I, xvii
Ventnor, Hannah at IV, 279
Venus de Medici, III, 263
Vernon, Archbishop Edward, V, 397n
Vernon, James, *Letters Illustrative of the Reign of William III*, III, 326n
Verona, VI, 26, TBM at 57; described 58-9; 60, 114, 230n
Verona, Congress of, I, 179, 183
Versailles, I, 284, IV, 148, 159
Verulam, Lord: *see* Francis Bacon
Vespasian, IV, 74
Vestris, Lucia Elizabeth, II, *310*
Vesuvius, in eruption, III, 272
Veteran: see Junius
Veteran Battalion, Canada, TBM proposes III, 331-5
Veto Act: *see* Church of Scotland
Vevey, V, 349n, 352, 354
Vice-Chancellor: *see* Sir John Leach
Vicenza, VI, 26
Victoria, Australia, its prosperity VI, 172
Victoria, Princess Royal, birth of, III, 347; marriage VI, 138n
Victoria, Queen, II, 252, coronation of III, ix; birth of first child 34; her accession 223; 224, coronation of 246; 264, displeasure with Tories 289; and bedchamber crisis 289n; TBM presented to 304; 316, compliments TBM on speech 319n; shot at by Edward Oxford 326; 348, patronizes Leigh Hunt 371; visit to Edinburgh IV, 51, a 'bad business' 54; 137, visit to France 151, 154; visits exhibit of decorations for new House of Parliament 198; TBM attends 199; 272, and effort to form new ministry 273; 274, Russell resigns his trust to 278; 337, drawing room at St James's 366; visit to Ireland V, 66; approves TBM's Royal Academy appointment 96-7; Pius IX meant to annoy 132; 135, invites TBM to Windsor 148; at performance of *Not So Bad as We Seem* 163n; visits Paris exhibition 331n; 351, angered by *Morning Advertiser* 378; 386, TBM at her levee 391; 395, 415n, invites TBM to Windsor VI, 10; TBM recommends Ticknor's *History of Spanish Literature* to 46n; 100, to choose inscription for Scutari monument 104n; 113, TBM recommends Froude's *History* to 144n; address to on opening of Town Hall, Leeds 167; patron of Rifle Corps 214n
Victoria Memorial Hall, Calcutta, VI, 70
Victory, TBM visits V, 159n
Vienna, V, viii, Trevelyans at 282; negotiations at 455
Vierzon, IV, 142
Villari, Pasquale, *Le Opere di Cesare Beccaria*, V, 404*
Villiers, Charles Pelham, II, *157*, his annual motion against Corn Laws IV, 102n, 111, 114, 185; 190
Villiers, Edward, II, *157*
Villiers, George: *see* 4th Earl of Clarendon
Villiers, George, son of 1st Earl of Clarendon, II, 157n
Villiers, Mrs George, II, *157*
Villiers, Henry Montagu, Bishop of Carlisle, VI, *70*
Villiers, Lady, V, x
Villiers, Lord, V, x
Villiers, Thomas Hyde, II, *31*, TBM succeeds as Secretary of Board of Control 31n; 123, 137, Gordon quarrels with 140; 157, his stomach complaint 158; 168, 179, 194, very ill 196; death 208; 211, 213
Villiers family, II, 157, 292, can supply Lister with information about Clarendon 320
Vincatagherry, III, 46
Vinci, Leonardo da, V, 143
Virgil, I, 5*, Dryden's translation of 5n; 18*, 35, quoted by Morier II, 38; imitated in TBM's 'Political Georgics' 60; TBM amuses himself by translating 283; III, 62*, 153, V, 270, *Aeneid*, Dryden's translation II, 82; V, 273, *Eclogues*, III, 6n*, V, 106*, 223*, 254*, TBM suggests a parody of to Mahon 254, *Georgics*, I, 61*, Dryden's translation II, 62; 62*, TBM's explication of passage in V, 100*
Virginia, University of, I, 154n, 242n
Vitruvius Britannicus, I, 231
Vitry, De, 'impudent dog' I, 174
Vizetelly, Henry, publishes edition of TBM's Speeches, V, *339*; ballad on his hanging himself 347-8; mock broadside against 350; 'rascally bookseller' 350; 360, 366, proceedings against by William Hazlitt 367; threatens suit against TBM 370; in ludicrous situation 371; VI, 292
Voltaire, I, 77*, TBM's verses on 209; II, 327*, III, 9, TBM plans essay on 21; 142, 'L'Auteur Arrivant dans Sa Terre Près du Lac de Genève' 180*; 216, 218*, statuette

of 349; IV, 18, on Holland 220; his novels V, 181; 'Diatribe of Doctor Akakia' 347n; *Dictionnaire Philosophique*, III, 62*; *Lettres Philosophiques*, I, 239*
Voluntaries, at Edinburgh, IV, 341; V, 42
Voluntary System, III, 364
Von Martius, Dr Karl Friedrich Philipp, V, *218*
LETTER TO: V, 218
Vopiscus, V, 268*, 274*
Vreede, Georg Willem, V, *113*, *Correspondance Diplomatique . . . Marlborough etc.*, 118*; sends TBM information on Dutch archives 186
LETTERS TO: V, 113, 186
Vulcatius, V, 268*, 274*, 278*
Vyvyan, Sir Richard, IV, *133*

Wa-a-afers, Miss, one of Preston's sisters I, 41
Waagen, Gustav, *Treasures of Art in Great Britain*, I, 202n, V, 284n
Waddell, Mrs, II, 262
Waddington, George, I, 322, V, *390*, VI, 93
Waddington, Horace, I, *109*, 135, VI, 222n
Waghorn, Thomas, 'Truths Concerning Mahomet Ali,' III, 359
Wailes, George, II, *132*
LETTER TO: II, 132
Waithmann, Robert, I, *133*, in Queen Caroline riot 163; VI, 87
Wakefield, I, 208n, 230n, 231, TBM at 250; 252n, VI, 243
Wakefield, Edward Gibbon, trial at Lancaster I, *218*, Panizzi at 227n
Wakefield, Mary, II, 243
Wakefield, William, I, 218n, V, *199*
Wakefield family, I, 248n, IV, 333
Wakley, Thomas, IV, *35*, 338n, V, 235n
Waldegrave, 2nd Earl of, II, *337*
Waldegrave, 6th Earl of, II, *337*
Wales, Ellis in, II, 105; Hannah and Margaret plan tour in 145-6; Zachary Macaulay in, as Charity Commissioner 186
Walford, Edward, VI, *256*
LETTER TO: VI, 256
Walker, Mrs, a proper object of charity VI, *34*; TBM sends money to 34n
Walker, Obadiah, V, *7*
Walker, R. J. B., *Catalogue of Paintings, Drawings, Sculpture and Engravings in the Palace of Westminster*, II, 64n, V, 175n
Walker, William, II, 64n, asks TBM to sit to Reynolds II, *223*
Walker, William Sidney, contributes to *Knight's Quarterly*, I, *188n*; VI, 34
Wallace, Robert, IV, *114*
Wallace, William Bayley, III, *107*, challenges Napier to duel 171; TBM confident he will give no trouble 244; 252, duel with averted 253-4; IV, 90
Waller, Edmund, I, 57, his plot V, 146
Wallington Hall, Northumberland, TBM's library at, I, xxxiv; 46n, III, 349n, and Eddis portrait of TBM V, 138n
Walmesley, John, V, *70*
Walmsley, Sir Joshua, V, *233*
Walpole, Colonel Henry, III, *36*
Walpole, Horace, I, xxix, TBM lays it on him unsparingly II, 317; his letters to Mme Du Deffand 317n; Memoirs, dedicated to Miss Berry 317, 349; his *Mysterious Mother* praised by Byron 321; and Mary Berry 348-9; VI, 47n, papers of, known to TBM 52
Writings: Anecdotes of Painting in England, III, 257*, V, 86*, *Letters to Sir Horace Mann*, reviewed by TBM, II, 308n, 315*, IV, 159, 177, TBM will make subject of essay 199; 208, *Letters*, III, 348, IV, 28, 160, Memoirs of the Reign of George III, TBM consults in MS, IV, 212
Walpole, Sir Robert, I, 318, II, 70, III, 252, 275*, his reception at Lynn VI, 121
Walpole, Spencer, V, 157n, *298*, his decision on Order of Merit 303; VI, 29n, 213, *A History of England*, II, 87n, 230n, III, 154n, V, 152n, *Life of Lord John Russell*, IV, 362, VI, 146n
Walsh, Sir John, V, 210n
Walter, A. B., engraver, IV, 225n
Walton, Christopher, acquires MSS collected by Thomas Mills, VI, *36*
LETTER TO: VI, 36
Walworth, III, 56
Walworth, William, I, 85
Wandsworth Common, III, 45
Wanlip Hall, Leicestershire, near Rothley Temple, II, 40n
War of the Spanish Succession, TBM reviews Mahon's book on, II, 190
War Office, I, xvi, III, 302, 328, IV, 166
Warburton, Eliot, V, *49*, TBM suggests topics to 87-8; *The Crescent and the Cross* V, 49n, *Memoirs of Prince Rupert and the Cavaliers* 49*
LETTERS TO: V, 49, 87, 115
Warburton, Henry, III, *74*, and copyright IV, 25
Warburton, William, IV, 394, *The Divine Legation of Moses*, I, 146*

Ward, Edward Matthew, portrait of TBM III, 349n; V, *175*, his use of TBM's *History* in his paintings 175n; TBM suggests details to 176; sends engraving to TBM 228; TBM compliments 'Last Sleep of Argyll' 400; Russell's misunderstanding about his paintings for House of Commons 470; painting of Alice Lisle VI, 152; of Charles II and Jane Lane 152
LETTERS TO: V, 175, 228, 399, VI, 152
Ward, Sir Henry George, V, *5*, speech on Irish Church IV, 135
Ward, Humphry, *History of the Athenaeum*, I, 295n
Ward, Ned, *London Spy*, V, 10n
Wardell, James, *Municipal History of the Borough of Leeds*, IV, 371*
Warren, Samuel, V, *365*, impudent letter from 421; *Ten Thousand A Year*, 363, 365, presents to TBM 418*
Warton, Joseph, edition of Pope, V, *104*
Warwick, Countess of, II, 20, 169
Warwick, Earl of, II, 169
Warwick, Earldom of, V, 476
Warwick, Robert Rich, 1st Earl of, V, *476*
Warwick Castle, II, 30, 45, IV, 151, 331n, 370
Warwick and Holland, Earls of, V, 477
Warwickshire, IV, 109
Washington, Treaty of: *see* Ashburton Treaty
Washington, D.C., burning of, I, 55
Washington, George, and Major André, V, 410n; 447n, Randall sends autograph of to TBM VI, 74; contrasted to Jefferson 75; 171
Waterfield, Thomas Nelson, II, *318*
Waterhouse, Ellis K., *Reynolds*, VI, 83n
Waterloo, subject of Chancellor's Medal competition, I, 186n; IV, 8, V, 308
Waterpark, 2nd Baron, II, 43, 348n
Watkins, John, letter to V, 289
Watson, Richard, M. P., II, *216*
Watson, Richard, Wesleyan minister, II, *454*; *Life of Wesley* 454n
Watson, Robert, *History of the Reign of Philip the Second*, I, 38
Watson v. *Walker*, York Assizes, I, 223n
Watson-Gordon, Sir John, portrait of TBM, V, *110*
Watts, George Frederick, at Bowood, V, *369*
Watts, Isaac, *Divine Songs for Children*, V, 344
Waugh, F. G., *Members of the Athenaeum Club*, III, 314n
Way, Lewis, I, *218*
Weale, John, VI, *154*
LETTER TO: VI, 154
Webb, R. K., *The British Working Class Reader*, I, 323
Webster, Sir Charles, *The Foreign Policy of Palmerston*, III, 335n, 352
Webster, Daniel, IV, 74
Webster, George, IV, *135*
Webster, Noah, *Dictionary* V, 36n, 43n; his spelling system 37
Wedderburne, Alexander, 1st Earl of Roslyn, III, *220*
Wedgwood, Hensleigh, resigns as police magistrate II, *350*
Wedgwood, Mrs Hensleigh (Frances Mackintosh), II, 350
Weekes, Henry, IV, *112*, his bust of Zachary Macaulay 112
LETTER TO: IV, 112
Weeks, Daniel, 'Samuel Rogers: Man of Taste,' II, 55n
Weeks, Jordan, and Co., publishers, Boston, III, 338n
Weigel, Leipzig, publish translation of *History*, VI, 35n
Weimar, Grand Duke of, V, 432n
Weissembourg, M. de, called Dutch ambassador, II, 76
Wellesley, Sir Arthur, V, 78
Wellesley, Richard Colley, 1st Marquess, 'lavish,' I, 70; II, *53*, 71, 124n, wishes to meet TBM 258; described 258-9; III, 42, 48, 55, 76, V, 78, 337
Wellington, Arthur Wellesley, 1st Duke of, I, 21, fighting in Peninsula 39n; a hero 44; created Duke 47; at Congress of Verona 179n; Prime Minister 230n; remarks on abolition 'bad' 244; speech on abolition 245; on slavery 247; 283, ministry in a scrape 286; 293, ministry resigns 293n; II, 21, 53n, 55, his forming government occasion of TBM's 'Political Georgics' 60; 98, 99, 100, 137, 166, resolution on Portugal 251n; 289, 290, 291, alleged illegitimate son III, 33-4; 52, picture of 56; head of 61; 155n, IV, 29, 101, 'magni nominis umbra' 133; *Despatches* IV, 199; will be angered by Twiss's *Eldon* 202; supports Peel on Corn Laws 270; 271, 272n, to form new ministry? 279; on Outram's case 307; consulted on Chartist demonstration 363n; compliments TBM's *History* V, 25; his characteristic oath 31; 78, 137, on red coats in British army 165; as subject for sermon 286; death 286n; duel with Lord Winchelsea 295; Disraeli's eulogy on 301n; 303, excitement of his campaigns in days of TBM's boyhood 429; VI, 146, 287
Wells, VI, 76

Wensleydale, James Parke, 1st Baron, with TBM at Sydney Smith's I, *215*; 216n, 266, Baron of the Court of Exchequer V, 109; 427n, on Shrewsbury case VI, 151, 217; advises TBM to visit Toulouse and Bordeaux 159

LETTER TO: V, 109

Wentworth of Nettlestede, Henrietta, Baroness, and Monmouth, VI, 235n

Wentworth Park, III, 81

Wentworth Woodhouse, I, 241n, TBM dines at 251n

Wesley, John, IV, 176, Southey on V, 454; his sermon on predestination 455*; *Sermons on Several Occasions* 455n

West, Sir Algernon, *Recollections*, IV, 91n

West India Bill: *see* Anti-Slavery Movement, government plan of abolition

West Indian Colonies, select committee on commerce, TBM on II, 115; 230n

West Indian Committee on abolition, its report II, 175; 238n

West Indians, resistance to abolition I, 245

West Indies, II, 281, apprenticeship plan for fails 307n

West Riding, TBM proposed as candidate for IV, 348

West Riding Quarter Sessions, TBM attends I, 208n, 213, 222n; conflict with Durham assizes 225n; 229n, TBM attends 230; barristers at 'a tolerably well informed circle' 232; TBM attends 233, 234, 235, 243n, 246, 250, 252n; 253n

Westleys and Co., letters to, VI, 224, 235

Westmacott, Charles, I, 319n, II, *106*, portrayed by Bulwer 315; IV, 129n

Westmacott, Richard, III, 309n

Westminster, Robert Grosvenor, 1st Marquess of, II, 276n, *291*, 301, III, 171, 174, 208, 219, TBM dines with IV, 202

Westminster Review, attacks TBM and *ER* I, 254; praises Croker's Boswell II, 106; V, 321n

Westminster School, I, xviii, III, 286, annual play IV, 272

Westmorland, I, 212, II, 216, 290, III, 71, Hannah and family in VI, 222

Weston House, Warwickshire, Sir George Philips's residence II, 183n, 196, described 197; 348

Weston Zoyland, TBM at IV, 44n

Westover MSS, V, 143

Westwood, Alfred, letter to, V, 44

Wetherby, I, 208n, 230n, 252n

Wetherell, Sir Charles, I, *221*, II, 62, his 'cursed lungs' 105

Wethey, H., *The Paintings of Titian*, VI, 61n

Weybridge, TBM thinks of settling at V, 418; living of given to Edward Rose 458; VI, 52, Trevelyans at 155, 156; 161, TBM at 162; 167, TBM at 170; 179n, TBM at 231n, 240n

Weymouth, Viscount: *see* Marquess of Bath

Whale, General Sir Charles, I, *47*

Whalley, Richard Chapple, 'It Is All True,' V, *275*

Wharncliffe, James Stuart-Wortley-Mackenzie, 1st Baron, I, *246*, his death IV 277

Wharncliffe, John Wortley, 2nd Baron, IV, *277*

Wharton, Thomas, III, 154

Wharton's Law Lexicon, I, 208n

Whately, Richard, Archbishop of Dublin, IV, *166*, no business to be at Edinburgh and talk nonsense 320-1; V, 65, TBM refuses invitation from 67

Whewell, William, Master of Trinity, I, *316*, II, 196n, sends book to TBM III, 277; attacked by Brewster IV, 20-1; 21, 22, entertains TBM at Cambridge 181; 323n, 331n, 361, TBM dines with 367; V, ix, 42n, 110n, 157n, TBM asks for information about Newton 209, 212; 313n, proposals for university reform 385n; TBM introduces Montalembert to 456; compliments TBM on *History* VI, 12; TBM advises on candidate for statue in antechapel 67-9; statue to Bacon put up by 69; sends TBM his articles on Plato 84*; 85n, 124, 125, pamphlet on new statutes for Trinity 136; 150n, pays too little attention to undergraduates 214; entertains TBM's party 214; thinks *Laches* genuine 255

Writings: English Hexameter Translations, IV, 333*, *History of the Inductive Sciences*, I, 317n, III, 247, *Lectures on Systematic Morality*, IV, 298-9*, 'Of the Platonic Theory of Ideas,' VI, 82-3*, *The Philosophy of Discovery*, VI, 84n, *Philosophy of the Inductive Sciences*, I, 317n, *Platonic Dialogues*, sent to TBM, VI, 250*

LETTERS TO: I, 316, III, 247, 277, IV, 117, 298, 333, 367, V, 37, 48, 48, 209, 210, 212, 299, 299, 384, 456, VI, 12, 67, 82, 84, 125, 136, 150, 222, 240, 267, 270

Whewell, Mrs William (Cordelia Marshall), IV, 117, V, 38, 209, 211, 212, death VI, 214n

Whewell, Mrs William (Everina, Lady Affleck, second wife), VI, *214*, 241, 252, 270

Whigs, I, viii, reasons for defeat in 1807 226; leaders in Commons weak II, 87-8, 89n; TBM has no confidence in ministry 99-100, 106; have the honour of Reform Bill 124; dismissed 140n; will soon turn Radicals III, 150; return to office 164; TBM fears a coalition 167; 176, abused by Brougham 250, 255n; and Bedchamber crisis 289; have advanced religious liberty 351; elections against 362; propose fixed duty 373n; defeated 381n; resign 385n; unable to carry any really good measure IV, 26; disgraced by affair of Auckland and Ellenborough 99; deserved Brougham's abuse 100; relation of *ER* to 163; should not be identified as war party 231, 232-3; leave Ellenborough alone 247n; anomalous position in succeeding to Peel 273-4; 'staid in when we ought to have gone out, and now we stay out when we ought to have gone in' 278n; may efface remembrance of 'folly and perverseness' 280; Lord John Russell treats too favourably 287; split over Ten Hours Bill 299; gap widening between them and Peelites V, 156; long closely allied with *ER* 304; 333, must remain in office if Reform Bill loses VI, 275-6

Whish, General Sir William Sampson, V, *272*, 280

Whish, Lady, V, 280

Whishaw, John, II, *43*, described 45-6; 146

Whiskey, TBM drinks a daily glass at Jeffrey's, I, 240; 'too good to last' III, 369; 372, 378, from Islay IV, 83; black seal and red seal expected from Napier 97; comes safe 99

Whitbread, Samuel, II, *44*, V, 212n

Whitbread's Brewery, II, 44, V, 212n

White, Captain, III, 51, 53

White, Francis, I, 147n

White, Henry Kirke, *Poetical Works*, I, 36*, 'To the Herb Rosemary' 36*

White, Lydia, I, *239*

White and Parson, *Leeds Directory*, II, 177n

White Surrey, TBM's horse?, I, 135

Whitefield, George, V, *454*

Whitehead, William, V, 131

Whitelocke, Bulstrode, *Journal of Swedish Embassy*, TBM presents to Edinburgh Philosophical Institution, V, 463; *Memorials of English Affairs*, V, 63*, 146

Whittingham, William, V, *21*

Whitty, E. M., *St Stephen's in the Fifties*, V, 336n

Whitty, Michael James, sentenced by Ramshay, V, *205*

Whitworth, Sir Charles, ed., *Political and Commercial Works of Charles Davenant*, VI, 55n

Widmore, near Bromley, Ellis's house at, V, 121n; manor house destroyed by fire 454

Widmore Court, built by Telford sisters V, 455n

Wieland, Christoph Martin, V, 27

Wigan, election riot at II, 93

Wigham, John, IV, 100, 102, *103*, 105, 215

LETTER TO: IV, 103

Wightwick, George, V, *265*

Wigram, William, II, *322*, objects to TBM's appointment 323; succeeds Marjoribanks 327; resigns 328

Wigton, TBM invited to stand for IV, 348

Wilberforce, Henry, II, *286*, 295, V, 96n

Wilberforce, Robert, I, 321, asks to use TBM's franking privilege II, *295*; attacks Clarkson III, 273; VI, 279

LETTER TO: VI, 279

Wilberforce, Robert and Samuel, eds., *Correspondence of William Wilberforce*, IV, 205n, *The Life of William Wilberforce*, I, 278n, II, 295n, III, 259n, 273n, IV, 205n, V, 434*, 437

Wilberforce, Samuel, Bishop of Oxford, I, 321, II, *286*, 295n, attacks Clarkson III, 273; elected to Athanaeum 314n; IV, 15n, 352, V, ix, x, TBM defends his view of episcopacy to 7-8; appointed Bishop of Oxford 7n; 49n, tells story of father taking tea in a brothel 110n; V, 157n, 168n, 172n, 234n, TBM's impatience with his part in Convocation 297; 328n, 329n, 402n, TBM on his late rising 458; VI, 37n, 90n, TBM dines with 91; 152n, 200n, speech on Marriage Bill 201; 216n, 222n

LETTERS TO: III, 314, V, 7, 110, 111, 119, 398, 407, 457, VI, 34, 45, 150, 151, 152, 195, 216, 236, 267

Wilberforce, William, I, xvii, xxi, xxiv, and Christian missions in India 25n; education in India 26n; 44, 50n, compared to Henry Thornton 55n; 60, and anti-slavery work on Continent 73n; 74n, 176n, and attacks on Zachary Macaulay 194; *Correspondence* 220n; his daily dose of opium 235; 237, compared to Jeffrey 238; 253n, losses through his son's failure 278n; II, 68, his house in Knightsbridge 156; death of 284; 285, his deathbed 286; to be buried in Westminster Abbey 289; burial described 290, 291; his *Life* 295; his marriage 326n;

toasted at Leeds 333n; and Mortlock's charity 363n; IV, 75, on Lord Thurlow's behaviour 205; letter to Lord Muncaster 206; 207, 352, portrait by Richmond V, 56n; story of his drinking tea in a brothel 110n; 156, 454n, his kindness to William Sydney Walker VI, 34; 195n, TBM on his death 279

Wilberforce, William, the younger, I, *14*, 15, 17, 18, kind to TBM at school 19; 22, 23, 26, 28, 33, 34, 40n, 55, TBM sees little of at Cambridge 103; studies law with TBM 172n; 196n, going to stand for Hull 277; his career as 'Cow Keeper' 277n; 'reprobate' 286; only expectations what he can wring from Macaulay and Babington 300; living at free quarter on George Babington 326; 366, greets TBM at Malvern V, 190; about to apostatize 196; 'something between a pettifogging attorney and one of the swell mob' 196

Wilberforce, Mrs William (Barbara Spooner), 'vixen' II, 286; blamed for faults of her children 326n; VI, 280

Wilbraham, George IV, *63*, 90, 91, 93, 97, he and Burney family pleased by 'Madame D'Arblay' 97
  LETTER TO: IV, 64

Wild cats, in Rome, IV, 65

Wilde, Oscar, V, 66n

Wilde, Sir Thomas: *see* Lord Truro

Wilde, Sir William Robert Wills, visits the Boyne with TBM V, *66n*; *Beauties of the Boyne and Blackwater* dedicated to TBM 66n; reports on Fingall MS VI, 223n
  LETTERS TO: VI, 223, 224

Wilkes, John, IV, 198

Wilkie, Sir David, II, *282*

Wilkie, William, *The Epigoniad*, III, 62

Wilks, Rev. S. C., editor of *Christian Observer*, I, 197n, 322, II, 154

William the Conqueror, IV, 256

William, Duke of Gloucester, IV, 257, 258n

William and Mary, V, 338n, 409

William Rufus, King, IV, 255, 256

William III, King, and Kensington Palace II, 169; 309, IV, ix, 15, 255, 257, 375, V, xi, 76, preferred Kensington to Whitehall 112-13; 146, 173, letters to Heinsius 186; 360, 433n, Fleming's panegyric on VI, 13; and meaning of 'extirpate' 145

William IV, King, proclaimed I, 275; TBM will see him prorogue Parliament 278; speech from throne 312n; his illegitimate children II, 16n; promises Garter to Grey 19; 42n, leads procession on opening of Parliament 49; TBM describes in presence-chamber, St James's 53; plan for coronation of 65; opens London Bridge 82; coronation of 94; described 96-9; his 'low, clumsy bearing' at coronation 98-9; does not give royal assent in person to Reform Bill 124; 134, in better temper with his ministers 136; stone thrown at him 141; TBM kisses his hand at levee 142; 251, will stand by Reform ministry 256; question of safety or 'general destruction' depends on him 257; won't create peers in Irish Church Bill crisis 269; 273, 339, TBM receives warrant for Indian appointment from 358; III, ix, 18, 43, 140n, V, 59, 74, 76, coronation of 233

William, TBM's clerk?, I, 212

William: *see* William Williams

Williams, Basil, *Stanhope*, VI, 53

Williams, Deacon's Bank, I, 6n, III, 262, 313, IV, 7, 69, V, 220, 225, 232, VI, 24n, 199

Williams, Elizabeth, TBM's servant, III, 341n, V, *183*, James Mills writes to 198; 270, prepares TBM's lunch 271; 283, to be pensioned off VI, 141n; TBM buys annuity for 163; succeeded by Mrs Kent 165n; compared to Mrs Kent as cook 170

Williams, John, I, 267n

Williams, Sir John, IV, 69n

Williams, Lady, TBM sends *Lays* to IV, *69*

Williams, Sydney, V, *338*
  LETTER TO: V, 338

Williams, Theodore, I, *19*

Williams, Thomas, imprisoned for selling *Age of Reason*, V, 359

Williams, Thomas Jay, *Priscilla Lydia Sellon*, V, 227n

Williams, William (M.P.), IV, *114*, 232

Williams, William, TBM's servant, III, *341*, V, 71, 123, 183n, 189, 190, 191, 192, freeholder of Herefordshire 241; leaves for Herefordshire 249; 251, 265, 271, turns James Mills away 272; 281n, to put TBM's London rooms in order 283; 304, 346, 366, 384, his niece's illness 425, 427; VI, 56, 63, 114, 'My Lords' TBM 115; goes with TBM to Malvern 117; 120, ill 141; to be pensioned off 141n; was in serious danger 143; TBM buys annuity for 163; succeeded by Gray 170

Williams, Zephaniah, IV, *293*

Williams and Norgate, firm, V, 338n

Williams's Library, Dr, VI, 36n

Willinck, Arthur, V, *199*

Willmott, Robert A., *Conversations at Cambridge*, I, 184n

Willock, Sir Henry, IV, *171*

Wilson, bullied TBM at school I, 57
Wilson, Daniel, Bishop of Calcutta, II, *33*, receives Hannah at Calcutta III, 35; 60, 67, 69, 71, 72, 132
Wilson, Horace Hayman, III, 122n
Wilson, J. M., II, *375n*
Wilson, James, TBM consults on budget question V, *332*
Wilson, John ('Christopher North'), attacks TBM in *Blackwoods*, I, 262n, 318n; *319*, insulting description of TBM II, 81; defends Croker against TBM 108n, 110; contest with him would be degrading 111; and *Lays* IV, 79; 80, 82, votes for TBM in 1852 election V, 252; TBM succeeds as President of Edinburgh Philosophical Institution 399n
Writings: City of the Plague, V, 252, *Isle of Palms*, V, 252, *Noctes Ambrosianae*, V, 348*
Wilson, General Sir Robert, II, *36*
Wilson, Thomas, V, 116
Wilson-Patten, John, bill on sale of beer on Sundays, V, 461
Wilton, TBM at IV, 247
Wiltshire, II, 97, IV, 188, TBM in 247; 353, pauperised labourers in V, 78; VI, 86
Wimbledon, TBM thinks of staying at, V, 455
Wimsatt, W. K., *The Portraits of Alexander Pope*, II, 54n
Winchelsea, George William Finch-Hatton, 10th Earl of, V, *295*
Winchester, Charles Grant at II, 331; TBM at V, 159n
Winchester, Marquesses of, IV, 246
Windermere, compared to Killarney V, 69; Low Wood Hotel, Hannah and family at VI, 216n
Windham, William, III, 136
Windsor Castle, II, 194, III, 301, 302, TBM dates letter from 303; 304, TBM dines at 315; IV, 274, 278, TBM at V, 148; 378, 409, consults Stuart Papers at 422; arms of Garter Knights at 426; TBM invited to VI, 10, 12; 13
Windsor Forest, III, 58, 61
Windsor Uniform, I, 275, 279
Wine, Burgundy, at breakfast at Duc de Broglie's I, 302; Lord Essex's fine II, 215; Champagne, Hock, Constantia served at Jeffrey's I, 240; Champagne at Holland House II, 144; Pease takes too much of Grillion's excellent stuff 265; 286, V, 248, Malden does justice to, 276; TBM offers to Ellis 302; good quality for Ellis 343; VI, 95, Trevelyan elated as if he had drunk three bottles 188; TBM not the worse for after dining with Lords and Ladies 200; Claret, at Holland House II, 144; drinks only claret in India III, 97; Chateau Lafite, at TBM's Clarendon dinner V, 148; special stock for Ellis at Richmond 459; toast to the conquerors of Delhi to be drunk in VI, 129; a toast to the charming Harriet in 149; Hockheimer, I, 219, served by the manufacturers of Leeds II, 188; special stock for Ellis V, 262, 276; Johannisberg, for TBM's dinner at Clarendon V, 148; 'glorious' at Heidelberg 351; superb at Rothschild's VI, 228; Madeira, a sum in I, 7n; presented after soup at French dinners 302; at Holland House, II, 144; destruction of vineyards at Madeira VI, 227; Majorca, at Holland House II, 144; Moselle, at Empson's cold collation II, 83; Port, at Holland House II, 144; TBM takes at 4 as physic 172; Sherry, at Holland House II, 144, Louis Philippe sends a fine cask of to Sir Edward Codrington 250; bad Sherry at Malvern makes Ellis ill V, 188n; special stock laid in for Ellis 262; for lunch with poached egg 271; for Ellis 343, 459; Wine, general: boys receive a Sunday glass at Preston's school I, 29; vintner's bill at Cambridge 152; TBM begs supply from home 180; Jeffrey's remarkably good 240; light wine in Dieppe for 18 pence 288; service of at Duc de Broglie's 302; intermediate wines linking Hock and Burgundy at Littleton's II, 79; Lord Stanley recommends warm negus as a nightcap 90; TBM will have good wine for Ellis at Ventnor V, 122; Dr Symonds prescribes it for TBM 271; stock laid in for Ellis at Tunbridge Wells 339; TBM brings his own to Brighton lodgings 366; good wine and plenty of it for Ellis at Thames Ditton 412
Winstanley, D. A., *Early Victorian Cambridge*, I, 40n, 113n, 141n, IV, 331n, 360n, V, 384, 385n, 462, VI, 29n, 67n, 93n
Winterbottom, Thomas, *Account of the Native Africans in the Neighbourhood of Sierra Leone*, III, *96*
Wise, Dr Thomas Alexander, III, *144*
Witness (Edinburgh), IV, 55n
Woburn Abbey, TBM visits IV, 172; 392, TBM at V, 142n, V, 425, 427; VI, 235
Wodehouse, Edmond, I, *286*
Wodehouse, John, 3rd Baron, V, *217*, 312n
Wodrow, Robert, *History of the Sufferings of the Church of Scotland*, IV, 375n

Woffington, Peg, II, 309, 310

Wolf, Friedrich August, *Prolegomena ad Homerum*, 'absurd,' IV, 207*

Wolff, Sir Henry Drummond, VI, *210*

Wolff, Joseph, I, *218*, 'most inveterate liar' III, 273; VI, 210n, *Researches and Missionary Labours*, 2nd edn, III, 372n

Wolmar, courier, V, 349, 418

Wolsey, Cardinal Thomas, IV, 246, V, 409

Wolverhampton, IV, 213

Wolverton, Buckinghamshire, V, 186n

Wood, Sir Charles: *see* Lord Halifax

Wood, John, I, *213*, 232, 236n, 246n, 267, 267n

Wood, Lady Mary: *see* Lady Halifax

Wood, Matthew, Lord Mayor of London, I, 85

Wood, Sir William Page, afterwards Baron Hatherley, appointed Vice-Chancellor V, *305*; 306n, VI, 181n

Woodcock Hall, III, 65n

Woodham, Henry Annesley, IV, *373*

Woodham-Smith, Cecil, *The Great Hunger*, IV, 310n, 328n

Woodhouse, Robert, *Treatise on Plane and Spherical Trigonometry*, I, *123*

Woodrow, Henry, 'Macaulay's Educational Minutes,' VI, 299, *Macaulay's Minutes on Education in India* 144n, 299

Woodward, Sir Llewellyn, *The Age of Reform*, V, 387n

Woolcombe, Mr, and index to *History*, V, 38n

Woolner, Thomas, his statue of TBM, I, 317n

Worcester, IV, 144, TBM at 298n; imbecile waiter at V, 174; 176, 177, 179, 191

Worcester, battle of, TBM supposed to be writing about V, 200; Charles's escape from VI, 152

Worcester, Cathedral, V, 175, 179, 180, 183

Worcester, Musical Festival, V, 175n, TBM attends 184

Worcestershire, V, 194

Wordsworth, Christopher, Master of Trinity, I, *150*, 173n, 'unutterable baseness and dirtiness' III, 112

Wordsworth, William, I, xxxiii, TBM and Derwent Coleridge do daily battle over 178; II, 28n, 60, Byron's mistaken judgment of 321; Poet Laureate III, 369n; portrait by Inman IV, 225; dying V, 108; succeeded by Tennyson 131n; 223n, would have spoiled subject of happy children 285; TBM visits his tomb VI, 230

Writings: The Excursion, I, 56*, II, 60n, V, 118, *The Prelude*, reason why Wordsworth kept it back V, 118*; 280*, *White Doe of Rylstone*, I, 90*, 'silly' 218

Wortley, John: *see* 2nd Baron Wharncliffe

Wotton, I, 124

Wotton, Sir Henry, VI, 238, 'A Hymn to My God in a Night of Late Sickness' 238n

Wraxall, Nathaniel, VI, 195, on news of Yorktown 196; TBM's opinion of 197; *Historical Memoirs of My Own Time*, doubtful authority of 179

Wrekin, The, V, 177

Wren, Sir Christopher, I, 294, 297, IV, 152

Wright, J. M. F., *Alma Mater*, I, 113n, 114n, 134n, 150n

Wright, Ichabod, II, 32n, trans. of Dante 277

Wright, Thomas, ed., *Correspondence of William Cowper*, II, 38n

Wright, Rev. William, VI, *229*

LETTER TO: VI, 229

Wrightson, William Battie, I, *246*

Wrington, Somerset (near Barley Wood), I, 13, V, 273

Writ of Right, at York, I, 208

Writers to the Signet, library, IV, 384

Wrottesley, Lady Caroline, libelled after her death, V, 363

Wrottesley, Sir John, wins suit for libel against his dead wife V, *363*

Wyatt, James, VI, 47n

Wycherley, William, III, 340, 344, 354, 358

Wye, River, I, 156, described V, 187, 188

Wykeham, William of, IV, 246

Wynn, Charles Watkin Williams, I, *312*, compliments TBM on India speech II, 268; on precedents of House of Commons 313; TBM's verses on 313n; 342, at India Board 366

Wyse, Sir Thomas, II, *78*, on Fine Arts Commission IV, 246

Xenophon, I, 17*, 242n, III, 132, 159*, *Ephesiaca*, 200*; 237*, V, 345, VI, 246, *Anabasis*, examination subject, I, 32; III, 196, 236, *Hellenics*, III, 177*, 180-1*

Yale University, V, 394n

Yankee clergyman, III, 263

Yarborough, 2nd Earl of, IV, *319*

Yates, Edmund, his quarrel with Thackeray, VI, 221n

Yeomen of the Guard, Edwin Pearson an Exon of, II, 142n

York, I, 218, 227, 247, 249, 266, TBM at 268; 290, II, 305, TBM at IV, 334; 371, Ellis at V, 99; 223, TBM plans to meet Ellis at 241; 244, 268, 291, 342, 387, Easter tour to 390n,

York,—*cont.*
TBM at 390n; 394n, Ellis at VI, 227; Cathedral II, 186
York, Duchess of: *see* Mary of Modena
York, Duke of: *see* James II
York, Frederica, Duchess of, and her dogs at Oatlands VI, 52
York, Frederick, Duke of, IV, 89n, V, 21
York Assizes, TBM attends, I, 208-10, 213, 217n, 222-5, TBM receives 1st brief at 223; TBM passes up 233n; attends 243, 252n, 253, 266n, election prevents him from attending 277
York Courant, II, 11n
York Herald, I, 223n, 266n
Yorkshire, II, 103n, Cromwell on IV, 165; seat for West Riding 277, *see also* West Riding Quarter Sessions
Yorktown, British defeat at, VI, 196
Young, Captain, I, 78n
Young, Edward, *Night Thoughts*, IV, 351*, displaced by Cowper V, 152
Young, G. M., ed., *Early Victorian England*, V, 430n, *Macaulay: Prose and Poetry*, III, 326n; on TBM I, x
Young, Colonel James, III, *209*
LETTER TO: III, 209
Young England, IV, 133n
Young Ireland Party, IV, 259n
Yoxall Lodge, Staffordshire, home of Thomas Gisborne, II, 191n

Zetland, Fanny sends news of, V, 272
Zetland, Thomas Dundas, 2nd Earl of, IV, 362n, *363*, 378
Zola, Émile, V, 339n
Zurich, VI, 26
Zwaan, J. A. de, of Dutch archives, IV, *354*